VW Passat
Service and Repair Manual

RM Jex and IM Coomber

Models covered

(3498 - 360 - 5AC2)

VW Passat front-wheel drive models with four-cylinder petrol and diesel engines, including special/limited editions; Saloon and Estate

1.8 litre (1781 cc) & 2.0 litre (1984 cc) SOHC petrol engines
1.9 litre (1896 cc) Turbo diesel engines (TD and TDi)

Does NOT cover 16-valve engine, 2792 cc VR6 engine or 1.6 litre Diesel engines

© Haynes Publishing 1999

A book in the **Haynes Service and Repair Manual Series**

ISBN 1 85960 498 6

British Library Cataloguing in Publication Data
A catalogue record for this book is available from the British Library.

ABCDE
FGHIJ
KLMNO
P

Printed in the USA

Haynes Publishing
Sparkford, Nr Yeovil, Somerset BA22 7JJ, England

Haynes North America, Inc
861 Lawrence Drive, Newbury Park, California 91320, USA

Editions Haynes S.A.
Tour Aurore - IBC, 18 Place des Reflets,
92975 Paris La Défense 2, Cedex, France

Haynes Publishing Nordiska AB
Box 1504, 751 45 Uppsala, Sverige

Contents

LIVING WITH YOUR VW PASSAT

Roadside repairs

Weekly checks

Lubricants, fluids and tyre pressures

MAINTENANCE

Routine maintenance and servicing

Contents

The VW Passat range covered by this Manual was introduced to the UK market in May 1988. Originally, the Passat was available with a choice of 1.8 litre (1781cc) and 2.0 litre (1984cc) petrol engines, in four-door Saloon and five-door Estate form. The new range broke the tradition set by the previous range in having a transversely-mounted engine, which liberated a great deal more interior space.

In September 1992, the 1.9 litre (1896cc) Turbo diesel (TD) engine was introduced. At the time of its introduction, the "Umwelt" or "Environment" engine was fairly unique in using a turbocharger more to reduce diesel emissions than to produce outright power.

For 1994, the range received a fairly substantial facelift, including a radiator grille for the first time. An updated Umwelt diesel (TDi) engine was also introduced, with direct injection and electronic diesel engine management for even lower emissions.

All engines are derived from the well-proven engines which have appeared in many VW/Audi vehicles. The engine is of four-cylinder overhead camshaft design, mounted transversely, with the transmission mounted on the left-hand side. All models have a five-speed manual transmission or four-speed automatic transmission.

All models have fully-independent front suspension. The rear suspension is semi-independent, with suspension struts and trailing arms. Self-levelling rear suspension was fitted to some Estate models.

A wide range of standard and optional equipment is available within the Passat range to suit most tastes, including central locking, electric windows, and an electric sunroof. On later facelifted models, air bags, seat belt tensioners, ABS and air conditioning system were fitted, or were available as options.

Provided that regular servicing is carried out in accordance with the manufacturer's recommendations, the VW Passat should prove a reliable and economical family car. The engine compartment is well-designed, and most of the items needing frequent attention are easily accessible.

Your VW Passat manual

The aim of this Manual is to help you get the best value from your vehicle. It can do so in several ways. It can help you decide what work must be done (even should you choose to get it done by a garage). It will also provide information on routine maintenance and servicing, and give a logical course of action and diagnosis when random faults occur. However, it is hoped that you will use the manual by tackling the work yourself. On simpler jobs it may even be quicker than booking the car into a garage and going there twice, to leave and collect it. Perhaps most important, a lot of money can be saved by avoiding the costs a garage must charge to cover its labour and overheads.

VW Passat 1.8 GL Saloon (1990 model)

VW Passat 1.9 CL Turbo diesel Estate (1994 model)

The VW Passat Team

Haynes manuals are produced by dedicated and enthusiastic people working in close co-operation. The team responsible for the creation of this book included:

Authors	R.M. Jex I.M Coomber
Sub-editor	Sophie Yar
Editor & Page Make-up	Steve Churchill
Workshop manager	Paul Buckland
Photo Scans	John Martin
Cover illustration & Line Art	Roger Healing
Wiring diagrams	Matthew Marke

We hope the book will help you to get the maximum enjoyment from your car. By carrying out routine maintenance as described you will ensure your car's reliability and preserve its resale value.

The manual has drawings and descriptions to show the function of the various components so that their layout can be understood. Tasks are described and photographed in a clear step-by-step sequence. The illustrations are numbered by the Section number and paragraph number to which they relate - if there is more than one illustration per paragraph, the sequence is denoted alphabetically.

References to the "left" or "right" of the vehicle are in the sense of a person in the driver's seat, facing forwards.

Acknowledgements

Thanks are due to Champion Spark Plug, who supplied the illustrations showing spark plug conditions, and to Duckhams Oils, who provided lubrication data. Special thanks to Autotechnics of Gillingham for assistance with the supply of project vehicles. Thanks are also due to Draper Tools Limited, who provided some of the workshop tools, and to all those people at Sparkford who helped in the production of this manual.

This manual is not a direct reproduction of the vehicle manufacturers' data, and its publication should not be taken as implying any technical approval by the vehicle manufacturers or importers.

We take great pride in the accuracy of information given in this manual, but vehicle manufacturers make alterations and design changes during the production run of a particular vehicle of which they do not inform us. No liability can be accepted by the authors or publishers for loss, damage or injury caused by any errors in, or omissions from, the information given.

Working on your car can be dangerous. This page shows just some of the potential risks and hazards, with the aim of creating a safety-conscious attitude.

General hazards

Scalding

• Don't remove the radiator or expansion tank cap while the engine is hot.
• Engine oil, automatic transmission fluid or power steering fluid may also be dangerously hot if the engine has recently been running.

Burning

• Beware of burns from the exhaust system and from any part of the engine. Brake discs and drums can also be extremely hot immediately after use.

Crushing

• When working under or near a raised vehicle, always supplement the jack with axle stands, or use drive-on ramps. *Never venture under a car which is only supported by a jack.*

• Take care if loosening or tightening high-torque nuts when the vehicle is on stands. Initial loosening and final tightening should be done with the wheels on the ground.

Fire

• Fuel is highly flammable; fuel vapour is explosive.
• Don't let fuel spill onto a hot engine.
• Do not smoke or allow naked lights (including pilot lights) anywhere near a vehicle being worked on. Also beware of creating sparks (electrically or by use of tools).
• Fuel vapour is heavier than air, so don't work on the fuel system with the vehicle over an inspection pit.
• Another cause of fire is an electrical overload or short-circuit. Take care when repairing or modifying the vehicle wiring.
• Keep a fire extinguisher handy, of a type suitable for use on fuel and electrical fires.

Electric shock

• Ignition HT voltage can be dangerous, especially to people with heart problems or a pacemaker. Don't work on or near the ignition system with the engine running or the ignition switched on.

• Mains voltage is also dangerous. Make sure that any mains-operated equipment is correctly earthed. Mains power points should be protected by a residual current device (RCD) circuit breaker.

Fume or gas intoxication

• Exhaust fumes are poisonous; they often contain carbon monoxide, which is rapidly fatal if inhaled. Never run the engine in a confined space such as a garage with the doors shut.

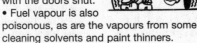

• Fuel vapour is also poisonous, as are the vapours from some cleaning solvents and paint thinners.

Poisonous or irritant substances

• Avoid skin contact with battery acid and with any fuel, fluid or lubricant, especially antifreeze, brake hydraulic fluid and Diesel fuel. Don't syphon them by mouth. If such a substance is swallowed or gets into the eyes, seek medical advice.
• Prolonged contact with used engine oil can cause skin cancer. Wear gloves or use a barrier cream if necessary. Change out of oil-soaked clothes and do not keep oily rags in your pocket.
• Air conditioning refrigerant forms a poisonous gas if exposed to a naked flame (including a cigarette). It can also cause skin burns on contact.

Asbestos

• Asbestos dust can cause cancer if inhaled or swallowed. Asbestos may be found in gaskets and in brake and clutch linings. When dealing with such components it is safest to assume that they contain asbestos.

Special hazards

Hydrofluoric acid

• This extremely corrosive acid is formed when certain types of synthetic rubber, found in some O-rings, oil seals, fuel hoses etc, are exposed to temperatures above 400°C. The rubber changes into a charred or sticky substance containing the acid. *Once formed, the acid remains dangerous for years. If it gets onto the skin, it may be necessary to amputate the limb concerned.*
• When dealing with a vehicle which has suffered a fire, or with components salvaged from such a vehicle, wear protective gloves and discard them after use.

The battery

• Batteries contain sulphuric acid, which attacks clothing, eyes and skin. Take care when topping-up or carrying the battery.
• The hydrogen gas given off by the battery is highly explosive. Never cause a spark or allow a naked light nearby. Be careful when connecting and disconnecting battery chargers or jump leads.

Air bags

• Air bags can cause injury if they go off accidentally. Take care when removing the steering wheel and/or facia. Special storage instructions may apply.

Diesel injection equipment

• Diesel injection pumps supply fuel at very high pressure. Take care when working on the fuel injectors and fuel pipes.

⚠ *Warning: Never expose the hands, face or any other part of the body to injector spray; the fuel can penetrate the skin with potentially fatal results.*

Remember...

DO

• Do use eye protection when using power tools, and when working under the vehicle.

• Do wear gloves or use barrier cream to protect your hands when necessary.

• Do get someone to check periodically that all is well when working alone on the vehicle.

• Do keep loose clothing and long hair well out of the way of moving mechanical parts.

• Do remove rings, wristwatch etc, before working on the vehicle – especially the electrical system.

• Do ensure that any lifting or jacking equipment has a safe working load rating adequate for the job.

DON'T

• Don't attempt to lift a heavy component which may be beyond your capability – get assistance.

• Don't rush to finish a job, or take unverified short cuts.

• Don't use ill-fitting tools which may slip and cause injury.

• Don't leave tools or parts lying around where someone can trip over them. Mop up oil and fuel spills at once.

• Don't allow children or pets to play in or near a vehicle being worked on.

The following pages are intended to help in dealing with common roadside emergencies and breakdowns. You will find more detailed fault finding information at the back of the manual, and repair information in the main chapters.

If your car won't start and the starter motor doesn't turn

☐ If it's a model with automatic transmission, make sure the selector is in 'P' or 'N'.
☐ Open the bonnet and make sure that the battery terminals are clean and tight.
☐ Switch on the headlights and try to start the engine. If the headlights go very dim when you're trying to start, the battery is probably flat. Get out of trouble by jump starting (see next page) using a friend's car.

If your car won't start even though the starter motor turns as normal

☐ Is there fuel in the tank?
☐ Is there moisture on electrical components under the bonnet? Switch off the ignition, then wipe off any obvious dampness with a dry cloth. Spray a water-repellent aerosol product (WD-40 or equivalent) on ignition and fuel system electrical connectors like those shown in the photos. Pay special attention to the ignition coil wiring connector and HT leads. (Note that Diesel engines don't normally suffer from damp.)

A Check the security and condition of the battery terminals.

B Check that the diesel fuel cut-off/"stop" solenoid valve wiring plug is securely connected.

C Check that the diesel glow plug control unit wiring plugs are secure, and that the main fusible link (under the plastic cover) has not blown.

Check that electrical connections are secure (with the ignition switched off). On petrol engine models, check the four spark plug leads and the ignition coil connections at the rear of the engine compartment. Spray the connector plugs with a water-dispersant spray like WD40 if you suspect a problem due to damp

D Check that the airflow meter wiring plug is securely connected.

E Check the remaining engine compartment wiring connectors (as applicable).

Jump starting

When jump-starting a car using a booster battery, observe the following precautions:

✔ Before connecting the booster battery, make sure that the ignition is switched off.

✔ Ensure that all electrical equipment (lights, heater, wipers, etc) is switched off.

✔ Take note of any special precautions printed on the battery case.

✔ Make sure that the booster battery is the same voltage as the discharged one in the vehicle.

✔ If the battery is being jump-started from the battery in another vehicle, the two vehicles MUST NOT TOUCH each other.

✔ Make sure that the transmission is in neutral (or PARK, in the case of automatic transmission).

1 Connect one end of the red jump lead to the positive (+) terminal of the flat battery

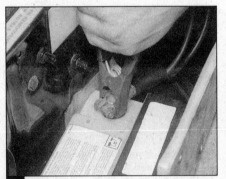

2 Connect the other end of the red lead to the positive (+) terminal of the booster battery.

3 Connect one end of the black jump lead to the negative (-) terminal of the booster battery

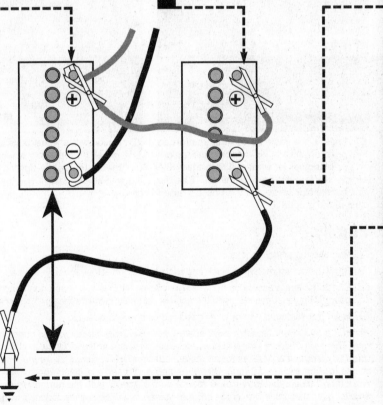

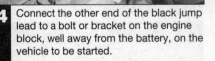

4 Connect the other end of the black jump lead to a bolt or bracket on the engine block, well away from the battery, on the vehicle to be started.

5 Make sure that the jump leads will not come into contact with the fan, drive-belts or other moving parts of the engine.

6 Start the engine using the booster battery and run it at idle speed. Switch on the lights, rear window demister and heater blower motor, then disconnect the jump leads in the reverse order of connection. Turn off the lights etc.

Wheel changing

Some of the details shown here will vary according to model. For instance, the location of the spare wheel and jack is not the same on all cars. However, the basic principles apply to all vehicles.

 Warning: Do not change a wheel in a situation where you risk being hit by another vehicle. On busy roads, try to stop in a lay-by or a gateway. Be wary of passing traffic while changing the wheel - it is easy to become distracted by the job in hand.

Preparation

☐ When a puncture occurs, stop as soon as it is safe to do so.

☐ Park on firm level ground, if possible, and well out of the way of other traffic.

☐ Use hazard warning lights if necessary.

☐ If you have one, use a warning triangle to alert other drivers of your presence.

☐ Apply the handbrake and engage first or reverse gear (or Park on models with automatic transmission.

☐ Chock the wheel diagonally opposite the one being removed – a couple of large stones will do for this.

☐ If the ground is soft, use a flat piece of wood to spread the load under the jack.

Changing the wheel

1 The spare wheel and tools are stored in the luggage compartment, under the floor. A warning triangle may be provided on the left-hand side of the luggage compartment, behind a trim panel on Estate models.

2 Release the retaining strap, and lift out the jack and wheel changing tools out from the centre of the wheel. Unscrew the retaining nut and lift the wheel out of the vehicle.

3 Remove the wheel trim/hub cap (on some models, a wire hook is provided, which is inserted through one of the holes in the wheel trim, and used with the wheelbrace handle to pull off the trim).

4 Slacken each wheel bolt by a half turn, using the wheelbrace. If the bolts are too tight, DON'T stand on the wheelbrace to undo them - call for assistance from one of the motoring organisations.

5 Locate the jack below the reinforced point on the sill, indicated by the square or triangular indentations (don't jack the vehicle at any other point of the sill). Turn the jack handle clockwise until the wheel is raised clear of the ground.

6 Unscrew the wheel bolts and remove the wheel. Fit the spare wheel, and screw in the bolts. Lightly tighten the bolts with the wheelbrace then lower the vehicle to the ground.

Finally...

☐ Remove the wheel chocks.

☐ Stow the punctured wheel, jack and tools in the correct locations in the car.

☐ Check the tyre pressure on the wheel just fitted. If it is low, or if you don't have a pressure gauge with you, drive slowly to the nearest garage and inflate the tyre to the right pressure.

☐ Have the damaged tyre or wheel repaired as soon as possible.

Note: If a temporary "space-saver" spare wheel has been fitted, special conditions apply to its use. This type of spare wheel is only intended for use in an emergency, and should not remain fitted any longer than it takes to get the punctured wheel repaired. While the temporary wheel is in use, do not exceed 50 mph (80 km/h), and avoid harsh acceleration, braking or cornering. Note that, besides being narrower than a normal roadwheel, the temporary spare wheel is of smaller diameter; therefore, since ground clearance will be slightly reduced with the temporary spare in use, take care when travelling over rough ground.

7 Securely tighten the wheel bolts in the sequence shown, then refit the wheel trim/hub cap. The wheel bolts should be slackened and retightened to the correct torque at the earliest possible opportunity.

Identifying leaks

Puddles on the garage floor or drive, or obvious wetness under the bonnet or underneath the car, suggest a leak that needs investigating. It can sometimes be difficult to decide where the leak is coming from, especially if the engine bay is very dirty already. Leaking oil or fluid can also be blown rearwards by the passage of air under the car, giving a false impression of where the problem lies.

 Warning: Most automotive oils and fluids are poisonous. Wash them off skin, and change out of contaminated clothing, without delay.

 The smell of a fluid leaking from the car may provide a clue to what's leaking. Some fluids are distinctively coloured. It may help to clean the car carefully and to park it over some clean paper overnight as an aid to locating the source of the leak.

Remember that some leaks may only occur while the engine is running.

Sump oil

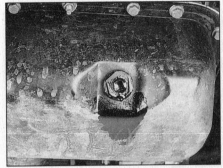

Engine oil may leak from the drain plug...

Oil from filter

...or from the base of the oil filter.

Gearbox oil

Gearbox oil can leak from the seals at the inboard ends of the driveshafts.

Antifreeze

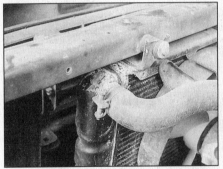

Leaking antifreeze often leaves a crystalline deposit like this.

Brake fluid

A leak occurring at a wheel is almost certainly brake fluid.

Power steering fluid

Power steering fluid may leak from the pipe connectors on the steering rack.

Towing

When all else fails, you may find yourself having to get a tow home – or of course you may be helping somebody else. Long-distance recovery should only be done by a garage or breakdown service. For shorter distances, DIY towing using another car is easy enough, but observe the following points:
☐ Use a proper tow-rope – they are not expensive. The vehicle being towed must display an 'ON TOW' sign in its rear window.
☐ Always turn the ignition key to the 'on' position when the vehicle is being towed, so

that the steering lock is released, and that the direction indicator and brake lights will work.
☐ Only attach the tow-rope to the towing eyes provided.
☐ Before being towed, release the handbrake and select neutral on the transmission.
☐ Note that greater-than-usual pedal pressure will be required to operate the brakes, since the vacuum servo unit is only operational with the engine running.
☐ On models with power steering, greater-than-usual steering effort will also be required.

☐ The driver of the car being towed must keep the tow-rope taut at all times to avoid snatching.
☐ Make sure that both drivers know the route before setting off.
☐ Only drive at moderate speeds and keep the distance towed to a minimum. Drive smoothly and allow plenty of time for slowing down at junctions.
☐ On models with automatic transmission, special precautions apply. If in doubt, do not tow, or transmission damage may result.

Introduction

There are some very simple checks which need only take a few minutes to carry out, but which could save you a lot of inconvenience and expense.

These "Weekly checks" require no great skill or special tools, and the small amount of time they take to perform could prove to be very well spent, for example;

☐ Keeping an eye on tyre condition and pressures, will not only help to stop them wearing out prematurely, but could also save your life.

☐ Many breakdowns are caused by electrical problems. Battery-related faults are particularly common, and a quick check on a regular basis will often prevent the majority of these.

☐ If your car develops a brake fluid leak, the first time you might know about it is when your brakes don't work properly. Checking the level regularly will give advance warning of this kind of problem.

☐ If the oil or coolant levels run low, the cost of repairing any engine damage will be far greater than fixing the leak, for example.

Underbonnet check points

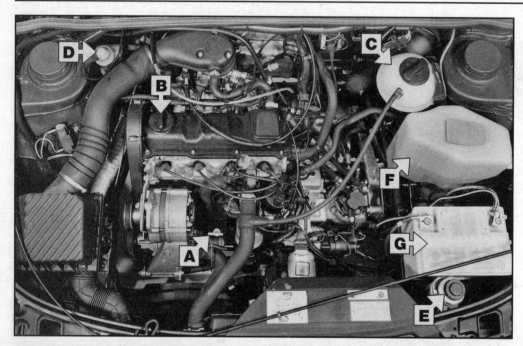

◀ 1.8 litre petrol

A *Engine oil level dipstick*

B *Engine oil filler cap*

C *Coolant expansion tank*

D *Brake and clutch fluid reservoir*

E *Power steering fluid reservoir*

F *Screen washer fluid reservoir*

G *Battery*

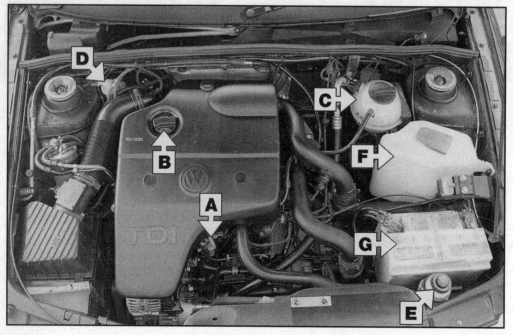

◀ Turbo diesel

A *Engine oil level dipstick*

B *Engine oil filler cap*

C *Coolant expansion tank*

D *Brake fluid reservoir*

E *Power steering fluid reservoir*

F *Screen washer fluid reservoir*

G *Battery*

Engine oil level

Before you start
✔ Make sure that your car is on level ground.
✔ Check the oil level before the car is driven, or at least 5 minutes after the engine has been switched off.

 If the oil is checked immediately after driving the vehicle, some of the oil will remain in the upper engine components, resulting in an inaccurate reading on the dipstick!

The correct oil
Modern engines place great demands on their oil. It is very important that the correct oil for your car is used (See "Lubricants, fluids and tyre pressures").

Car Care
● If you have to add oil frequently, you should check whether you have any oil leaks. Place some clean paper under the car overnight, and check for stains in the morning. If there are no leaks, the engine may be burning oil *(see "Fault Finding").*

● Always maintain the level between the upper and lower dipstick marks (see photo 3). If the level is too low severe engine damage may occur. Oil seal failure may result if the engine is overfilled by adding too much oil.

1 The dipstick top is often brightly coloured for easy identification (see *"Underbonnet check points"* on page 0•10 for exact location). Withdraw the dipstick.

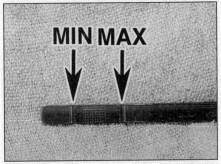

3 Note the oil level on the end of the dipstick, which should be within the hatched area marked. If the oil level is at the bottom of, or below, the hatched area, topping-up is required.

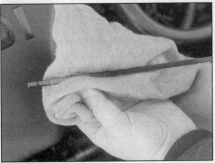

2 Using a clean rag or paper towel remove all oil from the dipstick. Insert the clean dipstick into the tube as far as it will go, then withdraw it again.

4 Oil is added through the filler cap. Unscrew the cap and top-up the level. Add the oil slowly, checking the level on the dipstick often, and allowing time for the oil to fall to the sump. Add oil until the level is at the top of the hatched area on the dipstick - don't overfill (see *Car Care* left).

Coolant level

⚠ **Warning: DO NOT attempt to remove the expansion tank pressure cap when the engine is hot, as there is a very great risk of scalding. Do not leave open containers of coolant about, as it is poisonous.**

Car Care
● With a sealed-type cooling system, adding coolant should not be necessary on a regular basis. If frequent topping-up is required, it is likely there is a leak. Check the radiator, all hoses and joint faces for signs of staining or wetness, and rectify as necessary.

● It is important that antifreeze is used in the cooling system all year round, not just during the winter months. Don't top-up with water alone, as the antifreeze will become too diluted.

1 The coolant level varies with the temperature of the engine. When the engine is cold, the coolant level should be between the "MAX" and "MIN" marks. When the engine is hot, the level may rise slightly above the "MAX" mark.

2 If topping up is necessary, **wait until the engine is cold**. Slowly unscrew the expansion tank cap, to release any pressure present in the cooling system, and remove it.

3 Add a mixture of water and antifreeze to the expansion tank until the coolant level is halfway between the level marks. Refit the cap and tighten it securely.

Brake (and clutch*) fluid level

*On models with a hydraulically-operated clutch, this information is also applicable to the clutch fluid level

Warning:
● Brake fluid can harm your eyes and damage painted surfaces, so use extreme caution when handling and pouring it.
● Do not use fluid that has been standing open for some time, as it absorbs moisture from the air, which can cause a dangerous loss of braking effectiveness.

 HAYNES HiNT
● Make sure that your car is on level ground.
● The fluid level in the reservoir will drop slightly as the brake pads wear down, but the fluid level must never be allowed to drop below the "MIN" mark.

1 The brake and clutch fluid reservoir is located on the right-hand side of the engine compartment, next to the suspension strut top mounting.

Before you start:
✔ Park the vehicle on level ground.
✔ On models with ABS, switch on the ignition and wait for one minute before proceeding.

Safety First!
● If the reservoir requires repeated topping-up this is an indication of a fluid leak somewhere in the system, which should be investigated immediately.

● If a leak is suspected, the car should not be driven until the braking system has been checked. Never take any risks where brakes are concerned.

2 The "MAX" and "MIN" marks are indicated on the front of the reservoir. The fluid level must be kept between the marks at all times. If topping-up is necessary, first wipe clean the area around the filler cap to prevent dirt entering the hydraulic system. Unscrew the reservoir cap and carefully lift it out of position, taking care not to damage the level switch float. Place the cap and float on a piece of clean rag.

3 Inspect the reservoir; if the fluid is dirty, the hydraulic system should be drained and refilled (see Chapter 1). Carefully add fluid, taking care not to spill it onto the surrounding components. Use only the specified fluid; mixing different types can cause damage to the system. After topping-up to the correct level, securely refit the cap and wipe off any spilt fluid.

Screen washer fluid level*

*On models with a headlight washer system, the screen wash is also used to clean the headlights. On Estate models, the underbonnet reservoir also serves the tailgate washer.

Screenwash additives not only keep the winscreen clean during foul weather, they also prevent the washer system freezing in cold weather - which is when you are likely to need it most. Don't top up using plain water as the screenwash will become too diluted, and will freeze during cold weather. **On no account use coolant antifreeze in the washer system - this could discolour or damage paintwork.**

1 The screen washer fluid reservoir is located in the front left-hand corner of the engine compartment, next to the battery. It is marked in litres, to assist in mixing quantities of screenwash additive and water.

2 The screen washer level can be seen through the reservoir body. If topping-up is necessary, open the cap.

3 When topping-up the reservoir, add a screenwash additive in the quantities recommended on the bottle.

Power steering fluid level

Before you start:

✔ Park the vehicle on level ground.

✔ Set the steering wheel straight-ahead.

✔ The engine should be turned off.

 HAYNES HiNT *For the check to be accurate, the steering must not be turned once the engine has been stopped.*

Safety First!

● The need for frequent topping-up indicates a leak, which should be investigated immediately.

1 The reservoir is located in the front left-hand corner of the engine compartment, next to the battery. The fluid level is visible through the reservoir, and should always be between the "MAX" and "MIN" marks.

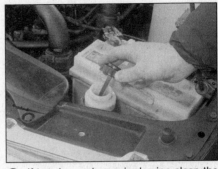

2 If topping-up is required, wipe clean the area around the reservoir filler neck and unscrew the filler cap/dipstick from the reservoir.

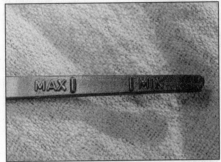

3 Dip the fluid with the reservoir cap/dipstick (do not screw the cap into position). When the engine is cold, the fluid level should be up to the "MIN" mark; when hot, it should be on the "MAX" mark.

4 When topping-up, use **only** the specified type of fluid and do not overfill the reservoir. When the level is correct, securely refit the cap.

Wiper blades

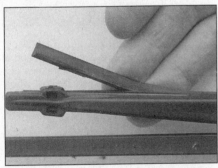

1 Check the condition of the wiper blades; if they are cracked or show any signs of deterioration, or if the glass swept area is smeared, renew them. Wiper blades should be renewed annually.

2 To remove a windscreen wiper blade, pull the arm fully away from the screen until it locks. Swivel the blade through 90°, press the locking tab with your fingers and slide the blade out of the arm's hooked end.

3 On Estate models, don't forget to check the tailgate wiper blade as well. To remove the blade, depress the retaining tab and slide the blade out of the hooked end of the arm.

Tyre condition and pressure

It is very important that tyres are in good condition, and at the correct pressure - having a tyre failure at any speed is highly dangerous. Tyre wear is influenced by driving style - harsh braking and acceleration, or fast cornering, will all produce more rapid tyre wear. As a general rule, the front tyres wear out faster than the rears. Interchanging the tyres from front to rear ("rotating" the tyres) may result in more even wear. However, if this is completely effective, you may have the expense of replacing all four tyres at once! Remove any nails or stones embedded in the tread before they penetrate the tyre to cause deflation. If removal of a nail does reveal that the tyre has been punctured, refit the nail so that its point of penetration is marked. Then immediately change the wheel, and have the tyre repaired by a tyre dealer.

Regularly check the tyres for damage in the form of cuts or bulges, especially in the sidewalls. Periodically remove the wheels, and clean any dirt or mud from the inside and outside surfaces. Examine the wheel rims for signs of rusting, corrosion or other damage. Light alloy wheels are easily damaged by "kerbing" whilst parking; steel wheels may also become dented or buckled. A new wheel is very often the only way to overcome severe damage.

New tyres should be balanced when they are fitted, but it may become necessary to re-balance them as they wear, or if the balance weights fitted to the wheel rim should fall off. Unbalanced tyres will wear more quickly, as will the steering and suspension components. Wheel imbalance is normally signified by vibration, particularly at a certain speed (typically around 50 mph). If this vibration is felt only through the steering, then it is likely that just the front wheels need balancing. If, however, the vibration is felt through the whole car, the rear wheels could be out of balance. Wheel balancing should be carried out by a tyre dealer or garage.

1 Tread Depth - visual check
The original tyres have tread wear safety bands (B), which will appear when the tread depth reaches approximately 1.6 mm. The band positions are indicated by a triangular mark on the tyre sidewall (A).

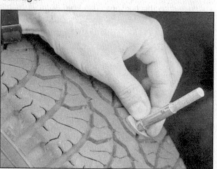

2 Tread Depth - manual check
Alternatively, tread wear can be monitored with a simple, inexpensive device known as a tread depth indicator gauge.

3 Tyre Pressure Check
Check the tyre pressures regularly with the tyres cold. Do not adjust the tyre pressures immediately after the vehicle has been used, or an inaccurate setting will result. The recommended pressures are on page 0•16

Tyre tread wear patterns

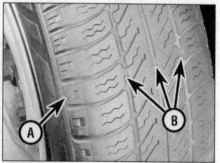

Shoulder Wear

Underinflation (wear on both sides)
Under-inflation will cause overheating of the tyre, because the tyre will flex too much, and the tread will not sit correctly on the road surface. This will cause a loss of grip and excessive wear, not to mention the danger of sudden tyre failure due to heat build-up.
Check and adjust pressures
Incorrect wheel camber (wear on one side)
Repair or renew suspension parts
Hard cornering
Reduce speed!

Centre Wear

Overinflation
Over-inflation will cause rapid wear of the centre part of the tyre tread, coupled with reduced grip, harsher ride, and the danger of shock damage occurring in the tyre casing.
Check and adjust pressures

If you sometimes have to inflate your car's tyres to the higher pressures specified for maximum load or sustained high speed, don't forget to reduce the pressures to normal afterwards.

Uneven Wear

Front tyres may wear unevenly as a result of wheel misalignment. Most tyre dealers and garages can check and adjust the wheel alignment (or "tracking") for a modest charge.
Incorrect camber or castor
Repair or renew suspension parts
Malfunctioning suspension
Repair or renew suspension parts
Unbalanced wheel
Balance tyres
Incorrect toe setting
Adjust front wheel alignment
Note: *The feathered edge of the tread which typifies toe wear is best checked by feel.*

Battery

Caution: Before carrying out any work on the vehicle battery, read the precautions given in "Safety first" at the start of this manual.

✔ Make sure that the battery tray is in good condition, and that the clamp is tight. Corrosion on the tray, retaining clamp and the battery itself can be removed with a solution of water and baking soda. Thoroughly rinse all cleaned areas with water. Any metal parts damaged by corrosion should be covered with a zinc-based primer, then painted.

✔ Periodically (approximately every three months), check the charge condition of the battery as described in Chapter 5A.

✔ If the battery is flat, and you need to jump start your vehicle, see **Roadside Repairs.**

1 The battery is located on the left-hand side of the engine compartment. The exterior of the battery should be inspected periodically for damage such as a cracked case or cover.

2 Check the tightness of battery clamps to ensure good electrical connections. You should not be able to move them. Also check each cable for cracks and frayed conductors.

HAYNES HiNT

Battery corrosion can be kept to a minimum by applying a layer of petroleum jelly to the clamps and terminals after they are reconnected.

3 If corrosion (white, fluffy deposits) is evident, remove the cables from the battery terminals, clean them with a small wire brush, then refit them. Automotive stores sell a tool for cleaning the battery post . . .

4 . . . as well as the battery cable clamps

Bulbs and fuses

✔ Check all external lights and the horn. Refer to the appropriate Sections of Chapter 12 for details if any of the circuits are found to be inoperative.

✔ Visually check all accessible wiring connectors, harnesses and retaining clips for security, and for signs of chafing or damage.

HAYNES HiNT *If you need to check your brake lights and indicators unaided, back up to a wall or garage door and operate the lights. The reflected light should show if they are working properly.*

1 If a single indicator light, stop-light or headlight has failed, it is likely that a bulb has blown and will need to be replaced. Refer to Chapter 12 for details. If both stop-lights have failed, it is possible that the switch has failed (see Chapter 9).

2 If more than one indicator light or tail light has failed it is likely that either a fuse has blown or that there is a fault in the circuit (see Chapter 12). The fuses are located behind a panel on the bottom of the driver's side lower facia panel.

3 The main fuses are in a row at the bottom of the combined fuse and relay panel. To replace a blown fuse, simply pull it out and fit a new fuse of the correct rating (see Chapter 12). If the fuse blows again, it is important that you find out why - a complete checking procedure is given in Chapter 12.

Lubricants and fluids

Engine (petrol) . . . . Multigrade engine oil, viscosity SAE 15W/40, 15W/50 or 20W/50, to VW spec 500 00
(Duckhams QXR Premium Petrol Engine Oil)

Engine (Diesel) . . . . Multigrade engine oil, viscosity SAE 15W/40, 15W/50 or 20W/50
(Duckhams QXR Premium Diesel Engine Oil, or Duckhams Hypergrade Diesel Engine Oil)

Cooling system . . . . Ethylene glycol-based antifreeze with corrosion inhibitor
(Duckhams Antifreeze & Summer Coolant)

Manual transmission and final drive . . . . Gear oil, viscosity SAE 80, to API GL4, or
VW gear oil G50, SAE 75W/90
(Duckhams Hypoid Gear Oil 80W GL-4 or Duckhams Hypoid Gear Oil 75W-90 GL-4)

Automatic transmission:
  Type 096 transmission . . . . Dexron II type ATF
(Duckhams ATF Autotrans III)
  Type 01M transmission (1995 onwards) . . . . VW ATF G 052 162 A1*
Final drive (Type 096 transmission) . . . . VW gear oil G50, SAE 75W/90
(Duckhams Hypoid Gear Oil 75W-90 GL-4)

Final drive (Type 01M transmission) . . . . VW ATF G 052 162 A1*
Brake and clutch hydraulic system . . . . Hydraulic fluid to FMVSS 116 DOT 4
(Duckhams Universal Brake & Clutch Fluid)

Power steering:
  To February 1989 . . . . Dexron II type ATF
(Duckhams ATF Autotrans III)
  February 1989 on . . . . VW hydraulic oil G 002 000

*See Chapter 1A, Section 7.

Tyre pressures

Saloon models	Front	Rear
Up to half load ("normal" usage):		
1.8 litre and 1.9 TD models	2.0 bar (29 psi)	2.0 bar (29 psi)
1.9 TDi and 2.0 litre models	2.2 bar (32 psi)	2.2 bar (32 psi)
Up to full load:		
1.8 litre and 1.9 TD models	2.2 bar (32 psi)	2.6 bar (38 psi)
1.9 TDi and 2.0 litre models	2.4 bar (35 psi)	2.7 bar (39 psi)
Estate models		
Up to half load ("normal" usage):		
1.8 litre and 1.9 litre TD models	2.0 bar (29 psi)	2.0 bar (29 psi)
1.9 litre TDi models	2.1 bar (30 psi)	2.3 bar (33 psi)
2.0 litre models	2.2 bar (32 psi)	2.2 bar (32 psi)
Up to full load:		
1.8 litre and 1.9 litre TD models	2.2 bar (32 psi)	2.8 bar (41 psi)
1.9 litre TDi models	2.7 bar (39 psi)	3.3 bar (48 psi)
2.0 litre models	2.4 bar (35 psi)	3.0 bar (44 psi)

Note 1: *Pressures apply to original-equipment tyres, and may vary if any other make of tyre is fitted; check with the tyre manufacturer or supplier for the correct pressures if necessary. Note that the correct pressures for each individual vehicle are given on a sticker which is either inside of the glovebox lid or inside the fuel filler flap. The information on this sticker may vary slightly with that quoted above - if so, consult your VW dealer for the latest recommendations.*

Note 2: *The spare wheel may be of conventional or "space-saver" type. A conventional spare wheel should be maintained at the highest full-load pressure for the vehicle. The "space-saver" spare runs at a pressure of 4.2 bar (61 psi) - this pressure should be marked on the tyre sidewall.*

Chapter 1 Part A:
Routine maintenance & servicing - petrol models

Contents

1A

Degrees of difficulty

Easy, suitable for novice with little experience

Fairly easy, suitable for beginner with some experience

Fairly difficult, suitable for competent DIY mechanic

Difficult, suitable for experienced DIY mechanic

Very difficult, suitable for expert DIY or professional

Lubricants and fluids

Refer to end of *"Weekly checks"*

Capacities

Engine oil (including filter)
All engines . . . . 3.8 litres

Cooling system (approximate)
Without air conditioning . . . . 5.0 litres
With air conditioning . . . . 5.6 litres

Transmission
Manual transmission . . . . 2.0 litres
Automatic transmission:
   Transmission (initial fill):
      Type 096 . . . . 5.6 litres
      Type 01M . . . . 5.3 litres
   Transmission (fluid change) . . . . 3.0 litres
   Final drive . . . . 0.75 litres

Power-assisted steering
All models (approximate) . . . . 1.5 litres

Fuel tank
All models (approximate) . . . . 70 litres

Washer reservoirs
Models with headlight washers . . . . 8.0 litres
Models without headlight washers . . . . 5.0 litres

Engine
Oil filter:
   All petrol engines except codes ADY and AGG . . . . Champion C160
   Engine codes ADY and AGG . . . . Champion C149

Cooling system
Antifreeze mixture:
   40% antifreeze . . . . Protection down to -25°C
   50% antifreeze . . . . Protection down to -35°C
Note: *Refer to antifreeze manufacturer for latest recommendations.*

Fuel system
Air filter element . . . . Champion U572
Fuel filter . . . . Champion L206

Ignition system
Ignition timing . . . . Refer to Chapter 5B
Spark plugs*:
   Engine codes PB, PF, RP and ABS . . . . Champion N7BYC
   Engine code 2E . . . . Champion N7BMC
   Engine codes ADY, ADZ and AGG . . . . Champion RN8VTYC4
   Engine code AAM . . . . Champion RN10VTYC4
Electrode gap* . . . . Not adjustable
The spark plug recommendations are those supplied by Champion Spark Plug. If spark plugs of any other type are to be fitted, consult their manufacturers for plug gap information.

Brakes
Brake pad minimum thickness (including backing plate) . . . . 7.0 mm
Brake shoe friction material minimum thickness . . . . 2.5 mm

Torque wrench settings

	Nm	lbf ft
Manual transmission filler/level and drain plugs	25	18
Roadwheel bolts	110	81
Spark plugs	25	18
Sump drain plug	30	22

The maintenance intervals in this manual are provided with the assumption that you, not the dealer, will be carrying out the work. These are the minimum intervals recommended by us for vehicles driven daily.

If you wish to keep your vehicle in peak condition at all times, you may wish to perform some of these procedures more often. We encourage frequent maintenance, since it enhances the efficiency, performance and resale value of your vehicle.

When the vehicle is new, it should be serviced by a dealer service department, in order to preserve the factory warranty.

Every 250 miles (400 km) or weekly

☐ Refer to *"Weekly checks"*

Every 5000 miles (7500 km)

☐ Renew the engine oil and filter (Section 3)

Every 10 000 miles (15 000 km)

☐ Check the front brake pad thickness (Section 4)
☐ Renew the pollen filter element (Section 5)

Every 12 months

Note: *If the vehicle is covering less than 10 000 miles (15 000 km) a year, also carry out the tasks listed above*

☐ Check the operation of all lights and horn (Section 6)
☐ Check the automatic transmission fluid level (Section 7)
☐ Check the condition of the airbag unit(s) (Section 8)
☐ Check the operation of the washer system(s) (Section 9)
☐ Check all underbonnet components and hoses for fluid leaks (Section 10)
☐ Check the battery electrolyte level - where applicable (Section 11)
☐ Lubricate all hinges, locks and door check straps (Section 12)
☐ Check the steering and suspension components for condition and security (Section 13)
☐ Check the condition of the driveshaft gaiters (Section 14)
☐ Check the braking system for leaks and damage (Section 15)
☐ Check the condition of the exhaust system and its mountings (Section 16)
☐ Check the rear brake pad thickness - rear disc brake models (Section 17)
☐ Check the rear brake shoe lining thickness - rear drum brake models (Section 18)
☐ Check the automatic transmission for fault codes (Section 19)
☐ Check the headlight beam adjustment (Section 20)
☐ Carry out a road test (Section 21)

Every 20 000 miles (30 000 km)

Note: *If the vehicle is covering more than 20 000 miles (30 000 km) a year, also carry out all the operations described above*

☐ Check the condition of the auxiliary drivebelt(s), and renew if necessary (Section 22)
☐ Renew the spark plugs (Section 23)
☐ Renew the air filter element (Section 24)
☐ Check the timing belt condition and tension (Section 25)
☐ Check the manual transmission oil level (Section 26)
☐ Check the transmission for leaks and damage (Section 27)
☐ Check the underbody protection for damage (Section 28)

Every 40 000 miles (60 000 km)

☐ Renew the automatic transmission fluid and filter (Section 29)
☐ Renew the fuel filter (Section 30)
☐ Renew the timing belt (Section 31)

Note: *VW specify a timing belt renewal interval of 60 000 miles (90 000 km). However, if the vehicle is used mainly for short journeys or a lot of stop-start driving, we recommend that this shorter interval is adhered to. The actual belt renewal interval is very much up to the individual owner but, bearing in mind that severe engine damage will result if the belt breaks in use, we recommend you err on the side of caution.*

Every 2 years (regardless of mileage)

☐ Renew the coolant (Section 32)
☐ Renew the brake fluid (Section 33)
☐ Check exhaust emissions (Section 34)

Underbonnet view of an early 1.8 litre model (2.0 litre similar)

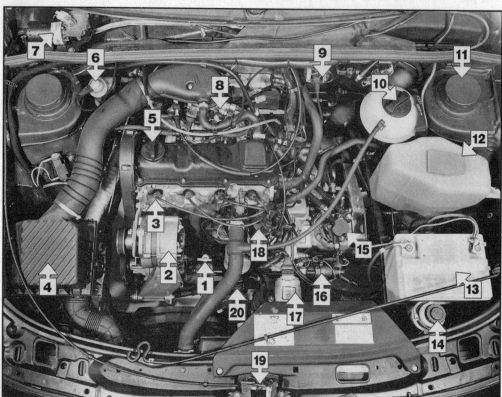

1 Engine oil dipstick
2 Alternator
3 No 1 spark plug
4 Air cleaner housing
5 Engine oil filler cap
6 Brake/clutch fluid reservoir
7 Windscreen wiper motor
8 Injector unit
9 Ignition HT coil
10 Coolant expansion tank
11 Suspension strut upper mounting
12 Washer fluid reservoir
13 Battery
14 Power steering fluid reservoir
15 Gear selector control unit (manual transmission)
16 Starter motor
17 Cooling fan motor
18 Distributor
19 Bonnet lock
20 Oil filter

Front underbody view (1.8 litre model shown - 2.0 litre similar)

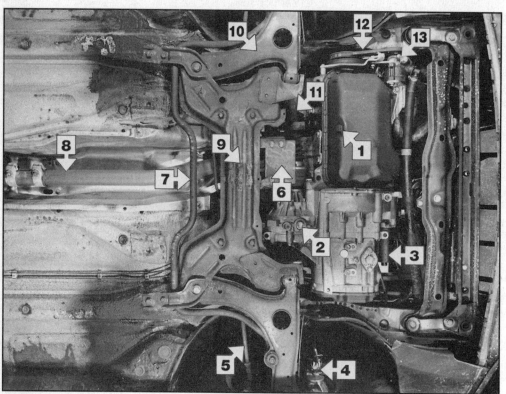

1 Engine oil drain plug
2 Manual transmission oil drain plug
3 Starter motor
4 Front brake caliper
5 Track rod
6 Damper
7 Anti-roll bar
8 Exhaust front pipe
9 Front suspension subframe (crossmember)
10 Front suspension arm
11 Driveshaft
12 Power steering pump drivebelt
13 Power steering pump

Rear underbody view

1   *Exhaust pipe and centre silencer*
2   *Brake regulator*
3   *Handbrake cable*
4   *Suspension strut lower mounting*
5   *Rear silencer*
6   *Exhaust mounting*
7   *Fuel tank*
8   *Rear axle*
9   *Rear axle/suspension pivot mounting*
10 *Fuel filter*

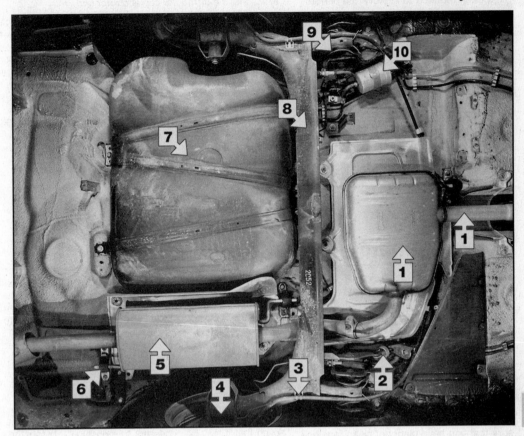

1A

Maintenance procedures - petrol models

1   Introduction

This Chapter is designed to help the home mechanic maintain his/her vehicle for safety, economy, long life and peak performance.

The Chapter contains a master maintenance schedule, followed by Sections dealing specifically with each task in the schedule. Visual checks, adjustments, component renewal and other helpful items are included. Refer to the accompanying illustrations of the engine compartment and the underside of the vehicle for the locations of the various components.

Servicing your vehicle in accordance with the mileage/time maintenance schedule and the following Sections will provide a planned maintenance programme, which should result in a long and reliable service life. This is a comprehensive plan, so maintaining some items but not others at the specified service intervals, will not produce the same results.

As you service your vehicle, you will discover that many of the procedures can - and should - be grouped together, because of the particular procedure being performed, or because of the proximity of two otherwise unrelated components to one another. For example, if the vehicle is raised for any reason, the exhaust can be inspected at the same time as the suspension and steering components.

The first step in this maintenance programme is to prepare yourself before the actual work begins. Read through all the Sections relevant to the work to be carried out, then make a list and gather all the parts and tools required. If a problem is encountered, seek advice from a parts specialist, or a dealer service department.

2   Intensive maintenance

1 If, from the time the vehicle is new, the routine maintenance schedule is followed closely, and frequent checks are made of fluid levels and high-wear items, as suggested throughout this manual, the engine will be kept in relatively good running condition, and the need for additional work will be minimised.

2 It is possible that there will be times when the engine is running poorly due to the lack of regular maintenance. This is even more likely if a used vehicle, which has not received regular and frequent maintenance checks, is purchased. In such cases, additional work may need to be carried out, outside of the regular maintenance intervals.

3 If engine wear is suspected, a compression test (refer to the relevant Part of Chapter 2) will provide valuable information regarding the overall performance of the main internal components. Such a test can be used as a basis to decide on the extent of the work to be carried out. If, for example, a compression test indicates serious internal engine wear, conventional maintenance as described in this Chapter will not greatly improve the performance of the engine, and may prove a waste of time and money, unless extensive overhaul work is carried out first.

4 The following series of operations are those most often required to improve the performance of a generally poor-running engine:

Primary operations

a) Clean, inspect and test the battery (See "Weekly checks" and Section 11, where applicable).

b) Check all the engine-related fluids (See "Weekly checks" and Section 7, where applicable).

c) Check the condition and tension of the auxiliary drivebelt (Section 22).

d) Renew the spark plugs (Section 23).

e) Inspect the distributor cap and rotor arm (see Chapter 5B).

f) Check the condition of the air filter, and renew if necessary (Section 24).

g) Check the fuel filter (Section 30).

h) Check the condition of all hoses, and check for fluid leaks (Section 10).

i) Check the exhaust gas emissions (Section 34).

5 If the above operations do not prove fully effective, carry out the following secondary operations:

Secondary operations

All items listed under "Primary operations", plus the following:

a) Check the charging system (see Chapter 5A).

b) Check the ignition system (see Chapter 5B).

c) Check the fuel system (see relevant Part of Chapter 4).

d) Renew the distributor cap and rotor arm (see Chapter 5B).

e) Renew the ignition HT leads (see Chapter 5B).

Every 5000 miles (7500 km)

3 Engine oil and filter renewal

1 Frequent oil and filter changes are the most important maintenance procedures which can be undertaken by the DIY owner. As engine oil ages, it becomes diluted and contaminated, which leads to premature engine wear.

2 Before starting this procedure, gather all the necessary tools and materials. Also make sure that you have plenty of clean rags and newspapers handy, to mop up any spills. Ideally, the engine oil should be warm, as it will drain better, and more built-up sludge will be removed with it. Take care, however, not to touch the exhaust or any other hot parts of the engine when working under the vehicle. To avoid any possibility of scalding, and to protect yourself from possible skin irritants and other harmful contaminants in used engine oils, it is advisable to wear gloves when carrying out this work.

3 Access to the underside of the vehicle will be greatly improved if it can be raised on a lift, driven onto ramps, or jacked up and supported on axle stands (see "Jacking and vehicle support"). Whichever method is

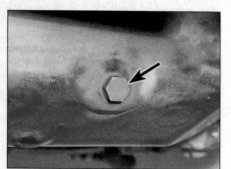

3.4 Engine oil drain plug (arrowed)

chosen, make sure that the vehicle remains level, or if it is at an angle, that the drain plug is at the lowest point. Where applicable, release the fasteners and remove the engine lower splash shield.

4 Using a socket and wrench or a ring spanner, slacken the drain plug about half a turn **(see illustration)**. Position the draining container under the drain plug, then remove the plug completely **(see Haynes Hint)**. Recover the sealing ring from the drain plug.

5 Allow some time for the old oil to drain, noting that it may be necessary to reposition the container as the oil flow slows to a trickle.

6 After all the oil has drained, wipe off the drain plug with a clean rag, and fit a new sealing washer. Clean the area around the drain plug opening, and refit the plug. Tighten the plug securely.

7 Move the container into position under the oil filter, which is located on the front of the cylinder block.

8 Using an oil filter removal tool if necessary, slacken the filter initially, then unscrew it by hand the rest of the way. Empty the oil in the filter into the container.

9 Use a clean rag to remove all oil, dirt and sludge from the filter sealing area on the engine. Check the old filter to make sure that the rubber sealing ring has not stuck to the engine. If it has, carefully remove it.

10 Apply a light coating of clean engine oil to the sealing ring on the new filter, then screw it into position on the engine. Tighten the filter firmly by hand only - **do not** use any tools.

11 Remove the old oil and all tools from under the car then lower the car to the ground (if applicable).

12 Remove the dipstick, then unscrew the oil filler cap from the cylinder head cover. Fill the engine, using the correct grade and type of oil (see "Lubricants and fluids"). An oil can spout or funnel may help to reduce spillage. Pour in half the specified quantity of oil first, then wait a few minutes for the oil to fall to the sump.

Continue adding oil a small quantity at a time until the level is up to the lower mark on the dipstick. Adding around 1.0 litre will bring the level up to the upper mark on the dipstick. Refit the filler cap.

13 Start the engine and run it for a few minutes; check for leaks around the oil filter seal and the sump drain plug. Note that there may be a few seconds delay before the oil pressure warning light goes out when the engine is started, as the oil circulates through the engine oil galleries and the new oil filter before the pressure builds up.

14 Switch off the engine, and wait a few minutes for the oil to settle in the sump once more. With the new oil circulated and the filter completely full, recheck the level on the dipstick, and add more oil as necessary.

15 Dispose of the used engine oil safely, with reference to "General repair procedures" in the Reference section of this manual.

Keep the drain plug pressed into the sump while unscrewing it by hand the last couple of turns. As the plug releases, move it away sharply so the stream of oil issuing from the sump runs into the container, not up your sleeve!

Every 10 000 miles (15 000 km)

4 Front brake pad check

1 Firmly apply the handbrake, loosen the front roadwheel bolts, then jack up the front of the car and support it securely on axle stands (see "*Jacking and vehicle support*"). Remove the front roadwheels.

2 For a comprehensive check, the brake pads should be removed and cleaned. The operation of the caliper can then also be checked, and the condition of the brake disc itself can be fully examined on both sides. Refer to Chapter 9 (**see Haynes Hint**).

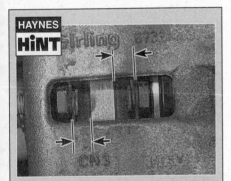

For a quick check, the thickness of the friction material on each brake pad can be measured through the aperture in the caliper body

3 If any pad's friction material is worn to the specified thickness or less, *all four pads must be renewed as a set.*

5 Pollen filter renewal

1 The pollen filter (where fitted) is located beneath the windscreen cowl panels; it is located on the left side on right-hand-drive models, and the right side on left-hand drive models (**see illustration**).
2 Release the filter cover fasteners by turning them as necessary (**see illustrations**).
3 Peel back the rubber seal from the relevant end of the top of the engine compartment bulkhead (**see illustration**).

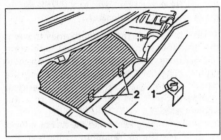

5.1 Pollen filter location - left-hand drive models

1 Fastener
2 Element retaining clips

Right-hand-drive models

4 Lift off the thermotronic sensor mounting bracket, and place it and the sensor to one side (**see illustration**).
5 Although not strictly necessary, access is improved by disconnecting the left-hand washer supply tube (**see illustration**). Place the tubing to one side, out of the way.

All models

6 Lift out the pollen filter cover panel (**see illustration**).
7 Release the two spring clips at the front or at the sides to release the element, and pivot the pollen filter upwards and out from its location (**see illustration**).
8 Wipe clean the filter housing, then fit the new filter. Clip the filter securely in position and refit the cover.
9 Refitting is a reversal of removal.

5.2a Pollen filter cover panel fasteners (arrowed)

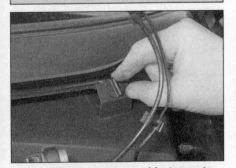

5.2b Turn the cover panel fasteners to release

5.3 Peel back the rubber seal from the top of the bulkhead

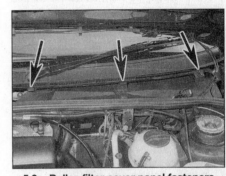

5.4 Lift off the thermotronic sensor and mounting bracket

5.5 Disconnect the windscreen washer tubing at the bulkhead

5.6 Lift out the pollen filter cover panel

5.7 Release the spring clips and lift out the pollen filter element

1A

Every 12 months

6 Lights and horn operation check

1 With the ignition switched on where necessary, check the operation of all exterior lights.
2 Check the brake lights with the help of an assistant, or by reversing up close to a reflective door. Make sure that all the rear lights are capable of operating independently, without affecting any of the other lights - for example, switch on as many rear lights as possible, then try the brake lights. If any unusual results are found, this is usually due to an earth fault at that rear light unit.
3 Again with the help of an assistant or using a reflective surface, check as far as possible that the headlights work on both main and dipped beam.
4 Replace any defective bulbs with reference to Chapter 12.

> **HAYNES HiNT**
> *Particularly on older vehicles, bulbs can stop working as a result of corrosion build-up on the bulb or its holder - fitting a new bulb may not cure the problem in this instance. When replacing any bulb, if you find any green or white-coloured powdery deposits, these should be cleaned off using emery cloth.*

5 Check the operation of all interior lights. Switch on the ignition, and check that all relevant warning lights come on as expected - the vehicle handbook should give details of these. Now start the engine, and check that the appropriate lights go out. When you are next driving at night, check that all the instrument panel and facia lighting works correctly. If any problems are found, refer to Chapter 12.

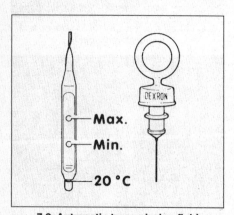

7.2 Automatic transmission fluid dipstick markings

6 Finally, choose an appropriate time of day to test the operation of the horn.

7 Automatic transmission fluid level check

Note: *Checking the fluid level by the DIY mechanic is only possible on the Type 096 transmission, which can be identified by the fact that it has a dipstick on the front of the transmission. Models from 1995 onwards may be fitted with the Type 01M transmission, on which fluid level checking requires the use of dedicated VW test equipment, and an involved procedure requiring accurate measurement of fluid temperature. In view of this, models fitted with the Type 01M transmission must be taken to a VW dealer for the fluid level to be checked.*

1 Take the vehicle on a short journey to warm the transmission up to normal operating temperature, then park the vehicle on level ground. The fluid level is checked using the dipstick located at the front of the engine compartment, on the front of the transmission.
2 With the engine idling and the selector lever in the "P" (Park) position, withdraw the dipstick from the tube, and wipe all the fluid from its end with a clean rag or paper towel. Insert the clean dipstick back into the tube as far as it will go, then withdraw it once more. Note the fluid level on the end of the dipstick; it should be between the "MAX" and "MIN" marks **(see illustration)**.

Note: *If the engine has not been warmed up, the fluid level should be at the 20°C mark.*

3 If topping-up is necessary, add the required quantity of the specified fluid to the transmission through the dipstick tube. Use a funnel with a fine mesh gauze, to avoid spillage and to ensure that no foreign matter enters the transmission. **Note:** *Never overfill the transmission so that the fluid level is above the upper mark.*

4 After topping-up, take the vehicle on a short run to distribute the fresh fluid, then recheck the level again, topping-up if necessary.

5 Always maintain the level between the two dipstick marks. If the level is allowed to fall below the lower mark, fluid starvation may result, which could lead to severe transmission damage. If the level is too high, the excess fluid may be ejected. In either case, an incorrect level will adversely affect the operation of the transmission.

6 Frequent need for topping-up indicates that there is a leak, which should be found and corrected before it becomes serious.

8 Airbag unit check

Where fitted, inspect the airbag(s) exterior condition checking for signs of damage or deterioration. If an airbag shows signs of obvious damage, it must be renewed (see Chapter 12).

9 Washer system(s) check

Check that each of the washer jet nozzles is clear, and that each nozzle provides a strong jet of washer fluid. The tailgate and headlight jets (where applicable) should be aimed to spray at a point slightly above the centre of the screen/headlight. The windscreen washer nozzles have two jets; aim one of the jets slightly above the centre of the screen and the other just below to ensure complete coverage of the screen. If necessary, adjust the jets using a pin.

10 Hose and fluid leak check

1 Visually inspect the engine joint faces, gaskets and seals for any signs of water or oil leaks. Pay particular attention to the areas around the camshaft cover, cylinder head, oil filter and sump joint faces. Bear in mind that, over a period of time, some very slight seepage from these areas is to be expected - what you are really looking for is any indication of a serious leak **(see Haynes Hint)**. Should a leak be found, renew the offending gasket or oil seal by referring to the appropriate Chapters in this manual.

A leak in the cooling system will usually show up as white- or rust-coloured deposits on the area adjoining the leak

2 Also check the security and condition of all the engine-related pipes and hoses. Ensure that all cable-ties or securing clips are in place and in good condition. Clips that are broken or missing can lead to chafing of the hoses, pipes or wiring, which could cause more serious problems in the future.

3 Carefully check the radiator hoses and heater hoses along their entire length. Renew any hose that is cracked, swollen or deteriorated. Cracks will show up better if the hose is squeezed. Pay close attention to the hose clips that secure the hoses to the cooling system components. Hose clips can pinch and puncture hoses, resulting in cooling system leaks.

4 Inspect all the cooling system components (hoses, joint faces etc.) for leaks. A leak in the cooling system will usually show up as white- or rust-coloured deposits on the area adjoining the leak. Where any problems of this nature are found on system components, renew the component or gasket with reference to Chapter 3.

5 Where applicable, inspect the automatic transmission fluid cooler hoses for leaks or deterioration.

6 With the vehicle raised, inspect the fuel tank and filler neck for punctures, cracks and other damage. The connection between the filler neck and tank is especially critical. Sometimes a rubber filler neck or connecting hose will leak due to loose retaining clamps or deteriorated rubber.

7 Carefully check all rubber hoses and metal fuel lines leading away from the fuel tank. Check for loose connections, deteriorated hoses, crimped lines, and other damage. Pay particular attention to the vent pipes and hoses, which often loop up around the filler neck and can become blocked or crimped. Follow the lines to the front of the vehicle, carefully inspecting them all the way. Renew damaged sections as necessary.

8 From within the engine compartment, check the security of all fuel hose attachments and pipe unions, and inspect the fuel hoses and vacuum hoses for kinks, chafing and deterioration.

9 Where applicable, check the condition of the power steering fluid hoses and pipes.

11 Battery electrolyte level check

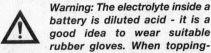

> ⚠ *Warning: The electrolyte inside a battery is diluted acid - it is a good idea to wear suitable rubber gloves. When topping-up, don't overfill the cells so that the electrolyte overflows. In the event of any spillage, rinse the electrolyte off without delay. Refit the cell covers and rinse the battery with copious quantities of clean water. Don't attempt to siphon out any excess electrolyte.*

1 Most models covered by this Manual were fitted with a maintenance-free battery as standard equipment. If the battery in your vehicle is marked "Freedom", "Maintenance-Free" or similar, no electrolyte level checking is required (the battery is often completely sealed, preventing any topping-up).

2 It is possible that a replacement battery may have been fitted which is not of maintenance-free type. These can be recognised by the presence of removable covers over the six battery cells - the battery casing is also sometimes translucent, so that the electrolyte level can be more easily checked. Make sure you do not have a maintenance-free battery before attempting to top up the electrolyte level.

3 Remove the cell covers and either look down inside the battery to see the level, or check the level using any markings provided on the battery casing. The electrolyte should at least cover the battery plates. If necessary, top up a little at a time with distilled (deionised) water until the level in all six cells is correct - don't fill the cells up to the brim. Wipe up any spillage, then refit the cell covers.

12 Hinge and lock lubrication

Lubricate the hinges of the bonnet, doors and tailgate with light general-purpose oil. Similarly, lubricate all latches, locks and lock strikers, and the door check straps. At the same time, check the security and operation of all the locks, adjusting them if necessary (see Chapter 11).

Lightly lubricate the bonnet release mechanism and cable with suitable grease.
Caution: Do not attempt to lubricate the steering lock.

13 Steering and suspension check

Front suspension and steering check

1 Raise the front of the vehicle, and securely support it on axle stands (see "*Jacking and vehicle support*").

2 Visually inspect the balljoint dust covers and the steering rack-and-pinion gaiters for splits, chafing or deterioration. Any wear of these components will cause loss of lubricant, together with dirt and water entry, resulting in rapid deterioration of the balljoints or steering gear.

3 On vehicles with power steering, check the fluid hoses for chafing or deterioration, and the pipe and hose unions for fluid leaks. Also check for signs of fluid leakage under pressure from the steering gear rubber gaiters, which would indicate failed fluid seals within the steering gear.

4 Grasp the roadwheel at the 12 o'clock and 6 o'clock positions, and try to rock it (see illustration). Very slight free play may be felt, but if the movement is appreciable, further investigation is necessary to determine the source. Continue rocking the wheel while an assistant depresses the footbrake. If the movement is now eliminated or significantly reduced, it is likely that the hub bearings are at fault. If the free play is still evident with the footbrake depressed, then there is wear in the suspension joints or mountings. Before condemning any components, however, check that the roadwheel bolts are tightened to the specified torque.

5 Now grasp the wheel at the 9 o'clock and 3 o'clock positions, and try to rock it as before. Any movement felt now may again be caused by wear in the hub bearings or the steering track-rod balljoints. If the inner or outer balljoint is worn, the visual movement will be obvious.

6 Using a large screwdriver or flat bar, check for wear in the suspension mounting bushes by levering between the relevant suspension component and its attachment point. Some movement is to be expected as the mountings are made of rubber, but excessive wear should be obvious. Also check the condition of any visible rubber bushes, looking for splits, cracks or contamination of the rubber.

7 With the car standing on its wheels, have an assistant turn the steering wheel back and forth about an eighth of a turn each way. There should be very little, if any, lost movement between the steering wheel and roadwheels. If this is not the case, closely observe the joints and mountings previously described, but in addition, check the steering column universal joints for wear, and the rack-and-pinion steering gear itself.

Suspension strut/ shock absorber check

8 Check for any signs of fluid leakage around the suspension strut/shock absorber body, or from the rubber gaiter around the piston rod. Should any fluid be noticed, the suspension strut/shock absorber is defective internally, and should be renewed.

13.4 Check for wear in the hub bearings by grasping the wheel and trying to rock it

1A

14.1 Check the condition of the driveshaft gaiters (arrowed)

Note: *Suspension struts/shock absorbers should always be renewed in pairs on the same axle.*

9 The efficiency of the suspension strut/shock absorber may be checked by bouncing the vehicle at each corner. Generally speaking, the body will return to its normal position and stop after being depressed. If it rises and returns on a rebound, the suspension strut/shock absorber is probably suspect. Examine also the suspension strut/shock absorber upper and lower mountings for any signs of wear.

14 Driveshaft gaiter and CV joint check

1 With the vehicle raised and securely supported on stands (see *"Jacking and vehicle support"*), turn the steering onto full lock, then slowly rotate the roadwheel. Inspect the condition of the outer constant velocity (CV) joint rubber gaiters, squeezing the gaiters to open out the folds. Check for signs of cracking, splits or deterioration of the rubber, which may allow the grease to escape, and lead to water and grit entry into the joint. Also check the security and condition of the retaining clips. Repeat these checks on the inner CV joints **(see illustration)**. If any damage or deterioration is found, the gaiters should be renewed (see Chapter 8).
2 At the same time, check the general condition of the CV joints themselves by first

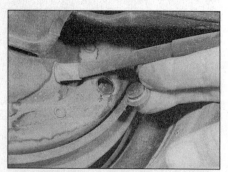

18.2 Remove the rubber plug and check the brake friction material thickness through the backplate aperture

holding the driveshaft and attempting to rotate the wheel. Repeat this check by holding the inner joint and attempting to rotate the driveshaft. Any appreciable movement indicates wear in the joints, wear in the driveshaft splines, or a loose driveshaft retaining nut.

15 Braking system check

1 Starting under the bonnet, examine the brake fluid reservoir and master cylinder for leaks. When a brake fluid leak occurs, it is normal to find blistered or wrinkled paint in the area of the leak. Check the metal pipes from the master cylinder for damage, and check the brake pressure regulator, servo/ABS unit and fluid unions for leaks.
2 With the vehicle raised and securely supported on axle stands (see *"Jacking and vehicle support"*), first inspect each front brake caliper. In particular, check the flexible hose leading to the caliper for signs of damage or leaks, especially where the hose enters the metal end fitting. Make sure that the hose is not twisted or kinked, and that it cannot come into contact with any other components when the steering is on full lock.
3 From the caliper, trace the metal brake pipes back along the car. Again, look for leaks from the fluid unions or signs of damage, but additionally check the pipes for signs of corrosion. Make sure the pipes are securely located by the clips provided on the vehicle underside.
4 At the rear of the vehicle, inspect each rear brake and its flexible hose, where applicable. Examine the handbrake cable, tracing it back from each rear brake and checking for frayed cables or other damage. Lubricate the handbrake cable guides, pivots and other moving parts with general-purpose grease.
5 If any damage is found, refer to Chapter 9 for further information.

16 Exhaust system check

1 With the engine cold (at least an hour after the vehicle has been driven), check the complete exhaust system from the engine to the end of the tailpipe. The exhaust system is most easily checked with the vehicle raised on a hoist, or suitably supported on axle stands (see *"Jacking and vehicle support"*), so that the exhaust components are readily visible and accessible.
2 Check the exhaust pipes and connections for evidence of leaks, severe corrosion and damage. Make sure that all brackets and mountings are in good condition, and that all relevant nuts and bolts are tight. Leakage at any of the joints or in other parts of the system will usually show up as a black sooty stain in the vicinity of the leak.

3 Rattles and other noises can often be traced to the exhaust system, especially the brackets and mountings. Try to move the pipes and silencers. If the components are able to come into contact with the body or suspension parts, secure the system with new mountings. Otherwise separate the joints (if possible) and twist the pipes as necessary to provide additional clearance.

17 Rear brake pad check - models with rear disc brakes

1 Chock the front wheels, then jack up the rear of the vehicle and support it on axle stands (see *"Jacking and vehicle support"*).
2 For a quick check, the thickness of friction material remaining on each brake pad can be seen through the rear wheel. If preferred, remove the rear wheels to make inspection easier. If any pad's friction material is worn to the specified thickness or less, all four pads must be renewed as a set.
3 For a comprehensive check, the brake pads should be removed and cleaned. This will permit the operation of the caliper to be checked, and the condition of the brake disc itself to be fully examined on both sides. Refer to Chapter 9 for further information.

18 Rear brake shoe check - models with rear drum brakes

1 Chock the front wheels, then jack up the rear of the vehicle, and support it securely on axle stands (see *"Jacking and vehicle support"*).
2 For a quick check, the thickness of friction material remaining on one of the brake shoes can be observed through the hole in the brake backplate which is exposed by prising out the sealing grommet **(see illustration)**. If a rod of the same diameter as the specified minimum friction material thickness is placed against the shoe friction material, the amount of wear can be assessed. A torch or inspection light will probably be required. If the friction material on any shoe is worn down to the specified minimum thickness or less, all four shoes must be renewed as a set.
3 For a comprehensive check, the brake drum should be removed and cleaned. This will allow the wheel cylinders to be checked, and the condition of the brake drum itself to be fully examined (see Chapter 9).

19 Automatic transmission fault code check

1 This check is part of the manufacturer's maintenance schedule, and involves "interrogating" the transmission control unit using special dedicated test equipment.

Such testing will allow the test equipment to read any fault codes stored in the electronic control unit memory.

2 Unless a fault is suspected, this test is not essential, although it should be noted that it is recommended by the manufacturers.

20 Headlight beam alignment check

Accurate adjustment of the headlight beam is only possible using optical beam-setting equipment, and this work should therefore be carried out by a VW dealer or service station with the necessary facilities. Headlight alignment is checked as part of the MoT test.

Basic adjustments can be carried out in an emergency, and further details are given in Chapter 12.

21 Road test

Instruments and electrical equipment

1 Check the operation of all instruments and electrical equipment.
2 Make sure that all instruments read correctly, and switch on all electrical equipment in turn, to check that it functions properly.

Steering and suspension

3 Check for any abnormalities in the steering, suspension, handling or road "feel".
4 Drive the vehicle, and check that there are no unusual vibrations or noises.
5 Check that the steering feels positive, with no excessive "sloppiness", or roughness, and check for any suspension noises when cornering and driving over bumps.

Drivetrain

6 Check the performance of the engine, clutch (where applicable), transmission and driveshafts.
7 Listen for any unusual noises from the engine, clutch and transmission.
8 Make sure the engine runs smoothly at idle, and there is no hesitation on accelerating.
9 Check that, where applicable, the clutch action is smooth and progressive, that the drive is taken up smoothly, and that the pedal travel is not excessive. Also listen for any noises when the clutch pedal is depressed.
10 On manual transmission models, check that all gears can be engaged smoothly without noise, and that the gear lever action is not abnormally vague or "notchy".
11 On automatic transmission models, make sure that all gearchanges occur smoothly, without snatching, and without an increase in engine speed between changes. Check that all the gear positions can be selected with the vehicle at rest. If any problems are found, they should be referred to a VW dealer.

12 Listen for a metallic clicking sound from the front of the vehicle, as the vehicle is driven slowly in a circle with the steering on full-lock. Carry out this check in both directions. If a clicking noise is heard, this indicates wear in a driveshaft joint, in which case renew the joint if necessary.

Braking system

13 Make sure that the vehicle does not pull to one side when braking, and that the wheels do not lock prematurely when braking hard.
14 Check that there is no vibration through the steering when braking.
15 Check that the handbrake operates correctly without excessive movement of the lever, and that it holds the vehicle stationary on a slope.
16 Test the operation of the brake servo unit as follows. With the engine off, depress the footbrake four or five times to exhaust the vacuum. Hold the brake pedal depressed, then start the engine. As the engine starts, there should be a noticeable "give" in the brake pedal as vacuum builds up. Allow the engine to run for at least two minutes, and then switch it off. If the brake pedal is depressed now, it should be possible to detect a hiss from the servo as the pedal is depressed. After about four or five applications, no further hissing should be heard, and the pedal should feel considerably harder.

1A

Every 20 000 miles (30 000 km)

22 Auxiliary drivebelt check and renewal

Checking

1 Disconnect the battery negative cable and position it away from the terminal. **Note:** *If the vehicle has a security-coded radio, check that you have a copy of the code number before disconnecting the battery. Refer to your VW dealer if in doubt.*
2 Park the vehicle on a level surface, apply the handbrake and chock the rear wheels. Loosen the right-hand front wheel bolts.
3 Raise the front of the vehicle, rest it securely on axle stands (see "*Jacking and vehicle support*") and remove the right-hand front roadwheel.
4 Turn the steering to full right-hand lock. Where applicable, remove the screws and clips, and lower the undertray away from the engine bay.

5 Using a socket and wrench on the crankshaft sprocket bolt, rotate the crankshaft so that the full length of the auxiliary drivebelts can be examined. Depending on the level of equipment fitted, there may be as many as three drivebelts to be checked. Look for cracks, splitting and fraying on the surface of the belt; check also for signs of glazing (shiny patches) and separation of the belt plies. If damage or wear is visible, the belt should be renewed.
6 Check the drivebelt tension by pressing on the belt at a point midway between two pulleys. Depending on the type of belt, it should move by approximately 5 to 10 mm. If the drivebelt appears excessively taut or slack, refer to Chapter 2A and adjust the belt tension.

Renewal

7 For details of auxiliary drivebelt renewal, refer to the relevant part of Chapter 2A.

23 Spark plug renewal

1 The correct functioning of the spark plugs is vital for the correct running and efficiency of the engine. It is essential that the plugs fitted are appropriate for the engine (a suitable type is specified at the beginning of this Chapter). If this type is used and the engine is in good condition, the spark plugs should not need attention between scheduled replacement intervals. Spark plug cleaning is rarely necessary, and should not be attempted unless specialised equipment is available, as damage can easily be caused to the firing ends.
2 Before removing the spark plugs, allow the engine time to cool.
3 If the marks on the original-equipment spark plug (HT) leads cannot be seen, mark the leads "1" to "4", to correspond to the cylinder the lead serves (No 1 cylinder is at the

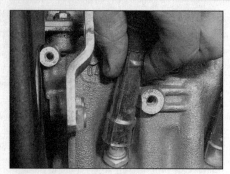

23.3 Pull the HT leads from the plugs by gripping the end fitting, not the lead, or the lead connection may be fractured

23.4 Using a clean brush to remove the dirt from the spark plug recesses

23.5 Removing a spark plug (engine code 2E shown)

timing belt end of the engine). Where metal heat shields are fitted to the lead end fittings, take care not to burn your hands if the engine is still warm. Pull the leads from the plugs by gripping the end fitting, not the lead, otherwise the lead connection may be fractured **(see illustration)**.

4 It is advisable to remove the dirt from the spark plug recesses using a clean brush, vacuum cleaner or compressed air before removing the plugs, to prevent dirt dropping into the cylinders **(see illustration)**.

5 Unscrew the plugs using a spark plug spanner, suitable box spanner or a deep socket and extension bar. Keep the socket aligned with the spark plug - if it is forcibly moved to one side, the ceramic insulator may be broken off **(see illustration)**. As each plug is removed, examine it as follows.

6 Examination of the spark plugs will give a good indication of the condition of the engine. If the insulator nose of the spark plug is clean and white, with no deposits, this is indicative of a weak mixture or too hot a plug (a hot plug transfers heat away from the electrode slowly, a cold plug transfers heat away quickly).

7 If the tip and insulator nose are covered with hard black-looking deposits, then this is indicative that the mixture is too rich. Should the plug be black and oily, then it is likely that the engine is fairly worn, as well as the mixture being too rich.

8 If the insulator nose is covered with light tan to greyish-brown deposits, then the mixture is correct and it is likely that the engine is in good condition.

9 The spark plug electrode gap is of considerable importance as, if it is too large or too small, the size of the spark and its efficiency will be seriously impaired. **Note:** *Spark plugs with multiple earth electrodes are becoming an increasingly common fitment, especially to vehicles equipped with catalytic converters. Unless there is clear information to the contrary, no attempt should be made to adjust the plug gap on a spark plug with more than one earth electrode.*

10 To set the gap, measure it with a feeler blade and then bend open, or closed, the outer plug electrode until the correct gap is achieved. The centre electrode should never be bent, as this may crack the insulator and cause plug failure, if nothing worse. If using feeler blades, the gap is correct when the appropriate-size blade is a firm sliding fit **(see illustration)**.

11 Special spark plug electrode gap adjusting tools are available from most motor accessory shops, or from some spark plug manufacturers.

12 Before fitting the spark plugs, check that

the threaded connector sleeves are tight, and that the plug exterior surfaces and threads are clean. It's often difficult to screw in new spark plugs without cross-threading them - this can be avoided using a piece of rubber hose **(see Haynes Hint)**.

13 Remove the rubber hose (if used), and tighten the plug to the specified torque using the spark plug socket and a torque wrench. If a torque wrench is not available, tighten the plug by hand until it just seats, then tighten it by no more than a quarter of a turn further with the plug socket and handle. Refit the remaining spark plugs in the same manner.

14 Connect the HT leads in their correct order, and refit any components removed for access.

24 Air filter renewal

1 Prise open the spring clips and lift off the air cleaner top cover. **Caution: On certain models, the airflow meter is integral with the air cleaner top cover. Handle the airflow meter very carefully, as it easily damaged.** The cover need only be lifted to allow the element to be withdrawn, but depending on the system type, it may be necessary to detach the inlet duct and/or associated vacuum or fuel system components.

2 Lift out the filter element **(see illustration)**.

23.10 Adjusting a spark plug electrode gap

HAYNES HiNT

It is very often difficult to insert spark plugs into their holes without cross-threading them. To avoid this possibility, fit a short length of ⅝ inch internal diameter rubber hose over the end of the spark plug. The flexible hose acts as a universal joint to help align the plug with the plug hole. Should the plug begin to cross-thread, the hose will slip on the spark plug, preventing thread damage to the aluminium cylinder head

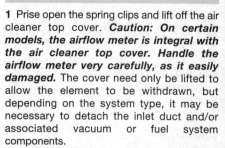

24.2 Lifting out the air cleaner element

3 Remove any debris that may have collected inside the air cleaner.

4 Fit a new air filter element in position, noting any direction-of-fitting markings and ensuring that the edges are securely seated.

5 Refit the air cleaner top cover and snap the retaining clips into position.

25 Timing belt condition and tension check

1 Refer to Chapter 2A and remove the timing belt covers for access to the timing belt

2 Examine the belt for signs of cracking or splitting, especially around the "roots" of the teeth, and for signs of fraying or separation of the belt plies. If any damage is noted, the belt should be renewed as described in Chapter 2A.

3 If there is any sign that the belt is being contaminated with oil or other fluid, the belt should be changed and the source of the leak found and fixed, otherwise the new belt will quickly go the same way.

4 The timing belt tension can be checked by twisting the belt at a point midway along its longest run. It should just be possible to turn the belt through 90° (quarter-turn). The belt tension is critical - if it is slack, there is a danger that the belt might jump a tooth, while a belt which is too tight might wear prematurely.

26 Manual transmission oil level check

1 Park the car on a level surface. The oil level must be checked before the car is driven, or at least 5 minutes after the engine has been switched off. If the oil is checked immediately after driving the car, some of the oil will remain distributed around the transmission components, resulting in an inaccurate level reading.

2 Where applicable, remove the retaining clips and screws, then lower the undertray away from the engine bay.

3 Wipe clean the area around the filler/level plug, which is situated on the front of the differential casing (**see illustration**). A special hexagonal socket (or a large Allen key) will be required to remove the plug, which will probably be quite tight.

4 The oil level should reach the lower edge of the filler/level hole. A certain amount of oil will have gathered behind the filler/level plug, and will trickle out when it is removed; this does **not** necessarily indicate that the level is correct. To ensure that a true level is established, wait until the initial trickle has stopped, then add oil as necessary until a trickle of new oil can be seen emerging. The level will be correct when the flow ceases; use only good-quality oil of the specified type (**see illustration**).

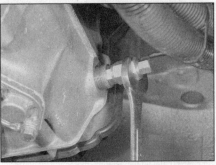

26.3 Manual transmission oil filler/level plug removal

5 Filling the transmission with oil is an extremely awkward operation; above all, allow plenty of time for the oil level to settle properly before checking it. If a large amount is added to the transmission, and a large amount flows out on checking the level, refit the filler/level plug; take the vehicle on a short journey so that the new oil is distributed fully around the transmission components, then recheck the level when it has settled again.

6 If the transmission has been overfilled so that oil flows out when the filler/level plug is removed, check that the car is completely level (front-to-rear and side-to-side), and allow the surplus to drain off into a suitable container.

7 When the level is correct, fit a new sealing washer to the filler/level plug. Refit the plug, tightening it securely, and wipe off any spilt oil. Where applicable, refit the engine bay undertray, securing it in position with the retaining clips and screws.

27 Transmission - general maintenance

1 Raise the front of the vehicle and support on axle stands (see "*Jacking and vehicle support*"). Alternatively, drive the car onto ramps.

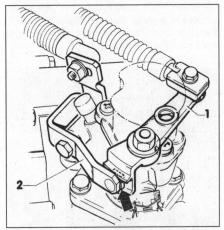

27.3 Lubrication point (arrowed) for the gearchange lever (1) and relay lever (2)

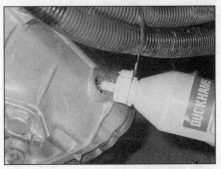

26.4 Topping-up manual transmission oil

2 Inspect around the transmission for any sign of leaks or damage. In particular, check the area around the driveshaft oil/fluid seals for leakage. Slight seepage should not be of great concern, but a serious leak should be investigated further, with reference to the relevant Part of Chapter 7.

Manual transmission

3 Periodically lubricate the gearchange/relay lever with grease at the points indicated (**see illustration**).

4 Although not included in the maintenance schedule by the manufacturers, it is a good idea to drain and renew the manual transmission oil on a regular basis. The frequency with which this needs to be carried out can be left to the individual, but it is certainly advisable on a vehicle that has covered a high mileage.

5 The transmission oil drain plug is located in the base of the differential housing (**see illustration**) - like the oil filler/level plug, a special hexagonal socket (or large Allen key) will be required for removal.

6 When refilling the transmission, remember that the vehicle must be level for the oil level to be correct (see Section 26).

Automatic transmission

7 Check the security and condition of the wiring and wiring plugs on the transmission housing.

8 Check for any sign of leakage from the transmission fluid filter on top of the transmission.

1A

27.5 Manual transmission oil drain plug

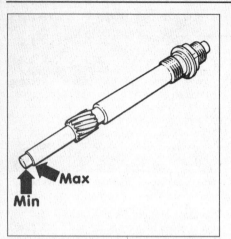

27.10 Differential housing oil level markings on the base of the speedometer driveshaft

9 The oil in the differential housing of the automatic transmission is separate from the transmission, and is "filled for life". It therefore does not normally require its oil to be renewed.

10 However, the differential oil/fluid level should be checked by disconnecting the speedometer drive cable, and unscrewing and removing the cable drivegear unit from the differential housing. The oil/fluid level must be between the "MAX" and "MIN" marks on the base of the speedometer driveshaft **(see illustration)**. Wipe the driveshaft clean, reinsert it into the differential housing, then withdraw it and observe the level. If required, the oil/fluid level can be topped up through the speedometer drive aperture, but take care not to overfill. The difference between the "MAX" and "MIN" marks is only 0.1 litres.

11 Refit the drivegear and reconnect the cable to complete.

28 Underbody protection check

Raise and support the vehicle on axle stands (see "*Jacking and vehicle support*"). Using an electric torch or lead light, inspect the entire underside of the vehicle, paying particular attention to the wheel arches. Look for any damage to the flexible underbody coating, which may crack or flake off with age, leading to corrosion. Also check that the wheel arch liners (where fitted) are securely attached with any clips provided - if they come loose, dirt may get in behind the liners and defeat their purpose. If there is any damage to the underseal, or any corrosion, it should be repaired before the damage gets too serious.

Every 40 000 miles (60 000 km)

29 Automatic transmission fluid and filter renewal

1 The Type 096 automatic transmission is not fitted with a drain plug, so the transmission fluid must be drawn out through the dipstick tube using a special adapter.

2 The Type 01M automatic transmission can be drained, but the fluid level cannot be accurately established without the use of dedicated VW test equipment (see Section 7).

3 For the above reasons, it is recommended that a VW dealer carry out automatic transmission fluid renewal.

30 Fuel filter renewal

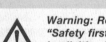

⚠ **Warning: Refer to the notes in "Safety first!", and follow them implicitly. Petrol is a highly-dangerous and volatile liquid, and the precautions necessary when handling it cannot be overstressed.**

1 The fuel filter is situated underneath the rear of the vehicle, on the right-hand side in front of the fuel tank **(see illustration)**. To gain access to the filter, chock the front wheels, then jack up the rear of the vehicle and support it on axle stands (see "*Jacking and vehicle support*").

2 Depressurise the fuel system with reference to the relevant Part of Chapter 4.

3 Release the retaining clips and remove the protective undershield to allow access to the filter.

4 If you have them, fit hose clamps to the filter inlet and outlet hoses. These are not essential, but even with the system depressurised, there will still be an amount of petrol in the pipes (and the old filter), and this will siphon out when the pipes are disconnected. Even with hose clamps fitted, the old filter will contain some fuel, so have some rags ready to soak up any spillage.

5 Release the hose clips and detach the hoses from the filter. If crimp-type clips are used, discard them and fit proper petrol pipe clips when reassembling. Similarly, if the fuel hoses show any sign of perishing or cracking, particularly at the hose ends or where the hose enters the metal end fitting, renew the hoses.

6 Before removing the filter, note any direction-of-flow markings on the filter body, and check against the new filter - the arrow should point towards the front of the vehicle, away from the fuel tank.

30.1 Fuel filter location

7 Undo the retaining clamp screw and remove the old filter.

8 Fit the new filter into position, with the flow marking arrow pointing towards the front of the vehicle, and secure with the retaining clamp.

9 Reconnect the fuel hoses using new clips if necessary. Ensure that no dirt is allowed to enter the hoses or filter connections. Release the hose clamps.

10 Start the engine (there may be a delay as the system re-pressurises and the new filter fills with fuel). Let the engine run for several minutes while you check the filter hose connections for leaks.

11 Fit the protective undershield and secure with the retaining clips, then lower the vehicle to the ground.

⚠ **Warning: Dispose safely of the old filter; it will be highly flammable, and may explode if thrown on a fire.**

31 Timing belt renewal

Refer to Chapter 2A.

Note: *VW specify a timing belt renewal interval of 60 000 miles (90 000 km). However, if the vehicle is used mainly for short journeys or a lot of stop-start driving, we recommend that this shorter interval is adhered to. The actual belt renewal interval is very much up to the individual owner but, bearing in mind that severe engine damage will result if the belt breaks in use, we recommend you err on the side of caution.*

Every 2 years (regardless of mileage)

32 Coolant renewal

Cooling system draining

 Warning: Wait until the engine is cold before starting this procedure. Do not allow antifreeze to come in contact with your skin, or with the painted surfaces of the vehicle. Rinse off spills immediately with plenty of water. Never leave antifreeze lying around in an open container, or in a puddle in the driveway or on the garage floor. Children and pets are attracted by its sweet smell, but antifreeze can be fatal if ingested.

1 With the engine completely cold, cover the expansion tank cap with a wad of rag, and slowly turn the cap anti-clockwise to relieve the pressure in the cooling system (a hissing sound will normally be heard). Wait until any pressure remaining in the system is released, then continue to turn the cap until it can be removed.

2 Where necessary, release the fasteners and remove the engine lower splash shield. Position a suitable container beneath the radiator bottom hose connection, then release the retaining clip and ease the hose from the radiator stub. If the hose joint has not been disturbed for some time, it will be necessary to gently manipulate the hose to break the joint. Do not use excessive force, or the radiator stub could be damaged. Allow the coolant to drain into the container.

3 If the coolant has been drained for a reason other than renewal, then provided it is clean and less than two years old, it can be re-used, though this is not recommended.

4 Once all the coolant has drained, reconnect the hose to the radiator and secure it in position with the retaining clip.

Cooling system flushing

5 If coolant renewal has been neglected, or if the antifreeze mixture has become diluted, then in time, the cooling system may gradually lose efficiency, as the coolant passages become restricted due to rust, scale deposits, and other sediment. Flushing the system clean can restore the cooling system efficiency.

6 The radiator should be flushed independently of the engine, to avoid unnecessary contamination.

Radiator flushing

7 To flush the radiator, disconnect the top and bottom hoses and any other relevant hoses from the radiator, with reference to Chapter 3.

8 Insert a garden hose into the radiator top inlet. Direct a flow of clean water through the radiator, and continue flushing until clean water emerges from the radiator bottom outlet.

9 If after a reasonable period, the water still does not run clear, the radiator can be flushed with a good proprietary cooling system cleaning agent. It is important that their manufacturer's instructions are followed carefully. If the contamination is particularly bad, insert the hose in the radiator bottom outlet, and reverse-flush the radiator.

Engine flushing

10 To flush the engine, remove the thermostat as described in Chapter 3, then temporarily refit the thermostat cover.

11 With the top and bottom hoses disconnected from the radiator, insert a garden hose into the radiator top hose. Direct a clean flow of water through the engine, and continue flushing until clean water emerges from the radiator bottom hose.

12 On completion of flushing, refit the thermostat and reconnect the hoses with reference to Chapter 3.

Cooling system filling

13 Before attempting to fill the cooling system, make sure that all hoses and clips are in good condition, and that the clips are tight. Note that an antifreeze mixture must be used all year round, to prevent corrosion of the engine components (see following sub-Section).

14 Remove the expansion tank filler cap, and fill the system by slowly pouring the coolant into the expansion tank to prevent airlocks from forming.

15 If the coolant is being renewed, begin by pouring in a couple of litres of water, followed by the correct quantity of antifreeze, then top-up with more water.

16 Once the level in the expansion tank starts to rise, squeeze the radiator top and bottom hoses to help expel any trapped air in the system. Once all the air is expelled, top-up coolant level to the "MAX" mark and refit the expansion tank cap.

17 Start the engine and run it until it reaches normal operating temperature, then stop the engine and allow it to cool.

18 Check for leaks, particularly around disturbed components. Check the coolant level in the expansion tank, and top-up if necessary. Note that the system must be cold before an accurate level is indicated in the expansion tank. If the expansion tank cap is removed while the engine is still warm, cover the cap with a thick cloth, and unscrew the cap slowly to gradually relieve the system pressure (a hissing sound will normally be heard). Wait until any pressure remaining in the system is released, then continue to turn the cap until it can be removed.

Antifreeze mixture

19 The antifreeze should always be renewed at the specified intervals. This is necessary not only to maintain the antifreeze properties, but also to prevent corrosion which would otherwise occur as the corrosion inhibitors become progressively less effective.

20 Always use ethylene-glycol-based antifreeze suitable for use in mixed-metal cooling systems. The quantity of antifreeze and levels of protection are indicated in the Specifications.

21 Before adding antifreeze, the cooling system should be completely drained, preferably flushed, and all hoses checked for condition and security.

22 After filling with antifreeze, a label should be attached to the expansion tank, stating the type and concentration of antifreeze used, and the date installed. Any subsequent topping-up should be made with the same type and concentration of antifreeze.

23 Do not use engine antifreeze in the windscreen/tailgate washer system, as it will cause damage to the vehicle paintwork.

33 Brake/clutch fluid renewal

 Warning: Brake hydraulic fluid can harm your eyes and damage painted surfaces, so use extreme caution when handling and pouring it. Do not use fluid that has been standing open for some time, as it absorbs moisture from the air. Excess moisture can cause a dangerous loss of braking effectiveness.

1 The procedure is similar to that for the bleeding of the hydraulic system as described in Chapter 9. The brake fluid reservoir should be emptied by siphoning, using a clean poultry baster or similar before starting, and allowance should be made for the old fluid to be expelled when bleeding a section of the circuit.

2 Working as described in Chapter 9, open the first bleed screw in the sequence, and pump the brake pedal gently until nearly all the old fluid has been emptied from the master cylinder reservoir.

3 Top-up to the "MAX" level with new fluid, and continue pumping until only the new fluid remains in the reservoir, and new fluid can be seen emerging from the bleed screw. Tighten the screw, and top the reservoir level up to the "MAX" level line.

 Old hydraulic fluid is often much darker in colour than the new, making it easy to distinguish the two.

1A

4 Work through all the remaining bleed screws in the sequence until new fluid can be seen at all of them. Be careful to keep the master cylinder reservoir topped-up to above the "MIN" level at all times, or air may enter the system and greatly increase the length of the task.

5 When the operation is complete, check that all bleed screws are securely tightened, and that their dust caps are refitted. Wash off all traces of spilt fluid, and recheck the fluid level.

6 Check the operation of the brakes before taking the car on the road.

34 Exhaust emissions check

This check is part of the manufacturer's maintenance schedule, and involves testing the exhaust emissions using an exhaust gas analyser. Unless a fault is suspected, this test is not essential, although it should be noted that it is recommended by the manufacturers. In the majority of cases, adjusting the idle speed and mixture is either not possible, or requires access to dedicated VW test equipment (the exception to this is the early Digifant system - see Chapter 4B). Exhaust emissions testing is included as part of the MoT test.

Chapter 1 Part B:
Routine maintenance & servicing - diesel models

Contents

Degrees of difficulty

| Easy, suitable for novice with little experience | Fairly easy, suitable for beginner with some experience | Fairly difficult, suitable for competent DIY mechanic | Difficult, suitable for experienced DIY mechanic | Very difficult, suitable for expert DIY or professional |

Lubricants and fluids

Refer to end of *"Weekly checks"*

Capacities

Engine oil (including filter)

All engines . . . .   4.5 litres

Cooling system (approximate)

Without air conditioning . . . .   5.0 litres
With air conditioning . . . .   5.6 litres

Transmission

All models (approximate) . . . .   2.0 litres

Power-assisted steering

All models (approximate) . . . .   1.5 litres

Fuel tank

All models (approximate) . . . .   70 litres

Washer reservoirs

Models with headlight washers . . . .   8.0 litres
Models without headlight washers . . . .   5.0 litres

Engine

Oil filter:
   Engine codes AAZ and 1Z . . . .   Champion C150
   Engine code AHU . . . .   Champion C122
   Engine code AFN . . . .   Champion type not available

Cooling system

Antifreeze mixture:
   40% antifreeze . . . .   Protection down to -25°C
   50% antifreeze . . . .   Protection down to -35°C
Note: *Refer to antifreeze manufacturer for latest recommendations.*

Fuel system

Air filter element:
   Engine code AHU . . . .   Champion U567
   All other engines . . . .   Champion U572
Fuel filter:
   Engine codes AAZ and 1Z . . . .   Champion L114
   All other engines . . . .   Champion type not available
Idle speed (engine code AAZ) . . . .   900 ± 30 rpm

Brakes

Brake pad minimum thickness (including backing plate) . . . .   7.0 mm
Brake shoe friction material minimum thickness . . . .   2.5 mm

Torque wrench settings

	Nm	lbf ft
Roadwheel bolts	110	81
Sump drain plug	30	22
Transmission filler/level and drain plugs	25	18

The maintenance intervals in this manual are provided with the assumption that you, not the dealer, will be carrying out the work. These are the minimum intervals recommended by us for vehicles driven daily.

If you wish to keep your vehicle in peak condition at all times, you may wish to perform some of these procedures more often. We encourage frequent maintenance, since it enhances the efficiency, performance and resale value of your vehicle.

When the vehicle is new, it should be serviced by a dealer service department, in order to preserve the factory warranty.

Every 250 miles (400 km) or weekly
☐ Refer to *"Weekly checks"*

Every 5000 miles (7500 km)
☐ Renew the engine oil and filter (Section 3)

Every 10 000 miles (15 000 km)
☐ Check the front brake pad thickness (Section 4)
☐ Renew the pollen filter element (Section 5)
☐ Drain water from fuel filter (Section 6)

Every 12 months
Note: *If the vehicle is covering less than 10 000 miles (15 000 km) a year, also carry out the tasks listed above*
☐ Check the operation of all lights and horn (Section 7)
☐ Check the condition of the airbag unit(s) (Section 8)
☐ Check the operation of the washer system(s) (Section 9)
☐ Check all underbonnet components and hoses for fluid leaks (Section 10)
☐ Check the battery electrolyte level - where applicable (Section 11)
☐ Lubricate all hinges, locks and door check straps (Section 12)
☐ Check the steering and suspension components for condition and security (Section 13)
☐ Check the condition of the driveshaft gaiters (Section 14)
☐ Check the braking system for leaks and damage (Section 15)
☐ Check the condition of the exhaust system and its mountings (Section 16)
☐ Check the rear brake shoe lining thickness (Section 17)
☐ Check the idle speed (Section 18)
☐ Check the headlight beam adjustment (Section 19)
☐ Carry out a road test (Section 20)

Every 20 000 miles (30 000 km)
Note: *If the vehicle is covering more than 20 000 miles (30 000 km) a year, also carry out all the operations described above*
☐ Check the condition of the auxiliary drivebelt(s), and renew if necessary (Section 21)
☐ Renew the air filter element (Section 22)
☐ Check the timing belt condition and tension (Section 23)
☐ Renew the fuel filter (Section 24)
☐ Check the transmission oil level (Section 25)
☐ Check the transmission for leaks and damage (Section 26)
☐ Check the underbody protection for damage (Section 27)

Every 40 000 miles (60 000 km)
☐ Renew the timing belt (and tensioner on all engines except code AAZ) (Section 28)
Note: *VW specify a timing belt renewal interval of 60 000 miles (90 000 km). However, if the vehicle is used mainly for short journeys or a lot of stop-start driving, we recommend that this shorter interval is adhered to. The actual belt renewal interval is very much up to the individual owner but, bearing in mind that severe engine damage will result if the belt breaks in use, we recommend you err on the side of caution.*

Every 2 years (regardless of mileage)
☐ Renew the coolant (Section 29)
☐ Renew the brake fluid (Section 30)
☐ Check the exhaust emissions (Section 31)

1B

Underbonnet view of later diesel

1 Engine oil filler cap
2 Engine oil dipstick
3 Brake fluid reservoir
4 Fuel filter
5 Air cleaner housing
6 Alternator
7 Coolant expansion tank
8 Washer fluid reservoir
9 Suspension strut upper
  mounting
10 Pollen filter cover
11 Wiper motor
12 Intercooler air hoses
13 Glow plug control unit
14 Battery
15 Power steering fluid
   reservoir
16 Radiator top hose

Front underbody view

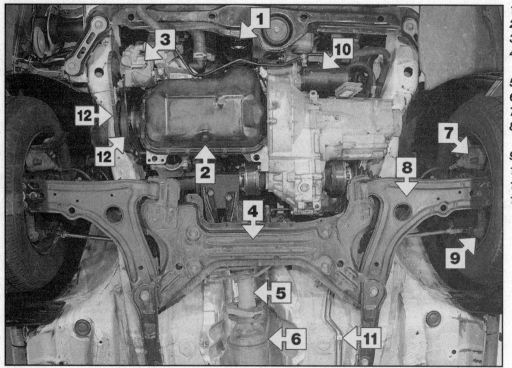

1 Engine oil filter
2 Sump drain plug
3 Power steering pump
4 Front suspension
  subframe
5 Exhaust front pipe
6 Catalytic converter
7 Front brake caliper
8 Front suspension lower
  arm
9 Track rod balljoint
10 Starter motor
11 Brake pipes
12 Auxiliary drivebelts

Rear underbody view

1 Fuel tank
2 Exhaust tailpipe
3 Rear axle assembly
4 Fuel pipes
5 Handbrake cable
6 Rear brake pressure regulating valve
7 Suspension strut lower mounting

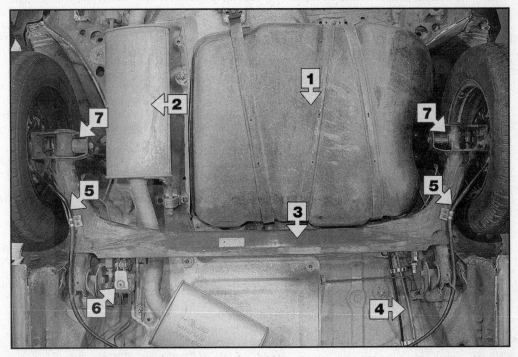

Maintenance procedures - diesel models

1 Introduction

This Chapter is designed to help the home mechanic maintain his/her vehicle for safety, economy, long life and peak performance.

The Chapter contains a master maintenance schedule, followed by Sections dealing specifically with each task in the schedule. Visual checks, adjustments, component renewal and other helpful items are included. Refer to the accompanying illustrations of the engine compartment and the underside of the vehicle for the locations of the various components.

Servicing your vehicle in accordance with the mileage/time maintenance schedule and the following Sections will provide a planned maintenance programme, which should result in a long and reliable service life. This is a comprehensive plan, so maintaining some items but not others at the specified service intervals, will not produce the same results.

As you service your vehicle, you will discover that many of the procedures can - and should - be grouped together, because of the particular procedure being performed, or because of the proximity of two otherwise unrelated components to one another. For example, if the vehicle is raised for any reason, the exhaust can be inspected at the same time as the suspension and steering components.

The first step in this maintenance programme is to prepare yourself before the actual work begins. Read through all the Sections relevant to the work to be carried out, then make a list and gather all the parts and tools required. If a problem is encountered, seek advice from a parts specialist, or a dealer service department.

2 Intensive maintenance

1 If, from the time the vehicle is new, the routine maintenance schedule is followed closely, and frequent checks are made of fluid levels and high-wear items, as suggested throughout this manual, the engine will be kept in relatively good running condition, and the need for additional work will be minimised.
2 It is possible that there will be times when the engine is running poorly due to the lack of regular maintenance. This is even more likely if a used vehicle, which has not received regular and frequent maintenance checks, is purchased. In such cases, additional work may need to be carried out, outside of the regular maintenance intervals.
3 If engine wear is suspected, a compression test (refer to the relevant Part of Chapter 2) will provide valuable information regarding the overall performance of the main internal components. Such a test can be used as a basis to decide on the extent of the work to be carried out. If, for example, a compression test indicates serious internal engine wear, conventional maintenance as described in this Chapter will not greatly improve the performance of the engine, and may prove a waste of time and money, unless extensive overhaul work is carried out first.
4 The following series of operations are those most often required to improve the performance of a generally poor-running engine:

Primary operations

a) Clean, inspect and test the battery (See "Weekly checks").
b) Check all the engine-related fluids (See "Weekly checks").
c) Drain the water from the fuel filter (Section 6).
d) Check the condition and tension of the auxiliary drivebelt(s) (Section 21).
e) Check the condition of the air filter, and renew if necessary (Section 22).
f) Check the condition of all hoses, and check for fluid leaks (Section 10).
g) Check the engine idle speed setting (Section 18 or Chapter 4C).
h) Check the exhaust gas emissions (Section 31).

5 If the above operations do not prove fully effective, carry out the following secondary operations:

Secondary operations

All items listed under "Primary operations", plus the following:

a) Check the charging system (see Chapter 5A).
b) Check the preheating system (see Chapter 5C).
c) Renew the fuel filter (Section 24) and check the fuel system (see Chapter 4C).

1B

Every 5000 miles (7500 km)

3 Engine oil and filter renewal

1 Frequent oil and filter changes are the most important maintenance procedures which can be undertaken by the DIY owner. As engine oil ages, it becomes diluted and contaminated, which leads to premature engine wear.

2 Before starting this procedure, gather all the necessary tools and materials. Also make sure that you have plenty of clean rags and newspapers handy, to mop up any spills. Ideally, the engine oil should be warm, as it will drain better, and more built-up sludge will be removed with it. Take care, however, not to touch the exhaust or any other hot parts of the engine when working under the vehicle. To avoid any possibility of scalding, and to protect yourself from possible skin irritants and other harmful contaminants in used engine oils, it is advisable to wear gloves when carrying out this work.

3 Access to the underside of the vehicle will be greatly improved if it can be raised on a lift, driven onto ramps, or jacked up and supported on axle stands (see "*Jacking and vehicle support*"). Whichever method is chosen, make sure that the vehicle remains level, or if it is at an angle, that the drain plug is at the lowest point. Where applicable, release the fasteners and remove the engine lower splash shield.

4 Using a socket and wrench or a ring spanner, slacken the drain plug about half a turn **(see illustration)**. Position the draining container under the drain plug, then remove the plug completely **(see Haynes Hint)**. Recover the sealing ring from the drain plug.

5 Allow some time for the old oil to drain, noting that it may be necessary to reposition the container as the oil flow slows to a trickle.

6 After all the oil has drained, wipe off the drain plug with a clean rag, and fit a new sealing washer. Clean the area around the drain plug opening, and refit the plug. Tighten the plug securely.

7 Move the container into position under the oil filter, which is located on the front of the cylinder block.

8 Using an oil filter removal tool if necessary, slacken the filter initially, then unscrew it by hand the rest of the way. Empty the oil in the filter into the container.

9 Use a clean rag to remove all oil, dirt and sludge from the filter sealing area on the engine. Check the old filter to make sure that the rubber sealing ring has not stuck to the engine. If it has, carefully remove it.

10 Apply a light coating of clean engine oil to the sealing ring on the new filter, then screw it

HAYNES HINT

Keep the drain plug pressed into the sump while unscrewing it by hand the last couple of turns. As the plug releases, move it away sharply so the stream of oil issuing from the sump runs into the container, not up your sleeve!

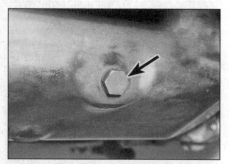

3.4 Engine oil drain plug (arrowed)

into position on the engine **(see illustration)**. Tighten the filter firmly by hand only - **do not use any tools**.

11 Remove the old oil and all tools from under the car then lower the car to the ground (if applicable).

12 Remove the dipstick, then unscrew the oil filler cap from the cylinder head cover. Fill the engine, using the correct grade and type of oil (see "*Lubricants and fluids*"). An oil can spout or funnel may help to reduce spillage. Pour in half the specified quantity of oil first, then wait a few minutes for the oil to fall to the sump. Continue adding oil a small quantity at a time until the level is up to the lower mark on the dipstick. Adding around 1.0 litre will bring the level up to the upper mark on the dipstick. Refit the filler cap.

13 Start the engine and run it for a few minutes; check for leaks around the oil filter seal and the sump drain plug. Note that there may be a few seconds delay before the oil pressure warning light goes out when the engine is started, as the oil circulates through the engine oil galleries and the new oil filter before the pressure builds up.

14 Switch off the engine, and wait a few minutes for the oil to settle in the sump once more. With the new oil circulated and the filter completely full, recheck the level on the dipstick, and add more oil as necessary.

15 Dispose of the used engine oil safely, with reference to "*General repair procedures*" in the *Reference* section of this manual.

3.10 Fitting a new oil filter

Every 10 000 miles (15 000 km)

4 Front brake pad check

1 Firmly apply the handbrake, loosen the front roadwheel bolts, then jack up the front of the car and support it securely on axle stands (see "*Jacking and vehicle support*"). Remove the front roadwheels.

2 For a comprehensive check, the brake pads should be removed and cleaned. The operation of the caliper can then also be checked, and the condition of the brake disc itself can be fully examined on both sides.

Refer to Chapter 9 **(see Haynes Hint)**.

3 If any pad's friction material is worn to the

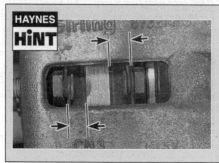

HAYNES HINT

specified thickness or less, *all four pads must be renewed as a set*.

For a quick check, the thickness of the friction material on each brake pad can be measured through the aperture in the caliper body

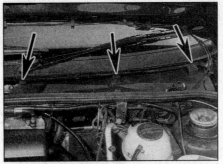

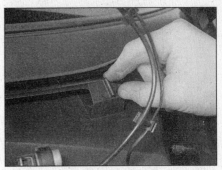

5.1 Pollen filter location - left-hand drive models

1 Fastener
2 Element retaining clips

5.2a Pollen filter cover panel fasteners (arrowed)

5.2b Turn the cover panel fasteners to release

5 Pollen filter renewal

1 The pollen filter (where fitted) is located beneath the windscreen cowl panels; it is located on the left side on right-hand-drive models, and the right side on left-hand drive models **(see illustration)**.
2 Release the filter cover fasteners by turning them as necessary **(see illustrations)**.
3 Peel back the rubber seal from the relevant end of the top of the engine compartment bulkhead **(see illustration)**.

Right-hand-drive models

4 Lift off the thermotronic sensor mounting bracket, and place it and the sensor to one side **(see illustration)**.
5 Although not strictly necessary, access is improved by disconnecting the left-hand washer supply tube **(see illustration)**. Place the tubing to one side, out of the way.

All models

6 Lift out the pollen filter cover panel **(see illustration)**.
7 Release the two spring clips at the front or at the sides to release the element, and pivot the pollen filter upwards and out from its location **(see illustration)**.
8 Wipe clean the filter housing, then fit the new filter. Clip the filter securely in position and refit the cover.
9 Refitting is a reversal of removal.

6 Fuel filter water draining

1 From time to time, the water collected from the fuel by the filter unit must be drained out.
2 The fuel filter is mounted on the inner wing, behind the air cleaner. At the top of the filter unit, release the clip and lift out the control valve, leaving the fuel hoses attached.

3 Slacken the retaining bracket screw and lift the filter up slightly.
4 Position a container below the filter unit, and pad the surrounding area with rags to absorb any fuel that may be spilt.
5 Unscrew the drain valve at the base of the filter unit, until fuel starts to run out into the container **(see illustration)**. Keep the valve open until about 100 cc of fuel has been collected.
6 Refit the control valve to the top of the filter and insert the retaining clip. Close the drain valve and wipe off any surplus fuel from the nozzle.
7 Remove the collecting container and rags, then push the filter unit back into the retaining bracket and tighten the bracket screw.
8 Run the engine at idle, and check around the fuel filter for fuel leaks.
9 Raise the engine speed to about 2000 rpm several times, then allow the engine to idle again. Observe the fuel flow through the transparent hose leading to the fuel injection pump and check that it is free of air bubbles.

1B

5.3 Peel back the rubber seal from the top of the bulkhead

5.4 Lift off the thermotronic sensor and mounting bracket

5.5 Disconnect the windscreen washer tubing at the bulkhead

5.6 Lift out the pollen filter cover panel

5.7 Release the spring clips and lift out the pollen filter element

6.5 Unscrew the drain valve (arrowed) at the base of the filter unit

Every 12 months

7 Lights and horn operation check

1 With the ignition switched on where necessary, check the operation of all exterior lights.
2 Check the brake lights with the help of an assistant, or by reversing up close to a reflective door. Make sure that all the rear lights are capable of operating independently, without affecting any of the other lights - for example, switch on as many rear lights as possible, then try the brake lights. If any unusual results are found, this is usually due to an earth fault at that rear light unit.
3 Again with the help of an assistant or using a reflective surface, check as far as possible that the headlights work on both main and dipped beam.
4 Replace any defective bulbs with reference to Chapter 12.

Particularly on older vehicles, bulbs can stop working as a result of corrosion build-up on the bulb or its holder - fitting a new bulb may not cure the problem in this instance. When replacing any bulb, if you find any green or white-coloured powdery deposits, these should be cleaned off using emery cloth.

5 Check the operation of all interior lights. Switch on the ignition, and check that all relevant warning lights come on as expected - the vehicle handbook should give details of these. Now start the engine, and check that the appropriate lights go out. When you are next driving at night, check that all the instrument panel and facia lighting works correctly. If any problems are found, refer to Chapter 12.
6 Finally, choose an appropriate time of day to test the operation of the horn.

A leak in the cooling system will usually show up as white- or rust-coloured deposits on the area adjoining the leak

8 Airbag unit check

Where fitted, inspect the airbag(s) exterior condition checking for signs of damage or deterioration. If an airbag shows signs of obvious damage, it must be renewed (see Chapter 12).

9 Washer system(s) check

Check that each of the washer jet nozzles is clear, and that each nozzle provides a strong jet of washer fluid. The tailgate and headlight jets (where applicable) should be aimed to spray at a point slightly above the centre of the screen/headlight. The windscreen washer nozzles have two jets; aim one of the jets slightly above the centre of the screen and the other just below to ensure complete coverage of the screen. If necessary, adjust the jets using a pin.

10 Hose and fluid leak check

1 Visually inspect the engine joint faces, gaskets and seals for any signs of water or oil leaks. Pay particular attention to the areas around the camshaft cover, cylinder head, oil filter and sump joint faces. Bear in mind that, over a period of time, some very slight seepage from these areas is to be expected - what you are really looking for is any indication of a serious leak **(see Haynes Hint)**. Should a leak be found, renew the offending gasket or oil seal by referring to the appropriate Chapters in this manual.
2 Also check the security and condition of all the engine-related pipes and hoses. Ensure that all cable-ties or securing clips are in place and in good condition. Clips that are broken or missing can lead to chafing of the hoses, pipes or wiring, which could cause more serious problems in the future.
3 Carefully check the radiator hoses and heater hoses along their entire length. Renew any hose that is cracked, swollen or deteriorated. Cracks will show up better if the hose is squeezed. Pay close attention to the hose clips that secure the hoses to the cooling system components. Hose clips can pinch and puncture hoses, resulting in cooling system leaks.
4 Inspect all the cooling system components (hoses, joint faces etc.) for leaks. A leak in the cooling system will usually show up as white- or rust-coloured deposits on the area adjoining the leak. Where any problems of this nature are found on system components, renew the component or gasket (see Chapter 3).

5 With the vehicle raised, inspect the fuel tank and filler neck for punctures, cracks and other damage. The connection between the filler neck and tank is especially critical. Sometimes a rubber filler neck or connecting hose will leak due to loose retaining clamps or deteriorated rubber.
6 Carefully check all rubber hoses and metal fuel lines leading away from the fuel tank. Check for loose connections, deteriorated hoses, crimped lines, and other damage. Pay particular attention to the vent pipes and hoses, which often loop up around the filler neck and can become blocked or crimped. Follow the lines to the front of the vehicle, carefully inspecting them all the way. Renew damaged sections as necessary.
7 From within the engine compartment, check the security of all fuel hose attachments and pipe unions, and inspect the fuel hoses and vacuum hoses for kinks, chafing and deterioration.
8 Where applicable, check the condition of the power steering fluid hoses and pipes.

11 Battery electrolyte level check

⚠ *Warning: The electrolyte inside a battery is diluted acid - it is a good idea to wear suitable rubber gloves. When topping-up, don't overfill the cells so that the electrolyte overflows. In the event of any spillage, rinse the electrolyte off without delay. Refit the cell covers and rinse the battery with copious quantities of clean water. Don't attempt to siphon out any excess electrolyte.*

1 Most models covered by this Manual were fitted with a maintenance-free battery as standard equipment. If the battery in your vehicle is marked "Freedom", "Maintenance-Free" or similar, no electrolyte level checking is required (the battery is often completely sealed, preventing any topping-up).
2 It is possible that a replacement battery may have been fitted which is not of maintenance-free type. These can be recognised by the presence of removable covers over the six battery cells - the battery casing is also sometimes translucent, so that the electrolyte level can be more easily checked. Make sure you do not have a maintenance-free battery before attempting to top up the electrolyte level.
3 Remove the cell covers and either look down inside the battery to see the level, or check the level using any markings provided on the battery casing. The electrolyte should at least cover the battery plates. If necessary, top up a little at a time with distilled (deionised) water until the level in all six cells is correct - don't fill the cells up to the brim. Wipe up any spillage, then refit the cell covers.

12 Hinge and lock lubrication

Lubricate the hinges of the bonnet, doors and tailgate with light general-purpose oil. Similarly, lubricate all latches, locks and lock strikers, and the door check straps. At the same time, check the security and operation of all the locks, adjusting them if necessary (see Chapter 11).

Lightly lubricate the bonnet release mechanism and cable with suitable grease. *Caution: Do not attempt to lubricate the steering lock.*

13 Steering and suspension check

Front suspension and steering check

1 Raise the front of the vehicle, and securely support it on axle stands (see "*Jacking and vehicle support*").
2 Visually inspect the balljoint dust covers and the steering rack-and-pinion gaiters for splits, chafing or deterioration. Any wear of these components will cause loss of lubricant, together with dirt and water entry, resulting in deterioration of the balljoints or steering gear.
3 On vehicles with power steering, check the fluid hoses for chafing or deterioration, and the pipe and hose unions for fluid leaks. Also check for signs of fluid leakage under pressure from the steering gear rubber gaiters, which would indicate failed fluid seals within the steering gear.
4 Grasp the roadwheel at the 12 o'clock and 6 o'clock positions, and try to rock it (see illustration). Very slight free play may be felt, but if the movement is appreciable, further investigation is necessary to determine the source. Continue rocking the wheel while an assistant depresses the footbrake. If the movement is now eliminated or significantly reduced, it is likely that the hub bearings are at fault. If the free play is still evident with the

footbrake depressed, then there is wear in the suspension joints or mountings.
5 Now grasp the wheel at the 9 o'clock and 3 o'clock positions, and try to rock it as before. Any movement felt now may again be caused by wear in the hub bearings or the steering track-rod balljoints. If the inner or outer balljoint is worn, the visual movement will be obvious.
6 Using a large screwdriver or flat bar, check for wear in the suspension mounting bushes by levering between the relevant suspension component and its attachment point. Some movement is to be expected as the mountings are made of rubber, but excessive wear should be obvious. Also check the condition of any visible rubber bushes, looking for splits, cracks or contamination of the rubber.
7 With the car standing on its wheels, have an assistant turn the steering wheel back and forth about an eighth of a turn each way. There should be very little, if any, lost movement between the steering wheel and roadwheels. If this is not the case, closely observe the joints and mountings previously described, but in addition, check the steering column universal joints for wear, and the rack-and-pinion steering gear itself.

Suspension strut/ shock absorber check

8 Check for any signs of fluid leakage around the suspension strut/shock absorber body, or from the rubber gaiter around the piston rod. Should any fluid be noticed, the suspension strut/shock absorber is defective internally, and should be renewed. **Note:** *Suspension struts/shock absorbers should always be renewed in pairs on the same axle.*
9 The efficiency of the suspension strut/shock absorber may be checked by bouncing the vehicle at each corner. Generally speaking, the body will return to its normal position and stop after being depressed. If it rises and returns on a rebound, the suspension strut/shock absorber is probably suspect. Examine also the suspension strut/shock absorber upper and lower mountings for any signs of wear.

14 Driveshaft gaiter and CV joint check

1 With the vehicle raised and securely supported on axle stands (see "*Jacking and vehicle support*"), turn the steering onto full lock, then slowly rotate the roadwheel. Inspect the condition of the outer constant velocity (CV) joint rubber gaiters, squeezing the gaiters to open out the folds. Check for signs of cracking, splits or deterioration of the rubber, which may allow the grease to escape, and lead to water and grit entry into the joint. Also check the security and condition of the retaining clips. Repeat these checks on the inner CV joints (see illustration). If any damage or deterioration is

found, the gaiters should be renewed (see Chapter 8).
2 At the same time, check the general condition of the CV joints themselves by first holding the driveshaft and attempting to rotate the wheel. Repeat this check by holding the inner joint and attempting to rotate the drive-shaft. Any appreciable movement indicates wear in the joints, wear in the driveshaft splines, or a loose driveshaft retaining nut.

15 Braking system check

1 Starting under the bonnet, examine the brake fluid reservoir and master cylinder for leaks. When a brake fluid leak occurs, it is normal to find blistered or wrinkled paint in the area of the leak. Check the metal pipes from the master cylinder for damage, and check the brake pressure regulator, servo/ABS unit and fluid unions for leaks.
2 With the vehicle raised and securely supported on axle stands (see "*Jacking and vehicle support*"), first inspect each front brake caliper. In particular, check the flexible hose leading to the caliper for signs of damage or leaks, especially where the hose enters the metal end fitting. Make sure that the hose is not twisted or kinked, and that it cannot come into contact with any other components when the steering is on full lock.
3 From the caliper, trace the metal brake pipes back along the car. Again, look for leaks from the fluid unions or signs of damage, but additionally check the pipes for signs of corrosion. Make sure the pipes are securely located by the clips provided on the vehicle underside.
4 At the rear of the vehicle, inspect each rear brake and its flexible hose, where applicable. Examine the handbrake cable, tracing it back from each rear brake and checking for frayed cables or other damage. Lubricate the handbrake cable guides, pivots and other moving parts with general-purpose grease.
5 If any damage is found, refer to Chapter 9 for further information.

1B

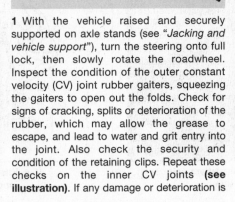

13.4 Check for wear in the hub bearings by grasping the wheel and trying to rock it

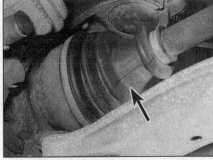

14.1 Check the condition of the driveshaft gaiters (arrowed)

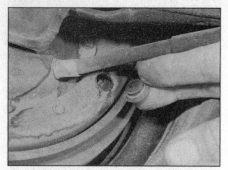

17.2 Remove the rubber plug and check the brake friction material thickness through the backplate aperture

16 Exhaust system check

1 With the engine cold (at least an hour after the vehicle has been driven), check the complete exhaust system from the engine to the end of the tailpipe. The exhaust system is most easily checked with the vehicle raised on a hoist, or suitably supported on axle stands (see "*Jacking and vehicle support*"), so that the exhaust components are readily visible and accessible.

2 Check the exhaust pipes and connections for evidence of leaks, severe corrosion and damage. Make sure that all brackets and mountings are in good condition, and that all relevant nuts and bolts are tight. Leakage at any of the joints or in other parts of the system will usually show up as a black sooty stain in the vicinity of the leak.

3 Rattles and other noises can often be traced to the exhaust system, especially the brackets and mountings. Try to move the pipes and silencers. If the components are able to come into contact with the body or suspension parts, secure the system with new mountings. Otherwise separate the joints (if possible) and twist the pipes as necessary to provide additional clearance.

17 Rear brake shoe check

1 Chock the front wheels, then jack up the rear of the vehicle, and support it securely on axle stands (see "*Jacking and vehicle support*").

2 For a quick check, the thickness of friction material remaining on one of the brake shoes can be observed through the hole in the brake backplate which is exposed by prising out the sealing grommet **(see illustration)**. If a rod of the same diameter as the specified minimum friction material thickness is placed against the shoe friction material, the amount of wear can be assessed. A torch or inspection light will probably be required. If the friction material on any shoe is worn down to the specified minimum thickness or less, all four shoes must be renewed as a set.

3 For a comprehensive check, the brake drum should be removed and cleaned. This will allow the wheel cylinders to be checked, and the condition of the brake drum itself to be fully examined (see Chapter 9).

18 Idle speed check

Engine code AAZ

1 Start the engine and run it until it reaches its normal operating temperature. With the handbrake applied and the transmission in neutral, allow the engine to idle. Check that the cold start knob is pushed into the fully 'off' position.

2 Using a diesel tachometer, check the idle speed against the Specifications at the start of this Chapter.

Models without air conditioning

3 If necessary, adjust the engine idle speed by rotating the adjustment spindle at the fuel injection pump **(see illustration)**. If the idle speed cannot be lowered using the adjustment spindle, loosen the locknut on the idle speed stop screw, and turn back the stop screw by a few turns. Now adjust the idle speed using the adjustment spindle. On completion, screw the idle speed stop screw back down until it just touches its lever, then tighten the locknut.

Models with air conditioning

4 To adjust the idle speed, loosen the locknut on the idle speed stop screw, then adjust the screw as necessary **(see illustration)**. On completion, tighten the locknut.

All other engines

5 The idle speed must be checked by a VW dealer using dedicated electronic test equipment.

19 Headlight beam alignment check

Accurate adjustment of the headlight beam is only possible using optical beam-setting equipment, and this work should therefore be carried out by a VW dealer or service station with the necessary facilities. Headlight alignment is checked as part of the MoT test.

Basic adjustments can be carried out in an emergency, and further details are given in Chapter 12.

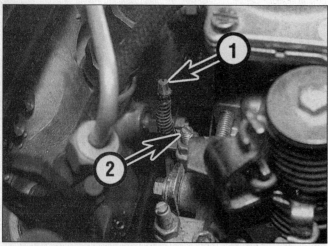

18.3 Adjust the idle speed by rotating the adjustment spindle (1) - idle speed stop screw (2) also shown

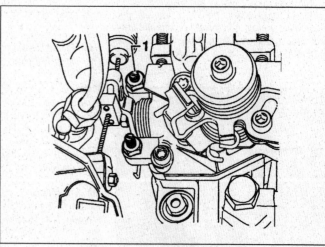

18.4 Idle speed adjustment screw (1) - models with air conditioning

20 Road test

Instruments and electrical equipment

1 Check the operation of all instruments and electrical equipment.
2 Make sure that all instruments read correctly, and switch on all electrical equipment in turn, to check that it functions properly.

Steering and suspension

3 Check for any abnormalities in the steering, suspension, handling or road "feel".
4 Drive the vehicle, and check that there are no unusual vibrations or noises.
5 Check that the steering feels positive, with no excessive "sloppiness", or roughness, and check for any suspension noises when cornering and driving over bumps.

Drivetrain

6 Check the performance of the engine, clutch, transmission and driveshafts.
7 Listen for any unusual noises from the engine, clutch and transmission.
8 Make sure the engine runs smoothly at idle, and there is no hesitation on accelerating.
9 Check that the clutch action is smooth and progressive, that the drive is taken up smoothly, and that the pedal travel is not excessive. Also listen for any noises when the clutch pedal is depressed.
10 Check that all gears can be engaged smoothly without noise, and that the gear lever action is not abnormally vague or "notchy".
11 Listen for a metallic clicking sound from the front of the vehicle, as the vehicle is driven slowly in a circle with the steering on full-lock. Carry out this check in both directions. If a clicking noise is heard, this indicates wear in a driveshaft joint, in which case renew the joint if necessary.

Braking system

12 Make sure that the vehicle does not pull to one side when braking, and that the wheels do not lock prematurely when braking hard.
13 Check that there is no vibration through the steering when braking.
14 Check that the handbrake operates correctly without excessive movement of the lever, and that it holds the vehicle stationary on a slope.
15 Test the operation of the brake servo unit as follows. With the engine off, depress the footbrake four or five times to exhaust the vacuum. Hold the brake pedal depressed, then start the engine. As the engine starts, there should be a noticeable "give" in the brake pedal as vacuum builds up. Allow the engine to run for at least two minutes, and then switch it off. If the brake pedal is depressed now, it should be possible to detect a hiss from the servo as the pedal is depressed. After about four or five applications, no further hissing should be heard, and the pedal should feel considerably harder.

Every 20 000 miles (30 000 km)

21 Auxiliary drivebelt check and renewal

Checking

1 Disconnect the battery negative cable and position it away from the terminal. **Note:** *If the vehicle has a security-coded radio, check that you have a copy of the code number before disconnecting the battery. Refer to your VW dealer if in doubt.*
2 Park the vehicle on a level surface, apply the handbrake and chock the rear wheels. Loosen the right-hand front wheel bolts.
3 Raise the front of the vehicle, rest it securely on axle stands (see "*Jacking and vehicle support*") and remove the right-hand front roadwheel.
4 Turn the steering to full right-hand lock. Where applicable, remove the screws and clips, and lower the undertray away from the engine bay.
5 Using a socket and wrench on the crankshaft sprocket bolt, rotate the crankshaft so that the full length of the auxiliary drivebelts can be examined. Depending on the level of equipment fitted, there may be as many as three drivebelts to be checked. Look for cracks, splitting and fraying on the surface of the belt; check also for signs of glazing (shiny patches) and separation of the belt plies. If damage or wear is visible, the belt should be renewed.
6 Check the drivebelt tension by pressing on the belt at a point midway between two pulleys. Depending on the type of belt, it should move by approximately 5 to 10 mm. If

the drivebelt appears excessively taut or slack, refer to Chapter 2B and adjust the belt tension.

Renewal

7 For details of auxiliary drivebelt renewal, refer to Chapter 2B.

22 Air filter renewal

1 Prise open the spring clips and lift off the air cleaner top cover (**see illustration**). *Caution: On certain models, the airflow meter is integral with the air cleaner top cover. Handle the airflow meter very carefully, as it easily damaged.* The cover need only be lifted to allow the element to be withdrawn, but depending on the system type, it may be necessary to detach the inlet duct and/or associated fuel system components.

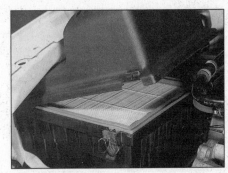

22.1 Prise open the spring clips, and lift off the air cleaner top cover

2 Lift out the filter element.
3 Remove any debris that may have collected inside the air cleaner.
4 Fit a new air filter element in position, noting any direction-of-fitting markings and ensuring that the edges are securely seated (**see illustration**).
5 Refit the air cleaner top cover and snap the retaining clips into position.

23 Timing belt condition and tension check

1 Refer to Chapter 2B and remove the timing belt covers for access to the timing belt.
2 Examine the belt for signs of cracking or splitting, especially around the "roots" of the teeth, and for signs of fraying or separation of the belt plies. If any damage is noted, the belt should be renewed as described in Chapter 2B.

22.4 Fit a new air filter element in position, ensuring the edges are securely seated

1B

24.2a Release the clip . . .

24.2b . . . and lift out the control valve, leaving the fuel hoses attached to it

24.4a Slacken the screw . . .

3 If there is any sign that the belt is being contaminated with oil or other fluid, the belt should be changed and the source of the leak found and fixed, otherwise the new belt will quickly go the same way.

4 The timing belt tension can be checked by twisting the belt at a point midway along its longest run. It should just be possible to turn the belt through 90° (quarter-turn). The belt tension is critical - if it is slack, there is a danger that the belt might jump a tooth, while a belt which is too tight might wear prematurely.

24 Fuel filter renewal

1 The fuel filter is mounted on the inner wing, behind the air cleaner. Position a container underneath the filter unit, and pad the surrounding area with rags to absorb any fuel that may be spilt.

2 At the top of the filter unit, release the clip and lift out the control valve, leaving the fuel hoses attached to it **(see illustrations)**.

3 Slacken the hose clips and pull the fuel supply and delivery hoses from the ports on the top of the filter unit. If crimp-type clips are fitted, cut them off using snips, and use proper fuel hose clips on refitting. Note the fitted position of each hose, to aid correct refitting.

Caution: Be prepared for an amount of fuel loss.

4 Slacken the retaining bracket screw and lift the filter out **(see illustrations)**.

24.4b . . . and lift the filter out of its retaining bracket

5 Fit a new fuel filter into the retaining bracket, and tighten the screw.

6 Refit the control valve to the top of the filter, and insert the retaining clip.

7 Reconnect the fuel supply and delivery hoses, using the notes made during removal - note the fuel flow arrow markings next to each port. Where crimp-type hoses were originally fitted, use screw-type clips on refitting **(see illustration)**. Remove the collecting container and rags.

8 Start and run the engine at idle, then check around the fuel filter for fuel leaks. **Note:** *It may take a few seconds of cranking before the engine starts.*

9 Raise the engine speed to about 2000 rpm several times, then allow the engine to idle again. Observe the fuel flow through the transparent hose leading to the fuel injection pump, and check that it is free of air bubbles.

24.7 Reconnect the fuel supply and delivery hoses

25 Transmission oil level check

1 Park the car on a level surface. The oil level must be checked before the car is driven, or at least 5 minutes after the engine has been switched off. If the oil is checked just after driving the car, some of the oil will remain distributed around the transmission components, resulting in an inaccurate level reading.

2 Where applicable, remove the retaining clips and screws, then lower the undertray away from the engine bay.

3 Wipe clean the area around the filler/level plug, which is situated on the front of the differential casing **(see illustration)**. A special hexagonal socket (or a large Allen key) will be required to remove the plug, which will probably be quite tight.

4 The oil level should reach the lower edge of the filler/level hole. A certain amount of oil will have gathered behind the filler/level plug, and will trickle out when it is removed; this does **not** necessarily indicate that the level is correct. To ensure that a true level is established, wait until the initial trickle has stopped, then add oil as necessary until a trickle of new oil can be seen emerging. The level will be correct when the flow ceases; use only good-quality oil of the specified type **(see illustration)**.

5 Filling the transmission with oil is an extremely awkward operation; above all, allow plenty of time for the oil level to settle properly before checking it. If a large amount is added

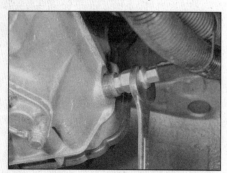

25.3 Transmission filler/level plug removal

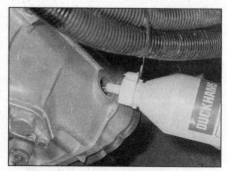

25.4 Topping-up transmission oil

to the transmission, and a large amount flows out on checking the level, refit the filler/level plug; take the vehicle on a short journey so that the new oil is distributed fully around the transmission components, then recheck the level when it has settled again.

6 If the transmission has been overfilled so that oil flows out when the filler/level plug is removed, check that the car is completely level (front-to-rear and side-to-side), and allow the surplus to drain off into a suitable container.

7 When the level is correct, fit a new sealing washer to the filler/level plug. Refit the plug, tightening it securely, and wipe off any spilt oil. Where applicable, refit the engine bay undertray, securing it in position with the retaining clips and screws.

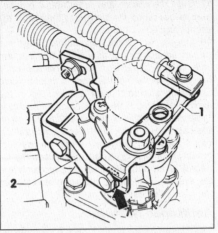

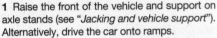

26.3 Lubrication point (arrowed) for the gearchange lever (1) and relay lever (2)

26.5 Transmission oil drain plug

26 Transmission - general maintenance

1 Raise the front of the vehicle and support on axle stands (see "*Jacking and vehicle support*"). Alternatively, drive the car onto ramps.

2 Inspect around the transmission for any sign of leaks or damage. In particular, check the area around the driveshaft oil seals for leakage. Slight seepage should not be of great concern, but a serious leak should be investigated further, with reference to the relevant Part of Chapter 7.

3 Periodically lubricate the gearchange/relay lever with grease at the points indicated (see illustration).

4 Although not included in the maintenance schedule by the manufacturers, it is a good idea to drain and renew the transmission oil on a regular basis. The frequency with which this needs to be carried out can be left to the individual, but it is certainly advisable on a vehicle that has covered a high mileage.

5 The transmission oil drain plug is located in the base of the differential housing (see illustration) - like the oil filler/level plug, a special hexagonal socket (or large Allen key) will be required for removal.

6 When refilling the transmission, remember that the vehicle must be level for the oil level to be correct (see Section 25).

27 Underbody protection check

Raise and support the vehicle on axle stands (see "*Jacking and vehicle support*"). Using an electric torch or lead light, inspect the entire underside of the vehicle, paying particular attention to the wheel arches. Look for any damage to the flexible underbody coating, which may crack or flake off with age, leading to corrosion. Also check that the wheel arch liners (where fitted) are securely attached with any clips provided - if they come loose, dirt may get in behind the liners and defeat their purpose. If there is any damage to the underseal, or any corrosion, it should be repaired before the damage gets too serious.

1B

Every 40 000 miles (60 000 km)

28 Timing belt and tensioner renewal

Refer to Chapter 2B.

Note: *VW specify a timing belt renewal interval of 60 000 miles (90 000 km). However, if the vehicle is used mainly for short journeys or a lot of stop-start driving, we recommend that this shorter interval is adhered to. The actual belt renewal interval is very much up to the individual owner but, bearing in mind that severe engine damage will result if the belt breaks in use, we recommend you err on the side of caution.*

Every 2 years (regardless of mileage)

29 Coolant renewal

Cooling system draining

⚠ *Warning: Wait until the engine is cold before starting this procedure. Do not allow antifreeze to come in contact with your skin, or with the painted surfaces of the vehicle. Rinse off spills immediately with plenty of water. Never leave antifreeze lying around in an open container, or in a puddle in the driveway or on the garage floor. Children and pets are attracted by its sweet smell, but antifreeze can be fatal if ingested.*

1 With the engine completely cold, cover the expansion tank cap with a wad of rag, and slowly turn the cap anti-clockwise to relieve the pressure in the cooling system (a hissing sound will normally be heard). Wait until any pressure remaining in the system is released, then continue to turn the cap until it can be removed.

2 Where necessary, release the fasteners and remove the engine lower splash shield. Position a suitable container beneath the radiator bottom hose connection, then release the retaining clip and ease the hose from the radiator stub. If the hose joint has not been disturbed for some time, it will be necessary to gently manipulate the hose to break the joint. Do not use excessive force, or the radiator stub could be damaged. Allow the coolant to drain into the container.

3 If the coolant has been drained for a reason other than renewal, then provided it is clean and less than two years old, it can be re-used, though this is not recommended.

4 Once all the coolant has drained, reconnect the hose to the radiator and secure it in position with the retaining clip.

Cooling system flushing

5 If coolant renewal has been neglected, or if the antifreeze mixture has become diluted, then in time, the cooling system may gradually lose efficiency, as the coolant passages become restricted due to rust, scale deposits, and other sediment. Flushing the system clean can restore the cooling system efficiency.

6 The radiator should be flushed independently of the engine, to avoid unnecessary contamination.

Radiator flushing

7 To flush the radiator, disconnect the top and bottom hoses and any other relevant hoses from the radiator, with reference to Chapter 3.

8 Insert a garden hose into the radiator top inlet. Direct a flow of clean water through the radiator, and continue flushing until clean water emerges from the radiator bottom outlet.

9 If after a reasonable period, the water still does not run clear, the radiator can be flushed with a good proprietary cooling system cleaning agent. It is important that their manufacturer's instructions are followed carefully. If the contamination is particularly bad, insert the hose in the radiator bottom outlet, and reverse-flush the radiator.

Engine flushing

10 To flush the engine, remove the thermostat as described in Chapter 3, then temporarily refit the thermostat cover.

11 With the top and bottom hoses disconnected from the radiator, insert a garden hose into the radiator top hose. Direct a clean flow of water through the engine, and continue flushing until clean water emerges from the radiator bottom hose.

12 On completion of flushing, refit the thermostat and reconnect the hoses with reference to Chapter 3.

Cooling system filling

13 Before attempting to fill the cooling system, make sure that all hoses and clips are in good condition, and that the clips are tight. Note that an antifreeze mixture must be used all year round, to prevent corrosion of the engine components (see following sub-Section).

14 Remove the expansion tank filler cap, and fill the system by slowly pouring the coolant into the expansion tank to prevent airlocks from forming.

15 If the coolant is being renewed, begin by pouring in a couple of litres of water, followed by the correct quantity of antifreeze, then top-up with more water.

16 Once the level in the expansion tank starts to rise, squeeze the radiator top and bottom hoses to help expel any trapped air in the system. Once all the air is expelled, top-up the coolant level to the "MAX" mark and refit the expansion tank cap.

17 Start the engine and run it until it reaches normal operating temperature, then stop the engine and allow it to cool.

18 Check for leaks, particularly around disturbed components. Check the coolant level in the expansion tank, and top-up if necessary. Note that the system must be cold before an accurate level is indicated in the expansion tank. If the expansion tank cap is removed while the engine is still warm, cover the cap with a thick cloth, and unscrew the cap slowly to gradually relieve the system pressure (a hissing sound will normally be heard). Wait until any pressure remaining in the system is released, then continue to turn the cap until it can be removed.

Antifreeze mixture

19 The antifreeze should always be renewed at the specified intervals. This is necessary not only to maintain the antifreeze properties, but also to prevent corrosion which would otherwise occur as the corrosion inhibitors become progressively less effective.

20 Always use ethylene-glycol-based antifreeze suitable for use in mixed-metal cooling systems. The quantity of antifreeze and levels of protection are indicated in the Specifications.

21 Before adding antifreeze, the cooling system should be completely drained, preferably flushed, and all hoses checked for condition and security.

22 After filling with antifreeze, a label should be attached to the expansion tank, stating the type and concentration of antifreeze used, and the date installed. Any subsequent topping-up should be made with the same type and concentration of antifreeze.

23 Do not use engine antifreeze in the windscreen/tailgate washer system, as it will cause damage to the vehicle paintwork.

---

30 Brake fluid renewal

 Warning: Brake hydraulic fluid can harm your eyes and damage painted surfaces, so use extreme caution when handling and pouring it. Do not use fluid that has been standing open for some time, as it absorbs moisture from the air. Excess moisture can cause a dangerous loss of braking effectiveness.

1 The procedure is similar to that for the bleeding of the hydraulic system as described in Chapter 9. The brake fluid reservoir should be emptied by siphoning, using a clean poultry baster or similar before starting, and allowance should be made for the old fluid to be expelled when bleeding a section of the circuit.

2 Working as described in Chapter 9, open the first bleed screw in the sequence, and pump the brake pedal gently until nearly all the old fluid has been emptied from the master cylinder reservoir.

> **HAYNES HINT** *Old hydraulic fluid is often much darker in colour than the new, making it easy to distinguish the two.*

3 Top-up to the "MAX" level with new fluid, and continue pumping until only the new fluid remains in the reservoir, and new fluid can be seen emerging from the bleed screw. Tighten the screw, and top the reservoir level up to the "MAX" level line.

4 Work through all the remaining bleed screws in the sequence until new fluid can be seen at all of them. Be careful to keep the master cylinder reservoir topped-up to above the "MIN" level at all times, or air may enter the system and greatly increase the length of the task.

5 When the operation is complete, check that all bleed screws are securely tightened, and that their dust caps are refitted. Wash off all traces of spilt fluid, and recheck the fluid level.

6 Check the operation of the brakes before taking the car on the road.

---

31 Exhaust emissions check

This check is part of the manufacturer's maintenance schedule, and involves testing the exhaust emissions using a diesel exhaust gas analyser. Unless a fault is suspected, this test is not essential, although it should be noted that it is recommended by the manufacturers. Exhaust emissions testing is included as part of the MoT test.

Chapter 2 Part A:
Petrol engine in-car repair procedures

Contents

Degrees of difficulty

Easy, suitable for novice with little experience | **Fairly easy,** suitable for beginner with some experience | **Fairly difficult,** suitable for competent DIY mechanic | **Difficult,** suitable for experienced DIY mechanic | **Very difficult,** suitable for expert DIY or professional

Specifications

General

Engine code*
1.8 litre (1781cc):
  Digifant multi-point injection, non-catalyst, 82kW .... PB
  Digifant multi-point injection, 79kW .... PF
  Bosch Mono-Jetronic injection, 66kW .... RP
  Bosch Mono-Motronic injection, 55kW, 10/93 on .... AAM
  Bosch Mono-Motronic injection, 66kW, to 10/94 .... ABS
  Bosch Mono-Motronic injection, 66kW, 10/94 on .... ADZ
2.0 litre (1984cc):
  Digifant multi-point injection, 85kW, to 10/94 .... 2E
  Simos multi-point injection, 85kW, 10/94 on .... ADY
  Simos multi-point injection, 85kW, 08/95 on .... AGG

*Note: See "Buying spare parts and vehicle identification" for the location of code marking on the engine.

	1.8 litre	2.0 litre
Bore	81.0 mm	82.5 mm
Stroke	86.4 mm	92.8 mm

Compression ratio:
  RP and AAM 9.0:1
  AGG 9.6:1
  All other engines 10.0:1
Compression pressures (minimum):
  RP and AAM .... 7.0 bar
  All other engines .... 7.5 bar
Firing order .... 1 - 3 - 4 - 2
No 1 cylinder location .... Timing belt end

Auxiliary drivebelts

V-belt tension (deflection at mid-point between pulleys):
  New belt .... 2 mm
  Used belt .... 5 mm

Lubrication system

Oil pump type .... Sump-mounted, driven indirectly from intermediate shaft
Normal operating oil pressure .... 2.0 bar minimum (at 2000 rpm, oil temperature 80°C)
Oil pump backlash .... 0.20 mm (wear limit)
Oil pump axial clearance .... 0.15 mm (wear limit)

Torque wrench settings

	Nm	lbf ft
Alternator mounting bolts	25	18
Auxiliary belt tensioner-to-bracket bolts	20	15
Auxiliary belt tensioner pulley bolt	20	15
Auxiliary belt pulley bolts	25	18
Camshaft cover retaining screws/nuts	10	7
Camshaft sprocket bolt	80	59
Crankshaft oil seal housing bolts	10	7
Crankshaft sprocket bolt (hex type)	180	133
Crankshaft sprocket bolt (splined type)*:		
Stage 1	90	66
Stage 2 (angle-tighten)	Angle-tighten a further 90°	
Cylinder head bolts*:		
Stage 1	40	30
Stage 2	60	44
Stage 3	Angle-tighten a further 90°	
Stage 4	Angle-tighten a further 90°	
Engine mountings **(see illustration 14.13b on page 2A•15):**		
a	25	18
b	30	22
c	80	59
d	50	37
e	60	44
f	70	52
g	55	41
Exhaust manifold nuts		
M8 nuts	25	18
M10 nuts	40	30
Flywheel mounting bolts*:		
Stage 1	60	44
Stage 2	Angle-tighten a further 90°	
Intermediate shaft sealing flange bolts	25	18
Intermediate shaft sprocket bolt	80	59
Knock sensor bolt	20	15
Oil pickup-to-oil pump bolts	10	7
Oil pressure switch	25	18
Oil pump cover bolts	10	7
Oil pump-to-crankcase bolts	25	18
Power steering pump mounting bolts	25	18
Power steering pump upper pivot bolt	45	33
Sump retaining bolts	20	15
Timing belt cover bolts	10	7
Timing belt inner cover bolts	20	15
Timing belt tensioner centre nut/bolt	45	33
Torque converter driveplate bolts*:		
Stage 1	60	44
Stage 2	Angle-tighten a further 90°	

*Use new bolt(s)

1 General information

Using this Chapter

Chapter 2 is divided into three Parts; A, B and C. Repair operations that can be carried out with the engine in the vehicle are described in Parts A (petrol engines) and B (diesel engines). Part C covers the removal of the engine/transmission as a unit, and describes the engine dismantling and overhaul procedures.

In Parts A and B, the assumption is made that the engine is installed in the vehicle, with all ancillaries connected. If the engine has been removed for overhaul, the preliminary dismantling information which precedes each operation may be ignored.

Access to the engine bay can be improved by removing the bonnet and the front lock carrier assembly; for details, see Chapter 11.

Engine description

Throughout this Chapter, engines are identified and referred to by the manufacturer's code letters, rather than capacity. A listing of all engines covered, together with their code letters, is given in the Specifications.

The engines are water-cooled, single camshaft, in-line four-cylinder units, with cast-iron cylinder blocks and aluminium-alloy cylinder heads. All are mounted transversely at the front of the vehicle, with the transmission bolted to the left-hand side of the engine.

The cylinder head carries the camshaft, which is driven by a toothed timing belt. It also houses the inlet and exhaust valves, which are closed by single or double coil springs, and which run in guides pressed into the cylinder head. The camshaft actuates the valves directly via hydraulic tappets, mounted in the cylinder head. The cylinder head contains integral oilways which supply and lubricate the tappets.

The crankshaft is supported by five main bearings, and endfloat is controlled by a thrust bearing fitted between cylinder Nos 2 and 3.

Engine coolant is circulated by a pump, driven by the auxiliary drivebelt. For details of the cooling system, refer to Chapter 3.

All engines are fitted with a timing belt-driven intermediate shaft, which provides drive for the distributor and the oil pump.

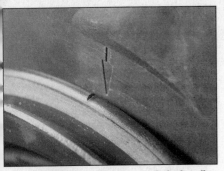

2.5a TDC timing marks on crankshaft pulley
and lower timing cover - early models

2.5b Crankshaft/intermediate shaft
sprocket timing marks - all models

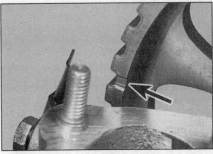

2.6a Camshaft sprocket rear timing mark
aligned with front of cylinder head (or
camshaft cover, if still fitted) - early models

Lubricant is circulated under pressure by a pump, driven by the intermediate shaft. Oil is drawn from the sump through a strainer, and then forced through an externally-mounted, replaceable screw-on filter. From there, it is distributed to the cylinder head, where it lubricates the camshaft journals and hydraulic tappets, and also to the crankcase, where it lubricates the main bearings, connecting rod big- and small-ends, gudgeon pins and cylinder bores. Some engines are fitted with oil jets, mounted at the base of each cylinder - these spray oil onto the underside of the pistons, to improve cooling. An oil cooler, supplied with engine coolant, reduces the temperature of the oil before it re-enters the engine.

Repairs possible with the engine installed in the vehicle

The following operations can be performed without removing the engine:-

a) Auxiliary drivebelts - removal and refitting.
b) Camshaft - removal and refitting. *
c) Camshaft oil seal - renewal.
d) Camshaft sprocket - removal and refitting.
e) Coolant pump - removal and refitting (refer to Chapter 3)
f) Crankshaft oil seals - renewal.
g) Crankshaft sprocket - removal and refitting.
h) Cylinder head - removal and refitting. *
i) Engine mountings - inspection and renewal.
j) Intermediate shaft oil seal - renewal.
k) Oil pump and pickup assembly - removal and refitting.

l) Sump - removal and refitting.
m)Timing belt, sprockets and cover - removal, inspection and refitting.
*Cylinder head dismantling procedures are detailed in Chapter 2C, with details of camshaft and hydraulic tappet removal.
Note: *It is possible to remove the pistons and connecting rods (after removing the cylinder head and sump) without removing the engine. However, this is not recommended. Work of this nature is more easily and thoroughly completed with the engine on the bench, as described in Chapter 2C.*

2 Engine assembly and valve timing marks - general information and usage

General information

Note: *This sub-section has been written with the assumption that the distributor, HT leads and timing belt are correctly fitted.*

1 The crankshaft, camshaft and intermediate shaft sprockets are driven by the timing belt, and rotate in phase with each other. When the timing belt is removed during servicing or repair, it is possible for the shafts to rotate independently of each other, and the correct phasing is then lost.
2 The design of the engines covered in this Chapter is such that potentially damaging piston-to-valve contact may occur if the camshaft is rotated when any of the pistons are stationary at, or near, the top of its stroke.
3 For this reason, it is important that the

correct phasing between the camshaft, crankshaft and intermediate shaft is preserved whilst the timing belt is off the engine. This is achieved by setting the engine in a reference condition (known as Top Dead Centre or TDC) before the timing belt is removed, and then preventing the shafts from rotating until the belt is refitted. Similarly, if the engine has been dismantled for overhaul, the engine can be set to TDC during reassembly to ensure that the correct shaft phasing is restored.
4 TDC is the highest position a piston reaches within its respective cylinder - in a four-stroke engine, each piston reaches TDC twice per cycle; once on the compression stroke, and once on the exhaust stroke. In general, TDC normally refers to No 1 cylinder on the compression stroke. (Note that the cylinders are numbered 1 to 4, starting from the timing belt end of the engine).
5 The crankshaft sprocket is equipped with a marking which, when aligned with a reference marking on the timing belt cover or intermediate shaft sprocket, indicates that No 1 cylinder (and hence also No 4 cylinder) is at TDC **(see illustrations)**.
6 The camshaft sprocket is also equipped with a timing mark - when this is similarly aligned, the engine is correctly synchronised, and the timing belt can then be refitted and tensioned **(see illustrations)**.
7 Early models are also equipped with a TDC mark on the flywheel, which may be viewed after removing the rubber inspection plug from the transmission housing **(see illustrations)**.

2A

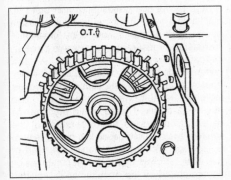

2.6b Camshaft sprocket timing marks -
all models

2.7a Remove the inspection plug from the
transmission housing . . .

2.7b . . . to view the flywheel timing marks
- early models

8 The following sub-Sections describe setting the engine to TDC on No 1 cylinder.

Setting TDC on No 1 cylinder - timing belt fitted

All engines

9 Before starting work, disconnect the battery negative lead. **Note:** *If the vehicle has a security-coded radio, check that you have a copy of the code number before disconnecting the battery. Refer to your VW dealer if in doubt.* Disable the ignition system by removing the distributor centre HT lead and grounding it on the cylinder block, using a jumper wire. Prevent any vehicle movement by putting the transmission in neutral, applying the handbrake and chocking the rear wheels.

10 On the distributor cap, note the position of the No 1 cylinder HT terminal with respect to the distributor body. On some models, the manufacturer provides a marking in the form of a small cut-out. If the terminal is not marked, follow the HT lead from the No 1 cylinder spark plug back to the distributor cap - No 1 cylinder is at the timing end of the engine - and using chalk or a pen (*not* a pencil), place a mark on the distributor body directly under the terminal.

11 Remove the distributor cap, as described in Chapter 5B.

12 Disconnect the HT leads from the spark plugs, noting their order of connection.

13 To bring any piston up to TDC, it will be necessary to rotate the crankshaft manually. This can be done by using a wrench and socket on the bolt that retains the crankshaft pulley (refer to Section 5 for more detail).

14 Rotate the crankshaft in its normal direction of rotation until the distributor rotor arm electrode begins to approach the mark that was made on the distributor body.

Remove all four spark plugs; this will make the engine easier to turn; refer to Chapter 1A for details.

15 With reference to Section 4, remove the upper timing belt outer covers to expose the camshaft timing belt sprocket beneath. Identify the timing marks on the camshaft sprocket and the inner section of the timing belt cover/top of the camshaft cover (see illustration 2.6a or b). Continue turning the crankshaft clockwise until these marks are exactly aligned with each other.

16 At this point, identify the timing marks on the crankshaft pulley and the timing belt cover/intermediate shaft sprocket, and check that they are correctly aligned; refer to illustration 2.5a or b. **Note:** *The outer part of the lower timing belt cover must be removed to expose the intermediate shaft sprocket timing marks.*

17 On early models, remove the inspection plug from the transmission housing and check

that the flywheel mark is aligned at TDC; refer to illustrations 2.7a and b.

18 Check that the centre of the distributor rotor arm electrode is now aligned with the No 1 terminal mark on the distributor body. If it proves impossible to align the rotor arm with the No 1 terminal whilst maintaining the alignment of the camshaft timing marks, refer to Chapter 5B and check that the distributor has been fitted correctly.

19 When all the above steps have been completed successfully, the engine will be set to TDC on No 1 cylinder.

Caution: If the timing belt is to be removed, ensure that the crankshaft, camshaft and intermediate shaft alignment is preserved by preventing the sprockets from rotating with respect to each other.

Setting TDC on No 1 cylinder - timing belt removed

20 This procedure has been written with the assumption that the timing belt has been removed and that the alignment between the camshaft, crankshaft and intermediate shaft has been lost - for example, following engine removal and overhaul.

21 On all the engines covered in this manual, it is possible for damage to be caused by the piston crowns striking the valve heads, if the camshaft is rotated with the timing belt removed and the crankshaft set to TDC. For this reason, the TDC setting procedure must be carried out in a particular order, as described in the following paragraphs.

22 Before the cylinder head is refitted, use a wrench and socket on the crankshaft pulley centre bolt to turn the crankshaft in its normal direction of rotation, until all four pistons are positioned **halfway down** their bores, with No 1 piston on its upstroke - i.e. around 90° before TDC.

23 With the cylinder head and camshaft sprocket fitted, identify the timing marks on the camshaft sprocket and the inner section of the timing belt cover/top of the cylinder head (see illustration 2.6a or b).

24 Turn the camshaft sprocket in its normal direction of rotation until the timing marks on the sprocket and timing belt inner cover/top of the cylinder head are exactly aligned.

25 Identify the timing marks on the crankshaft pulley and the intermediate shaft (refer to illustration 2.5b). Using a socket and wrench on the crankshaft sprocket retaining bolt, turn the crankshaft through 90° (quarter of a turn) in its normal direction of rotation, to bring the timing marks into alignment.

26 On early models, remove the inspection plug from the transmission housing and check that the flywheel mark is aligned at TDC; refer to illustrations 2.7a and b.

27 Check that the centre of the distributor rotor arm electrode is now aligned with No 1 cylinder terminal marking on the distributor body. If it proves impossible to align the rotor arm with the No 1 terminal whilst maintaining the alignment of the camshaft timing marks,

refer to Chapter 5B and check that the distributor has been fitted correctly.

28 When all the above steps have been completed successfully, the engine will be set at TDC on No 1 cylinder. The timing belt can now be fitted as described in Section 4.

Caution: Until the timing belt is fitted, ensure that the crankshaft, camshaft and intermediate shaft alignment is preserved by preventing the sprockets from rotating with respect to each other.

3 Cylinder compression test

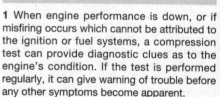

1 When engine performance is down, or if misfiring occurs which cannot be attributed to the ignition or fuel systems, a compression test can provide diagnostic clues as to the engine's condition. If the test is performed regularly, it can give warning of trouble before any other symptoms become apparent.

2 The engine must be fully warmed-up to normal operating temperature, the battery must be fully charged, and all the spark plugs must be removed (refer to Chapter 1A). The aid of an assistant will also be required.

3 Disable the ignition system by disconnecting the ignition HT coil lead from the distributor cap and earthing it on the cylinder block. Use a jumper lead or similar wire to make a good connection. Disable the fuel system by removing the fuel pump relay from its socket, or by removing the fuel pump fuse.

4 Fit a compression tester to the No 1 cylinder spark plug hole - the type of tester which screws into the plug thread is preferable.

5 Have an assistant hold the throttle wide open, then crank the engine on the starter motor; after one or two revolutions, the compression pressure should build up to a maximum figure, and then stabilise. Record the highest reading obtained.

6 Repeat the test on the remaining cylinders, recording the pressure in each. Keep the throttle wide open.

7 All cylinders should produce very similar pressures; a difference of more than 2 bar between any two cylinders indicates a fault. Note that the compression should build up quickly in a healthy engine; low compression on the first stroke, followed by gradually-increasing pressure on successive strokes, indicates worn piston rings. A low compression reading on the first stroke, which does not build up during successive strokes, indicates leaking valves or a blown head gasket (a cracked head could also be the cause). Deposits on the undersides of the valve heads can also cause low compression.

8 The Specifications section at the start of this Chapter gives the minimum compression figures stated by the manufacturer; provided the figures obtained are higher, all should be well.

9 If the pressure in any cylinder is low, carry out the following test to isolate the cause. Introduce a teaspoonful of clean oil into that cylinder through its spark plug hole, and repeat the test.

10 If the addition of oil temporarily improves the compression pressure, this indicates that bore or piston wear is responsible for the pressure loss. No improvement suggests that leaking or burnt valves, or a blown head gasket, may be to blame.

11 A low reading from two adjacent cylinders is almost certainly due to the head gasket having blown between them; the presence of coolant in the engine oil will confirm this.

12 If one cylinder is about 20 percent lower than the others and the engine has a slightly rough idle, a worn camshaft lobe could be the cause.

13 If the compression reading is unusually high, the combustion chambers are probably coated with carbon deposits. If this is the case, the cylinder head should be removed and decarbonised.

14 On completion of the test, refit the spark plugs and restore the ignition system.

4 Timing belt and outer covers - removal and refitting

1 The primary function of the toothed timing belt is to drive the camshaft(s), but it is also used to drive the coolant pump or intermediate shaft, depending on the engine specification. Should the belt slip or break in service, the valve timing will be disturbed and piston-to-valve contact may occur, resulting in serious engine damage.

2 For this reason, it is important that the timing belt is tensioned correctly, and inspected regularly for signs of wear or deterioration.

3 Note that the removal of the *inner* section of the timing belt cover is described as part of the cylinder head removal procedure; see Section 11 later in this Chapter.

Removal

4 Before starting work, immobilise the engine and vehicle as follows:
 a) *Disable the ignition system by removing the distributor centre HT lead and grounding it on the cylinder block, using a jumper wire.*
 b) *Disable the fuel system by removing the fuel pump relay from its socket, or by removing the fuel pump fuse.*
 c) *Disconnect the battery negative lead, and position the lead away from the battery.* **Note:** *If the vehicle has a security-coded radio, check that you have a copy of the code number before disconnecting the battery. Refer to your VW dealer if in doubt.*
 d) *Prevent any vehicle movement by applying the handbrake and chocking the rear wheels.*

4.6a Release the retaining clips . . .

5 Access to the timing belt covers can be improved by removing the air cleaner housing-to-throttle body ducting, and by removing the crankcase breather hose. Access from below can be improved by jacking up and supporting the front of the vehicle, and removing the right-hand front roadwheel. Some later models may be fitted with plastic panels which will need to be unclipped for access to the engine through the wheel arch.

6 Release the uppermost part of the timing belt cover by prising open the metal spring clips and where applicable, removing the retaining screws. Lift the cover away from the engine **(see illustrations)**.

7 With reference to Section 6, remove the auxiliary drive V-belt and/or the ribbed auxiliary drivebelt.

8 Refer to Section 2 and using the engine alignment markings, set the engine to TDC on No 1 cylinder.

9 Slacken and withdraw the retaining screws, then remove the pulley(s) for the auxiliary drivebelt(s) from the crankshaft sprocket. On completion, check that the engine is still set to TDC.

> **HAYNES HiNT** *To prevent the auxiliary drivebelt pulley from rotating whilst the mounting bolts are being slackened, select top gear (manual transmission) or 'PARK' (automatic transmission) and get an assistant to apply the footbrake firmly. Failing this, grip the sprocket by wrapping a length of old rubber hose or inner tube around it.*

10 Unscrew the bolts and remove the coolant pump pulley to allow removal of the timing belt lower cover.

11 Remove the retaining screws and clips, and lift off the timing belt lower cover.

12 Refer to Section 5 and relieve the tension on the timing belt by slackening the tensioner mounting nut slightly, allowing it to pivot away from the belt **(see illustration)**.

13 Examine the timing belt for manufacturer's markings that indicate the direction of rotation. If none are present, make your own using typist's correction fluid.

4.6b . . . and remove the timing belt upper cover (seen with engine removed for clarity)

Caution: If the belt appears to be in good condition and can be re-used, it is essential that it is refitted the same way around, otherwise accelerated wear will result, leading to premature failure.

14 Slide the belt off the sprockets, taking care to avoid twisting or kinking it excessively. Ensure that the sprockets remain aligned with their respective timing markings once the timing belt has been removed.

Caution: It is potentially damaging to allow the camshaft to turn with the timing belt removed and the engine set at TDC, as piston-to-valve contact may occur.

15 Examine the belt for evidence of contamination by coolant or lubricant. If this is the case, identify the source of the contamination before progressing any further. Check the belt for signs of wear or damage, particularly around the leading edges of the belt teeth. Renew the belt if its condition is in doubt; the cost of belt renewal is negligible compared with potential cost of the engine repairs, should the belt fail in service. Similarly, if the belt is known to have covered more than 36 000 miles, it is prudent to renew it regardless of condition, as a precautionary measure.

16 If the timing belt is not going to be refitted for some time, it is a wise precaution to hang a warning label on the steering wheel, to remind yourself (and others) not to attempt starting the engine.

4.12 Relieve the tension on the timing belt by slackening the tensioner mounting nut (arrowed) - engine code 2E shown

2A

4.22 Tension the belt by turning the tensioner clockwise using circlip pliers

Refitting

17 Ensure that the timing marks are still correctly aligned in the TDC on No 1 cylinder position, as described in Section 2.

18 Loop the timing belt under the crankshaft sprocket loosely, observing the direction of rotation markings.

19 Temporarily refit the pulley for the auxiliary drivebelt to the crankshaft sprocket, using two of the retaining screws - note that the offset mounting holes allow only one fitting position.

20 Engage the timing belt teeth with the crankshaft sprocket, then manoeuvre it into position over the intermediate shaft and camshaft sprockets. Take great care not to move the sprockets as this is done. Observe the direction of rotation markings on the belt.

21 Pass the flat side of the belt over the tensioner roller - avoid bending the belt back on itself or twisting it excessively as you do this. Ensure that the 'front run' of the belt is taut - ie all the slack should be in the section of the belt that passes over the tensioner roller.

22 Tension the belt by turning the eccentrically-mounted tensioner clockwise; two holes are provided in the side of the tensioner hub for this purpose - a pair of sturdy right-angled circlip pliers is a suitable substitute for the correct VW tool **(see illustration)**.

23 Test the timing belt tension by grasping it between the fingers at a point mid-way between the intermediate shaft and camshaft sprockets and twisting it; the belt tension is correct when it can just be twisted through 90° (quarter of a turn) and no further.

5.5 Slide the tensioner off its mounting stud

24 When the correct belt tension has been achieved, tighten the tensioner nut to the specified torque.

25 Using a spanner or wrench and socket on the crankshaft pulley centre bolt, rotate the crankshaft through two complete revolutions. Reset the engine to TDC on No 1 cylinder with reference to Section 2, and check that the timing marks are re-aligned. Re-check the timing belt tension and adjust it, if necessary.

26 Remove the pulley for the auxiliary drivebelt from the crankshaft sprocket, to allow the lower section of the outer timing belt cover to be refitted, then refit the pulley(s), noting that the offset of the mounting holes allows only one fitting position. Insert and tighten the pulley bolts to the specified torque.

27 Refer to Chapter 3 and refit the coolant pump pulley.

28 Working from Section 6, refit and tension the auxiliary drivebelt(s).

29 Restore the ignition system by reconnecting the HT lead to the distributor cap, then restore the fuelling system by refitting the fuel pump relay or fuel pump fuse. Reconnect the battery negative lead. If removed, refit the right-hand front roadwheel and plastic panels from the wheel arch.

---

5 Timing belt sprockets and tensioner - removal, inspection and refitting

1 Before starting work, immobilise the engine and vehicle as follows:
 a) *Disable the ignition system by removing the distributor centre HT lead and grounding it on the cylinder block, using a jumper wire.*
 b) *Disable the fuelling system by removing the fuel pump relay from its socket, or by removing the fuel pump fuse.*
 c) *Disconnect the battery negative lead, and position the lead away from the battery.* **Note:** *If the vehicle has a security-coded radio, check that you have a copy of the code number before disconnecting the battery. Refer to your VW dealer if in doubt.*
 d) *Prevent any vehicle movement by applying the handbrake and chocking the rear wheels.*

2 To gain access to the components detailed in this Section, carry out the following:
 a) *Refer to Section 6 and remove the auxiliary drivebelt(s).*
 b) *Refer to Chapter 3 and remove the coolant pump pulley.*

Timing belt tensioner

Removal

3 With reference to the relevant paragraphs of Sections 2 and 4, set the engine to TDC on No 1 cylinder, then remove the timing belt upper and lower covers.

4 Slacken the retaining nut at the hub of the tensioner pulley, and allow the assembly to rotate anti-clockwise, relieving the tension on the timing belt. Remove the nut and recover the washer.

5 Slide the tensioner off its mounting stud **(see illustration)**.

Inspection

6 Wipe the tensioner clean, but do not use solvents that may contaminate the bearings. Spin the tensioner pulley on its hub by hand. Stiff movement or excessive freeplay is an indication of severe wear; the tensioner is not a serviceable component, and should be renewed.

Refitting

7 Slide the tensioner pulley over the mounting stud, then refit the washer and retaining nut - do not fully tighten the nut at this stage.

8 With reference to Section 4, tension the timing belt and refit the timing belt covers.

9 Restore the ignition and fuelling systems by reconnecting the distributor HT lead and refitting the fuel pump relay (or fuse).

Camshaft timing belt sprocket

Removal

10 With reference to Sections 2 and 4, remove the timing belt covers and set the engine to TDC on No 1 cylinder. Slacken the tensioner centre nut and rotate it anti-clockwise to relieve the tension on the timing belt. Carefully slide the timing belt off the camshaft sprocket.

11 The camshaft sprocket must be held stationary whilst its retaining bolt is slackened; if access to the correct VW special tool is not possible, a simple home-made tool using basic materials may be fabricated **(see Tool Tip)**.

To make a camshaft sprocket holding tool, obtain two lengths of steel strip about 6mm thick by 30 mm wide or similar, one 600 mm long, the other 200 mm long (all dimensions approximate). Bolt the two strips together to form a forked end, leaving the bolt slack so that the shorter strip can pivot freely. At the end of each 'prong' of the fork, secure a bolt with a nut and a locknut, to act as the fulcrums; these will engage with the cut-outs in the sprocket, and should protrude by about 30mm

12 Using the home-made tool, brace the camshaft sprocket. Slacken and remove the retaining bolt; recover the washer (if fitted).
13 Slide the camshaft sprocket from the end of the camshaft. Where applicable, recover the Woodruff key from the keyway.

Inspection

14 With the sprocket removed, examine the camshaft oil seal for signs of leaking. If necessary, refer to Section 8 and renew it.
15 Wipe the sprocket and camshaft mating surfaces clean.

Refitting

16 Where applicable, fit the Woodruff key into the keyway, with the plain surface facing upwards. Offer up the sprocket to the camshaft, engaging the slot in the sprocket with the Woodruff key. On engines where a key is not used, ensure that the lug in the sprocket hub engages with recess in the end of the camshaft.
17 Working from Section 2, check that the engine is still set to TDC on No 1 cylinder, then refit and tension the timing belt. Refit the timing belt covers.
18 Refit the crankshaft auxiliary belt pulley(s), then insert the retaining bolts and tighten them to the specified torque.
19 With reference to Section 6, refit and tension the auxiliary drivebelt(s).

Crankshaft timing belt sprocket

Removal

20 With reference to Sections 2 and 4, remove the timing belt covers and set the engine to TDC on No 1 cylinder. Slacken the tensioner centre nut and rotate it anti-clockwise to relieve the tension on the timing belt. Carefully slide the timing belt off the crankshaft sprocket.
21 The crankshaft sprocket must be held stationary whilst its retaining bolt is slackened. If access to the correct VW flywheel locking tool is not available, lock the crankshaft in position by removing the starter motor, as described in Chapter 5A, to expose the flywheel ring gear. Then get an assistant insert a stout lever between the gear teeth and the transmission bellhousing whilst the sprocket retaining bolt is slackened.
22 Withdraw the bolt, recover the washer and lift off the sprocket **(see illustration)**.

Inspection

23 With the sprocket removed, examine the crankshaft oil seal for signs of leaking. If necessary, refer to Section 10 and renew it.
24 Wipe the sprocket and crankshaft mating surfaces clean.

Refitting

25 Offer up the sprocket, engaging the lug on the inside of the sprocket with the recess in the end of the crankshaft. Insert the bolt and tighten it to the specified torque.
26 Working from Section 4, check that the engine is still set to TDC on No 1 cylinder,

5.22 Removing the crankshaft sprocket

then refit and tension the timing belt. Refit the timing belt covers.
27 Refit the crankshaft auxiliary belt pulley(s), then insert the retaining bolts and tighten them to the specified torque.
28 With reference to Section 6, refit and tension the auxiliary drivebelt(s).

Intermediate shaft sprocket

Removal

29 With reference to Sections 2 and 4, remove the timing belt covers, and set the engine to TDC on No 1 cylinder. Slacken the tensioner centre nut, and rotate it anti-clockwise to relieve the tension on the timing belt. Carefully slide the timing belt off the intermediate shaft sprocket.
30 The intermediate shaft sprocket must be held stationary whilst its retaining bolt is slackened; if access to the correct VW special tool is not possible, a simple home-made tool using basic materials may be fabricated as described in the camshaft sprocket removal sub-Section.
31 Using the home-made tool, brace the intermediate shaft sprocket and slacken and remove the retaining bolt; recover the washer where fitted.
32 Slide the sprocket from the end of the intermediate shaft. Where applicable, recover the Woodruff key from the keyway.

Inspection

33 With the sprocket removed, examine the intermediate shaft oil seal for signs of leaking. If necessary, refer to Section 9 and renew it.
34 Wipe the sprocket and shaft mating surfaces clean.

Refitting

35 Where applicable, fit the Woodruff key into the keyway, with the plain surface facing upwards. Offer up the sprocket to the intermediate shaft, engaging the slot in the sprocket with the Woodruff key.
36 With reference to Section 2, check that the engine is still set to TDC on No 1 cylinder. Where applicable, align the intermediate shaft sprocket with the crankshaft pulley timing marks.
37 Tighten the sprocket retaining bolt to the specified torque; hold the sprocket using the method employed during removal.

38 With reference to Section 4, refit and tension the timing belt, then refit the timing belt covers.
39 Refit the crankshaft auxiliary belt pulley(s), then insert the retaining bolts and tighten them to the specified torque.
40 With reference to Section 6, refit and tension the auxiliary drivebelt(s).

6 Auxiliary drivebelts - removal, refitting and tensioning

1 Depending on the vehicle specification and engine type, one or two auxiliary drivebelts may be fitted. Both are driven from pulleys mounted on the crankshaft, and provide drive for the alternator, coolant pump, power steering pump and on vehicles with air conditioning, the refrigerant compressor.
2 The run of the belts and the components they drive is also dependent on vehicle specification and engine type.
3 Most models up to 1994 are equipped with V-belts only. The alternator/coolant pump drivebelt is tensioned by pivoting the alternator on its mountings - a rack-and-pinion adjuster is provided to tension the belt **(see illustration overleaf)**. The power steering pump V-belt is tensioned by pivoting the power steering pump on its mounting.
4 Models after 1994 are equipped with a ribbed auxiliary belt, which may be fitted with an automatic tensioning device, depending on its run (and hence the number of components it is driving). Otherwise, a ribbed belt is tensioned by the alternator mountings, which have an in-built tensioning spring. Later models still have a V-belt driving the power steering pump.
5 The auxiliary belts must be tensioned correctly, to ensure correct operation under all conditions and prolonged service life.

Auxiliary V-belts

Alternator drivebelt

6 Park the vehicle on a level surface, and apply the handbrake. Disconnect the battery negative terminal, and position the lead away from the battery. **Note:** *If the vehicle has a security-coded radio, check that you have a copy of the code number before disconnecting the battery. Refer to your VW dealer if in doubt.* Jack up the front of the vehicle and rest it securely on axle stands - refer to *"Jacking and vehicle support"*.
7 Turn the steering to full right lock. To provide better access, the right-hand front wheel can be removed if wished. Some later models may be fitted with plastic panels which will need to be unclipped for access to the engine through the wheel arch.
8 Loosen the alternator pivot and adjustment bolts, then turn the tensioner rack bolt to swivel the alternator towards the engine.
9 On models with power steering, it will be necessary to remove the power steering pump V-belt first, in order to pass the alternator belt over the crankshaft pulley.

2A

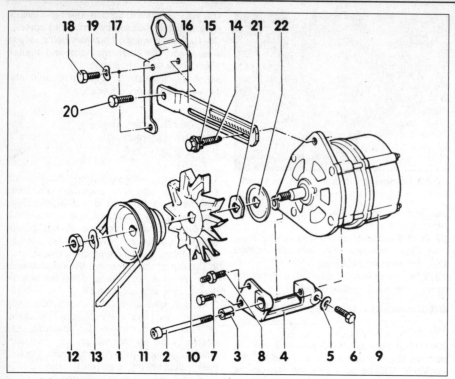

6.3 Alternator and its mounting components - early models with V-belt drive

1	Drivebelt	6	Bolt
2	Socket-head bolt	7	Bolt
		8	Stud
3	Sleeve	9	Alternator
4	Bracket	10	Fan wheel
5	Washer	11	Pulley

12	Nut	17	Lifting eye
13	Washer	18	Bolt
14	Bolt	19	Washer
15	Tensioner pinion	20	Bolt
16	Tensioner rack	21	Spacer
		22	Washer

6.13a Checking the alternator V-belt tension

6.13b Adjusting the V-belt tension

10 Slip the alternator belt off the alternator, crankshaft and coolant pump pulleys (as applicable).
11 Examine the belt for signs of wear or damage, and renew it if necessary.
12 Fit the new drivebelt over the relevant pulleys, ensuring the belt seats properly in the pulley grooves.
13 Tension the belt by turning the tensioner rack bolt until the belt deflection midway between the longest pulley run is as specified at the start of this Chapter (see illustrations). When adjustment is complete, tighten the alternator pivot and adjustment bolts.
14 Rotate the crankshaft in its normal

direction of rotation through two turns, then re-check and if necessary adjust the tension. Refit the right-hand front wheel and any plastic panels from the wheel arch (if removed) then lower the car to the ground. If removed, fit and tension the power steering pump drivebelt as described in the next sub-Section. Reconnect the battery negative lead.

Power steering pump drivebelt

15 Refer to paragraphs 6 and 7 to gain access to the drivebelt.
16 With reference to Chapter 10, slacken the power steering pump mounting bolts and allow the pump body to pivot around its uppermost mounting towards the engine.

17 Guide the V-belt off the power steering pump pulley and where applicable, the coolant pump pulley.
18 Examine the belt for signs or wear or damage, and renew it if necessary.
19 Refit the belt by reversing the removal procedure, ensuring that it seats evenly in the pulleys.

Early models
20 The belt tension is set using a tensioning bolt and a locking bolt (see illustrations). With all the pump mounting nuts and bolts slackened, turn the tensioning bolt until the belt tension is correct, and then tighten the locking bolt. Tighten all the remaining mounting bolts securely on completion.

Later models
21 The belt tension on later models is most easily set by grasping the underside of the power steering pump and drawing it towards the front of the vehicle. Tighten the power steering pump mounting bolts to the specified torque on completion.

All models
22 Rotate the crankshaft in its normal direction of rotation through two turns, then re-check and if necessary adjust the tension. Refit the right-hand front wheel and any plastic panels from the wheel arch (if removed) then lower the car to the ground. Reconnect the battery negative lead.

Air conditioning compressor drivebelt
23 The procedure for tensioning the air conditioning compressor drivebelt is identical to that for the alternator drivebelt in paragraphs 6 to 14.

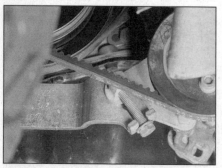

6.20a Power steering pump drivebelt tensioning bolt

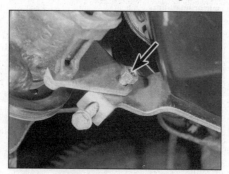

6.20b Power steering pump tensioner locking bolt (arrowed)

6.27 Rotate the tensioner roller arm clockwise using an adjustable spanner

Auxiliary ribbed belt

Removal

24 Park the vehicle on a level surface, and apply the handbrake. Disconnect the battery negative terminal, and position the lead away from the battery. **Note:** *If the vehicle has a security-coded radio, check that you have a copy of the code number before disconnecting the battery. Refer to your VW dealer if in doubt.* Jack up the front of the vehicle and rest it on axle stands - refer to *"Jacking and vehicle support"*.

25 Turn the steering to full right lock. To provide better access, the right-hand front wheel can be removed if wished. Some later models may be fitted with plastic panels which will need to be unclipped for access to the engine through the wheel arch. Where applicable, remove the auxiliary V-belt as described in the previous sub-Section.

26 Examine the ribbed belt for manufacturer's markings, indicating the direction of rotation. If none are present, make some using typist's correction fluid or a dab of paint - do not cut or score the belt in any way.

Vehicles with a roller-arm automatic tensioning device

27 Rotate the tensioner roller arm clockwise against its spring tension, so that the roller is forced away from the belt - use an adjustable spanner as a lever **(see illustration)**.

Vehicles with a rotary automatic tensioning device

28 Fit a ring spanner to the tensioner centre nut, and rotate the assembly anti-clockwise, against its spring tension.

Vehicles without an automatic tensioning device

29 Slacken the alternator upper and lower mounting bolts by between one and two turns.

30 Push the alternator down to its stop against the spring tension, so that it rotates around its uppermost mounting.

All vehicles

31 Pull the belt off the alternator pulley, then release it from the remaining pulleys.

32 Examine the belt for signs or wear or damage, and renew it if necessary.

33 Pass the ribbed belt underneath the crankshaft pulley, ensuring that the ribs seat in the channels on the surface of the pulley.

Caution: Observe the manufacturer's direction of rotation markings on the belt, when refitting.

Vehicles with a roller-arm automatic tensioning device

34 Rotate the tensioner roller arm clockwise against its spring tension - use an adjustable spanner as a lever.

35 Pass the belt around the coolant pump pulley or air conditioning refrigerant pump pulley (as applicable), then fit it over the alternator pulley.

36 Release the tensioner pulley arm, and allow the roller to bear against the flat surface of the belt.

Vehicles with a rotary automatic tensioning device

37 Fit a ring spanner to the tensioner centre nut, and rotate the assembly anti-clockwise, against its spring tension.

38 Pass the flat side of the belt underneath the tensioner roller, then fit it over the power steering pump and alternator pulleys.

39 Release the spanner and allow the tensioner roller to bear against the flat side of the belt.

Vehicles without an automatic tensioning device

40 Repeatedly push the alternator down to its stop against the spring tension, so that it rotates around its uppermost mounting, and check that it moves back freely when released. If necessary, slacken the alternator mounting bolts by a further half a turn.

41 Keep the alternator pushed down against its stop, pass the belt over the alternator pulley, then release the alternator and allow it to tension the belt.

42 Reconnect the battery negative lead, then without tightening the alternator mountings, start the engine and allow it to idle for about 10 seconds.

43 Switch the engine off, then tighten first the lower, then the upper alternator mounting bolts to the specified torque.

All vehicles

44 Where applicable, refer to the previous sub-Section and refit the auxiliary V-belt.

45 If removed, refit the right-hand front wheel and any plastic panels removed for access, then lower the vehicle to the ground. If not already done, reconnect the battery negative lead.

7 Camshaft cover - removal and refitting

Removal

1 Immobilise the engine by:
  a) *Unplugging the fuel pump relay from its socket, or by removing the fuel pump fuse.*
  b) *Disconnecting the HT king lead from the distributor and earthing it on the engine block using a jumper wire.*
  c) *Disconnecting the battery negative terminal, and positioning the lead away from the battery. **Note:** If the vehicle has a security-coded radio, check that you have a copy of the code number before disconnecting the battery. Refer to your VW dealer if in doubt.*

2 Disconnect the crankcase breather hose(s) from the top of the camshaft cover. If crimp-type hose clips are used, cut them off and replace them with standard worm-drive clips on refitting. On models with a pressure regulator valve mounted on top of the camshaft cover (two breather hoses), slacken and withdraw the retaining screws and remove the regulator valve.

3 On later models with engine code 2E, access may be improved by removing the idling stabilisation valve; refer to Chapter 4B.

4 Where applicable, to gain greater working space, refer to Chapter 4A and disconnect the throttle cable from the throttle housing.

5 Working around the edge of the camshaft cover, progressively slacken and remove the retaining nuts.

6 Where fitted, lift off the reinforcement strips, then lift the cover away from the cylinder head **(see illustrations)**. If it sticks, do not attempt to lever it off with an implement - instead free it by working around the cover and tapping it lightly with a soft-faced mallet.

2A

7.6a Remove the reinforcement strips . . .

7.6b . . . and lift off the camshaft cover

7.7 Where fitted, lift off the baffle plate . . .

7.8 . . . and recover the gasket

7 Where fitted, lift the baffle plate off the camshaft bearing caps **(see illustration)**.

8 Recover the camshaft cover gasket **(see illustration)**. Note that the gasket may be made up of several pieces, depending on engine specification. Inspect the gasket carefully - renew the gasket if damage or deterioration is evident, or if the gasket has seen extended service. Where a multi-piece gasket is used, VW state that the gasket must be renewed whenever it is disturbed, regardless of condition.

9 Clean the mating surfaces of the cylinder head and camshaft cover thoroughly, removing all traces of oil and old gasket. Take care, however, not to damage the surfaces.

Refitting

10 Refit the camshaft cover by following the removal procedure in reverse, noting the following points:

a) *Ensure that all sections of the gasket are correctly seated on the cylinder head, and take care to avoid displacing it as the camshaft cover is lowered into position.*

b) *Tighten the camshaft cover retaining screws/nuts to the specified torque.*

c) *When refitting hoses that were originally secured with crimp-type clips, use standard worm-drive clips in their place on refitting.*

11 On completion, restore the fuel and ignition systems by refitting the fuel pump relay (or fuse) and reconnecting the distributor HT lead. Refit any components removed for access, and reconnect the battery negative lead.

8.8 Drive the camshaft oil seal squarely into its housing

8 Camshaft oil seal - renewal

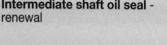

1 Immobilise the engine by:

a) *Unplugging the fuel pump relay from its socket, or by removing the fuel pump fuse.*

b) *Disconnecting the HT king lead from the distributor and earthing it on the engine block using a jumper wire.*

c) *Disconnecting the battery negative terminal, and positioning the lead away from the battery.* **Note:** *If the vehicle has a security-coded radio, check that you have a copy of the code number before disconnecting the battery. Refer to your VW dealer if in doubt.*

2 Refer to Section 6 and remove the auxiliary drivebelt(s).

3 With reference to Sections 2, 4 and 5 of this Chapter, remove the auxiliary belt pulleys and timing belt cover, then set the engine to TDC on No 1 cylinder and remove the timing belt, timing belt tensioner and camshaft sprocket.

4 After removing the retaining screws, lift the timing belt inner cover away from the engine block - this will expose the oil seal.

5 Drill two small holes into the existing oil seal, diagonally opposite each other. Thread two self-tapping screws into the holes, and using two pairs of pliers, pull on the heads of the screws to extract oil seal. Take great care to avoid drilling through into the seal housing or camshaft sealing surface.

6 Clean out the seal housing and sealing surface of the camshaft by wiping it with a lint-free cloth - avoid using solvents that may enter the cylinder head and affect component lubrication. Remove any swarf or burrs that may cause the seal to leak.

7 Lubricate the lip of the new oil seal with clean engine oil, and push it over the camshaft until it is positioned above its housing.

8 Using a hammer and a socket of suitable diameter, drive the seal squarely into its housing **(see illustration)**. Note: *Select a socket that bears only on the hard outer surface of the seal, not the inner lip, which can easily be damaged.*

9 With reference to Sections 2, 4 and 5 of this Chapter, refit the timing belt inner cover and the timing sprockets, then refit and tension the timing belt. On completion, refit the timing belt outer cover.

10 With reference to Section 6, refit and tension the auxiliary drivebelt(s).

11 On completion, restore the fuel and ignition systems by refitting the fuel pump relay (or fuse) and reconnecting the distributor HT lead. Reconnect the battery negative lead.

9 Intermediate shaft oil seal - renewal

1 Immobilise the engine by:

a) *Unplugging the fuel pump relay from its socket, or by removing the fuel pump fuse.*

b) *Disconnecting the HT king lead from the distributor and earthing it on the engine block using a jumper wire.*

c) *Disconnecting the battery negative terminal, and positioning the lead away from the battery.* **Note:** *If the vehicle has a security-coded radio, check that you have a copy of the code number before disconnecting the battery. Refer to your VW dealer if in doubt.*

2 Refer to Section 6 and remove the auxiliary drivebelt(s).

3 With reference to Sections 4 and 5 of this Chapter, remove the auxiliary belt pulleys, timing belt outer cover, timing belt, tensioner and intermediate shaft sprocket.

4 After removing the retaining screws, lift the timing belt inner cover away from the engine block - this will expose the intermediate shaft sealing flange.

5 With reference to Section 7 of Chapter 2C, remove the intermediate shaft flange, and renew the shaft and flange oil seals.

6 Referring to Sections 4 and 5 of this Chapter, carry out the following:

a) *Refit the timing belt inner cover.*

b) *Refit the intermediate shaft timing belt sprocket.*

c) *Refit and tension the timing belt.*

d) *Refit the timing belt outer cover.*

7 With reference to Section 6 of this Chapter, refit and tension the auxiliary drivebelt(s).

10 Crankshaft oil seals - renewal

Crankshaft front oil seal

1 Immobilise the engine by:

a) *Unplugging the fuel pump relay from its socket, or by removing the fuel pump fuse.*

b) *Disconnecting the HT king lead from the distributor and earthing it on the engine block using a jumper wire.*

c) Disconnecting the battery negative terminal, and positioning the lead away from the battery. **Note:** *If the vehicle has a security-coded radio, check that you have a copy of the code number before disconnecting the battery. Refer to your VW dealer if in doubt.*

2 Drain the engine oil - see Chapter 1A.

3 With reference to *"Jacking and vehicle support"*, raise the front of the vehicle and rest it securely on axle stands.

4 Turn the steering to full right lock. To provide better access, the right-hand front wheel can be removed if wished. Some later models may be fitted with plastic panels which will need to be unclipped for access to the engine through the wheel arch.

5 Remove the auxiliary drivebelt(s), see Section 6.

6 With reference to Sections 2, 4 and 5 of this Chapter, remove the auxiliary belt pulleys, timing belt outer covers, timing belt and crankshaft sprocket.

7 Remove the oil seal, using the same method as that described for the camshaft oil seal removal, in Section 8.

8 Clean out the seal housing and sealing surface of the crankshaft by wiping it with a lint-free cloth - avoid using solvents that may enter the crankcase and affect component lubrication. Remove any swarf or burrs that could cause the seal to leak.

9 Lubricate the lip of the new oil seal with clean engine oil, and position it over the housing **(see illustration)**.

10 Using a hammer and a socket of suitable diameter, drive the seal squarely into its housing **(see illustration)**. **Note:** *Select a socket that bears only on the hard outer surface of the seal, not the inner lip, which can easily be damaged.*

11 With reference to Sections 2, 4 and 5 of this Chapter, refit the crankshaft timing belt sprocket, then refit and tension the timing belt. On completion, refit the timing belt outer cover, and auxiliary drivebelt pulley(s).

12 The remainder of the refitting procedure is a reversal of removal, as follows:

a) *With reference to Section 6, refit and tension the auxiliary drivebelt(s).*

b) *Refit the right-hand front roadwheel (where removed).*

c) *Refer to Chapter 1A and refill the engine with the correct grade and quantity of oil.*

d) *Restore the ignition and fuel systems.*

Crankshaft front oil seal housing - gasket renewal

13 Proceed as described in paragraphs 1 to 6 above, then refer to Section 15 and remove the sump.

14 Progressively slacken and then remove the oil seal housing retaining bolts.

15 Lift the housing away from the cylinder block, together with the crankshaft oil seal, using a twisting motion to ease the seal along the shaft.

16 Recover the old gasket from the seal housing on the cylinder block. If it has disintegrated, scrape the remains off with a trimming knife blade. Take care to avoid damaging the mating surfaces.

17 Prise the old oil seal from the housing using a stout screwdriver.

18 Wipe the oil seal housing clean, and check it visually for signs of distortion or cracking. Lay the housing on a work surface, with the mating surface face down. Press in a new oil seal, using a block of wood as a press to ensure that the seal enters the housing squarely.

19 Smear the crankcase mating surface with non-hardening jointing compound, and lay the new gasket in position.

20 Pad the end of the crankshaft with a layer of PVC tape; this will protect the oil seal as it is being fitted.

21 Lubricate the inner lip of the crankshaft oil seal with clean engine oil, then offer up the seal and its housing to the end of the crankshaft. Ease the seal along the shaft using a twisting motion, until the housing is flush with the crankcase.

22 Insert the retaining bolts and tighten them progressively to the specified torque **(see illustration)**.

Caution: The housing is fabricated from a light alloy, and may be distorted if the bolts are not tightened progressively.

23 Refer to Section 15 and refit the sump.

24 With reference to Sections 2, 4 and 5 of this Chapter, refit the crankshaft timing belt sprocket, then refit and tension the timing belt. On completion, refit the timing belt outer cover, and auxiliary drivebelt pulley(s).

25 The remainder of the refitting procedure is a reversal of removal, as follows:

a) *With reference to Section 6, refit and tension the auxiliary drivebelt(s).*

b) *Refit the right-hand front wheel and any plastic panels removed for access.*

c) *Refer to Chapter 1A and refill the engine with the correct grade and quantity of oil.*

d) *Restore the ignition and fuel systems.*

Crankshaft rear oil seal (flywheel end)

Note: *Check availability of the oil seal before proceeding*

26 Proceed as described in paragraphs 1 to 3 above, then refer to Section 15 and remove the sump.

10.9 Lubricate the new crankshaft oil seal, and position it over the housing

27 Turn the steering to full left lock. To provide better access, the left-hand front wheel can be removed if wished. Some later models may be fitted with plastic panels which will need to be unclipped for access to the engine through the wheel arch.

28 Refer to Chapter 7A or B as applicable, and remove the transmission from the engine.

29 On vehicles with manual transmission, refer to Section 13 of this Chapter and remove the flywheel, then refer to Chapter 6 and remove the clutch friction plate and pressure plate.

30 On vehicles with automatic transmission, refer to Section 13 of this Chapter and remove the driveplate from the crankshaft.

31 Where applicable, remove the retaining bolts and lift the intermediate plate away from the cylinder block.

32 Progressively slacken and then remove the oil seal housing retaining bolts.

33 Lift the housing away from the cylinder block, together with the crankshaft oil seal, using a twisting motion to ease the seal along the shaft.

34 Recover the old gasket from the seal housing on the cylinder block. If it has disintegrated, scrape the remains off with a trimming knife blade. Take care to avoid damaging the mating surfaces.

35 Prise the old oil seal from the housing using a stout screwdriver.

36 Wipe the oil seal housing clean, and check it visually for signs of distortion or cracking. Lay the housing on a work surface, with the mating surface face down. Press in a new oil seal, using a block of wood as a press to ensure that the seal enters the housing squarely.

10.10 Using a hammer and a socket, drive the seal squarely into its housing

10.22 Tighten the front oil seal housing bolts to the specified torque

2A

37 Smear the crankcase mating surface with non-hardening jointing compound, and lay the new gasket in position.

38 A protective plastic cap is supplied with genuine VW crankshaft oil seals; when fitted over the end of the crankshaft, the cap prevents damage to the inner lip of the oil seal as it is being fitted. Use PVC tape to pad the end of the crankshaft if a cap is not available.

39 Lubricate the inner lip of the crankshaft oil seal with clean engine oil, then offer up the seal and its housing to the end of the crankshaft. Ease the seal along the shaft using a twisting motion, until the housing is flush with the crankcase.

40 Insert the retaining bolts and tighten them progressively to the specified torque **(see illustration)**.

Caution: The housing is fabricated from a light alloy, and may be distorted if the bolts are not tightened progressively.

41 Refer to Section 15 and refit the sump.

42 Fit the intermediate plate to the cylinder block, then insert and tighten the bolts.

43 On vehicles with automatic transmission, work from Section 13 of this Chapter and refit the driveplate to the crankshaft.

44 On vehicles with manual transmission, refer to Section 13 of this Chapter and refit the flywheel, then refer to Chapter 6 and refit the clutch friction plate and pressure plate.

45 Referring to Chapter 7A or B as applicable, refit the transmission to the engine.

46 The remainder of the refitting procedure is a reversal of removal, as follows:
a) Refit the left-hand front wheel and any plastic panels removed for access.
b) Refer to Chapter 1A and refill the engine with the correct grade and quantity of oil.
c) Restore the ignition and fuel systems.

11 Cylinder head and manifolds - removal, separation and refitting

Note 1: *From March 1995, a metal cylinder head gasket has been fitted, replacing the previous type. At the same time, modified cylinder head bolts, identifiable by the presence of three raised "pips" on the bolt heads, were also introduced. From this date, the later gasket will be supplied for all engines, meaning that the cylinder head bolts must now be replaced as a set for bolts of the later type.*

Note 2: *On vehicles with engine code RP, the exhaust manifold-to-downpipe joint incorporates two spring clips, which are almost impossible to remove without the special VW service tool (4140A/2). Refer to Chapter 4D, Section 7 for further details.*

Removal

1 Select a solid, level surface to park the vehicle upon. Give yourself enough space to move around it easily.

10.40 Tighten the rear oil seal housing bolts to the specified torque

2 Refer to Chapter 11 and remove the bonnet from its hinges.

3 Disconnect the battery negative lead, and position it away from the terminal. **Note:** *If the vehicle has a security-coded radio, check that you have a copy of the code number before disconnecting the battery. Refer to your VW dealer if in doubt.*

4 Referring to Chapter 1A, carry out the following :
a) Drain the engine oil.
b) Drain the cooling system.

5 Refer to Section 6 and remove the auxiliary drivebelt(s).

6 With reference to Section 2, set the engine to TDC on No 1 cylinder.

7 Refer to Chapter 3 and perform the following:
a) Slacken the clips and disconnect the radiator hoses from the engine and coolant pump/thermostat housing (as applicable).
b) Slacken the clips and disconnect the expansion tank and cabin heater inlet and outlet coolant hoses from the ports on the cylinder head.

8 The "lock carrier" is a panel assembly comprising the headlight units, radiator grille (later models), and bonnet lock mechanism. Although its removal is not essential, its does give greatly-improved access to the engine; see Chapter 11.

9 With reference to Chapter 4A or 4B, unplug the lambda sensor wiring from the main harness at the multiway connector (where applicable).

10 With reference to Chapter 1A, remove the HT leads from the spark plugs and the distributor.

11 On multi-point fuel-injected models, refer to Chapter 4B and remove the throttle housing, the fuel rail and the fuel injectors.

12 On single-point fuel-injected models, remove the throttle body air box, and then remove the throttle body with reference to Chapter 4A.

13 With reference to Sections 2, 4 and 7, carry out the following:
a) Remove the camshaft cover.
b) Remove the timing belt outer covers, and disengage the timing belt from the camshaft sprocket.

14 Slacken and withdraw the retaining screws, or release the clips, and lift off the inner timing belt cover(s).

15 With reference to Chapter 4A or B as applicable, unplug the wiring harness from the coolant temperature sensor at the connector.

16 Refer to Chapter 4D and separate the exhaust downpipe from the exhaust manifold flange.

17 Where applicable, detach the warm air inlet hose from the exhaust manifold heat shield.

18 Slacken and remove the bolt securing the engine oil dipstick tube to the cylinder head.

19 Remove the retaining screw and detach the engine harness connector bracket from the cylinder head.

20 Following the reverse of the tightening sequence (see *"Refitting"*), progressively slacken the cylinder head bolts, by half a turn at a time, until all bolts can be unscrewed by hand.

21 Check that nothing remains connected to the cylinder head, then lift the head away from the cylinder block; seek assistance if possible as it is a heavy assembly, especially if it is being removed complete with the manifolds.

22 Remove the gasket from the top of the block, noting the locating dowels. If the dowels are a loose fit, remove them and store them with the head for safe-keeping. Do not discard the gasket - on some models it will be needed for identification purposes.

23 If the cylinder head is to be dismantled for overhaul, refer to Chapter 2C.

Manifold separation

24 Inlet manifold removal and refitting is described in Chapter 4A or B as applicable.

25 Progressively slacken and remove the exhaust manifold retaining nuts. Lift the manifold away from the cylinder head and recover the gaskets. Where applicable, slacken the union and detach the CO sampling pipe from the manifold.

26 Ensure that the mating surfaces are completely clean, then refit the exhaust manifold, using new gaskets. Tighten the retaining nuts to the specified torque.

Preparation for refitting

27 The mating faces of the cylinder head and cylinder block/crankcase must be perfectly clean before refitting the head. Use a hard plastic or wood scraper to remove all traces of gasket and carbon; also clean the piston crowns. Take particular care during the cleaning operations, as aluminium alloy is easily damaged. Also, make sure that the carbon is not allowed to enter the oil and water passages - this is particularly important for the lubrication system, as carbon could block the oil supply to the engine's components. Using adhesive tape and paper, seal the water, oil and bolt holes in the cylinder block/crankcase.

28 Check the mating surfaces of the cylinder block/crankcase and the cylinder head for nicks, deep scratches and other damage. If slight, they may be removed carefully with a file, but if excessive, machining may be the only alternative to renewal.

29 If warpage of the cylinder head gasket surface is suspected, use a straight-edge to check it for distortion. Refer to Part C of this Chapter if necessary.

30 On all the engines covered in this Chapter, it is possible for the piston crowns to strike and damage the valve heads, if the camshaft is rotated with the timing belt removed and the crankshaft set to TDC. For this reason, the crankshaft must be set to a position other than TDC on No 1 cylinder, before the cylinder head is refitted: use a wrench and socket on the crankshaft pulley centre bolt to turn the crankshaft in its normal direction of rotation, until all four pistons are positioned halfway down their bores, with No 1 piston on its upstroke - ie 90° before TDC.

Refitting

31 Lay a new head gasket on the cylinder block, engaging it with the locating dowels. Handle the metal gasket with great care while fitting - any damage caused to the silicone coating or beading will result in leaks. Ensure that the manufacturer's "TOP" and part number markings are face up **(see illustrations)**.

32 With the help of an assistant, place the cylinder head and manifolds centrally on the cylinder block, ensuring that the locating dowels engage with the recesses in the cylinder head. Check that the head gasket is correctly seated before allowing the weight the full weight of the cylinder head to rest upon it.

33 Apply a smear of grease to the threads, and to the underside of the heads, of the new cylinder head bolts; use a good-quality high-melting point grease.

34 Carefully enter each bolt into its relevant hole (*do not drop them in*) and screw in, by hand only, until finger-tight.

35 Working progressively and in the sequence shown, tighten the cylinder head bolts to their Stage 1 torque setting, using a torque wrench and suitable socket **(see illustration)**. Repeat the exercise in the same sequence for the Stage 2 torque setting.

36 Once all the bolts have been tightened to their Stage 2 settings, working again in the given sequence, angle-tighten the bolts through the specified Stage 3 angle, using a socket and extension bar. It is recommended that an angle-measuring gauge is used during this stage of the tightening, to ensure accuracy. If a gauge is not available, use white paint to make alignment marks between the bolt head and cylinder head prior to tightening; the marks can then be used to check that the bolt has been rotated through the correct angle during tightening. Repeat the exercise for the Stage 4 setting.

37 Refit the timing belt inner cover, tightening the retaining screws securely.

11.31a Lay a new head gasket on the block, engaging it with the locating dowels - earlier type gasket shown

38 Refer to Section 2 and follow the procedure for setting the engine to TDC on No 1 cylinder with the timing belt removed. On completion, refer to Section 4 and refit the camshaft timing belt.

39 The remainder of the refitting sequence is a reversal of the removal procedure, as follows:

a) *Bolt the engine dipstick tube to the cylinder head, where applicable.*
b) *Refer to Chapter 4D and reconnect the exhaust downpipe to the exhaust manifold.*
c) *On multipoint fuel-injected systems, refer to Chapter 4B and refit the fuel injectors, fuel rail, and the throttle body.*
d) *On single-point fuel-injected models, refer to Chapter 4A and refit the throttle body and air box.*
e) *Refer to Chapter 1A and refit the ignition HT leads.*
f) *Refer to Section 7 and refit the camshaft cover.*
g) *With reference to the information in Chapter 11, refit the lock carrier assembly, if it was removed for greater access.*
h) *Reconnect the coolant hoses to the radiator, expansion tank and heater, referring to Chapter 3 for guidance. Reconnect the coolant temperature sensor wiring.*
i) *Refer to Section 6 and refit the auxiliary drivebelt(s).*
j) *Restore the battery connection.*
k) *Refer to Chapter 11 and refit the bonnet.*

40 On completion, refer to Chapter 1A and carry out the following:

a) *Refill the engine cooling system with the correct quantity of new coolant.*

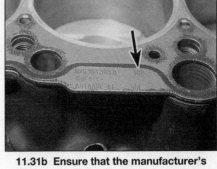

11.31b Ensure that the manufacturer's "TOP" mark and part number are face up

b) *Refill the engine lubrication system with the correct grade and quantity of oil.*

12 Hydraulic tappets - operation check

> **Warning: After fitting hydraulic tappets, wait a minimum of 30 minutes (or preferably, leave overnight) before starting the engine, to allow the tappets time to settle, otherwise the pistons may strike the valve heads.**

1 The hydraulic tappets are self-adjusting, and require no attention whilst in service.

2 If the hydraulic tappets become excessively noisy, their operation can be checked as described below.

3 Run the engine until it reaches its normal operating temperature. Switch off the engine, then refer to Section 7 and remove the camshaft cover.

4 Rotate the camshaft by turning the crankshaft with a socket and wrench, until the first cam lobe over No 1 cylinder is pointing upwards.

5 Using a feeler blade, measure the clearance between the base of the cam lobe and the top of the tappet. If the clearance is greater than 0.1mm, then the tappet is defective and must be renewed.

6 If the clearance is less than 0.1 mm, press down on the top of the tappet, until it is felt to contact the top of the valve stem **(see illustration)**. Use a wooden or plastic

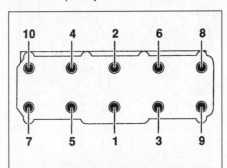

11.35 Cylinder head bolt tightening sequence

10 4 2 6 8
7 5 1 3 9

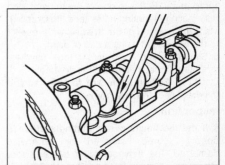

12.6 Press down on the tappet, until it contacts the top of the valve stem

13.4 Flywheel locked in position with a home-made tool

13.9 If necessary, apply locking compound to the new flywheel bolts

13.11 Tighten the flywheel bolts to the specified torque

implement that will not damage the surface of the tappet.

7 If the tappet travels more than 0.1 mm before making contact, then it is defective and must be renewed.

8 Hydraulic tappet removal and refitting is described as part of the cylinder head overhaul sequence - see Chapter 2C for details.

13 Flywheel/driveplate -
removal, inspection and refitting

General information

Manual transmission models

1 The flywheel is mounted on the crankshaft, with the pressure plate bolted to it. Removal of the flywheel is as described below.

Automatic transmission models

2 The torque converter driveplate is bolted directly to the end of the crankshaft; removal is as described below. Removal of the automatic transmission and torque converter is described in Chapter 7B.

Flywheel

Removal

3 Remove the transmission and clutch as described in Chapter 7A and Chapter 6 respectively.

4 Lock the flywheel in position using a home-made locking tool, fabricated from a piece of scrap metal. Bolt it to one of the transmission bellhousing mounting holes **(see illustration)**. Mark the position of the flywheel with respect to the crankshaft using a dab of paint.

5 Slacken and withdraw the flywheel mounting bolts, then lift off the flywheel.
Caution: Get an assistant to help, as the flywheel is extremely heavy.

Inspection

6 If the flywheel's clutch mating surface is deeply scored, cracked or otherwise damaged, the flywheel must be renewed. However, it may be possible to have it surface-ground; seek the advice of a VW dealer or engine reconditioning specialist.

7 If the ring gear is badly worn or has missing teeth, the flywheel must be renewed.

Refitting

8 Clean the mating surfaces of the flywheel and crankshaft. Remove any remaining locking compound from the threads of the crankshaft holes, using the correct-size tap, if available.

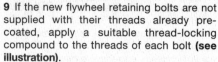
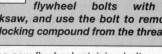

If a suitable tap is not available, cut two slots down the threads of one of the old flywheel bolts with a hacksaw, and use the bolt to remove the locking compound from the threads.

9 If the new flywheel retaining bolts are not supplied with their threads already pre-coated, apply a suitable thread-locking compound to the threads of each bolt **(see illustration)**.

10 Offer up the flywheel to the crankshaft, using the alignment marks made during removal, and fit the new retaining bolts.

11 Lock the flywheel using the method employed on dismantling, and tighten the retaining bolts to the specified torque **(see illustration)**.

12 Refit the clutch as described in Chapter 6. Remove the locking tool, and refit the transmission as described in Chapter 7A.

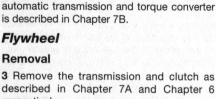

13.15 Driveplate components

1 *Packing plate*   3 *Mounting bolt*
2 *Shim*

Driveplate

Removal

13 Remove the transmission (Chapter 7B).

14 Lock the driveplate in position by bolting a piece of scrap metal between the driveplate and one of the transmission bellhousing mounting holes. Mark the position of the driveplate with respect to the crankshaft using a dab of paint.

15 Slacken and withdraw the driveplate mounting bolts, then lift off the driveplate. Recover the packing plate and the shim (where applicable) **(see illustration)**.

Refitting

16 Refitting is a reversal of removal, using the alignment marks made during removal. Fit new mounting bolts and tighten them to the specified torque. Remove the locking tool, and refit the transmission as described in Chapter 7B.

14 Engine mountings -
inspection and renewal

Inspection

1 If improved access is required, raise the front of the car and support it securely on axle stands (see "*Jacking and vehicle support*").

2 Check the mounting rubbers to see if they are cracked, hardened or separated from the metal at any point; renew the mounting if any such damage or deterioration is evident.

3 Check that all the mounting's fasteners are securely tightened; use a torque wrench to check if possible.

4 Using a large screwdriver or a crowbar, check for wear in the mounting by carefully levering against it to check for free play. Where this is not possible, enlist the aid of an assistant to move the engine/transmission back and forth, or from side to side, while you watch the mounting. While some free play is to be expected even from new components, excessive wear should be obvious. If excessive free play is found, check first that the fasteners are correctly secured, then renew any worn components as described below.

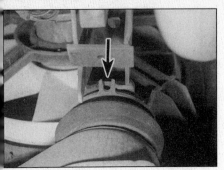

14.13a Lug (arrowed) on top of the mounting block engages in the recess in the bracket

Renewal

Front engine mounting

5 Disconnect the battery negative cable, and position it away from the terminal.

6 Position a trolley jack underneath the engine and position it such that the jack head is directly underneath the engine/bellhousing mating surface.

7 Raise the jack until it just takes the weight of the engine off the front engine mounting.

8 Slacken and withdraw the engine mounting through-bolt.

9 Refer to Chapter 5A and remove the starter motor.

10 Slacken and withdraw the engine mounting-to-transmission bellhousing bolts and remove the bracket.

11 Working under the engine mounting front crossmember, remove the engine mounting block retaining screw.

12 Lift the engine mounting block out of the crossmember cup.

13 Refitting is a reversal of removal, noting the following points:

a) *Ensure that the orientation lug that protrudes from the top of surface of the engine mounting block engages with the recess in the mounting bracket (see illustration).*

b) *Tighten all bolts to the specified torque (see illustration).*

Rear right-hand engine mounting

14 Disconnect the battery negative cable.

15 Mount an engine lifting beam across the engine bay, and attach the jib to the engine lifting eyes on the cylinder head. Alternatively, an engine hoist can be used. Raise the hoist/lifting beam jib to take the weight of the engine off the engine mounting.

16 Slacken and withdraw the engine mounting through-bolt.

17 Unbolt the engine mounting bracket from the cylinder block.

18 Unbolt the engine mounting block from the body, and remove it from the engine bay.

19 Refitting is a reversal of removal, noting the following points:

a) *Ensure that the orientation lug that protrudes from the top of surface of the engine mounting block engages with the*

14.13b Engine mountings and retaining bolts - refer to the Specifications for torque wrench settings

recess in the mounting bracket.

b) *Tighten all bolts to the specified torque (see illustration 14.13b).*

Rear left-hand mounting

20 Disconnect the battery negative cable, and position it away from the terminal.

21 Position a trolley jack below the engine, with the jack head directly underneath the engine/bellhousing mating surface.

22 Raise the jack until it just takes the weight of the engine off the rear right-hand engine mounting.

23 Slacken and withdraw the engine mounting through-bolt.

24 Unbolt the engine mounting bracket from the end of the transmission casing.

25 Unbolt the engine mounting block from the body, and remove it from the engine bay (see illustration).

26 Refitting is a reversal of removal, noting the following points:

a) *Ensure that the orientation lug that protrudes from the top of surface of the engine mounting block engages with the recess in the mounting bracket.*

b) *Tighten all bolts to the specified torque (see illustration 14.13b).*

14.25 Removing the rear left-hand engine mounting block

2A

15.5 Removing the sump bolts (engine removed and inverted for clarity)

15 Sump - removal and refitting

Removal

1 Disconnect the battery negative lead, and position it away from the terminal. **Note:** *If the vehicle has a security-coded radio, check that you have a copy of the code number before disconnecting the battery. Refer to your VW dealer if in doubt.* Refer to Chapter 1A and drain the engine oil. Where applicable, remove the screws and lower the engine undertray away from the vehicle.

2 Park the vehicle on a level surface, apply the handbrake and chock the rear wheels.

3 Raise the front of the vehicle, rest it securely on axle stands or wheel ramps; refer to "Jacking and vehicle support".

4 To improve access to the sump, refer to Chapter 8 and disconnect the right-hand driveshaft from the transmission output flange. Where necessary, release the fasteners and remove the engine lower splash shield.

5 Working around the outside of the sump, progressively slacken and withdraw the sump retaining bolts **(see illustration)**. Where applicable, unbolt and remove the flywheel cover plate from the transmission to gain access to the left-hand sump fixings.

6 Break the joint by striking the sump with the palm of your hand, then lower the sump and withdraw it from underneath the vehicle. Recover and discard the sump gasket. Where a baffle plate is fitted, note that it can only be removed once the oil pump has been unbolted (see Section 16).

7 While the sump is removed, take the opportunity to check the oil pump pick-up/strainer for signs of clogging or disintegration. If necessary, remove the pump as described in Section 16, and clean or renew the strainer.

Refitting

8 Clean all traces of sealant from the mating surfaces of the cylinder block/crankcase and sump, then use a clean rag to wipe out the sump.

9 Ensure that the sump and cylinder block/crankcase mating surfaces are clean and dry, then apply a coating of suitable sealant to the sump and crankcase mating surfaces.

10 Lay a new sump gasket in position on the sump mating surface, then offer up the sump and refit the retaining bolts. Tighten the nuts and bolts evenly and progressively to the specified torque.

11 Where applicable, refit the driveshaft and engine bay undertray.

12 Refer to Chapter 1A and refill the engine with the specified grade and quantity of oil.

13 Restore the battery connection.

16 Oil pump and pickup - removal, inspection and refitting

1 The oil pump and pickup are both mounted in the sump. Drive is taken from the intermediate shaft, which rotates at half crankshaft speed.

Removal

2 Refer to Section 15 and remove the sump from the crankcase.

3 Slacken and remove the bolts securing the oil pump to the base of the crankcase **(see illustration)**.

4 Lower the oil pump and pickup away from the crankcase. Where applicable, recover the baffle plate.

Inspection

5 Remove the screws from the mating flange, and lift off the pickup tube. Recover the O-ring seal. Slacken and withdraw the screws, then remove the oil pump cover.

6 Clean the pump thoroughly, and inspect the gear teeth for signs of damage or wear.

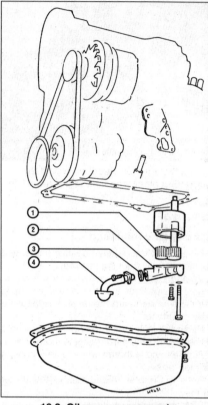

16.3 Oil pump components

1 Oil pump gears	3 O-ring seal
2 Oil pump cover	4 Pickup tube

7 Where applicable, check the condition of the oil pump drive chain; if the links appear excessively worn or are particularly loose, renew the chain.

8 Check the pump backlash by inserting a feeler blade between the meshed gear teeth; rotate the gears against each other slightly, to give the maximum clearance **(see illustration)**. Compare the measurement with the limit quoted in Specifications.

9 Check the pump axial clearance as follows. Lay an engineer's straight edge across the oil pump casing, then using a feeler blade, measure the clearance between the straight edge and the pump gears **(see illustration)**. Compare the measurement with the limit quoted in Specifications.

10 If either measurement is outside of the specified limit, this indicates that the pump is worn and must be renewed.

Refitting

11 Refit the oil pump cover, then fit and tighten the screws to the specified torque.

12 Reassemble the oil pickup to the oil pump, using a new O-ring seal. Tighten the retaining screws to the specified torque.

13 Where applicable, fit the crankcase baffle plate in place.

14 Offer up the oil pump to the crankcase, then fit the mounting bolts and tighten them to the specified torque.

15 Refer to Section 15 and refit the sump.

16.8 Checking the oil pump backlash (engine code 2E shown)

16.9 Checking the oil pump axial clearance (engine code 2E shown)

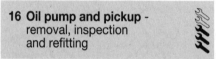

Chapter 2 Part B:
Diesel engine in-car repair procedures

Contents

Degrees of difficulty

| Easy, suitable for novice with little experience | Fairly easy, suitable for beginner with some experience | Fairly difficult, suitable for competent DIY mechanic | Difficult, suitable for experienced DIY mechanic | Very difficult, suitable for expert DIY or professional |

Specifications

General

Engine code: *
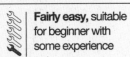

1896 cc, mechanical injection, turbocharged, 55 kW	AAZ
1896 cc, electronic direct injection, turbocharged, 66 kW	1Z or AHU
1896 cc, electronic direct injection, turbocharged, 81 kW (01/96 on) . .	AFN

*Note: See "Buying spare parts and vehicle identification" for the location of the code marking on the engine.

Bore	79.5 mm
Stroke	95.5 mm
Compression ratio:	
AAZ	22.5:1
All other engines	19.5:1
Compression pressures (wear limit):	
AAZ	26 bar
All other engines	19 bar
Firing order	1 - 3 - 4 - 2
No 1 cylinder location	Timing belt end

Lubrication system

Oil pump type	Sump-mounted, driven indirectly from intermediate shaft
Normal operating oil pressure	2.0 bar minimum (at 2000 rpm, oil temperature 80°C)
Oil pump backlash	0.20 mm (wear limit)
Oil pump axial clearance	0.15 mm (wear limit)

Auxiliary drivebelts

V-belt tension (deflection at mid-point between pulleys):
New belt	2 mm
Used belt	5 mm

Torque wrench settings

	Nm	lbf ft
Alternator mounting bolts	25	18
Auxiliary belt tensioner-to-bracket bolts	20	15
Auxiliary belt tensioner pulley bolt	20	15
Auxiliary belt pulley bolts	25	18
Camshaft cover nuts	10	7
Camshaft sprocket bolt	45	33
Crankshaft auxiliary belt pulley screws	25	18
Crankshaft front oil seal housing bolts	25	18
Crankshaft rear oil seal housing bolts	10	7
Crankshaft sprocket bolt:		
Stage 1	90	66
Stage 2	Angle-tighten a further 90°	
Cylinder head bolts*:		
Stage 1	40	30
Stage 2	60	44
Stage 3	Angle-tighten a further 90°	
Stage 4	Angle-tighten a further 90°	
Engine mountings **(see illustration 14.13b on page 2B•16)**:		
a	25	18
b	30	22
c	80	59
d	50	37
e	60	44
f	70	52
g	55	41
Exhaust manifold nuts	25	18
Flywheel mounting bolts*:		
Stage 1	60	44
Stage 2	Angle-tighten a further 90°	
Glow plugs:		
Engine code AAZ	25	18
All other engines	15	11
Idler roller to timing belt cover (not engine code AAZ)	25	18
Injection pump sprocket bolts (engine code AAZ, 10/94 on)	25	18
Injection pump sprocket nut:		
Engine code AAZ	45	33
All other engines	55	41
Injector pipe unions	25	18
Inlet manifold bolts	25	18
Intermediate shaft sprocket bolt	45	33
Oil cooler retaining nut	25	18
Oil filter bracket-to-engine bolts	25	18
Oil pressure switch	25	18
Oil pump cover screws	10	7
Oil pump mounting bolts	25	18
Oil pump pickup tube screws	10	7
Power steering pump mounting bolts	25	18
Sump cover bolts (engine code AFN)	10	7
Sump retaining bolts	20	15
Timing belt tensioner locknut (see text):		
Normal tensioner	45	33
Semi-automatic tensioner	20	15
Turbocharger oil feed pipe-to-turbocharger union (engine code AFN only)	10	7
Turbocharger oil feed union bolts	25	18
Turbocharger oil return union bolts	30	22
Turbocharger-to-exhaust manifold nuts/bolts:		
Engine code AAZ*	45	33
Engine codes 1Z and AHU	35	26
Engine code AFN*	25	18

*Use new nuts/bolt(s)

1 General information

Using this Chapter

Chapter 2 is divided into three parts; A, B and C. Repair operations that can be carried out with the engine in the vehicle are described in Parts A (petrol engines) and B (diesel engines). Part C covers the removal of the engine/ transmission as a unit and describes the engine dismantling and overhaul procedures.

In Parts A and B, the assumption is made that the engine is installed in the vehicle, with all ancillaries connected. If the engine has been removed for overhaul, the preliminary dismantling information which precedes each operation may be ignored.

Access to the engine bay can be improved by removing the bonnet and the front lock carrier assembly; these procedures are described in Chapter 11.

Engine description

Throughout this Chapter, engines are identified and referred to by manufacturer's code letters, rather than capacity. A listing of all engines covered, together with their code letters, is given in the Specifications at the start of this Chapter.

The engines are water-cooled, single overhead camshaft, in-line four cylinder units with cast-iron cylinder blocks and aluminium-alloy cylinder heads. All are mounted transversely at the front of the vehicle, with the transmission bolted to the left-hand side of the engine.

The cylinder head carries the camshaft(s), which are driven by a toothed timing belt. It also houses the inlet and exhaust valves, which are closed by single or double coil springs, and which run in guides pressed into the cylinder head. The camshaft actuates the valves directly via hydraulic tappets, mounted in the cylinder head. The cylinder head contains integral oilways which supply and lubricate the tappets.

On engine code AAZ (indirect injection engine), the cylinder head incorporates renewable swirl chambers. On all other engines (direct injection), the piston crowns are shaped to form combustion chambers.

The crankshaft is supported by five main bearings, and endfloat is controlled by a thrust bearing fitted between cylinders No 2 and 3.

All diesel engines are fitted with a timing belt-driven intermediate shaft, which provides drive for the brake servo vacuum pump and the oil pump.

Engine coolant is circulated by a pump, driven by the auxiliary drivebelt. For details of the cooling system, refer to Chapter 3.

Lubricant is circulated under pressure by a pump, driven by the intermediate shaft. Oil is drawn from the sump through a strainer, and then forced through an externally-mounted, replaceable screw-on filter. From there, it is distributed to the cylinder head, where it lubricates the camshaft journals and hydraulic tappets, and also to the crankcase, where it lubricates the main bearings, connecting rod big- and small-ends, gudgeon pins and cylinder bores. Oil jets are fitted to the base of each cylinder - these spray oil onto the underside of the pistons, to improve cooling. An oil cooler, supplied with engine coolant, reduces the temperature of the oil before it re-enters the engine.

Repairs possible with the engine installed in the vehicle

The following operations can be performed without removing the engine:

a) Auxiliary drivebelts - removal and refitting.
b) Camshaft(s) - removal and refitting. *
c) Camshaft oil seal - renewal.
d) Camshaft sprocket - removal and refitting.
e) Coolant pump - removal and refitting (refer to Chapter 3)
f) Crankshaft oil seals - renewal.
g) Crankshaft sprocket - removal and refitting.
h) Cylinder head - removal and refitting. *
i) Engine mountings - inspection and renewal.
j) Intermediate shaft oil seal - renewal.
k) Oil pump and pickup assembly - removal and refitting.
l) Sump - removal and refitting.
m) Timing belt, sprockets and cover - removal, inspection and refitting.

*Cylinder head dismantling procedures are in Chapter 2C, and also contain details of camshaft and hydraulic tappet removal.

Note: It is possible to remove the pistons and connecting rods (after removing the cylinder head and sump) without removing the engine from the vehicle. However, this procedure is not recommended. Work of this nature is more easily and thoroughly completed with the engine on the bench - refer to Chapter 2C.

2 Location of TDC on No 1 cylinder

1 Remove the engine top cover (where applicable), camshaft cover, auxiliary drivebelts and timing belt outer covers as described in Sections 17, 7, 6 and 4 respectively.

2 Remove the inspection bung from the transmission bellhousing. Rotate the crankshaft clockwise with a wrench and socket, or a spanner, until the timing mark machined onto the edge of the flywheel lines up with the pointer on the bellhousing casting **(see illustrations)**.

3 To lock the engine in the TDC position, the camshaft (not the sprocket) and fuel injection pump sprocket must be secured in a reference position, using special locking tools. Improvised tools may be fabricated, but due to the exact measurements and machining involved, it is strongly recommended that a kit of locking tools is either borrowed or hired from a VW dealer, or purchased from a reputable tool manufacturer - for example, Sykes Pickavant produce a kit of camshaft and fuel injection pump sprocket locking tools specifically for the range of engines covered in this Chapter **(see illustration)**.

4 Engage the edge of the locking bar with the slot in the end of the camshaft **(see illustration)**.

2B

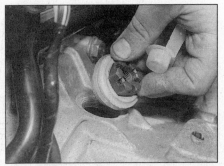

2.2a Remove the inspection bung from the transmission bellhousing

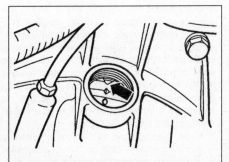

2.2b Timing mark on the edge of the flywheel (arrowed) lined up with pointer on bellhousing casting

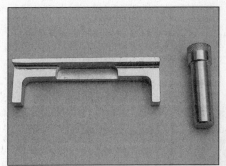

2.3 Engine locking tools

2.4 Engage the locking bar with the slot in the camshaft

2.6 Camshaft centred and locked using locking bar and feeler gauges

2.7 Injection pump sprocket locked using locking pin (arrowed) - engine code AAZ

5 With the locking bar still inserted, turn the camshaft slightly (by turning the crankshaft clockwise, as before), so that the locking bar rocks to one side, allowing one end of the bar to contact the cylinder head surface. At the other side of the locking bar, measure the gap between the end of the bar and the cylinder head using a feeler blade.

6 Turn the camshaft back slightly, then pull out the feeler blade. The idea now is to level the locking bar by inserting two feeler blades, each with a thickness equal to *half* the originally measured gap, on either side of the camshaft between each end of the locking bar and the cylinder head. This centres the camshaft, and sets the valve timing in reference condition **(see illustration)**.

7 Insert the locking pin through the fuel injection pump sprocket alignment hole, and thread it into the support bracket behind the sprocket. This locks the fuel injection pump in a reference condition **(see illustration)**.

8 The engine is now set to TDC on No 1 cylinder.

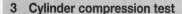

3 Cylinder compression test

Compression test

Note: *A compression tester specifically designed for diesel engines must be used for this test.*

1 When engine performance is down, or if misfiring occurs, a compression test can provide diagnostic clues as to the engine's condition. If the test is performed regularly, it can give warning of trouble before any other symptoms become apparent.

2 A compression tester specifically intended for diesel engines must be used, because of the higher pressures involved. The tester is connected to an adapter which screws into the glow plug or injector hole. It is unlikely to be worthwhile buying such a tester for occasional use, but it may be possible to borrow or hire one - if not, have the test performed by a garage.

3 Unless specific instructions to the contrary are supplied with the tester, observe the

following points:

a) *The battery must be in a good state of charge, the air filter must be clean, and the engine should be at normal operating temperature.*

b) *On engine code AFN, remove the engine top cover (Section 17).*

c) *All the injectors OR glow plugs (depending on the type of tester used) should be removed before starting the test. If removing the injectors, also remove the flame shield washers, otherwise they may be blown out.*

d) *The stop solenoid must be disconnected, to prevent the engine from running or fuel from being discharged.*

4 There is no need to hold the accelerator pedal down during the test, because the diesel engine air inlet is not throttled.

5 VW specify wear limits for compression pressures - refer to the Specifications. Seek the advice of a VW dealer or other diesel specialist if in doubt as to whether a particular pressure reading is acceptable.

6 The cause of poor compression is less easy to establish on a diesel engine than on a petrol one. The effect of introducing oil into the cylinders ("wet" testing) is not conclusive, because there is a risk that the oil will sit in the swirl chamber or in the recess on the piston crown, instead of passing to the rings. However, the following can be used as a rough guide to diagnosis.

7 All cylinders should produce very similar pressures; a difference of more than 5 Bar between any two cylinders indicates the existence of a fault. Note that the compression should build up quickly in a healthy engine; low compression on the first stroke, followed by gradually-increasing pressure on successive strokes, indicates worn piston rings. A low compression reading on the first stroke, which does not build up during successive strokes, indicates leaking valves or a blown head gasket (a cracked head could also be the cause).

8 A low reading from two adjacent cylinders is almost certainly due to the head gasket having blown between them; the presence of coolant in the engine oil will confirm this.

9 If the compression reading is unusually high, the cylinder head surfaces, valves and

pistons are probably coated with carbon deposits. If this is the case, the cylinder head should be removed and decarbonised (refer to Part C of this Chapter).

Leakdown test

10 A leakdown test measures the rate at which compressed air fed into the cylinder is lost. It is an alternative to a compression test, and in many ways it is better, since the escaping air provides easy identification of where pressure loss is occurring (piston rings, valves or head gasket).

11 The equipment needed for leakdown testing is unlikely to be available to the home mechanic. If poor compression is suspected, have the test performed by a suitably-equipped garage.

4 Timing belt and outer covers - removal and refitting

General information

1 The primary function of the toothed timing belt is to drive the camshaft(s), but it is also used to drive the fuel injection pump and intermediate shaft. Should the belt slip or break in service, the valve timing will be disturbed and piston-to-valve contact may occur, resulting in serious engine damage.

2 For this reason, it is important that the timing belt is tensioned correctly, and inspected regularly for signs of wear or deterioration.

3 Note that the removal of the *inner* section of the timing belt cover is described as part of the cylinder head removal procedure; see Section 11 later in this Chapter.

Removal

4 Before starting work, immobilise the engine by disconnecting the fuel cut-off solenoid (see Chapter 4C). Prevent any vehicle movement by applying the handbrake and chocking the rear wheels.

5 Access to the timing belt covers can be improved by removing the air cleaner housing - refer to Chapter 4C. On engine code AFN, remove the engine top cover (Section 17).

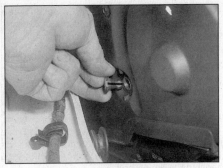

4.6 Removing the press-stud fixings from the timing belt upper cover

4.9 Removing the crankshaft auxiliary belt pulleys

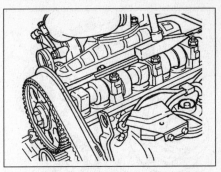

4.19 Releasing the camshaft sprocket from the taper using a pin punch

6 Release the uppermost part of the timing belt outer cover by prising open the metal spring clips and where applicable, removing the press-stud fixings **(see illustration)**. Lift the cover away from the engine

7 With reference to Section 6, remove the auxiliary drivebelt(s). Slacken and withdraw the screws, and lift off the coolant pump pulley.

8 Refer to Section 2, and using the engine alignment markings, set the engine to TDC on No 1 cylinder.

9 Slacken and withdraw the retaining screws, then remove the pulley for the ribbed auxiliary belt (together with the V-belt pulley, where fitted) from the crankshaft sprocket **(see illustration)**. On completion, check that the engine is still set to TDC.

> **HAYNES HiNT**
> *To prevent the auxiliary belt pulley from rotating whilst the mounting bolts are being slackened, select top gear) and get an assistant to apply the footbrake firmly. Failing this, grip the sprocket by wrapping a length of old rubber hose or inner tube around it.*

10 Remove the retaining screws and clips, and lift off the timing belt lower cover.

11 On the AAZ engine with a two-part fuel injection pump sprocket, ensure that the sprocket locking pin is firmly in position (see Section 2), then loosen the outer sprocket securing bolts by half a turn.

Caution: Do not loosen the sprocket centre bolt, as this will alter the fuel injection pump's basic timing setting.

12 With reference to Section 5, relieve the tension on the timing belt by slackening the tensioner mounting nut slightly, allowing it to pivot away from the belt.

13 On all engines except code AAZ, slacken and withdraw the bolt and remove the idler roller from the timing belt inner cover.

14 Examine the timing belt for manufacturer's markings that indicate the direction of rotation. If none are present, make your own using typist's correction fluid or a dab of paint - do not cut or score the belt in any way.

Caution: If the belt appears to be in good condition and can be re-used, it is essential that it is refitted the same way around, otherwise accelerated wear will result, leading to premature failure.

15 Slide the belt off the sprockets, taking care to avoid twisting or kinking it excessively.

16 Examine the belt for evidence of contamination by coolant or lubricant. If this is the case, find the source of the contamination before progressing any further. Check the belt for signs of wear or damage, particularly around the leading edges of the belt teeth. Renew the belt if its condition is in doubt; the cost of belt renewal is negligible compared with potential cost of the engine repairs, should the belt fail in service. Similarly, if the belt is known to have covered more than 36 000 miles, it is prudent to renew it regardless of condition, as a precautionary measure.

17 If the timing belt is not going to be refitted for some time, it is a wise precaution to hang a warning label on the steering wheel, to remind yourself (and others) not to start the engine.

Refitting

18 Ensure that the crankshaft is still set to TDC on No 1 cylinder, as described in Section 2.

19 Refer to Section 5 and slacken the camshaft sprocket bolt by half a turn. Release the sprocket from the camshaft taper mounting by carefully tapping it with a pin punch, inserted through the hole provided in the timing belt inner cover **(see illustration)**.

20 Loop the timing belt loosely under the crankshaft sprocket.

Caution: Observe the direction of rotation markings on the belt.

21 Engage the timing belt teeth with the crankshaft sprocket, then manoeuvre it into position over the camshaft and injection pump sprockets. Ensure the belt teeth seat correctly on the sprockets. **Note:** *Slight adjustments to the position of the camshaft sprocket (and where applicable, injection pump sprocket) may be necessary to achieve this.*

22 Pass the flat side of the belt over the intermediate shaft pulley and tensioner roller - avoid bending the belt back on itself or twisting it excessively as you do this.

23 On all engines except code AAZ, refit the idler roller to the timing belt inner cover, and tighten the retaining bolt to the specified torque.

24 On engines with a single-part fuel injection pump sprocket, remove the locking pin from the fuel injection pump sprocket (see Section 2).

25 Ensure that the "front run" of the belt is taut - ie all the slack should be in the section of the belt that passes over the tensioner roller.

26 Tension the belt by turning the eccentrically-mounted tensioner clockwise; two holes are provided in the side of the tensioner hub for this purpose - a pair of sturdy right-angled circlip pliers is a suitable substitute for the correct VW tool. **(see illustrations).**

4.26a Tensioning the timing belt using a pair of circlip pliers in the belt tensioner

4.26b Timing belt correctly fitted

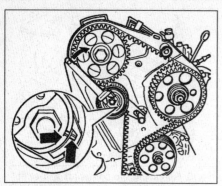

4.27 Alignment marks on pulley and hub - engines with semi-automatic tensioner

27 On engines with a semi-automatic belt tensioner, turn the tensioner clockwise until the alignment markings on the pulley and hub are lined up **(see illustration)**.

28 Test the timing belt tension by grasping it between the fingers at a point mid-way between the intermediate shaft and camshaft sprockets, and twisting it. The belt tension is correct when the belt can just be twisted through 90° (quarter of a turn) and no further.

29 When the correct belt tension has been achieved, tighten the tensioner locknut to the specified torque.

30 On engines without a semi-automatic tensioner, the belt tension must be accurately checked, and if necessary adjusted - this involves the use of dedicated belt tension measuring device, and it is advisable to have this operation carried out by a VW dealer.

31 At this point, check the crankshaft is still set to TDC on No 1 cylinder (see Section 2).

32 Refer to Section 5 and tighten the camshaft sprocket bolt to the specified torque.

33 On the AAZ engine with a two-part fuel injection pump sprocket, tighten the outer sprocket bolts, then remove the sprocket locking pin.

34 With reference to Section 2, remove the camshaft locking bar.

35 Using a spanner or wrench and socket on the crankshaft pulley centre bolt, rotate the crankshaft through two complete revolutions. Reset the engine to TDC on No 1 cylinder, with reference to Section 2 and check that the fuel injection pump sprocket locking pin can

be inserted. Re-check the timing belt tension and adjust it, if necessary.

36 Refit the upper and lower sections of the timing belt outer cover, tightening the retaining screws securely.

37 Refit the coolant pump pulley and tighten the retaining screws to the specified torque.

38 Refit the crankshaft auxiliary belt pulley and tighten the retaining screws to the specified torque, using the method employed during removal. Note that the offset of the pulley mounting holes allows only one fitting position.

39 Working from Section 6, refit and tension the auxiliary drivebelt(s).

40 Restore the fuelling system by reconnecting the fuel cut-off solenoid wiring (see Chapter 4C).

41 On completion, refer to Chapter 4C and check the fuel injection pump timing.

---

5 Timing belt tensioner and sprockets - removal and refitting

1 Before starting work, disable the fuelling system by disconnecting the wiring from the fuel cut-off solenoid (see Chapter 4C). Prevent any vehicle movement by applying the handbrake and chocking the rear wheels.

2 To gain access to the components detailed in this Section, refer to Section 6 and remove the auxiliary drivebelt(s).

Timing belt tensioner

Removal

3 With reference to the relevant paragraphs of Sections 2 and 4, set the engine to TDC on No 1 cylinder, then remove the upper and lower sections of the timing belt outer cover.

4 Slacken the retaining nut at the hub of the tensioner pulley and allow the assembly to rotate anti-clockwise, relieving the tension on the timing belt. Remove the nut and recover the washer **(see illustration)**.

5 Slide the tensioner off its mounting stud **(see illustration)**.

Inspection

6 Wipe the tensioner clean, but do not use solvents that may contaminate the bearings. Spin the tensioner pulley on its hub by hand.

Stiff movement or excessive freeplay is an indication of severe wear; the tensioner is not a serviceable component, and should be renewed.

Refitting

7 Slide the tensioner pulley over the mounting stud. On engines with a semi-automatic tensioner, engage the forked end of the backplate with the timing belt pillar.

8 Refit the tensioner washer and retaining nut - do not fully tighten the nut at this stage.

9 With reference to Section 4, refit and tension the timing belt.

10 On engines with a semi-automatic tensioner, the operation of the tensioner can be tested as follows: apply finger pressure to the timing belt at a point mid-way between the camshaft and crankshaft sprockets. The tensioner pulley alignment marks should move apart as pressure is applied, and then move back and line up again as the pressure is removed **(refer to illustration 4.27)**.

11 Restore the fuelling system by reconnecting the fuel cut-off solenoid wiring.

12 Refer to Section 4 and refit the timing belt covers.

Camshaft timing belt sprocket

Removal

13 Refer to Section 2 and 4, set the engine to TDC on No 1 cylinder, then remove the timing belt outer covers. With reference to the previous sub-Section, slacken the tensioner centre nut and allow it to rotate anti-clockwise, to relieve the tension on the timing belt. Carefully slide the timing belt off the camshaft sprocket.

14 The camshaft sprocket must be held stationary whilst its retaining bolt is slackened; if access to the correct VW special tool is not possible, a simple home-made tool using basic materials may be fabricated **(see Tool Tip)**.

TOOL TIP

To make a camshaft sprocket holding tool, obtain two lengths of steel strip about 6mm thick by 30 mm wide or similar, one 600 mm long, the other 200 mm long (all dimensions approximate). Bolt the two strips together to form a forked end, leaving the bolt slack so that the shorter strip can pivot freely. At the end of each 'prong' of the fork, secure a bolt with a nut and a locknut, to act as the fulcrums; these will engage with the cut-outs in the sprocket, and should protrude by about 30mm

5.4 Remove the tensioner nut and recover the washer

5.5 Slide the tensioner off its mounting stud

15 Using the home-made tool, brace the camshaft sprocket and slacken and remove the retaining bolt; recover the washer where fitted.

16 Slide the camshaft sprocket from the end of the camshaft **(see illustration)**. Where applicable, recover the Woodruff key from the keyway.

17 With the sprocket removed, examine the camshaft oil seal for signs of leaking. If necessary, refer to Section 8 and renew it.

18 Wipe the sprocket and camshaft mating surfaces clean.

Refitting

19 Where applicable, fit the Woodruff key into the keyway with the plain surface facing upwards. Fit the sprocket to the camshaft, engaging the slot in the sprocket with the Woodruff key. Where a key is not used, ensure the lug in the sprocket hub engages with recess in the end of the camshaft.

20 Working from Sections 2 and 4, check that the engine is still set to TDC on No 1 cylinder, then refit and tension the timing belt. Refit the timing belt covers.

21 Refit the crankshaft auxiliary belt pulley(s), then insert the retaining screws and tighten them to the specified torque.

22 With reference to Section 6, refit and tension the auxiliary drivebelt(s).

Crankshaft timing belt sprocket

Removal

23 Referring to Sections 2 and 4, set the engine to TDC on No 1 cylinder, then remove the timing belt outer covers. With reference to the previous sub-Section, slacken the tensioner centre hut and allow it to rotate anti-clockwise, to relieve the tension on the timing belt. Carefully slide the timing belt off the camshaft sprocket.

24 The crankshaft sprocket must be held stationary whilst its retaining bolt is slackened. If access to the correct VW flywheel locking tool is not available, lock the crankshaft in position by removing the starter motor, as described in Chapter 5A, to expose the flywheel ring gear. Get an assistant to insert a stout lever between the ring gear teeth and the transmission bellhousing whilst the sprocket retaining bolt is slackened.

5.16 Removing the camshaft sprocket

25 Withdraw the bolt, recover the washer and lift off the sprocket.

26 With the sprocket removed, examine the crankshaft oil seal for signs of leaking. If necessary, refer to Section 10 and renew it.

27 Wipe the sprocket and crankshaft mating surfaces clean.

Refitting

28 Offer up the sprocket to the crankshaft, engaging the lug on the inside of the sprocket with the recess in the end of the crankshaft. Insert the retaining bolt and tighten it to the specified torque **(see illustrations)**.

29 Working from Sections 2 and 4, check that the engine is still set to TDC on No 1 cylinder, then refit and tension the timing belt. Refit the timing belt covers.

30 Refit the crankshaft auxiliary belt pulley(s).

31 With reference to Section 6, refit and tension the auxiliary drivebelt(s).

Intermediate shaft sprocket

Removal

32 With reference to Sections 2 and 4, remove the timing belt covers and set the engine to TDC on No 1 cylinder. Slacken the tensioner centre nut and rotate it anti-clockwise to relieve the tension on the timing belt. Carefully slide the timing belt off the camshaft sprocket.

33 The intermediate shaft sprocket must be held stationary whilst its retaining bolt is slackened; if access to the correct VW special tool is not possible, a simple home-made tool using basic materials may be fabricated as

5.28a Insert the crankshaft sprocket bolt . . .

described in the camshaft sprocket removal sub-Section.

34 Using a socket and extension bar, brace the intermediate shaft sprocket. Slacken and remove the retaining bolt; recover the washer, where fitted **(see illustration)**.

35 Slide the sprocket from the end of the intermediate shaft. Where applicable, recover the Woodruff key from the keyway.

36 With the sprocket removed, examine the intermediate shaft oil seal for signs of leaking. If necessary, refer to Section 9 and renew it.

37 Wipe the sprocket and shaft mating surfaces clean.

Refitting

38 Where applicable, fit the Woodruff key into the keyway with the plain surface facing upwards. Offer up the sprocket to the intermediate shaft, engaging the slot in the sprocket with the Woodruff key.

39 Tighten the sprocket retaining bolt to the specified torque; hold the sprocket using the method employed during removal.

40 With reference to Section 2, check that the engine is still set to TDC on No 1 cylinder. Working from Section 4, refit and tension the timing belt, then refit the timing belt covers.

41 Refit the crankshaft auxiliary belt pulley(s), then insert the retaining screws and tighten them to the specified torque.

42 With reference to Section 6, refit and tension the auxiliary drivebelt(s).

Fuel injection pump sprocket

43 Refer to Chapter 4C.

5.28b . . . tighten it to the Stage 1 torque . . .

5.28c . . . then through the Stage 2 angle

5.34 Brace the intermediate shaft sprocket, then remove the retaining bolt

2B

6.9 Removing the auxiliary V-belt

6.12a Power steering pump drivebelt tensioning bolt

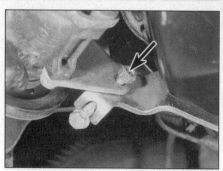

6.12b Power steering pump tensioner locking bolt (arrowed)

6 Auxiliary drivebelts - removal, refitting and tensioning

General information

1 Depending on the vehicle specification and engine type, one or two auxiliary drivebelts may be fitted. Both are driven from pulleys mounted on the crankshaft, and provide drive for the alternator, coolant pump, power steering pump and on vehicles with air conditioning, the refrigerant compressor.
2 The run of the belts and the components they drive is also dependent on vehicle specification and engine type. Because of this, the coolant pump and power steering pump may have pulleys to suit either a ribbed belt or a V-belt.
3 The ribbed auxiliary belt may have an automatic tensioner, depending on its run (and hence the number of components it is driving). Otherwise, the belt is tensioned by the alternator mountings, which have an in-built tensioning spring. The V-belt is tensioned by pivoting the power steering pump on its mounting.
4 On refitting, the auxiliary belt must be tensioned correctly to ensure correct operation and prolonged service life.

Auxiliary V-belt

Removal

5 Park the vehicle on a level surface and apply the handbrake. Disconnect the battery

6.13 Tightening the power steering pump bolt

negative terminal, and position the lead away from the battery. **Note:** *If the vehicle has a security-coded radio, check that you have a copy of the code number before disconnecting the battery. Refer to your VW dealer if in doubt.* Jack up the front of the vehicle and rest it on axle stands - refer to *"Jacking and vehicle support"*.
6 Access can be improved by removing the air cleaner housing - refer to Chapter 4C. On engine code AFN, remove the engine top cover (Section 17).
7 Turn the steering to full right lock. To provide better access, the right-hand front wheel can be removed if wished. Some later models may be fitted with plastic panels which will need to be unclipped for access to the engine through the wheel arch.
8 With reference to Chapter 10, slacken the power steering pump mounting bolts and allow the pump body to pivot around its uppermost mounting towards the engine.
9 Guide the V-belt off the power steering pump pulley and where applicable, the coolant pump pulley **(see illustration)**.
10 Examine the belt for signs or wear or damage, and renew it if necessary.

Refitting and tensioning

11 Refit the belt by reversing the removal procedure. Ensure it seats evenly in the pulleys.

Early models

12 The belt tension is set using a tensioning bolt and a locking bolt **(see illustrations)**. With all the pump mounting nuts and bolts

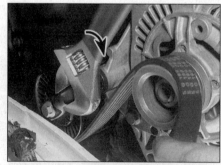

6.18 Rotate the tensioner roller arm clockwise - use an adjustable spanner - and remove the belt

slackened, turn the tensioning bolt until the belt tension is correct, and then tighten the locking bolt. Tighten all the remaining mounting bolts securely on completion.

Later models

13 Set the belt tension by grasping the underside of the power steering pump and drawing it towards the front of the vehicle. The tension is correct when the midpoint of the belt's longest run can be deflected by no more than the amount specified at the start of this Chapter. Tighten the power steering pump bolt to the correct torque **(see illustration)**.

All models

14 Rotate the crankshaft in its normal direction of rotation through two turns, then re-check and if necessary adjust the tension.

Auxiliary ribbed belt

Removal

15 Park the vehicle on a level surface and apply the handbrake. Disconnect the battery negative terminal, and position the lead away from the battery. **Note:** *If the vehicle has a security-coded radio, check that you have a copy of the code number before disconnecting the battery. Refer to your VW dealer if in doubt.* Jack up the front of the vehicle and rest it on axle stands - refer to *"Jacking and vehicle support"*.
16 Turn the steering to full right lock. To provide better access, the right-hand front wheel can be removed if wished. Some later models may be fitted with plastic panels which will need to be unclipped for access to the engine through the wheel arch. Where applicable, remove the auxiliary V-belt as described in the previous sub-Section.
17 Examine the ribbed belt for manufacturer's markings, indicating the direction of rotation. If none are present, make some using typist's correction fluid or a dab of paint - do not cut or score the belt in any way.

Vehicles with a roller-arm automatic tensioning device

18 Rotate the tensioner roller arm clockwise against its spring tension so that the roller is forced away from the belt - use an adjustable spanner as a lever **(see illustration)**.

Vehicles with a rotary automatic tensioning device

19 Fit a ring spanner to the tensioner centre nut and rotate the assembly anti-clockwise, against its spring tension.

Vehicles without an automatic tensioning device

20 Slacken the alternator upper and lower mounting bolts by between one and two turns.

21 Push the alternator down to its stop against the spring tension, so that it rotates around its uppermost mounting.

All vehicles

22 Pull the belt off the alternator pulley, then release it from the remaining pulleys.

Refitting and tensioning

Caution: Observe the manufacturer's direction of rotation markings on the belt, when refitting.

23 Pass the ribbed belt underneath the crank-shaft pulley, ensuring that the ribs seat securely in the channels on the surface of the pulley.

Vehicles with a roller-arm automatic tensioning device

24 Rotate the tensioner roller arm clockwise against its spring tension - use an adjustable spanner as a lever (refer to illustration 6.18).

25 Pass the belt around the coolant pump pulley or air conditioning refrigerant pump pulley (as applicable), then fit it over the alternator pulley.

26 Release the tensioner pulley arm and allow the roller to bear against the flat surface of the belt.

Vehicles with a rotary automatic tensioning device

27 Fit a ring spanner to the tensioner centre nut and rotate the assembly anti-clockwise, against its spring tension.

28 Pass the flat side of the belt underneath the tensioner roller, then fit it over the power steering pump and alternator pulleys.

29 Release the spanner, and let the tensioner roller bear against the flat side of the belt.

Vehicles without an automatic tensioning device

30 Repeatedly push the alternator down to its stop against the spring tension, so that it rotates around its uppermost mounting and check that it moves back freely when

7.3 Crankcase breather regulator valve

released. If necessary, slacken the alternator mounting bolts by a further half a turn.

31 Keep the alternator pushed down against its stop, pass the belt over the alternator pulley, then release the alternator and allow it to tension the belt.

32 Reconnect the battery negative lead, then without tightening the mounting bolts, start the engine and allow it to idle for approximately ten seconds.

33 Switch the engine off, then tighten first the lower, then the alternator upper mounting bolts to the specified torque. If removed, fit and tension the power steering pump drivebelt as described in the previous sub-Section.

All vehicles

34 Where applicable, refer to the previous sub-Section and refit the auxiliary V-belt.

35 If removed, refit the right-hand front wheel and any plastic panels removed for access, then lower the vehicle to the ground. If not already done, reconnect the battery negative lead.

7 Camshaft cover - removal and refitting

Removal

1 On engine code AFN, take off the engine top cover (Section 17).

2 Immobilise the engine by unplugging the electrical wiring from the fuel cut-off solenoid at the connector; refer to Chapter 4C for guidance.

7.4 Camshaft cover retaining nut

3 Disconnect the crankcase breather hose and regulator valve from the camshaft cover (see illustration).

4 Slacken and withdraw the three camshaft cover retaining nuts - recover the washers and seals (see illustration).

5 Lift the cover away from the cylinder head (see illustration); if it sticks, do not attempt to lever it off - instead free it by working around the cover and tapping it lightly with a soft-faced mallet.

6 Recover the camshaft cover gasket (see illustration). Inspect the gasket carefully, and renew it if damage or deterioration is evident.

7 Clean the mating surfaces of the cylinder head and camshaft cover thoroughly, removing all traces of oil and old gasket - take care to avoid damaging the surfaces as you do this.

Refitting

8 Refit the camshaft cover by following the removal procedure in reverse, noting the following points:

a) Ensure that the gasket is correctly seated on the cylinder head, and take care to avoid displacing it as the camshaft cover is lowered into position (see illustration).

b) Tighten the camshaft cover retaining nuts to the specified torque.

c) When refitting hoses that were originally secured with crimp-type clips, use standard worm-drive clips in their place on refitting.

9 On completion, restore the fuelling system by reconnecting the fuel cut-off solenoid lead.

10 On engine code AFN, refit the engine top cover.

2B

7.5 Lift the camshaft cover away from the cylinder head

7.6 Recover the camshaft cover gasket

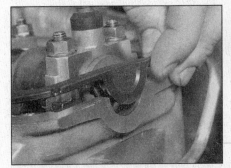
7.8 Ensure that the camshaft cover gasket is correctly seated on the cylinder head

8 Camshaft oil seal - renewal

1 On engine code AFN, remove the engine top cover (Section 17).
2 Immobilise the engine by unplugging the electrical wiring from the fuel cut-off solenoid at the connector; refer to Chapter 4C for guidance.
3 Refer to Section 6 and remove the auxiliary drivebelt(s).
4 With reference to Sections 2, 4 and 5 of this Chapter, remove the auxiliary belt pulleys and timing belt cover; set the engine to TDC on No 1 cylinder and remove the timing belt, timing belt tensioner (where applicable) and camshaft sprocket.
5 After removing the retaining screws, lift the timing belt inner cover away from the engine block.
6 Working from the relevant Section of Chapter 2C, carry out the following:
 a) *Unbolt the camshaft No 1 bearing cap, and slide off the old camshaft oil seal.*
 b) *Lubricate the surface of a new camshaft oil seal with clean engine oil, and fit it over the end of the camshaft.*
 c) *Apply a suitable sealant to the mating surface of the bearing cap, then refit it and tighten its mounting nuts progressively to the specified torque* **(see illustration)**.
7 Refer to Section 7 and refit the camshaft cover.
8 With reference to Sections 2, 4 and 5 of this Chapter, refit the timing belt inner cover and timing sprockets, then refit and tension the timing belt. On completion, refit the timing belt outer cover.
9 With reference to Section 6, refit and tension the auxiliary drivebelt(s).
10 Where applicable, refit the engine top cover.

9 Intermediate shaft oil seal - renewal

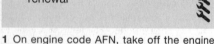

1 On engine code AFN, take off the engine top cover (Section 17).
2 Immobilise the engine by unplugging the electrical wiring from the fuel cut-off solenoid at the connector; refer to Chapter 4C for guidance.
3 Refer to Section 6 and remove the auxiliary drivebelt(s).
4 With reference to Sections 4 and 5 of this Chapter, remove the auxiliary belt pulleys, timing belt outer cover, timing belt, tensioner (where applicable) and intermediate shaft sprocket.
5 After removing the retaining screws, lift the inner timing belt cover away from the engine block - this will expose the intermediate shaft sealing flange.

8.6 Refitting the camshaft bearing cap

6 With reference to Section 7 of Chapter 2C, remove the intermediate shaft flange and renew the shaft and flange oil seals.
7 Refer to Sections 4 and 5 of this Chapter, carry out the following:
 a) *Refit the timing belt inner cover.*
 b) *Refit the intermediate shaft timing belt sprocket.*
 c) *Refit and tension the timing belt.*
 d) *Refit the timing belt outer cover.*
8 With reference to Section 6 of this Chapter, refit and tension the auxiliary drivebelt(s).

10 Crankshaft oil seals - renewal

Crankshaft front oil seal

1 On engine code AFN, take off the engine top cover (Section 17).
2 Immobilise the engine by unplugging the electrical wiring from the fuel cut-off solenoid at the connector; refer to Chapter 4C for guidance.
3 Refer to Chapter 1B and drain the engine oil.
4 With reference to *"Jacking and vehicle support"*, raise the front of the vehicle and rest it securely on axle stands.
5 Refer to Section 6 and remove the auxiliary drivebelt(s).
6 With reference to Sections 4 and 5 of this Chapter, remove the auxiliary belt pulleys, timing belt outer covers, timing belt and crankshaft sprocket.

10.7 Removing the crankshaft front oil seal using self-tapping screws

7 Drill two small holes into the existing oil seal, diagonally opposite each other. Thread two self-tapping screws into the holes and using two pairs of pliers, pull on the heads of the screws to extract the oil seal **(see illustration)**. Take great care to avoid drilling through into the seal housing or crankshaft sealing surface.
8 Clean out the seal housing and sealing surface of the crankshaft by wiping it with a lint-free cloth - avoid using solvents that may enter the crankcase and affect component lubrication. Remove any swarf or burrs that could cause the seal to leak.
9 Smear the lip of the new oil seal with clean engine oil, and position it over the housing.
10 Using a hammer and a socket of suitable diameter, drive the seal squarely into its housing. **Note:** *Select a socket that bears only on the hard outer surface of the seal, not the inner lip, which can easily be damaged.*
11 With reference to Sections 2, 4 and 5 of this Chapter, refit the crankshaft timing belt sprocket, then refit and tension the timing belt. On completion, refit the timing belt outer cover, and auxiliary drivebelt pulley(s).
12 The remainder of the refitting procedure is a reversal of removal, as follows:
 a) *With reference to Section 6, refit and tension the auxiliary drivebelt(s).*
 b) *Refer to Chapter 1B and refill the engine with the correct grade and quantity of oil.*
 c) *Restore the fuelling system.*
 d) *On engine code AFN, refit the engine top cover.*

Crankshaft front oil seal housing - gasket renewal

13 Proceed as described in paragraphs 1 to 6 above, then refer to Section 15 and remove the sump.
14 Progressively slacken and then remove the oil seal housing retaining bolts.
15 Lift the housing away from the cylinder block, together with the crankshaft oil seal, using a twisting motion to ease the seal along the shaft.
16 Recover the old gasket from the seal housing on the cylinder block. If it has disintegrated, scrape the remains off with a trimming knife blade. Take care to avoid damaging the mating surfaces.

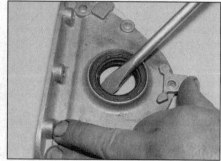

10.17 Prise the old oil seal from the housing

10.19 Locate the new crankshaft front oil seal housing gasket in position

10.21 Offer up the seal and its housing to the end of the crankshaft - note tape around the end of the crankshaft, to protect the oil seal as it passes over the crankshaft

17 If necessary, prise the old oil seal from the housing using a stout screwdriver **(see illustration)**.

18 Wipe the oil seal housing clean, and check it visually for signs of distortion or cracking. Lay the housing on a work surface, with the mating surface face down. If removed, press in a new oil seal, using a block of wood as a press to ensure that the seal enters the housing squarely.

19 Smear the crankcase mating surface with multi-purpose grease, and lay the new gasket in position **(see illustration)**.

20 Pad the end of the crankshaft with a layer of PVC tape; this will protect the oil seal as it is being fitted.

21 Lubricate the inner lip of the crankshaft oil seal with clean engine oil, then offer up the seal and its housing to the end of the crankshaft. Ease the seal along the shaft using a twisting motion, until the housing is flush with the crankcase **(see illustration)**.

22 Insert the bolts and tighten them to the specified torque.

Caution: The housing is light alloy, and may be distorted if the bolts are not tightened progressively.

23 Refer to Section 15 and refit the sump.

24 With reference to Sections 2, 4 and 5 of this Chapter, refit the crankshaft timing belt sprocket, then refit and tension the timing belt. On completion, refit the timing belt outer cover, and auxiliary drivebelt pulley(s).

25 The remainder of the refitting procedure is a reversal of removal, as follows:

  a) With reference to Section 6, refit and tension the auxiliary drivebelt(s).

  b) Refer to Chapter 1B and refill the engine with the correct grade and quantity of oil.

  c) Restore the fuelling system.

  d) On engine code AFN, refit the engine top cover.

Crankshaft rear oil seal (flywheel end)

Note: *Check the availability of oil seal before commencing work.*

26 Proceed as described in paragraphs 1 to 3 above, then refer to Section 15 and remove the sump.

27 Refer to Chapter 7A or B as applicable, and remove the transmission from the engine.

28 Refer to Section 13 and remove the flywheel; refer to Chapter 6 and remove the clutch friction plate and pressure plate.

29 Where applicable, remove the retaining bolts and lift the intermediate plate away from the cylinder block.

30 Progressively slacken and then remove the oil seal housing retaining bolts.

31 Lift the housing away from the cylinder block, together with the crankshaft oil seal, using a twisting motion to ease the seal along the shaft.

32 Recover the old gasket from the seal housing cylinder block. If it has disintegrated, scrape the remains off with a trimming knife blade. Take care to avoid damaging the mating surfaces.

33 Prise the old oil seal from the housing using a stout screwdriver **(see illustration)**.

34 Wipe the oil seal housing clean, and check it visually for signs of distortion or cracking. Lay the housing on a work surface, with the mating surface face down. Press in a new oil seal, using a block of wood as a press to ensure that the seal enters the housing squarely **(see illustration)**.

35 Smear the crankcase mating surface with non-hardening jointing compound, and lay the new gasket in position **(see illustration)**.

36 A protective plastic cap is supplied with genuine VW crankshaft oil seals; when fitted over the end of the crankshaft, the cap prevents damage to the inner lip of the oil seal as it is being fitted **(see illustration)**. Use PVC tape to pad the end of the crankshaft if a cap is not available.

2B

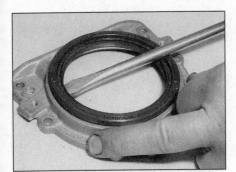

10.33 Prise the crankshaft rear oil seal from the housing

10.34 Press in a new oil seal, using a block of wood

10.35 Locate the new crankshaft rear oil seal housing gasket in position

10.36 A protective plastic cap is supplied with genuine VW crankshaft oil seals

10.37 Fitting the crankshaft rear oil seal and housing

10.38 Tightening the crankshaft rear oil seal housing retaining bolts

37 Lubricate the inner lip of the crankshaft oil seal with clean engine oil, then offer up the seal and its housing to the end of the crankshaft. Ease the seal along the shaft using a twisting motion, until the housing is flush with the crankcase **(see illustration)**.

38 Insert the retaining bolts and tighten them progressively to the specified torque **(see illustration)**.

Caution: The housing is light alloy, and may be distorted if the bolts are not tightened progressively.

39 Refer to Section 15 and refit the sump.

40 Fit the intermediate plate to the cylinder block, then insert and tighten the retaining bolts.

41 Refer to Chapter 6 and refit the flywheel, pressure plate and clutch friction plate.

42 With reference to Chapter 7A, refit the transmission to the engine.

11.7 Disconnect the heater coolant hoses from the ports on the cylinder head

43 The remainder of the refitting procedure is a reversal of removal, as follows:

a) *Refer to Chapter 1B and refill the engine with the correct grade and quantity of oil.*

b) *Restore the fuelling system.*

c) *On engine code AFN, refit the engine top cover.*

11 Cylinder head, inlet and exhaust manifolds - removal, separation and refitting

Removal

1 Select a level surface to park the vehicle upon. Give yourself enough space to move around it easily.

2 Refer to Chapter 11 and remove the bonnet from its hinges.

3 Disconnect the battery negative cable, and position It away from the terminal. **Note:** *If the vehicle has a security-coded radio, check that you have a copy of the code number before disconnecting the battery cable.*

4 With reference to Chapter 1B, carry out the following:

a) *Drain the engine oil.*

b) *Drain the cooling system.*

5 Refer to Section 6 and remove the auxiliary drivebelt(s).

6 With reference to Section 2, set the engine to TDC on No 1 cylinder.

7 Refer to Chapter 3 and perform the following:

a) *Slacken the clips and disconnect the radiator hoses from the ports on the cylinder head.*

b) *Slacken the clips and disconnect the expansion tank hose, and the heater inlet and outlet coolant hoses, from the ports on the cylinder head* **(see illustration)**.

8 The "lock carrier" is a panel assembly comprising the headlight units, radiator grille (later models), and bonnet lock mechanism. Although its removal is not essential, its does give greatly-improved access to the engine - refer to Chapter 11 for details.

9 Refer to Chapter 4C and carry out the following:

a) *Disconnect and remove the injector fuel supply hoses from the injectors and the injection pump head.*

b) *Disconnect the injector bleed hose from the injection pump fuel return port.*

c) *Unplug all fuel system electrical cabling at the relevant connectors, labelling each cable to aid refitting later.*

10 With reference to Sections 2, 4 and 7, carry out the following:

a) *Remove the camshaft cover.*

b) *Remove the timing belt outer covers, and disengage the timing belt from the camshaft sprocket.*

c) *Remove the timing belt tensioner, camshaft sprocket and fuel injection pump sprocket.*

11 Slacken and withdraw the retaining screws and lift off the timing belt inner covers **(see illustrations)**.

12 With reference to Chapter 3 and 4C (as applicable), disconnect the wiring plug from the coolant temperature sensor **(see illustration)**.

11.11a Slacken and withdraw the retaining screws . . .

11.11b . . . and lift off the timing belt inner covers

11.12 Disconnect the wiring plug from the coolant temperature sensor

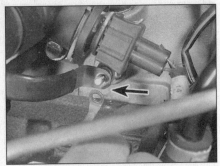

11.13 Unbolt the electrical supply cable from No 4 cylinder glow plug

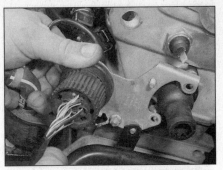

11.14 Removing the engine harness connector bracket from the cylinder head

11.16 Lifting the cylinder head away from the engine

13 Refer to Chapter 4D and carry out the following:
a) *Remove the bolts and separate the exhaust downpipe from the exhaust manifold flange.*
b) *Remove the turbocharger from the exhaust manifold.*
c) *Where applicable, remove the EGR valve and its connecting pipework from the inlet and exhaust manifolds.*
d) *Unbolt the supply cable from the glow plug in cylinder No 4 (see illustration).*

14 Remove the retaining screw and detach the engine harness connector bracket from the cylinder head **(see illustration)**.

15 Following the reverse of the tightening sequence (see *"Refitting"*), progressively slacken the cylinder head bolts, by half a turn at a time, until all bolts can be unscrewed by hand. Discard the bolts - new ones must be fitted on reassembly.

16 Check that nothing remains connected to the cylinder head, then lift the head away from the cylinder block; seek assistance if possible, as it is a heavy assembly, especially if it is being removed complete with the manifolds **(see illustration)**.

17 Remove the gasket from the top of the block, noting the locating dowels. If the dowels are a loose fit, remove them and store them with the head for safe-keeping. Do not discard the gasket yet - it will be needed for identification purposes.

18 If the cylinder head is to be dismantled for overhaul, refer to Chapter 2C.

Manifold separation

19 With the cylinder head on a work surface, slacken and withdraw the inlet manifold securing bolts. Lift the manifold away, and recover the gasket.

20 Unbolt the heat shield **(see illustration)**, then progressively slacken and remove the exhaust manifold retaining nuts. Lift the manifold away from the cylinder head, and recover the gaskets.

21 Ensure that the inlet and exhaust manifold mating surfaces are completely clean. Refit the exhaust manifold, using new gaskets. Ensure that the gaskets are fitted the correct way around, otherwise they will obstruct the inlet manifold gasket. Tighten the exhaust manifold retaining nuts to the specified torque **(see illustrations)**.

22 Refit the heat shield to the studs on the exhaust manifold, then fit and tighten the retaining nuts.

23 Fit a new inlet manifold gasket to the cylinder head, then lift the inlet manifold into position. Insert the retaining bolts and tighten them to the specified toque **(see illustrations)**.

2B

11.20 Unbolt and remove the exhaust manifold heat shield

11.21a Fit the exhaust manifold gaskets . . .

11.21b . . . then refit the exhaust manifold. Tighten the nuts to the specified torque

11.23a Fit a new inlet manifold gasket to the cylinder head . . .

11.23b . . . then lift the inlet manifold into position

11.23c Insert the retaining bolts and tighten them to the specified toque

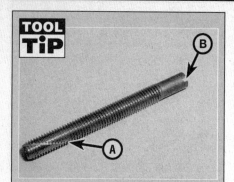

TOOL TiP

If a tap is not available, make a home-made substitute by cutting a slot (A) down the threads of one of the old cylinder head bolts. After use, the bolt head can be cut off, and the shank can then be used as an alignment dowel to assist cylinder head refitting. Cut a screwdriver slot (B) in the top of the bolt, to allow it to be unscrewed

Preparation for refitting

24 The mating faces of the cylinder head and cylinder block/crankcase must be perfectly clean before refitting the head. Use a hard plastic or wood scraper to remove all traces of gasket and carbon; also clean the piston crowns. Take particular care during the cleaning operations, as aluminium alloy is easily damaged. Also, make sure that the carbon is not allowed to enter the oil and water passages - this is particularly important for the lubrication system, as carbon could block the oil supply to the engine's components. Using adhesive tape and paper, seal the water, oil and bolt holes in the cylinder block/crankcase.

25 Check the mating surfaces of the cylinder block/crankcase and the cylinder head for nicks, deep scratches and other damage. If slight, they may be removed carefully with abrasive paper, but note that head machining will not be possible - refer to Chapter 2C.

26 If warpage of the cylinder head gasket surface is suspected, use a straight-edge to check it for distortion. Refer to Part C of this Chapter if necessary.

27 Clean out the cylinder head bolt drillings

11.36 Oil the cylinder head bolt threads, then place each bolt into its relevant hole

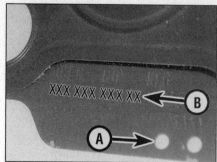

11.29 Cylinder head gasket punched holes (A) and part number (B)

using a suitable tap. If a tap is not available, make a home-made substitute **(see Tool Tip)**.

28 On all the engines covered in this Chapter, it is possible for the piston crowns to strike and damage the valve heads, if the camshaft is rotated with the timing belt removed and the crankshaft set to TDC. For this reason, the crankshaft must be set to a position other than TDC on No 1 cylinder, before the cylinder head is refitted. Use a wrench and socket on the crankshaft pulley centre bolt to turn the crankshaft in its normal direction of rotation, until all four pistons are positioned halfway down their bores, with No 1 piston on its upstroke - approximately 90° before TDC.

Refitting

29 Examine the old cylinder head gasket for manufacturer's identification markings. These will either be in the form of punched holes or a part number, on the edge of the gasket **(see illustration)**. Unless new pistons have been fitted, the new cylinder head gasket must be the same type as the old one.

30 If new piston assemblies have been fitted as part of an engine overhaul, before purchasing the new cylinder head gasket, refer to Section 13 of Chapter 2C and measure the piston projection. Purchase a new gasket according to the results of the measurement (see Chapter 2C Specifications).

31 Lay the new head gasket on the cylinder block, engaging it with the locating dowels. Ensure that the manufacturer's "TOP" and part number markings are face up.

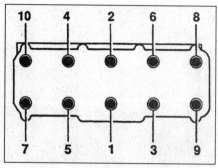

11.37a Cylinder head bolt tightening sequence

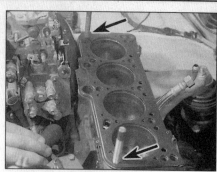

11.32 Two of the old head bolts (arrowed) used as cylinder head alignment dowels

32 Cut the heads from two of the old cylinder head bolts. Cut a slot, big enough for a screwdriver blade, in the end of each bolt. These can be used as alignment dowels to assist in cylinder head refitting **(see illustration)**.

33 With the help of an assistant, place the cylinder head and manifolds centrally on the cylinder block, ensuring that the locating dowels engage with the recesses in the cylinder head. Check that the head gasket is correctly seated before allowing the full weight of the cylinder head to rest upon it.

34 Unscrew the home-made alignment dowels, using a flat-bladed screwdriver.

35 Apply a smear of grease to the threads, and to the underside of the heads, of the new cylinder head bolts.

36 Oil the bolt threads, then carefully enter each bolt into its relevant hole (*do not drop them in*) and screw in, by hand only, until finger-tight **(see illustration)**.

37 Working progressively and in the sequence shown, tighten the cylinder head bolts to their Stage 1 torque setting, using a torque wrench and suitable socket **(see illustrations)**. Repeat the exercise in the same sequence for the Stage 2 torque setting.

38 Once all the bolts have been tightened to their Stage 2 settings, working again in the given sequence, angle-tighten the bolts through the specified Stage 3 angle, using a socket and extension bar. It is recommended that an angle-measuring gauge is used during this stage of the tightening, to ensure accuracy. If a gauge is not available, use white paint to make alignment marks between the

11.37b Tightening the cylinder head bolts using a torque wrench and socket

bolt head and cylinder head prior to tightening; the marks can then be used to check the bolt has been rotated through the correct angle during tightening. Repeat for the Stage 4 setting (see illustration).

39 Refit the timing belt inner cover, tightening the retaining screws securely.

40 With reference to Sections 2 and 5, refit the timing belt tensioner and sprockets.

41 Refer to Section 2 and set the engine to TDC on No 1 cylinder. On completion, refer to Section 4 and refit the camshaft timing belt and outer covers.

42 The remainder of refitting is a reversal of the removal procedure, as follows:

a) *Refer to Chapter 4D and refit the turbocharger, the exhaust downpipe, the EGR valve (where applicable) and the glow plug cabling.*

b) *Refer to Chapter 4C and refit the injector fuel supply hoses to the injectors and the injection pump head. Reconnect all fuel system electrical cabling. Refit the injector bleed hose to the injection pump fuel return port.*

c) *Refit the engine harness connector bracket to the cylinder head.*

d) *Refit the camshaft cover (see Section 7).*

e) *With reference to the information in Chapter 11, refit the lock carrier assembly, if it was removed for greater access.*

f) *Reconnect the radiator, expansion tank and heater coolant hoses, referring to Chapter 3 for guidance. Reconnect the coolant temperature sensor wiring.*

g) *Refer to Section 6 and refit the auxiliary drivebelt(s).*

h) *Restore the battery connection.*

i) *Refer to Chapter 11 and refit the bonnet.*

j) *On engine code AFN, refit the engine top cover.*

43 On completion, refer to Chapter 1B and carry out the following:

a) *Refill the engine cooling system with the correct quantity of new coolant.*

b) *Refill the engine lubrication system with the correct grade and quantity of oil.*

Note: *No further tightening of the cylinder head bolts is required.*

12 Hydraulic tappets - operation check

1 The hydraulic tappets are self-adjusting, and require no attention whilst in service.

2 If the hydraulic tappets become excessively noisy, their operation can be checked as described below.

3 Run the engine until it reaches its normal operating temperature. Switch off the engine, then refer to Section 7 and remove the camshaft cover.

11.38 Angle-tightening a cylinder head bolt

4 Rotate the camshaft by turning the crankshaft with a socket and wrench, until the first cam lobe over No 1 cylinder is pointing upwards.

5 Using a feeler blade, measure the clearance between the base of the cam lobe and the top of the tappet. If the clearance is greater than 0.1mm, then the tappet is defective and must be renewed.

6 If the clearance is less than 0.1 mm, press down on the top of the tappet, until it is felt to contact the top of the valve stem. Use a wooden or plastic implement that will not damage the surface of the tappet.

7 If the tappet travels more than 1.0 mm before making contact, then it is defective and must be renewed.

8 Hydraulic tappet removal and refitting is described as part of the cylinder head overhaul sequence - see Chapter 2C for details.

⚠ *Warning: After fitting hydraulic tappets, wait a minimum of 30 minutes (or leave overnight) before starting the engine, to allow the tappets time to settle, otherwise the pistons may strike the valve heads.*

13 Flywheel/driveplate - removal, inspection and refitting

Removal of the flywheel is as described in Section 13 of Chapter 2A.

14.10a Remove the engine mounting-to-transmission bellhousing bolts . . .

14 Engine mountings - inspection and renewal

Inspection

1 If improved access is required, raise the front of the car and support it securely on axle stands (see "*Jacking and vehicle support*").

2 Check the mounting rubbers to see if they are cracked, hardened or separated from the metal at any point; renew the mounting if any such damage or deterioration is evident.

3 Check that all the mounting's fasteners are securely tightened; use a torque wrench to check if possible.

4 Using a large screwdriver or a crowbar, check for wear in the mounting by carefully levering against it to check for free play. Where this is not possible, enlist the aid of an assistant to move the engine/transmission back and forth, or from side to side, while you watch the mounting. While some free play is to be expected even from new components, excessive wear should be obvious. If excessive free play is found, check first that the fasteners are correctly secured, then renew any worn components as described below.

Renewal

Front engine mounting

5 Disconnect the battery negative lead, and position it away from the terminal. **Note:** *If the vehicle has a security-coded radio, check that you have a copy of the code number before disconnecting the battery. Refer to your VW dealer if in doubt.*

6 Position a trolley jack underneath the engine, and position it such that the jack head is directly underneath the engine/bellhousing mating surface.

7 Raise the jack until it just takes the weight of the engine off the front engine mounting.

8 Slacken and withdraw the engine mounting through-bolt.

9 Refer to Chapter 5A and remove the starter motor.

10 Slacken and withdraw the engine mounting-to-transmission bellhousing bolts, and remove the bracket (see illustrations).

14.10b . . . and remove the bracket

2B

14.11 Remove the engine mounting block retaining bolt

14.12 Lift the engine mounting block out of the crossmember cup

14.13a Lug (arrowed) on top of the mounting engages with the recess in the bracket

11 Working under the engine mounting front crossmember, remove the engine mounting block retaining bolt **(see illustration)**.

12 Lift the engine mounting block out of the crossmember cup **(see illustration)**.

13 Refitting is a reversal of removal, noting the following points:

a) *Ensure that the orientation lug that protrudes from the top of surface of the engine mounting block engages with the recess in the mounting bracket* **(see illustration)**.

b) *Tighten all bolts to the specified torque* **(see illustration)**.

Rear right-hand engine mounting

14 Disconnect the battery negative lead, and position it away from the terminal. **Note:** *If the vehicle has a security-coded radio, check that you have a copy of the code number before disconnecting the battery. Refer to your VW dealer if in doubt.*

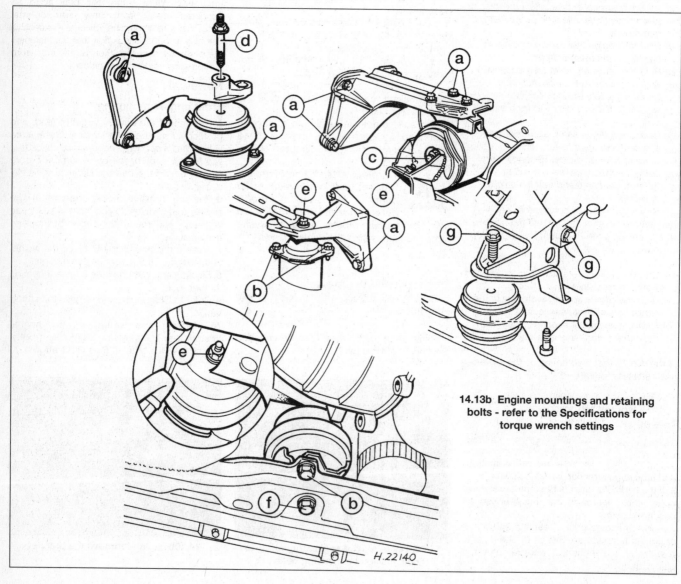

14.13b Engine mountings and retaining bolts - refer to the Specifications for torque wrench settings

H.22140

15 Mount an engine lifting beam across the engine bay, and attach the jib to the engine lifting eyes on the cylinder head. Alternatively, an engine hoist can be used. Raise the hoist/lifting beam jib to take the weight of the engine off the engine mounting.

16 Slacken and withdraw the engine mounting through-bolt.

17 Unbolt the engine mounting bracket from the cylinder block.

18 Unbolt the engine mounting block from the body, and remove it from the engine bay.

19 Refitting is a reversal of removal, noting the following points:

a) *Ensure that the orientation lug that protrudes from the top of surface of the engine mounting block engages with the recess in the mounting bracket.*

b) *Tighten all bolts to the specified torque (see illustration 14.13b).*

Rear left-hand mounting

20 Disconnect the battery negative cable, and position it away from the terminal. **Note:** *If the vehicle has a security-coded radio, check that you have a copy of the code number before disconnecting the battery. Refer to your VW dealer if in doubt.*

21 Position a trolley jack underneath the engine, and position it such that the jack head is directly underneath the engine/bellhousing mating surface.

22 Raise the jack until it just takes the weight of the engine off the rear right-hand engine mounting.

23 Slacken and withdraw the engine mounting through-bolt.

24 Unbolt the engine mounting bracket from the end of the transmission casing.

25 Unbolt the engine mounting block from the body, and remove it from the engine bay.

26 Refitting is a reversal of removal, noting the following points:

a) *Ensure that the orientation lug that protrudes from the top of surface of the engine mounting block engages with the recess in the mounting bracket.*

b) *Tighten all bolts to the specified torque (see illustration 14.13b).*

15 Sump -
removal, inspection and refitting

Removal

1 Disconnect the battery negative cable, and position it away from the terminal. **Note:** *If the vehicle has a security-coded radio, check that you have a copy of the code number before disconnecting the battery. Refer to your VW dealer if in doubt.* Refer to Chapter 1B and drain the engine oil. Where applicable, remove the screws and lower the engine undertray away from the vehicle.

2 Park the vehicle on a level surface, apply the handbrake and chock the rear wheels.

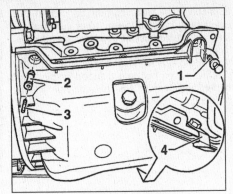

15.5 Sump cover fasteners - engine code AFN

1 Bolt
2 Securing clip
3 Spreader pin
4 Spring clip

3 Raise the front of the vehicle, rest it securely on axle stands or wheel ramps; refer to *"Jacking and vehicle support"*.

4 To improve access to the sump, refer to Chapter 8 and disconnect the right-hand driveshaft from the transmission output flange. Where necessary, release the fasteners and remove the engine lower splash shield.

5 On models with the AFN engine, the sump cover must be removed for access to the sump. Unscrew the two bolts, extract the spreader pins from the securing clips, and remove the clips. The cover is further secured by a spring clip at the front edge - release the clip and lower the sump cover **(see illustration)**.

6 Working around the outside of the sump, progressively slacken and withdraw the sump retaining bolts. Where applicable, unbolt and remove the flywheel cover plate from the transmission to gain access to the left-hand sump fixings.

7 Break the joint by striking the sump with the palm of your hand, then lower the sump and withdraw it from underneath the vehicle. Recover and discard the sump gasket. Where a baffle plate is fitted, note that it can only be removed once the oil pump has been unbolted (see Section 16).

8 While the sump is removed, take the opportunity to check the oil pump pick-up/strainer for signs of clogging or disintegration. If necessary, remove the pump

as described in Section 16, and clean or renew the strainer.

Refitting

9 Clean all traces of sealant from the mating surfaces of the cylinder block/crankcase and sump, then use a piece of clean rag to wipe out the sump.

10 Ensure that the sump and cylinder block/crankcase mating surfaces are clean and dry, then apply a coating of suitable sealant to the sump and crankcase mating surfaces.

11 Lay a new sump gasket in position on the sump mating surface, then offer up the sump and refit the retaining bolts. Tighten the nuts and bolts evenly and progressively to the specified torque.

12 Where applicable, refit the driveshaft and engine undertray.

13 On models with the AFN engine, refit the sump cover.

14 Refer to Chapter 1B and refill the engine with the specified grade and quantity of oil.

15 Restore the battery connection.

16 Oil pump and pickup -
removal and refitting

1 The oil pump and pickup are both mounted in the sump. Drive is taken from the intermediate shaft, which rotates at half crankshaft speed.

2 The oil pump arrangement is identical to that described for petrol engines; refer to Chapter 2A for further details.

17 Engine top cover
(engine code AFN) -
removal and refitting

1 Models with the later engine code AFN have a large plastic cover fitted over the top of the engine, which acts as an acoustic shroud. Removing this cover gives greatly-improved access to many components.

2 Using a suitable screwdriver or similar tool, prise out the plastic covers fitted over the retaining nuts **(see illustrations)**.

2B

17.2a Prise out the covers . . .

17.2b . . . for access to the retaining nuts

17.3a Unscrew the retaining nuts . . .

3 Unscrew the retaining nuts and lift off the cover **(see illustrations)**. Take care not to lose any of the rubber spacers fitted to the locating studs as the cover is removed.

4 Refitting is a reversal of removal. Ensure that no hoses become trapped or pinched under the cover as it is refitted. Tighten the retaining nuts securely.

17.3b . . . and lift off the top cover

Chapter 2 Part C:
Engine removal and overhaul procedures

Contents

Degrees of difficulty

| Easy, suitable for novice with little experience | | Fairly easy, suitable for beginner with some experience | | Fairly difficult, suitable for competent DIY mechanic | | Difficult, suitable for experienced DIY mechanic | | Very difficult, suitable for expert DIY or professional | |

Specifications

Engine codes
See Chapter 2A or B.

Cylinder head
Cylinder head gasket surface, maximum distortion .... 0.1 mm
Minimum cylinder head height:
  Petrol engines .... 132.6 mm
  Diesel engines .... Head reworking not possible
Maximum swirl chamber projection (diesel engines) .... 0.07 mm

Cylinder head gasket
Identification markings (punched holes), diesel engines only*:
  All diesel engines except engine code AAZ:
    Piston projection:
      0.91 to 1.00 mm .... 1 hole
      1.01 to 1.10 mm .... 2 holes
      1.11 to 1.20 mm .... 3 holes
  Engine code AAZ:
    Piston projection:
      0.66 to 0.86 mm .... 1 hole
      0.87 to 0.90 mm .... 2 holes
      0.91 to 1.02 mm .... 3 holes
*Note: See text in Chapter 2B and in Sections 4 and 13 of this Chapter for details.

Valves

	Inlet	Exhaust
Valve stem diameter:		
Engine codes AAM, ADZ, ADY, AGG:		
Up to November 1994	7.97 mm	7.95 mm
From December 1994	6.92 ± 0.02 mm	6.92 ± 0.02 mm
All other engines	7.97 mm	7.95 mm
Maximum valve head deflection (end of valve stem flush with top of guide):		
Diesel engines	1.3 mm	1.3 mm
Petrol engines	1.0 mm	1.3 mm

Camshaft

Endfloat, all engine codes	0.15 mm
Maximum runout, all engine codes	0.01 mm
Maximum running clearance:	
Diesel engines	0.11 mm
Petrol engines	0.10 mm
Camshaft identification codes:	
Engine codes PB, PF	G 026
Engine code RP	N or Q 026
Engine codes 1Z, AHU and AFN	W 028F
Engine code AAZ	W 028D
Engine code AAM	M 026
Engine codes ABS, ADZ	Q 026
Engine code 2E	A 026
Engine code ADY	D 048
Engine code AGG	A 050

Intermediate shaft

Maximum endfloat:	
Petrol engines	0.25 mm
Diesel engines	N/A

Cylinder block

Bore diameter:	
1.8 litre engines:	
Standard	81.01 mm
1st oversize	81.26 mm
2nd oversize	81.51 mm
Maximum bore wear	0.08 mm
2.0 litre engines:	
Standard	82.51 mm
1st oversize	82.76 mm
2nd oversize	83.01 mm
Maximum bore wear	0.08 mm
Diesel engines:	
Standard	79.51 mm
1st oversize	79.76 mm
2nd oversize	80.01 mm
Maximum bore wear	0.10 mm

Pistons and piston rings

Piston diameter:	
2.0 litre engines:	
Standard	82.485 mm
1st oversize	82.735 mm
2nd oversize	82.985 mm
Maximum deviation	0.04 mm
1.8 litre engines:	
Standard	80.985 mm
1st oversize	81.235 mm
2nd oversize	81.485 mm
Maximum deviation	0.04 mm
Engine code AAZ:	
Standard	79.48 mm
1st oversize	79.73 mm
2nd oversize	79.98 mm
Maximum deviation	0.04 mm
Engine code 1Z, AHU, AFN:	
Standard	79.47 mm
1st oversize	79.92 mm
2nd oversize	79.97 mm
Maximum deviation	0.04 mm
Gudgeon pin external diameter:	
Diesel engines	26.0 mm
Petrol engines:	
1.8 litre	20.0 mm
2.0 litre	21.0 mm

Piston ring-to-groove wall clearance:
  Petrol engines:
    Top compression ring:
      Standard . . . . 0.02 to 0.05 mm
      Service limit . . . . 0.15 mm
    2nd compression ring:
      Standard . . . . 0.02 to 0.05 mm
      Service limit . . . . 0.15 mm
    Oil scraper ring:
      Standard . . . . 0.02 to 0.05 mm
      Service limit . . . . 0.15 mm
  Engine codes 1Z, AHU and AFN:
    Top compression ring:
      Standard . . . . 0.06 to 0.09 mm
      Service limit . . . . 0.25 mm
    2nd compression ring:
      Standard . . . . 0.05 to 0.08 mm
      Service limit . . . . 0.25 mm
    Oil scraper ring:
      Standard . . . . 0.03 to 0.06 mm
      Service limit . . . . 0.15 mm
  Engine code AAZ:
    Top compression ring:
      Standard . . . . 0.09 to 0.12 mm
      Service limit . . . . 0.25 mm
    2nd compression ring:
      Standard . . . . 0.05 to 0.08 mm
      Service limit . . . . 0.25 mm
    Oil scraper ring:
      Standard . . . . 0.03 to 0.06 mm
      Service limit . . . . 0.15 mm
Piston ring end gap:
  All engines except AAZ:
    Top compression ring:
      Standard . . . . 0.20 to 0.40 mm
      Service limit . . . . 1.0 mm
    2nd compression ring:
      Standard . . . . 0.20 to 0.40 mm
      Service limit . . . . 1.0 mm
    Oil scraper ring (two-part):
      Standard . . . . 0.25 to 0.50 mm
      Service limit . . . . 1.0 mm
    Oil scraper ring (three-part):
      Standard . . . . 0.40 to 0.50 mm
      Service limit . . . . 1.0 mm
  Engine code AAZ:
    Top compression ring:
      Standard . . . . 0.20 to 0.40 mm
      Service limit . . . . 1.2 mm
    2nd compression ring:
      Standard . . . . 0.20 to 0.40 mm
      Service limit . . . . 0.6 mm
    Oil scraper ring:
      Standard . . . . 0.25 to 0.50 mm
      Service limit . . . . 1.2 mm

Connecting rods

Length:
  Diesel engines . . . . 144 mm
  Petrol engines . . . . N/A
Big-end thrust clearance:
  Petrol engines:
    Standard . . . . 0.05 to 0.31 mm
    Service limit . . . . 0.37 mm
  Diesel engines:
    Standard . . . . N/A
    Service limit . . . . 0.37 mm

Crankshaft

Maximum shaft runout	N/A
Maximum endfloat:	
Petrol engines:	
Standard	0.07 to 0.17 mm
Service limit	0.25 mm
Diesel engines:	
Standard	0.07 to 0.17 mm
Service limit	0.37 mm
Main bearing journal diameters:	
All engine codes:	
Standard	54.00 mm
1st undersize	53.75 mm
2nd undersize	53.50 mm
3rd undersize	53.25 mm
Tolerance	-0.022 to -0.042 mm
Main bearing running clearances:	
Petrol engines:	
Standard	0.02 to 0.06 mm
Service limit	0.17 mm
Diesel engines:	
Standard	0.03 to 0.08 mm
Service limit	0.17 mm
Crankpin journal diameters:	
Standard	47.80 mm
1st undersize	47.55 mm
2nd undersize	47.30 mm
3rd undersize	47.05 mm
Tolerance	-0.022 to -0.042 mm
Big-end running clearance:	
Petrol engines:	
Standard	0.01 to 0.06 mm
Service limit	0.12 mm
Diesel engines:	
Standard	N/A
Service limit	0.08 mm

Torque wrench settings

	Nm	lbf ft
Big-end bearing caps bolts/nuts*:		
Stage 1	30	22
Stage 2	Angle-tighten a further 90°	
Camshaft bearing cap nuts*	20	15
Crankshaft main bearing cap bolts*:		
Engine codes AAZ, 1Z, AHU, AFN, ADZ, ADY, AGG:		
Stage 1	65	48
Stage 2	Angle-tighten a further 90°	
Engine codes PB, PF, RP, AAM, ABS, 2E	65	48
Driveshaft flange bolts	45	33
Engine carrier-to-body bolts	80	59
Exhaust pipe-to-manifold (petrol)	40	30
Exhaust pipe-to-turbo (diesel)	25	18
Flywheel cover plate	10	7
Intermediate shaft flange bolts	25	18
Intermediate shaft sprocket bolt:		
Diesel engines	45	33
Petrol engines	80	59
Lock carrier retaining bolts	5	4
Piston oil jet/pressure relief valve	27	19
Torque converter to driveplate nuts	60	44
Transmission bellhousing to engine:		
M10 screws	60	44
M12 screws	80	59

*Use new nuts/bolts

1 Engine and transmission removal - preparation and precautions

If you have decided that the engine must be removed for overhaul or major repair work, several preliminary steps should be taken.

Locating a suitable place to work is extremely important. Adequate work space, along with storage space for the vehicle, will be needed. If a workshop or garage is not available, at the very least a solid, level, clean work surface is required.

If possible, clear some shelving close to the work area and use it to store the engine components and ancillaries as they are removed and dismantled. In this manner, the components stand a better chance of staying clean and undamaged during the overhaul. Laying out components in groups together with their fixings bolts, screws etc will save time and avoid confusion when the engine is refitted.

Clean the engine compartment and engine/transmission before beginning the removal procedure; this will help visibility and help to keep tools clean.

The help of an assistant should be available; there are certain instances when one person cannot safely perform all of the operations required to remove the engine from the vehicle. Safety is of primary importance, considering the potential hazards involved in this kind of operation. A second person should always be in attendance to offer help in an emergency. If this is the first time you have removed an engine, advice and aid from someone more experienced would also be beneficial.

2.5a Radiator top hose connection to engine

Plan the operation ahead of time. Before starting work, obtain (or arrange for the hire of) all of the tools and equipment you will need. Access to the following items will allow the task of removing and refitting the engine/transmission to be completed safely and with relative ease: a heavy-duty trolley jack - rated in excess of the combined weight of the engine and transmission, complete sets of spanners and sockets as described in the front of this manual, wooden blocks, and plenty of rags and cleaning solvent for mopping up spilled oil, coolant and fuel. A selection of different sized plastic storage bins will also prove useful for keeping dismantled components grouped together. If any of the equipment must be hired, make sure that you arrange for it in advance, and perform all of the operations possible without it beforehand; this may save you time and money.

Plan on the vehicle being out of use for quite a while, especially if you intend to carry out an engine overhaul. Read through the whole of this Section and work out a strategy based on your own experience and the tools, time and workspace available to you. Some of the overhaul processes may have to carried out by a VW dealer or an engineering works - these establishments often have busy schedules, so it would be prudent to consult them before removing or dismantling the engine, to get an idea of the amount of time required to carry out the work.

When removing the engine from the vehicle, be methodical about the disconnection of external components. Labelling cables and hoses as they are removed will greatly assist the refitting process.

Always be extremely careful when lifting the engine/transmission assembly from the engine bay. Serious injury can result from careless actions. If help is required, it is better to wait until it is available rather than risk personal injury and/or damage to components by continuing alone. By planning ahead and taking your time, a job of this nature, although major, can be accomplished successfully and without incident.

On all models described in this manual, the engine and transmission are removed as a complete assembly, upwards and forwards. This involves the removal of the lock carrier, which is the panel assembly that forms the

upper front part of the engine bay. Although the lock carrier is a large assembly, its removal is not difficult, and the benefits in terms of ease of access are well worth the effort involved.

Note that the engine and transmission should ideally be removed with the vehicle standing on all four roadwheels, but access to the driveshafts and exhaust system downpipe will be improved if the vehicle can be temporarily raised onto axle stands.

Note: *On vehicles with engine code RP, the exhaust manifold-to-downpipe joint incorporates two spring clips, which are almost impossible to remove without the special VW service tool (4140A/2). Refer to Chapter 4D, Section 7 for further details.*

2 Engine and transmission - removal, separation and refitting

Removal

All models

1 Select a solid, level surface to park the vehicle upon. Give yourself enough space to move around it easily.

2 Refer to Chapter 11 and remove the bonnet from its hinges. Also remove the lock carrier and the engine lower splash shield (where fitted).

3 Disconnect the battery negative lead, and position it away from the terminal. **Note:** *If the vehicle has a security-coded radio, check that you have a copy of the code number before disconnecting the battery cable; refer to Chapter 12 for details.*

4 With reference to Chapter 1A or B as applicable, carry out the following:

a) *If the engine is to be dismantled, drain the engine oil.*

b) *Drain the cooling system.*

c) *Remove the auxiliary drivebelt(s).*

5 Refer to Chapter 3 and perform the following:

a) *Slacken the clips and disconnect the radiator hoses from the engine (see illustration), and from the thermostat housing/coolant pump (as applicable).*

b) *Disconnect the coolant hoses from the expansion tank and heater pipes (see illustrations).*

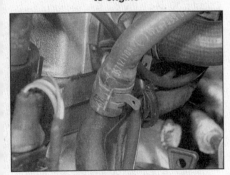

2.5b Heater hose connection at rear of engine

2.5c Expansion tank overflow hose

2.5d Expansion tank lower hose connection

2C

c) *Disconnect the wiring connectors from the radiator and cooling fan motor(s).*

d) *Disconnect the top and bottom hoses from the radiator. Lift the radiator, complete with fan(s) from its lower mountings and remove it from the vehicle.*

6 On vehicles with air conditioning, refer to Chapter 3 and carry out the following additional operations:

a) *Unbolt the air conditioning fluid reservoir from its mountings, and allow it to hang free.*

b) *Remove the retaining bolts from the clips securing the refrigerant condenser supply and return pipes.*

c) *Unbolt the air conditioning compressor from the engine, and allow it to rest on the floor with the radiator. Make sure the refrigerant hoses are not under strain.*

7 Remove the air cleaner housing and air inlet duct, with reference to the appropriate Part of Chapter 4.

Petrol models

8 On catalyst models, with reference to Chapter 4D, unplug the lambda sensor cabling from the main harness at the multiway connector.

9 Disconnect the ignition HT king lead from the centre terminal of the distributor cap, and tie it back away from the engine.

10 Refer to Chapter 9 and disconnect the brake servo vacuum hose from the port on the inlet manifold.

11 On vehicles with an Exhaust Gas Recirculation (EGR) system, refer to Chapter 4D and disconnect the vacuum hoses from the connection points on the EGR valve, brake servo vacuum hose, and air inlet hose. Make a careful note of the order of connection to ensure correct refitting.

12 On vehicles with an activated charcoal canister emission control system, refer to Chapter 4D and disconnect the vacuum hose from the port on the throttle body. Make a careful note of the point of connection to ensure correct refitting.

Single-point injection models

13 With reference to Chapter 4A, carry out the following operations:

a) *Depressurise the fuel system.*

b) *Remove the exhaust manifold-to-air*

cleaner and throttle body airbox-to-air cleaner ducting from the engine bay.

c) *Remove the airbox from the top of the throttle body; make a note of the vacuum hose connections to ensure correct refitting later.*

d) *Disconnect the accelerator cable from the throttle spindle lever.*

e) *Disconnect the fuel supply and return hoses from the throttle body - observe the precautions at the start of Chapter 4A.*

Multi-point injection models

14 With reference to Chapter 4B, carry out the following operations:

a) *Depressurise the fuel system.*

b) *Slacken the clips and remove the exhaust manifold-to-air cleaner and throttle body-to-airflow meter ducting from the engine bay.*

c) *Disconnect the accelerator cable from the throttle spindle lever.*

d) *Disconnect the fuel supply and return hoses from the throttle body - observe the precautions at the start of Chapter 4B.*

15 On vehicles with automatic transmission, extra clearance is required when removing the engine and transmission as one assembly. Removing the ribbed auxiliary belt pulleys from the crankshaft and where applicable, coolant pump achieves this - see Chapter 2A.

Diesel models

⚠ **Warning: When dismantling any part of the air inlet system on a turbocharged vehicle, ensure that no foreign material can get into the turbo air inlet port; cover the opening with a sheet of plastic, secured with an elastic band. The turbocharger compressor blades could be severely damaged on restarting if debris is allowed to enter.**

16 On engine code AFN, remove the engine top cover. To save it from being damaged, it's a good idea to remove the sump cover also.

17 Refer to Chapter 9 and disconnect the brake servo vacuum hose from the vacuum pump.

18 On vehicles with an Exhaust Gas Recirculation (EGR) system, refer to Chapter 4D and disconnect the vacuum hoses from the connection points on the EGR valve,

brake servo vacuum hose, air inlet hose and where applicable, fuel injection pump. Make a careful note of the order of connection to ensure correct refitting.

19 Refer to Chapter 4C and carry out the following operations:

a) *Slacken and withdraw the banjo bolts, then disconnect the fuel supply and return hoses from the fuel injection pump.*

b) *Release the clip, then disconnect the injector bleed hose from the port on the fuel return union.*

Engine code AAZ

c) *Slacken the clips and remove the inlet air hose from the air cleaner, crankcase ventilation hose or turbocharger inlet, as applicable.*

d) *Disconnect the accelerator cable from the fuel injection pump.*

e) *Where applicable, disconnect the cold start accelerator cable from the fuel injection pump.*

Engine codes 1Z, AHU and AFN

f) *Slacken the clips and remove the inlet air hose from the air mass meter, turbocharger inlet and crankcase ventilation hose.*

g) *Slacken the clips and remove the supply and return inlet air hoses that run from the turbocharger to the intercooler and back. It will be necessary to unplug the cabling from the inlet air temperature sensor at the connector.*

h) *Disconnect the vacuum control hose from the port on the boost pressure control diaphragm, at the side of the turbocharger; refer to Chapter 4D for details.*

All models

20 Refer to Chapter 5A and disconnect the wiring from the alternator, starter motor and solenoid.

21 With reference to Chapter 5B and Chapter 4A, B or C as applicable, identify those sections of the engine, ignition and fuelling system electrical harness that remain connected to sensors and actuators on the engine. Label each connector carefully to ensure correct refitting **(see illustrations)**.

22 On vehicles with power steering, refer to Chapter 10 and carry out the following:

a) *Slacken the retaining screws and release the clips securing the power steering supply and return pipes.*

b) *Remove the power steering fluid reservoir retaining screws and lower it away, allowing it to rest so that the fluid pipes are not strained.*

c) *Unbolt the power steering pump, together with its mounting brackets, from the engine. Support it so that the pipes are not strained.* **Note:** *The power steering hoses can remain connected to the pump and reservoir, so there is no need to drain the hydraulic fluid from the system.*

2.21a Disconnecting the high oil pressure . . .

2.21b . . . and low oil pressure switch wiring

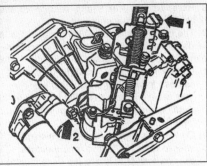

2.23a Electronic speedometer sender (1) and reversing light switch (2) wiring plugs

2.23b On models with a mechanical speedometer, disconnect the speedometer drive cable

2.23c Disconnect the selector and gearchange cables

23 On manual transmission models, refer to Chapter 7A and carry out the following:

a) *At the top of the transmission casing, disconnect the wiring from the reversing light switch. On models with an electronic speedometer, disconnect the wiring plug from the speedometer sender on top of the transmission (see illustration).*

b) *On models with a conventional speedometer, unscrew the retaining collar and disconnect the speedometer cable from the transmission (see illustration).*

c) *Disconnect the gear selection mechanism from the transmission (see illustration).*

d) *On vehicles with a cable-operated clutch, refer to Chapter 6 and disconnect the clutch cable from the release mechanism at the front of the transmission casing.*

e) *On vehicles with a hydraulically-operated clutch, slacken the selector relay lever through-bolt, then remove the retaining bolts and withdraw the clutch slave cylinder from the transmission casing. Leave the hydraulic line connected to the cylinder, and position the cylinder out of the way.*

24 On automatic transmission models, refer to Chapter 7B and carry out the following:

a) *Select position "P", then release the selector cable from the selector lever at the top of the transmission casing.*

b) *Clamp the coolant hoses leading to the transmission fluid cooler, then release the clips and disconnect the hoses from the cooler ports.*

c) *Unplug the wiring harness from the*

transmission at the connectors; label each connector to aid refitting later.

25 Refer to Chapter 8 and separate the driveshafts from the transmission differential output shafts.

26 With reference to Chapter 4D, unbolt the exhaust downpipe from the exhaust manifold (or turbocharger). Recover and discard the gasket. On vehicles with engine code RP, special tools will be needed to separate the two spring clips either side of the manifold-to-downpipe joint - refer to the note at the end of Section 1.

27 Unbolt the engine and transmission earthing straps from the bodywork.

28 If not already done, raise the front of the vehicle and support it on axle stands (see "Jacking and vehicle support").

29 Unbolt and remove the vibration damper from the subframe.

30 Unbolt and remove the right-hand driveshaft shield from the engine.

31 Connect a hoist and raise it so that the weight of the engine and transmission are just supported. Arrange the hoist and sling so that the engine and transmission are kept level when they are being withdrawn from the vehicle.

32 Unscrew and remove the engine and transmission mounting bolts. Where possible, leave the bonded rubber mountings attached to the support points; this will avoid the need for realignment during refitting.

33 Check around the engine and transmission assembly to ensure that all associated attachments are disconnected

and positioned out of the way. Engage the services of an assistant to help in guiding the assembly clear of surrounding components, then carefully raise the engine/transmission assembly so that it is clear of the mountings, then when at a suitable height, remove the assembly from the front of the vehicle **(see illustration)**.

34 Once the engine/transmission assembly is clear of the vehicle, move it to an area where it can be cleaned and worked on.

Separation

35 Rest the engine and transmission assembly on a firm, flat surface, and use wooden blocks as wedges to keep the unit steady.

Manual transmission models

36 The transmission is secured to the engine by a combination of machine screws and studs, threaded into the cylinder block and bellhousing - the total number of fixings depends on the type of transmission and vehicle specification. Note that two of these fixings also serve as mountings for the starter motor and the front engine mounting.

37 Starting at the bottom, remove all the screws and nuts then carefully draw the transmission away from the engine, resting it securely on wooden blocks **(see illustrations)**. Collect the locating dowels if they are loose enough to be extracted.

Caution: Take care to prevent the transmission from tilting, until the input shaft is fully disengaged from the clutch friction plate.

2C

2.33 Engine and transmission assembly removal

2.37a Remove the engine-to-transmission screws . . .

2.37b . . . and the side cover plate (where applicable) . . .

2.37c . . . then separate the transmission from the engine

38 Refer to Chapter 6, and remove the clutch release mechanism, pressure plate and friction plate.

Automatic transmission models

39 Unbolt the skid plate from the underside of the transmission oil pan.

40 Unbolt the protection plate from the bottom of the transmission bellhousing; this will expose the rear face of the driveplate.

41 Mark the position of the torque converter with respect to the driveplate, using chalk or a marker pen. Remove the three nuts that secure the driveplate to the torque converter; turn the engine over using a socket and wrench on the crankshaft sprocket to rotate the driveplate and expose each nut in turn.

42 The transmission is secured to the engine by a combination of machine screws and studs with nuts, threaded into the cylinder block and bellhousing - the total number of fixings depends on the type of transmission and vehicle specification. Note that two of these fixings also serve as mountings for the starter motor.

43 Starting at the bottom, remove all the screws and nuts then carefully draw the transmission away from the engine, resting it securely on wooden blocks. Collect the locating dowels if they are loose enough to be extracted.

Caution: Take care to prevent the torque converter from sliding off the transmission input shaft - hold it in place as the transmission is withdrawn.

44 Place a length of batten across the open face of the bellhousing, fastening it with cable-ties, to keep the torque converter in place in its housing.

Refitting

45 If the engine and transmission have not been separated, go to paragraph 50.

Manual transmission

46 Smear a little high-melting-point grease on the splines of the transmission input shaft. Do not use an excessive amount, as there is the risk of contaminating the clutch friction plate. Carefully offer up the transmission to the cylinder block, guiding the dowels into the mounting holes in cylinder block.

47 Refit the bellhousing bolts and nuts, hand tightening them to secure the transmission in

position. **Note:** *Do not tighten them to force the engine and transmission together.* Ensure that the bellhousing and cylinder block mating faces will butt together evenly without obstruction, before tightening the bolts and nuts to their specified torque.

Automatic transmission

48 Remove the torque converter restraint from the face of the bellhousing. Check that the drive lugs on the torque converter hub are correctly engaged with the recesses in the inner wheel of the automatic transmission fluid pump.

49 Carefully offer up the transmission to the cylinder block, guiding the dowels into the mounting holes in cylinder block. Observe the markings made during the removal, to ensure correct alignment between the torque converter and the driveplate.

50 Refit the bellhousing bolts and nuts, hand-tightening them to secure the transmission in position. **Note:** *Do not tighten them to force the engine and transmission together.* Ensure that the bellhousing and cylinder block mating faces will butt together evenly without obstruction, before tightening the bolts and nuts to their specified torque.

All models

51 With reference to Chapter 5A, refit the starter motor, together with the front engine mounting bracket, and tighten the retaining bolts to the specified torque.

52 Attach the jib of an engine hoist to the lifting eyelets on the cylinder head, and raise the engine and transmission from the ground.

53 Wheel the hoist up to the front of the vehicle and with the help of an assistant, guide the engine and transmission in through the front of the engine bay. Rotate the assembly slightly so that the transmission casing enters first, then guide the auxiliary belt pulleys past the bodywork.

54 Align the rear engine mounting brackets with the mounting points on the body. Note that alignment lugs protrude from the metal discs that are bonded to the top of each of each engine mounting; these must engage with the recesses on the underside of the engine mounting brackets (Chapter 2A or 2B).

55 Fit the front engine mounting rubber block into the cup in the crossmember, then insert the retaining bolt through the underside of the crossmember and tighten it to the specified torque.

56 Lower the engine and transmission into position, ensuring that the locating lugs on the front engine mounting engage with the recess in the mounting bracket. Insert the front and rear engine mounting through-bolts, tightening them by hand initially.

57 Detach the engine hoist jib from the lifting eyelets.

58 Settle the engine and transmission assembly on its mountings by rocking it backwards and forwards, then tighten the mounting through-bolts to the specified torque.

59 Refer to Chapter 8 and reconnect the driveshafts to the transmission.

60 The remainder of the refitting sequence is the direct reverse of the removal procedure, noting the following points:

a) *Ensure that all sections of the wiring harness follow their original routing; use new cable-ties to secure the harness in position, keeping it away from sources of heat and abrasion.*

b) *On vehicles with manual transmission, refer to Chapter 7A and reconnect the gear shift mechanism to the transmission, then check the overall operation of the gear shift mechanism. If necessary, adjust the gear shift rod/cables.*

c) *On vehicles with a hydraulically-operated clutch, refer to Chapter 6 and refit the slave cylinder. Provided the pipe unions were not disturbed, there should be no need to bleed the clutch hydraulic system.*

d) *On vehicles with a cable-operated clutch, refer to Chapter 6 and reconnect the cable to the transmission, then check the operation of the automatic adjustment mechanism.*

e) *On vehicles with automatic transmission, refer to Chapter 7B and reconnect the selector cable to the transmission, then check (and if necessary adjust) the overall operation of the gear selection mechanism.*

f) *Refer to Chapter 11 and refit the lock carrier assembly to the front of the vehicle; ensure that all wiring harness connections are remade correctly and tighten the retaining fixings to the specified torque.*

g) *Ensure that all hoses are correctly routed and are secured with the correct hose clips, where applicable. If the hose clips originally fitted were of the crimp variety, they cannot be used again; proprietary worm drive clips must be fitted in their place, unless otherwise specified.*

h) *Refill the cooling system as described in Chapter 1A or B.*

i) *Refill the engine with appropriate grades and quantities of oil (Chapter 1A or B).*

Diesel models

j) *Engine code AAZ: with reference to Chapter 4D, after reconnecting the cold start accelerator cable to the fuel injection pump, check and if necessary adjust the operation of the cold start acceleration system.*

Petrol models

k) *With reference to Chapter 4A or B as applicable, reconnect the throttle cable and adjust it as necessary.*

All models

61 When the engine is started for the first time, check for air, coolant, lubricant and fuel leaks from manifolds, hoses etc. If the engine has been overhauled, read the notes in Section 14 before attempting to start it.

3 Engine overhaul -
preliminary information

It is much easier to dismantle and work on the engine if it is mounted on a portable engine stand. These stands can often be hired from a tool hire shop. Before the engine is mounted on a stand, the flywheel should be removed, so that the stand bolts can be tightened into the end of the cylinder block/ crankcase.

If a stand is not available, it is possible to dismantle the engine with it blocked up on a sturdy workbench, or on the floor. Be very careful not to tip or drop the engine when working without a stand.

If you intend to obtain a reconditioned engine, all ancillaries must be removed first, to be transferred to the replacement engine (just as they will if you are doing a complete engine overhaul yourself). These components include the following:

Petrol engines

a) Power steering pump (Chapter 10) - where applicable.
b) Air conditioning compressor (Chapter 3) - where applicable.
c) Alternator (including mounting brackets)and starter motor (Chapter 5A).
d) The ignition system and HT components including all sensors, distributor, HT leads and spark plugs (Chapters 1A and 5B).
e) The fuel injection system components (Chapter 4A and B)
f) All electrical switches, actuators and sensors, and the engine wiring harness (Chapter 4A and B, Chapter 5B).
g) Inlet and exhaust manifolds (Chapter 2C).
h) Engine oil dipstick and tube (Chapter 2A)
i) Engine mountings (Chapter 2A).
j) Flywheel/driveplate (Chapter 2C)
k) Clutch components (Chapter 6) - manual transmission

Diesel engines

a) Power steering pump (Chapter 10) - where applicable.
b) Air conditioning compressor (Chapter 3) - where applicable.
c) Alternator (including mounting brackets)and starter motor (Chapter 5A).
d) The glow plug/pre-heating system components (Chapter 5C)
e) All fuel system components, including the fuel injection pump, all sensors and actuators (Chapter 4C)
f) The brake vacuum pump (Chapter 9)
g) All electrical switches, actuators and sensors, and the engine wiring harness (Chapter 4A and B, Chapter 5A).
h) Inlet and exhaust manifolds and where applicable, the turbocharger (Chapter 4D).
i) The engine oil level dipstick and its tube (Chapter 2C)
j) Engine mountings (Chapter 2B).

k) Flywheel/driveplate (Chapter 2C).
l) Clutch components (Chapter 6) - manual transmission.

Note: When removing the external components from the engine, pay close attention to details that may be helpful or important during refitting. Note the fitted position of gaskets, seals, spacers, pins, washers, bolts, and other small components.

If you are obtaining a "short" engine (the engine cylinder block/ crankcase, crankshaft, pistons and connecting rods, all fully assembled), then the cylinder head, sump and baffle plate, oil pump, timing belt (together with its tensioner and covers), auxiliary belt (together with its tensioner), coolant pump, thermostat housing, coolant outlet elbows, oil filter housing and where applicable oil cooler will also have to be removed.

If you are planning a full overhaul, the engine can be dismantled in the order given below:

a) Inlet and exhaust manifolds.
b) Timing belt, sprockets and tensioner.
c) Cylinder head.
d) Flywheel/driveplate.
e) Sump.
f) Oil pump.
g) Piston/connecting rod assemblies.
h) Crankshaft.

4 Cylinder head -
dismantling, cleaning, inspection and reassembly

Note: New and reconditioned cylinder heads are available from VW dealers, and from engine specialists. Specialist tools are required for the dismantling and inspection procedures, and new components may not be readily available. It may, therefore, be more practical for the home mechanic to buy a reconditioned head, rather than to dismantle, inspect and recondition the original head.

Dismantling

1 Remove the cylinder head from the engine block, and separate the inlet and exhaust manifolds from it (Part A or B of this Chapter).
2 On diesel models, remove the injectors and glow plugs (see Chapter 4C and Chapter 5C).
3 Refer to Chapter 3 and remove the coolant outlet elbow together with its gasket/O-ring.
4 Where applicable, unscrew the coolant sensor and oil pressure switch from the cylinder head.
5 Remove the timing belt sprocket from the camshaft (Part A or B of this Chapter).
6 It is important that groups of components are kept together when they are removed and, if still serviceable, refitted in the same groups. If they are refitted randomly, accelerated wear leading to early failure will occur. Stowing groups of components in plastic bags or storage bins will help to keep everything in the right order - label them

4.6 Keep groups of components together in labelled bags or boxes

according to their fitted location, eg 'No 1 exhaust', 'No 2 inlet', etc **(see illustration)**. (Note that No 1 cylinder is nearest the timing belt end of the engine.)
7 Check that the manufacturer's identification markings are visible on camshaft bearing caps; if none can be found, make your own using a scriber or centre-punch.
8 The camshaft bearing cap nuts must be removed progressively and in sequence to avoid stressing the camshaft, as follows.

Diesel engines

9 Slacken the nuts from bearing caps Nos 5, 1 and 3 first, then at bearing caps 2 and 4. Slacken the nuts alternately and diagonally half a turn at a time until they can be removed by hand. **Note:** Camshaft bearing caps are numbered 1 to 5 from the timing belt end.

Petrol engines

10 Slacken and remove the retaining nuts from bearing caps Nos 1 and 3 first, then bearing caps 2 and 5. Slacken the nuts alternately and diagonally half a turn at a time until they can be removed by hand. **Note:** Camshaft bearing caps are numbered 1 to 5 from the timing belt end - there is no bearing cap fitted at cylinder No 4 **(see illustration overleaf)**.

All engines

11 Slide the oil seal from the timing sprocket end of the camshaft and discard it; a new one must be used on reassembly.
12 Carefully lift the camshaft from the cylinder head - do not tilt it. Support both ends as it is removed so that the journals and lobes are not damaged.
13 Lift the hydraulic tappets from their bores and store them with the valve contact surface facing downwards, to prevent the oil from draining out. Alternatively, place the tappets in a tray full of oil, sufficiently deep to prevent the tappets draining. Make a note of the position of each tappet, as they must be fitted to the same valves on reassembly - accelerated wear leading to early failure will result if they are interchanged.
14 Turn the cylinder head over, and rest it on one side. Using a valve spring compressor, compress each valve spring in turn, extracting the split collets when the upper valve spring seat has been pushed far enough down the

2C

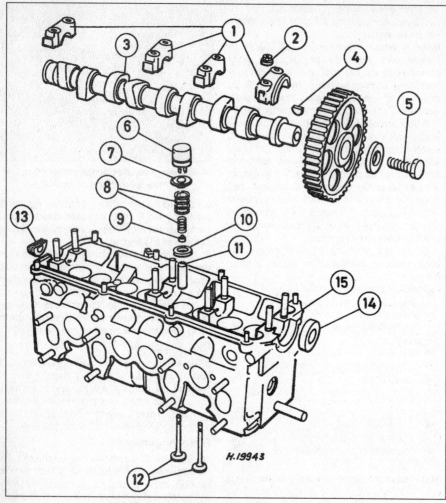

4.14 Compress the valve springs and remove the collets

4.15a Lift out the valve spring cover . . .

4.15b . . . inner valve spring . . .

4.10 Cylinder head components - petrol engines

1 Camshaft bearing cap	6 Hydraulic tappet	11 Valve guides
2 Nut	7 Valve spring upper seat	12 Valves
3 Camshaft	8 Valve springs	13 Plug
4 Woodruff key	9 Valve stem seals	14 Camshaft oil seal
5 Camshaft sprocket bolt	10 Valve spring lower seat	15 Cylinder head casting

valve stem to free them. If the spring seat sticks, tap the upper jaw of the compressor with a hammer to free it (see illustration).
15 Release the valve spring compressor and remove the upper spring seat, valve spring(s) and lower spring seat (see illustrations).

Note: *Depending on age and specification, engines may have concentric double valve springs, or single valve springs with no lower spring seat.*
16 Use a pair of pliers to extract the valve stem oil seal. Withdraw the valve itself from the

head gasket side of the cylinder head. If the valve sticks in the guide, carefully deburr the end face with fine abrasive paper. Repeat this process for the remaining valves.
17 On engine code AAZ, if the swirl chambers are badly coked or burned and are

4.15c . . . outer valve spring . . .

4.15d . . . and valve

4.15e Remove valve spring seat

4.17 Swirl chamber removal (diesel engine code AAZ)

4.21 Look for cracking between the valve seats

4.23 Measuring the distortion of the cylinder head gasketed surface

in need of renewal, insert a pin punch through each injector hole, and carefully drive out the swirl chambers using a mallet **(see illustration)**.

Cleaning

18 Using a suitable degreasing agent, remove all traces of oil deposits from the cylinder head, paying particular attention to the journal bearings, hydraulic tappet bores, valve guides and oilways. Scrape off any traces of old gasket from the mating surfaces, taking care not to score or gouge them. If using emery paper, do not use a grade of less than 100. Turn the head over and using a blunt blade, scrape any carbon deposits from the combustion chambers and ports.
Caution: Do not erode the sealing surface of the valve seat. Finally, wash the entire head casting with a suitable solvent to remove the remaining debris.
19 Clean the valve heads and stems using a fine wire brush. If the valve is heavily coked, scrape off the majority of the deposits with a blunt blade first, then use the wire brush.
Caution: Do not erode the sealing surface of the valve face.
20 Thoroughly clean the remainder of the components using solvent and allow them to dry completely. Discard the oil seals, as new items must be fitted when the cylinder head is reassembled.

Inspection

Cylinder head casting

Note: *On diesel engines the cylinder heads and valves cannot be reworked (although valves may be lapped in); new or exchange units must be obtained.*
21 Examine the head casting closely to identify any damage sustained or cracks that may have developed **(see illustration)**. Pay particular attention to the areas around the mounting holes, valve seats and spark plug holes. If cracking is discovered between the valve seats, Volkswagen state that the cylinder head may be re-used, provided the cracks are no larger than 0.5 mm wide. More serious damage will mean the renewal of the cylinder head casting.
22 Moderately pitted and scorched valve seats can be repaired by lapping the valves in

during reassembly, as described later in this Chapter. Badly worn or damaged valve seats may be restored by recutting; this is a highly specialised operation involving precision machining and accurate angle measurement and as such should be entrusted to a professional cylinder head re-builder.
23 Measure any distortion of the gasketed surfaces using a straight edge and a set of feeler blades. Take one measurement longitudinally on both the inlet and exhaust manifold mating surfaces. Take several measurements across the head gasket surface, to assess the level of distortion in all planes **(see illustration)**. Compare the measurements with the figures in the Specifications. On petrol engines, if the head is distorted out of specification, it may be possible to repair it by smoothing down any high-spots on the surface with fine abrasive paper.
24 Minimum cylinder head heights (measured between the cylinder head gasket surface and the cylinder head cover gasket surface), where quoted by the manufacturer, are listed in Specifications. If the cylinder head is to be professionally machined, bear in mind the following:
a) *The minimum cylinder head height dimension (where specified) must be adhered to.*
b) *The valve seats will need to be recut to suit the new height of the cylinder head, otherwise valve-to-piston crown contact may occur.*
c) *Before the valve seats can be recut, check that there is enough material left on the cylinder head to allow repair; if too much material is removed, the valve stem may protrude too far above the top of the valve guide and this would prevent the hydraulic tappets from operating correctly. Refer to a professional head rebuilder or machine shop for advice.* **Note:** *Depending on engine type, it may be possible to obtain new valves with shorter valve stems - refer to your VW dealer for advice.*

Camshaft

25 The camshaft is identified by means of markings stamped onto the side of the shaft, between the inlet and exhaust lobes - refer to the Specifications for details **(see illustration)**.

26 Visually inspect the camshaft for evidence of wear on the surfaces of the lobes and journals. Normally their surfaces should be smooth and have a dull shine; look for scoring, erosion or pitting and areas that appear highly polished - these are signs that wear has begun to occur. Accelerated wear will occur once the hardened exterior of the camshaft has been damaged, so always renew worn items. **Note:** *If these symptoms are visible on the tips of the camshaft lobes, check the corresponding tappet, as it will probably be worn as well.*
27 Where applicable, examine the distributor drive gear for signs of wear or damage. Slack in the drive caused by worn gear teeth will affect ignition timing.
28 If the machined surfaces of the camshaft appear discoloured or "blued", it is likely that it has been overheated at some point, probably due to inadequate lubrication. This may have distorted the shaft, so check the runout as follows: place the camshaft between two V-blocks and using a DTI gauge, measure the runout at the centre journal. If it exceeds the figure quoted in the Specifications at the start of this Chapter, camshaft renewal should be considered.
29 To measure the camshaft endfloat, temporarily refit the camshaft to the cylinder head, then fit the first and last bearing caps and tighten the retaining nuts to the specified first stage torque setting - refer to *"Reassembly"* for details. Anchor a DTI gauge to the timing pulley end of the cylinder head, and align the gauge probe with the camshaft axis. Push the camshaft to one end of the

4.25 Camshaft identification markings

2C

4.29 Checking camshaft endfloat using a DTI gauge

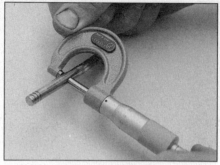

4.42 Measure the diameter of a valve stem with a micrometer

cylinder head as far as it will travel, then rest the DTI gauge probe on the end of the camshaft, and zero the gauge display. Push the camshaft as far as it will go to the other end of the cylinder head, and record the gauge reading. Verify the reading by pushing the camshaft back to its original position and checking that the gauge indicates zero again **(see illustration). Note:** *The hydraulic tappets must **not** be fitted to the cylinder whilst this measurement is being taken.*

30 Check that the camshaft endfloat measurement is within the limit listed in the Specifications. Wear outside of this limit is unlikely to be confined to any one component, so renewal of the camshaft, cylinder head and bearing caps must be considered; seek the advice of a cylinder head rebuilding specialist.

31 The difference between the outside diameters of the camshaft bearing surfaces and the internal diameters formed by the bearing caps and the cylinder head must now be measured, this dimension is known as the camshaft "running clearance".

32 The dimensions of the camshaft bearing journals are not quoted by the manufacturer, so running clearance measurement by means of a micrometer and a bore gauge or internal vernier calipers cannot be recommended in this case.

33 Another (more accurate) method of measuring the running clearance involves the use of Plastigauge. This is a soft, plastic material supplied in thin "sticks" of about the same diameter as a sewing needle. Lengths of Plastigauge are cut to length as required, laid on the camshaft bearing journals and crushed

as the bearing caps are temporarily fitted and tightened. The Plastigauge spreads widthways as it is crushed; the running clearance can then be determined by measuring the increase in width using the card gauge supplied with the Plastigauge kit.

34 The following paragraphs describe this measurement procedure step by step, but note that a similar method is used to measure the crankshaft running clearances; refer to the illustrations in Section 11 for further guidance.

35 Ensure that the cylinder head, bearing cap and camshaft bearing surfaces are completely clean and dry. Lay the camshaft in position in the cylinder head.

36 Lay a length of Plastigauge on top of each of the camshaft bearing journals.

37 Lubricate each bearing cap with a little silicone release agent, then place them in position over the camshaft and tighten the retaining nuts down to the specified torque - refer to *Reassembly* later in this Section for guidance. **Note:** *Where the torque setting is expressed in several stages, tighten the cap fixings to the first stage only. Do not rotate the camshaft whilst the bearing caps are in place, as the measurements will be affected.*

38 Carefully remove the bearing caps again, lifting them vertically away from the camshaft to avoid disturbing the Plastigauge. The Plastigauge should remain on the camshaft bearing surface, squashed into a uniform sausage shape. If it disintegrates as the bearing caps are removed, re-clean the components and repeat the exercise, using a little more release agent on the bearing cap.

39 Hold the scale card supplied with the kit

against each bearing journal, and match the width of the crushed Plastigauge with the graduated markings on the card; use this to determine the running clearances.

40 Compare the camshaft running clearance measurements with those listed in the Specifications; if any are outside the specified tolerance, the camshaft and cylinder head should be renewed. Note that undersize camshafts with bearing shells may be obtained from VW dealers, but only as part of an exchange cylinder head package.

41 On completion, remove the bearing caps and camshaft, and clean of all remaining traces of Plastigauge and silicone release agent.

Valves and associated components

Note: *On all engines, the valve heads cannot be re-cut (although they may be lapped in); new or exchange units must be obtained.*

42 Examine each valve closely for signs of wear. Inspect the valve stems for wear ridges, scoring or variations in diameter; measure their diameters at several points along their lengths with a micrometer **(see illustration)**.

43 The valve heads should not be cracked, badly pitted or charred. Note that light pitting of the valve head can be rectified by grinding-in the valves during reassembly, as described later in this Section.

44 Check that the valve stem end face is free from excessive pitting or indentation; this would be caused by defective hydraulic tappets.

45 Place the valves in a V-block and using a DTI gauge, measure the runout at the valve head. A maximum figure is not quoted by the manufacturer, but the valve should be renewed if the runout appears excessive.

46 Insert each valve into its respective guide in the cylinder head, and set up a DTI gauge against the edge of the valve head. With the valve end face flush with the top of the valve guide, measure the maximum side-to-side deflection of the valve in its guide **(see illustration)**.

47 If the measurement is out of tolerance, the valve and valve guide should be renewed as a pair. **Note:** *Valve guides are an interference fit in the cylinder head and their removal requires access to a hydraulic press. For this reason, it would be wise to entrust the job to an engineering workshop or head rebuilding specialist.*

48 Using vernier calipers, measure the free length of each of the valve springs. As a manufacturer's figure is not quoted, the only way to check the length of the springs is by comparison with a new component. Note that valve springs are usually renewed during a major engine overhaul **(see illustration)**.

49 Stand each spring on its end on a flat surface, against an engineer's square **(see illustration)**. Check the squareness of the spring visually; if it appears distorted, renew the spring. No squareness limits are specified by the manufacturers.

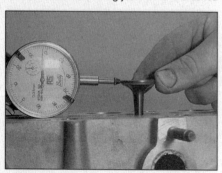

4.46 Measure the maximum deflection of the valve in its guide, using a DTI gauge

4.48 Measure the free length of each of the valve springs

4.49 Checking the squareness of a valve spring

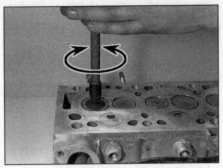

4.52 Grinding-in a valve

4.57a Fitting a swirl chamber (diesel engine code AAZ)

50 Measuring valve spring pre-load involves compressing the valve by applying a specified weight and measuring the reduction in length. This may be a difficult operation to conduct in the home workshop, so it would be wise to approach your local garage or engineering workshop for assistance. Weakened valve springs will at best, increase engine running noise and at worst, cause poor compression, so defective items should be renewed.

Reassembly

Caution: Unless all new components are to be used, maintain groups when refitting valve train components - do not mix components between cylinders, and ensure that components are refitted in their original positions.

51 To achieve a gas-tight seal between the valves and their seats, it will be necessary to

4.57b Swirl chamber locating recess

grind, or 'lap', the valves in. To complete this process, you will need a quantity of fine/coarse grinding paste and a grinding tool - this can either be of the dowel and rubber sucker type, or the automatic type which are driven by a rotary power tool.

52 Smear a small quantity of *fine* grinding paste on the sealing face of the valve head. Turn the cylinder head over so that the combustion chambers are facing upwards, and insert the valve into the correct guide. Attach the grinding tool to the valve head and using a backward/forward rotary action, grind the valve head into its seat. Periodically lift the valve and rotate it to redistribute the grinding paste (see illustration).

53 Continue this process until the contact between valve and seat produces an unbroken, matt grey ring of uniform width, on both faces. Repeat the operation for the remaining valves.

54 If the valves and seats are so badly pitted that coarse grinding paste must be used, check first that there is enough material left on both components to make this operation worthwhile - if too little material is left remaining, the valve stems may protrude too far above their guides, impeding the correct operation of the hydraulic tappets. Refer to a machine shop or cylinder head rebuilding specialist for advice.

55 Assuming the repair is feasible, work as described in the previous paragraph but use the coarse grinding paste initially, to achieve a dull finish on the valve face and seat. Then,

wash off coarse paste with solvent and repeat the process using fine grinding paste to obtain the correct finish.

56 When all the valves have been ground in, remove all traces of grinding paste from the cylinder head and valves with solvent, and allow them to dry completely.

57 Where necessary on engine code AAZ, fit new swirl chambers by driving them squarely into their housings with a mallet - use a block of wood to protect the face of the swirl chamber. Note the locating recess on the side of the chamber and the corresponding groove in the housing (see illustrations).

58 On completion, the projection of the swirl chamber from the face of the cylinder head must be measured using a DTI gauge and compared with the limit quoted in the Specifications (see illustration). If this limit is exceeded, there is a risk that the chamber may be struck by the piston, and in this case the advice of a professional cylinder head rebuilder or machine shop should be sought.

59 Turn the head over and place it on a stand, or wooden blocks. Where applicable, fit the first lower spring seat into place, with the convex side facing the cylinder head (see illustration).

60 Working on one valve at a time, lubricate the valve stem with clean engine oil, and insert it into the guide. Fit one of the protective plastic sleeves supplied with the new valve stem oil seals over the valve end face - this will protect the oil seal whilst it is being fitted (see illustrations).

2C

4.58 Measuring swirl chamber projection using a DTI gauge

4.59 Fit the lower spring seat in place, with the convex side facing the cylinder head

4.60a Lubricate the valve stem with clean engine oil and insert it into the guide

4.60b Fit one of the protective plastic sleeves over the valve end face

4.61a Fit a new valve stem seal over the valve

4.61b Use a long-reach socket to press on the oil seal

61 Dip a new valve stem seal in clean engine oil, and carefully push it over the valve and onto the top of the valve guide - take care not to damage the stem seal as it passes over the valve end face. Use a suitable long-reach socket to press it firmly into position **(see illustrations)**.

62 Locate the valve spring(s) over the valve stem **(see illustration)**. Where a lower spring seat is fitted, ensure that the springs locate squarely on the stepped surface of the seat. **Note:** *Depending on age and specification, engines may have either concentric double valve springs, or single valve springs with no lower spring seat.*

63 Fit the upper seat over the top of the springs, then using a valve spring compressor, compress the springs until the upper seat is pushed beyond the collet grooves in the valve stem. Refit the split collet, using a dab of grease to hold the two

halves in the grooves **(see illustrations)**. Gradually release the spring compressor, checking that the collet remains correctly seated as the spring extends. When correctly seated, the upper seat should force the two halves of the collet together, and hold them securely in the grooves in the end of the valve.

64 Repeat this process for the remaining sets of valve components. To settle the components after installation, strike the end of each valve stem with a mallet, using a block of wood to protect the stem from damage. Check before progressing any further that the spilt collets remain firmly held in the end of the valve stem by the upper spring seat.

65 Smear some clean engine oil onto the sides of the hydraulic tappets, and fit them into position in their bores in the cylinder head. Push them down until they contact the valves, then lubricate the camshaft lobe contact surfaces **(see illustration)**.

66 Lubricate the camshaft and cylinder head bearing journals with clean engine oil, then carefully lower the camshaft into position on the cylinder head. Support the ends of the shaft as it is inserted, to avoid damaging the lobes and journals **(see illustrations)**.

67 On diesel engines, with reference to Chapter 2B, lubricate the lip of a new camshaft oil seal with clean engine oil and locate it over the end of the camshaft. Slide the seal along the camshaft until it locates in the lower half of its housing in the cylinder head **(see illustration)**.

68 Oil the upper surfaces of the camshaft bearing journals, then fit the bearing caps in place. Ensure that they fitted the right way around and in the correct locations, then fit and tighten the retaining nuts, as follows: **Note:** *New bearing cap retaining nuts must be used on reassembly for all engine codes.*

4.62 Fitting a valve spring

4.63a Fit the upper seat over the top of the valve spring

4.63b Use grease to hold the two halves of the split collet in the groove

4.65 Fit the tappets into their bores in the cylinder head

4.66a Lubricate the camshaft bearings with clean engine oil . . .

4.66b . . . then lower the camshaft into position on the cylinder head

4.67 Fitting the camshaft oil seal (diesel engines)

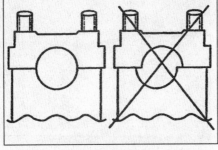

4.69 The camshaft bearing cap holes are drilled off-centre

4.72 Fitting a new camshaft oil seal

Petrol engines

69 The bearing cap mounting holes are drilled off-centre; ensure they are fitted the correct way round **(see illustration)**.

70 Fit caps Nos 2 and 5 over the camshaft and tighten the retaining nuts alternately and diagonally to the specified torque.

71 Smear the mating surfaces of cap No 1 with sealant. Locate caps No 1 and No 3 over the camshaft, then fit and tighten the nuts to the specified torque **(refer to illustration 4.75)**.

72 With reference to Chapter 2A or B as applicable, lubricate the lip of a new camshaft oil seal with clean engine oil, and locate it over the end of the camshaft. Using a mallet and a long-reach socket of an appropriate diameter, drive the seal squarely into its housing until it bears against the inner stop - do not attempt to force it in any further **(see illustration)**.

Diesel engines

73 The bearing cap mounting holes are drilled off-centre; ensure that they are fitted the correct way around **(see illustration 4.69)**.

74 Fit caps Nos 2 and 4 over the camshaft, and tighten the retaining nuts alternately and diagonally to the specified torque.

75 Smear the mating surfaces of cap No 1 with sealant then fit it, together with cap Nos 3 and 5, over the camshaft and tighten the nuts to the specified torque **(see illustration)**.

All engines

76 Refit the coolant outlet elbow, using a new gasket/O-ring as necessary **(see illustration)**.

77 Refit the coolant sensor and oil pressure switch.

78 With reference to Chapter 2A or B as applicable, carry out the following:
 a) *Refit the timing belt sprocket to the camshaft.*
 b) *Refit the inlet and exhaust manifolds, complete with new gaskets.*

79 On diesel engines, refit the fuel injectors and glow plugs, with reference to Chapter 4C and 5C.

80 Refer to Chapter 2A or B as applicable refit the cylinder head to the cylinder block.

4.75 Smear the mating surfaces of cap No 1 with sealant

4.76 Fit the coolant elbow, using a new O-ring or gasket

5 Pistons and connecting rods
- removal and inspection

Removal

1 Refer to Part A or B of this Chapter (as applicable) and remove the cylinder head, flywheel, sump and baffle plate, oil pump and pickup.

2 Inspect the tops of the cylinder bores; any wear ridges found at the point where the pistons reach top dead centre must be removed; otherwise the pistons may be damaged when they are pushed out of their bores. This can be accomplished with a scraper or ridge reamer.

3 Scribe the number of each piston on its crown, to allow identification later; note that No 1 is at the timing belt end of the engine.

4 Using a set of feeler blades, measure the big-end to crankpin web thrust clearance at each connecting rod, and record the measurements for later reference.

5 Where applicable, remove the retaining screw and withdraw the piston cooling jets from their mounting holes. On engine code 2E, the jet mounting incorporates a pressure relief valve, take care to avoid damaging it during removal **(see illustrations)**.

6 Rotate the crankshaft until pistons No 1 and 4 are at bottom dead centre. Unless they are already identified, mark the big-end bearing caps and connecting rods with their respective piston numbers, using a centre-punch or a scribe **(see illustration)**. Note the orientation of the bearing caps in relation to the connecting rod; it may be difficult to see the manufacturer's markings at this stage, so scribe alignment arrows on them both to ensure correct reassembly. Unbolt the

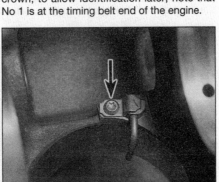

5.5a Remove the piston cooling jet retaining screw (arrowed) . . .

5.5b . . . and withdraw the jet from its mounting hole

2C

5.6 Mark the big-end caps and connecting rods with their piston numbers (arrowed)

5.7 Pad the bolt threads with tape

soft. **Note:** *Take care to preserve the pisto* *number markings that were made durir* *removal.*

14 Once the deposits have been remove clean the pistons and connecting rods wi paraffin or a suitable solvent, and d thoroughly. Make sure that the oil return hole in the ring grooves are clear.

15 Examine the piston for signs of termin wear or damage. Some normal wear will b apparent, in the form of a vertical 'grain' c the piston thrust surfaces and a sligh looseness of the top compression ring in i groove. Abnormal wear should be careful examined, to assess whether the componen is still serviceable and what the cause of th wear might be.

16 Scuffing or scoring of the piston skirt ma indicate that the engine has been overheating through inadequate cooling, lubrication c abnormal combustion temperatures. Scorc marks on the skirt indicate that blow - by ha occurred, perhaps caused by worn bores c piston rings. Burnt areas on the piston crow are usually an indication of pre-ignitior pinking or detonation. In extreme cases, th piston crown may be melted by operatin under these conditions. Corrosion pit marks the piston crown indicate that coolant ha seeped into the combustion chamber and/c the crankcase. The faults causing thes symptoms must be corrected before th engine is brought back into service, or th same damage will recur.

17 Check the pistons, connecting rods gudgeon pins and bearing caps for cracks Lay the connecting rods on a flat surface, an look along the length to see if it appears ber or twisted. If you have doubts about the condition, get them measured at a engineering workshop. Inspect the small-en bush bearing for signs of wear or cracking.

18 Using a micrometer, measure th diameter of all four pistons at a point 10 mr from the bottom of the skirt, at right-angles t the gudgeon pin axis **(see illustration)** Compare the measurements with those liste in the Specifications. If the piston diameter i out of the tolerance band listed for it particular size, then it must be renewed. Note *If the cylinder block was re-bored during previous overhaul, oversize pistons may hav*

bearing cap bolts/nuts, half a turn at a time, until they can be removed by hand. Recover the bottom shell bearing, and tape it to the cap for safe keeping. Note that if the shell bearings are to be re-used, they must be refitted to the same connecting rod.

7 On certain engines, the bearing cap bolts will remain in the connecting rod; in this case the threads of the bolts should be padded with insulating tape, to prevent them from scratching the crankpins when the pistons are removed from their bores **(see illustration)**.

8 Drive the pistons out of the top of their bores by pushing on the underside of the piston crown with a piece of dowel or a hammer handle. As the piston and connecting rod emerge, recover the top shell bearing and tape it to the connecting rod for safekeeping.

9 Turn the crankshaft through half a turn and working as described above, remove No 2 and 3 pistons and connecting rods.

5.10a Insert a small screwdriver into the slot and prise off the gudgeon pin circlips

Remember to maintain the components in their cylinder groups, whilst they are in a dismantled state.

10 Insert a small flat-bladed screwdriver into the removal slot and prise the gudgeon pin circlips from each piston. Push out the gudgeon pin, and separate the piston and connecting rod **(see illustrations)**. Discard the circlips as new items must be fitted on reassembly. If the pin proves difficult to remove, heat the piston to 60°C with hot water - the resulting expansion will then allow the two components to be separated.

Inspection

11 Before an inspection of the pistons can be carried out, the existing piston rings must be removed, using a removal/installation tool, or an old feeler blade if such a tool is not available. Always remove the upper piston rings first, expanding them to clear the piston crown. The rings are very brittle and will snap if they are stretched too much - sharp edges are produced when this happens, so protect your eyes and hands. Discard the rings on removal, as new items must be fitted when the engine is reassembled **(see illustration)**.

12 Use a section of old piston ring to scrape the carbon deposits out of the ring grooves, taking care not to score or gouge the edges of the groove.

13 Carefully scrape away all traces of carbon from the top of the piston. A hand-held wire brush (or a piece of fine emery cloth) can be used, once the majority of the deposits have been scraped away. Be careful not to remove any metal from the piston, as it is relatively

5.10b Push out the gudgeon pin and separate the piston and connecting rod

5.11 Piston rings can be removed using an old feeler blade

5.18 Using a micrometer, measure the diameter of all four pistons

5.19 Measuring the piston ring-to-groove clearance using a feeler blade

been fitted. Record the measurements and use them to check the piston clearances when the cylinder bores are measured, later in this Chapter.

19 Hold a new piston ring in the appropriate groove and measure the ring-to-groove clearance using a feeler blade **(see illustration)**. Note that the rings are of different widths, so use the correct ring for the groove. Compare the measurements with those listed; if the clearances are outside of the tolerance band, then the piston must be renewed. Confirm this by checking the width of the piston ring with a micrometer.

20 Using internal/external vernier calipers, measure the connecting rod small-end internal diameter and the gudgeon pin external diameter. Subtract the gudgeon pin diameter from the small-end diameter to obtain the clearance. If this measurement is outside its specification (where given), then the piston and connecting rod bush will have to be resized and a new gudgeon pin installed. An engineering workshop will have the equipment needed to undertake a job of this nature.

21 The orientation of the piston with respect to the connecting rod must be correct when the two are reassembled. The piston crown is marked with an arrow (which may be obscured by carbon deposits); this must point towards the timing belt end of the engine when the piston is installed. The connecting rod and its bearing cap both have recesses machined into them, close to their mating surfaces - these recesses must both face the same way as the arrow on the piston crown (ie towards the timing belt end of the engine) when correctly installed **(see illustration)**. Reassemble the two components to satisfy this requirement. **Note:** *On certain engines, the connecting rod big-ends are provided with offset dowels which locate in holes in the bearing caps.*

22 Lubricate the gudgeon pin and small-end bush with clean engine oil. Slide the pin into the piston, engaging the connecting rod small-end. Fit two new circlips to the piston at either end of the gudgeon pin, such that their open ends are facing 180° away from the removal slot in the piston. Repeat this operation for the remaining pistons.

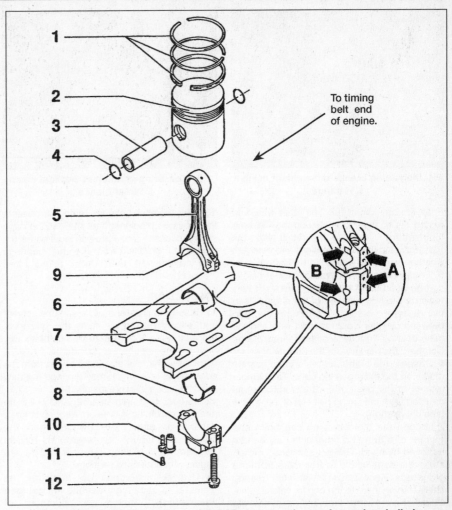

To timing belt end of engine.

5.21 Piston assembly (engine code AAZ shown - other engine codes similar)

1 Piston rings	6 Big-end bearing shell	10 Oil jet for piston cooling
2 Piston	7 Top of cylinder block	(where applicable)
3 Gudgeon pin	8 Big-end bearing cap	11 Oil jet retaining screw
4 Circlip	9 Locating dowel (where	12 Big-end bearing cap
5 Connecting rod	applicable)	bolts

A Connecting rod/bearing cap identification marks
B Connecting rod/bearing cap orientation marks

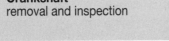

**6 Crankshaft -
removal and inspection**

Removal

1 **Note:** *If no work is to be done on the pistons and connecting rods, then removal of the cylinder head and pistons will not be necessary. Instead, the pistons need only be pushed far enough up the bores so that they are positioned clear of the crankpins. The use of an engine stand is strongly recommended.*

2 With reference to Chapter 2A or B as applicable, carry out the following:
a) *Remove the crankshaft timing belt sprocket.*

b) *Remove the clutch components and flywheel.*
c) *Remove the sump, baffle plate, oil pump and pickup.*
d) *Remove the front and rear crankshaft oil seals and their housings.*

3 Remove the pistons and connecting rods, as described in Section 5 (refer to the Note above).

4 Carry out a check of the crankshaft endfloat, as follows. **Note:** *This can only be accomplished when the crankshaft is still installed in the cylinder block/crankcase, but is free to move.* Set up a DTI gauge so that the probe is in line with the crankshaft axis and is in contact with a fixed point on end of the crankshaft. Push the crankshaft along its axis to the end of its travel, and then zero the gauge.

2C

6.4 Measuring crankshaft endfloat using a DTI gauge

6.5 Measuring crankshaft endfloat using feeler blades

6.6 Manufacturer's identification markings on the main bearing caps (arrowed)

Push the crankshaft fully the other way, and record the endfloat indicated on the dial (**see illustration**). Compare the result with the figure given in the Specifications and establish whether new thrustwashers are required.

5 If a dial gauge is not available, feeler blades can be used. First push the crankshaft fully towards the flywheel end of the engine, then use a feeler blade to measure the gap between cylinder No 2 crankpin web and the main bearing thrustwasher (**see illustration**). Compare the results with the Specifications.

6 Observe the manufacturer's identification marks on the main bearing caps. The number relates to the position in the crankcase, as counted from the timing belt end of the engine (**see illustration**).

7 Loosen the main bearing cap bolts one quarter of a turn at a time, until they can be removed by hand. Using a soft-faced mallet, strike the caps lightly to free them from the crankcase. Recover the lower main bearing shells, taping them to the cap for safekeeping. Mark them with indelible ink to aid identification, but do not score or scratch them in any way.

8 Carefully lift the crankshaft out, taking care not to dislodge the upper main bearing shells (**see illustration**). It would be wise to get an assistant's help, as the crankshaft is heavy. Set it down on a clean, level surface and chock it with blocks to prevent it from rolling.

9 Extract the upper main bearing shells from the crankcase, and tape them to their respective bearing caps. Remove the two thrustwasher bearings from either side of No 3 crank web.

10 With the shell bearings removed, observe the recesses machined into the bearing caps and crankcase - these provide location for the lugs which protrude from the shell bearings and so prevent them from being fitted incorrectly.

Inspection

11 Wash the crankshaft in a suitable solvent and allow it to dry. Flush the oil holes thoroughly, to ensure that are not blocked - use a pipe cleaner or a needle brush if necessary. Remove any sharp edges from the edge of the hole which may damage the new bearings when they are installed.

12 Inspect the main bearing and crankpin journals carefully; if uneven wear, cracking, scoring or pitting are evident then the crankshaft should be reground by an engineering workshop, and refitted to the engine with undersize bearings.

13 Use a micrometer to measure the diameter of each main bearing journal (**see illustration**). Taking a number of measurements on the surface of each journal will reveal if it is worn unevenly. Differences in diameter measured at 90° intervals indicate that the journal is out of round. Differences in diameter measured along the length of the journal, indicate that the journal is tapered. Again, if wear is detected, the crankshaft must be reground by an engineering workshop, and undersize bearings will be needed (refer to "Reassembly").

14 Check the oil seal journals at either end of the crankshaft. If they appear excessively scored or damaged, they may cause the new

seals to leak when the engine is reassembled. It may be possible to repair the journal; seek the advice of an engineering workshop or your VW dealer.

15 Measure the crankshaft runout by setting up a DTI gauge on the centre main bearing and rotating the shaft in V-blocks. The maximum deflection of the gauge will indicate the runout. Take precautions to protect the bearing journals and oil seal mating surfaces from damage during this procedure. A maximum runout figure is not quoted by the manufacturer, but use the figure of 0.05 mm as a rough guide. If the runout exceeds this figure, crankshaft renewal should be considered - consult your VW dealer or an engine rebuilding specialist for advice.

16 Refer to Section 9 for details of main and big-end bearing inspection.

7 Intermediate shaft - removal and refitting

Removal

1 Refer to Chapter 1A or B and carry out the following:
  a) Remove the timing belt.
  b) Remove the intermediate shaft sprocket.

2 Before the shaft is removed, the endfloat must be checked. Anchor a DTI gauge to the cylinder block, with its probe in line with the intermediate shaft centre axis. Push the shaft into the cylinder block to the end of its travel, zero the DTI gauge and then draw the shaft out to the opposite end of its travel. Record the maximum deflection and compare the figure with that listed in Specifications - renew the shaft if the endfloat exceeds this limit (**see illustration**).

3 Slacken the retaining bolts and withdraw the intermediate shaft flange. Recover the O-ring seal, then press out the oil seal (**see illustrations**).

4 Withdraw the intermediate shaft from the cylinder block, and inspect the drive gear at the end of the shaft; if the teeth show signs of excessive wear, or are damaged in any way, the shaft should be renewed.

6.8 Lifting the crankshaft from the crankcase

6.13 Use a micrometer to measure the diameter of each main bearing journal

7.2 Check the intermediate shaft endfloat using a DTI gauge

7.3a Slacken the retaining bolts (arrowed) . . .

7.3b . . . and withdraw the intermediate shaft flange

5 If the oil seal has been leaking, check the shaft mating surface for signs of scoring or damage.

Refitting

6 Liberally oil the intermediate shaft bearing surfaces and drive gear, then carefully guide the shaft into the cylinder block and engage the journal at the leading end with its support bearing.

7 Press a new shaft oil seal into its housing in the intermediate shaft flange and fit a new O-ring seal to the inner sealing surface of the flange.

8 Lubricate the inner lip of the seal with clean engine oil, and slide the flange and seal over the end of the intermediate shaft. Ensure that the O-ring is correctly seated, then fit the flange retaining bolts and tighten them to the specified torque. Check that the intermediate shaft can rotate freely.

9 With reference to Chapter 2A or B, carry out the following:

a) Refit the timing belt sprocket to the intermediate shaft and tighten the centre bolt to the specified torque.

b) Refit the timing belt. Where applicable on petrol models, follow the intermediate sprocket alignment instructions carefully to ensure that the distributor drive gear alignment is preserved.

8 Cylinder block/ crankcase casting - cleaning and inspection

Cleaning

1 Remove all external components and electrical switches/sensors from the block. For complete cleaning, the core plugs should ideally be removed. Drill a small hole in the plugs, then insert a self-tapping screw into the hole. Extract the plugs by pulling on the screw with a pair of grips, or by using a slide hammer.

2 Scrape all traces of gasket and sealant from the cylinder block/crankcase, taking care not to damage the sealing surfaces.

3 Remove all oil gallery plugs (where fitted). The plugs are usually very tight - they may

7.3c Press out the oil seal . . .

have to be drilled out, and the holes re-tapped. Use new plugs when the engine is reassembled.

4 If the casting is extremely dirty, it should be steam-cleaned. After this, clean all oil holes and galleries one more time. Flush all internal passages with warm water until the water runs clear. Dry thoroughly, and apply a light film of oil to all mating surfaces and cylinder bores, to prevent rusting. If you have access to compressed air, use it to speed up the drying process, and to blow out all the oil holes and galleries.

⚠ **Warning: Wear eye protection when using compressed air!**

5 If the castings are not very dirty, you can do an adequate cleaning job with hot, soapy water and a stiff brush. Take plenty of time, and do a thorough job. Regardless of the cleaning method used, be sure to clean all oil holes and galleries very thoroughly, and to dry all components well. Protect the cylinder bores as described above, to prevent rusting.

6 All threaded holes must be clean, to ensure accurate torque readings during reassembly. To clean the threads, run the correct-size tap into each of the holes to remove rust, corrosion, thread sealant or sludge, and to restore damaged threads **(see illustration)**. If possible, use compressed air to clear the holes of debris produced by this operation. **Note:** Take extra care to exclude all cleaning liquid from blind tapped holes, as the casting may be cracked by hydraulic action if a bolt is threaded into a hole containing liquid.

7.3d . . . then recover the O-ring seal

7 Apply suitable sealant to the new oil gallery plugs, and insert them into the holes in the block. Tighten them securely.

8 If the engine is not going to be reassembled immediately, cover it with a large plastic bag to keep it clean; protect all mating surfaces and the cylinder bores as described above, to prevent rusting.

Inspection

9 Visually check the casting for cracks and corrosion. Look for stripped threads in the threaded holes. If there has been any history of internal water leakage, it may be worthwhile having an engine overhaul specialist check the cylinder block/crankcase with professional equipment. If defects are found, have them renewed or if possible, repaired.

10 Check the cylinder bores for scuffing or scoring. Any evidence of this kind of damage should be cross-checked with an inspection

8.6 To clean the cylinder block threads, run a correct-size tap into the holes

2C

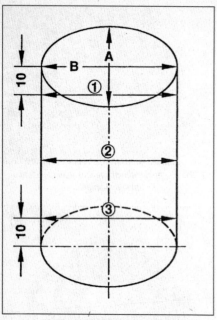

8.12 Bore measurement points

of the pistons: see Section 5 of this Chapter. If the damage is in its early stages, it may be possible to repair the block by reboring it. Seek the advice of an engineering workshop before you progress.

11 To allow an accurate assessment of the wear in the cylinder bores to be made, their diameter must be measured at a number of points, as follows. Insert a bore gauge into bore No 1 and take three measurements in line with the crankshaft axis; one at the top of the bore, roughly 10 mm below the bottom of the wear ridge, one halfway down the bore and one at a point roughly 10 mm the bottom of the bore. **Note:** *Stand the cylinder block squarely on a workbench during this procedure, inaccurate results may be obtained if the measurements are taken when the engine mounted on a stand.*

12 Rotate the bore gauge through 90°, so that it is at right-angles to the crankshaft axis

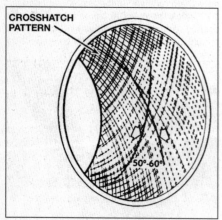

8.17 Cylinder bore honing pattern

and repeat the measurements detailed in paragraph 11 **(see illustration)**. Record all six measurements, and compare them with the data listed in the Specifications. If the difference in diameter between any two cylinders exceeds the wear limit, or if any one cylinder exceeds its maximum bore diameter, then *all four* cylinders will have to be rebored and oversize pistons will have to be fitted. Note that the imbalances produced by not reboring all the cylinders together would render the engine unusable.

13 Use the piston diameter measurements recorded earlier (see Section 5) to calculate the piston-to-bore clearances. Figures are not available from the manufacturer, so seek the advice of your VW dealer or engine reconditioning specialist.

14 Place the cylinder block on a level work surface, crankcase downwards. Use a straight edge and a set of feeler blades to measure the distortion of the cylinder head mating surface in both planes. A maximum figure is not quoted by the manufacturer, but use the figure of 0.05 mm as a rough guide. If the measurement exceeds this figure, repair may be possible by machining - consult your dealer for advice.

15 Before the engine can be reassembled, the cylinder bores must be honed. This process involves using an abrasive tool to produce a fine, cross-hatch pattern on the inner surface of the bore. This has the effect of seating the piston rings, resulting in a good seal between the piston and cylinder. There are two types of honing tool available to the home mechanic, both are driven by a rotary power tool, such as a drill. The 'bottle brush' hone is a stiff, cylindrical brush with abrasive stones bonded to its bristles. The more conventional surfacing hone has abrasive stones mounted on spring-loaded legs. For the inexperienced home mechanic, satisfactory results will be achieved more easily using the bottle brush hone. **Note:** *If you are unwilling to tackle cylinder bore honing, an engineering workshop will be able to carry out the job for you at a reasonable cost.*

16 Carry out the honing as follows; you will need one of the honing tools described above, a power drill/air wrench, a supply of clean rags, some honing oil and a pair of safety glasses.

17 Fit the honing tool in the drill chuck. Lubricate the cylinder bores with honing oil and insert the honing tool into the first bore, compressing the stones to allow it to fit. Turn on the drill and as the tool rotates, move it up and down in the bore at a rate that produces a fine cross-hatch pattern on the surface. The lines of the pattern should ideally cross at about 50 to 60° **(see illustration)**, although some piston ring manufacturer's may quote a different angle; check the literature supplied with the new rings.

 Warning: Wear safety glasses to protect your eyes from debris flying off the honing tool.

18 Use plenty of oil during the honing process. Do not remove any more material than is necessary to produce the required finish. When removing the hone tool from the bore, do not pull it out whilst it is still rotating; maintain the up/down movement until the chuck has stopped, then withdraw the tool whilst rotating the chuck by hand, in the normal direction of rotation.

19 Wipe out the oil and swarf with a rag and proceed to the next bore. When all four bores have been honed, thoroughly clean the whole cylinder block in hot soapy water to remove all traces of honing oil and debris. The block is clean when a clean rag, moistened with new engine oil does not pick up any grey residue when wiped along the bore.

20 Apply a light coating of engine oil to the mating surfaces and cylinder bores to prevent rust forming. Store the block in a plastic bag until reassembly.

9 Main and big-end bearings - inspection and selection

Inspection

1 Even though the main and big-end bearings should be renewed during the engine overhaul, the old bearings should be retained for close examination, as they may reveal valuable information about the condition of the engine **(see illustration)**.

2 Bearing failure can occur due to lack of lubrication, the presence of dirt or other foreign particles, overloading the engine, or corrosion. Regardless of the cause of bearing failure, the cause must be corrected before the engine is reassembled, to prevent it from happening again.

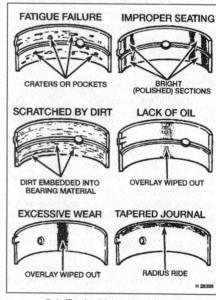

9.1 Typical bearing failures

3 When examining the bearing shells, remove them from the cylinder block/crankcase, the main bearing caps, the connecting rods and the connecting rod big-end bearing caps. Lay them out on a clean surface in the same general position as their location in the engine. This will enable you to match any bearing problems with the corresponding crankshaft journal. *Do not* touch any shell's internal bearing surface with your fingers while checking it, or the delicate surface may be scratched.

4 Dirt and other foreign matter gets into the engine in a variety of ways. It may be left in the engine during assembly, or it may pass through filters or the crankcase ventilation system. It may get into the oil, and from there into the bearings. Metal chips from machining operations and normal engine wear are often present. Abrasives are sometimes left in engine components after reconditioning, especially when parts are not thoroughly cleaned using the proper cleaning methods. Whatever the source, these foreign objects often end up embedded in the soft bearing material, and are easily recognised. Large particles will not embed in the bearing, but will score or gouge the bearing and journal. The best prevention for this cause of bearing failure is to clean all parts thoroughly, and keep everything spotlessly-clean during engine assembly. Frequent and regular engine oil and filter changes are also recommended.

5 Lack of lubrication (or lubrication breakdown) has a number of interrelated causes. Excessive heat (which thins the oil), overloading (which squeezes the oil from the bearing face) and oil leakage (from excessive bearing clearances, worn oil pump or high engine speeds) all contribute to lubrication breakdown. Blocked oil passages, which usually are the result of misaligned oil holes in a bearing shell, will also oil-starve a bearing, and destroy it. When lack of lubrication is the cause of bearing failure, the bearing material is wiped or extruded from the steel backing of the bearing. Temperatures may increase to the point where the steel backing turns blue from overheating.

6 Driving habits can have a definite effect on bearing life. Full-throttle, low-speed operation (labouring the engine) puts very high loads on bearings, tending to squeeze out the oil film. These loads cause the bearings to flex, which produces fine cracks in the bearing face (fatigue failure). Eventually, the bearing material will loosen in pieces, and tear away from the steel backing.

7 Short-distance driving leads to corrosion of bearings, because insufficient engine heat is produced to drive off the condensed water and corrosive gases. These products collect in the engine oil, forming acid and sludge. As the oil is carried to the engine bearings, the acid attacks and corrodes the bearing material.

8 Incorrect bearing installation during engine assembly will lead to bearing failure as well.

Tight-fitting bearings leave insufficient bearing running clearance, and will result in oil starvation. Dirt or foreign particles trapped behind a bearing shell result in high spots on the bearing, which lead to failure.

9 *Do not* touch any shell's internal bearing surface with your fingers during reassembly; there is a risk of scratching the delicate surface, or of depositing particles of dirt on it.

10 As mentioned at the beginning of this Section, the bearing shells should be renewed as a matter of course during engine overhaul; to do otherwise is false economy.

Selection - main and big-end bearings

11 Main and big-end bearings for the engines described in this Chapter are available in standard sizes and a range of undersizes to suit reground crankshafts - refer to Specifications for details.

12 The running clearances will need to be checked when the crankshaft is refitted with its new bearings (see Section 11).

10 Engine overhaul - reassembly sequence

1 Before reassembly begins, ensure that all new parts have been obtained, and that all necessary tools are available. Read through the entire procedure to familiarise yourself with the work involved, and to ensure that all items necessary for reassembly of the engine are at hand. In addition to all normal tools and materials, thread-locking compound will be needed. A suitable tube of liquid sealant will also be required for the joint faces that are without gaskets. It is recommended that the manufacturer's own products are used, which are specially formulated for this purpose; the relevant product names are quoted in the text of each Section where they are required.

2 In order to save time and avoid problems, engine reassembly should ideally be carried out in the following order:
a) Crankshaft
b) Piston/connecting rod assemblies
c) Oil pump (see Chapter 2A or B)
d) Sump (see Chapter 2A or B)
e) Flywheel (see Chapter 2A or B)
f) Cylinder head and gasket (see Chapter 2A or B)
g) Timing belt tensioner, sprockets and timing belt (see Chapter 2A or B)
h) Engine external components and ancillaries
i) Auxiliary drivebelts, pulleys and tensioners (see Chapter 2A or B)

3 At this stage, all engine components should be absolutely clean and dry, with all faults repaired. The components should be laid out (or in individual containers) on a completely clean work surface.

11 Crankshaft - refitting and running clearance check

1 Crankshaft refitting is the first stage of engine reassembly following overhaul. At this point, it is assumed that the crankshaft, cylinder block/crankcase and bearings have been cleaned, inspected and reconditioned or renewed.

2 Place the cylinder block on a clean, level work surface, with the crankcase facing upwards. Unbolt the bearing caps and carefully release them from the crankcase; lay them out in order to ensure correct reassembly. If they are still in place, remove the bearing shells from the caps and the crankcase, and wipe out the inner surfaces with a clean rag - they must be kept spotlessly clean.

3 Clean the rear surface of the new bearing shells with a rag and lay them on the bearing saddles. Ensure that the orientation lugs on the shells engage with the recesses in the saddles, and that the oil holes are correctly aligned **(see illustration)**. Do not hammer or otherwise force the bearing shells into place. It is critically important that the surfaces of the bearings are kept free from damage and contamination.

4 Give the newly-fitted bearing shells and the crankshaft journals a final clean with a rag. Check that the oil holes in the crankshaft are free from dirt, as any left here will become embedded in the new bearings when the engine is first started.

5 Carefully lay the crankshaft in the crankcase, taking care not to dislodge the bearing shells.

Running clearance check

6 When the crankshaft and bearings are refitted, a clearance must exist between them to allow lubricant to circulate. This clearance is impossible to check using feeler blades, so Plastigauge is used. This is a thin strip of soft plastic that is crushed between the bearing shells and journals when the bearing caps are tightened up. The change in its width then indicates the size of the clearance gap.

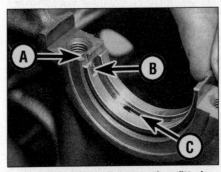

11.3 Bearing shells correctly refitted

A Recess in bearing saddle
B Lug on bearing shell
C Oil hole

2C

11.7 Lay a piece of Plastigauge (arrowed) on each journal, in line with the crankshaft axis

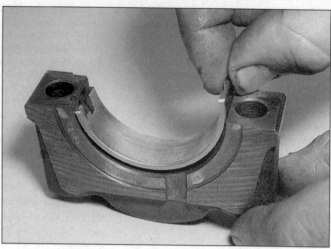

11.8 Fit the new lower half main bearing shells to the main bearing caps

7 Cut off five pieces of Plastigauge, just shorter than the length of the crankshaft journal. Lay a piece on each journal, in line with its axis **(see illustration)**.

8 Wipe off the rear surfaces of the new lower half main bearing shells and fit them to the main bearing caps, ensuring the locating lugs engage correctly **(see illustration)**.

9 Wipe the front surfaces of the bearing shells and give them a light coating of silicone release agent - this will prevent the Plastigauge from sticking to the shell. Fit the caps in their correct locations on the bearing saddles, using the manufacturer's markings as a guide. Ensure that they are correctly orientated - the caps should be fitted such that the recesses for the bearing shell locating lugs are on the same side as those in the bearing saddle.

10 Working from the centre bearing cap, tighten the bolts one half turn at a time until they are all correctly torqued *to their first stage only*. Do not let the crankshaft turn at all whilst the Plastigauge is in place. Progressively unbolt the bearing caps and remove them, taking care not to dislodge the Plastigauge.

11 The width of the crushed Plastigauge can now be measured, using the scale provided **(see illustration)**. Use the correct scale, as

both imperial and metric are printed. This measurement indicates the running clearance - compare it with that listed in Specifications. If the clearance is outside the tolerance, it may be due to dirt or debris trapped under the bearing surface; try cleaning them again and repeat the clearance check. If the results are still unacceptable, re-check the journal diameters and the bearing sizes. If the Plastigauge is thicker at one end, the journals may be tapered, and will require regrinding.

12 When you are satisfied that the clearances are correct, carefully remove the remains of the Plastigauge from the journals and bearings faces. Use a soft, plastic or wooden scraper as anything metallic is likely to damage the surfaces.

Crankshaft - final refitting

13 Lift the crankshaft out of the crankcase. Wipe off the surfaces of the bearings in the crankcase and the bearing caps. Fit the thrust bearings either side of the No 3 bearing saddle, between cylinders No 2 and 3. Use a small quantity of grease to hold them in place; ensure that they are seated correctly in the machined recesses, with the oil grooves facing outwards

14 Liberally coat the bearing shells in the crankcase with clean engine oil of the appropriate grade.

15 Lower the crankshaft into position so that No 2 and 3 cylinder crankpins are at TDC; No 1 and 4 cylinder crankpins will then be at BDC, ready for fitting No 1 piston.

16 Lubricate the lower bearing shells in the main bearing caps with clean engine oil, then fit the thrustwashers to either side of bearing cap No 3, noting that the lugs protruding from the washers engage the recesses in the side of the bearing cap **(see illustration)**. Make sure that the locating lugs on the shells are still engaged with the corresponding recesses in the caps.

17 Fit the main bearing caps in the correct order and orientation - No 1 bearing cap must be at the timing belt end of the engine, and the bearing shell locating recesses in the bearing saddles and caps must be adjacent to each other **(see illustration)**. Insert the bearing cap bolts and hand tighten them only.

18 Working from the centre bearing cap outwards, tighten the retaining bolts to their specified torques. Where the torque is expressed in several stages, tighten all the bolts to the first stage, then repeat the exercise in the same sequence for the subsequent stage(s) **(see illustration)**.

19 Refit the crankshaft rear oil seal housing, together with a new oil seal; refer to Part A or B (as applicable) of this Chapter for details.

11.11 Measure the width of the crushed Plastigauge using the scale provided

11.16 Fitting the thrustwashers to No 3 bearing cap

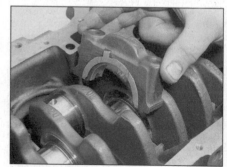

11.17 Fitting a main bearing cap in place

11.18 Tighten the bearing cap bolts to the specified torque

20 Check that the crankshaft rotates freely by turning it by manually. If resistance is felt, re-check the running clearances, as described above.

21 Carry out a check of the crankshaft endfloat as described at the beginning of Section 6. If the thrust surfaces of the crankshaft have been checked and new thrust bearings have been fitted, then the endfloat should be within specification.

12 Pistons and piston rings - assembly

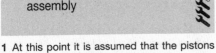

1 At this point it is assumed that the pistons have been correctly assembled to their respective connecting rods, and that the piston ring-to-groove clearances have been checked. If not, refer to the end of Section 5.

2 Before the rings can be fitted to the pistons, the end gaps must be checked with the rings fitted into the cylinder bores.

3 Lay out the piston assemblies and the new ring sets on a clean work surface so that the components are kept together in their groups during and after end gap checking. Place the crankcase on the work surface on its side, allowing access to the top and bottom of the bores.

4 Take the No 1 piston top ring and insert it into the top of the bore. Using the No 1 piston as a ram, push the ring close to the bottom of the bore, at the lowest point of the piston travel. Ensure that it is perfectly square in the bore by pushing firmly against the piston crown.

5 Use a set of feeler blades to measure the gap between the ends of the piston ring; the correct blade will just pass through the gap with a minimal amount of resistance **(see illustration)**. Compare this measurement with that listed in Specifications. Check that you have the correct ring before deciding that a gap is incorrect. Repeat the operation for all twelve rings.

6 If new rings are being fitted, it is unlikely that the end gaps will be too small. If a measurement is found to be undersize, it must be corrected or there is the risk that the ends of the ring may contact each other during

operation, possibly resulting in engine damage. This is achieved by gradually filing down the ends of the ring, using a file clamped in a vice. Fit the ring over the file such that both its ends contact opposite faces of the file. Move the ring along the file, removing small amounts of material at a time. Take great care as the rings are brittle and form sharp edges if they fracture. Remember to keep the rings and piston assemblies in the correct order.

7 When all the piston ring end gaps have been verified, they can be fitted to the pistons. Work from the lowest ring groove (oil control ring) upwards. Note that the oil control ring comprises two side rails separated by a expander ring. Note also that the two compression rings are different in cross-section, and so must be fitted in the correct groove and the right way up, using a piston ring fitting tool. Both of the compression rings have marks stamped on one side to indicate the top facing surface. Ensure that these marks face up when the rings are fitted **(see illustration)**.

8 Distribute the end gaps around the piston, spaced at 120° intervals to the each other. **Note:** *If the piston ring manufacturer supplies specific fitting instructions with the rings, follow these exclusively.*

13 Piston and connecting rod assemblies - refitting and big-end bearing clearance check

Big-end running clearance check

Note: *At this point, it is assumed that the crankshaft has been fitted to the engine, as described in Section 11.*

1 As with the main bearings (Section 11), a running clearance must exist between the big-end crankpin and its bearing shells to allow oil to circulate. There are two methods of checking the size of the running clearance, as described in the following paragraphs.

2 Place the cylinder block on a clean, level work surface, with the crankcase facing upwards. Position the crankshaft such that crankpins No 1 and 4 are at BDC.

3 The first method is the least accurate and involves bolting bearing caps to the big-ends, away from the crankshaft, with the bearing shells in place. **Note:** *Correct orientation of the bearing caps is critical; refer to the notes in Section 5. The internal diameter formed by the assembled big-end is then measured using internal vernier calipers. The diameter of the respective crankpin is then subtracted from this measurement and the result is the running clearance.*

4 The second method of carrying out this check involves the use of Plastigauge, in the same manner as the main bearing running clearance check (see Section 11) and is much more accurate than the previous method. Clean all four crankpins with a clean rag. With crankpins No 1 and 4 at BDC initially, place a strand of Plastigauge on each crankpin journal.

5 Fit the upper big-end bearing shells to the connecting rods, ensuring that the locating lugs and recesses engage correctly. Temporarily refit the piston/connecting rod assemblies to the crankshaft; refit the big-end bearing caps, using the manufacturer's markings to ensure that they are fitted the correct way around - refer to *"Final refitting"* for details.

6 Tighten the bearing cap nuts/bolts as described below. Take care not to disturb the Plastigauge or rotate the connecting rod during the tightening process.

7 Dismantle the assemblies without rotating the connecting rods. Use the scale printed on the Plastigauge envelope to determine the big-end bearing running clearance and compare it with the figures listed in Specifications.

8 If the clearance is significantly different from that expected, the bearing shells may be the wrong size (or excessively worn, if the original shells are being re-used). Make sure that no dirt or oil was trapped between the bearing shells and the caps or connecting rods when the clearance was measured. Re-check the diameters of the crankpins. Note that if the Plastigauge was wider at one end than at the other, the crankpins may be tapered. When the problem is identified, fit new bearing shells or have the crankpins reground to a listed undersize, as appropriate.

2C

12.5 Checking a piston ring end gap using a feeler blade

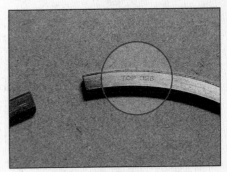

12.7 Piston ring "TOP" marking

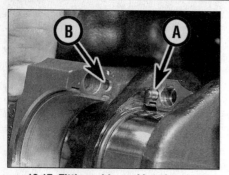

13.17 Fitting a big-end bearing cap

A Dowel
B Locating hole

9 Upon completion, carefully scrape away all traces of the Plastigauge material from the crankshaft and bearing shells. Use a plastic or wooden scraper, which will be soft enough to prevent scoring of the bearing surfaces.

Piston and connecting rod assemblies - final refitting

10 Note that the following procedure assumes that the crankshaft main bearing caps are in place (see Section 11).
11 Ensure that the bearing shells are correctly fitted, as described at the beginning of this Section. If new shells are being fitted, ensure that all traces of the protective grease are cleaned off using paraffin. Wipe dry the shells and connecting rods with a lint-free cloth.
12 Lubricate the cylinder bores, the pistons, and piston rings with clean engine oil. Lay out each piston/connecting rod assembly in order on a work surface. On engines where the big-end bolts are captive in the connecting rods, fit short sections of rubber hose or tape over the bolt threads, to protect the cylinder bores during reassembly.
13 Start with piston/connecting rod assembly No 1. Make sure that the piston rings are still spaced as described in Section 12, then clamp them in position with a piston ring compressor.
14 Insert the piston/connecting rod assembly into the top of cylinder No 1. Lower the big-end in first, guiding it to protect the big-end bolts and the cylinder bores.

15 Ensure that the orientation of the piston in its cylinder is correct - the piston crown, connecting rods and big-end bearing caps have markings, which must point towards the timing belt end of the engine when the piston is installed in the bore - refer to Section 5 for details.
16 Using a block of wood or hammer handle against the piston crown, tap the assembly into the cylinder until the piston crown is flush with the top of the cylinder.
17 Ensure that the bearing shell is still correctly installed. Liberally lubricate the crankpin and both bearing shells with clean engine oil. Taking care not to mark the cylinder bores, tap the piston/connecting rod assembly down the bore and onto the crankpin. Refit the big-end bearing cap, tightening its retaining nuts/bolts finger-tight at first **(see illustration)**. Note that the orientation of the bearing cap with respect to the connecting rod must be correct when the two components are reassembled. The connecting rod and its corresponding bearing cap both have recesses machined into them, close to their mating surfaces - these recesses must both face in the same direction as the arrow on the piston crown (ie towards the timing belt end of the engine) when correctly installed - refer to the illustrations in Section 5 for details. **Note:** *On certain engines, the connecting rod big-ends are provided with offset dowels which locate in holes in the bearing caps.*
18 On engine codes 1Z, AHU and AFN (direct injection diesel engines), the piston crowns are specially shaped. Because of this, pistons 1 and 2 are different to pistons 3 and 4. When correctly fitted, the larger inlet valve chambers on pistons 1 and 2 must face the flywheel end of the engine, and the larger inlet valve chambers on pistons 3 and 4 must face the timing belt end of the engine. New pistons have number markings on their crowns to indicate their type - "1/2" denotes piston 1 or 2, "3/4" indicates piston 3 or 4 **(see illustration)**.
19 Working progressively around each bearing cap, tighten the retaining nuts half a turn at a time to the specified torque **(see illustrations)**.

20 Refit the remaining three piston/connecting rod assemblies in the same way.
21 Rotate the crankshaft by hand. Check that it turns freely; some stiffness is to be expected if new parts have been fitted, but there should be no binding or tight spots.

Diesel engines

22 If new pistons are to be fitted, or if a new short engine is to be installed, the projection of the piston crowns above the cylinder head at TDC must be measured, to determine the type of head gasket that should be fitted.
23 Turn the cylinder block over (so that the crankcase is facing downwards) and rest it on a stand or wooden blocks. Anchor a DTI gauge to the cylinder block, and zero it on the head gasket mating surface. Rest the gauge probe on No 1 piston crown and turn the crankshaft slowly by hand so that the piston reaches and then passes through TDC. Measure and record the maximum deflection at TDC.
24 Repeat the measurement at piston No 4, then turn the crankshaft through 180° and take measurements at pistons Nos 2 and 3.
25 If the measurements differ from piston to piston, take the highest figure and use this to determine the head gasket type that must be used - refer to the Specifications for details.
26 Note that if the original pistons have been refitted, then a new head gasket of the same type as the original item must be fitted; refer to Chapter 2B for details of how to identify different head gasket types.

14 Engine - initial start-up after overhaul and reassembly

1 Refit the remainder of the engine components in the order listed in Section 10 of this Chapter, referring to Part A or B where necessary. Refit the engine (and transmission) to the vehicle as described in Section 2 of this Chapter. Double-check the engine oil and coolant levels and make a final check that everything has been reconnected. Make sure that there are no tools or rags left in the engine compartment.

13.18 Piston orientation and fitting order (engine codes 1Z, AHU and AFN)

13.19a Tightening the big-end bearing cap bolts to the Stage 1 . . .

13.19b . . . and Stage 2 torque settings

Petrol models

2 Remove the spark plugs, referring to Chapter 1A for details.

3 The engine must be immobilised such that it can be turned over using the starter motor, without starting - disable the fuel pump by unplugging the fuel pump power relay from the relay board; refer to the relevant Part of Chapter 4 for details. Alternatively, identify and remove the fuel pump fuse.

Caution: If the vehicle has a catalytic converter, it is potentially damaging to immobilise the engine by disabling the ignition system without first disabling the fuel system, as unburnt fuel could be supplied to the catalyst.

4 Turn the engine using the starter motor until the oil pressure warning lamp goes out. If the lamp fails to extinguish after several seconds of cranking, check the engine oil level and that the oil filter is secure. Assuming these are correct, check the security of the oil pressure switch wiring - do not progress any further until you are satisfied that oil is being pumped around the engine at sufficient pressure.

5 Refit the spark plugs, and reconnect the fuel pump relay (or refit the fuel pump fuse).

Diesel models

6 Disconnect the electrical cable from the fuel cut-off valve (stop solenoid) at the fuel injection pump - refer to Chapter 4C for details.

7 Turn the engine using the starter motor until the oil pressure warning lamp goes out.

8 If the lamp fails to extinguish after several seconds of cranking, check the engine oil level and that the oil filter is secure. Assuming these are correct, check the security of the oil pressure switch wiring - do not progress any further until you are satisfied that oil is being pumped around the engine at sufficient pressure.

9 Reconnect the fuel cut-off valve cable.

All models

10 Start the engine, but be aware that as fuel system components have been disturbed, the cranking time may be a little longer than usual.

11 While the engine is idling, check for fuel, water and oil leaks. Don't be alarmed if there are some odd smells and the occasional plume of smoke as components heat up and burn off oil deposits.

12 Assuming all is well, keep the engine idling until hot water is felt circulating through the top hose.

13 On diesel models, check the fuel injection pump timing and engine idle speed, as described in Chapter 4C and/or Chapter 1B.

14 After a few minutes, recheck the oil and coolant levels, and top-up as necessary.

15 On all the engines described in this Chapter, there is no need to re-tighten the cylinder head bolts once the engine has been run following reassembly.

16 If new pistons, rings or crankshaft bearings have been fitted, the engine must be treated as new, and run-in for the first 600 miles (1000 km). *Do not* operate the engine at full-throttle, or allow it to labour at low engine speeds in any gear. It is recommended that the engine oil and filter are changed at the end of this period.

Notes

Chapter 3
Cooling, heating and ventilation systems

Contents

Degrees of difficulty

Easy, suitable for novice with little experience	**Fairly easy,** suitable for beginner with some experience	**Fairly difficult,** suitable for competent DIY mechanic

Difficult, suitable for experienced DIY mechanic

Very difficult, suitable for expert DIY or professional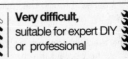

Specifications

System type .... Pressurised, radiator, thermostat and expansion tank, belt-driven coolant pump. Thermostatically controlled electric cooling fan

System operating pressure .... 1.2 to 1.5 bar (17.4 to 21.8 lbf/in²)

Thermostat
Starts to open .... 85°C (185°F)
Fully open .... 105°C (221°F)
Stroke (minimum) .... 7 mm

Electric cooling fan thermo-switch
Operating temperature:
  Speed 1 on .... 92 to 97°C (198 to 207°F)
  Speed 1 off .... 84 to 91°C (183 to 196°F)
  Speed 2 on .... 99 to 105°C (210 to 221°F)
  Speed 2 off .... 91 to 98°C (196 to 208°F)
Fan run-on switch (injector cooling, later models):
  Switches on .... 100°C (212°F)
  Switches off .... 90°C (194°F)

Torque wrench settings	**Nm**	**lbf ft**
Air conditioning compressor mounting bolts:		
M8	25	18
M10	45	33
Coolant pump pulley socket-head bolts	25	18
Coolant pump mounting bolts to engine block:		
Models with V-belt drive	20	15
Models with ribbed belt drive*:		
Stage 1	20	15
Stage 2 (angle-tighten)	Angle-tighten a further 90°	
Coolant pump-to-housing bolts	10	7
Radiator-to-lock carrier bolts	10	7
Thermo-switch (cooling fan)	35	26
Thermostat cover bolts	10	7

*Use new bolts

3

1 General description

The cooling system is of the pressurised type and includes a front-mounted radiator, a coolant pump driven by an auxiliary drivebelt, a thermostat (located in the coolant pump housing) and a thermostatically-controlled electric cooling fan. A remote expansion tank is fitted to all models and the system pressure is regulated by the pressure/filler cap fitted in the expansion tank.

The system functions as follows. With the engine cold, the thermostat is shut, and the coolant pump forces the water through the internal passages, then via the bypass hose and heater circuit over the thermostat capsule, and to the coolant pump inlet again. This circulation of water cools the cylinder bores, combustion surfaces and valve seats. However, when the coolant reaches the predetermined temperature, the thermostat begins to open and the coolant circulates through the top hose to the top of the radiator. As it passes through the radiator matrix, it is cooled by the inrush of air when the car is in forward motion, supplemented by the action of the electric cooling fan when necessary. Finally, the coolant is returned to the coolant pump via the bottom hose, and through the open thermostat.

The electric cooling fan is controlled by a thermo-switch, located in the lower left-hand side of the radiator. In addition to the normal coolant temperature gauge sender unit, thermo-switches and temperature sender units are fitted to actuate components of the fuel injection and ignition systems.

A conventional heating system is fitted whereby the engine coolant is circulated through a matrix within the heater body. An air conditioning system is fitted to later models and where this is the case the precautionary notes outlined in Section 14 should be observed before working on any part of the system.

⚠️ *Warning: Do not attempt to remove the expansion tank filler cap or disturb any part of the cooling system while the engine is hot, as there is a high risk of scalding. If the expansion tank filler cap must be removed before the engine and radiator have fully cooled (even though this is not recommended) the pressure in the cooling system must first be relieved. Cover the cap with a thick layer of cloth, to avoid scalding, and slowly unscrew the filler cap until a hissing sound can be heard. When the hissing has stopped, indicating that the pressure has reduced, slowly unscrew the filler cap until it can be removed; if more hissing sounds are heard, wait until they have stopped before unscrewing the cap completely. At all times keep well away from the filler cap opening.*

Do not allow antifreeze to come into contact with skin or painted surfaces of the vehicle. Rinse off spills immediately with plenty of water. Never leave antifreeze lying around in an open container or in a puddle in the driveway or on the garage floor. Children and pets are attracted by its sweet smell. Antifreeze can be fatal if ingested.

If the engine is hot, the electric cooling fan may start rotating even if the engine is not running, so be careful to keep hands, hair and loose clothing well clear when working in the engine compartment.

Refer to Section 14 for precautions to be observed when working on models with air conditioning.

2 Cooling system hoses - disconnection and renewal

Note: *Refer to the warnings given in Section 1 of this Chapter before proceeding.*

1 If the checks described in Chapter 1 reveal a faulty hose, it must be renewed as follows.

2 First drain the cooling system (see Chapter 1). If the coolant is not due for renewal, it may be re-used if it is collected in a clean container.

3 To disconnect a hose, release its retaining clips, then move them along the hose, clear of the relevant inlet/outlet union **(see illustration)**. Carefully work the hose free. While the hoses can be removed with relative ease when new or hot, **do not** attempt to disconnect any part of the system while it is still hot.

4 Note that the radiator inlet and outlet unions are fragile; do not use excessive force when attempting to remove the hoses. If a hose proves to be difficult to remove, try to release it by rotating the hose ends before attempting to free it.

> **HAYNES HiNT** *If all else fails, cut the hose with a sharp knife, then slit it so that it can be peeled off in two pieces. Although this may prove expensive if the hose is otherwise undamaged, it is preferable to buying a new radiator.*

5 When fitting a hose, first slide the clips onto the hose, then work the hose into position. If clamp type clips were originally fitted, it is a good idea to replace them with screw type clips when refitting the hose. If the hose is stiff, use a little soapy water as a lubricant, or soften the hose by soaking it in hot water.

6 Work the hose into position, checking that it is correctly routed, then slide each clip along the hose until it passes over the flared end of the relevant inlet/outlet union, before securing it in position with the retaining clip.

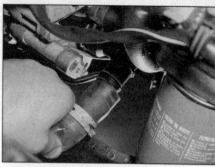

2.3 Disconnecting the thermostat housing hose (diesel engine shown)

7 Refill the cooling system (see Chapter 1).

8 Check thoroughly for leaks as soon as possible after disturbing any part of the cooling system.

3 Radiator - removal and refitting

Removal

> **HAYNES HiNT** *If leakage is the reason for wanting to remove the radiator, bear in mind that minor leaks can often be cured using a radiator sealant with the radiator in situ.*

1 Disconnect the battery earth lead. **Note:** *If the vehicle has a security-coded radio, check that you have a copy of the code number before disconnecting the battery. Refer to your VW dealer if in doubt.*

2 Drain the cooling system as described in Chapter 1.

3 Refer to Chapter 11 for details and remove the front lock carrier complete with headlight units from the vehicle.

4 Slacken their retaining clips and detach the top and bottom hoses from the radiator **(see illustrations)**.

5 Disconnect the wiring connection from the cooling fan thermo-switch **(see illustration)**.

6 On models equipped with air conditioning, in order to gain the clearance required to remove the radiator, carry out the following. Unscrew the retaining nuts and release the air conditioning system fluid reservoir/drier assembly from its mounting bracket. Release the refrigerant lines from all the relevant retaining clips, then undo the retaining bolts and move the condenser forwards as far as possible, taking great care not to place any excess strain on the refrigerant lines. **Do not** disconnect the refrigerant lines from the condenser (refer to the warnings given in Section 14).

7 Check that all connections are clear, then lift the radiator carefully from the vehicle **(see illustration)**.

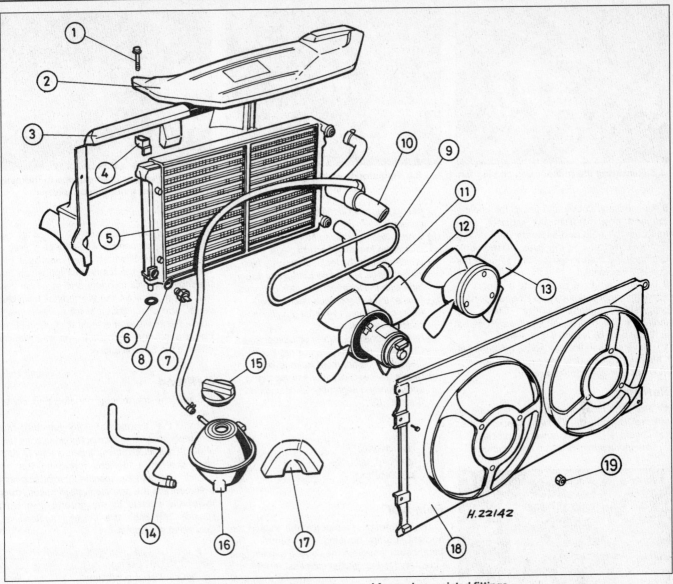

3.4a Cooling system radiator, two-speed fan and associated fittings

1 Bolt	6 Rubber washer	11 Bottom hose	15 Filler/pressure cap
2 Cover panel	7 Fan thermo-switch	12 Fan	16 Expansion tank
3 Air duct	8 Seal ring	13 Secondary fan (where	17 Cover
4 Bracket	9 Drivebelt	fitted)	18 Fan cowl
5 Radiator	10 Top hose	14 Coolant pipe hose	19 Nut

3

3.4b Radiator top hose connection

3.4c Radiator bottom hose connection

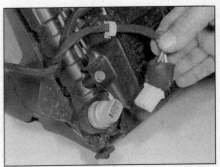

3.5 Cooling fan thermo-switch and wire connector

3.7 Removing the radiator and cooling fan

3.8 Radiator-to-cooling fan shroud retaining bolt

3.11 Lock carrier bolts engage in radiator upper mounting brackets

8 If necessary, unbolt and unclip the cooling fan and cowling from the radiator, then unscrew the nuts and separate the fan and motor from the cowling **(see illustration)**. Unscrew the thermo-switch, and remove the gasket if necessary.
9 Radiator repair is best left to a specialist, although minor leaks may be stopped using a proprietary coolant additive. Clean the radiator matrix of flies and small leaves with a soft brush, or by hosing with water.
10 Reverse-flush the radiator as described in Chapter 1, and renew the hoses and clips if they are damaged or deteriorated.

Refitting

11 Refit the radiator in the reverse order of removal, but note the following special points:
  a) *If worn or perished, renew the rubber mounting washers which are located on*

4.2a Undo the two retaining bolts to remove thermostat cover . . .

the engagement pegs on the base of the radiator.
  b) *When lowering the radiator into position, locate the two engagement pegs.*
  c) *When refitting the lock carrier unit, take care to engage the two bolts in its upper face with the location recesses in the top face of the radiator (see illustration). Refer to Chapter 11 for full details on refitting the lock carrier.*
  d) *Refill the cooling system as described in Chapter 1. If a new radiator has been fitted, the coolant must be renewed.*
  e) *Check the headlights for satisfactory operation and alignment as described in Chapter 12.*

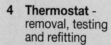

4 Thermostat - removal, testing and refitting

Removal

1 The thermostat is located in the base of the coolant pump housing. To remove the thermostat, first drain the cooling system (see Chapter 1). For easier access, apply the handbrake, chock the rear wheels, then jack up the front of the vehicle and support on axle stands (see *"Jacking and vehicle support"*).
2 Undo the two retaining bolts to remove the thermostat cover, then extract the thermostat and O-ring from its housing in the base of the coolant pump **(see illustrations)**.

Testing

3 To test whether the thermostat is serviceable, suspend it with a piece of string in a container of water. Gradually heat the water, and note the temperature at which the thermostat starts to open, and at which it is fully open. Remove the thermostat from the water, and check that it is fully closed when cold. Renew the thermostat if it fails to operate in accordance with the information given in the Specifications.

Refitting

4 Clean the thermostat housing and cover faces.
5 Refit the thermostat into its housing, ensuring that it is correctly orientated as shown **(see illustration)**. Insert a new O-ring seal, then refit the cover and tighten its retaining bolts to the specified torque setting.
6 Reconnect the cooling system hoses, then lower the vehicle to the ground (if it was raised) and refill the cooling system as described in Chapter 1.

5 Coolant pump - removal and refitting

Removal

1 Drain the cooling system as described in Chapter 1.

4.2b . . . then remove the O-ring . . .

4.2c . . . and the thermostat

4.5 Thermostat orientation and O-ring location in cover

5.5a Unscrew the socket-head bolts . . .

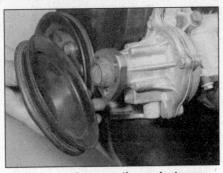

5.5b . . . and remove the coolant pump drive pulley (V-belt drive pulley shown)

5.6 Disconnecting the bypass hose

2 Remove the alternator and its drivebelt as described in Chapter 5A.

3 Where fitted, remove the power steering pump as described in Chapter 10.

4 On models equipped with air conditioning, unbolt the compressor from its mounting bracket, and position it clear of the engine. **Note:** *Do not disconnect the refrigerant lines from the compressor (see Section 14).*

5 Unbolt the pulley from the coolant pump drive flange, using an Allen key **(see illustrations)**.

6 Loosen the clips, and disconnect the hoses from the coolant pump housing **(see illustration)**.

7 Unscrew the nut, and remove the special bolt retaining the lower timing cover to the coolant pump assembly **(see illustration)**.

8 Unbolt the coolant pump assembly from the cylinder block, and remove the sealing O-ring **(see illustrations)**.

9 Unscrew the bolts, and remove the coolant pump from its housing **(see illustrations)**. If it is tight, carefully tap it free using a wooden mallet. Remove the gasket.

10 If the coolant pump is faulty, renew it complete; individual components are not available. Clean the mating faces of the coolant pump and housing.

Refitting

11 Refitting is a reversal of removal, but use a new gasket or sealing O-ring, as applicable. Fill the cooling system with reference to Chapter 1. Tension the auxiliary drivebelt(s) as described in Chapter 2.

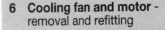

6 Cooling fan and motor - removal and refitting

Removal

1 Disconnect the battery negative lead. **Note:** *If the vehicle has a security-coded radio, check that you have a copy of the code number before disconnecting the battery. Refer to your VW dealer if in doubt.*

2 Disconnect the wiring from the cooling fan motor and the support frame **(see illustration)**.

3 Remove the bolts and screws. and lift the cowl together with the cooling fan and motor from the radiator.

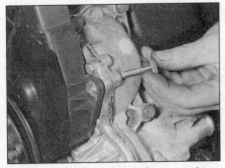

5.7 Remove the lower timing cover-to-coolant pump bolt

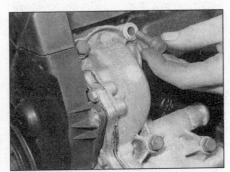

5.8a Remove the mounting bolts . . .

5.8b . . . and withdraw the coolant pump

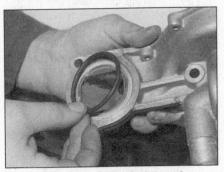

5.8c Remove the O-ring seal

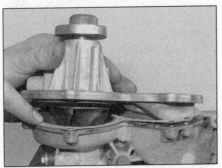

5.9a Remove the coolant pump from its housing

5.9b Coolant pump removed

3

6.2 Single cooling fan and motor attachment to radiator and cowl

6.4 Twin cooling fans and drivebelt

4 Remove the nuts to separate the cooling fan and motor from the cowl and support frame. Where twin cooling fans are fitted, detach the drivebelt from the pulley on the front of each fan **(see illustration)**.

Refitting

5 Refit in the reverse order of removal. Check for satisfactory operation on completion.

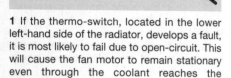

7 Cooling fan thermo-switch - testing, removal and refitting

1 If the thermo-switch, located in the lower left-hand side of the radiator, develops a fault, it is most likely to fail due to open-circuit. This will cause the fan motor to remain stationary even through the coolant reaches the operating temperature.

Testing

2 To test the thermo-switch for an open-circuit fault, disconnect the wiring, and connect a length of wire or suitable metal object between the earth and live wires. The fan should operate (even without the ignition switch on), if not, the thermo-switch is proved faulty and must be renewed.

Removal

3 Either drain the cooling system to below the level of the switch (as described in Chapter 1), or have ready a suitable plug which can be used to plug the switch aperture in the

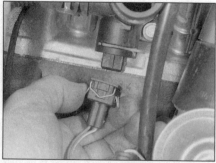

8.4 Detaching the wiring connector from the coolant temperature gauge sender - RP engine shown

radiator whilst the switch is removed. If a plug is used, take great care not to damage the radiator, and do not use anything which will allow foreign matter to enter the radiator.
4 Disconnect the battery negative lead. **Note:** *If the vehicle has a security-coded radio, check that you have a copy of the code number before disconnecting the battery. Refer to your VW dealer if in doubt.*
5 Disconnect the wiring, then unscrew the thermo-switch from the radiator and remove its sealing washer.
6 To check the operating temperature of the thermo-switch, suspend it in a pan of water so that only the screwed end of the switch is immersed and the electrical contacts are clear of the water. Either connect an ohmmeter between the switch terminals, or connect up a torch battery and bulb in series with the switch. With a thermometer placed in the pan, heat the water, and note the temperature at which the switch contacts close, so that the ohmmeter reads zero, or the bulb lights. Allow the water to cool, and note the temperature at which switch contacts open. Discard the switch and fit a new one if the operating temperatures are not within the specified limits.

Refitting

7 Refitting is a reversal of removal, but always fit a new sealing washer. Fill the cooling system as described in Chapter 1, or top up as described in *"Weekly checks"*.

8 Coolant temperature gauge sender unit - testing, removal and refitting

Testing

1 The coolant temperature gauge, mounted in the instrument panel, is fed with a stabilised voltage supply from the instrument panel feed (through the ignition switch and a fuse), and its earth is controlled by the sender.
2 The sender unit is screwed or clipped into the coolant outlet elbow on the front of the cylinder head; it may be fitted on top of the elbow, or underneath it. The sender contains a thermistor, which consists of an electronic component whose electrical resistance decreases at a predetermined rate as its

temperature rises. When the coolant is cold, the sensor resistance is high, current flow through the gauge is reduced, and the gauge needle points towards the "cold" end of the scale. If the sender is faulty, it must be renewed.
3 If the gauge develops a fault, first check the other instruments; if they do not work at all, check the instrument panel electrical feed. If the readings are erratic, there may be a fault in the instrument panel assembly. If the fault lies in the temperature gauge alone, check it as follows.
4 If the gauge needle remains at the "cold" end of the scale, disconnect the wiring connector from the sensor unit, and earth the temperature gauge wire (see *"Wiring diagrams"* for details) to the cylinder head **(see illustration)**. If the needle then deflects when the ignition is switched on, the sensor unit is proved faulty, and should be renewed. If the needle still does not move, remove the instrument panel (Chapter 12) and check the continuity of the wiring between the sensor unit and the gauge, and the feed to the gauge unit. If continuity is shown, and the fault still exists, then the gauge is faulty and should be renewed.

Removal

5 Either partially drain the cooling system (as described in Chapter 1) to just below the level of the sender or have ready a suitable plug which can be used to plug the sender aperture whilst it is removed. If a plug is used, take great care not to damage the sender unit aperture, and do not use anything which will allow foreign matter to enter the cooling system.
6 Disconnect the battery negative lead. **Note:** *If the vehicle has a security-coded radio, check that you have a copy of the code number before disconnecting the battery. Refer to your VW dealer if in doubt.*
7 Disconnect the wiring from the sender.
8 Either depress the sender unit and slide out its retaining clip, or unscrew the sender. Withdraw the sender from the coolant elbow and recover its sealing ring or washer.

Refitting

9 Fit a new sealing ring or washer to the sender unit and fit it to the elbow, tightening it securely or retaining it in position with the clip.
10 Reconnect the wiring connector then refill the cooling system as described in Chapter 1 or top-up as described in *"Weekly checks"*.

9 Fuel system temperature switches - general information, removal and refitting

General information

1 According to model, various additional temperature switches/senders may be fitted to the coolant elbow, for use in conjunction with the fuel system. They are as follows:

a) *PB and PF engine codes: The coolant temperature sender for the airflow meter is located on the outer end of the coolant elbow, on the side of the cylinder head. It has a blue wiring connector.*

b) *2E engine code: The thermo-switch for the injection/ignition system is located on the coolant elbow, on the side of the cylinder head (inboard end). It has a blue wiring connector.*

c) *RP engine code: The thermo-switch for the inlet manifold preheater is located on the outboard end of the coolant elbow, on the side of the cylinder head. It has a red wiring connector. In addition a thermo-switch for the injection system is fitted to the inboard end of the coolant elbow on the side of the cylinder head. Its wiring connector is coloured blue.*

2 On later models, this multiple switch arrangement has been dropped, and one unit performs all coolant temperature sensing functions. On diesel engine models, the coolant temperature sender unit provides information which is used to operate the preheater system. Coolant temperature sender information is also used by the air conditioning system.

Removal

3 In each case, the removal of these switch/sender units is the same. Either partially drain the cooling system (as described in Chapter 1) to just below the level of the sender or have ready a suitable plug which can be used to plug the sender aperture whilst it is removed. If a plug is used, take great care not to damage the sender unit aperture, and do not use anything which will allow foreign matter to enter the cooling system.

4 Disconnect the battery negative lead. **Note:** *If the vehicle has a security-coded radio, check that you have a copy of the code number before disconnecting the battery. Refer to your VW dealer if in doubt.*

5 Detach the wiring connector from the switch/sender concerned, then release its retaining clip, and remove the switch/sender unit, together with its O-ring seal **(see illustrations)**.

6 To remove the coolant elbow, detach the

9.5a Inlet manifold thermo-switch/sender removal - RP engine. Disconnect the wiring connector . . .

switch/sender wiring connectors, disconnect the coolant hoses from the elbow, then undo its retaining bolts and remove the elbow. Note that it is sealed at the cylinder head by an O-ring seal **(see illustration)**.

Refitting

7 Refit in the reverse order of removal; always renew the O-ring seal. Refill the cooling system as described in Chapter 1, or top up as described in *"Weekly checks"*.

10 Core plug - renewal

1 In the event of a core plug leaking, it may be renewed as follows. First drain the cooling system, as described in Chapter 1.

2 Measure and record the fitted depth of the core plug.

3 Drill one or two small holes through the core plug, and use self-tapping screws and a pair of grips to pull out the plug. If the plug is rusted in position, drill a larger hole, and use a lever to remove it.

4 Clean the seating in the cylinder block, then smear a little non-setting sealant around it. Use sealant suitable for use on cooling system components.

5 Using a large socket or piece of metal tubing, tap the new core plug squarely into the block, to the previously-recorded depth.

6 Fill the cooling system as described in Chapter 1.

9.5b . . . withdraw the retaining clip . . .

11 Heating and ventilation system - general information

The heating/ventilation system consists of a four-speed blower motor (housed in the passenger compartment), face-level vents in the centre and at each end of the facia, and air ducts to the front and rear footwells.

The control unit is located in the facia, and the controls operate flap valves to deflect and mix the air flowing through the various parts of the heating/ventilation system. The flap valves are contained in the air distribution housing, which acts as a central distribution unit, passing air to the various ducts and vents.

Cold air enters the system through the grille at the rear of the engine compartment. On later models, a pollen filter is fitted to the ventilation inlet to filter out dust, soot, pollen and spores from the air entering the vehicle.

The airflow, which can be boosted by the blower, then flows through the various ducts, according to the settings of the controls. Stale air is expelled through ducts at the rear of the vehicle. If warm air is required, the cold air is passed through the heater matrix, which is heated by the engine coolant.

If necessary, the outside air supply can be closed off, allowing the air inside the vehicle to be recirculated. This can be useful to prevent unpleasant odours entering from outside the vehicle, but should only be used briefly, as the recirculated air inside the vehicle will soon deteriorate.

3

9.5c . . . extract the thermo-switch/ sender . . .

9.5d . . . and O-ring seal

9.6 Coolant elbow removal - RP engine. Note O-ring seal location

Later models were available with an automatic heat regulator system, called "Thermotronic". The system effectively replaces the normal hot-cold heat control - the central heater control is now marked with temperature settings. The system uses two sensors - one next to the radio/cassette unit, and one in the fresh air inlet duct on the top of the engine compartment bulkhead - and an electronic control unit behind the heater control panel, to regulate the temperature to the selected setting automatically.

For details of the air conditioning system, see Section 14.

Certain models may be fitted with heated front seats. The heat is produced by electrically-heated mats in the seat and backrest cushions (see Chapter 12). The

12.3 Heater coolant supply and return hose connections at the bulkhead

temperature is regulated automatically by a thermostat, and cannot be adjusted.

12 Heater/ventilation components - removal and refitting

Models without air conditioning

Heater/ventilation control unit and heater matrix

1 Disconnect the battery earth lead. **Note:** *If the vehicle has a security-coded radio, check that you have a copy of the code number before disconnecting the battery. Refer to your VW dealer if in doubt.*

2 Drain the cooling system as described in Chapter 1.

3 Release the retaining clips and detach the coolant supply and return hoses from their connections to the heater on the engine side of the bulkhead **(see illustration)**.

4 Remove the steering wheel as described in Chapter 10.

5 Refer to the appropriate Sections in Chapters 11 and 12 to detach and remove the facia, its associated trim, and the control panels **(see illustration)**. As they are disconnected, take note of their respective wiring connections and the routing of the harnesses.

a) *Centre console*
b) *Lower the facia trim panels on the right and left-hand side*
c) *Radio/cassette unit*
d) *Heater control panel, leaving the control cables attached to the control panel and heater. With the control unit detached from the facia, it can be withdrawn with the heater unit (then disconnected if required)*
e) *Glovebox*
f) *Right and left-hand air vent housings*
g) *Instrument panel*
h) *Complete facia panel*

6 If still in position, detach and remove the insulation panel from the underside of the heater blower motor.

7 Unscrew and remove the two heater unit retaining nuts **(see illustration)** on the engine side of the bulkhead. Lift the flap in the insulation panel for access to the lower retaining nut.

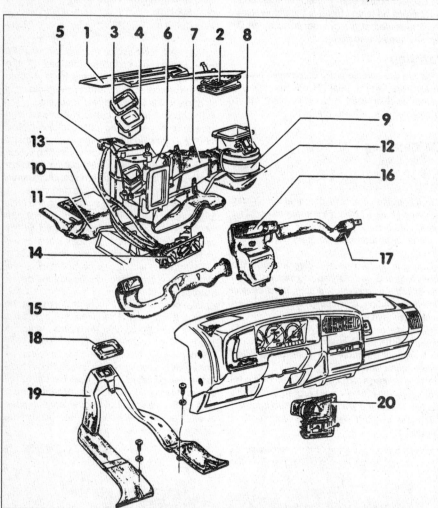

12.5 Heater unit and associated fittings

1 Plastic water deflector cover	7 Air duct and cut-off flap	14 Hot air and fresh air control unit
2 Air inlet grille	8 Resistor	15 Air duct
3 Seal	9 Fresh air blower	16 Air distributor
4 Intermediate piece	10 Pedal cover	17 Air duct
5 Heater matrix	11 Footwell outlets	18 Rear duct seal
6 Air distribution housing	12 Air duct cover	19 Rear duct
	13 Cables	20 Vent housing

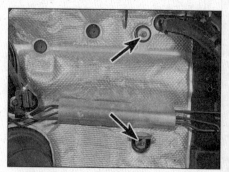

12.7 Heater retaining nuts (arrowed)

8 Check that all wiring and associate fittings are clear, then with the help of an assistant, partially withdraw the heater unit and detach the air duct between the heater and the blower unit. As the heater is withdrawn, take care not to tilt it down at the front too much or any residual coolant will be expelled.

9 Pull on the matrix to withdraw it from the heater unit for inspection **(see illustration)**.

10 If the control cables are to be detached, note how each is attached to its valve (or lever) as a guide for refitting **(see illustrations)**.

11 If required, the heater casings can be dismantled by releasing the retaining clips and undoing the screws **(see illustrations)**.

12 Refitting is a reversal of the removal procedure. Ensure that all seals and gaskets are in good condition and correctly seated. Also ensure that the control cables are correctly attached and that they operate the control flaps in satisfactory manner before fitting the heater into position.

13 As the heater unit is refitted, ensure that the pegs engage in the locating holes.

14 Ensure that all wiring connections are correctly and securely made. When the battery is reconnected, check the operation of all switches and controls.

12.9 Heater matrix removal

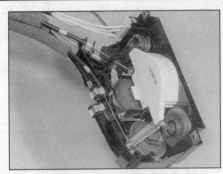

12.10a Heater and cable connections

12.10b Heater cable attachments

12.11a Heater casing retaining clip and screw

15 Refill the cooling system as described in Chapter 1 and check for any sign of leakage from the heater hose connections.

Heater control panel and cables

16 Disconnect the battery earth lead. **Note:** *If the vehicle has a security-coded radio, check that you have a copy of the code number before disconnecting the battery. Refer to your VW dealer if in doubt.*

17 Carefully prise free and release the trim panel from the front of the control panel **(see illustration)**.

18 Remove the centre console as described in Chapter 11.

19 Undo the four retaining screws and press the heater/fresh air control panel inwards, then downwards, and withdraw it from under

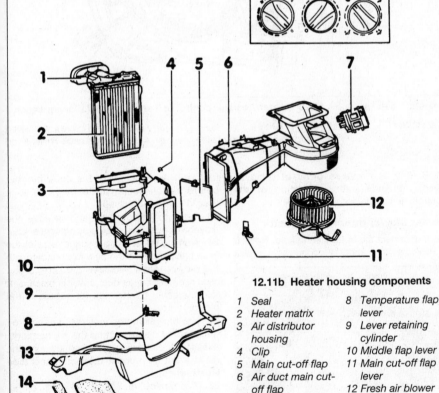

12.11b Heater housing components

1 Seal
2 Heater matrix
3 Air distributor housing
4 Clip
5 Main cut-off flap
6 Air duct main cut-off flap
7 Resistor
8 Temperature flap lever
9 Lever retaining cylinder
10 Middle flap lever
11 Main cut-off flap lever
12 Fresh air blower
13 Footwell outlet
14 Pedal cover

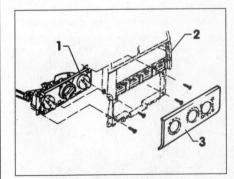

12.17 Heater/fresh air control panel

1 Control unit
2 Facia
3 Control panel trim

3

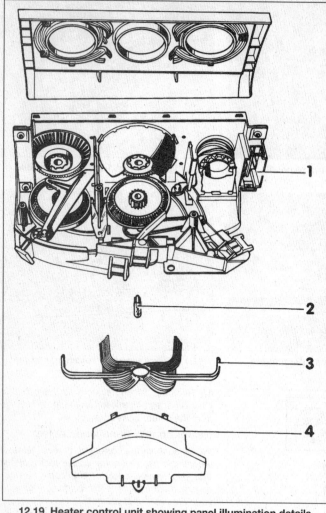

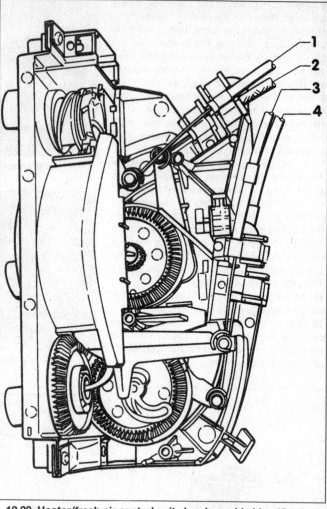

12.19 Heater control unit showing panel illumination details

1 Regulator
2 Illumination bulb
3 Light transmitter
4 Cap

12.20 Heater/fresh air control unit showing cable identification

1 Blower cable
2 Temperature control cable
3 Air distribution cable (upper lever)
4 Air distribution cable (lower lever)

the facia. Access can now be gained to its wiring and control cable connections **(see illustration)**.

20 If the cables are to be disconnected from the control panel, note their respective connections to avoid the possibility of confusion when refitting **(see illustration)**.

21 Refit in the reverse order of removal. Check for satisfactory operation of the controls on completion.

Heater blower motor and resistor

22 Disconnect the battery earth lead. **Note:** *If the vehicle has a security-coded radio, check*

that you have a copy of the code number before disconnecting the battery. Refer to your VW dealer if in doubt.

23 Refer to Chapter 11 and remove the glovebox or passenger side oddments shelf.

24 Working under the passenger side of the facia panel, remove the plug from underneath the blower motor. Remove the screws and clips retaining the air duct cover in place, and fold the cover to one side for access to the blower motor.

25 The blower motor resistor may now be removed by disconnecting the wiring plugs, releasing the retaining clips and lowering the resistor out from under the facia panel **(see illustrations)**.

26 Disconnect the motor wiring plugs. Release the retaining clip, then twist the motor assembly and lower the motor out from under the facia panel **(see illustrations)**.

27 If a replacement motor is being fitted, reconnect the wiring plug to the new motor,

12.25a Heater blower motor resistor (seen with heater removed)

12.25b Release the retaining clips and withdraw the resistor

12.26a Heater blower motor location

12.26b Release the retaining clip, then twist the blower motor to remove it from the housing

12.29 Thermotronic inlet air temperature sensor

temporarily reconnect the battery, and check the motor operation before refitting the trim. Refit in the reverse order of removal, checking for satisfactory operation again on completion.

Thermotronic sensors

28 To remove the interior temperature sensor, refer to Section 13.
29 The inlet air temperature sensor is mounted on top of the engine compartment bulkhead, on the passenger side **(see illustration)**. To remove the sensor, unclip it from its mounting bracket and disconnect the wiring plug. Refitting is a reversal of removal.

Models with air conditioning

Note: *The following information is only applicable to manually controlled air conditioning systems. At the time of writing no information was available on models with the automatic "Climatronic" system, which in any case does not appear to have been fitted to UK models.*

Heater matrix

30 On models equipped with air conditioning, it is not possible to remove the heater matrix without opening the refrigerant circuit (See Section 14). Therefore this task must be entrusted to a VW dealer.

Heater control panel and cables

31 Refer to the information given in paragraphs 16 to 21.

Heater blower motor and resistor

32 Carry out the operations described in paragraphs 22 and 23.
33 The blower motor resistor may now be removed if required. Pull off the four-wire multi-plug and remove the screws. Withdraw the resistor from under the facia panel.
34 Disconnect the wiring connector from the motor. Undo the retaining screws and lower the motor assembly out of position.
35 If a replacement motor is being fitted, reconnect the wiring plug to the new motor, temporarily reconnect the battery, and check the motor operation before refitting the trim. Refit in the reverse order of removal, checking for satisfactory operation again on completion.

13 Heater vents and housings - removal and refitting

Vent grilles

1 All vent grilles can be carefully levered out of position with a small flat-bladed screwdriver, taking great care not to mark the vent housing **(see illustration)**.
2 On refitting, carefully manoeuvre the grille back into position ensuring it is correctly engaged with the locating pegs.

Instrument panel surround - later models

3 On later models, the instrument panel surround must be removed for access to the driver's side and central vent housings.
4 First remove the three vent grilles from the driver's side and central vent housings. Remove the rotary lighting switch (see Chapter 12).
5 Unclip the trim panel immediately behind the left-hand side of the steering wheel.
6 Remove four screws - one behind each vent grille, and one behind the trim panel removed in paragraph 5 - and take out the instrument panel surround **(see illustration)**.
7 Refitting is the reverse of removal.

Driver's side facia vent housing

8 On later models, remove the instrument panel surround as described in paragraphs 3 to 6.

13.1 Removing a facia vent grille

9 Remove the lighting switch as described in Chapter 12.
10 If not already done, remove the vent grille from the driver's side vent housing. Undo the retaining screw and remove the vent housing from the facia.
11 Refitting is the reverse of removal.

Central facia vent housing

12 On later models, remove the instrument panel surround as described in paragraphs 3 to 6.
13 Remove the radio/cassette unit as described in Chapter 12.
14 If not already done, remove the vent grilles from the central vent housing. Unclip and remove the switch and heater control panel surrounds.
15 For access to the two vent housing retaining screws - below the heater control panel - it may be necessary to refer to Chapter 11 and loosen the centre console front section fixings.
16 Remove the housing retaining screws and withdraw the housing from the facia.
17 Refitting is the reverse of removal.

Passenger side facia vent housing

18 Remove the vent grille from the passenger side vent housing.
19 Undo the retaining screw and withdraw the vent housing from the facia.
20 Refitting is the reverse of removal.

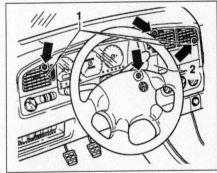

13.6 Instrument panel surround securing screws - arrowed (later models)

1 Vent grilles   2 Trim panel

3

Thermotronic sensor housing/trim panel

21 Refer to Chapter 12 and remove the radio/cassette unit.
22 Working through the radio/cassette aperture as necessary, pull off the housing/trim panel for the thermotronic sensor.
23 If required, the sensor can be removed through the radio/cassette aperture, after releasing the plastic retaining clips each side of the sensor with a suitable screwdriver, and unplugging the wiring connector.
24 Refitting is the reverse of removal.

14 Air conditioning system - general information, precautions and maintenance

General information

1 An air conditioning system is available on certain models. It enables the temperature of incoming air to be lowered, and dehumidifies the air, which makes for rapid demisting and increased comfort (**see illustration**).
2 The cooling side of the system works in the same way as a domestic refrigerator. Refrigerant gas is drawn into a belt-driven compressor and passes into a condenser mounted in front of the radiator, where it loses heat and becomes liquid. The liquid passes through an expansion valve to an evaporator, where it changes from liquid under high pressure to gas under low pressure. This change is accompanied by a drop in temperature, which cools the evaporator. The refrigerant returns to the compressor and the cycle begins again.

3 Air blown through the evaporator passes to the air distribution unit, where it is mixed with hot air blown through the heater matrix to achieve the desired temperature in the passenger compartment.
4 The heating side of the system works in the same way as on models without air conditioning (see Section 11).
5 The operation of the system is controlled electronically by coolant temperature switches and pressure switches which are screwed into the compressor high-pressure line. Any problems with the system should be referred to a VW dealer.

Precautions

 Warning: The refrigeration circuit contains a liquid refrigerant (Freon) and it is therefore dangerous to disconnect any part of the system without specialised knowledge and equipment. The refrigerant is potentially dangerous and should only be handled by qualified persons. If it is splashed onto the skin it can cause frostbite. It is not itself poisonous, but in the presence of a naked flame (including a cigarette) it forms a poisonous gas. Uncontrolled discharging of the refrigerant is dangerous and potentially damaging to the environment.

6 Do not operate the air conditioning system if it is known to be short of refrigerant, as this may damage the compressor.
7 Where the compressor or condenser obstruct other mechanical operations such as engine removal, then it is permissible to unbolt their mountings and move them to the limit of their flexible hose deflection, but **not** to disconnect the hoses. If there is still

insufficient room to carry out the required work, then the system must be discharged before disconnecting and removing the assemblies. The system will, of course, have to be recharged on completion.
8 The system will also need to be discharged if the vehicle is to be welded in the vicinity of the system or its hoses, or if the area is to be heated in excess of 80°C (176°F) in a repaint booth, as the increase in the temperature can cause the system to burst.
9 Do not work on a vehicle which has a refrigerant leak, particularly in a closed, non-ventilated workshop. Ventilate the workshop and have the system discharged before proceeding with any other repairs. The refrigerant is colourless and odourless. It can cause suffocation in a non-ventilated area and if it comes into contact with the skin, can cause frostbite.
10 In the event of an accidental discharge of the refrigerant (R12 Freon), rinse the affected part of the body in cold water for a minimum period of fifteen minutes and seek medical advice immediately. This is particularly important where the refrigerant has come into contact with the eyes. Bathe them in cold water for fifteen minutes, apply eye drops and have them checked by a doctor immediately, even though they may not be in pain.

Maintenance

11 Regularly check the condenser - behind the radiator - for clogging. Hose away any flies and dirt with water or compressed air.

 Warning: Wear eye protection when using compressed air!

12 Check the tension and condition of the compressor drivebelt as described in Chapters 1 and 2.

15 Air conditioning system components - removal and refitting

 Warning: Do not attempt to open the refrigerant circuit. Refer to the precautions given in Section 14.

1 The only operation which can be carried out easily without discharging the refrigerant is the renewal of the compressor drivebelt, which is covered in Chapter 2. All other operations must be referred to a VW dealer or an air conditioning specialist.
2 If necessary the compressor can be unbolted and moved aside, without disconnecting its flexible hoses, after removing the drivebelt.

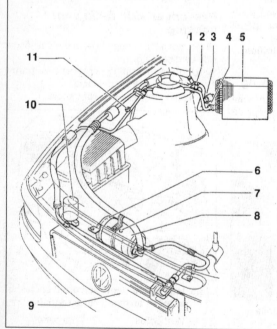

14.1 Air conditioning system components

1 *Evacuating and charging valve (low-pressure side)*
2 *Evacuating and charging valve (high-pressure side)*
3 *Air conditioning pressure switch*
4 *Expansion valve*
5 *Evaporator*
6 *Compressor magnetic coupling*
7 *Compressor oil filling/draining plug*
8 *Compressor*
9 *Condenser*
10 *Fluid container with drier*
11 *Sight glass (discontinued on later models)*

Chapter 4 Part A:
Fuel system - single-point petrol injection

Contents

Degrees of difficulty

Easy, suitable for novice with little experience	**Fairly easy,** suitable for beginner with some experience	**Fairly difficult,** suitable for competent DIY mechanic 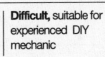	**Difficult,** suitable for experienced DIY mechanic	**Very difficult,** suitable for expert DIY or professional

Specifications

System type
Engine code RP (to 08/90) . . . . Bosch Mono-Jetronic
Engine codes AAM, ABS, ADZ and RP (08/90 on) . . . . Bosch Mono-Motronic

Fuel system data
Fuel pump type . . . . Electric, immersed in fuel tank
Fuel pump delivery rate . . . . 1000 cm³ / min (battery voltage of 12.5 V)
Regulated fuel pressure . . . . 0.8 to 1.2 bar
Engine idle speed . . . . 700-1000 rpm (non-adjustable, electronically controlled)
Maximum engine speed . . . . 6300 rpm (governed electronically)
Injector electrical resistance:
  Mono-Jetronic system . . . . 3.0 to 4.0 ohms
  Mono-Motronic system . . . . 1.2 to 1.6 ohms at 15°C

Recommended fuel
Minimum octane rating:
  Engine codes RP and AAM . . . . 91 RON unleaded
  Engine codes ABS and ADZ . . . . 95 RON unleaded

Torque wrench settings

	Nm	lbf ft
CO sampling pipe bracket to inlet manifold	20	15
Fuel tank retaining strap bolts	25	18
Injector cap/inlet air temperature sensor housing screw	5	4
Inlet manifold heater retaining screws	10	7
Inlet manifold retaining nuts/bolts	25	18
Lambda sensor	50	37
Throttle body air box retaining screw	10	7
Throttle body retaining screws	10	7
Throttle valve positioning module screws	6	4
Warm-air collection plate to inlet manifold	20	15

4A

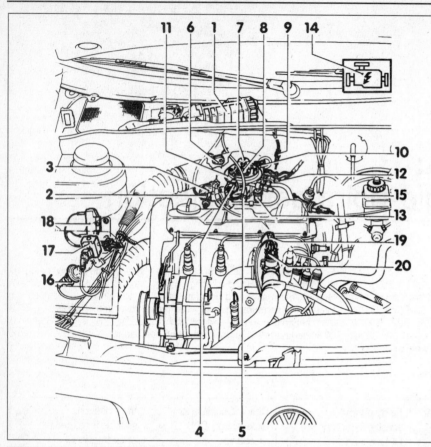

1.1 Mono-Jetronic system and associated components

1 Mono-Jetronic electronic control unit (ECU)
2 Throttle valve positioner and throttle valve switch connector
3 Throttle damper
4 Injector and air inlet temperature sender connector
5 Throttle valve positioner and switch
6 Inlet air pre-heating temperature regulator
7 Injector and inlet air temperature sender
8 Fuel pressure regulator
9 Inlet manifold pre-heater connector
10 Ignition timing vacuum control valve
11 Injector unit/throttle body
12 Throttle valve potentiometer
13 Throttle valve potentiometer water deflector
14 Self-diagnosis fault warning lamp
15 Plug and socket for lambda probe
16 Activated charcoal filter solenoid (valve I) grey
17 Activated charcoal filter solenoid (valve II) black
18 Injector series resistor
19 Injection system temperature sender
20 Inlet manifold pre-heater thermo switch

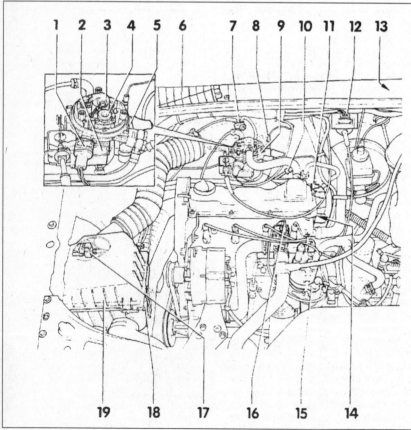

1.2 Mono-Motronic system and associated components

1 Injector/inlet air temperature sender connector
2 Throttle valve positioner and idle switch
3 Injector and inlet air temperature sender
4 Fuel pressure regulator
5 Throttle valve potentiometer
6 Electronic control unit (ECU)
7 Temperature regulator
8 Plug connection
9 Injection unit/throttle body
10 CO measuring pipe
11 Lambda probe connector
12 Ignition coil
13 Inlet air preheating relay (in driver's footwell)
14 Engine earth connection
15 Distributor
16 Coolant temperature sender
17 Charcoal filter solenoid valve
18 Vacuum unit for inlet air preheating
19 Air cleaner

1 General information and precautions

General information

The Bosch Mono-Jetronic system is a single-point or throttle body injection system, with a single fuel injector mounted on the inlet manifold, rather like a carburettor (see illustration). Electronic sensors monitor engine speed, load and temperature, and the signals are processed by an Electronic Control Unit (ECU). The Hall-effect ignition system operates independently of the injection system - see Chapter 5B.

The later Bosch Mono-Motronic system is very similar to the earlier Mono-Jetronic system, but is a self-contained engine management system, which controls both the fuel injection and ignition (see illustration). This Chapter deals with the fuel injection system components only - refer to Chapter 5B for details of the ignition system components.

The fuel injection system comprises a fuel tank, an electric fuel pump, a fuel filter, fuel supply and return lines, a throttle body with an integral electronic fuel injector, and an Electronic Control Unit (ECU) together with its associated sensors, actuators and wiring.

The fuel pump delivers a constant supply of fuel through a cartridge filter to the throttle body, at a slightly higher pressure than required - the fuel pressure regulator (integral with the throttle body) maintains a constant fuel pressure at the fuel injector and returns excess fuel to the tank via the return line. This constant flow system also helps to reduce fuel temperature and prevents vaporisation.

The fuel injector is opened and closed by an Electronic Control Unit (ECU), which calculates the injection timing and duration according to engine speed, throttle position and rate of opening, inlet air temperature, coolant temperature, road speed and exhaust gas oxygen content information, received from sensors mounted on the engine.

Inlet air is drawn into the engine through the air cleaner, which contains a renewable paper filter element. The inlet air temperature is regulated by a vacuum operated valve mounted in the air cleaner, which blends air at ambient temperature with hot air, drawn from over the exhaust manifold.

Idle speed control is achieved by an electronic throttle positioning module, mounted on the side of the throttle body. On the Mono-Motronic system, additional idle speed control is achieved through the ignition system, which gives fine control of the idle speed by altering the ignition timing. As a result, manual adjustment of the engine idle speed is not necessary (or possible, without access to dedicated VW test equipment).

To improve cold starting and idling (and fuel economy), an electric heating element is mounted on the underside of the inlet manifold; this prevents fuel vapour condensation when the engine is cold. Power is supplied to the heater by a relay, which is in turn controlled by the ECU.

The exhaust gas oxygen content is constantly monitored by the ECU via the Lambda sensor, which is mounted in the exhaust pipe. The ECU then uses this information to modify the injection timing and duration to maintain the optimum air/fuel ratio - a result of this is that manual adjustment of the idle exhaust CO content is not necessary. In addition, all models are fitted with an exhaust catalyst - see Chapter 4D for details.

In addition, the ECU controls the operation of the activated charcoal filter evaporative loss system - refer to Chapter 4D for further details.

It should be noted that fault diagnosis is only possible with dedicated electronic test equipment. Problems with the system's operation should therefore be referred to a VW dealer for assessment. Once the fault has been identified, the removal/refitting sequences detailed in the following Sections will then allow the appropriate component(s) to be renewed as required.

Note: *Throughout this Chapter, vehicles are frequently referred to by their engine code, rather than by their engine capacity - refer to Chapter 2A for engine code listings.*

Precautions

Warning: Petrol is extremely flammable - great care must be taken when working on any part of the fuel system.

Do not smoke, or allow any naked flames or uncovered light bulbs near the work area. Note that gas powered domestic appliances with pilot flames, such as heaters boilers and tumble-dryers, also present a fire hazard - bear this in mind if you are working in an area where such appliances are present. Always keep a suitable fire extinguisher close to the work area and familiarise yourself with its operation before starting work. Wear eye protection when working on fuel systems and wash off any fuel spilt on bare skin immediately with soap and water. Note that fuel vapour is just as dangerous as liquid fuel; a vessel that has been emptied of liquid fuel will still contain vapour and can be potentially explosive.

Many of the operations described in this Chapter involve the disconnection of fuel lines, which may cause an amount of fuel spillage. Before commencing work, refer to the above Warning and the information in "Safety first!" at the beginning of this manual.

Residual fuel pressure always remain in the fuel system, long after the engine has been switched off. This pressure must be relieved in a controlled manner before work can commence on any component in the fuel system - refer to Section 8 for details.

When working with fuel system components, pay particular attention to cleanliness - dirt entering the fuel system may cause blockages which will lead to poor running.

In the interests of personal safety and equipment protection, many of the procedures in this Chapter suggest that the negative lead be removed from the battery terminal. This firstly eliminates the possibility of accidental short circuits being caused as the vehicle is being worked upon, and secondly prevents damage to electronic components (eg sensors, actuators, ECUs) which are particularly sensitive to the power surges caused by disconnection or reconnection of the wiring harness whilst they are still "live".

It should be noted, however, that the systems described in this Chapter (and Chapter 5B) have a "learning" capability, that allows the system to adapt to the engine's running characteristics as it wears with use. This "learnt" information is lost when the battery is disconnected, and the system may then take a short period of time to "re-learn" the engine's characteristics - this may be manifested (temporarily) as rough idling, reduced throttle response and possibly a slight increase in fuel consumption, until the system re-adapts. The re-adaptation time will depend on how often the vehicle is used and the driving conditions encountered.

2 Air cleaner and inlet system - removal and refitting

Removal

1 Slacken the worm-drive clips and disconnect the air ducting from the air cleaner assembly.

2 Lift off the plastic cap, remove the retaining screws (see illustration) and lift off the throttle body air box, recovering the seal.

3 Disconnect the vacuum hoses from the inlet air temperature regulator vacuum switch, noting their order of fitment.

2.2 Remove the throttle body air box retaining screws (arrowed)

4A

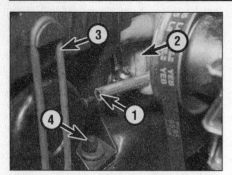

2.4 Air cleaner vacuum hose (1), warm air duct (2), retaining strap (3) and housing location peg (4)

4 Unhook the rubber retaining straps from the lugs on the chassis member **(see illustration)**.
5 Pull the air cleaner towards the engine and detach the air inlet hose.
6 Lift the air cleaner clear of its locating pegs and out of the engine bay.
7 If required, prise open the retaining clips and lift the top cover from the air cleaner. Remove the air cleaner filter element (see Chapter 1A for more details).

Refitting

8 Refit the air cleaner by reversing the removal procedure.

---

3 Inlet air temperature regulator - testing, removal and refitting

Testing

1 This check must be made with the engine cold, and with the air intake temperature below 40°C (104°F). Detach and remove the air cleaner cover from the air cleaner body, and extract the cleaner element.
2 Check that the air regulator flap in the air cleaner body moves freely, and when cold with the engine stopped, shuts off the warm air channel **(see illustration)**. Start the engine, allow it to idle, then check to see that the flap has moved to close off the cold air channel.

4.2 Accelerator cable-to-pedal attachment (arrowed)

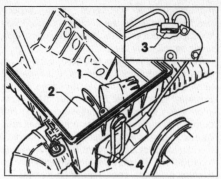

3.2 Temperature regulator operation check

1 Warm air channel	3 Temperature regulator
2 Cold air channel	4 Vacuum unit

3 If the flap does not operate as specified, detach the temperature regulator lines and connect them together. The vacuum unit is faulty if the warm air channel remains shut. If the flap seals off the cold air channel, the temperature regulator is at fault. Renew as necessary.
4 When the engine is running, the position of the regulator flap is set by the temperature regulator. The regulator should be open and the cool air channel closed off when the air temperature is under 35°C (95°F). When the air temperature rises above 45°C (113°F), the regulator should close and the cold air channel should open.

Removal

5 Disconnect the vacuum hoses from the temperature regulator, noting their locations.
6 Remove the throttle body air box/air cleaner, as described in Section 2.
7 Prise off the metal retaining plate and remove the temperature regulator from inside the throttle body air box **(see illustrations)**. Recover the gasket.

Refitting

8 Refit the regulator by reversing the removal procedure.

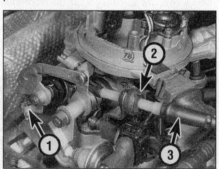

4.3a Accelerator cable-to-throttle housing connection

1 Inner cable and nipple/retaining clip	2 Cable adjuster and support
	3 Outer cable

3.7a Temperature regulator metal retaining plate

3.7b Temperature regulator unit in throttle body air box

---

4 Accelerator cable - removal, refitting and adjustment

Removal

1 Remove the lower facia panels on the driver's side to allow access to the accelerator cable attachment to the pedal.
2 Detach the cable from the pedal arm by pushing through the rubber bush **(see illustration)**.
3 Open and support the bonnet. Disconnect the cable at the throttle valve end by prising free the cable retainer from the quadrant, then disengaging the inner cable nipple from the quadrant **(see illustrations)**. Pull the outer

4.3b Release the inner cable retainer clip (arrowed) . . .

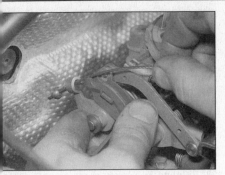

4.3c . . . to disengage the nipple from the quadrant

4.6 Accelerator cable adjuster clip and ferrule

cable upwards to disengage it from the support bracket. Note that the U-shaped clip in front of the support bracket sets the cable adjustment, and if this is to be removed, first measure its fitted position as a guide to adjustment when refitting the cable.

4 Note the routing of the cable, and then withdraw it through the bulkhead and remove it from the engine side.

Refitting

5 Refitting is a reversal of the removal procedure. When refitted, check that the throttle valve opens and closes fully, and operates freely throughout its movement.

Adjustment

Manual transmission models

6 The adjuster clip must be positioned on the ferrule so that the throttle is fully open when the accelerator pedal is fully depressed (see illustration). When the pedal is fully released, the inner cable clearance must not exceed 1.0 mm (0.04 in).

Automatic transmission models

7 Insert a block of wood 15 mm (0.6 in) thick between the accelerator pedal and the stop (see illustration). At the throttle valve end of

the cable, pull the cable sleeve to fully open the throttle, then lock it in this position by inserting the adjuster clip. Release the pedal and remove the spacer. Check the kickdown switch for satisfactory operation by connecting up a multimeter to the kickdown switch terminals. With the accelerator pedal in the fully-released position, the reading should be infinity. Depress the pedal slowly down to the kickdown pressure point (just clear of the stop). The resistance reading must now be zero ohms.

5 Fuel injection system components - removal and refitting

Note: *Observe the precautions in Section 1 before working on any component in the fuel system.*

Throttle body

Removal

1 Refer to Section 2 and remove the air cleaner/throttle body air box.

2 Refer to Section 8 and depressurise the fuel system, then disconnect the battery negative lead and position it away from the terminal.

Note: *If the vehicle has a security-coded radio, check that you have a copy of the code number before disconnecting the battery. Refer to your VW dealer if in doubt.*

3 Disconnect the fuel supply and return hoses from the ports on the side of the throttle body. Note the arrows that denote the direction of fuel flow, and mark the hoses accordingly (see illustration).

4 Unplug the wiring harness from the throttle body at the connectors, labelling them to aid correct refitting later.

5 Refer to Section 4 and disconnect the accelerator cable from the throttle body.

6 Remove the through-bolts and lift the throttle body away from the inlet manifold, recovering the gasket.

Refitting

7 Refitting is a reversal of removal; renew all gaskets where appropriate. On completion, check and if necessary adjust the accelerator cable. If the lower section of the throttle body has been renewed (with integral throttle potentiometer) in vehicles with electronic automatic transmission control, the new potentiometer must be matched to the transmission ECU; refer to a VW dealer for advice as this operation requires access to dedicated test equipment.

Fuel injector

Note: *If a faulty injector is suspected, before removing or condemning the injector, it is worth trying the effect of one of the proprietary injector-cleaning treatments which can be added to the fuel tank.*

Removal

8 Refer to Section 2 and remove the air cleaner/throttle body air box.

9 Refer to Section 8 and depressurise the fuel system. Disconnect the battery negative lead and position it away from the terminal (see paragraph 2).

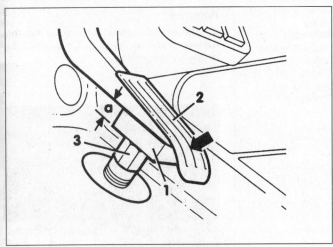

4.7 Accelerator cable adjustment – automatic transmission models

1 *Spacer*   2 *Pedal*   3 *Stop*   a = 15 mm

5.3 Throttle body fuel supply and return ports

10 Unplug the wiring harness from the injector at the connector(s), labelling them to aid correct refitting later.

11 Remove the screw and lift off the injector retaining cap/inlet air temperature sensor housing.

12 Lift the injector out of the throttle body, recovering the O-ring seals **(see illustration)**.

13 Check the injector electrical resistance using a multimeter and compare the result with the Specifications.

Refitting

14 Refit the injector by reversing the removal procedure, renewing all O-ring seals. Tighten the retaining screw to the specified torque.

Inlet air temperature sensor

15 The inlet air temperature sensor is an integral part of the injector retaining cap. Removal is as described in the previous sub-Section. Check its electrical resistance using a multimeter with a resistance measurement function **(refer to illustration 5.12)**.

Fuel pressure regulator

Removal

16 If the operation of the fuel pressure regulator is in question, dismantle the unit as described below, then check the cleanliness and integrity of the internal components.

17 Remove the air cleaner/throttle body air box, with reference to Section 2.

18 Refer to Section 8 and depressurise the fuel system. Disconnect the battery negative lead and position it away from the terminal (see paragraph 2).

19 With reference to the relevant sub-Section, remove the screw and lift off the inlet air temperature/injector cap.

20 Slacken and withdraw the retaining screws and lift off the fuel pressure regulator retaining frame **(refer to illustration 5.12)**.

21 Lift out the upper cover, spring and diaphragm.

22 Clean all the components thoroughly, then inspect the diaphragm for cracks or splits - renew it if necessary.

Refitting

23 Reassemble the pressure regulator by reversing the removal procedure.

Throttle valve positioning module

Removal

24 Disconnect the battery negative lead and position it away from the terminal (see paragraph 2). Remove the air cleaner/throttle body air box, with reference to Section 2.

25 Refer to Section 4 and disconnect the accelerator cable from the throttle body.

26 Unplug the connector from the side of the throttle valve positioning module **(see illustration)**.

27 Remove the retaining screws and lift the module together with the accelerator cable outer mounting bracket away from the throttle body.

Refitting

28 Refitting is a reversal of removal. Note that if a new module has been fitted, the adjustment of the idle switch will need to be checked - refer to a VW dealer for advice as this operation requires access to dedicated test equipment.

Throttle valve potentiometer

29 Refer to the relevant sub-Section and remove the throttle body. The throttle valve potentiometer is an integral part of the lower section of the throttle body, and cannot be renewed separately.

30 Where a new lower throttle body (with throttle potentiometer) has been fitted in vehicles with electronic automatic transmission control, the potentiometer must be matched to the transmission ECU; refer to a VW dealer for advice as this operation requires access to dedicated test equipment.

Idle switch

31 Refer to the relevant sub-Section and remove the throttle valve positioning module. The idle switch is an integral part of the module and cannot be renewed separately.

32 Where a new throttle valve positioning module has been fitted, the adjustment of the idle switch will need to be checked - refer to a VW dealer for advice as this operation requires access to dedicated test equipment.

Lambda sensor

Removal

33 The lambda sensor is threaded into the exhaust manifold. Refer to Chapter 4D for details on its operation.

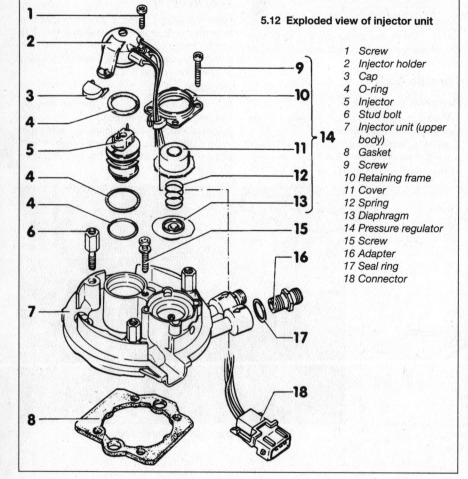

5.12 Exploded view of injector unit

1 Screw
2 Injector holder
3 Cap
4 O-ring
5 Injector
6 Stud bolt
7 Injector unit (upper body)
8 Gasket
9 Screw
10 Retaining frame
11 Cover
12 Spring
13 Diaphragm
14 Pressure regulator
15 Screw
16 Adapter
17 Seal ring
18 Connector

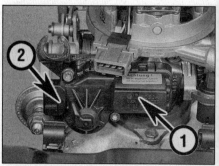

5.26 Throttle valve positioner unit (1) and wiring connector (2)

34 Disconnect the battery negative lead and position it away from the terminal (see paragraph 2). Unplug the wiring harness from the lambda sensor at the connector.

35 Note: *As a flying lead remains connected to the sensor after it has been disconnected, if the correct size spanner is not available, a slotted socket will be required to remove the sensor.* Working under the vehicle, slacken and withdraw the sensor, taking care to avoid damaging the sensor probe as it is removed.

Refitting

36 Apply a little anti-seize grease to the sensor threads only - keep the probe tip clean.
37 Refit the sensor to its housing, tightening it to the correct torque. Restore the harness connection. Note that the type of lambda sensor fitted depends on vehicle specification - if the sensor is being renewed, be sure to obtain the correct part.

Coolant temperature sensor

Removal

38 Disconnect the battery negative lead and position it away from the terminal (see paragraph 2). Refer to Chapter 1A and drain approximately one quarter of the coolant from the engine.
39 The sensor is mounted at the top coolant outlet elbow, at the front of the cylinder head.
40 Unscrew/unclip the sensor from its housing and recover the sealing washer(s) and O-ring - be prepared for an amount of coolant loss.

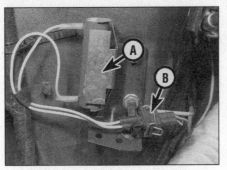

5.42 Series resistor (A) and wiring connector (B)

Refitting

41 Refit the sensor by reversing the removal procedure, using new sealing washers and rings where appropriate. Refer to Chapter 1A or *"Weekly checks"* and top-up the cooling system.

Injector series resistor - early models only

Removal

42 Detach the wiring connector **(see illustration)**.
43 Undo the retaining nuts, and remove the resistor from the suspension turret.

Refitting

44 Refit in the reverse order to removal.

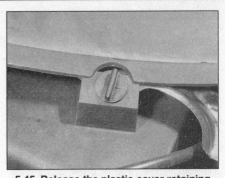

5.45 Release the plastic cover retaining clip by turning through 90°

Electronic control unit (ECU)

Removal

45 This unit is located in cavity to the rear of the bulkhead. To gain access to it, remove the plastic cover by turning the retaining clips a quarter of a turn **(see illustration)**, and then prise the cover free from the top of the bulkhead.
46 Check that the ignition is switched off (take out the key). Undo the single retaining nut, then withdraw the unit from the clevis type securing posts **(see illustrations)**.
47 Detach the wiring multi-plug(s) from the ECU, then remove it from the cavity, complete with its support plate. The support plate can be detached from the unit retaining lugs after undoing the single retaining screw **(see illustrations)**.

4A

5.46a Undo the retaining nut . . .

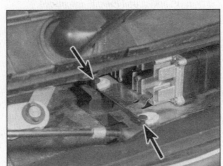

5.46b . . . and detach the ECU support plate from the location posts (arrowed)

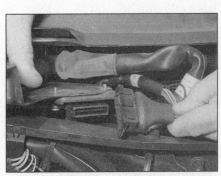

5.47a Disconnect the TCI-H multi-plug (early models only) . . .

5.47b . . . and the ECU multi-plug

5.47c Undo the screw (arrowed) . . .

5.47d . . . and disengage the ECU from the retaining lugs (arrowed)

Refitting

48 Refit in the reverse order to removal.

Inlet manifold pre-heater

49 This device is located on the underside of the inlet manifold, and access to it for removal is best obtained by first removing the manifold, as described in Section 9.
50 Detach the wiring connector, undo the retaining screws, and remove the pre-heater unit from the manifold **(see illustration)**. Remove the gasket.
51 Refit in the reverse order of removal. Ensure that the mating surfaces are clean, and use a new gasket.

5.50 Inlet manifold pre-heater

6 Fuel pump and fuel gauge sender unit - removal and refitting

Note: *Observe the precautions in Section 1 before working on any component in the fuel system.*

 Warning: Avoid direct skin contact with fuel - wear protective clothing and gloves when handling fuel system components. Ensure that the work area is well ventilated to prevent the build-up of fuel vapour - do not carry out this procedure over an inspection pit.

General information

1 The fuel pump and gauge sender unit are combined in one assembly, which is mounted

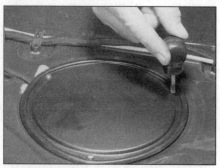

6.5 Slacken and withdraw the access hatch screws from the floorpan

6.6 Unplug the wiring harness connector from the pump/sender unit

on the top of the fuel tank. Access is via a hatch provided in the load space floor. The unit protrudes into the fuel tank and its removal involves exposing the contents of the tank to the atmosphere.

Removal

2 Depressurise the fuel system (Section 8).
3 Ensure that the vehicle is parked on a level surface. Disconnect the battery negative lead and position it away from the terminal. **Note:** *If the vehicle has a security-coded radio, check that you have a copy of the code number before disconnecting the battery. Refer to your VW dealer if in doubt.*
4 Refer to Chapter 11 as necessary and remove the trim from the load space floor.
5 Slacken and withdraw the access hatch screws and lift the hatch away from the floorpan **(see illustration)**.
6 Unplug the wiring harness connector from the pump/sender unit **(see illustration)**.
7 Pad the area around the supply and return fuel hoses with rags to absorb any spilt fuel, then slacken the hose clips and remove them from the ports at the sender unit. Observe the supply and return arrow markings on the ports - label the fuel hoses accordingly to ensure correct refitting later.
8 Unscrew the plastic securing ring and lift it out. Use a pair of water pump pliers to grip and rotate the plastic securing ring.
9 Turn the pump/sender unit to the left to release it from its bayonet fitting and lift it out, holding it above the level of the fuel in the tank until the excess fuel has drained out. Recover the rubber seal.

10 Remove the pump/sender unit from the vehicle, and lay it on an absorbent card or rag. Inspect the float at the end of the sender unit swinging arm for punctures and fuel ingress - renew the unit if it appears damaged.
11 The fuel pick-up incorporated in the assembly is spring-loaded to ensure that it always draws fuel from the lowest part of the tank. Check that the pick-up is free to move under spring tension with respect to the sender unit body.
12 Inspect the rubber seal from the fuel tank aperture for signs of fatigue - renew it if necessary.
13 Inspect the sender unit wiper and track, clean off any dirt and debris that may have accumulated, and look for breaks in the track.

Refitting

14 Refit the sender unit by following the removal procedure in reverse, noting the following points:
a) *The arrow markings on the sender unit body and the fuel tank must be aligned **(see illustration)**.*
b) *Smear the tank aperture rubber seal with clean fuel before fitting it in position.*
c) *Reconnect the fuel hoses to the correct ports - observe the direction-of-flow arrow markings **(see illustration)**.*

7 Fuel tank - removal and refitting

Note: *Observe the precautions in Section 1 before working on any component in the fuel system.*

Removal

1 Before the tank can be removed, it must be drained of as much fuel as possible. As no drain plug is provided, it is preferable to carry out this operation with the tank almost empty.
2 Disconnect the battery negative lead and position it away from the terminal. **Note:** *If the vehicle has a security-coded radio, check that you have a copy of the code number before disconnecting the battery. Refer to your VW dealer if in doubt.* Using a hand pump or siphon, remove any remaining fuel from the bottom of the tank.

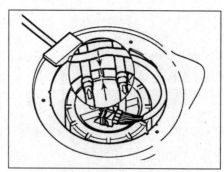

6.14a Arrow markings on the sender unit body and the fuel tank must be aligned

6.14b Reconnect the fuel hoses to the correct ports - observe the direction-of-flow arrow markings

3 Refer to Section 6 and carry out the following:
 a) *Disconnect the wiring harness from the top of the pump/sender unit at the multiway connector.*
 b) *Disconnect the fuel supply and return hoses from the pump/sender unit.*

4 Position a trolley jack under the centre of the tank. Insert a block of wood between the jack head and the tank to prevent damage to the tank surface. Raise the jack until it just takes the weight of the tank.

5 Working inside the right-hand rear wheelarch, slacken and withdraw the screws that secure the tank filler neck inside of the wheelarch. Open the fuel filler flap and peel the rubber sealing flange away from the bodywork **(see illustrations)**.

6 Remove the retaining bolts from the tank securing straps **(see illustrations)**, keeping one hand on the tank to steady it, as it is released from its mountings.

7 Lower the jack and tank away from the underside of the vehicle; disconnect the charcoal canister vent pipe from the port on the filler neck as it is exposed. Locate the earthing strap and disconnect it from the terminal at the filler neck.

8 If the tank is contaminated with sediment or water, remove the fuel pump/sender unit (see Section 6) and swill the tank out with clean fuel. The tank is injection-moulded from a synthetic material and if damaged, it should be renewed. However, in certain cases it may be possible to have small leaks or minor damage repaired. Seek the advice of a specialist before attempting to repair the fuel tank.

Refitting

9 Refitting is the reverse of the removal procedure noting the following points:
 a) *When lifting the tank back into position, make sure the mounting rubbers are correctly positioned, and take care to ensure none of the hoses get trapped between the tank and vehicle body.*
 b) *Ensure that all pipes and hoses are correctly routed and securely held in position with their retaining clips.*
 c) *Reconnect the earth strap to its terminal on the filler neck.*
 d) *Tighten the tank retaining strap bolts to the specified torque.*

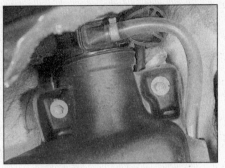

7.5a Filler neck retaining bolts

 e) *On completion, refill the tank with fuel and exhaustively check for signs of leakage prior to taking the vehicle out on the road.*

8 Fuel injection system - depressurisation

Note: *Observe the precautions in Section 1 before working on any component in the fuel system.*

 Warning: The following procedure will merely relieve the pressure in the fuel system - remember that fuel will still be present in the system components and take precautions accordingly before disconnecting any of them.

1 The fuel system referred to in this Section is defined as the tank-mounted fuel pump, the fuel filter, the fuel injector, the throttle body-mounted fuel pressure regulator, and the metal pipes and flexible hoses of the fuel lines between these components. All these contain fuel which will be under pressure while the engine is running and/or while the ignition is switched on. The pressure will remain for some time after the ignition has been switched off, and must be relieved before any of these components are disturbed for servicing work. Ideally, the engine should be allowed to cool completely before work commences.

2 Refer to Chapter 12 and locate the fuel pump relay or fuel pump fuse. Remove the fuse or relay, then crank the engine for a few seconds. The engine may fire and run for a

7.5b Remove the filler neck retaining ring and grommet

while, but continue cranking until it stops. The fuel injector should have opened enough times during cranking to considerably reduce the line fuel pressure.

3 Disconnect the battery negative lead, and position the lead away from the battery. **Note:** *If the vehicle has a security-coded radio, check that you have a copy of the code number before disconnecting the battery. Refer to your VW dealer if in doubt.*

4 Place a suitable container beneath the relevant connection/union to be disconnected, and have a large rag ready to soak up any escaping fuel not being caught by the container.

5 Slowly loosen the connection or union nut (as applicable) to avoid a sudden release of pressure, and position the rag around the connection to catch any fuel spray which may be expelled. Once the pressure has been released, disconnect the fuel line. Insert plugs to minimise fuel loss and prevent the entry of dirt into the fuel system.

9 Inlet manifold - removal and refitting

Note: *Observe the precautions in Section 1 before working on any component in the fuel system.*

Removal

1 Disconnect the battery negative lead and position it away from the terminal. **Note:** *If the vehicle has a security-coded radio, check that*

4A

7.6a Fuel tank strap retaining bolts (front)

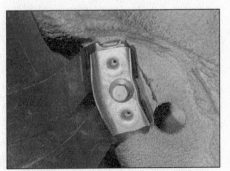

7.6b Fuel tank strap retaining bolt (right-hand rear)

7.6c Fuel tank strap retaining bolt (left-hand rear)

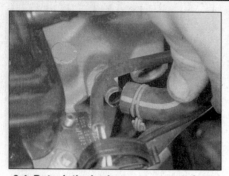

9.4 Detach the brake servo vacuum hose from the inlet manifold

9.6a Disconnect the warm air duct . . .

9.6b . . . and remove the collector plate

you have a copy of the code number before disconnecting the battery. Refer to your VW dealer if in doubt. Refer to Chapter 1A and drain the coolant from the engine.

2 With reference to Section 5, remove the throttle body from the inlet manifold. Recover and discard the gasket and where applicable, remove the intermediate flange.

3 Slacken the clips and remove the coolant hoses from the inlet manifold.

4 Refer to Chapter 9 and disconnect the brake servo vacuum hose from the port on the inlet manifold (see illustration).

5 Disconnect the harness wiring from the inlet manifold heater at the connector.

6 From the underside of the manifold, unbolt and detach the warm air duct and the CO measuring pipe where it is attached to the support bracket on the manifold (see illustrations).

7 Progressively slacken and unscrew the manifold retaining nuts/bolts, and withdraw the manifold from the cylinder head (see illustrations). Remove the manifold gasket and the coolant passage seal.

8 If required, remove the retaining screws and lift out the manifold heater unit (refer to Section 5).

Refitting

9 Refitting is the reverse of the removal procedure, noting the following points:

a) Ensure that the manifold and cylinder head mating surfaces are clean and dry. Install the manifold with a new gasket and seal (see illustrations), and tighten its

9.6c Unbolt and remove the CO measuring pipe and the support bracket

retaining nuts/bolts to the specified torque setting.

b) Ensure that all relevant hoses are reconnected to their original positions and are securely held (where necessary) by their retaining clips.

c) Refit the throttle body as described in Section 5.

d) On completion, refill the cooling system as described in Chapter 1A.

10 Fuel injection system - testing and adjustment

1 If a fault appears in the fuel injection system, first ensure that all the system wiring connectors are securely connected and free of corrosion. Then ensure that the fault is not

9.7a Unscrew and remove the inlet manifold and inlet-to-exhaust manifold retaining nuts and bolts . . .

due to poor maintenance; ie, check that the air cleaner filter element is clean, the spark plugs are in good condition and correctly gapped, the cylinder compression pressures are correct, the ignition timing is correct and the engine breather hoses are clear and undamaged, referring to Chapter 1A, Chapter 2A and Chapter 5B for further information.

2 If these checks fail to reveal the cause of the problem, the vehicle should be taken to a suitably-equipped VW dealer for testing. A diagnostic connector is incorporated in the engine management system wiring harness into which a dedicated electronic test equipment can be plugged. The test equipment is capable of "interrogating" the engine management system ECU electronically and accessing its internal fault log. In this manner, faults can be pinpointed quickly and simply, even if their occurrence is

9.7b . . . and remove the inlet manifold

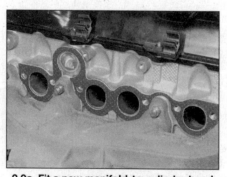

9.9a Fit a new manifold-to-cylinder head gasket . . .

9.9b . . . and a new coolant passage seal

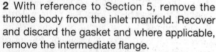
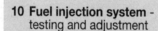

intermittent. Testing all the system components individually in an attempt to locate the fault by elimination is a time-consuming operation that is unlikely to be fruitful (particularly if the fault occurs dynamically) and carries high risk of damage to the ECU's internal components.

3 Experienced home mechanics equipped with an accurate tachometer and a carefully-calibrated exhaust gas analyser may be able to check the exhaust gas CO content and the engine idle speed; if these are found to be out of specification, then the vehicle must be taken to a suitably-equipped VW dealer for assessment. Neither the air/fuel mixture (exhaust gas CO content) nor the engine idle speed are manually adjustable; incorrect test results indicate a fault within the fuel injection system.

11 Unleaded petrol - general information and usage

Note: *The information given in this Chapter is correct at the time of writing, and applies only to petrols currently available in the UK. Check with a VW dealer, as more up-to-date information may be available. If travelling abroad, consult one of the motoring organisations (or a similar authority) for advice on the petrols available and their suitability for your vehicle.*

1 The fuel recommended by VW is given in the Specifications of this Chapter.

2 All vehicles equipped with a catalytic converter ("catalyst" or "cat") should be run on unleaded petrol **only**. Use of leaded petrol will damage the catalytic converter.

3 RON and MON are different testing standards; RON stands for Research Octane Number (also written as RM), while MON stands for Motor Octane Number (also written as MM).

4A

Notes

Chapter 4 Part B:
Fuel system - multi-point petrol injection

Contents

Degrees of difficulty

Easy, suitable for novice with little experience	Fairly easy, suitable for beginner with some experience	Fairly difficult, suitable for competent DIY mechanic	Difficult, suitable for experienced DIY mechanic	Very difficult, suitable for expert DIY or professional 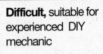

Specifications

System type

Engine codes PB, PF and 2E	Digifant
Engine codes ADY and AGG	Simos

Fuel system data

Fuel pump type	Electric, immersed in fuel tank
Fuel pump delivery rate	1100 cm^3 / min (battery voltage of 12.6 V)
Regulated fuel pressure	2.5 bar
Engine idle speed (not adjustable on Simos system)	750 to 850 rpm
Idle CO content:	
Engine code PB	0.5 to 1.5%
Engine codes PF and 2E	0.3 to 1.1%
Engine codes ADY and AGG	N/A
Injector electrical resistance	15 to 20 ohms

Recommended fuel

Minimum octane rating:	
All engines except code PB (non-catalyst)	95 RON
Engine code PB (non-catalyst)	98 RON

Torque wrench settings

	Nm	lbf ft
Fuel pressure regulator bolts	15	11
Fuel rail screws/bolts:		
Except engine codes ADY and AGG	10	7
Engine codes ADY and AGG:		
M6 bolts	10	7
M8 bolts	20	15
Injector inserts (engine codes PB and PF only)	20	15
Inlet manifold to cylinder head	25	18
Inlet/exhaust manifold support bracket:		
Engine codes PB and PF	15	11
Engine code 2E	20	15
Lambda sensor	50	37
Stabilisation valve bracket (to inlet manifold)	10	7
Throttle damper nut	20	15
Throttle housing through-bolts (M6 bolts)	10	7
Throttle housing through-bolts (M8 bolts)	20	15
Warm air collector plate:		
Engine codes PB, PF and 2E	20	15
Engine codes ADY and AGG	30	22

4B

1 General information and precautions

General information

The Bosch Digifant and Simos systems are self-contained engine management systems, which control both the fuel injection and ignition. This Chapter deals with the fuel system components only - see Chapter 5B for details of the ignition system.

The fuel injection system comprises a fuel tank, an electric fuel pump, a fuel filter, fuel supply and return lines, a throttle housing, a fuel rail, a fuel pressure regulator, four electronic fuel injectors, and an Electronic Control Unit (ECU) together with its associated sensors, actuators and wiring. The component layout varies from system to system - refer to the relevant Section for details.

The fuel pump delivers a constant supply of fuel through a cartridge filter to the fuel rail, at a slightly higher pressure than required - the fuel pressure regulator maintains a constant fuel pressure to the fuel injectors and returns excess fuel to the tank via the return line. This constant flow system also helps to reduce fuel temperature and prevents vaporisation.

The fuel injectors are opened and closed by an Electronic Control Unit (ECU), which calculates the injection timing and duration according to engine speed, crankshaft position, throttle position and rate of opening, inlet manifold depression (or inlet air volume flow rate, depending on system type), inlet air temperature, coolant temperature, road speed and exhaust gas oxygen content information, received from sensors mounted on and around the engine. Refer to the relevant Section for specific details of the components utilised in each system.

Inlet air is drawn into the engine through the air cleaner, which contains a renewable paper filter element. On Digifant systems, the inlet air temperature is regulated by a vacuum-operated valve mounted in the air cleaner, which blends air at ambient temperature with hot air, drawn from over the exhaust manifold. On the Simos system, inlet air temperature is monitored by a sensor in the air cleaner housing.

Idle speed control is achieved partly by an electronic throttle valve positioning module, on the side of the throttle housing and partly by the ignition system, which gives fine control of the idle speed by altering the ignition timing. On the Digifant system up to July 1992, idle and ignition timing basic settings are adjustable - see Section 5 and Chapter 5B.

The exhaust gas oxygen content is constantly monitored by the ECU via the Lambda sensor, which is mounted in the exhaust pipe. The ECU then uses this information to modify the injection timing and duration to maintain the optimum air/fuel ratio. In addition, most models are fitted with an exhaust catalyst - see Chapter 4D.

Where fitted, the ECU controls the operation of the activated charcoal filter evaporative loss system - refer to Chapter 4D for further details.

It should be noted that fault diagnosis of all the engine management systems described in this Chapter is only possible with dedicated electronic test equipment. Problems with the systems operation should therefore be referred to a VAG dealer for assessment. Once the fault has been identified, the removal/refitting sequences detailed in the following Sections will then allow the appropriate component(s) to be renewed as required.

Note: *Throughout this Chapter, vehicles are frequently referred to by their engine code, rather than by engine capacity - refer to Chapter 2A for engine code listings.*

Precautions

 Warning: Petrol is extremely flammable - great care must be taken when working on any part of the fuel system.

Do not smoke, or allow any naked flames or uncovered light bulbs near the work area. Note that gas powered domestic appliances with pilot flames, such as heaters, boilers and tumble-dryers, also present a fire hazard - bear this in mind if you are working in an area where such appliances are present. Always keep a suitable fire extinguisher to hand and familiarise yourself with its operation before starting work. Wear eye protection when working on fuel systems and wash off any fuel spilt on bare skin immediately with soap and water. Note that fuel vapour is just as dangerous as liquid fuel; a vessel that has been emptied of liquid fuel will still contain vapour and can be potentially explosive.

Many of the operations described in this Chapter involve the disconnection of fuel lines, which may cause some fuel spillage. Before commencing work, refer to the above Warning and the information in "Safety first!" at the start of this manual.

Residual fuel pressure always remain in the fuel system, long after the engine has been switched off. This pressure must be relieved in a controlled manner before work can commence on any component in the fuel system - refer to Section 10 for details.

When working with fuel system components, pay particular attention to cleanliness - dirt entering the fuel system may cause blockages which will lead to poor running.

In the interests of personal safety and equipment protection, many of the procedures in this Chapter suggest that the negative cable be removed from the battery terminal. This firstly eliminates the possibility of accidental short-circuits being caused as the vehicle is being worked upon, and secondly prevents damage to electronic components (eg sensors, actuators, ECUs) which are very sensitive to the power surges caused by disconnection or reconnection of the wiring harness whilst they are still "live".

It should be noted, however, that the engine management systems described in this Chapter (and Chapter 5B) have a "learning" capability, that allows the system to adapt to the engine's running characteristics as it wears with normal use. This "learnt" information is lost when the battery is disconnected and on reconnection, the system will then take a short period of time to "re-learn" the engine's characteristics - this may be manifested (temporarily) as rough idling, reduced throttle response and possibly a slight increase in fuel consumption, until the system re-adapts. The re-adaptation time will depend on how often the vehicle is used and the driving conditions encountered.

2 Air cleaner and inlet system - removal and refitting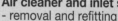

Removal

1 Slacken the worm-drive clips and disconnect the air ducting from the air cleaner assembly.

2 Where applicable, slacken the clip and disconnect the warm air duct from the base of the air cleaner.

3 Refer to Section 6 or 7 as applicable and remove the airflow meter from the air cleaner. **Caution: The airflow meter is a delicate component - handle it carefully.**

4 Disconnect the vacuum hoses from the inlet air temperature regulator vacuum switch, noting their order of fitment.

5 Unhook the rubber straps from the lugs on the chassis member.

6 Pull the air cleaner towards the engine and detach the air inlet hose.

7 Lift the air cleaner clear of its locating pegs and out of the engine bay. Recover the rubber retaining straps.

8 If required, prise open the retaining clips and lift the top cover from the air cleaner. Remove the air cleaner filter element (see Chapter 1A for more details).

Refitting

9 Refit the air cleaner by reversing the removal procedure.

3 Inlet air temperature regulation system - general information and component renewal

Note: *This system is only fitted to vehicles with the Digifant engine management system (engine codes PB, PF and 2E).*

General information

1 The inlet air regulation system consists of a temperature-controlled vacuum switch, mounted in the air cleaner housing, a vacuum-operated flap valve, several lengths of interconnecting vacuum hose, and a warm air hose from the exhaust manifold. The switch senses the temperature of the inlet air, and opens when a preset lower limit is reached. It then directs the manifold vacuum to the flap valve which opens, allowing warm air drawn from around the exhaust manifold to blend with the inlet air.

Testing

2 Detach the vacuum hose from the temperature regulator vacuum unit.
3 Detach and lift the top cover from the air cleaner body, then extract the element. Check that the air regulator flap in the lower body is shutting off the warm air channel.
4 Attach a suitable length of hose to the vacuum unit hose, and apply suction through it. Check that the regulator flap operates freely and shuts off the cool air channel.
5 Start the engine, and run it at idle speed. Connect the extension tube to the brass pipe, and check the temperature regulator operation. Depending on the temperature of the regulator, the regulator flap position after twenty seconds should be either: (a) cool air channel closed off when the temperature is under 20°C (68°F), or (b) warm air channel closed off when the temperature is 30°C (86°F) or over.

Component renewal

Temperature switch

6 With reference to Section 2, release the clips and remove the top cover from the air cleaner.
7 Disconnect the vacuum hoses from the temperature switch, noting their order of connection to ensure correct refitting.
8 Prise the metal retaining clip off the temperature switch ports, then press the switch body through into the top of the air cleaner. Recover the gasket.
9 Refitting is a reversal of removal.

Flap valve

10 The flap valve is integral with the lower section of the air cleaner and cannot be renewed separately.

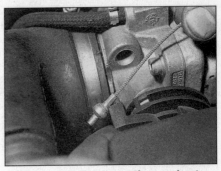

4.2a At the throttle housing, prise off the clip . . .

4 Accelerator cable - removal, refitting and adjustment

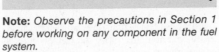

Note: *Observe the precautions in Section 1 before working on any component in the fuel system.*

Removal

1 Remove the air cleaner as described in Section 2.
2 At the throttle housing, prise off the clip and disconnect the accelerator cable inner from the throttle valve spindle **(see illustrations)**.
3 Remove the metal clip and extract the cable outer from the mounting bracket **(see illustrations)**.
4 Refer to Chapter 11 and remove the facia trim panels from underneath the steering column.
5 Depress the accelerator pedal slightly, then unclip the accelerator cable end from the pedal extension lever.
6 At the point where the cable passes through the bulkhead, unscrew the cap from the two-piece grommet so that the cable can move freely.
7 Release the cable from its securing clips and guide it out through the bulkhead grommet.

4.3a Remove the metal clip . . .

4.2b . . . and disconnect the accelerator cable inner from the throttle valve

Refitting

8 Refit the accelerator cable by reversing the removal procedure.

Adjustment

Vehicles with manual transmission

9 At the throttle housing, fix the position of the cable outer in its mounting bracket by inserting the metal clip in one of the locating slots, such that when the accelerator is depressed fully, the throttle valve is held wide open to its end stop.

Vehicles with automatic transmission

10 On vehicles with automatic transmission, place a block of wood 15 mm thick between the underside of the accelerator pedal and the stop on the floorpan, then hold the accelerator pedal down onto the block of wood.
11 At the throttle housing, fix the position of the cable outer in its bracket by inserting the metal clip in one of the locating slots, such that when the accelerator is depressed fully (onto the block of wood), the throttle valve is held wide open to its end stop.
12 Remove the block of wood and release the accelerator pedal. Refer to Chapter 7B and using a continuity tester, check that the kick-down switch contacts close as the accelerator pedal is depressed past the full throttle position, just before it contacts the stop on the floorpan.

4.3b . . . and extract the cable outer from the bracket (engine code 2E shown)

4B

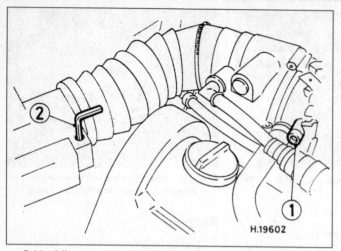

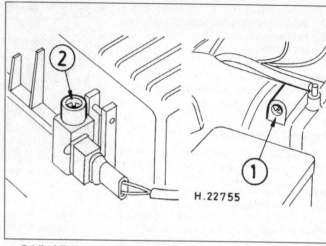

5.14a Idle speed (1) and CO/mixture (2) adjustment points - engine codes PB and PF

5.14b Idle speed (1) and CO/mixture (2) adjustment points - engine code 2E

5 Digifant system - idle speed and mixture (CO) checks and adjustments

Note: *On the Digifant system up to July 1992, the idle speed and mixture should not normally require adjustment on a regular basis. In any case, manual adjustment only provides a basic setting, from which the Digifant control unit can provide settings suitable for all running conditions. The idle speed and mixture cannot be adjusted on vehicles with the Digifant system after August 1992, or those fitted with the Simos engine management system.*

1 A tachometer and exhaust gas analyser will be required for the following checks. Where adjustment is necessary, a key to fit the adjuster screws will be required.
2 The engine must be at normal operating temperature.
3 All electrical components must be switched off, and the radiator cooling fan must not be running during the adjustment.
4 The exhaust system must be in good condition.
5 The ignition timing must be correct - see Chapter 5B.
6 Where fitted, the lambda control must be operating correctly.
7 On automatic transmission models, the kickdown function must be operating in a satisfactory manner.
8 The throttle valve must be at its normal idle position.
9 If the injector pipes have been detached, the engine must be run at 3000 rpm several times, then allowed to idle for at least two minutes prior to making adjustments.
10 The air conditioning system (where fitted) must be switched off.
11 With the ignition switched off, connect up a tachometer and an exhaust gas analyser in accordance with the equipment manufacturer's

instructions. The exhaust gas analyser is fitted to the exhaust tail pipe, except on the PF engine model, where if a suitable connector is available, it can be attached to the CO measuring pipe at the manifold end.
12 Disconnect the crankcase ventilation hose from the pressure regulating valve, and plug the hose.
13 Start the engine, and allow it to run at idle speed for one minute, then pull the blue connector from the coolant temperature sender. Open and close the throttle three times. Each time it is opened, the engine speed must exceed 3000 rpm.
14 Allow the engine to idle again, and now check the idle speed and the CO content. If adjustment is required, remove the tamperproof plug(s) (where fitted) and using a suitable key, turn the idle speed screw and the CO adjuster to obtain the specified settings **(see illustrations)**.
15 Re-attach the temperature sender connector, then open the throttle sharply another three times (exceeding 3000 rpm), then allow the engine to run at idle speed again, and recheck that the idle speed and CO content settings are as specified.
16 When the crankcase ventilation hose is reattached, the CO content may increase. This is most probably due to the nature of the adjustment procedure. A journey in the vehicle will reduce the fuel build-up in the engine oil, and the CO content will return to normal. Further adjustment should not therefore be required.
17 On catalyst engines only, check the lambda control. Ensure that the blue temperature sender plug is reconnected, then pull the throttle housing pressure regulator hose free, and keep it closed off. The CO content reading should momentarily increase, then drop back to normal.
18 If the idle speed and CO content adjustments are satisfactory, reconnect the hoses, and detach the tachometer and the CO

analyser. If the adjustments are not as required, have the idling switch (manual transmission models) or the throttle valve potentiometer (automatic transmission models) checked by a VW dealer. Special equipment is required to test these items.

6 Digifant system components - removal and refitting

Note: *Observe the precautions in Section 1 before working on any component in the fuel system.*

Airflow meter

Removal

1 Disconnect the battery negative lead and position it away from the terminal. **Note:** *If the vehicle has a security-coded radio, check that you have a copy of the code number before disconnecting the battery. Refer to your VW dealer if in doubt.*
2 With reference to Section 2, slacken the clips and disconnect the air ducting from the airflow meter, at the rear of the air cleaner housing.
3 Unplug the harness connector from the airflow meter **(see illustration)**.

6.3 Unplug the harness connector from the airflow meter (engine code 2E only)

4 Remove the retaining screws and extract the meter from the air cleaner housing. Recover the seal.
Caution: Handle the airflow meter carefully - its internal components are easily damaged.

Refitting

5 Refitting is a reversal of removal. Renew the O-ring seal if it appears damaged. **Note:** *On completion, the airflow meter must be "matched" electronically to the Digifant Electronic Control Unit (ECU) - this operation requires access to dedicated electronic test equipment, refer to a VAG dealer for advice.*

Throttle valve potentiometer

Removal

6 Disconnect the battery negative lead and position it away from the terminal (see paragraph 1).
7 Unplug the harness connector from the potentiometer **(see illustration)**.
8 Remove the retaining screws and lift the potentiometer away from the throttle housing. Where applicable, recover the O-ring seal.

Refitting

9 Refitting is a reversal of removal, noting the following:
  a) *Where applicable, renew the O-ring seal if it appears damaged.*
  b) *Ensure that the potentiometer drive engages correctly with the throttle spindle extension.*
  c) *On completion, the potentiometer must be "matched" electronically to the Digifant Electronic Control Unit (ECU) - this operation requires access to dedicated electronic test equipment, refer to a VAG dealer for advice.*
  d) *On vehicles with automatic transmission, the potentiometer must be matched to the automatic transmission Electronic Control Unit (ECU) - this operation requires access to dedicated electronic*

test equipment, refer to a VAG dealer for advice.

Inlet air temperature sensor

10 The sensor is an integral part of the airflow meter and cannot be renewed separately.

Idling stabilisation valve

Removal

11 The valve is mounted on a bracket on the inlet manifold, above the camshaft cover.
12 Disconnect the battery negative lead and position it away from the terminal (see paragraph 1). Unplug the harness connector from the valve **(see illustration)**.
13 Slacken the clip and disconnect the inlet air duct hose from the port on the idle stabilisation valve.
14 Slacken the mounting bracket retaining clip and carefully extract the valve from the inlet manifold.

Refitting

15 Refitting is a reversal of removal.

Road speed sensor (later models only)

16 The road speed sensor is combined with the electronic speedometer sender and is mounted on the transmission - refer to Chapter 7A, Section 6.

Coolant temperature sensor

Removal

17 The coolant temperature sensor is mounted in the coolant outlet elbow on the front of the cylinder head (see Chapter 3).
18 Disconnect the battery negative lead and position it away from the terminal (see paragraph 1). Unplug the harness connector from the sensor **(see illustration)**.
19 Refer to Chapter 1A and drain approximately one quarter of the coolant from the engine.

6.7 Unplug the harness connector (arrowed) from the throttle potentiometer - inlet air duct removed for clarity

20 Extract the retaining clip and lift the sensor from the coolant elbow - be prepared for an amount of coolant loss. Recover the O-ring.

Refitting

21 Refit the sensor by reversing the removal procedure, using a new O-ring/sealing washer as applicable. Refer to Chapter 1A or *"Weekly checks"* and top-up the cooling system.

Engine speed sensor (later models)

Removal

22 The engine speed sensor is mounted on the front of the cylinder block, adjacent to the mating surface of the block and transmission bellhousing.
23 Disconnect the battery negative lead and position it away from the terminal (see paragraph 1). Unplug the harness connector from the sensor.
24 Remove the sensor retaining screw, and carefully withdraw the sensor from the cylinder block.

Refitting

25 Refit the sensor by reversing the removal procedure.

4B

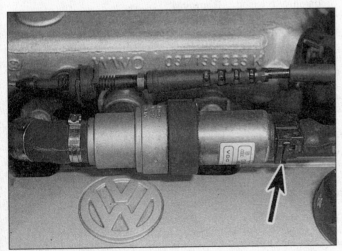

6.12 Idling stabilisation valve harness connector (arrowed)

6.18 Unplug the harness connector (arrowed) from the coolant temperature sensor (engine code 2E shown)

6.36 Throttle housing upper through-bolts (arrowed)

Cold start valve (engine code 2E up to July 1993)

Removal

26 Refer to Section 10 and depressurise the fuel system.
27 Disconnect the battery negative lead and position it away from the terminal (see paragraph 1).
28 Unplug the harness connection from the cold start valve.
29 Slacken the clip and pull the fuel hose off the port at the rear of the cold start valve.
30 Remove the retaining screw and withdraw the cold start valve from the inlet manifold. Recover and discard the gasket.

Refitting

31 Refit the cold start valve by reversing the removal procedure, using a new gasket.

Throttle housing

Removal

32 Refer to Section 4 and detach the accelerator cable from the throttle valve lever.
33 Slacken the clips and detach the inlet air ducting from the throttle housing.
34 Disconnect the battery negative lead and position it away from the terminal (see paragraph 1). Unplug the harness connector from the throttle potentiometer.
35 Disconnect the vacuum hoses from the ports on the throttle housing, noting their order of fitment. Release the wiring harness from the guide clip.
36 Slacken and withdraw the upper and lower through-bolts **(see illustration)**, then lift the throttle housing away from the inlet manifold. Recover and discard the gasket.
37 If required, refer to the relevant sub-Section and remove the throttle potentiometer.

Refitting

38 Refitting is a reversal of removal, noting the following:
a) Use a new throttle housing-to-inlet manifold gasket.
b) Observe the correct tightening torque when refitting the throttle housing through-bolts.
c) Ensure that all vacuum hoses and electrical connectors are refitted securely.

d) With reference to Section 4, check and if necessary adjust the accelerator cable.

Fuel injectors and fuel rail

Note: If faulty injectors are suspected, before removing or condemning the injectors, it is worth trying the effect of one of the proprietary injector-cleaning treatments which can be added to the fuel tank.

Removal

39 Disconnect the battery negative lead and position it away from the terminal (see paragraph 1).
40 Refer to the relevant sub-Section in this Chapter and remove the throttle housing.
41 Unplug the injector harness at the multiway connector.
42 Refer to Section 10 and depressurise the fuel system.
43 Disconnect the vacuum hose from the port on the top of the fuel pressure regulator.
44 Slacken the clips and disconnect the fuel supply and return hoses from the end of the fuel rail. *Carefully* note the fitted positions of the hoses - the supply hose is colour-coded black/white and the return hose is colour-coded blue.
45 Slacken and withdraw the fuel rail retaining screws, then carefully lift the fuel rail away from the inlet manifold, together with the injectors. Recover the injector lower O-ring seals as they emerge from the manifold.

Engine codes PB and PF

46 Detach the wiring connectors from the injectors, and release the harness from the fuel rail. The injectors can now be removed individually by releasing the retaining clip from each injector, noting how it is fitted. Recover the upper O-ring seal from each injector. If required, the injector inserts can be unscrewed from the cylinder head.

Engine code 2E

47 Remove the retaining screw and separate the upper section of the fuel rail from the lower section; recover and discard the gasket. The injectors can now be carefully pressed from the fuel rail individually. Recover the injector upper O-ring seals.

All engines

48 If required, remove the fuel pressure regulator, referring to the relevant sub-Section for guidance.
49 Check the electrical resistance of the injectors using a multimeter set to the resistance measurement function connected across the injector terminals and compare it with the Specifications.

Refitting

50 Refit the injectors and fuel rail by reversing the removal procedure, noting the following points:
a) Renew the injector O-ring seals (and/or injector inserts, where applicable) if they appear worn or damaged. Apply a light coating of engine oil to the O-rings, to aid refitting.

b) On engine code 2E, use a new gasket between the upper and lower sections of the fuel rail, and tighten the retaining screw to the specified torque.
c) Ensure that the injector retaining clips (where applicable) are securely seated.
d) Check that the fuel supply and return hoses are reconnected correctly - refer to the colour coding described in "Removal".
e) Check that all connections are remade correctly and securely.
f) On completion, check exhaustively for fuel leaks before bringing the vehicle back into service.

Fuel pressure regulator

Removal

51 Disconnect the battery negative lead and position it away from the terminal (see paragraph 1).
52 Refer to Section 10 and depressurise the fuel system.
53 Disconnect the vacuum hose from the port on top of the fuel pressure regulator.
54 Slacken the clip and disconnect the fuel supply hose from the end of the fuel rail. This will allow the majority of fuel in the regulator to drain out. Be prepared for an amount of fuel loss - position a small container and some old rags underneath the fuel regulator housing.
55 Extract the retaining clip from the side of the regulator housing and lift out the regulator body, recovering the O-ring seal.

Refitting

56 Refit the fuel pressure regulator by reversing the removal procedure, noting the following points:
a) Renew the O-ring seals if they appear worn or damaged.
b) Ensure that the regulator retaining clip is securely seated.
c) Refit the regulator vacuum hose securely.

Lambda sensor (catalyst models)

Removal

57 The lambda sensor is threaded into the exhaust pipe, at the front of the catalyst converter. Refer to Chapter 4D for details.
58 Disconnect the battery negative lead and position it away from the terminal (see paragraph 1). Unplug the wiring harness from the lambda sensor at the connector.
59 Working under the vehicle, slacken and withdraw the sensor, taking care to avoid damaging the sensor probe as it is removed. **Note:** *As a flying lead remains connected to the sensor after is has been disconnected, if the correct size spanner is not available, a slotted socket will be required to remove the sensor.*

Refitting

60 Apply a little anti-seize grease to the sensor threads - avoid contaminating the probe tip.
61 Refit the sensor to its housing, tightening it to the correct torque. Restore the harness connection.

7 Simos system components - removal and refitting

Note: *Observe the precautions in Section 1 before working on any component in the fuel system.*

Airflow meter

Removal

1 Disconnect the battery negative lead and position it away from the terminal. **Note:** *If the vehicle has a security-coded radio, check that you have a copy of the code number before disconnecting the battery. Refer to your VW dealer if in doubt.*

2 With reference to Section 2, slacken the clips and disconnect the air ducting from the airflow meter, at the rear of the air cleaner housing.

3 Unplug the harness connector from the airflow meter **(see illustration)**.

4 Remove the retaining screws and extract the meter from the air cleaner housing. Recover the O-ring seal.

Caution: Handle the airflow meter carefully - its internal components are easily damaged.

Refitting

5 Refitting is a reversal of removal. Renew the O-ring seal if it appears damaged.

Throttle valve potentiometer

6 The throttle valve potentiometer is an integral part of the throttle housing - refer to the information in the relevant sub-Section.

Inlet air temperature sensor

Removal

7 The sensor is mounted on the side of the air cleaner housing.

8 Disconnect the battery negative lead and position it away from the terminal (see paragraph 1). Unplug the harness connector from the sensor.

9 Extract the retaining clip and withdraw the sensor from its housing.

Refitting

10 Refitting is a reversal of removal.

Road speed sensor

11 The road speed sensor is combined with the electronic speedometer sender and is mounted on the transmission - refer to Chapter 7A, Section 6.

Coolant temperature sensor

Removal

12 The coolant temperature sensor is mounted in the coolant outlet elbow on the front of the cylinder head (see Chapter 3).

13 Disconnect the battery negative lead and position it away from the terminal (see paragraph 1). Unplug the harness connector from the sensor.

14 Refer to Chapter 1A, and drain approximately one quarter of the coolant from the engine.

15 Extract the retaining clip and lift the sensor from the coolant elbow - be prepared for an amount of coolant loss. Recover the O-ring.

Refitting

16 Refit the sensor by reversing the removal procedure, using a new O-ring. Refer to Chapter 1A or *"Weekly checks"* and top-up the cooling system.

Engine speed sensor

Removal

17 The engine speed sensor is mounted on the front of the cylinder block, adjacent to the mating surface of the block and transmission bellhousing. If necessary, drain the engine oil and remove the oil filter (and where applicable oil cooler) to improve access - see Chapter 1A for details.

18 Disconnect the battery negative lead and position it away from the terminal (see paragraph 1). Unplug the harness connector from the sensor.

19 Remove the retaining screw and withdraw the sensor from the cylinder block.

Refitting

20 Refit the sensor by reversing the removal procedure.

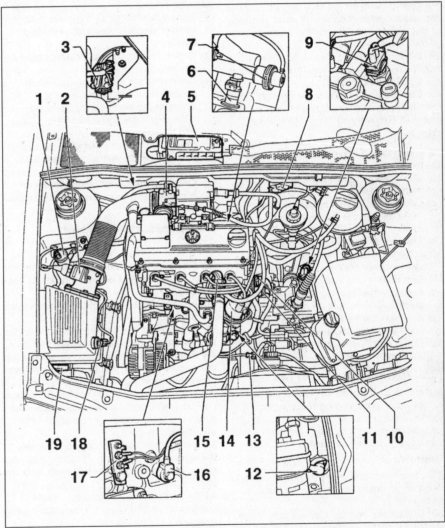

7.3 Simos engine management system components

1 Charcoal filter solenoid valve	7 Fuel pressure regulator	14 Distributor
2 Airflow meter	8 Ignition coil	15 Coolant temperature sender
3 Lambda sensor connector	9 Speedometer sender	16 Knock sensor
4 Throttle housing	10 Knock sensor connector	17 Earth connection
5 ECU	11 Wiring harness connector	18 Inlet air temperature sensor
6 Injector	12 Engine speed sensor	19 Charcoal filter
	13 Engine speed sensor connector	

4B

Throttle housing

Removal

21 Refer to Section 4 and detach the accelerator cable from the throttle valve lever.

22 Slacken the clips and detach the inlet air ducting from the throttle housing.

23 Disconnect the battery negative lead and position it away from the terminal (see paragraph 1). Unplug the harness connector from the throttle positioning valve module, mounted at the rear of the throttle housing.

24 Disconnect the vacuum hose from the port on the throttle housing, then release the wiring harness from the guide clip.

25 Refer to Chapter 1A, and drain approximately one quarter of the coolant from the engine. Slacken the clips and disconnect the coolant hoses from the ports at the base of the throttle housing, making a careful note of their fitted positions.

26 Disconnect the charcoal filter emission control system vacuum hose from the port at the top of the throttle housing.

27 Slacken and withdraw the through-bolts, then lift the throttle housing away from the inlet manifold. Recover and discard the gasket.

Refitting

28 Refitting is a reversal of removal, noting the following:
a) Use a new throttle housing-to-inlet manifold gasket.
b) Observe the correct tightening torque when refitting the throttle housing through-bolts.
c) Ensure that the coolant hoses are correctly refitted - the hose from the cylinder head connects to the port furthest from the inlet manifold.
d) Ensure that all the vacuum hoses and electrical connectors are refitted securely.
e) Refer to Chapter 1A or "Weekly checks" and top-up the cooling system.
f) Check and if necessary adjust the accelerator cable.

Fuel injectors and fuel rail

Note: *If faulty injectors are suspected, before removing or condemning the injectors, it is worth trying the effect of one of the proprietary injector-cleaning treatments which can be added to the fuel tank.*

Removal

29 Disconnect the battery negative cable and position it away from the terminal (see paragraph 1).

30 Unplug the injector harness connectors, labelling them to aid correct refitting later.

31 Depressurise the fuel system (Section 10).

32 Disconnect the vacuum hose from the port on the top of the fuel pressure regulator.

33 Slacken the clips and disconnect the fuel supply and return hoses from the end of the fuel rail. *Carefully* note the fitted positions of the hoses and label them to aid refitting later.

34 Slacken and withdraw the fuel rail screws, then carefully lift the rail away from the inlet

manifold, together with the injectors. Recover the injector inserts and lower O-ring seals as they emerge from the manifold.

35 The injectors can be removed individually from the fuel rail by extracting the relevant metal clip and easing the injector out of the rail. Recover the injector upper O-ring seals.

36 If required, remove the fuel pressure regulator, referring to the relevant sub-Section for guidance.

37 Check the electrical resistance of the injectors using a multimeter and compare it with the Specifications.

Refitting

38 Refit the injectors and fuel rail by following the removal procedure in reverse, noting the following points:
a) Renew the injector O-ring seals (and/or injector inserts) if they appear worn or damaged.
b) Ensure that the injector retaining clips are securely seated.
c) Check that the fuel supply and return hoses are reconnected correctly, according to the notes made during "Removal" - the fuel return port faces downwards.
d) Check that all vacuum and electrical connections are remade correctly and securely.
e) On completion, check exhaustively for fuel leaks before bringing the vehicle back into service.

Fuel pressure regulator

Removal

39 Disconnect the battery negative lead and position it away from the terminal (see paragraph 1).

40 Refer to Section 10 and depressurise the fuel system.

41 Disconnect the vacuum hose from the port on the top of the fuel pressure regulator.

42 Slacken the clip and disconnect the fuel return hose from the end of the fuel rail. **Note:** *The return port faces downwards.* This will allow the majority of fuel in the fuel rail to drain out. Be prepared for an amount of fuel loss - position a small container and some old rags underneath the port.

43 Extract the retaining clip from the side of the regulator housing and lift out the regulator body, recovering the O-ring seals and the strainer plate.

44 Examine the strainer plate for contamination and clean it if necessary, using neat fuel.

Refitting

45 Refit the fuel pressure regulator by following the removal procedure in reverse, noting the following points:
a) Renew the O-ring seals if they appear worn or damaged.
b) Ensure that the regulator retaining clip is securely seated.
c) Refit the regulator vacuum hose securely.

Lambda sensor

Removal

46 The lambda sensor is threaded into the exhaust pipe, at the front of the catalytic converter. Refer to Chapter 4D for details.

47 Disconnect the battery negative lead and position it away from the terminal (see paragraph 1). Unplug the wiring harness from the lambda sensor at the connector.

48 Working under the car, slacken and withdraw the sensor, taking care to avoid damaging the sensor probe as it is removed. **Note:** *As a flying lead remains connected to the sensor after is has been disconnected, if the correct spanner is not available, a slotted socket will be required to remove the sensor.*

Refitting

49 Apply a little anti-seize grease to the sensor threads - avoid contaminating the probe tip.

50 Refit the sensor to its housing, tightening it to the correct torque. Restore the harness connection.

---

8 Fuel pump and fuel gauge sender unit - removal and refitting

Refer to the information in Chapter 4A, Section 6.

9 Fuel tank - removal and refitting

Refer to the information in Chapter 4A, Section 7.

10 Fuel injection system - depressurisation

Refer to the information in Chapter 4A, Section 8.

11 Inlet manifold - removal and refitting

Removal

1 Refer to Section 10 and depressurise the fuel system, then disconnect the battery negative lead and position it away from the terminal. **Note:** *If the vehicle has a security-coded radio, check that you have a copy of the code number before disconnecting the battery. Refer to your VW dealer if in doubt.*

2 Refer to Section 2 and disconnect the air inlet ducting from the throttle housing.

3 Refer to Section 6 or 7 as applicable and remove the throttle housing from the inlet manifold.

4 Detach the throttle cable from its bracket on the manifold.

5 Disconnect the brake servo vacuum hose from the port on the side of the inlet manifold.

6 Refer to Section 6 or 7 as applicable and remove the fuel rail and fuel injectors, together with the fuel pressure regulator. **Note:** *The fuel rail may be moved to one side, leaving the fuel lines connected to it, but take care to avoid straining them.*

Engine codes PB, PF and 2E

7 Disconnect the idle speed stabilisation valve from the manifold, complete with its mounting bracket.

8 Disconnect the CO measuring pipe from the underside of the manifold, by unscrewing its retaining clip screw. Move the pipe so that it is clear of the manifold, but take care not to distort or fracture it.

9 Unbolt and detach the support plate between the inlet and exhaust manifold.

10 Undo the retaining bolt, and detach the earth strap from the manifold.

11 As necessary, detach the wiring connectors from the idle and full-throttle switches, or from the throttle valve potentiometer, as applicable.

Engine codes ADY and AGG

12 Unplug the wiring harness from the temperature switch at the side of the inlet manifold.

All engines

13 Progressively slacken and remove the inlet manifold-to-cylinder head bolts. Lift the manifold away from the head and recover the gasket.

Refitting

14 Refit the inlet manifold by following the removal procedure in reverse, noting the following points:

  a) *Use a new manifold-to-cylinder head gasket.*

  b) *Tighten the manifold-to-cylinder head bolts to the specified torque.*

  c) *Check that all vacuum and electrical connections are remade correctly and securely.*

  d) *On completion, check exhaustively for fuel leaks before bringing the vehicle back into service.*

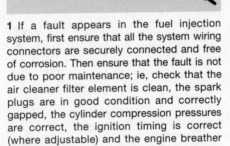

12 Fuel injection system - testing and adjustment

1 If a fault appears in the fuel injection system, first ensure that all the system wiring connectors are securely connected and free of corrosion. Then ensure that the fault is not due to poor maintenance; ie, check that the air cleaner filter element is clean, the spark plugs are in good condition and correctly gapped, the cylinder compression pressures are correct, the ignition timing is correct (where adjustable) and the engine breather hoses are clear and undamaged, referring to Chapter 1A, Chapter 2A and Chapter 5B.

2 If these checks fail to reveal the cause of the problem the vehicle should be taken to a suitably-equipped VW dealer for testing. A diagnostic connector is incorporated in the engine management system wiring harness, into which a dedicated electronic test equipment can be plugged. The test equipment is capable of "interrogating" the engine management system ECU electronically and accessing its internal fault log. In this manner, faults can be pinpointed quickly and simply, even if their occurrence is intermittent. Testing all the system components individually in an attempt to locate the fault by elimination is a time-consuming operation that is unlikely to be fruitful (particularly if the fault occurs dynamically) and carries high risk of damage

to the ECU's internal components.

3 Experienced home mechanics equipped with an accurate tachometer and a carefully-calibrated exhaust gas analyser may be able to check the exhaust gas CO content and the engine idle speed. However, if these are found to be significantly out of specification, then the vehicle must be taken to a suitably-equipped VAG dealer for assessment. Only on the Digifant system is it possible to adjust the idle speed and mixture settings, and then only to provide a basic setting from which the system can automatically set the ideal values for all operating conditions. Serious deviation from values which might reasonably be expected indicates a fault within the fuel injection system.

13 Unleaded petrol - general information and usage

Note: *The information given in this Chapter is correct at the time of writing and applies only to petrols currently available in the UK. Check with a VW dealer as more up-to-date information may be available. If travelling abroad, consult one of the motoring organisations (or a similar authority) for advice on the petrols available and their suitability for your vehicle.*

1 The fuel recommended by VW is given in the Specifications of this Chapter.

2 All vehicles equipped with a catalytic converter ("catalyst" or "cat") should be run on unleaded petrol **only**. Use of leaded petrol will damage the catalytic converter.

3 RON and MON are different testing standards; RON stands for Research Octane Number (also written as RM), while MON stands for Motor Octane Number (also written as MM).

4B

Chapter 4 Part C:
Fuel system - diesel

Contents

Degrees of difficulty

| Easy, suitable for novice with little experience | | Fairly easy, suitable for beginner with some experience | | Fairly difficult, suitable for competent DIY mechanic | | Difficult, suitable for experienced DIY mechanic | | Very difficult, suitable for expert DIY or professional | |

Specifications

Engine codes
See Chapter 2B Specifications.

General
Firing order 1-3-4-2
Maximum engine speed (engine code AAZ) . . . . 5200 ± 100 rpm
Engine idle speed (engine code AAZ) . . . . 900 ± 30 rpm
Engine fast idle speed (engine code AAZ) . . . . 1050 ± 50 rpm

Fuel injection pump
Injection pump timing, DTI reading (engine code AAZ):
  Checking . . . . 0.83 to 0.97 mm
  Setting . . . . 0.90 ± 0.02 mm

Torque wrench settings

	Nm	lbf ft
Fuel tank retaining strap bolts	25	18
Injection pump fuel supply and return banjo bolts	25	18
Injection pump fuel union lock nuts	20	15
Injection pump head fuel unions	25	18
Injection pump sprocket bolts (engine code AAZ, 10/94 on)	25	18
Injection pump sprocket nut:		
Engine code AAZ	45	33
All other engines	55	41
Injection pump timing plug	15	11
Injection pump-to-front support bracket bolts	25	18
Injection pump-to-rear support bracket bolts	25	18
Injection pump top cover screws (not engine code AAZ)	10	7
Injector fuel pipe unions	25	18
Injectors	70	52

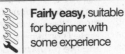

4C

1 General information and precautions

General information

Engine code AAZ

The fuel system comprises a fuel tank, a fuel injection pump, an engine-bay mounted fuel filter with an integral water separator, fuel supply and return lines and four fuel injectors.

The injection pump is driven at half crankshaft speed by the camshaft timing belt. Fuel is drawn from the fuel tank, through the filter by the injection pump, which then distributes the fuel under very high pressure to the injectors via separate delivery pipes.

The injectors are spring-loaded mechanical valves, which open when the pressure of the fuel supplied to them exceeds a specific limit. Fuel is then sprayed from the injector nozzle into the cylinder via a swirl chamber (indirect injection). Engine code AAZ is fitted with two-stage injectors which open in steps as the supplied fuel pressure rises; this improves the engine's combustion characteristics, making for smoother running and improved efficiency.

The basic injection timing is set by the position of the injection pump on its mounting bracket. When the engine is running, the injection timing is advanced and retarded mechanically by the injection pump itself, and is influenced primarily by the accelerator position and engine speed.

The engine is stopped by means of a solenoid-operated fuel cut-off valve which interrupts the flow of fuel to the injection pump when de-activated.

On early models, when starting from cold, the engine idle speed can be raised manually by means of a cold start accelerator cable, controlled via a control on the facia. On later models, the cold start accelerator cable may be replaced by an automatic idle boost actuator, mounted on the side of the injection pump.

Again on later models, the fuel injection pump is equipped with an electronic self-diagnosis and fault logging system. Servicing of this system is only possible with dedicated electronic test equipment. Problems with the system's operation should therefore be referred to a VW dealer for assessment. Once the fault has been identified, the removal/refitting sequences detailed in the following Sections will then allow the appropriate component(s) to be renewed as required.

Later models are equipped with an immobiliser which cuts off the fuel supply to the injection pump when activated. The fuel cut-off valve is attached to the injection pump by two shear-head bolts. This immobiliser can be retro-fitted to early models, but this work must be carried out by a VW dealer, since the valve must be matched to the diesel electronic control unit.

Engine codes 1Z, AHU and AFN

The direct-injection fuelling system is controlled electronically by a diesel engine management system, comprising an Electronic Control Unit (ECU) and its associated sensors, actuators and wiring.

Basic injection timing is set mechanically by the position of the pump on its mounting bracket. Dynamic timing and injection duration are controlled by the ECU, and are dependent on engine speed, throttle position and rate of opening, inlet air flow, inlet air temperature, coolant temperature, fuel temperature, ambient pressure (altitude) and manifold depression information, received from sensors mounted on and around the engine. Closed-loop control of the injection timing is achieved by means of an injector needle lift sensor. Note that injector No 3 is fitted with the needle lift sensor.

Two-stage injectors are used, which improve the engine's combustion characteristics, leading to quieter running and better exhaust emissions.

In addition, the ECU manages the operation of the Exhaust Gas Recirculation (EGR) emission control system, the turbocharger boost pressure control system and the glow plug control system (Chapter 4D).

It should be noted that fault diagnosis of the diesel engine management system fitted to these engines is only possible with dedicated electronic test equipment. Problems with the system's operation should therefore be referred to a VW dealer for assessment. Once the fault has been identified, the removal/refitting sequences detailed in the following Sections will then allow the appropriate component(s) to be renewed as required.

Note: *Throughout this Chapter, vehicles are frequently referred to by their engine code, rather than by their engine capacity - refer to Chapter 2B for engine code listings.*

Precautions

Many of the operations described in this Chapter involve the disconnection of fuel lines, which may cause an amount of fuel spillage. Before commencing work, refer to the warnings below and the information in *"Safety first!"* at the beginning of this manual.

2.1 Disconnect the air ducting from the air cleaner assembly

Warning: *When working on any part of the fuel system, avoid direct contact skin contact with diesel fuel - wear protective clothing and gloves when handling fuel system components. Ensure that the work area is well ventilated to prevent the build up of diesel fuel vapour. Do not open the fuel system with the vehicle standing over an inspection pit, as the fuel vapour could build up in the pit.*

Fuel injectors operate at extremely high pressures - the jet of fuel produced at the nozzle is capable of piercing skin, with potentially fatal results. When working with pressurised injectors, take great to avoid exposing any part of the body to the fuel spray. It is recommended that any pressure-testing of the fuel system components should be carried out by a diesel fuel systems specialist.

Under no circumstances should diesel fuel be allowed to come into contact with coolant hoses - wipe off accidental spillage immediately. Hoses that have been contaminated with fuel for an extended period should be renewed. Diesel fuel systems are particularly sensitive to contamination from dirt, air and water. Pay particular attention to cleanliness when working on any part of the fuel system, to prevent the ingress of dirt. Thoroughly clean the area around fuel unions before disconnecting them. Store dismantled components in sealed containers to prevent contamination and the formation of condensation. Only use lint-free cloths and clean fuel for component cleaning. Avoid using compressed air when cleaning components in situ.

2 Air cleaner assembly - removal and refitting

Removal

1 Slacken the worm-drive clips and disconnect the air ducting from the air cleaner assembly (engine code AAZ) or airflow meter (all other engines) **(see illustration)**.
2 Unhook the rubber retaining straps from the lugs on the chassis member **(see illustration)**.

2.2 Unhook the rubber retaining straps from the lugs on the chassis member

3 Pull the air cleaner towards the engine and detach the air inlet hose.

4 Lift the air cleaner out of the engine bay. On engine codes 1Z, AHU and AFN, separate the airflow meter from the air cleaner by removing the retaining screws. *Caution: The airflow meter is a delicate component - handle it carefully.*

5 If required, prise open the retaining clips and lift the top cover from the air cleaner. Remove the air cleaner filter element (see Chapter 1B for more details).

Refitting

6 Refit the air cleaner by reversing the removal procedure. Where applicable, engage the mounting lug with the recess in the inner wing (see illustration).

3 Accelerator cable (engine code AAZ) - removal, refitting and adjustment

1 This Section only applies to engine code AAZ; all other engines are fitted with an electronic accelerator position sensor (see Section 13).

Removal

2 Refer to Chapter 11 and remove the facia trim panels from underneath the steering column.

3 Depress the accelerator pedal slightly, then unclip the accelerator cable end from the pedal extension lever (see illustration).

4 At the point where the cable passes through the bulkhead, unscrew the cap from the two-piece grommet so that the cable can move freely.

5 Working in the engine bay, remove the clip and detach the end of the accelerator cable inner from the fuel injection pump lever (see illustration).

6 Slide back the rubber grommet and extract the accelerator cable outer from the mounting bracket (see illustration).

7 Release the cable from its securing clips, and guide it out through the bulkhead grommet.

Refitting

8 Refit the accelerator cable by reversing the removal procedure.

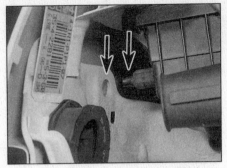

2.6 Engage the mounting lug with the recess (arrowed) in the inner wing

Adjustment

9 At the fuel injection pump, fix the position of the cable outer in its mounting bracket by inserting the metal clip in one of the locating slots, such that when the accelerator is depressed fully, the throttle lever is held wide open to its end stop.

4 Cold Start Accelerator (CSA) cable (engine code AAZ) - removal, refitting and adjustment

Removal

1 Working in the engine bay at the fuel injection pump, slacken the locking screw and disconnect the CSA cable inner from the injection pump lever.

2 Prise off the retaining clip and withdraw the cable outer from the mounting bracket on the side of the injection pump. Recover the washer.

3 Release the cable from the clips that secure it in position in the engine bay.

4 Remove the trim panels from underneath the steering column (see Chapter 11), to gain access to the inside of the facia.

5 Pull the cold start knob out to expose its rear surface, then prise off the clip and remove the knob from the cable inner.

6 Slacken and remove the retaining nut to release the cable outer from the facia.

7 Pull the cable through into the cabin, guiding it through the bulkhead grommet.

Refitting

8 Refit the CSA cable by reversing the removal procedure.

Adjustment

9 Push the cold start knob into the "fully off" position.

10 Thread the CSA cable inner through the drilling in the lever on the injection pump. Hold the injection pump cold start lever in the closed position, then pull the cable inner taut to take up the slack and tighten the locking screw.

11 Operate the cold start knob from the cabin, and check that it is possible to move the injection pump lever through its full range of travel.

12 Push the cold start knob in to its "fully off" position, then start the engine and check the idle speed, as described in Chapter 1B.

13 Pull the cold start knob fully out and check that the idle speed rises to approximately 1050 rpm. Adjust the cable if necessary.

5 Fuel tank sender unit - removal and refitting

1 The fuel tank sender unit is on the top of the fuel tank, and is accessible via a hatch in the load space floor. The unit provides a variable voltage signal that drives the facia-mounted fuel gauge; it also serves as a connection point for the fuel supply and return hoses.

2 The unit protrudes into the fuel tank, and its removal involves exposing the contents of the tank to the atmosphere.

 Warning: Avoid direct contact skin contact with diesel fuel - wear protective clothing and gloves when handling fuel system components. Ensure that the work area is well ventilated to prevent the build-up of diesel fuel vapour.

4C

Removal

3 Ensure that the vehicle is parked on a level surface, then disconnect the battery negative lead and position it away from the terminal. *Note: If the vehicle has a security-coded radio, check that you have a copy of the code number before disconnecting the battery. Refer to your VW dealer if in doubt.*

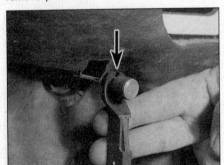

3.3 Unclip the accelerator cable end (arrowed) from the pedal extension lever

3.5 Detach the accelerator cable inner from the fuel injection pump lever

3.6 Extract the accelerator cable outer from the mounting bracket

5.5 Slacken the access hatch screws, and lift the hatch away from the floorpan

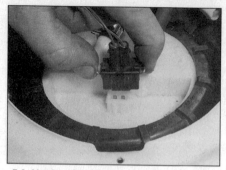

5.6 Unplug the wiring harness connector from the sender unit

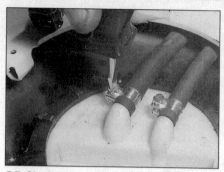

5.7 Slacken the hose clips and remove the fuel pipes from the ports at the sender unit

4 Remove the trim from the load space floor.

5 Slacken and withdraw the access hatch screws and lift the hatch away from the floorpan **(see illustration)**.

6 Unplug the wiring harness connector from the sender unit **(see illustration)**.

7 Pad the area around the supply and return fuel hoses with rags to absorb any spilt fuel, then slacken the hose clips and remove them from the ports at the sender unit **(see illustration)**. Observe the supply and return arrow markings on the ports - label the fuel hoses accordingly to ensure correct refitting.

8 Unscrew the plastic securing ring and lift it out **(see Tool Tip)**. Where applicable, turn the sender unit to left to release it from its bayonet fitting and lift it out, holding it above the level of the fuel in the tank until the excess fuel has

drained out. Recover the rubber seal **(see illustrations)**.

9 Remove the sender unit from the vehicle and lay it on an absorbent card or rag. Inspect the float at the end of the swinging arm for punctures and fuel ingress - renew the sender unit if it appears damaged.

10 The fuel pick-up incorporated in the sender unit is spring-loaded to ensure that it always draws fuel from the lowest part of the tank. Check that the pick-up is free to move under spring tension with respect to the sender unit body.

11 Recover the rubber seal from the fuel tank aperture and inspect for signs of damage or perishing - renew it if necessary **(see illustration 5.8c)**.

12 Inspect the sender unit wiper and track; clean off any dirt and debris that may have accumulated, and look for breaks in the track **(see illustration)**. An electrical specification

for the sender unit is not quoted by VW, but the integrity of the wiper and track may be verified by connecting a multimeter, set to the resistance function, across the sender unit connector terminals. The resistance should vary uniformly as the float arm is moved up and down; an open-circuit reading at any point indicates that the sender is faulty and should be renewed.

Refitting

13 Refitting is a reversal of removal, noting the following points:
- a) *The arrow markings on the sender unit body and the fuel tank must be aligned* **(see illustration)**.
- b) *Smear the tank aperture rubber seal with clean fuel before fitting it in position.*
- c) *Reconnect the fuel hoses to the correct ports - observe the direction-of-flow arrow markings as noted in paragraph 7.*

TOOL TIP

Use a pair of water pump pliers to grip and rotate the fuel tank sender unit plastic securing ring

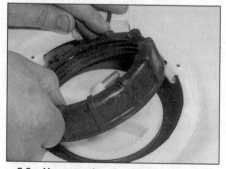

5.8a Unscrew the plastic securing ring and lift it out

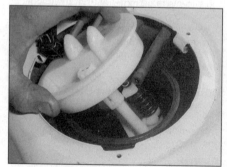

5.8b Lift out the sender unit . . .

5.8c . . . and recover the rubber seal

5.12 Look for breaks in the sender unit wiper track

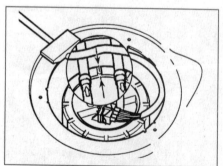

5.13 The arrow marks on the sender unit body and the fuel tank must be aligned

6 Fuel tank -
removal and refitting

Note: *Observe the precautions in Section 1 before working on any component in the fuel system.*

Removal

1 Before the tank can be removed, it must be drained of as much fuel as possible. As no drain plug is provided, it is preferable to carry out this operation with the tank almost empty. Take care, however, not to actually run out of fuel, as air will be drawn into the system, necessitating extended bleeding and possibly causing damage to the injection pump.
2 Disconnect the battery negative lead and position it away from the terminal. **Note:** *If the vehicle has a security-coded radio, check that you have a copy of the code number before disconnecting the battery. Refer to your VW dealer if in doubt.* Using a hand pump or siphon, remove any remaining fuel from the bottom of the tank.
3 Refer to Section 5 and carry out the following:
  a) *Disconnect the wiring harness from the top of the sender unit at the multiway connector.*
  b) *Disconnect the fuel supply and return hoses from the sender unit.*
4 Position a trolley jack under the centre of the tank. Insert a block of wood between the jack head and the tank to prevent damage to the tank surface. Raise the jack carefully until it just takes the weight of the tank (see "*Jacking and vehicle support*").
5 Working inside the right-hand rear wheelarch, slacken and withdraw the screws that secure the tank filler neck inside of the wheelarch. Open the fuel filler flap and peel the rubber sealing flange away from the bodywork.
6 Remove the retaining screws from the tank securing straps, keeping one hand on the tank to steady it, as it is released from its mountings.
7 Lower the jack and tank away from the underside of the vehicle; disconnect the breather hose(s) from the port on the filler neck as they are exposed. Locate the earthing strap and disconnect it from the terminal at the filler neck.
8 If the tank is contaminated with sediment or water, remove the sender unit (see Section 5) and swill the tank out with clean fuel. The tank is injection-moulded from a synthetic material and if damaged, it should be renewed. However, in certain cases it may be possible to have small leaks or minor damage repaired. Seek the advice of a suitable specialist before attempting to repair the fuel tank.

Refitting

9 Refitting is the reverse of the removal procedure, noting the following points:
  a) *When lifting the tank back into position, make sure the mounting rubbers are correctly positioned and take great care to ensure that none of the hoses become trapped between the tank and vehicle body.*
  b) *Ensure that all pipes and hoses are correctly routed and securely held in position with their retaining clips.*
  c) *Reconnect the earth strap to its terminal on the filler neck.*
  d) *Tighten the tank retaining strap bolts to the specified torque.*
  e) *On completion, refill the tank with fuel and exhaustively check for signs of leakage prior to taking the vehicle out on the road.*

7 Fuel injection pump -
removal and refitting

Note: *On engine codes 1Z, AHU and AFN, the injection pump commencement-of-injection setting must be checked and if necessary adjusted after refitting. The commencement of injection is controlled by the fuel injection ECU and is influenced by several other engine parameters, including coolant temperature, and engine speed/position. Although the adjustment is a mechanical operation, checking can only be carried out by a VW dealer, as dedicated electronic test equipment is needed to interface with the fuel injection ECU.*

Removal

1 Disconnect the battery negative lead and position it away from the terminal. **Note:** *If the vehicle has a security-coded radio, check that you have a copy of the code number before disconnecting the battery. Refer to your VW dealer if in doubt.*
2 With reference to Chapter 2B, carry out the following:
  a) *Remove the air cleaner (and airflow meter on engine codes 1Z, AHU and AFN) and the associated ducting.*
  b) *Remove the cylinder head cover and timing belt outer cover.*
  c) *Set the engine to TDC on cylinder No 1.*
  d) *Remove the timing belt from the camshaft and fuel injection pump sprockets.*
3 Loosen the nut or bolts (as applicable) that secure the timing belt sprocket to the injection pump shaft. The sprocket must be braced whilst its fixings are loosened - a home made tool can easily be fabricated for this purpose; refer to Section 5 of Chapter 2B for further details. *Caution: On engine codes AAZ and 1Y from October 1994 on, the sprocket is a two-piece assembly, secured with three bolts - on no account should the shaft centre nut be slackened, as this will alter the basic injection timing.*
4 Attach a two-legged puller to the injection pump sprocket, then gradually tighten the puller until the sprocket is under firm tension **(see illustration)**. *Caution: To prevent damage to the injection pump shaft, insert a flat piece of scrap metal between the end of the shaft and the puller centre bolt.*
5 Tap sharply on the puller centre bolt with a hammer - this will free the sprocket from the tapered shaft. Detach the puller, then fully slacken and remove the sprocket fixings, lift off the sprocket and recover the Woodruff key **(see illustration)**.
6 Using a pair of spanners, slacken the rigid fuel pipe unions at the rear of the injection pump and at each of the injectors, then lift the fuel pipe assembly away from the engine **(see illustrations)**. *Caution: Be prepared for some fuel leakage during this operation, position a small container under the union to be slackened and pad the area with old rags, to catch any spilt diesel. Take great care to avoid stressing the rigid fuel pipes as they are removed.*

4C

7.4 Attach a two-legged puller to the injection pump sprocket

7.5a Lift off the pump sprocket . . .

7.5b . . . and recover the Woodruff key

7.6a Slacken the rigid fuel pipe unions at the rear of the injection pump

7.6b Lift the fuel pipe assembly away from the engine

7 Cover the open pipes and ports to prevent the ingress of dirt and excess fuel leakage **(see Haynes Hint 1)**.

8 Slacken the fuel supply and return banjo bolts at the injection pump ports, again taking precautions to minimise fuel spillage. Cover the open pipes and ports to prevent the ingress of dirt and excess fuel leakage **(see Haynes Hint 2)**.

9 Disconnect the injector bleed hose from the port on the fuel return union **(see illustration)**.

10 Refer to Section 12 and disconnect the wiring from the stop control valve.

11 On engine code AAZ, with reference to Sections 3 and 4, disconnect the cold start accelerator cable (where fitted) from the injection pump.

12 On engine code AAZ, disconnect the accelerator cable from the injection pump.

13 On engine codes 1Z, AHU and AFN, unplug the electrical wiring from the fuel cut-off valve/commencement-of-injection valve and the quantity adjuster module at the connectors, labelling the wiring to aid refitting later.

14 On all engines except post-October 1994 engine code AAZ, if the existing injection pump is to be refitted later, use a scriber or a pen to mark the relationship between the injection pump body and the front mounting bracket. This will allow an approximate injection timing setting to be achieved when the pump is refitted.

Engine code AAZ, October 1994 onwards

15 Unplug the electrical wiring from the following components, labelling the connectors to aid refitting later:
a) *Commencement-of-injection valve.*
b) *Injection period sensor.*
c) *Boost pressure enrichment cut-off valve.*
d) *On vehicles without air conditioning, the idle speed boost actuator.*

16 On later models, where the injection pump wiring does not have individual connectors, free the engine harness multiway connector from its bracket, and unbolt the earth connection **(see illustration)**. Note: *New injection pumps are not supplied with harness multiway connector housings; if the pump is to be renewed, then the relevant spade terminal pins must be pushed out of the existing connector housing, to allow those from the new pump to be inserted.*

17 On vehicles with air conditioning, disconnect the vacuum hose from the idle speed boost actuator.

All models

18 Slacken and withdraw the bolt that secures the injection pump to the rear mounting bracket **(see illustration)**.
Caution: Do not slacken the pump distributor head bolts, as this could cause serious internal damage to the injection pump.

19 Slacken and withdraw the three nuts/bolts that secure the injection pump to the front mounting bracket. Note that where fixing bolts are used, the two outer bolts are held captive with metal brackets. Support the pump body as the last fixing is removed. Check that nothing remains connected to the injection pump, then lift it away from the engine.

Refitting

20 Offer up the injection pump to the engine, then insert the injection pump-to-rear support bracket bolt and tighten it to the specified torque.

21 Insert the injection pump-to-front support bracket bolts and tighten them to the specified torque. Note: *On all engines except post-October 1994 code AAZ, the mounting holes are elongated to allow adjustment - if a*

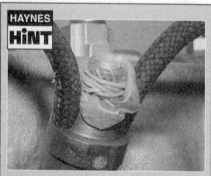

Hint 1: Cut the fingertips from an old pair of rubber gloves and secure them over the fuel ports with elastic bands

Hint 2: Fit a short length of hose over the banjo bolt (arrowed) so that the drillings are covered, then thread the bolt back into its injection pump port

7.9 Disconnect the injector bleed hose from the fuel return union port (arrowed)

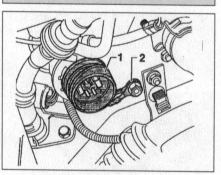

7.16 Injection pump multiway connector (1) and earth connection (2)

7.18 Withdraw the injection pump rear mounting bolt

new pump is being fitted, then mount it such that the bolts are initially at the centre of the holes, to allow the maximum range of pump timing adjustment. Alternatively, if the existing pump is being refitted, use the markings made during removal for alignment.

22 On all engines except pre-October 1994 code AAZ, where a new injection pump is being fitted, prime new injection pumps by fitting a small funnel to the fuel return pipe union and filling the cavity with clean diesel. Pad the area around the union with clean dry rags to absorb any spillage.

23 Reconnect the fuel injector delivery pipes to the injectors and injection pump head, then tighten the unions to the correct torque using a pair of spanners.

24 Reconnect the fuel supply and return pipes to the injection pump using new sealing washers, and tighten the banjo bolts to the specified torque. **Note:** *The inside diameter of the banjo bolt for the fuel return pipe is smaller than that of the fuel supply line, and is marked "OUT".*

25 Push the injector bleed hose onto the port on the return hose union.

26 Fit the timing belt sprocket to the injection pump shaft, ensuring that the Woodruff key is correctly seated. Fit the washer and retaining nut/bolts (as applicable), hand-tightening them only at this stage.

27 Lock the injection pump sprocket in position by inserting a bar or bolt through its alignment hole and into the drilling in the pump front mounting bracket. Ensure that there is minimal play in the sprocket, once it has been locked in position.

28 With reference to Chapter 2B, refit the timing belt, then check and adjust the injection pump-to-camshaft timing. On completion, tension the timing belt and tighten the fuel injection pump sprocket to the specified torque **(see illustration)**. Refit the timing belt outer cover and cylinder head cover, using a new gasket where necessary.

29 The rest of refitting is a direct reversal of removal, noting the following points:

a) *Reconnect all electrical connections to the pump, using the labels made during removal. When fitting a new injection pump to post-October 1994 engine code AAZ, push the pump wiring terminal pins into their respective locations in the existing engine harness multiway connector; refer to the wiring diagrams at the end of the Manual for assistance in identifying the wiring.*

b) *Refit the air cleaner (and airflow meter on engine codes 1Z, AHU and AFN) and its ducting.*

c) *Reconnect the battery negative lead.*

Engine codes 1Z, AHU and AFN

30 The commencement-of-injection must now be dynamically checked and if necessary adjusted by a VW dealer; refer to the note at the beginning of this Section.

Engine code AAZ

31 Carry out the following:

a) *Reconnect the accelerator cable and cold start accelerator cable to the pump and adjust them as necessary.*

b) *On pre-October 1994 engines, check and if necessary adjust the injection pump static timing as described in Section 10.*

c) *Check and if necessary adjust the idle speed as described in Chapter 1B.*

d) *Check and if necessary adjust the maximum engine speed, as described in Section 8.*

e) *Check and if necessary adjust the fast idle speed, as described in Section 9.*

8 Maximum engine speed (engine code AAZ) - checking and adjustment

⚠ **Warning: This operation should not be carried if the condition of the camshaft timing belt is at all** questionable. This check requires that the engine be run at maximum speed, which places considerable strain on the camshaft timing belt. Provided the belt is known to be in good condition, there should be no problem, but if the belt breaks, considerable engine damage would result.

Note: *Observe the precautions in Section 1 before working on any component in the fuel system.*

1 Start the engine and ensure that the handbrake is applied and the transmission is in neutral. Have an assistant depress the accelerator fully to the floor, building up to maximum speed over a period of a few seconds.

2 Using a diesel tachometer, check that the maximum engine speed is as quoted in the Specifications.

Caution: Do not maintain maximum engine speed for more than two or three seconds.

3 If necessary, adjust the maximum engine speed by slackening the locknut and rotating the adjusting screw **(see illustration)**.

4 On completion, tighten the locknut.

9 Fast idle speed (engine code AAZ) - checking and adjustment

Note: *Observe the precautions in Section 1 before working on any component in the fuel system.*

1 With reference to Chapter 1B, check and if necessary adjust the idle speed.

Models with facia-mounted cold start control

2 Pull the facia cold start control fully out and using a diesel tachometer, check that the idle speed rises to the fast idle value given in the Specifications.

3 If necessary, adjust the setting by slackening the locknut and rotating the fast idle adjusting screw **(see illustration)**.

7.28 Tightening the fuel injection pump sprocket, using a home-made locking tool

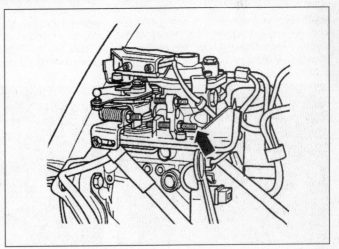

8.3 Maximum engine speed adjustment screw (engine code AAZ)

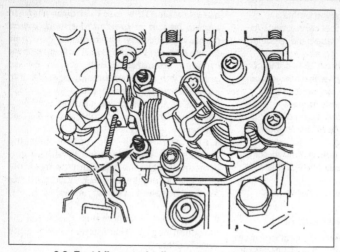

9.3 Fast idle speed adjustment screw (arrowed)

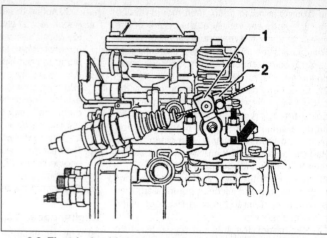

9.6 Electrical cold start actuator - idle speed lever (1) in
contact with fast idle speed screw (arrowed).
Cable clamping piece (2) also shown

4 On completion, tighten the locknut.

Models with cold start actuator

5 Where an electrical or pneumatic cold start actuator is used in place of a facia-mounted manual control, adjustment of the fast idle speed is carried out as follows.

6 Move the idle speed lever by hand so that it is in contact with the fast idle adjusting screw **(see illustration)**, and check that the fast idle speed is as specified.

7 If necessary, adjust the setting by slackening the locknut and rotating the fast idle adjusting screw **(refer to illustration 9.3)**.

8 On completion, tighten the locknut.

9 Check that there is no slack in the operating cable when the lever is held against the fast idle speed screw. If necessary, loosen the clamping piece at the end of the cable, eliminate the slack, then re-tighten the clamp.

---

10 Fuel injection pump timing (engine code AAZ) -
checking and adjustment

Note: *On engine codes 1Z, AHU and AFN, the fuel injection pump timing can only be tested and adjusted using dedicated test equipment. Refer to a VW dealer for advice.*

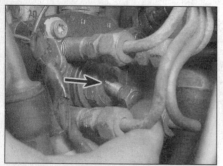

10.3 Unscrew the plug (arrowed) from the
pump head and recover the seal

Note: *Observe the precautions in Section 1 before working on any component in the fuel system.*

Checking

1 Disconnect the battery negative lead and position it away from the terminal. **Note:** *If the vehicle has a security-coded radio, check that you have a copy of the code number before disconnecting the battery. Refer to your VW dealer if in doubt.*

2 With reference to Chapter 2B, set the engine to TDC on cylinder No 1. Check the alignment of the injection pump and camshaft sprockets, adjusting if necessary. On completion, reset the engine to TDC on cylinder No 1.

3 At the rear of the injection pump, unscrew the timing plug from the pump head and recover the seal **(see illustration)**.

4 Using a suitably-threaded adapter, screw a DTI gauge into the pump head **(see illustration)**. Pre-load the gauge by a reading of approximately 2.5 mm.

5 Using a socket and wrench on the crankshaft bolt, slowly rotate the crankshaft anti-clockwise; the DTI gauge will indicate movement - keep turning the crankshaft until the movement just ceases.

6 Zero the DTI gauge with a pre-load of approximately 1.0 mm.

10.4 Screw a DTI gauge into the
pump head

7 Now turn the crankshaft clockwise to bring the engine back up to TDC on cylinder No 1. Observe the reading indicated by the DTI gauge, and compare it with the Specifications.

8 If the reading is within the checking tolerance quoted in the Specifications, remove the DTI gauge and refit the pump timing plug. Use a new seal and tighten the plug to the specified torque.

9 If the reading is out of tolerance, proceed as described in the next sub-Section.

Adjustment

10 Slacken the pump securing bolts at the front and rear brackets (see Section 7).

11 Rotate the injection pump body until the "Setting" reading (see Specifications) is indicated on the DTI gauge.

12 On completion, tighten the pump securing bolts to the specified torque.

13 Remove the DTI gauge and refit the pump timing plug. Use a new seal and tighten the plug to the specified torque.

---

11 Injectors -
general information,
removal and refitting

⚠️ *Warning: Exercise extreme caution when working on the fuel injectors. Never expose the hands or any part of the body to injector spray, as the high working pressure can cause the fuel to penetrate the skin, with possibly fatal results. You are strongly advised to have any work which involves testing the injectors under pressure carried out by a dealer or fuel injection specialist. Refer to the precautions given in Section 1 of this Chapter before proceeding.*

General information

1 Injectors do deteriorate with prolonged use, and it is reasonable to expect them to need

11.6 Removing an injector from the cylinder head

11.7 Recover the heat shield washer

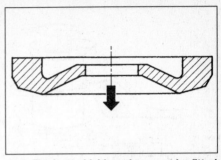

11.8 The heat shield washer must be fitted with its convex side facing downwards (arrow faces the cylinder head)

reconditioning or renewal after 60 000 miles (100 000 km) or so. Accurate testing, overhaul and calibration of the injectors must be left to a specialist. A defective injector which is causing knocking or smoking can be located without dismantling as follows.

2 Run the engine at a fast idle. Slacken each injector union in turn, placing rag around the union to catch spilt fuel, and being careful not to expose the skin to any spray. When the union on the defective injector is slackened, the knocking or smoking will stop.

Removal

Note: *Take great care not to allow dirt into the injectors or fuel pipes during this procedure. Do not drop the injectors or allow the needles at their tips to become damaged. The injectors are precision-made to fine limits, and must not be handled roughly.*

3 Disconnect the battery negative lead and place the lead away from the terminal. **Note:** *If the vehicle has a security-coded radio, check that you have a copy of the code number before disconnecting the battery. Refer to your VW dealer if in doubt.* Cover the alternator with a clean cloth or plastic bag to protect it if any fuel is spilt onto it.

4 Carefully clean around the injectors and pipe union nuts, and disconnect the return pipe from the injector.

5 Wipe clean the pipe unions, then slacken the union nut securing the relevant injector pipes to each injector and the relevant union nuts securing the pipes to the rear of the injection pump (pipes are removed as one

assembly). As each pump union nut is slackened, retain the adapter with a suitable open-ended spanner to prevent it being unscrewed from the pump. With the union nuts undone remove the injector pipes from the engine. Cover the injector and pipe unions to prevent the entry of dirt into the system.

  Cut the fingertips from an old rubber glove and secure them over the open unions with elastic bands to prevent dirt ingress (see Section 7).

6 Unscrew the injector, using a deep socket or box spanner, and remove it from the cylinder head **(see illustration)**.

7 Recover the heat shield washer **(see illustration)**.

Refitting

8 Fit a new heat shield washer to the cylinder head, noting that it must be fitted with its convex side facing downwards (towards the cylinder head) **(see illustration)**.

9 Screw the injector into position and tighten it to the specified torque **(see illustration)**.

10 Refit the injector pipes and tighten the union nuts to the specified torque setting. Position any clips attached to the pipes as noted before removal.

11 Reconnect the return pipe to the injector.

12 Restore the battery connection and check the running of the engine.

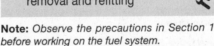

12 Fuel cut-off ("stop") solenoid valve - removal and refitting

Note: *Observe the precautions in Section 1 before working on the fuel system.*

Removal

1 The fuel cut-off solenoid valve is located at the rear of the injection pump.

2 Disconnect the battery negative lead and position it away from the terminal. **Note:** *If the vehicle has a security-coded radio, check that you have a copy of the code number before disconnecting the battery. Refer to your VW*

dealer if in doubt. Unplug the harness from the connector at the top of the valve **(see illustration)**.

3 Slacken and withdraw the valve body from the injection pump. Recover the sealing washer, O-ring seal and the plunger.

Refitting

4 Refitting is a reversal of removal. Use a new sealing washer and O-ring seal.

13 Diesel engine management system - component removal and refitting

Note: *This Section only applies to engine codes 1Z, AHU and AFN.*
Note: *Observe the precautions in Section 1 before working on the fuel system.*

Accelerator position sensor

Removal

1 Disconnect the battery negative lead and position it away from the terminal. **Note:** *If the vehicle has a security-coded radio, check that you have a copy of the code number before disconnecting the battery. Refer to your VW dealer if in doubt.*

2 Refer to Chapter 11 and remove the trim panels from under the steering column area of the facia, to gain access to the pedal cluster.

3 Prise the clip from the end of the accelerator pedal spindle, then withdraw the spindle and recover the bush and spring.

4C

11.9 Screw the injector into position and tighten it to the specified torque

12.2 Fuel cut-off ("stop") solenoid valve connector (arrowed)

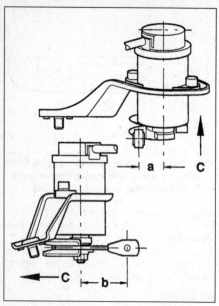

13.9 Mounting arrangement of accelerator position sensor cable cam plate

a 22 ± 0.5 mm	*C Towards front of*
b 41± 0.5 mm	*vehicle*

4 Lift the accelerator pedal clear of the pedal bracket, disengaging it from the position sensor cable cam plate.
5 Unplug the position sensor from the wiring harness at the connector.
6 Remove the screw that secures the position sensor bracket to the pedal bracket.
7 Remove the sensor from the pedal bracket, then remove the fixings and release it from the mounting bracket.
8 Slacken and remove the spindle nut, then pull the cable cam plate off the spindle.

Refitting

9 Refitting is a reversal of removal, noting the following points:
 a) *The cable cam plate must be fitted to the position sensor spindle according to the dimensions shown (see illustration).*
 b) *On completion, the adjustment of the position sensor must be verified electronically, using dedicated test equipment - refer to a VW dealer for advice.*

Coolant temperature sensor

Removal

10 Disconnect the battery negative lead and position it away from the terminal (see paragraph 1). Refer to Chapter 1B and drain approximately one quarter of the coolant from the engine.
11 The sensor is at the top coolant outlet elbow, at the front of the cylinder head. On engine code AFN, remove the engine top cover for access. Unplug the wiring from it at the connector.
12 Remove the securing clip and extract the sensor from its housing and recover the O-ring seal - be prepared for coolant loss.

Refitting

13 Refit the coolant temperature sensor by reversing the removal procedure, using a new O-ring seal. Refer to Chapter 1B or *"Weekly checks"* and top-up the cooling system.

Fuel temperature sensor

Removal

14 Disconnect the battery negative lead and position it away from the terminal (see paragraph 1). On engine code AFN, remove the engine top cover for access.
15 Slacken and withdraw the retaining screws and lift the top cover from the injection pump. Recover the gasket.
16 Remove the screws and lift out the fuel temperature sensor.

Refitting

17 Refitting is a reversal of removal. Tighten the pump top cover screws to the specified torque.

Inlet air temperature sensor

Removal

18 Disconnect the battery negative lead and position it away from the terminal (see paragraph 1).
19 The sensor is mounted in the air hose between the intercooler and the inlet manifold. Unplug the wiring harness from it at the connector.
20 Remove the securing clip and extract the sensor from its housing and recover the O-ring seal.

Refitting

21 Refit the inlet air temperature sensor by reversing the removal procedure, using a new O-ring seal.

Engine speed signal sensor

Removal

22 The engine speed sensor is mounted on the front cylinder block, adjacent to the mating surface of the block and transmission bellhousing.
23 Disconnect the battery negative lead and position it away from the terminal (see paragraph 1), then unplug the harness connector from the sensor.
24 Remove the retaining screw and withdraw the sensor from the cylinder block.

Refitting

25 Refit the sensor by reversing the removal procedure.

Airflow meter

Removal

26 Disconnect the battery negative lead and position it away from the terminal (see paragraph 1).
27 With reference to Section 2, slacken the clips and disconnect the air ducting from the airflow meter, at the rear of the air cleaner housing.

28 Unplug the harness connector from the airflow meter.
29 Remove the retaining screws and extract the meter from the air cleaner housing. Recover the O-ring seal.
Caution: Handle the airflow meter carefully - its internal components are easily damaged.

Refitting

30 Refitting is a reversal of removal. Renew the O-ring seal if it appears damaged.

Manifold pressure sensor

31 The manifold pressure sensor is an integral part of the electronic control unit, and hence cannot be renewed separately.

Absolute pressure (altitude) sensor

Vehicles up to August 1994

32 The sensor is mounted behind the facia, above the relay board. Refer to Chapter 11 and remove the relevant sections of the facia to gain access.
33 Disconnect the battery negative lead and position it away from the terminal (see paragraph 1). Unclip the sensor from its bracket and unplug it from the wiring harness at the connector.

Vehicles from August 1994 on

34 The absolute pressure sensor is an integral part of the electronic control unit and hence cannot be renewed separately.

Boost pressure valve

Removal

35 The boost pressure valve is mounted on the inner wing, to the rear of the air cleaner housing.
36 Disconnect the battery negative lead and position it away from the terminal (see paragraph 1). Unplug the wiring harness from it at the connector.
37 Remove the vacuum hoses from the ports on the boost control valve, noting their order of connection carefully to aid correct refitting.
38 Remove the retaining screw and lift the valve away from the inner wing. Refitting is a reversal of removal.

Electronic control unit (ECU)

39 The ECU is mounted underneath the

13.41 ECU location, showing multi-plug (arrowed)

windscreen cowl panels at the rear of the engine compartment.

40 Disconnect the battery negative lead and position it away from the terminal (see paragraph 1).

41 Refer to Chapter 1 and remove the pollen filter cover panel for access to the ECU (see illustration).

42 Unplug the ECU multi-plug, then undo the retaining nut and release the unit from its retaining bracket. Remove the ECU from the vehicle.

43 Refitting is a reversal of removal. When reconnecting the ECU multi-plug, make sure that the ignition switch is off (or that the battery negative lead is disconnected).

14 Intercooler - general information, component removal and refitting

General information

1 An intercooler is only fitted to engine codes 1Z, AHU and AFN. It is effectively an "air radiator", and its function is to cool the pressurised air from the turbocharger before it enters the inlet manifold.

2 The turbocharger is driven by hot exhaust gases, and will therefore rapidly become hot itself; this heat will be passed on to any air passing through it. The action of compressing the air taken in from the air cleaner will also heat it. As a result, the air reaching the inlet manifold would be considerably above ambient temperature.

3 With an intercooler system, the air from the turbocharger is directed through large-diameter pipes to the intercooler, which is very similar in appearance and function to the coolant radiator. The intercooler is mounted in the airflow at the front of the vehicle, on the left-hand side of the engine compartment (see illustration).

4 The heated air from the turbocharger is fed in at the bottom, is cooled by the airflow over the intercooler fins, and emerges appreciably cooler at the top, where it is then ducted into the inlet manifold. An air temperature sensor is mounted in the air hose to the inlet manifold, to provide information to the ECU (see illustration).

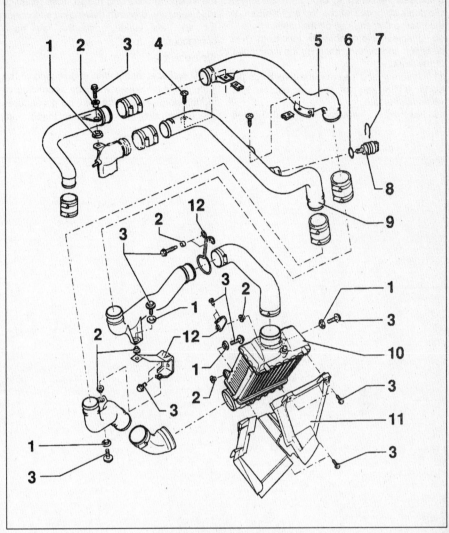

14.3 Intercooler and air hoses

1 Rubber mounting	5 Turbocharger-to-intercooler air hose	9 Intercooler-to-inlet manifold air hose
2 Spacer	6 O-ring	10 Intercooler
3 Mounting bolt	7 Retaining clip	11 Air ducting
4 Retaining screw	8 Inlet manifold temperature sender	12 Mounting bracket

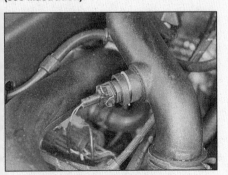

14.4 Inlet air temperature sensor in intercooler hose to inlet manifold

5 The benefit of cooling the inlet air is that cooler air is more dense, so that a greater effective amount of air is forced into the cylinders for combustion. This has the effect of increasing the engine's power output, without harming the fuel economy. Having a greater quantity of air in the cylinders also leads to more complete combustion, with fewer emissions.

Component removal and refitting

Intercooler

6 Disconnect the battery negative lead and position it away from the terminal. Note: If the vehicle has a security-coded radio, check that you have a copy of the code number before disconnecting the battery. Refer to your VW dealer if in doubt.

7 Depending on model, the underbonnet layout will dictate the easiest way to remove the intercooler. On most models, the unit will be withdrawn from below, while on others, it will be easier to manoeuvre the unit out upwards. If the unit is to be withdrawn from above, refer to Chapter 5A if necessary, and remove the battery from the engine compartment; if possible, also remove the battery support tray.

8 If the intercooler is to be withdrawn from below, apply the handbrake, then jack up the front of the vehicle and support on axle stands (see "Jacking and vehicle support"). Where applicable, release the fasteners and remove the engine lower splash shield.

9 Loosen the retaining clips from the large-diameter air hoses at the top and bottom of the intercooler, and pull off the hoses.

10 Unscrew and remove the four bolts (two bolts top and bottom) securing the intercooler at the front.

11 Unscrew and remove the two through-bolts at the rear of the intercooler, and withdraw the unit.

12 Refitting is a reversal of removal. Tighten the mounting bolts and the air hose retaining clips securely, then run the engine and check for any air leaks from the air hose connections.

Air hoses

13 The shape, orientation and routing of the intercooler air hoses will vary according to model, but removal and refitting procedures should be fairly self-evident on inspection. Label the hoses if necessary on removal, so that there is no confusion on refitting.

Caution: If removing the air hose from the turbocharger, cover the turbocharger duct to prevent debris entering. Always ensure that, on refitting, any securing bolts/screws are tight, and that the hose clips are securely tightened, so that there are no air leaks.

Chapter 4 Part D:
Emission control and exhaust systems

Contents

Degrees of difficulty

Easy, suitable for novice with little experience	Fairly easy, suitable for beginner with some experience	Fairly difficult, suitable for competent DIY mechanic	Difficult, suitable for experienced DIY mechanic	Very difficult, suitable for expert DIY or professional

Specifications

Turbocharger

Type	Garrett or KKK
Maximum boost pressure:	
Engine code AAZ	0.60 to 0.83 bar at 4000 rpm
Engine code 1Z/AHU	0.50 to 0.65 bar at 3500 to 4000 rpm
Engine code AFN	No information at time of writing

Torque wrench settings	Nm	lbf ft
EGR valve nuts/bolts	25	18
Exhaust downpipe-to-turbocharger nuts	25	18
Exhaust mounting bracket-to-body bolts	40	30
Exhaust system clamp bolts	25	18
Turbocharger-to-exhaust manifold nuts/bolts:		
Engine code AAZ*	45	33
Engine codes 1Z and AHU	35	26
Engine code AFN*	25	18
Turbocharger mounting bracket bolts:		
M8	25	18
M10	30	22
Turbocharger oil feed pipe-to-turbocharger		
union (engine code AFN only)	10	7
Turbocharger oil feed union bolts	25	18
Turbocharger oil return union bolts	30	22

*Use new nuts/bolt(s)

4D

---

1 General information

Emission control systems

All petrol models have the ability to use unleaded petrol (refer to a VW dealer if in doubt), and most are controlled by engine management systems that are "tuned" to give the best compromise between driveability, fuel consumption and exhaust emission production. In addition, other systems are fitted that help to minimise other harmful emissions. A crankcase emission control system that reduces the release of pollutants from the engine's lubrication system is fitted to all models. Catalytic converters that reduce exhaust gas pollutants are fitted to most models **(see illustration)**, as well as an evaporative loss emission control system that reduces the release of gaseous hydrocarbons from the fuel tank.

All diesel engined models also have a crankcase emission control system. In addition, all models are fitted with a catalytic converter and an Exhaust Gas Recirculation (EGR) system to reduce exhaust emissions.

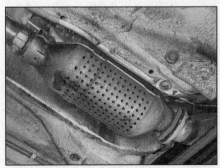

**1.1 Catalytic converter -
petrol engine model shown**

Crankcase emission control

To reduce the emission of unburned hydrocarbons from the crankcase into the atmosphere, the engine is sealed and the blow-by gases and oil vapour are drawn from inside the crankcase, through a wire-mesh oil separator, into the inlet tract to be burned by the engine during normal combustion.

Under conditions of high manifold depression (idling, deceleration) the gases will be sucked positively out of the crankcase. Under conditions of low manifold depression (acceleration, full-throttle running) the gases are forced out of the crankcase by the (relatively) higher crankcase pressure; if the engine is worn, the raised crankcase pressure (due to increased blow-by) will cause some of the flow to return under all manifold conditions. On certain engines, a pressure-regulating valve (on the camshaft cover) controls the flow of gases from the crankcase.

Exhaust emission control - petrol models

To minimise the amount of pollutants which escape into the atmosphere, most models are fitted with a catalytic converter in the exhaust system. On all models where a catalytic converter is fitted, the fuelling system is of the closed-loop type, in which a lambda sensor in the exhaust system provides the engine management system ECU with constant feedback, enabling the ECU to adjust the air/fuel mixture to optimise combustion.

The lambda sensor has a built-in heating element that is controlled by the ECU through the lambda sensor relay, to quickly bring the sensor's tip to its optimum operating temperature. The sensor's tip is sensitive to oxygen and sends a voltage signal to the ECU that varies according on the amount of oxygen in the exhaust gas. If the inlet air/fuel mixture is too rich, the exhaust gases are low in oxygen so the sensor sends a low-voltage signal, the voltage rising as the mixture weakens and the amount of oxygen rises in the exhaust gases. Peak conversion efficiency of all major pollutants occurs if the inlet air/fuel mixture is maintained at the chemically-correct ratio for the complete combustion of petrol of 14.7 parts (by weight) of air to 1 part of fuel (the 'stoichiometric' ratio). The sensor output voltage alters in a large step at this point, the ECU using the signal change as a reference point and correcting the inlet air/fuel mixture accordingly by altering the fuel injector pulse width. Details of lambda sensor removal and refitting are given in Chapter 4A or B as applicable.

Exhaust emission control - diesel models

An oxidation catalyst is fitted in the line with the exhaust system of all diesel engined models. This has the effect of removing a large proportion of the gaseous hydrocarbons, carbon monoxide and particles present in the exhaust gas.

An Exhaust Gas Recirculation (EGR) system is fitted to all diesel engined models. This reduces the level of nitrogen oxides produced during combustion by introducing a proportion of the exhaust gas back into the inlet manifold, under certain engine operating conditions, via a plunger valve. The system is controlled electronically by the glow plug control module on engine code AAZ, or by the diesel engine management ECU on other engines.

Evaporative emission control - petrol models

To minimise the escape of unburned hydrocarbons into the atmosphere, an evaporative loss emission control system is fitted to all petrol models with a catalytic converter. The fuel tank filler cap is sealed, and a charcoal canister is mounted underneath the right-hand wing to collect the petrol vapours released from the fuel contained in the fuel tank. It stores them until they can be drawn from the canister (under the control of the fuel-injection/ignition system ECU) via the purge valve(s) into the inlet tract, where they are then burned by the engine during normal combustion.

To ensure that the engine runs correctly when it is cold and/or idling and to protect the catalytic converter from the effects of an over-rich mixture, the purge control valve(s) are not opened by the ECU until the engine has warmed up, and the engine is under load; the valve solenoid is then modulated on and off to allow the stored vapour to pass into the inlet tract.

Exhaust systems

The exhaust system comprises the exhaust manifold, one or two silencers (depending on model and specification), a catalytic converter (where fitted), a number of mounting brackets and a series of connecting pipes.

On diesel engines, a turbocharger is fitted to the exhaust manifold - refer to Section 6 for further details.

---

2 Evaporative loss emission control system - information and component renewal

General information

1 The evaporative loss emission control system consists of the purge valve, the activated charcoal filter canister and a series of connecting vacuum hoses.
2 The purge valve is mounted on a bracket behind the air cleaner housing, and the charcoal canister is mounted on a bracket inside the right-hand front wheel housing.

Component renewal

Purge valve

3 The purge valve is located on top of the right-hand inner wing, behind the air cleaner. Ensure that the ignition is switched off, then

unplug the wiring harness from the purge valve at the connector **(see illustration)**.
4 Slacken the clips and pull the vacuum hoses off the purge valve ports. Make a note of their orientation to aid refitting later.
5 Slide the purge valve out of its retaining ring and remove it from the engine bay.
6 Refitting is a reversal of removal.

Charcoal canister

7 Locate the canister in the wheel housing. Depending on model, it may be necessary to remove the air cleaner housing for better access (refer to the appropriate Part of Chapter 4). Disconnect the vacuum hoses from the canister, noting which ports they connect to. Either unscrew the two bolts, or depress the locking tab on the side of the securing strap, and lift the canister out of the wheel housing.
8 Refitting is a reversal of removal.

---

3 Crankcase emission system - general information

The crankcase emission control system consists of a series of hoses that connect the crankcase vent to the camshaft cover vent and the air inlet, a pressure regulating valve (where applicable) and an oil separator.

The system requires no attention other than to check at regular intervals that the hose(s) are free of blockages and undamaged.

---

4 Exhaust Gas Recirculation (EGR) system (diesel models) - component renewal

1 The EGR system consists of the EGR valve and a series of connecting vacuum hoses.
2 On engine codes AAZ and 1Z, the EGR valve is mounted on a flange joint at the inlet manifold, and is connected to a second flange joint at the exhaust manifold by a semi-flexible pipe.
3 On engine code AFN, the EGR valve is an integral part of the inlet manifold, and cannot be replaced separately. A semi-flexible pipe connects the valve to the exhaust manifold.

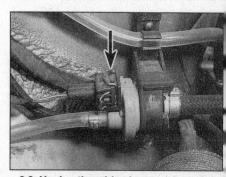

2.3 Unplug the wiring harness from the purge valve at the connector (arrowed)

Component renewal

EGR valve
(engine codes AAZ and 1Z only)

4 Disconnect the vacuum hose from the port at the top of the EGR valve.

5 Slacken and withdraw the bolts that secure the semi-flexible connecting pipe to the EGR valve flange **(see illustration)**. Recover and discard the gasket from the joint.

6 Remove the bolts that secure the EGR valve to the inlet manifold flange, and lift off the EGR valve. Recover and discard the gasket.

7 Refitting is a reversal of removal, noting the following points:

a) *Use new flange joint gaskets and self-locking nuts.*

b) *When reconnecting the semi-flexible pipe, fit the retaining bolts loosely and ensure that the pipe is unstressed before tightening the bolts to the specified torque.*

EGR valve-to-exhaust manifold pipe

8 Slacken and withdraw the bolts that secure the semi-flexible connecting pipe to the EGR valve flange. Recover and discard the gasket from the joint.

9 Remove the bolts that secure the pipe to the exhaust manifold, and lift the pipe away. Again, recover and discard the gasket from the exhaust manifold joint.

10 Refitting is a reversal of removal, noting the following points:

a) *Use new flange joint gaskets and self-locking nuts.*

b) *When reconnecting the semi-flexible pipe, fit the retaining bolts loosely and ensure that the pipe is unstressed before tightening the bolts to the specified torque.*

5 Exhaust manifold - removal and refitting

The exhaust manifold removal is described as part of the cylinder head dismantling sequence; refer to Chapter 2A or B as applicable. To separate the downpipe from the exhaust manifold, refer to the information in Section 7.

6.4a Slacken the clips . . .

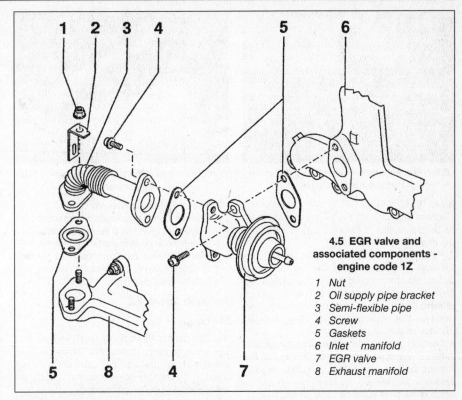

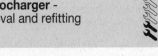

4.5 EGR valve and associated components - engine code 1Z

1 Nut
2 Oil supply pipe bracket
3 Semi-flexible pipe
4 Screw
5 Gaskets
6 Inlet manifold
7 EGR valve
8 Exhaust manifold

6 Turbocharger - removal and refitting

General information

1 A turbocharger is fitted to all diesel engines, and is mounted directly on the exhaust manifold. Lubrication is provided by a dedicated oil feed pipe that runs from the engine oil filter mounting. Oil is returned to the sump via a return pipe that connects to the side of the cylinder block. The turbocharger has an integral wastegate valve and vacuum actuator diaphragm, which is used to control the boost pressure applied to the inlet manifold.

2 The turbocharger's internal components rotate at very high speed, and as such are very sensitive to contamination; a great deal of damage can be caused by small particles

6.4b . . . and remove the turbocharger-to-inlet manifold ducting

of dirt, particularly if they strike the delicate turbine blades.

Caution: Thoroughly clean the area around all oil pipe unions before disconnecting them, to prevent the ingress of dirt. Store dismantled components in a sealed container to prevent contamination. Cover the turbocharger air inlet ducts to prevent debris entering, and clean using lint-free cloths only.

> ⚠️ **Warning: Do not run the engine with the turbocharger air inlet hose disconnected; the depression (vacuum) at the inlet can build up very suddenly if the engine speed is raised, and there is the risk of foreign objects being sucked in and ejected at very high speed.**

Engine code AAZ

Removal

3 Disconnect the battery negative lead and position it away from the terminal. **Note:** *If the vehicle has a security-coded radio, check that you have a copy of the code number before disconnecting the battery. Refer to your VW dealer if in doubt.*

4 Slacken the clips and remove the turbocharger-to-inlet manifold and air cleaner-to-turbocharger ducting **(see illustrations)**.

5 Disconnect the vacuum hoses from the wastegate actuator diaphragm housing; note their order of connection and colour coding to aid correct refitting later.

6 Loosen the unions and disconnect the oil feed and return pipes from the turbocharger

4D

6.6a Slackening the oil return pipe union at the turbocharger

6.6b Disconnecting the oil feed pipe at the turbocharger

(see illustrations). Recover the sealing washers and discard them - new items must be used on refitting. Free the supply pipe from the clip on the inlet manifold.

7 Remove the nuts and disconnect the exhaust downpipe from the turbocharger outlet. Recover and discard the gasket - a new item must be used on refitting **(see illustrations)**. Slacken the mountings and remove the downpipe from the exhaust manifold support bracket.

8 Slacken and withdraw the turbocharger-to-exhaust manifold bolts. **Note:** *Access to the lowest bolt is restricted; a universal-joint extension bar will ease its removal.* Discard the bolts - new ones must be used on refitting.

9 Lift the turbocharger away from the exhaust manifold.

Refitting

10 Refit the turbocharger by following the removal procedure in reverse, noting the following points:
a) *Offer up the turbocharger to the exhaust manifold, then fit and hand-tighten the exhaust downpipe nuts.*
b) *Apply high-temperature grease to the threads and heads of the new turbo-charger-to-exhaust manifold bolts, then fit and tighten them to the specified torque.*
c) *Tighten the exhaust downpipe nuts to the specified torque.*
d) *Prime the oil feed pipe and turbocharger oil inlet port with clean engine oil before reconnecting the union and tightening it to the specified torque.*
e) *Tighten the oil return union to the specified torque.*

f) *Reconnect the wastegate actuator vacuum hoses according to the notes made during removal* **(see illustration)**.
g) *When the engine is started after refitting, allow it idle for approximately one minute to give the oil time to circulate around the turbine shaft bearings.*

Engine code 1Z

Removal

11 Disconnect the battery negative lead and position it away from the terminal (see paragraph 3). Slacken the clips and remove the turbocharger-to-intercooler and air cleaner-to-turbocharger ducting.

12 Disconnect the boost control valve vacuum hoses from the wastegate actuator diaphragm housing; note their order of connection and colour coding to aid correct refitting later.

13 Remove the nuts and disconnect the exhaust downpipe from the turbocharger outlet. Recover and discard the gasket - a new item must be used on refitting.

14 Loosen the unions and disconnect the oil feed and return pipes from the turbocharger. Recover the sealing washers and discard them - new items must be used on refitting. Free the feed pipe from the clip on the inlet manifold.

15 Remove the retaining screws and detach the downpipe from the cylinder head support bracket.

16 Slacken and withdraw the two turbo-charger-to-inlet manifold bolts from above, then working underneath the exhaust manifold, slacken and remove the retaining nut.

17 Lift the turbocharger away from the exhaust manifold.

Refitting

18 Refit the turbocharger by following the removal procedure in reverse, noting the following points:
a) *Offer up the turbocharger to the exhaust manifold, then fit and initially hand-tighten the exhaust downpipe nuts.*
b) *Fit the exhaust manifold-to-turbocharger nut and tighten it to the specified torque.*
c) *Apply high-temperature grease to the threads and heads of the new turbo-charger-to-exhaust manifold bolts, then fit and tighten them to the specified torque.*
d) *Tighten the exhaust downpipe nuts to the specified torque.*
e) *Prime the oil feed pipe and turbocharger oil inlet port with clean engine oil before reconnecting the union and tightening it to the specified torque.*
f) *Fit a new seal to the oil return union and tighten it to the specified torque.*
g) *Reconnect the wastegate actuator vacuum hoses according to the notes made during removal* **(see illustration)**.
h) *When the engine is started after refitting, allow it idle for approximately one minute to give the oil time to circulate around the turbine shaft bearings.*

Engine code AFN

Removal

19 Disconnect the battery negative lead and position it away from the terminal (see paragraph 3). Remove the engine top cover. Slacken the clips and remove the turbo-charger-to-intercooler and air cleaner-to-turbocharger ducting.

20 Pull off the boost control valve vacuum hose from the wastegate actuator diaphragm housing.

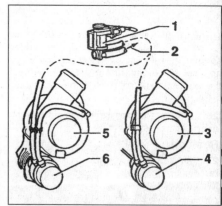

6.10 Wastegate vacuum hose connections - engine code AAZ

1 Two-way valve
2 To vacuum pump
3 Turbocharger
4 Wastegate actuator
5 Turbocharger (Garrett)
6 Wastegate actuator

6.7a Remove the nuts and disconnect the downpipe from the turbocharger outlet

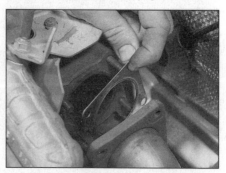

6.7b Recover and discard the gasket

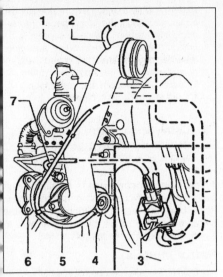

6.18 Wastegate vacuum hose connections - engine code 1Z

1 *Inlet hose*
2 *Hose colour-coded black*
3 *Boost pressure control solenoid*
4 *Wastegate actuator*
5 *Hose colour-coded blue*
6 *Turbocharger*
7 *Hose colour-coded red*

21 Loosen the union and disconnect the oil feed pipe from the turbocharger. Recover the O-ring from the pipe and discard it - a new one must be used on refitting. Unscrew the retaining nut and bolt, and release the feed pipe from the bracket on the inlet manifold.
22 Remove the nuts and disconnect the exhaust downpipe from the turbocharger outlet. Recover and discard the gasket - a new item must be used on refitting.
23 Unbolt the turbocharger mounting bracket from the turbocharger and the cylinder head.
24 Unscrew and remove the two bolts from the oil return connection on the base of the turbocharger. When the turbocharger is removed, recover and discard the gasket - a new one will be needed for reassembly.
25 Slacken and remove the two turbocharger-to-manifold nuts from below, then slacken and remove the retaining nut from above. Discard the nuts, as new items must be used on refitting.
26 Lift the turbocharger away from the exhaust manifold.

Refitting

27 Refit the turbocharger by following the removal procedure in reverse, noting the following points:
a) *Apply high-temperature grease to the threads of the turbocharger and exhaust manifold studs.*
b) *Offer the turbocharger up to the exhaust manifold, and secure with the top nut, hand-tight at this stage.*
c) *Working from below, fit the remaining two turbocharger-to-manifold nuts, and tighten to the specified torque.*

d) *Using a new gasket, fit the two oil return pipe bolts to the connection at the base of the turbocharger, and tighten to the specified torque.*
e) *Refit the turbocharger mounting bracket to the cylinder head and turbocharger, tightening the bolts to the specified torque.*
f) *Tighten the turbocharger-to-exhaust manifold top nut to the specified torque.*
g) *Fit a new gasket over the turbocharger studs, then assemble the exhaust downpipe and tighten the nuts to the specified torque.*
h) *Prime the turbocharger oil inlet port with clean engine oil. Fit a new O-ring to the oil feed pipe before reconnecting the union to the turbocharger and tightening it to the specified torque. Attach the oil feed pipe to the inlet manifold bracket.*
i) *Reconnect the wastegate actuator vacuum hose.*
j) *When the engine is started after refitting, allow it idle for approximately one minute to give the oil time to circulate around the turbine shaft bearings.*

7 Exhaust system - general information and component renewal

General information

1 The exhaust system is made up of the downpipe, the catalytic converter (or front silencer, depending on model), an intermediate silencer that runs across the vehicle, and the tail section which contains the rear silencer. On later models, the intermediate silencer and tail section are originally fitted as one section, but individual sections are available for repair.
2 On all models, the system is suspended throughout its entire length by rubber mountings, which are secured to the underside of the vehicle by metal brackets.

Removal

⚠️ *Warning: Allow ample time for the exhaust system to cool before starting work. In particular, the catalytic converter (where applicable) runs at very high temperatures, and severe burns will*

result if it is carelessly handled. If there is any chance that the system may still be hot, wear suitable gloves.

3 Each exhaust section can be removed individually or, alternatively, the complete system can be removed as a unit.
4 To remove the system or part of the system, first jack up the front or rear of the car and support it on axle stands (see "Jacking and vehicle support").
5 Alternatively, position the car over an inspection pit or on car ramps.

Downpipe - except vehicles with engine code RP

6 Place blocks of wood under the catalytic converter/front silencer to act as a support. Where applicable, refer to Chapter 4A or B and remove the lambda sensor from the exhaust pipe.
7 Slacken and remove the nuts securing the downpipe to the catalytic converter/front silencer (as applicable). Remove the bolts and recover the sealing olive from the joint.
8 Undo the nuts and separate the downpipe from the exhaust manifold. Recover the gasket then withdraw the downpipe from underneath the vehicle.

Downpipe - vehicles with engine code RP

9 On RP engine models, the exhaust manifold-to-downpipe joint is a flared joint secured together by two very rigid fixing clips. If available, VW special tool No. 41 40A/2 should be used to spread each clip in turn to allow its removal from the joint. This tool is basically a wedge-shaped plate, and in the absence of the VW tool, a suitable alternative can be easily fabricated so that it fits tightly into the clip. When the wedge is in the clip, move the exhaust pipe sideways towards the wedged clip, so that the joint clearance on that side is reduced, and the clip can be withdrawn **(see illustrations)**. It will probably be necessary to disconnect the exhaust downpipe mountings to enable the pipe to be moved sideways. Note that the clips are secured on the joint by seatings in the flanges. Once one of the clips is released, press the downpipe towards the other side, and repeat the procedure to remove the second clip. Lower the downpipe, and remove the joint seal. Note that it should not be necessary (and it is not recommended) to prise the clips free, as they are likely to fly off, and

4D

7.9a Fixing clip and spread wedge (RP engine)

7.9b Fixing clip with wedge inserted (RP engine)

personal injury could result. Removal of the damper weight from the steering subframe and exhaust heat shield is recommended, to allow additional access to the joint. This is not an easy joint to separate (or attach), so care and patience are necessary.

10 Separation of the downpipe on RP engine vehicles is otherwise as described in paragraphs 6 to 8.

Catalytic converter

11 Slacken and remove the nuts securing the downpipe to the catalytic converter. Remove the bolts and recover the sealing olive from the joint.

12 Slacken the catalytic converter-to-intermediate pipe clamping ring bolts.

13 Free the catalytic converter from the intermediate pipe, then withdraw it from underneath the vehicle. **Note:** *The catalytic converter is FRAGILE (and expensive to replace) - don't drop it! Treat it with care at all times.*

Intermediate silencer - early models

14 Slacken the clamping ring bolts and disengage the clamp from the intermediate pipe-to-tailpipe joint and the intermediate pipe-to-catalytic converter/front silencer joint.

15 Disengage the intermediate pipe from the tailpipe and the catalytic converter/front silencer and remove it from the vehicle.

Intermediate silencer - later models

16 Slacken the clamping ring bolts and disengage the clamp from the intermediate pipe-to-catalytic converter/front silencer joint.

17 Disengage the intermediate pipe from the catalytic converter/front silencer, and remove the intermediate and rear silencers from the vehicle.

18 If the intermediate silencer alone is to be renewed, it will be necessary to cut through the pipe joining the intermediate and rear silencers, which passes over the rear axle when installed. Two cutting points are marked by three indentations around the pipe - cut at the rearmost point when renewing the intermediate silencer. If a non-VW silencer is to be fitted, a different approach may be needed, so don't cut the pipe until the new silencer has been purchased. If in doubt, leave this operation to a VW dealer or exhaust specialist.

Tail section and rear silencer - early models

19 Slacken the clamping ring bolts and disengage the tailpipe at the joint between the intermediate and rear silencers.

20 Unhook the tailpipe from its mounting rubbers and remove it from the vehicle.

Tail section and rear silencer - later models

21 Slacken the clamping ring bolts and disengage the clamp from the intermediate pipe-to-catalytic converter/front silencer joint.

22 Disengage the intermediate pipe from the catalytic converter/front silencer, and remove the intermediate and rear silencers from the vehicle.

23 If the tail section alone is to be renewed, it will be necessary to cut through the pipe joining the intermediate and rear silencers, which passes over the rear axle when installed. Two cutting points are marked by three indentations around the pipe - cut at the front point when renewing the tail section. If a non-VW section is to be fitted, don't cut the pipe until the new section has been purchased. If in doubt, leave this operation to a VW dealer or exhaust specialist.

Complete system

24 Disconnect the front pipe from the manifold - see paragraphs 6 to 10.

25 With the aid of an assistant, free the system from all its mounting rubbers and manoeuvre it out from underneath the vehicle.

Heatshield(s)

26 The heatshields are secured to the underside of the body by a mixture of nuts, bolts and clips. Each shield can be removed once the relevant exhaust section has been removed. Note that if the shield is being removed to gain access to a component located behind it, in some cases it may prove sufficient to remove the retaining nuts and/or bolts and simply lower the shield, removing the need to disturb the exhaust system.

Refitting

27 Each section is refitted by a reverse of the removal sequence, noting the following points.

 a) *Ensure that all traces of corrosion have been removed from the flanges, and renew all necessary gaskets* **(see illustration)**.

 b) *Inspect the rubber mountings for signs of damage or deterioration and renew as necessary.*

 c) *Renew the sealing olive in the catalytic converter/front silencer-to-downpipe joint.*

 d) *On joints which are secured by clamping rings, apply a smear of exhaust system jointing paste to the joint mating surfaces to ensure an air-tight seal. Tighten the clamping ring nuts evenly and progressively to the specified torque so that the clearance between the clamp halves is equal on either side.*

 e) *Prior to tightening the exhaust system fasteners, ensure that all rubber mountings are correctly located and that there is adequate clearance between the exhaust system and vehicle underbody. Grasp the*

7.27 Manifold-to-downpipe seal - (RP engine)

system and try to move it from side to side on its mountings. Similarly, check for fore-and-aft movement. If there is contact with any underbody components, try loosening the offending component's clamps, and twist it relative to the rest of the system. A little practical thought and application should resolve any problems.

8 Catalytic converter - general information and precautions

1 The catalytic converter is a reliable and simple device which needs no maintenance in itself, but there are some facts of which an owner should be aware if the converter is to function properly for its full service life.

Petrol models

 a) *DO NOT use leaded petrol in a car with a catalytic converter - the lead will coat the precious metals' reagents, reducing their converting efficiency and will eventually destroy the converter.*

 b) *Always keep the ignition and fuel systems well-maintained in accordance with the manufacturer's schedule (see Chapter 1A).*

 c) *If the engine develops a misfire, do not drive the car at all (or at least as little as possible) until the fault is cured.*

 d) *DO NOT push- or tow-start the car - this will soak the catalytic converter in unburned fuel, causing it to overheat when the engine does start.*

 e) *DO NOT switch off the ignition at high engine speeds (ie, do not "blip" the throttle immediately before switching off the engine).*

 f) *In some cases a sulphurous smell (like that of rotten eggs) may be noticed from the exhaust. This is common to many catalytic converter-equipped cars and once the car has covered a few thousand miles the problem should disappear. Low-quality fuel with a high sulphur content will exacerbate this effect.*

 g) *The catalytic converter, used on a well-maintained and well-driven car, should last between 50 000 and 100 000 miles - if the converter is no longer effective, it must be renewed.*

Petrol and diesel models

 h) *DO NOT use fuel or engine oil additives - these may contain substances harmful to the catalytic converter.*

 i) *DO NOT continue to use the car if the engine burns oil to the extent of leaving a visible trail of blue smoke.*

 j) *Remember that the catalytic converter operates at very high temperatures. DO NOT, therefore, park the car in dry undergrowth, over long grass or piles of dead leaves after a long run.*

 k) *Remember that the catalytic converter is FRAGILE - do not strike it with tools during servicing work.*

Chapter 5 Part A:
Starting and charging systems

Contents

Degrees of difficulty

Easy, suitable for novice with little experience	Fairly easy, suitable for beginner with some experience	Fairly difficult, suitable for competent DIY mechanic	Difficult, suitable for experienced DIY mechanic	Very difficult, suitable for expert DIY or professional 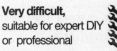

Specifications

General

System type . . . . 12 volt, negative earth

Starter motor

Rating:
    Petrol models . . . . 12V, 1.0 or 1.1 kW
    Diesel models . . . . 12V, 1.7 kW

Battery

Ratings . . . . 36 to 110 Ah (depending on model and market)

Alternator

Brush length (new) . . . . 12 mm
Minimum brush length . . . . 5 mm (tolerance +1mm, -0 mm)

Torque wrench settings

	Nm	lbf ft
Alternator mounting bolts	25	18
Battery clamp plate bolt	20	15
Battery terminal bolts	5	4
Starter motor mounting nuts/bolts:		
M8	10	7
M10	60	44
Starter motor-to-engine mounting bolt	55	41

5A

1 General information and precautions

General information

The engine electrical system consists mainly of the charging and starting systems. Because of their engine-related functions, these are covered separately from the body electrical devices such as the lights, instruments, etc (which are covered in Chapter 12). On petrol engine models refer to Part B of this Chapter for information on the ignition system, and on diesel models refer to Part C for the pre-heating system.

The electrical system is of the 12-volt negative earth type.

The battery may of the low maintenance or "maintenance-free" (sealed for life) type and is charged by the alternator, which is belt-driven from the crankshaft pulley.

The starter motor is of the pre-engaged type, with an integral solenoid. On starting, the solenoid moves the drive pinion into engagement with the flywheel ring gear before the starter motor is energised. Once the engine has started, a one-way clutch prevents the motor armature being driven by the engine until the pinion disengages from the flywheel.

Further details of the various systems are given in the relevant Sections of this Chapter. While some repair procedures are given, the usual course of action is to renew the component concerned. The owner whose interest extends beyond mere component renewal should obtain a copy of the "Automobile Electrical & Electronic Systems Manual", available from the publishers of this manual.

Precautions

Warning: It is necessary to take extra care when working on the electrical system to avoid damage to semi-conductor devices (diodes and transistors), and to avoid the risk of personal injury. In addition to the precautions given in "Safety first!", observe the following when working on the system:

Always remove rings, watches, etc before working on the electrical system. Even with the battery disconnected, capacitive discharge could occur if a component's live terminal is earthed through a metal object. This could cause a shock or nasty burn.

Do not reverse the battery connections. Components such as the alternator, electronic control units, or any other components having semi-conductor circuitry could be irreparably damaged.

Never disconnect the battery terminals, the alternator, any electrical wiring or any test instruments when the engine is running.

Do not allow the engine to turn the alternator when the alternator is not connected. Never "test" for alternator output by "flashing" the output lead to earth. Always ensure that the battery negative lead is disconnected when working on the electrical system.

If the engine is being started using jump leads and a slave battery, connect the batteries **positive-to-positive** and **negative-to-negative** (see "Booster battery (jump) starting"). This also applies when connecting a battery charger.

Never use an ohmmeter of the type incorporating a hand-cranked generator for circuit or continuity testing.

Before using electric-arc welding equipment on the car, **disconnect the battery, alternator and components such as the electronic control units** (where applicable) to protect them from the risk of damage.

Caution: Certain radio/cassettes fitted as standard equipment by VW have a built-in security code to deter thieves. If the power source to the unit is cut, the anti-theft system will activate. Even if the power source is immediately reconnected, the radio/cassette unit will not function until the correct security code has been entered. Therefore, if you do not know the correct security code for the radio/cassette unit do not disconnect the battery negative terminal of the battery or remove the radio/cassette unit from the vehicle. Refer to your VW dealer for further information on whether the unit fitted to your car has a security code.

2 Battery - testing and charging

Standard and low maintenance battery - testing

1 If the vehicle covers a small annual mileage it is worthwhile checking the specific gravity of the electrolyte every three months to determine the state of charge of the battery. Use a hydrometer to make the check and compare the results with the following table. The temperatures quoted are ambient (air temperatures. Note that the specific gravity readings assume an electrolyte temperature of 15°C; for every 10°C below 15°C add 0.007. For every 10°C above 15°C subtract 0.007.

	Above 25°C	Below 25°C
100% charged	1.210 to 1.230	1.270 to 1.290
70% charged	1.170 to 1.190	1.230 to 1.250
Discharged	1.050 to 1.070	1.110 to 1.130

2 If the battery condition is suspect, first check the specific gravity of electrolyte in each cell. A variation of 0.040 or more between any cells indicates loss of electrolyte or deterioration of the internal plates.

3 If the specific gravity variation is 0.040 or more, the battery should be renewed. If the cell variation is satisfactory but the battery is discharged, it should be charged as described later in this Section.

Maintenance-free battery - testing

4 In cases where a "sealed for life" maintenance-free battery is fitted, topping-up and testing of the electrolyte in each cell is not possible. The condition of the battery can therefore only be tested using a battery condition indicator or a voltmeter.

5 Certain models may be fitted with a maintenance-free battery, with a built-in charge condition indicator. The indicator is located in the top of the battery casing, and indicates the condition of the battery from its colour. If the indicator shows green, then the battery is in a good state of charge. If the indicator turns darker, eventually to black, then the battery requires charging, as described later in this Section. If the indicator shows clear/yellow, then the electrolyte level in the battery is too low to allow further use, and the battery should be renewed. **Do not** attempt to charge, load or jump start a battery when the indicator shows clear/yellow.

6 If testing the battery using a voltmeter, connect the voltmeter across the battery and note the voltage. The test is only accurate if the battery has not been subjected to any kind of charge for the previous six hours. If this is not the case, switch on the headlights for 30 seconds, then wait four to five minutes before testing the battery after switching off the headlights. All other electrical circuits must be switched off, so check that the doors and tailgate are fully shut when making the test.

7 If the voltage reading is less than 12.2 volts, then the battery is discharged, whilst a reading of 12.2 to 12.4 volts indicates a partially discharged condition.

8 If the battery is to be charged, remove it from the vehicle and charge it as described later in this Section.

Standard and low maintenance battery - charging

Note: The following is intended as a guide only. Always refer to the manufacturer's recommendations (often printed on a label attached to the battery) before charging a battery.

9 Charge the battery at a rate equivalent to 10% of the battery capacity (eg for a 45 Ah battery charge at 4.5 A) and continue to charge the battery at this rate until no further rise in specific gravity is noted over a four-hour period.

10 Alternatively, a trickle charger charging at the rate of 1.5 amps can safely be used overnight.

11 Specially rapid "boost" charges which are claimed to restore the power of the battery in 1 to 2 hours are not recommended, as they can cause serious damage to the battery plates through overheating.

12 While charging the battery, note that the temperature of the electrolyte should never exceed 37.8°C.

Maintenance-free battery - charging

Note: *The following is intended as a guide only. Always refer to the manufacturer's recommendations (often printed on a label attached to the battery) before charging a battery.*

13 This battery type takes considerably longer to fully recharge than the standard type, the time taken being dependent on the extent of discharge, but it can take anything up to three days.

14 A constant voltage type charger is required, to be set, when connected, to 13.9 to 14.9 volts with a charger current below 25 amps. Using this method, the battery should be useable within three hours, giving a voltage reading of 12.5 volts, but this is for a partially discharged battery and, as mentioned, full charging can take far longer.

15 If the battery is to be charged from a fully discharged state (condition reading less than 12.2 volts), have it recharged by your VW dealer or local automotive electrician, as the charge rate is higher and constant supervision during charging is necessary.

3 Battery -
removal and refitting

Removal

1 Note: *If the vehicle has a security-coded radio, check that you have a copy of the code number before disconnecting the battery lead; refer to the caution in Section 1.*

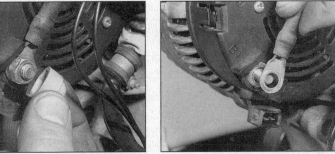

5.3 Unplug the sense cable from the alternator at the connector (later diesel engine model shown)

3.4 Battery clamp plate screw (arrowed)

2 Slacken the clamp screw and disconnect the battery negative lead from the terminal.
3 Unclip the plastic cover and disconnect the battery positive lead in the same manner.
4 At the base of the battery, slacken and withdraw the retaining bolt, then lift off the clamp plate **(see illustration)**.
5 Remove the battery from the engine bay.

Refitting

6 Refit the battery by following the removal procedure in reverse. Tighten the battery clamp plate bolt to the correct torque.

4 Alternator/charging system -
testing in vehicle

Note: *Refer to "Safety first!" and Section 1 of this Chapter before starting work.*

1 If the charge warning light fails to illuminate when the ignition is switched on, first check the alternator wiring connections for security. If satisfactory, check that the warning light bulb has not blown, and that the bulbholder is secure in its location in the instrument panel. If the light still fails to illuminate, check the continuity of the warning light feed wire from the alternator to the bulbholder. If all is satisfactory, the alternator is at fault, and should be renewed or taken to an auto-electrical specialist for testing and repair.

2 Similarly, if the charge warning light comes on with the ignition, but is then slow to go out when the engine is started, this may indicate an impending alternator problem. Check all the items listed in the preceding paragraph,

and refer to an auto-electrical specialist if no obvious faults are found.
3 If the ignition warning light illuminates when the engine is running, stop the engine and check that the drivebelt is correctly tensioned (see Chapter 2A or B) and that the alternator connections are secure. If all is so far satisfactory, check the alternator brushes and slip rings as described in Section 6. If the fault persists, the alternator should be renewed, or taken to an auto-electrical specialist for testing and repair.
4 If the alternator output is suspect even though the warning light functions correctly, the regulated voltage may be checked as follows.
5 Connect a voltmeter across the battery terminals and start the engine.
6 Increase the engine speed until the voltmeter reading remains steady; the reading should be approximately 12 to 13 volts, and no more than 14 volts.
7 Switch on as many electrical accessories (eg, the headlights, heated rear window and heater blower) as possible, and check that the alternator maintains the regulated voltage at around 13 to 14 volts.
8 If the regulated voltage is not as stated, this may be due to worn brushes, weak brush springs, a faulty voltage regulator, a faulty diode, a severed phase winding or worn or damaged slip rings. The brushes and slip rings may be checked (see Section 6), but if the fault persists, the alternator should be renewed or taken to an auto-electrical specialist.

5 Alternator -
removal and refitting

Removal

1 Disconnect the battery negative lead and position it away from the terminal (refer to the Caution in Section 1).
2 Remove the auxiliary drivebelt from the alternator pulley (see Chapter 2A or 2B).
3 Unplug the sense cable from the alternator at the connector **(see illustration)**.
4 Remove the protective cap, slacken and withdraw the nut and washers, then disconnect the power cable from the alternator at the screw terminal post. Where applicable, unbolt and remove the cable guide **(see illustrations)**.

5A

5.4a Remove the protective cap . . .

5.4b . . . remove the nut and washers, then disconnect the power cable

5.4c Where applicable, unbolt and remove the cable guide

5.5a Lifting the alternator away from its mounting bracket (diesel engine shown)

5.5b Alternator fitted to an early model, showing drivebelt adjustment link

5 Slacken and remove the lower, then the upper bolts, then lift the alternator away from its bracket **(see illustration)**. Where applicable, pivot the tensioner roller out of the way to gain access to the lower mounting bolt. Note also that it may be necessary to prise a plug from the timing cover for access to the pivot bolt. On early models, the adjustment link may be unbolted from the cylinder head if desired **(see illustration)**.

6 Refer to Section 6 if removal of the brush holder/voltage regulator module is required.

Refitting

7 Refitting is a reversal of removal. Refer to Chapter 2A or B as applicable for details of refitting and tensioning the auxiliary drivebelt.
8 On completion, tighten the alternator mounting bolts to the specified torque.

6 Alternator - brush holder/regulator module renewal

1 Access to the rear of the alternator is easy on most models, and the brushes and voltage regulator may be removed with the alternator on the engine.
2 Alternatively, remove the alternator, as described in Section 5, and place the alternator on a clean work surface, with the pulley facing down.
3 Where applicable, remove the retaining screws, then prise open the clips and lift the plastic cover from the rear of the alternator **(see illustrations)**.
4 Slacken and withdraw the brush holder/voltage regulator module screws, then lift the module away from the alternator **(see illustrations)**.

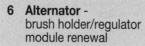

6.3a Where applicable, remove the retaining screws (arrowed) . . .

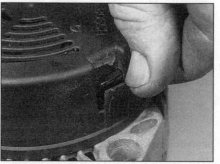

6.3b . . . then prise open the clips . . .

6.3c . . . and lift the plastic cover from the rear of the alternator

6.4a Remove the brush holder/voltage regulator module screws . . .

6.4b . . . then lift the module away from the alternator

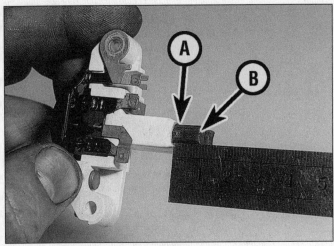

6.5 Measuring the alternator brush length - for A and B, see text

6.6 Inspect the surfaces of the slip rings (arrowed) at the end of the alternator shaft

5 Measure the free length of the brush contacts - take the measurement from the manufacturer's emblem (A) etched on the side of the brush contact, to the shallowest part of the curved end face of the brush (B) **(see illustration)**. Check the measurement with the Specifications; renew the module if the brushes are worn below the minimum limit.

6 Inspect the surfaces of the slip rings, at the end of the alternator shaft **(see illustration)**. If they appear excessively worn, burnt or pitted, then renewal must be considered; refer to an auto-electrical specialist for further guidance.

7 Reassemble the alternator by reversing the dismantling procedure. If the alternator was removed, refer to Section 5 and refit the alternator.

7 Starting system - testing

Note: *Refer to the precautions given in "Safety first!" and in Section 1 of this Chapter before starting work.*

1 If the starter motor fails to operate when the ignition key is turned to the appropriate position, the following possible causes may be to blame:
  a) *The battery is faulty.*
  b) *The electrical connections between the switch, solenoid, battery and starter motor are somewhere failing to pass the necessary current from the battery through the starter to earth.*
  c) *The solenoid is faulty.*
  d) *The starter motor is mechanically or electrically defective.*

2 To check the battery, switch on the headlights. If they dim after a few seconds, this indicates that the battery is discharged - recharge (see Section 2) or renew the battery. If the headlights glow brightly, operate the ignition switch and observe the lights. If they

dim, then this indicates that current is reaching the starter motor; therefore, the fault must lie in the starter motor. If the lights continue to glow brightly (and no clicking sound can be heard from the starter motor solenoid), this indicates that there is a fault in the circuit or solenoid. If the starter motor turns slowly when operated, then (if the battery is in good condition) this indicates that either the starter motor is faulty, or there is considerable resistance somewhere in the circuit.

3 If a fault in the circuit is suspected, disconnect the battery leads (including the earth connection to the body), the starter/solenoid wiring and the engine/transmission earth strap (refer to the Caution in Section 1). Thoroughly clean the connections, reconnect the leads and wiring, then use a voltmeter or test lamp to check that full battery voltage is available at the battery positive lead connection to the solenoid, and that the earth is sound. Smear petroleum jelly around the battery terminals to prevent corrosion - corroded connections are amongst the most frequent causes of electrical system faults.

4 If the battery and all connections are in good condition, check the circuit by disconnecting the wire from the solenoid blade terminal. Connect a voltmeter or test lamp between the wire end and a good earth (such as the battery negative terminal), and check that the wire is live when the ignition switch is turned to the "start" position. If it is, then the circuit is sound - if not the circuit wiring can be checked as described in Chapter 12.

5 The solenoid contacts can be checked by connecting a voltmeter or test lamp between the battery positive feed connection on the starter side of the solenoid, and earth. When the ignition switch is turned to the "start" position, there should be a reading or lighted bulb, as applicable. If there is no reading or lighted bulb, the solenoid is faulty and should be renewed.

6 If the circuit and solenoid are proved sound, the fault must lie in the starter motor. Begin checking the starter motor by removing it (see Section 8), and checking the brushes. If the fault does not lie in the brushes, the motor windings must be faulty. In this event, it may be possible to have the starter motor overhauled by a specialist, but check on the availability and cost of spares before proceeding, as it may prove more economical to obtain a new or exchange motor.

8 Starter motor - removal and refitting

1 The starter is situated on the bellhousing at the front of the engine, and shares one of its mounting bolts with the front engine mounting bracket. **Note:** *Removal of the starter motor-to-engine mounting bracket bolt involves supporting the engine whilst the bolt is removed - refer to Chapter 2A or B as applicable for greater detail.*

Removal

2 Disconnect the battery negative lead and position it away from the terminal (refer to the Caution in Section 1).

3 Referring to Chapter 2A or B as applicable, support the engine and remove the bolt securing the front engine mounting bracket to the starter motor.

4 If applicable, unhook the wiring connector from the cable guide above the solenoid housing, then remove the cable guide. Unplug the solenoid supply cabling at the connector **(see illustrations)**.

5 At the rear of the solenoid housing, remove the nut and washer from the power cable terminal post and take off the power cables **(see illustration)**.

6 Remove the starter upper mounting bolt, then slacken and remove the nut from the mounting stud underneath the starter motor.

8.4a Remove the cable guide from above the solenoid housing . . .

8.4b . . . then unplug the solenoid supply cabling at the connector

8.5 Remove the nut and washer, and take off the power cables

7 Guide the starter and solenoid assembly out of the bellhousing aperture **(see illustration)**.

Refitting

8 Refit the starter motor by following the removal procedure in reverse. Tighten the mounting bolts to the specified torque. Where applicable, refer to Chapter 2A or B and refit the bolt to the front engine mounting bracket.

9 Starter motor - testing and overhaul

If the starter motor is thought to be defective, it should be removed from the vehicle and taken to an auto-electrician for assessment. In the majority of cases, new starter motor brushes can be fitted at a reasonable cost. However, check the cost of repairs first as it may prove more economical to purchase a new or exchange motor.

8.7 Guide the starter and solenoid assembly out of the bellhousing aperture

Chapter 5 Part B:
Ignition system - petrol models

Contents

Degrees of difficulty

Easy, suitable for novice with little experience		Fairly easy, suitable for beginner with some experience		Fairly difficult, suitable for competent DIY mechanic		Difficult, suitable for experienced DIY mechanic		Very difficult, suitable for expert DIY or professional	

Specifications

General

System type:

Engine code RP (to 08/90)	Hall-effect (TCI-H), Bosch Mono-Jetronic
Engine codes AAM, ABS, ADZ and RP (08/90 on)	Bosch Mono-Motronic
Engine codes PB, PF and 2E	Digifant
Engine codes ADY and AGG	Simos

Ignition coil

Primary winding resistance (typical):

Except Simos system	0.5 to 0.8 ohms
Simos system	0.5 to 1.5 ohms

Secondary resistance (typical):

Coil with green sticker	2.4 to 3.5 kilohms
Coil with grey sticker	6.9 to 8.5 kilohms
All other coils	3 to 4 kilohms

Distributor

Type	Breakerless

Ignition timing:

Hall-effect system	6 ± 1° BTDC at idle, distributor vacuum hose disconnected and plugged
Digifant system up to 07/92	6 ± 1° BTDC at 2000 to 2500 rpm, coolant temperature sender blue connector plug disconnected
All other systems	Fluctuating at idle, controlled by engine management system - no adjustment possible without dedicated VW equipment

Spark plugs

See Chapter 1A Specifications

Torque wrench settings

	Nm	lbf ft
Distributor clamp plate bolt	25	18
Knock sensor mounting bolt	20	15

1 General information

Hall-effect system, TCI-H distributor

The transistor controlled ignition system incorporates an electronic sender unit in the distributor. A remote electronic switch controls the coil primary circuit.

The ignition timing is advanced and retarded automatically, to ensure that the spark occurs at just the right instant for the particular load at the prevailing engine speed. Ignition advance is controlled by the vacuum unit attached to the distributor body. The vacuum consists of a diaphragm, one side of which is connected via a small bore pipe to the inlet manifold, and the other side to the baseplate. Depression in the inlet manifold, which varies with engine speed and throttle opening, causes the diaphragm to move, so moving the baseplate, and advancing or retarding the spark. A fine degree of control is achieved by a spring in the vacuum assembly.

The low tension (LT) circuit is interrupted regularly by a Hall sender unit in the distributor, and this action causes the magnetic field around the coil primary windings to collapse. The coil secondary windings are located over the primary windings, and the magnetic field induces a high tension current. The current is fed to the spark plug via the distributor cap and rotor.

The exact timing of the HT spark is dependent on the speed of, and load on, the engine, to give the most efficient setting.

The distributor is mounted in the cylinder block and is driven through a skew gear by the intermediate shaft.

Digifant system up to July 1992

The Digifant ignition system up to July 1992 uses the Hall-effect system described above, but in addition it incorporates a knock sensor, which senses the onset of pre-ignition and retards the ignition timing accordingly. Ignition advance is automatically adjusted by the computerised control unit which also controls the fuel injection system, and because of this, there are no centrifugal advance weights in the distributor.

All other systems

The Bosch Mono-Motronic, later Digifant (August 1992 on) and Simos systems are self-contained engine management systems, which control both the fuel injection and ignition. This Chapter deals with the ignition system components only - refer to Chapter 4A or B for details of the fuel system components.

The basic operation is as follows: the ECU supplies a voltage to the input stage of the ignition coil which causes the primary windings in the coil to be energised. The supply voltage is periodically interrupted by the ECU and this results in the collapse of primary magnetic field, which then induces a much larger voltage in the secondary coil, called the HT voltage. This voltage is directed, by the distributor via the HT leads, to the spark plug in the cylinder currently on its ignition stroke. The spark plug electrodes form a gap small enough for the HT voltage to arc across, and the resulting spark ignites the fuel/air mixture in the cylinder. The timing of this sequence of events is critical and is regulated solely by the ECU.

The ECU calculates and controls the ignition timing and dwell angle primarily according to engine speed, crankshaft position and inlet manifold depression (or inlet air volume flow rate, depending on system type) information, received from sensors mounted on and around the engine. Other parameters that affect ignition timing are throttle position and rate of opening, inlet air temperature, coolant temperature and on certain systems, engine knock. Again, these are monitored via sensors mounted on the engine.

On systems where knock control is employed, knock sensor(s) are mounted on the cylinder block - these have the ability to detect engine pre-ignition (or 'pinking') before it actually becomes audible. If pre-ignition occurs, the ECU retards the ignition timing of the cylinder that is pre-igniting in steps until the pre-ignition ceases. The ECU then advances the ignition timing of that cylinder in steps until it is restored to normal, or until pre-ignition occurs again.

Idle speed control is achieved partly by an electronic throttle valve positioning module, mounted on the side of the throttle body and partly by the ignition system, which gives fine control of the idle speed by altering the ignition timing. As a result, manual adjustment of the engine idle speed is not necessary or possible.

On certain systems, the ECU has the ability to perform multiple ignition cycles during cold starting. During cranking, each spark plug fires several times per ignition stroke, until the engine starts. This greatly improves the engines cold starting performance.

It should be noted that comprehensive fault diagnosis of all the engine management systems described in this Chapter is only possible with dedicated electronic test equipment. Problems with a system's operation that cannot be pinpointed by following the basic guidelines in Section 2 should therefore be referred to a VW dealer for assessment. Once the fault has been identified, the removal/refitting sequences detailed in the following Sections will then allow the appropriate component(s) to renewed as required.

Note: *Throughout this Chapter, vehicles are frequently referred to by their engine code, rather than by engine capacity - refer to Chapter 2A for engine code listings.*

---

2 Ignition system - testing

> ⚠️ *Warning: Extreme care must be taken when working on the system with the ignition switched on; it is possible to get a substantial electric shock from a vehicle's ignition system. Persons with cardiac pacemaker devices should keep well clear of the ignition circuits, components and test equipment. Always switch off the ignition before disconnecting or connecting any component and when using a multi-meter to check resistances.*

General

1 Most ignition system faults are likely to be due to loose or dirty connections or to 'tracking' (unintentional earthing) of HT voltage due to dirt, dampness or damaged insulation, rather than by the failure of any of the system's components. **Always** check all wiring thoroughly before condemning an electrical component and work methodically to eliminate all other possibilities before deciding that a particular component is faulty.
2 The old practice of checking for a spark by holding the live end of an HT lead a short distance away from the engine is not recommended; not only is there a high risk of an electric shock, but the HT coil could be damaged. Similarly, **never** try to 'diagnose' misfires by pulling off one HT lead at a time.

Engine will not start

3 If the engine either will not turn over at all, or only turns very slowly, check the battery and starter motor. Connect a voltmeter across the battery terminals (meter positive probe to battery positive terminal), disconnect the ignition coil HT lead from the distributor cap and earth it, then note the voltage reading obtained while turning over the engine on the starter for (no more than) ten seconds. If the reading obtained is less than approximately 9.5 volts, first check the battery, starter motor and charging systems (see Chapter 5A).
4 If the engine turns over at normal speed but will not start, check the HT circuit by connecting a timing light (following the manufacturer's instructions) and turning the engine over on the starter motor; if the light flashes, voltage is reaching the spark plugs, so these should be checked first. If the light does not flash, check the HT leads themselves followed by the distributor cap, carbon brush and rotor arm using the information given in Chapter 1A.
5 If there is a spark, check the fuel system for faults referring to the relevant part of Chapter 4 for further information.
6 If there is still no spark, check the HT leads, ignition coil and distributor cap. If this does not reveal the problem, then the engine management system (where applicable) must be suspect. In these cases, the vehicle should be referred to a VW dealer for assessment.

Engine misfires

7 An irregular misfire suggests either a loose connection or intermittent fault on the primary circuit, or an HT fault on the coil side of the rotor arm.
8 With the ignition switched off, check carefully through the system ensuring that all connections are clean and securely fastened. If the equipment is available, check the LT circuit as described above.
9 Check that the HT coil, the distributor cap and the HT leads are clean and dry. Check the leads themselves and the spark plugs (by substitution, if necessary), then check the distributor cap, carbon brush and rotor arm as described later in this Section.
10 Regular misfiring is almost certainly due to a fault in the distributor cap, HT leads or spark plugs. Use a timing light (paragraph 4 above) to check whether HT voltage is present at all leads.
11 If HT voltage is not present on one particular lead, the fault will be in that lead or in the distributor cap. If HT is present on all leads, the fault will be in the spark plugs; check and renew them if there is any doubt about their condition.
12 If no HT voltage is present, check the HT coil; its secondary windings may be breaking down under load.

Other problems

13 Problems that cannot be pinpointed by following the guidelines in the preceding paragraphs should be referred to a VW dealer for assessment.

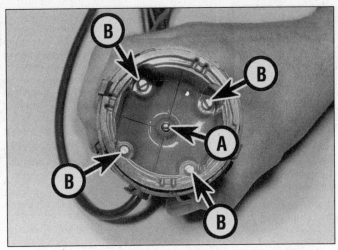

2.21 Distributor cap checking points - carbon brush (A) and HT lead segments (B)

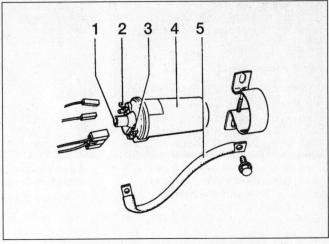

2.29a Ignition coil connections on early-type coil

1 Coil terminal 4 (HT "king"   3 Coil terminal 1 (-)
   lead connection)   4 Ignition coil
2 Coil terminal 15 (+)   5 Earth strap

Ignition component check

HT leads

14 The spark plug (HT) leads should be checked whenever new spark plugs are fitted (see Chapter 1A).

 HAYNES HINT *Ensure that the leads are numbered before removing them, to avoid confusion when refitting.*

15 Pull the leads from the plugs by gripping the end fitting, not the lead, otherwise the lead connection may be fractured.

16 Check inside the end fitting for signs of corrosion, which will look like a white crusty powder. Push the end fitting back onto the spark plug, ensuring that it is a tight fit on the plug. If not, remove the lead again and use pliers to carefully crimp the metal connector inside the end fitting until it fits securely on the end of the spark plug.

17 Using a clean rag, wipe the entire length of the lead to remove any built-up dirt and grease. Once the lead is clean, check for burns, cracks and other damage. Do not bend the lead too much, nor pull the lead length-ways - the conductor inside might break.

18 Disconnect the other end of the lead from the distributor cap. Again, pull only on the end fitting. Check for corrosion and a tight fit in the same manner as the spark plug end. If an ohmmeter is available, check the resistance of the lead by connecting the meter between the spark plug end of the lead and the segment inside the distributor cap. Refit the lead securely on completion.

19 Check the remaining leads one at a time, in the same way.

20 If new spark plug (HT) leads are required, buy a set for your specific car and engine.

Distributor cap

21 Unscrew its retaining screws or release the clips and remove the distributor cap. Wipe it clean, and carefully inspect it inside and out for signs of cracks, black carbon tracks (tracking) and worn, burned or loose contacts; check that the cap's carbon brush is unworn, free to move against spring pressure, and making good contact with the rotor arm **(see illustration)**. Also inspect the cap seal for signs of wear or damage, and renew if necessary.

22 Do not simultaneously remove all the leads from the old cap, or firing order confusion may occur. When refitting, tighten the cap retaining screws securely, or ensure that the cap clips engage correctly.

HAYNES HINT *When fitting a new cap, remove the leads from the old cap one at a time, and fit them to the new cap in the same location.*

23 Even with the ignition system in first-class condition, some engines may still occasionally experience poor starting attributable to damp ignition components. To disperse moisture, a water-dispersant aerosol should be liberally applied.

Rotor arm

24 With reference to the previous sub-Section, remove the distributor cap and its screening shield (where applicable).

25 Pull off the rotor arm from the distributor shaft and inspect the rotor arm. It is common practice to renew the cap and rotor arm whenever new spark plug (HT) leads are fitted.

26 Inspect the distributor shaft contacts and clean them if necessary.

27 Refitting is a reversal of removal - ensure that the rotor arm alignment lug engages with the recess in the distributor shaft, before refitting the distributor cap.

Ignition coil

28 Disconnect the wiring and cap from the ignition coil. If necessary, identify each wire for location.

29 Connect a multimeter between terminals 1(–) and 15(+), and check that the resistance of the primary windings is as given in the Specifications **(see illustrations)**.

30 Connect the multimeter between terminals 4 (HT) and 15(+), and check that the resistance of the secondary windings is as given in the Specifications.

31 Reconnect the wiring.

5B

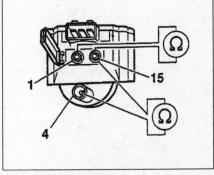

2.29b Checking ignition coil resistances on later-type coil

1 LT negative (-) connection
4 HT connection
15 LT positive (+) connection

3.3 Unplug the HT lead from the ignition coil at the connector - later-type coil shown

3.4 Disconnect the LT wiring from the ignition coil at the multiway connector

Note: For details of early-type coil, refer to illustration 2.29a

4.5 Detach the wiring connector from the distributor

3 Ignition HT coil - removal and refitting

Removal

1 On all models, the ignition coil is mounted at the rear of the engine compartment, near the coolant expansion tank.
2 Disconnect the battery negative lead and position it away from the terminal. **Note:** *If the vehicle has a security-coded radio, check that you have a copy of the code number before disconnecting the battery. Refer to your VW dealer if in doubt.*
3 Unplug the HT lead from the ignition coil at the connector **(see illustration)**.
4 Disconnect the LT cables from the ignition coil, or unplug the multiway connector **(see illustration)**.
5 Slacken and withdraw the mounting screws and remove the ignition coil.

Refitting

6 Refitting is a reversal of removal.

4 Distributor - removal, inspection and refitting

Removal

1 Disconnect the battery negative lead and position it away from the terminal. **Note:** *If the vehicle has a security-coded radio, check that you have a copy of the code number before disconnecting the battery. Refer to your VW dealer if in doubt.*
2 Set the engine to TDC on cylinder No 1, referring to Section 2 of Chapter 2A for guidance.
3 If required, unplug all five HT leads from the distributor cap, labelling them to aid refitting later.
4 Where applicable, remove the screws and lift off the screening cap.

5 Unplug the wiring plug from the distributor body at the connector **(see illustration)**.
6 Remove the screws/prise off the retaining clips (as applicable), then lift off the distributor cap. Check at this point that the centre of the rotor arm electrode is aligned with the cylinder No 1 marking on the rim of the distributor body **(see illustration)**.
7 Mark the relationship between the distributor body and the drive gear case flange by scribing arrows on each.
8 Slacken and remove the bolt, then lift off the clamp plate and withdraw the distributor body from the cylinder block **(see illustration)**. On engine code RP, disconnect the vacuum hose from the advance capsule, where applicable.

Inspection

9 Recover the O-ring seal(s) from the bottom of the distributor and inspect them **(see illustration)**. Renew them if they appear at all worn or damaged.

4.6 Rotor arm electrode aligned with timing mark on rim of distributor body

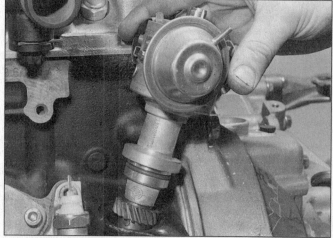

4.8 Slacken and remove the bolt, then lift out the distributor (early engine code RP type shown)

10 Inspect the teeth of the distributor drivegear for signs of wear or damage **(see illustration)**. Any slack in the distributor drive train will affect ignition timing. Renew the distributor if the teeth of the drivegear appear worn or chipped.

Refitting

11 Before progressing, check that the engine is still set to TDC on cylinder No 1.
12 On engine codes PB, PF, ADY, AGG and RP (up to August 1990), check at this point that the oil pump shaft drive tongue is aligned with the axis of the crankshaft **(see illustration)**.
13 On all other engines, the oil pump shaft drive tongue should be aligned with the threaded hole, adjacent to the distributor aperture **(see illustration)**.
14 Install the distributor, then loosely fit the clamp plate and securing bolt; it may be necessary to rotate the shaft slightly to allow it to engage with the intermediate shaft drive gear. Rotate the distributor body such that the alignment marks made during removal line up.
15 The shaft is engaged at the correct angle when the centre of the rotor arm electrode is pointing directly at the No 1 cylinder mark on the distributor body. It may take a few attempts to get this right, as the helical drive gears make the alignment difficult to judge. On engine codes ADY and AGG, the distributor is correctly installed when the two pins on the base of the distributor are aligned

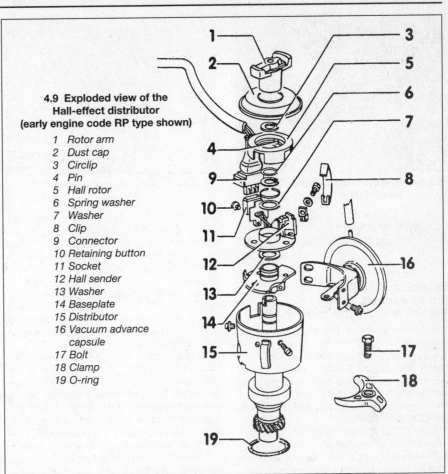

4.9 Exploded view of the Hall-effect distributor (early engine code RP type shown)

1 Rotor arm
2 Dust cap
3 Circlip
4 Pin
5 Hall rotor
6 Spring washer
7 Washer
8 Clip
9 Connector
10 Retaining button
11 Socket
12 Hall sender
13 Washer
14 Baseplate
15 Distributor
16 Vacuum advance capsule
17 Bolt
18 Clamp
19 O-ring

4.10 Check the condition of the drivegear and the O-ring seal (arrowed)

either side of the clamp bolt threaded hole **(see illustration)**.
Note: *If alignment proves impossible, check that the intermediate shaft sprocket is correctly aligned with the crankshaft pulley - refer to Chapter 2A for further guidance.*
16 When you are satisfied that the distributor is correctly installed, tighten the distributor clamp bolt to its specified torque.
17 Refit the distributor cap, pressing the retaining clips firmly into place/ tightening the retaining screws (as applicable).

18 Reconnect the wiring plug to the distributor.
19 Where applicable, refit the screening cap, tightening the screws securely.
20 Working from the No 1 terminal, connect the HT leads between the spark plugs and the distributor cap. The firing order is 1-3-4-2.
21 Fit the HT king lead between the coil and the centre terminal on the distributor cap.
22 It will now be necessary for the ignition timing to be checked and if necessary adjusted - refer to Section 5.

5B

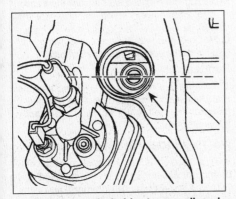

4.12 Oil pump shaft drive tongue aligned with the axis of the crankshaft

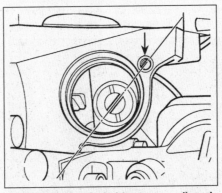

4.13 Oil pump shaft drive tongue aligned with the threaded hole (arrowed), adjacent to the distributor aperture

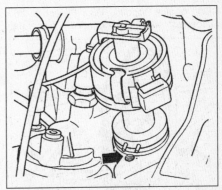

4.15 Pins on base of distributor must align either side of the clamp bolt threaded hole

5.3 Remove the inspection plug from the transmission housing . . .

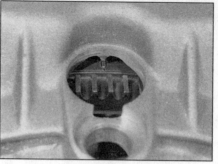

5.4a . . . to view the flywheel TDC "0" mark . . .

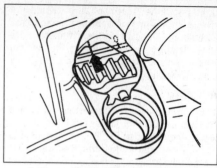

5.4b . . . and ignition timing mark (arrowed)

5 Ignition timing - checking and adjusting

Engine codes RP (up to August 1990), PB, PF and 2E (up to July 1992)

1 Before checking or adjusting the ignition timing, ensure that the rest of the ignition system is in good condition. In particular, check that all relevant leads are securely connected, and that the spark plugs are clean and correctly gapped. Also ensure that the fuel system is correctly adjusted (idle speed and CO/mixture settings).
2 Ensure that the air conditioning system (where fitted) is switched off.
3 Prise free the plug from the transmission housing access hole (see illustration).
4 Turn the engine using a spanner on the crankshaft pulley bolt, or by engaging top gear (manual transmission) and rolling the car backwards and forwards, until the flywheel timing marks are visible through the access hole (see illustrations). Using a dab of white quick-drying paint, highlight the ignition timing mark on the flywheel, and the inverted V-shaped notch in the lower edge of access hole.
5 Run the engine to normal operating temperature.
6 Stop the engine, and connect a stroboscopic timing light in accordance with the equipment manufacturer's instructions.
7 On engine codes PB, PF and 2E, disconnect the blue connector from the

temperature sender (see illustration). Start the engine, and run it at 2000 to 2500 rpm.
8 On engine code RP, disconnect and plug the vacuum hose to the distributor vacuum advance capsule. Start the engine, and allow it to idle.
9 Point the timing light into the access hole. If the ignition timing is correct, the previously-highlighted timing mark on the flywheel will appear in line with the notch in the lower edge of the access hole.
10 If adjustment is required, loosen the distributor clamp bolt (remove the tamperproof cap, if fitted) and turn the distributor as required to bring the timing marks into alignment. Tighten the bolt to the specified torque (and refit the cap, if applicable) after making any adjustment.
11 When the timing setting is satisfactory, stop the engine and refit the access hole plug. Disconnect the timing light, and reconnect the temperature sender plug or distributor vacuum hose (where removed). If the timing had to be altered significantly, it may now be necessary to adjust the idle settings (refer to Chapter 4A or B as applicable).

All other engines

12 The ignition timing is under the control of the engine management system ECU, and is not manually adjustable without access to dedicated electronic test equipment. A basic setting cannot be quoted because the ignition timing is constantly being altered to control engine idle speed (see Section 1 for details).
13 After the distributor has been disturbed, it will be necessary for the basic timing setting

to be verified. This can only be done by putting the system into basic setting mode, using VW test equipment.
14 The vehicle must be taken to a VW dealer if the timing requires checking or adjustment.

6 Ignition system sensors - removal and refitting

1 Many of the engine management system sensors provide signals for both the fuel injection and ignition systems. Those specific to the ignition system are detailed in this Section.
2 Those sensors that are common to both systems are detailed in Chapter 4A or B as applicable. These include the coolant temperature sensor, the inlet air temperature sensor, the air flow meter, the engine speed sensor, the throttle potentiometer, the idle switch and the lambda sensor.

Knock sensor

Removal

3 Disconnect the battery negative lead and position it away from the terminal. **Note:** *If the vehicle has a security-coded radio, check that you have a copy of the code number before disconnecting the battery. Refer to your VW dealer if in doubt.*
4 The knock sensor is located on the front of the cylinder block, below spark plug No 2.
5 Unplug the harness wiring from the sensor at the connector, which is next to the distributor.
6 Slacken and withdraw the mounting bolt and lift off the sensor (see illustration).

Refitting

7 Refitting is a reversal of removal, but note that the sensor's operation will be affected if its mounting bolt is not tightened to exactly the right torque.

No 1 cylinder Hall-effect sensor

8 This sensor is an integral part of the distributor assembly. It can be removed and renewed separately, but dismantling of the distributor will be necessary. It is therefore recommended that this operation is entrusted to a auto-electrical specialist.

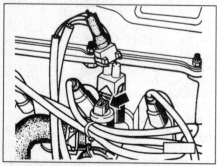

5.7 Blue connector plug (arrowed) on coolant temperature sender

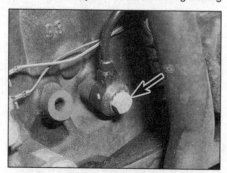

6.6 Slacken and withdraw the mounting bolt (arrowed) and lift off the knock sensor

Chapter 5 Part C:
Preheating system - diesel models

Contents

Degrees of difficulty

Easy, suitable for novice with little experience	Fairly easy, suitable for beginner with some experience	Fairly difficult, suitable for competent DIY mechanic	Difficult, suitable for experienced DIY mechanic	Very difficult, suitable for expert DIY or professional

Specifications

Glow plugs

Current consumption:

Engine code AAZ	8 amps (per glow plug)
All other engines	No information at time of writing

Torque wrench settings	Nm	lbf ft
Glow plug to cylinder head:		
Engine code AAZ	25	18
All other engines	15	11

1 General information

To assist cold starting, diesel models are fitted with a pre-heating system, which comprises four glow plugs, a glow plug control unit (incorporated in the diesel engine management ECU on many models), a facia-mounted warning lamp and the associated electrical wiring.

Ordinarily, a diesel engine achieves combustion from the heat generated by compressing the air in the cylinders; the diesel fuel is then injected into a high-temperature environment, and it ignites. When the engine is cold, this process is less easy, and the glow plugs are there to provide the missing heat. Faulty glow plugs are often the cause of poor starting, especially in cold weather. In warmer conditions, an engine may start reasonably well with one or two sub-standard glow plugs, but colder conditions will highlight any problems with the glow plug system.

The glow plugs are miniature electric heating elements, encapsulated in a metal case with a probe at one end and electrical connection at the other. Each swirl chamber/inlet tract has a glow plug threaded into it, and the glow plug probe is positioned directly in line with incoming spray of fuel. When the glow plug is energised, the fuel passing over it is heated, allowing its optimum combustion temperature to be achieved more readily when it reaches the cylinder.

The duration of the pre-heating period is governed by the glow plug control unit, which monitors the temperature of the engine via the coolant temperature sensor and alters the pre-heating time to suit the conditions.

A facia-mounted warning lamp informs the driver that pre-heating is taking place. The lamp extinguishes when sufficient pre-heating has taken place to allow the engine to be started, but power will still be supplied to the glow plugs for a further period until the engine is started. If no attempt is made to start the engine, the power supply to the glow plugs is switched off to prevent battery drain and glow plug burn-out. Note that on certain models, the warning lamp will also illuminate during normal driving if a pre-heating system malfunction occurs.

Generally, pre-heating is triggered by the ignition key being turned to the second position. However, the AAZ engine is equipped with a pre-heating system that activates when the driver's door is opened, then closed. Refer to the vehicle handbook for further information.

After the engine has been started, the glow plugs continue to operate for a further period. This helps to improve fuel combustion whilst the engine is warming up, resulting in quieter, smoother running and reduced exhaust emissions.

2.3 Glow plug control unit (later models)

3.2 Glow plug supply fusible link location

2 Glow plug control unit - removal and refitting

1 On engine codes 1Z, AHU and AFN, the pre-heating system is controlled by the diesel engine management system ECU - refer to Chapter 4C.

Removal

2 On early models, the glow plug control unit is located behind the facia, above the main relay box - refer to Chapter 11 and remove the relevant sections of trim to gain access.
3 On later models, the glow plug control unit is located in the engine compartment, next to the washer reservoir **(see illustration)**.
4 Disconnect the battery negative lead and position it away from the terminal. **Note:** *If the vehicle has a security-coded radio, check that you have a copy of the code number before disconnecting the battery. Refer to your VW dealer if in doubt.*
5 Unplug the wiring harness from the control unit at the connector.
6 Remove the retaining screws lift the control unit from its mounting bracket.

Refitting

7 Refitting is a reversal of removal.

3 Glow plugs - testing, removal and refitting

Testing

1 If the system malfunctions, testing is ultimately by substitution of known good units, but some preliminary checks may be made as described in the following paragraphs.
2 On models where the glow plug control unit is located in the engine compartment, the glow plug supply fusible link can be viewed through the plastic cover fitted over it **(see illustration)**. If this link has melted, this indicates a serious wiring fault - renewing the link should **not** be attempted without first diagnosing the reason why it failed. Refer to Chapter 12.
3 Connect a voltmeter or 12 volt test lamp to between the glow plug supply cable and a good earth point on the engine.
Caution: Make sure that the live connection is kept well clear of the engine and bodywork.
4 Have an assistant activate the pre-heating system (either using the ignition key, or by opening and closing the driver's door as applicable) and check that a battery voltage is applied to the glow plug electrical connection. (Note that the voltage will drop to zero when the pre-heating period ends).

5 If no supply voltage can be detected at the glow plug, then either the glow plug relay (where applicable) or the supply wiring must be faulty.
6 To locate a faulty glow plug, first disconnect the battery negative lead and position it away from the terminal. **Note:** *If the vehicle has a security-coded radio, check that you have a copy of the code number before disconnecting the battery. Refer to your VW dealer if in doubt.*
7 Refer to the next sub-Section and remove the supply wiring from the glow plug terminal. Measure the electrical resistance between the glow plug terminal and the engine earth. A reading of anything more than a few ohms indicates that the plug is defective.
8 If a suitable ammeter is available, connect it between the glow plug and its supply wire, and measure the steady-state current consumption (ignore the initial current surge which will be about 50% higher). Compare the result with the Specifications - high current consumption (or no current draw at all) indicates a faulty glow plug.
9 As a final check, remove the glow plugs and inspect them visually, as described in the next sub-Section.

Removal

10 If not already done, disconnect the battery negative lead and position it away from the terminal (see paragraph 5).
11 Remove the nuts and washers from the glow plug terminal. Lift off the bus bar **(see illustration)**.
12 Slacken and withdraw the glow plug **(see illustration)**.
13 Inspect the glow plug probe for signs of damage. A badly-burned or charred probe is usually an indication of a faulty fuel injector; refer to Chapter 4C.

Refitting

14 Refitting is a reversal of removal; tighten the glow plug to the specified torque **(see illustration)**.

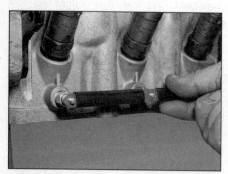

3.11 Remove the nuts and washers from the glow plug terminal. Lift off the bus bar

3.12 Slacken and withdraw the glow plug

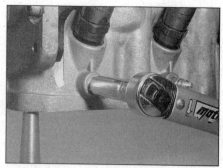

3.14 Tighten the glow plug to the specified torque

Chapter 6
Clutch

Contents

Degrees of difficulty

Easy, suitable for novice with little experience	**Fairly easy,** suitable for beginner with some experience	**Fairly difficult,** suitable for competent DIY mechanic	**Difficult,** suitable for experienced DIY mechanic	**Very difficult,** suitable for expert DIY or professional

Specifications

Type . . . . Single dry plate, diaphragm spring pressure plate, hydraulic or cable operation

Friction disc
Diameter . . . . 200 mm, 215 mm or 228 mm, depending on model
Run-out (maximum measured 2.5 mm from outer edge) . . . . 0.8 mm

Pressure plate
Maximum allowable distortion . . . . 0.2 mm

Diaphragm spring
Maximum allowable groove depth . . . . 0.3 mm

Hydraulic fluid type/specification . . . . Shared with braking system - see *"Lubricants and fluids"* on page 0•16

Torque wrench settings	**Nm**	**lbf ft**
Clutch cover bolts	20	15
Flywheel mounting bolts*:		
Stage 1	60	44
Stage 2	Angle-tighten a further 90°	
Hydraulic pipe union	20	15
Release lever ball stud	25	18
Slave cylinder bolts	25	18

*Use new bolt(s)

1 General description

The clutch is of single dry plate type, incorporating a diaphragm spring pressure plate, and is hydraulically or cable operated.

The clutch cover is bolted to the rear face of the flywheel, and the friction disc is located between the cover pressure plate and the flywheel friction surface. The disc hub is splined to the gearbox input shaft, and is free to slide along its splines. Friction lining material is riveted to each side of the disc, and the disc hub incorporates cushioning springs to absorb transmission shocks and ensure a smooth take-up of drive.

When the clutch pedal is depressed, the slave cylinder pushrod moves the release lever forwards, and the release bearing is forced onto the diaphragm spring fingers. As the centre of the spring is pushed in, the outer part of the spring moves out and releases the pressure plate from the friction disc. Drive then ceases to be transmitted to the gearbox.

When the clutch pedal is released, the diaphragm spring forces the pressure plate into contact with the linings on the friction disc, and at the same time pushes the disc slightly forward along the input shaft splines into engagement with the flywheel. The friction disc is now firmly sandwiched between the pressure plate and flywheel. This causes drive to be taken up.

As the linings wear on the friction disc, the pressure plate rest position moves closer to the flywheel resulting in the 'rest' position of the diaphragm spring fingers being raised. On cable-operated clutches, some form of adjustment is required, whereas the hydraulically-operated clutch requires no adjustment; the quantity of hydraulic fluid in the circuit automatically compensates for wear every time the clutch pedal is operated.

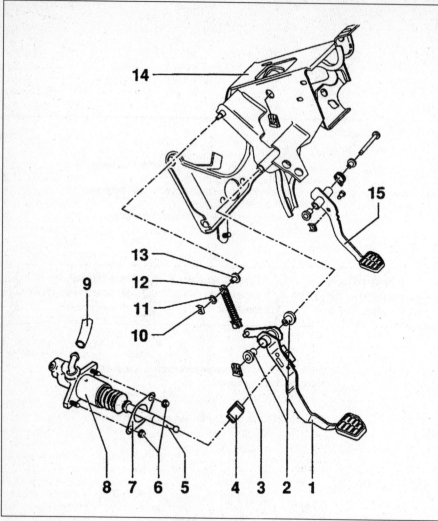

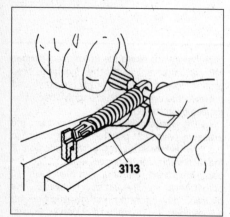

2.6 Clutch pedal components

1 Pedal	6 Self-locking nut	11 Washer
2 Bush	7 Gasket	12 Over-centre spring
3 Clip	8 Master cylinder	13 Bush
4 Retainer	9 Fluid supply hose	14 Mounting bracket
5 Clutch operating	10 Locking clip	15 Brake pedal
rod/master cylinder		

2.9 Setting the clutch over-centre spring using VW tool 3113

---

2   Clutch pedal - removal and refitting

Removal

1 Disconnect the battery negative lead and position it away from the terminal. **Note:** *If the vehicle has a security-coded radio, check that you have a copy of the code number before disconnecting the battery. Refer to your VW dealer if in doubt.*

2 Remove the cover from the fuse/relay unit, then undo the retaining screws and remove the facia underpanel and the insulation panel.

3 Undo the two retaining screws and remove the cover panel from the steering column lower end.

4 On hydraulically-operated clutches, release the retaining clip and extract the pedal to pushrod clevis pin.

5 On cable-operated clutches, refer to Section 6 and release the cable first from the operating lever end, then from the pedal end.

6 Reaching between the lower and upper heater ducts, release the retaining clip from the clutch/brake pedal pivot pin **(see illustration)**, and then push the pin to the right.

7 Disengage the pedal from the over-centre spring and remove the pedal. If the pedal bush is badly worn, it can be renewed by drifting it out, and pressing in a new bush between vice jaws.

8 The over-centre spring can be removed by releasing its retaining clip and washer.

Refitting

9 Refitting is a reversal of the removal procedure. When reassembling the over-centre spring, it will need to be preset for length using VW tool 3113 if available **(see illustration)**, or a similar method.

10 On cable-operated models, adjust the cable as described in Section 6.

---

3   Clutch hydraulic system - bleeding

1 If required, raise the front of the car and support it on axle stands, in order to gain better access to the bleed screw on the slave cylinder (see "*Jacking and vehicle support*").

2 First bleed the clutch master cylinder. **Note:** *Not all models have a bleed screw on the clutch master cylinder - in this case, proceed to paragraph 9 and bleed the slave cylinder.*

3 The clutch master cylinder is mounted at the rear of the engine compartment, next to the brake servo unit **(see illustration)**. Remove the rubber cap from the bleed screw on top of the cylinder.

4 Fit a bleed tube onto the bleed screw, and place the other end of the tube in a jar with some brake fluid in it.

5 Check that the fluid level in the brake/clutch reservoir is topped up to the maximum level, and have ready some fresh brake fluid for topping-up purposes.

6 Unscrew the bleed screw half a turn, and have an assistant fully depress the clutch pedal. As the pedal reaches the end of the downstroke close the bleed nipple. With the bleed nipple closed, release the clutch pedal. Repeat this procedure until the fluid entering the jar is free of air bubbles. Make sure that the fluid level in the reservoir does not drop to the level of the cylinder outlet, otherwise air will be drawn into the system.

7 Tighten the bleed screw with the clutch pedal depressed, release the pedal, then top up the fluid level as necessary.

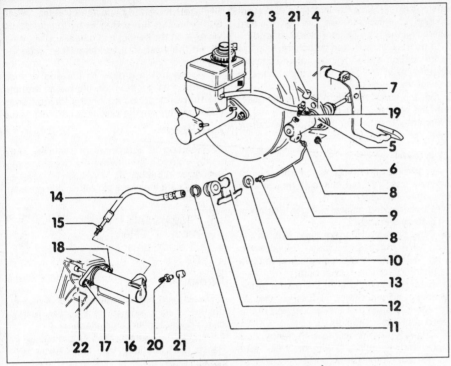

3.3 Clutch hydraulic system components

1 Fluid reservoir (brake and clutch system)	7 Clutch pedal	16 Slave cylinder
2 Supply hose	8 Pipe union	17 Nut
3 Brake servo unit and master cylinder	9 Pressure pipe	18 Nut
4 Clutch master cylinder/ brake servo mounting	10 Washer	19 Bleed screw (master cylinder) - not all models
5 Clutch master cylinder	11 Washer	20 Bleed screw (slave cylinder)
6 Nut	12 Bush	21 Dust cap
	13 Bracket	22 Transmission
	14 Hose	
	15 Pipe union	

8 Disconnect the bleed tube, and refit the rubber cap.

9 Remove the rubber cap from the slave cylinder bleed screw, connect the bleed tube to it, then repeat the procedure described above to bleed the air from the slave cylinder **(see illustration)**.

10 On completion, detach the bleed tube, refit the rubber cap and then lower the vehicle.

---

4 Clutch slave cylinder - removal, overhaul and refitting

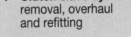

Removal

1 If a suitable hose clamp is available, clamp the slave cylinder's hydraulic hose at a point near its union. This will minimise fluid loss when the hose is detached and simplify the bleeding procedure when refitting.

2 Loosen the hydraulic pipe union on the slave cylinder and detach the hydraulic hose. If the hose is not clamped, plug the hose to minimise fluid loss and the possible ingress of dirt.

3 Unscrew the retaining bolts and withdraw the slave cylinder from the transmission **(see illustrations)**. It may be necessary to loosen off the gear selector unit from the transmission and withdraw it sufficiently to allow removal of the slave cylinder; leave the cables attached to the unit.

4 Do not operate the clutch pedal whilst the slave cylinder is removed.

Overhaul

5 At the time of writing, repair kits are not available from VW, but they may be available from other sources.

6 To overhaul the slave cylinder, first clean the exterior surfaces.

7 Prise off the rubber boot and remove the pushrod.

8 Extract the special spring clip from the mouth of the cylinder, and withdraw the piston and spring.

9 Clean the components, and examine them for wear and deterioration. If the piston and bore are worn excessively, or if corrosion is evident, renew the complete cylinder. If they are in good condition, remove the seal from the piston and renew it.

10 Dip the new seal in the hydraulic fluid, and fit it on the piston, using the fingers only to manipulate it into position (no tools). Make sure that the seal lip faces the spring end of the piston.

11 Insert the spring in the cylinder, then dip the piston in hydraulic fluid and carefully insert it.

12 Hold the piston depressed with a screwdriver, then press a new spring clip into the mouth of the cylinder, making sure that the legs of the clip grip the cylinder.

13 Fit the pushrod, then the rubber boot.

Refitting

14 Refitting is a reversal of removal, but bleed the system as described in Section 3. The end of the pushrod which contacts the release lever should be lightly lubricated with a molybdenum disulphide grease. Where a plastic support ring is fitted, the outer surface should also be lubricated with the same grease.

6

3.9 Bleeding the clutch slave cylinder

4.3a Unscrew the retaining bolts . . .

4.3b . . . and remove the clutch slave cylinder

5.6 Clutch master cylinder pushrod gaiter (1) and cylinder retaining nuts (2)

5 Clutch master cylinder - removal, overhaul and refitting

Removal

1 The clutch master cylinder is mounted at the rear of the engine compartment, next to the brake servo unit.

2 Working inside the car, remove the lower facia panel from under the steering column.

3 Prise off the clip, and extract the clevis pin securing the master cylinder pushrod to the clutch pedal.

4 If a suitable hose clamp is available, clamp the hydraulic hose from the combined brake/clutch cylinder reservoir at the clutch master cylinder end to prevent excess fluid loss, then detach the hose from the clutch master cylinder. Plug the fluid lines to prevent the ingress of dirt (and fluid loss from the fluid reservoir if the hose has not been clamped).

5 Undo the union nut and detach the fluid line to the clutch slave cylinder at the master cylinder. Plug the fluid line connections to prevent the ingress of dirt.

6 Working inside the car, prise free the gaiter from the bulkhead (see illustration).

7 Unscrew the mounting nuts and withdraw the clutch master cylinder.

Overhaul

8 At the time of writing, repair kits are not available from VW, but they may be available from other sources.

9 To overhaul the master cylinder, first clean the exterior surfaces.

10 Prise off the rubber boot and remove the pushrod. If necessary loosen the locknut, unscrew the clevis and locknut, and remove the pushrod from the rubber boot.

11 Extract the circlip from the mouth of the cylinder, and withdraw the washer, piston, and spring, noting that the smaller end of the spring contacts the piston.

12 Clean the components with methylated spirit, and examine them for wear and deterioration. If the piston and bore are worn excessively, renew the complete cylinder, but if they are in good condition, remove the seals from the piston and obtain new ones.

13 Dip the new seals in hydraulic fluid, and fit them on the piston, using the fingers only to manipulate them into position. Make sure that the seal lips face the spring end of the piston.

14 Insert the spring into the cylinder, large end first. Dip the piston in hydraulic fluid, locate it on the spring, and carefully insert it.

15 Fit the washer, then locate the circlip in the groove.

16 Apply a little grease to the end of the pushrod, then locate it on the piston and fit the rubber boot. Screw on the locknut and clevis and tighten the locknut.

Refitting

17 Refitting is a reversal of removal, but finally bleed the hydraulic system as described in Section 3.

18 Lubricate the clevis pin with a little grease.

6 Clutch cable - removal, refitting and adjustment

Removal

1 Detach and remove the lower facia panels on the driver's side to gain access to the clutch pedal and its cable attachment.

2 Depress the clutch pedal fully and release it. Repeat this a few times, then compress the self-adjusting mechanism by pressing the operating lever in reverse to its normal operating direction as far as its stop. Keep the adjustment mechanism compressed and disconnect the clutch cable from the lever. If it is impossible to compress the self-adjusting mechanism, it must be faulty and the cable must be cut to permit removal, using suitable cable cutters. Renewal of the cable will then be necessary on refitting. Do not dismantle the self-adjuster.

3 Prise free the cable from its supporting retainer on the coolant reservoir on the bulkhead (see illustration).

4 Disengage the inner cable from the pedal, then withdraw the cable from the engine compartment side.

Refitting and adjustment

5 Where a new cable is being fitted, the self-adjusting mechanism is held in compression by a strap. Do not release this strap at this stage (see illustration).

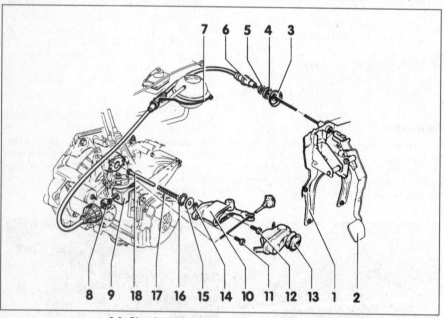

6.3 Clutch cable and associated components

1	Mounting bracket	7	Retainer	13	Seal boot
2	Clutch pedal	8	Rubber stop	14	Lock washer
3	Sleeve	9	Support	15	Washer
4	Clamping washer	10	Housing and lever	16	Star washer
5	Sealing rings	11	Bolt	17	Spring
6	Cable (and self-adjuster)	12	Bolt	18	Pushrod

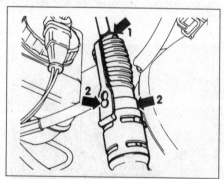

6.5 Clutch cable retaining strap (to hold adjuster mechanism in compression) showing upper (1) and lower (2) fixing points

Attach the cable to the clutch pedal, correctly re-route the cable in the engine compartment, but do not relocate it into the retainer yet.

Connect the cable to the clutch operating lever.

Where a new cable is being fitted, locate the cable in the retainer, then release the compression strap from the self-adjuster mechanism.

If the original cable is being refitted, compress the self-adjuster by moving the cable grommet back and forth a few times as far as possible (to the stop) so that the mechanism is compressed. **Note:** *Do not allow either end of the cable to become detached.* Now relocate the cable into the support by pressing the rubber buffer whilst simultaneously holding the self-adjuster mechanism in compression.

10 When refitted, ensure that the cable is clear of the gear selector unit on top of the transmission.

11 Initial adjustment of the clutch is made by fully depressing the pedal five times so that it touches its stop each time. Now move the lever about 10 mm in the opposite direction to its normal direction of travel, and check that it moves freely **(see illustration)**.

12 Refit the lower facia trim and insulation panels.

7 Clutch -
removal, inspection and refitting

Removal

1 Access to the clutch unit is gained by removing the engine and transmission combined, and then separating the two units as described in Chapter 2C, or by removing the transmission as described in Chapter 7. Unless it is wished to also carry out repairs to the engine, it is preferable to gain access by removing the transmission only. This is of particular advantage on RP engine models, as it eliminates the need to detach the exhaust manifold from the downpipe, which as mentioned in Chapter 4D, can be a difficult operation.

2 With the transmission separated from the engine, mark the clutch cover and flywheel in relation to each other as a guide for refitting.

3 Hold the flywheel stationary, then unscrew the clutch cover bolts progressively in diagonal sequence. With the bolts unscrewed two or three turns, check that the cover is not binding on the dowel pins. If necessary, use a screwdriver to release the cover.

4 Remove all the bolts, then lift the clutch cover and friction disc from the flywheel.

Inspection

Note: *Given the amount of dismantling work required to gain access to the clutch components, it is not advisable to refit any components unless they are known to have been recently fitted, or are obviously in as-new condition. Further, it is common practice when servicing the clutch to buy a complete kit (friction disc, pressure plate and release bearing) rather than just a new friction disc.*

5 Clean the cover, disc, and flywheel. *Do not inhale the dust, as it may contain asbestos which is dangerous to health.*

6 Examine the fingers of the diaphragm spring for wear or scoring. If the depth of any scoring exceeds the figure specified at the start of this Chapter, a new cover assembly must be fitted **(see illustration)**.

7 Examine the pressure plate for scoring, cracking and discoloration. Light scoring is acceptable, but if excessive, a new cover assembly must be fitted. Clutch pressure plate distortion must not exceed the figure specified at the start of this Chapter **(see illustration)**.

8 Examine the friction disc linings for wear, cracking, and for contamination with oil or grease. The linings are worn excessively if they are worn down to, or near, the rivets. Check the disc hub and splines for wear, by temporarily fitting it on the transmission input shaft. Renew the friction disc as necessary. If possible, check that the lateral run-out of the friction disc measured 2.5 mm from its outer edge does not exceed the specified amount.

9 If there is any evidence of contamination by oil or grease, the source of the leak should be traced and rectified before fitting new clutch

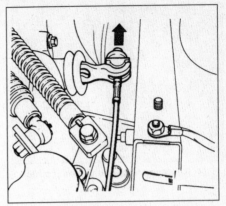

6.11 Clutch cable/mechanism check - move lever approximately 10 mm in direction indicated to check operation - see text

components, otherwise the new parts will quickly go the same way. There is no satisfactory way to de-grease the friction disc, once contaminated.

10 Examine the flywheel friction surface for scoring, cracking, and discoloration (caused by overheating). If excessive, it may be possible to have the flywheel machined by an engineering works, otherwise it should be renewed.

11 Before refitting the clutch, it is advisable to inspect the condition of the release bearing and lever as described in Section 8.

Refitting

12 Ensure that all parts are clean, and free of oil or grease, before reassembling. Apply just a small amount of high melting-point grease to the splines of the friction disc hub. Note that new pressure plates and clutch covers may be supplied coated with protective grease. It is only permissible to clean the grease away from the friction disc lining contact area. Removal of the grease from other areas will shorten the service life of the clutch.

13 Commence reassembly by locating the clutch disc on the flywheel, with the protruding hub of the disc towards the transmission **(see illustration)**.

6

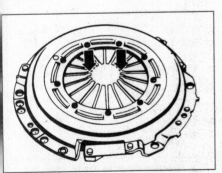

7.6 Check diaphragm spring fingers for excessive wear

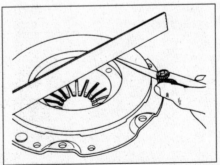

7.7 Check the pressure plate for excessive distortion

7.13 Clutch disc orientation

7.14 Refitting the clutch disc and clutch cover

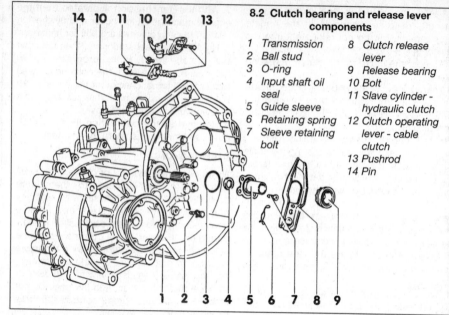

8.2 Clutch bearing and release lever components

1 Transmission
2 Ball stud
3 O-ring
4 Input shaft oil seal
5 Guide sleeve
6 Retaining spring
7 Sleeve retaining bolt
8 Clutch release lever
9 Release bearing
10 Bolt
11 Slave cylinder - hydraulic clutch
12 Clutch operating lever - cable clutch
13 Pushrod
14 Pin

14 Locate the clutch cover on the disc, and fit it onto the location dowels (see illustration). Hold the disc in its control position while doing this. If refitting the original cover, make sure that the previously-made marks are aligned.

15 Insert the bolts finger-tight to hold the cover in position, but to allow movement of the friction disc.

16 The friction disc must now be centralised, to ensure correct alignment of the transmission input shaft with the clutch components and the spigot bearing in the crankshaft. To do this, a proprietary tool may be used, or alternatively, use a wooden mandrel can be made to suit. Insert the tool through the friction disc into the spigot bearing, and make sure that it is central. Failure to centralise the friction disc will mean that the transmission input shaft will not be able to pass through the clutch components, making reconnecting the engine and transmission impossible. Time spent getting the centralisation correct will be well justified.

17 Tighten the clutch cover bolts progressively and in diagonal sequence, until the specified torque setting is reached, then remove the centralising tool.

18 Refit the engine and/or transmission with reference to Chapter 2C or 7, as applicable.

8 Release bearing and lever - removal and refitting

Removal

1 The release bearing and lever are only accessible once the engine and transmission have been separated - refer to paragraph 1 of the previous Section.

2 Using a screwdriver, prise the release lever from the ball stud on the gearbox housing (see illustration). If this proves difficult, push the spring from the release lever first. Remove the plastic pad from the stud.

3 Slide the release bearing, together with the lever, from the guide sleeve, and withdraw it over the transmission input shaft (see illustration).

4 Separate the release bearing from the lever (see illustration).

5 Spin the release bearing by hand, and check it for smooth running. Any tendency to seize or run rough will necessitate renewal of the bearing. If it is to be re-used, wipe it clean

with a dry cloth; on no account should the bearing be washed in a liquid solvent, otherwise the internal grease will be removed. Before deciding to re-use the bearing, refer to the Note in Section 7.

6 Clean the release lever, ball stud, and guide sleeve.

7 If a replacement release lever is to be fitted on cable-operated clutch models, insert the washers as shown (see illustration). The star washer must fit with its convex face towards the housing. Use a tube of suitable diameter to drive it into position but when fitted, ensure that the flat washer (B) is free to move.

Refitting

8 Refitting is a reversal of removal, but lubricate the ball stud with molybdenum disulphide grease. Smear a little grease on the release bearing surface which contacts the diaphragm spring fingers in the clutch cover. Fit the spring onto the release lever. Press the release lever onto the ball stud until the spring holds it in position.

9 Refit the engine and/or transmission with reference to Chapter 2C or 7, as applicable.

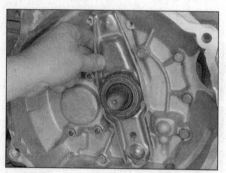

8.3 Clutch release lever and bearing removal

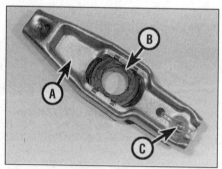

8.4 Clutch release lever (A), bearing (B) and ball stud socket (C)

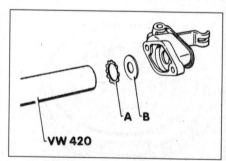

VW 420

8.7 Release lever on cable-operated clutch models showing star washer (A), flat washer (B) and the VW fitting tool

Chapter 7 Part A:
Manual transmission

Contents

Degrees of difficulty

Easy, suitable for novice with little experience	Fairly easy, suitable for beginner with some experience	Fairly difficult, suitable for competent DIY mechanic	Difficult, suitable for experienced DIY mechanic	Very difficult, suitable for expert DIY or professional

Specifications

General

Type . . . . Transverse mounted, front wheel drive layout with integral transaxle differential/final drive. 5 forward speeds with synchromesh, 1 reverse speed

Transmission type number 02A
Lubricant type . . . . See "Lubricants and fluids" on page 0•16
Lubricant capacity . . . . See Chapter 1A or 1B Specifications

Ratios (typical)

1st 3.778:1
2nd 2.105:1
3rd 1.345:1
4th 0.971:1
5th 0.795:1
Reverse 3.800:1
Final drive 3.944:1

Torque wrench settings

	Nm	lbf ft
Selector cables	25	18
Transmission bellhousing-to-engine bolts, M10	60	44
Transmission bellhousing-to-engine bolts, M12	80	59
Transmission filler/level and drain plugs	25	18
Transmission support bolts	60	44
Vibration damper-to-subframe	30	22

For other engine/transmission mountings, refer to Chapter 2A or 2B Specifications

7A

1 General information

The manual transmission is mounted transversely in the engine bay, bolted directly to the engine. This layout has the advantage of providing the shortest possible drive path to the front wheels, as well as locating the transmission in the airflow through engine bay, optimising cooling. The unit is cased in aluminium alloy.

Drive from the crankshaft is transmitted via the clutch to the gearbox input shaft, which is splined to accept the clutch friction plate.

All forward gears are fitted with syncromeshes. When a gear is selected, the movement of the cabin floor-mounted gear lever is communicated to the gearbox by a selector and shift cables. This in turn actuates a series of selector forks inside the gearbox which are slotted onto the synchromesh sleeves. The sleeves, which are locked to the gearbox shafts but can slide axially by means of splined hubs, press baulk rings into contact with the respective gear/pinion. The coned surfaces between the baulk rings and the pinion/gear act as a friction clutch, that progressively matches the speed of the synchromesh sleeve (and hence the gearbox

shaft) with that of the gear/pinion. The dog teeth on the outside of the baulk ring prevent the synchromesh sleeve ring from meshing with the gear/pinion until their speeds are exactly matched; this allows gearchanges to be carried out smoothly, and greatly reduces the noise and mechanical wear caused by rapid gearchanges.

Drive is transmitted to the differential crownwheel, which rotates the differential case and planetary gears, thus driving the sun gears and driveshafts. The rotation of the planetary gears on their shaft allows the inner roadwheel to rotate at a slower speed than the outer roadwheel during cornering.

2.2 Releasing a selector cable support bracket clip

2.4 Detach and remove the exhaust downpipe

2.5a Unscrew the retaining bolts . . .

2.5b . . . and the clamp washers to remove the heat shield

2.6 Undo the retaining bolts underneath the gear lever housing

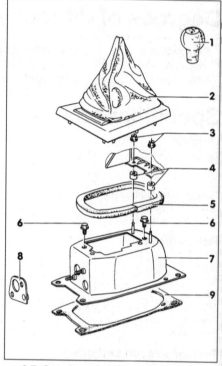

2.7 Gear lever housing components

1	Gear lever knob	5	Gasket
2	Gaiter	6	Bolt
3	Plastic nuts	7	Housing
4	Spacer sleeves	8	Gasket
		9	Gasket

2 Gear selector cables and lever - removal, refitting and adjustment

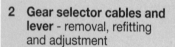

Removal

1 First disconnect the cables at the transmission **(see illustrations 3.9a to 3.9e)**.
2 Prise free the cable-to-support bracket clips **(see illustration)**, and release the cables from the bracket.
3 Raise and support the front of the vehicle at the front end on axle stands (see *"Jacking and vehicle support"*). Allow a suitable working clearance to remove the front section of the exhaust system.
4 Referring to Chapter 4D for details, detach and remove the exhaust downpipe **(see illustration)**.

5 Where applicable, detach and remove the heat shield from the underside of the transmission tunnel. It is attached by clamping washers at the front, and by two bolts at the rear **(see illustrations)**.
6 Undo the two selector mounting-to-floor retaining bolts at the rear **(see illustration)**.
7 Working inside the vehicle, unscrew the gear lever knob, and remove it **(see illustration)**.
8 Unclip and remove the gear lever gaiter. Detach the wiring from the connectors (where applicable).
9 Undo the two black plastic nuts, then lower the gear lever unit down, and remove it together with the cables from underneath the vehicle **(see illustrations)**.
10 To detach the cables from the gear selector unit, prise the lock tab from the housing on each side, and remove the bottom cover plate from the housing **(see illustration)**.

2.9a Working inside the vehicle, undo the plastic nuts . . .

2.9b . . . then lower the gear lever unit, and remove it from underneath

2.10 Remove the bottom cover plate for access to the selector housing

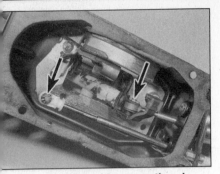

2.12 Selector cable connections in housing (arrowed)

1 Undo the cable-to-housing retaining nuts, then detach the cable locating plate from the housing.

2 Extract the retaining clips, and detach the cables from their connections to the gear lever and the gate selector lever **(see illustration)**. Withdraw the cables.

3 The lever housing component parts are as shown **(see illustration)**. To dismantle the unit, release the appropriate retaining clip/bolt(s). As it is dismantled, note the fitted position and orientation of the various components.

4 Renew any worn or defective parts. Note that some items were modified on later models, and it is important that the correct replacements are obtained.

5 Reassemble in the reverse order of removal. Note that the gate selector bush only fits in one position. Locate the trim securing sleeve so that it is distanced 40 mm from the lever knob. If a new cap is being fitted to the ball on the base of the selector housing, it helps if the cap is preheated in hot water to make it more malleable. Fit it by squeezing the cap together (to elongate the hole), then fit it from the side as shown **(see illustration)**.

6 When reconnecting the selector cable to the transmission mounting bracket, take care not to damage the cable-to-bracket bush.

Refitting and adjustment

7 The cables and gear lever refitting procedures are a reversal of the removal procedure. Where the cables and/or any parts of the selector unit have been renewed, the selector adjustment should be checked to ensure a satisfactory gearchange. A VW setting tool No 3192 is required for an accurate check/adjustment to be made, but in its absence, a basic check can be made by centralising the gear lever in its midway position in neutral. To achieve this, loosen off the gear lever and the relay lever-to-cable attachment bolt/nut, centralise the lever **(see illustration)**, and tighten the bolt/nut. Check for satisfactory adjustment of all gears. Further minor adjustment may be required.

8 Check the selector shaft stroke by engaging 1st gear and pressing the lever fully to the left. Now release it whilst an assistant measures the selector shaft movement at the transmission. The shaft should move about 1

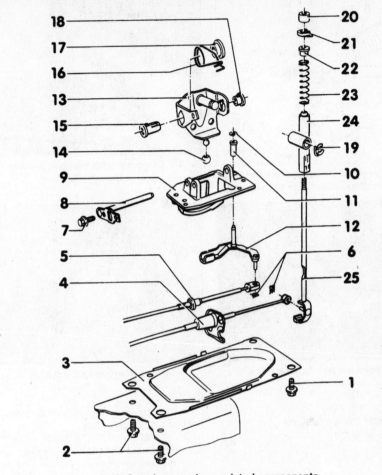

2.13 Gear lever and associated components

1 Bolt	8 Pin	14 Cap	20 Trim retaining
2 Bolt	9 Plate	15 Bush	sleeve
3 Cover	10 Lockwasher	16 Spring	21 Lockwasher
4 Gearchange cable	11 Bush	17 Guide bush	22 Spacer bush
5 Selector cable	12 Gate selector lever	18 Bush	23 Spring
6 Clips	13 Selector gate	19 Clip	24 Lever guide
7 Bolt	housing		25 Gear lever

mm. If adjustment is required, loosen off the relay lever-to-cable nut and take up the play by pressing the mounting pin towards the cable **(see illustration)**. Retighten the retaining nut.

19 It is advisable to have the gear selection adjustment checked at the earliest opportunity by a VW garage when a basic setting has been made.

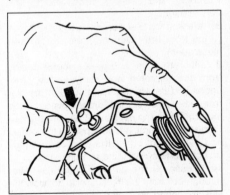

2.15 Fitting the selector housing ball cap

2.17 Insert drill or rod as shown to aid alignment when reconnecting and adjusting the selector cable bolt and nut

7A

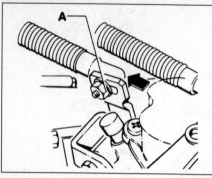

2.18 Loosen nut (A) and press mounting pin in direction indicated to take up play

3.6 Disconnecting the speedometer drive cable

3.8 Disconnecting the reversing light switch

3.9a Remove the bolt to detach the gear selector cable . . .

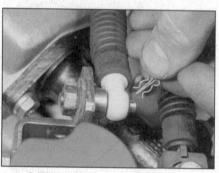

3.9b . . . then extract the clip . . .

3.9c . . . to detach the gate selector cable (early model shown)

3 Manual transmission - removal and refitting

Removal

1 Select a solid, level surface to park the vehicle upon. Give yourself enough space to move around it easily. Apply the handbrake and chock the rear wheels.
2 Disconnect the battery negative lead and position It away from the terminal. **Note:** *If the vehicle has a security-coded radio, check that you have a copy of the code number before*

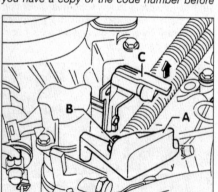

3.9d On models from October 1991, remove balance weight (A) and gear selector cable (B) from the gearshift lever. Gate selector cable (C) is removed by lifting the lug in the direction of the arrow

disconnecting the battery; refer to Chapter 5A, Section 1 for details.
3 The "lock carrier" is a panel assembly comprising the headlight units, radiator grille (later models) and bonnet lock mechanism. Although its removal is not essential, it does give greatly-improved access; see Chapter 11.
4 Where applicable, disconnect the clutch cable from the transmission release lever (see Chapter 6).
5 On diesel models, disconnect and remove as much of the intercooler pipework as required for better access - see Chapter 4C. On engine code AFN, remove the engine top cover.
6 Either unscrew the collar and disconnect the speedometer drive cable **(see illustration)**, or disconnect the wiring plug from the speed-ometer sender.
7 Unbolt the earth strap from the transmission.
8 Referring to Section 5, disconnect the wiring from the reversing light switch **(see illustration)**.
9 Detach the gear and gate selector cables from the gearshift and relay levers, then unbolt and detach the cable support bracket from the top of the transmission **(see illustrations)**. The cables can be left attached to the support bracket, but position the cables and the bracket out of the way, so that they do not interfere with transmission removal.
10 Loosen off the gear selector/relay lever through-bolt from the transmission, to allow the selector unit to be lifted a little, then undo the retaining bolts and withdraw the clutch slave

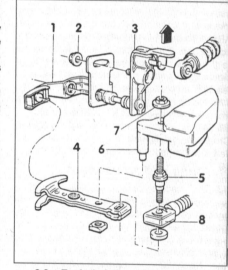

3.9e Exploded view of gearchange mechanism fitted on models from October 1991

1 Relay lever
2 Actuating arm-to-relay lever nut
3 Actuating arm - lift lug in direction of arrow to remove/refit gate selector cable
4 Gearshift lever
5 Gear selector cable/balance weight stud
6 Balance weight
7 Balance weight nut
8 Gear selector cable

cylinder from the clutch housing. Lift the gear selector to allow withdrawal of the cylinder. The hydraulic fluid hose can be left attached to the slave cylinder, but support it out of the way so that the hose is not stretched or distorted, and retain the pushrod fully in the cylinder.

1 Unscrew and remove the upper engine-to-transmission retaining bolts.

2 Raise and support the vehicle at the front end on axle stands (see "Jacking and vehicle support"). The transmission is removed from the underside of the vehicle, so allow sufficient clearance.

3 Undo the transmission oil drain plug from the differential housing, and drain the transmission oil into a suitable container. Refit the plug.

4 The weight of the engine must now be supported while the engine/transmission mountings are removed. To do this, attach a lift sling to the engine, and raise it with an engine crane just enough to support the weight of the engine, or support the engine securely from below, taking care not to damage the sump. Alternatively, use an engine support bracket similar to the type which VW mechanics use (see illustration).

5 Unscrew and remove the three retaining bolts from the right-hand engine mounting (at the rear).

6 Unscrew and remove the single retaining bolt from the transmission mounting at the rear, on the left-hand side. Where applicable, move the power steering hoses to one side so that they are out of the way. On models fitted with ABS, it may be necessary to remove the cooling system expansion tank to allow access to the mounting bolt. Move the hoses to one side, then using an extension bar and socket, reach down and unscrew the mounting bolt.

7 Unscrew and remove the nut retaining the front engine/transmission mounting.

8 Remove the starter motor, as described in Chapter 5A, positioning it out of the way (leave the wiring attached).

9 Unbolt and remove the front engine mounting bracket. Where necessary, relocate the power steering hoses over the mounting bushes, and secure them out of the way.

20 Working underneath the vehicle, unbolt and remove the vibration damper weight from the steering gear subframe. Support the weight securely as the four retaining bolts are unscrewed, and be prepared to support its considerable weight as it is removed.

21 Unbolt and remove the right-hand driveshaft inner CV joint heat shield from the engine.

22 Refer to Chapter 8 for full details, and unbolt the right- and left-hand driveshafts from the transmission output flanges. Tie the shafts up out of the way once they are detached.

23 Carefully move the engine and transmission to the right as much as possible, then lift them slightly on the left-hand side.

24 Undo the retaining bolts and remove the transmission support bracket arm (see illustration).

25 Push the engine towards the bulkhead, and then undo and remove the lower bolt ('C' in illustration 3.24) from the mounting bracket. Unscrew the remaining bolts, and remove the mounting bracket from the bulkhead.

26 Undo the retaining bolts, and remove the lower cover plate from the clutch housing.

27 Position a jack under the transmission housing to support its weight. A trolley jack with a suitable saddle should be used if available, for preference.

28 Unscrew and remove the lower engine-to-transmission retaining bolts.

29 Check that the respective transmission attachments are free and out of the way, then carefully prise free the transmission from the engine, so that it is clear of the location dowels on the engine rear flange face. The aid of an assistant should be enlisted if possible, to assist in steadying the transmission as it is withdrawn, lowered and removed.

⚠ **Warning: Support the transmission to ensure that it remains steady on the jack head. Keep the transmission level until the input shaft is fully withdrawn from the clutch friction plate.**

30 When the transmission is clear of the engine, lower and remove it from under the vehicle, but ensure that the engine remains fully supported.

Refitting

31 Before refitting the transmission, ensure that the location dowels are located in the engine rear face. Lightly lubricate the splines of the input shaft with a suitable high-melting-point grease.

32 Refitting is a reversal of the removal procedure, but note the following points:

a) Before lifting the transmission into position, extract the timing inspection plug from the bellhousing, then push the clutch release lever towards the transmission, and secure it in this position using an M8 x 22 bolt. Once the transmission is in position, extract the bolt to release the lever, and refit the plug.

b) Ensure that the engine and transmission mountings are free from stress before

tightening their retaining nuts and bolts. Tighten all fastenings to their specified torques, with reference to Chapter 2 as necessary.

c) Reconnect and adjust the gearchange and relay lever cables, as described in Section 2.

d) Fill the transmission with the specified type and quantity of oil on completion (see Chapter 1).

4 Manual transmission overhaul - general information

The overhaul of a manual transmission is a complex (and often expensive) engineering task for the DIY home mechanic to undertake, which requires access to specialist equipment. It involves dismantling and reassembly of many small components, measuring clearances precisely and if necessary, adjusting them by the selection shims and spacers. Internal transmission components are also often difficult to obtain and in many instances, extremely expensive. Because of this, if the transmission develops a fault or becomes noisy, the best course of action is to have the unit overhauled by a specialist repairer, or to obtain an exchange reconditioned unit.

Nevertheless, it is not impossible for the more experienced mechanic to overhaul the transmission if the special tools are available and the job is carried out in a deliberate step-by-step manner, to ensure that nothing is overlooked.

The tools necessary for an overhaul include internal and external circlip pliers, bearing pullers, a slide hammer, a set of pin punches, a dial test indicator and possibly a hydraulic press. In addition, a large, sturdy workbench and a vice will be required.

During dismantling of the transmission, make careful notes of how each component is fitted to make reassembly easier and accurate (see illustration overleaf).

Before dismantling the transmission, it will help if you have some idea of where the problem lies. Certain problems can be closely

7A

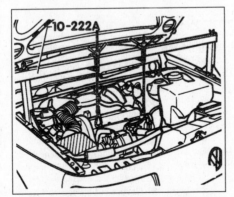

3.14 Using an engine support bracket to take the weight of the engine

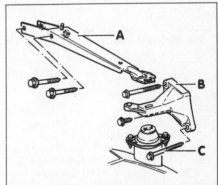

3.24 Transmission support arm (A), mounting bracket (B) and lower bolt (C)

related to specific areas in the transmission which can make component examination and renewal easier. Refer to the *"Fault diagnosis"* Section in this manual for more information.

5 Reversing light switch - testing, removal and refitting

Testing

1 Ensure that the ignition switch is turned to the 'OFF' position.

2 Unplug the wiring harness from the reversing light switch at the connector. The switch is located on the top of the transmission casing **(see illustration 3.8)**.

3 Connect the probes of a continuity tester, or multimeter set to the resistance measurement function, across the terminals of the reverse light switch.

4 The switch contacts are normally open, so with any gear other than reverse selected, the tester/meter should indicate an open-circuit. When reverse gear is then selected, the switch contacts should close, causing the tester/meter to indicate a short-circuit.

5 If the switch appears to be constantly open- or short-circuit, or is intermittent in its operation, it should be renewed.

Removal

6 Ensure that the ignition switch is turned to the 'OFF' position.

7 If not already done, unplug the wiring harness from the reversing light switch at the connector.

8 Slacken the switch body using a ring spanner and withdraw it from the transmission casing. Recover the sealing ring.

Refitting

9 Refit the switch by reversing the removal procedure. Tighten the switch securely, and check for satisfactory operation on completion.

6 Speedometer drive - removal and refitting

Mechanical speedometer

1 Early models are fitted with a conventional mechanical speedometer, driven by a cable and drivegear from the final drive.

2 Unscrew the retaining collar from the speedometer cable, then pull the cable end fitting from the drivegear.

3 The drivegear can now be unscrewed from the transmission using a suitable ring spanner.

4 Recover the sealing ring.

5 Refitting is a reversal of removal. Use a new O-ring, and tighten the drivegear securely. Insert the cable end fitting into the top of the drivegear, twisting it slightly until it locates and the retaining collar can be screwed on securely.

Electronic speedometer

6 Later transmissions are fitted with an electronic speedometer sender. This device measures the rotational speed of the transmission final drive and converts the information into an electronic signal, which is then sent to the speedometer module in the instrument panel. On certain models, the signal is also used as an input by the engine management system ECU.

7 Ensure that the ignition switch is turned to the 'OFF' position.

8 Locate the speed sender, at the top of the transmission casing. Unplug the wiring harness from the sender, at the connector.

9 Unscrew and withdraw the sender from the transmission casing.

10 Recover the sealing ring, where applicable.

11 Refit the sender by reversing the removal procedure, using a new sealing ring where applicable.

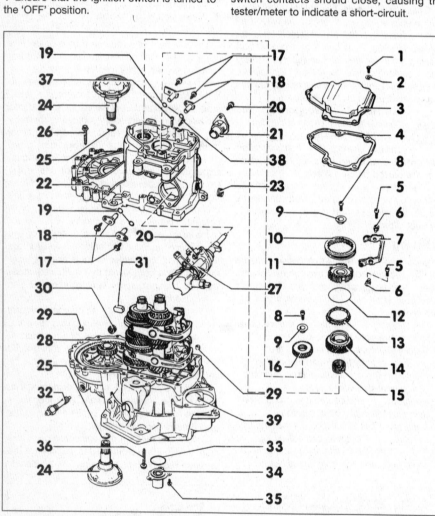

4.4 Exploded view of manual transmission housings and associated components

1 Bolt	14 5th gear	27 Gearchange unit
2 Washer	15 Needle bearing	28 Clutch/differential housing
3 End cover	16 5th gear (driven)	29 Sleeve
4 Gasket	17 Bolt	30 Filler/level plug
5 Bolt	18 Location pins	31 Magnet
6 Location pins	19 O-ring	32 Speedometer drive
7 5th gear selector fork	20 Bolt	33 O-ring
8 Bolt	21 Bearing sleeve cover	34 Guide sleeve and seal
9 Bush	22 Transmission housing	35 Bolt
10 5th gear lock ring	23 Drain plug	36 Bolt
11 5th gear synchro-hub	24 Drive flange	37 Reverse shaft support bolt
12 Spring	25 Circlip	38 Reverse shaft support bolt
13 5th gear synchro-ring	26 Bolt	39 Starter bush

Chapter 7 Part B:
Automatic transmission

Contents

Degrees of difficulty

Easy, suitable for novice with little experience 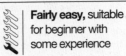	Fairly easy, suitable for beginner with some experience	Fairly difficult, suitable for competent DIY mechanic	Difficult, suitable for experienced DIY mechanic	Very difficult, suitable for expert DIY or professional

Specifications

General

Designation:

Up to January 1995	096
January 1995 on	01M

Description:

096 . . . . Electro-hydraulically controlled planetary gearbox providing four forward speeds and one reverse speed. Drive transmitted through hydrokinetic torque converter. Lock-up clutch on top two speeds, electronic control unit. Two selectable driving modes

01M . . . . As 096, but with lock-up clutch on all forward speeds, and "fuzzy logic" control unit giving infinitely variable gearchange points. Driving modes selected automatically by throttle position

Automatic transmission fluid type . . . . See "Lubricants and fluids" on Page 0•16

Automatic transmission fluid capacity . . . . See Chapter 1A Specifications

Ratios (typical)

1st	2.714:1
2nd	1.551:1
3rd	1.000:1
4th	0.679:1
Reverse	2.111:1
Final drive	4.222:1

Torque wrench settings

	Nm	lbf ft
Selector cable-to-transmission selector lever locking bolt	25	18
Torque converter shield plate	15	11
Torque converter-to-driveplate bolts	60	44
Transmission bellhousing-to-engine bolts, M10	60	44
Transmission bellhousing-to-engine bolts, M12	80	59

For engine/transmission mountings, refer to Chapter 2A Specifications

7B

1 General information

Type 096 transmission

The VW type 096 automatic transmission has four forward speeds (and one reverse). The automatic gear changes are electronically controlled, rather than hydraulically as with previous conventional types. The advantage of electronic management is to provide a faster gearchange response. A kick-down facility is also provided, to enable a faster acceleration response when required.

The transmission consists of three main assemblies, these being the torque converter, which is directly coupled to the engine; the final drive unit, which incorporates the differential unit; and the planetary gearbox, with its multi-disc clutches and brake bands. The final drive is lubricated independently, whilst the transmission is lubricated with automatic transmission fluid (ATF). A transmission fluid cooler and filter are fitted externally for ease of maintenance.

The torque converter incorporates an automatic lock-up feature which eliminates any possibility of converter slip in the top two gears; this aids performance and economy. In addition to the normal alternative of manual change, the two-position mode switch on the centre console (adjacent to the selector lever) provides either a "sport" or "economy" setting as required. In "sport" mode, upshifts are delayed longer, to make full use of engine power, while in "economy" mode, upshifts are taken as soon as possible, to permit optimum economy.

Another feature of this transmission is the selector lever lock, with which the selector lever can be set in the "P" or "N" position when the engine is running, below about 3 mph. Under these conditions, selection from "P" or "N" can only be made by depressing the brake pedal.

Type 01M transmission

The type 01M transmission fitted from January 1995 is very similar to the type 096 in terms of construction, features and general function, but its performance is enhanced by a number of refinements.

The torque converter lock-up facility has been extended to all forward speeds, for greater fuel economy. The electronic control unit now incorporates "fuzzy logic", allowing infinitely variable gearchange points to be determined in response to driver demands and driving conditions, for maximum performance or economy, as appropriate. In light of this development, the two-position "sport" and "economy" mode selector switch is no longer fitted - decisions as to operating mode are now determined by throttle position and its rate of change. In this way, gearchanges can be economy-orientated, but full acceleration is

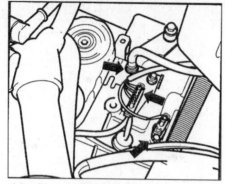

2.6a Disconnect the multiway connectors (arrowed) . . .

always available on demand. A further refinement is the inclusion of a gearchange map for gradients, allowing the control unit to select the most appropriate ratio to match gradient to engine output when climbing hills, and to allow adequate engine braking when descending.

All transmissions

A fault diagnosis system is integrated into the control unit, but analysis can only be undertaken with specialised equipment. If a malfunction should occur in the transmission electrical system, automatic gear selection will continue, but the changes will be noticeably jerky. In the event of automatic selection failure, the selection of gears can be made manually. In either instance, it is important that the transmission fault be identified and rectified at the earliest possible opportunity. Delay in doing so will only cause further problems.

Because of the need for special test equipment, the complexity of some of the parts, and the need for scrupulous cleanliness when servicing automatic transmissions, the amount which the owner can do is limited (this is especially the case with the type 01M transmission). Repairs to the final drive differential are also not recommended. Most major repairs and overhaul operations should be left to a VW dealer, who will be equipped with the necessary equipment for fault diagnosis and repair. The information in this

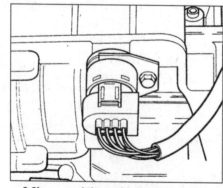

2.6b . . . and the multi-function switch

Chapter is therefore limited to a description of the removal and refitting of the transmission as a complete unit. The removal, refitting and adjustment of the selector cable is also described.

In the event of a transmission problem occurring, consult a VW dealer or transmission specialist before removing the transmission from the vehicle, since the majority of fault diagnosis is carried out with the transmission in situ.

2 Automatic transmission - removal and refitting

Removal

1 Select a solid, level surface to park the vehicle upon. Give yourself enough space to move around it easily. Apply the handbrake and chock the rear wheels.

2 Disconnect the battery negative lead and position it away from the terminal. **Note:** *If the vehicle has a security coded radio, check that you have a copy of the code number before disconnecting the battery; refer to Chapter 5A, Section 1 for details.*

3 The "lock carrier" is a panel assembly comprising the headlight units, radiator grille (later models), and bonnet lock mechanism. Although its removal is not essential, it does give greatly-improved access; see Chapter 11.

4 Raise the front of the vehicle and rest it securely on axle stands (see "*Jacking and vehicle support*"). Allow a suitable working clearance underneath for the eventual withdrawal of the transmission.

5 Disconnect the speedometer drive cable from the transmission, or unplug the speedometer sender.

6 Disconnect all the wiring connections from the transmission, labelling them if required for refitting **(see illustrations)**. Remove the multi-function switch.

7 Position the selector lever in the "P" position, then detach the selector cable from the lever on the transmission by unscrewing the shouldered retaining bolt. Detach the cable retaining clip, and move the cable out of the way.

8 Clamp the automatic transmission fluid cooler hoses as close to the cooler as possible **(see illustration)**, then detach the hoses from the cooler.

9 Disconnect the radiator cooling fan motor wiring plug.

10 Unscrew and remove the upper engine-to-transmission retaining bolts.

11 The weight of the engine must now be supported while the engine/transmission mountings are removed. To do this, attach a lift sling to the engine, and raise it with an engine crane just enough to support the weight of the engine, or support the engine securely from below, taking care not to damage the sump. Alternatively, use an

ngine support bracket similar to the type
which VW mechanics use.

2 Remove the starter motor, as described in
Chapter 5A, positioning it out of the way
leave the wiring attached).

3 Unbolt the coolant expansion tank, and
place it to one side, leaving the hoses
attached.

4 Unbolt and remove the engine/trans-
mission left-hand mounting.

5 Detach and remove the transmission fluid
pan protector plate.

6 Detach and remove the
engine/transmission front mounting.

7 Unscrew the flange bolts, and detach
the left- and right-hand driveshafts from the
transmission drive flanges. It will probably
be necessary to remove the left-hand
driveshaft completely (see Chapter 8 for
details). Suspend the right-hand driveshaft
as high as possible inside the engine using
cable-ties or wire. Turn the steering to full
right lock.

8 Refer to Chapter 10 and separate the left-
hand suspension lower arm from the lower
balljoint (see illustration).

9 Working underneath the vehicle, unbolt
and remove the vibration damper weight
(where fitted) from the steering gear subframe.
Support the weight securely as the four
retaining bolts are unscrewed, and be
prepared to support its considerable weight
as it is removed.

20 Unbolt and remove the torque converter
housing lower cover plate.

21 Working through the starter motor
aperture, slacken and withdraw each torque
converter-to-driveplate bolt in turn. As each
bolt is removed, rotate the crankshaft using a
wrench and socket on the crankshaft
sprocket to expose the next bolt. Repeat until
all the bolts are removed.

22 Lower the engine support bar, hoist or
jack (as applicable) as far as possible,
ensuring that the weight of the engine is still
supported. Locate a jack (trolley type if
available) under the transmission to support
its weight as it is separated from the engine.

23 Unscrew and remove the engine-to-
transmission lower retaining bolts.

24 Check that all fixings and attachments are
clear of the transmission. Enlist the aid of an
assistant to help in guiding and supporting the
transmission during its removal.

25 Pull the transmission clear of the engine,
and lower it so that it can be withdrawn from
under the front of the vehicle. The
transmission is located on engine alignment
dowels, and if stuck on them, it may be
necessary to carefully tap and prise the
transmission free of the dowels to allow
separation.

⚠️ Warning: Support the
transmission to ensure that it
remains steady on the jack
head. Ensure that the torque
converter remains in position on its shaft in
the torque converter housing.

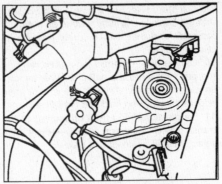

**2.8 Clamp off the coolant hoses leading to
and from the transmission fluid cooler unit**

26 With the transmission removed, bolt a
suitable bar and spacer across the front face
of the torque converter housing, to retain the
torque converter in position.

Refitting

27 Refitting is a reversal of the removal
procedure, but note the following special
points:
  a) When reconnecting the transmission to
     the engine, ensure that the location
     dowels are in position, and that the
     transmission is correctly aligned with
     them before pushing it fully into
     engagement with the engine. As the
     torque converter is refitted, ensure that
     the drive pins at the centre of the torque
     converter hub engage with the recesses
     in the automatic transmission fluid pump
     inner wheel.
  b) Tighten all retaining bolts to their
     specified torque wrench settings.
  c) Top up the transmission fluid level and
     the differential oil level with the specified
     lubricants.
  d) Reconnect and adjust the selector cable,
     as described in Section 4.
  e) Have the front wheel alignment checked
     at the earliest opportunity.

3 Automatic transmission overhaul - general information

In the event of a fault occurring, it will be
necessary to establish whether the fault is
electrical, mechanical or hydraulic in nature,
before repair work can be contemplated.
Diagnosis requires detailed knowledge of the
transmission's operation and construction, as
well as access to specialised test equipment,
and so is deemed to be beyond the scope of
this manual. It is therefore essential that
problems with the automatic transmission are
referred to a VW dealer for assessment.

Note that a faulty transmission should not
be removed before the vehicle has been
assessed by a dealer, as fault diagnosis is
carried out with the transmission *in situ*.

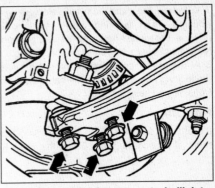

**2.18 Suspension lower arm-to-balljoint
bolts (arrowed)**

4 Selector cable - removal, refitting and adjustment

Removal

1 Disconnect the battery negative lead and
position It away from the terminal. **Note:** *If the
vehicle has a security-coded radio, check that
you have a copy of the code number before
disconnecting the battery; refer to Chapter 5A,
Section 1 for details.*

2 Raise and support the vehicle at the front
end on axle stands (see "*Jacking and vehicle
support*"). Allow a suitable working clearance
underneath the vehicle.

3 Move the selector lever to the "P" position.

4 Undo the grub screw in the end of the lever
handle, and lift the handle from the lever. On
the 096 transmission, note that the grub
screw is smeared with locking fluid, and this
makes it difficult to unscrew. When removed,
the threads of the grub screw must be
cleaned prior to refitting.

5 Detach and lift the selector cover up from
the centre console. As it is lifted clear, reach
underneath and detach the wiring from the
mode selector switch (096 type only) and the
illumination lamp.

6 Prise free the circlip and detach the cable
from the shift mechanism **(see illustration)**.

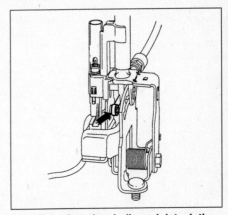

**4.6 Prise free the circlip and detach the
cable (arrowed) from the shift mechanism**

7B

7 Withdraw the cable from the selector lever housing, then working along its length, release the cable from the securing clips. Note the cable routing carefully for refitting.

8 At the transmission end of the cable, undo the locking bolt and detach the cable from the transmission selector shaft.

Refitting

9 Refit the selector cable by reversing the removal procedure. When fitting the cable to the selector lever, use a new circlip. Ensure that the cable is correctly routed, as noted on removal, and that it is securely held by its retaining clips.

10 On the 096 transmission, when refitting the grub screw to the selector lever handle, ensure the screw threads are clean, then apply a little locking fluid and tighten securely.

11 Before tightening the connection at the transmission selector shaft, adjust the selector cable as described below.

Adjustment

12 Move the selector lever to the "P" position

13 At the transmission, slacken the cable locking bolt on the side of the selector shaft lever. Push the selector shaft up against its end stop, corresponding to the "P" position, then tighten the locking bolt to the specified torque

14 Verify the operation of the selector lever by shifting through all gear positions and checking that every gear can be selected smoothly and without delay.

Chapter 8
Driveshafts

Contents

Degrees of difficulty

Easy, suitable for novice with little experience	Fairly easy, suitable for beginner with some experience	Fairly difficult, suitable for competent DIY mechanic	Difficult, suitable for experienced DIY mechanic	Very difficult, suitable for expert DIY or professional

Specifications

Type . . . . Steel shafts with ball-and-cage type constant velocity joint at each end (later automatic transmission models have a tripod type inner joint)

Torque wrench settings	Nm	lbf ft
Driveshaft retaining bolt:*		
M14 bolt:		
Stage 1	115	85
Stage 2	Angle-tighten a further 180°	
M16 bolt:		
Stage 1	190	140
Stage 2	Angle-tighten a further 90°	
Driveshaft retaining nut*	265	197
Inner CV joint-to-drive flange bolts:		
Driveshaft with tripod type inner joint (M10 bolt)	80	59
All other driveshafts	45	33
Lower arm balljoint retaining bolts	35	26
Roadwheel bolts	110	81

*Use new nut/bolt

8

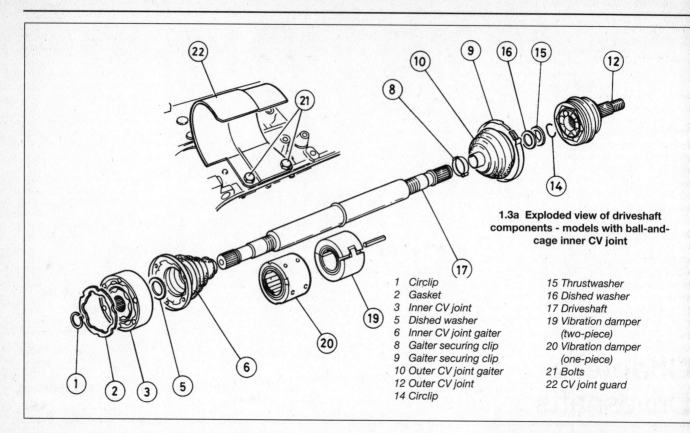

1.3a Exploded view of driveshaft components - models with ball-and-cage inner CV joint

1	Circlip	15	Thrustwasher
2	Gasket	16	Dished washer
3	Inner CV joint	17	Driveshaft
5	Dished washer	19	Vibration damper
6	Inner CV joint gaiter		(two-piece)
8	Gaiter securing clip	20	Vibration damper
9	Gaiter securing clip		(one-piece)
10	Outer CV joint gaiter	21	Bolts
12	Outer CV joint	22	CV joint guard
14	Circlip		

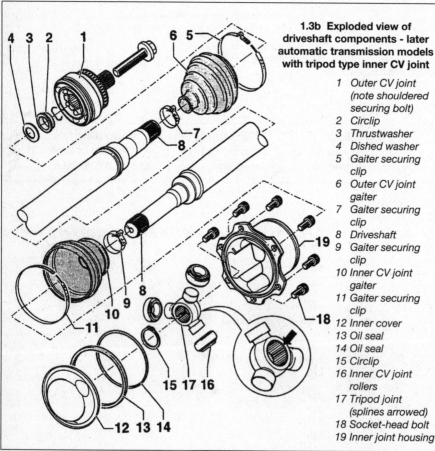

1.3b Exploded view of driveshaft components - later automatic transmission models with tripod type inner CV joint

1 Outer CV joint (note shouldered securing bolt)
2 Circlip
3 Thrustwasher
4 Dished washer
5 Gaiter securing clip
6 Outer CV joint gaiter
7 Gaiter securing clip
8 Driveshaft
9 Gaiter securing clip
10 Inner CV joint gaiter
11 Gaiter securing clip
12 Inner cover
13 Oil seal
14 Oil seal
15 Circlip
16 Inner CV joint rollers
17 Tripod joint (splines arrowed)
18 Socket-head bolt
19 Inner joint housing

1 General information

Drive is transmitted from the differential to the front wheels by means of two solid-steel driveshafts of unequal length. The right-hand driveshaft is longer than the left-hand, due to the position of the transmission.

Both driveshafts are splined at their outer ends to accept the wheel hubs, and are threaded so that each hub can be fastened by a large nut or bolt. The inner end of each driveshaft is bolted to the transmission drive flanges.

Constant velocity (CV) joints are fitted to each end of the driveshafts, to ensure the smooth and efficient transmission of drive at all the angles possible as the roadwheels move up and down with the suspension, and as they turn from side to side under steering. On manual transmission and early automatic transmission models, both inner and outer constant velocity joints are of the ball-and-cage type **(see illustration)**. On later automatic transmission models, the outer joint is of the ball-and-cage type, but the inner joint is of the tripod type **(see illustration)**. The later-type driveshaft can further be identified by having a shouldered bolt securing the outer end of the driveshaft to the wheel hub, rather than a nut.

2 Driveshaft -
removal and refitting

Note: *A new driveshaft retaining nut/bolt will be required on refitting.*

Removal

Note: *On later automatic transmission models with tripod type inner driveshaft joints (see Section 1, paragraph 3), in order to gain the necessary clearance required to withdraw the left-hand driveshaft, it may be necessary to unbolt the front and rear engine/transmission mountings (refer to Chapter 2A for details) and lift the engine slightly.*

1 Remove the wheel trim/hub cap (as applicable) and slacken the driveshaft retaining nut/bolt with the vehicle resting on its wheels **(see illustration)**. Also slacken the wheel bolts.

2 Chock the rear wheels of the car, firmly apply the handbrake, then jack up the front of the car and support it on axle stands (see "*Jacking and vehicle support*"). Remove the front roadwheel.

3 Slacken and remove the splined bolts securing the inner driveshaft joint to the transmission flange and, where necessary, recover the retaining plates from underneath the bolts **(see illustrations)**. Support the driveshaft by suspending it with wire or string - do not allow it to hang under its weight, or the joint may be damaged.

4 Using a suitable marker pen, draw around the end of the suspension lower arm, marking the correct fitted position of balljoint. Unscrew the balljoint retaining bolts and remove the retaining plate from the top of the lower arm **Note:** *On some models the balljoint inner retaining bolt hole is slotted; on these models the inner retaining bolt can be slackened, leaving the retaining plate and bolt in position in the arm, and the balljoint disengaged from the bolt.*

5 Access to the right-hand inner driveshaft joint is greatly improved by unbolting and removing the damper weight from the steering subframe, and the joint guard from the engine **(see illustration)**. Support the damper weight as it is unbolted and removed - it is quite heavy.

6 Unscrew the driveshaft retaining nut/bolt and (where necessary) remove its washer.

7 Carefully pull the swivel hub assembly outwards, and withdraw the driveshaft outer constant velocity joint from the hub assembly. The outer joint will be very tight, tap the joint out of the hub using a soft-faced mallet. If this fails to free it from the hub, the joint will have to be pressed out using a suitable tool which is bolted to the hub.

8 Manoeuvre the driveshaft out from underneath the vehicle and (where fitted) recover the gasket from the end of the inner constant velocity joint. Discard the gasket - a new one should be used on refitting.

2.1 Remove the trim/hub cap and slacken the driveshaft retaining nut

Caution: Do not allow the vehicle to rest on its wheels with one or both driveshaft(s) removed, as damage to the wheel bearing(s) may result.

9 If moving the vehicle is unavoidable, temporarily insert the outer end of the driveshaft(s) in the hub(s), and tighten the driveshaft retaining nut/bolt(s); in this case, the inner end(s) of the driveshaft(s) must be supported, for example by suspending with string from the vehicle underbody.

Caution: Do not allow the driveshaft to hang down under its weight, or the joint may be damaged.

Refitting

10 Ensure that the transmission flange and inner joint mating surfaces are clean and dry. Where necessary, fit a new gasket to the joint by peeling off its backing foil and sticking it in position.

11 Ensure that the outer joint and hub splines are clean and dry.

12 Manoeuvre the driveshaft into position, and engage the outer joint with the hub. Ensure that the threads are clean, and apply a smear of oil to the contact face of the new driveshaft retaining nut/bolt. Fit the washer (where fitted) and the nut/bolt, and draw the joint fully into position. Do not try to fully tighten the driveshaft nut/bolt until the vehicle is resting on its wheels.

13 Refit the suspension lower arm balljoint retaining bolts, and tighten them to the specified torque setting, using the marks made on removal to ensure that the balljoint is correctly positioned.

2.3b Using a suitable splined key or socket, slacken the inner joint retaining bolts, and recover the retaining plates

2.3a Inner driveshaft joint splined retaining bolts and retaining plates

14 Align the driveshaft inner joint with the transmission flange, and refit the retaining bolts and (where necessary) plates. Tighten the retaining bolts to the specified torque.

15 Ensure that the outer joint is drawn fully into position, then refit the roadwheel and lower the vehicle to the ground.

16 Tighten the driveshaft nut/bolt to the specified torque setting. Where a driveshaft bolt is fitted, use an angle gauge to ensure accuracy when tightening to the Stage 2 angle.

17 Once the driveshaft nut/bolt is correctly tightened, tighten the wheel bolts to the specified torque and refit the wheel trim/hub cap.

3 Driveshaft gaiters -
renewal

Outer CV joint gaiter

1 Remove the driveshaft (see Section 2).

2 Secure the driveshaft in a vice equipped with soft jaws, and release the two outer joint gaiter retaining clips. If necessary, the retaining clips can be cut to release them.

3 Slide the rubber gaiter down the shaft to expose the constant velocity joint, and scoop out excess grease.

4 Using a soft-faced mallet, tap the joint off the end of the driveshaft.

5 Remove the circlip from the driveshaft groove, and slide off the thrustwasher and dished washer, noting which way around it is fitted.

2.5 Removing the right-hand inner joint guard

8

6 Slide the rubber gaiter off the driveshaft and discard it.

7 Thoroughly clean the constant velocity joint(s) using paraffin, or a suitable solvent, and dry thoroughly. Carry out a visual inspection as follows.

8 Move the inner splined driving member from side to side to expose each ball in turn at the top of its track. Examine the balls for cracks, flat spots or signs of surface pitting.

9 Inspect the ball tracks on the inner and outer members. If the tracks have widened, the balls will no longer be a tight fit. At the same time, check the ball cage windows for wear or cracking between the windows.

10 If on inspection any of the constant velocity joint components are found to be worn or damaged, it will be necessary to renew the complete joint assembly. If the joint is in satisfactory condition, obtain a new gaiter and retaining clips, a constant velocity joint circlip and the correct type of grease. Grease is often supplied with the joint repair kit - if not, use a good-quality molybdenum disulphide grease.

11 Tape over the splines on the end of the driveshaft, to protect the new gaiter as it is slid into place.

12 Slide the new gaiter onto the end of the driveshaft, then remove the protective tape from the driveshaft splines.

13 Slide on the dished washer, making sure its convex side is innermost, followed by the thrustwasher.

14 Fit a new circlip to the driveshaft, then tap the joint onto the driveshaft until the circlip engages in its groove. Make sure that the joint is securely retained by the circlip.

15 Pack the joint with grease from the repair kit (where applicable) or with a suitable molybdenum disulphide grease. Work the grease well into the bearing tracks whilst twisting the joint, and fill the rubber gaiter with any excess.

16 Ease the gaiter over the joint, and ensure that the gaiter lips are correctly located on both the driveshaft and constant velocity joint. Lift the outer sealing lip of the gaiter to equalise air pressure within the gaiter.

17 Fit the large metal retaining clip to the gaiter. Pull the clip as tight as possible, and locate the hooks on the clip in their slots. Remove any slack in the gaiter retaining clip by carefully compressing the raised section of the clip. In the absence of the special tool, a pair of side cutters may be used, taking care not to cut the clip. Secure the small retaining clip using the same procedure.

18 Check the constant velocity joint moves freely in all directions, then refit the driveshaft to the vehicle, as described in Section 2.

Inner CV joint gaiter

19 A hydraulic press and several special tools are required to remove and refit the inner CV joint. Therefore it is recommended that gaiter renewal is entrusted to a VW dealer.

4 Driveshaft overhaul - general information

If any of the checks described in Chapter reveal wear in any driveshaft joint, first remo the roadwheel trim or centre cap (appropriate) and check that the drivesha retaining nut/bolt is tight.

If the nut/bolt is tight, refit the centre cap trim. Repeat this check on the remainin driveshaft nut/bolt.

Road test the vehicle, and listen for metallic clicking from the front as the vehic is driven slowly in a circle on full lock. If clicking noise is heard, this indicates wear the outer constant velocity joint. This mea that the joint must be renewed; reconditionin is not possible.

If vibration, consistent with road speed, felt through the car when accelerating, there a possibility of wear in the inner consta velocity joints.

To check the joints for wear, the drivesha must be dismantled. The outer consta velocity joint can be removed and checke but work on the inner joint should b entrusted to a VW dealer (see Section 3); any wear or free play is found, the affecte joint must be renewed.

Chapter 9
Braking system

Contents

Degrees of difficulty

| Easy, suitable for novice with little experience | | Fairly easy, suitable for beginner with some experience | | Fairly difficult, suitable for competent DIY mechanic | | Difficult, suitable for experienced DIY mechanic | | Very difficult, suitable for expert DIY or professional | |

Specifications

System type . . . . Front disc brakes, rear drums or discs. Dual-circuit; diagonally-split hydraulic system with vacuum servo assistance. Engine-driven vacuum pump on diesel engine models. Mechanical pressure regulator for rear brakes fitted to rear axle. Cable-operated handbrake to rear wheels. Anti-lock Braking System (ABS) on some models

Anti-lock Braking System (ABS)
System type:
  Left-hand-drive models up to July 1995 . . . . Teves 02 system - hydraulically-assisted (no servo)
  Right-hand-drive models up to July 1995 . . . . Teves 04 system - vacuum-assisted (remote servo)
  All models from July 1995 . . . . Teves 20 GI system - vacuum-assisted; mechanical pressure regulator no longer fitted

Front brakes
Disc diameter . . . . 256 mm
Disc thickness:
  New (unventilated) . . . . 13 mm
  New (ventilated) . . . . 20 mm
  Wear limit (unventilated) . . . . 11 mm
  Wear limit (ventilated) . . . . 18 mm
Allowable thickness tolerance . . . . 0.01 mm
Allowable run-out . . . . 0.03 mm
Disc pad thickness:
  New (unventilated) . . . . 14 mm
  New (ventilated) . . . . 11 mm
  Wear limit (including backing plate) . . . . 7 mm

9

Rear drum brakes

Drum diameter:
New .... 200 mm or 230 mm
   Maximum diameter .... 201.0 mm or 231.5 mm
Maximum drum out-of-round .... 0.1 mm
Brake shoe friction material thickness:
New .... 5.0 mm
Minimum .... 2.5 mm

Rear disc brakes

Disc diameter .... 226 mm
Disc thickness:
New .... 10 mm
Minimum .... 8 mm
Maximum disc runout .... 0.1 mm
Brake pad thickness:
New .... 12 mm
Minimum .... 7 mm

Torque wrench settings

	Nm	lbf ft
ABS hydraulic unit mounting nuts:		
Up to July 1995 (Teves 02/04)	25	18
July 1995 on (Teves 20 GI)	10	7
ABS hydraulic unit bracket-to-body nuts	25	18
ABS wheel sensor retaining bolts	10	7
Brake pipe unions:		
M10	15	11
M12	18	13
Front brake caliper:		
VW caliper mounting bolts	25	18
Girling caliper:		
Guide pin bolts	35	26
Mounting bracket bolts	125	92
Front brake splash shield bolts	10	7
Master cylinder mounting nuts:		
Non-ABS models	20	15
ABS models	25	18
Rear brake backplate bolts	60	44
Rear brake caliper:		
Guide pin bolts	35	26
Mounting bracket bolts	65	48
Rear brake wheel cylinder bolts	10	7
Roadwheel bolts	110	81
Servo unit mounting nuts	20	15
Vacuum pump clamp bolt	20	15

1 General information

The braking system is of the servo-assisted, dual-circuit hydraulic type. The arrangement of the hydraulic system is such that each circuit operates one front and one rear brake from a tandem master cylinder. Under normal circumstances, both circuits operate in unison. However, if there is hydraulic failure in one circuit, full braking force will still be available at two wheels.

All 2.0 litre engine models have disc brakes all round as standard; all other models are fitted with front disc brakes and rear drum brakes. ABS is fitted as standard to some models, and was offered as an option on most other models (refer to Section 22 for further information on ABS operation).

The front disc brakes are actuated by single-piston sliding type calipers, which ensure that equal pressure is applied to each disc pad.

On models with rear drum brakes, the rear brakes incorporate leading and trailing shoes, which are actuated by twin-piston wheel cylinders. A self-adjust mechanism is incorporated, to compensate for brake shoe wear.

On models with rear disc brakes, the brakes are actuated by single-piston sliding calipers which incorporate mechanical handbrake mechanisms.

A pressure-regulating set-up is incorporated in the braking system; this helps to prevent rear wheel lock-up during emergency braking. The system is controlled by a single load-dependent valve which is linked to the rear axle.

The handbrake provides an independent mechanical means of rear brake application.

On diesel engine models, an engine-driven vacuum pump provides a vacuum supply for the vacuum servo unit. On petrol engine models, the vacuum supply for the servo is taken via a drilling in the inlet manifold.

Note: *When servicing any part of the system, work carefully and methodically; also observe scrupulous cleanliness when overhauling any part of the hydraulic system. Always renew components (in axle sets, where applicable) if in doubt about their condition, and use only genuine VW replacement parts, or at least those of known good quality. Note the warnings given in "Safety first!" and at relevant points in this Chapter concerning the dangers of asbestos dust and hydraulic fluid.*

2 Hydraulic system - bleeding

⚠️ *Warning: Hydraulic fluid is poisonous; wash off immediately and thoroughly in the case of skin contact, and seek immediate medical advice if any fluid is swallowed or gets into the eyes. Certain types of hydraulic fluid are flammable, and may ignite when allowed into contact with hot components; when servicing any hydraulic system, it is safest to assume that the fluid is flammable, and to take precautions against the risk of fire as though it is petrol that is being handled. Hydraulic fluid is also an effective paint stripper, and will attack plastics; if any is spilt, it should be washed off immediately, using copious quantities of fresh water. Finally, it is hygroscopic (it absorbs moisture from the air) - old fluid may be contaminated and unfit for further use. When topping-up or renewing the fluid, always use the recommended type, and ensure that it comes from a freshly-opened sealed container.*

General

1 The correct operation of any hydraulic system is only possible after removing all air from the components and circuit; this is achieved by bleeding the system.

2 During the bleeding procedure, add only clean, unused hydraulic fluid of the recommended type; never re-use fluid that has already been bled from the system. Ensure that sufficient fluid is available before starting work.

3 If there is any possibility of incorrect fluid being already in the system, the brake components and circuit must be flushed completely with uncontaminated, correct fluid, and new seals should be fitted to the various components.

4 If hydraulic fluid has been lost from the system, or air has entered because of a leak, ensure that the fault is cured before continuing further.

5 Park the vehicle on level ground, switch off

2.14 Dust cap (arrowed) over the bleed screw on a rear brake wheel cylinder - models with rear drum brakes

the engine and select first or reverse gear, then chock the wheels and release the handbrake.

6 Check that all pipes and hoses are secure, unions tight and bleed screws closed. Clean any dirt from around the bleed screws.

7 Referring to *"Weekly checks"* if necessary, unscrew the master cylinder reservoir cap, and top the master cylinder reservoir up to the "MAX" level line. Refit the cap loosely, and remember to maintain the fluid level at least above the "MIN" level line throughout the procedure, or there is a risk of further air entering the system.

All models except left-hand-drive models with Teves 02 ABS

8 There are a number of one-man, do-it-yourself brake bleeding kits currently available from motor accessory shops. It is recommended that one of these kits is used whenever possible, as they greatly simplify the bleeding operation, and reduce the risk of expelled air and fluid being drawn back into the system. If such a kit is not available, the basic (two-man) method must be used, which is described in detail below.

9 If a kit is to be used, prepare the vehicle as described previously, and follow the kit manufacturer's instructions, as the procedure may vary slightly according to the type being used; generally, they are as outlined below in the relevant sub-section.

10 Whichever method is used, the same sequence must be followed (paragraphs 11 and 12) to ensure the removal of all air from the system.

Bleeding sequence

11 If the system has been only partially disconnected, and suitable precautions were taken to minimise fluid loss, it should be necessary only to bleed that part of the system (ie the primary or secondary circuit).

12 If the complete system is to be bled, then it should be done working in the following sequence:

a) *Right-hand rear brake.*
b) *Left-hand rear brake.*
c) *Right-hand front brake.*
d) *Left-hand front brake.*

Note: *When bleeding the rear brakes, an assistant working under the car should push the brake pressure regulating valve lever (where fitted) towards the rear axle.*

⚠️ *Warning: On models with ABS, under no circumstances should the hydraulic unit bleed screws be opened.*

Bleeding - basic (two-man) method

13 Collect together a clean glass jar of reasonable size, a suitable length of plastic or rubber tubing which is a tight fit over the bleed screw, and a ring spanner to fit the screw. The help of an assistant will also be required.

14 Remove the dust cap from the first screw in the sequence **(see illustration)**. Fit the spanner and tube to the screw, place the other end of the tube in the jar, and pour in

sufficient fluid to cover the end of the tube.

15 Ensure that the master cylinder reservoir fluid level is maintained at least above the "MIN" level line throughout the procedure.

16 Have the assistant fully depress the brake pedal several times to build up pressure, then maintain it on the final downstroke.

17 While pedal pressure is maintained, unscrew the bleed screw (approximately one turn) and allow the compressed fluid and air to flow into the jar. The assistant should maintain pedal pressure, following it down to the floor if necessary, and should not release it until instructed to do so. When the flow stops, tighten the bleed screw again, have the assistant release the pedal slowly, and recheck the reservoir fluid level.

18 Repeat the steps given in paragraphs 16 and 17 until the fluid emerging from the bleed screw is free from air bubbles. If the master cylinder has been drained and refilled, and air is being bled from the first screw in the sequence, allow approximately five seconds between cycles for the master cylinder passages to refill.

19 When no more air bubbles appear, tighten the bleed screw securely, remove the tube and spanner, and refit the dust cap. Do not overtighten the bleed screw.

20 Repeat the procedure on the remaining screws in the sequence, until all air is removed from the system and the brake pedal feels firm again.

Bleeding - using a one-way valve kit

21 As their name implies, these kits consist of a length of tubing with a one-way valve fitted, to prevent expelled air and fluid being drawn back into the system; some kits include a translucent container, which can be positioned so that the air bubbles can be more easily seen flowing from the end of the tube.

22 The kit is connected to the bleed screw, which is then opened. The user returns to the driver's seat, depresses the brake pedal with a smooth, steady stroke, and slowly releases it; this is repeated until the expelled fluid is clear of air bubbles **(see illustration)**.

23 Note that these kits simplify work so much that it is easy to forget the master cylinder reservoir fluid level; ensure that this is maintained at least above the "MIN" level line at all times.

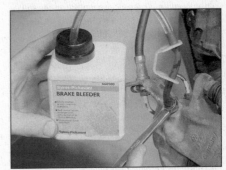

2.22 Brake bleeding using a 'one-man' kit

9

Bleeding - using a pressure-bleeding kit

24 These kits are usually operated by the reservoir of pressurised air contained in the spare tyre. However, note that it will probably be necessary to reduce the pressure to a lower level than normal; refer to the instructions supplied with the kit.

25 By connecting a pressurised, fluid-filled container to the master cylinder reservoir, bleeding can be carried out simply by opening each screw in turn (in the specified sequence), and allowing the fluid to flow out until no more air bubbles can be seen in the expelled fluid.

26 This method has the advantage that the large reservoir of fluid provides an additional safeguard against air being drawn into the system during bleeding.

27 Pressure-bleeding is particularly effective when bleeding "difficult" systems, or when bleeding the complete system at the time of routine fluid renewal.

All methods

28 When bleeding is complete, and firm pedal feel is restored, wash off any spilt fluid, tighten the bleed screws securely, and refit their dust caps.

29 Check the hydraulic fluid level in the master cylinder reservoir, and top-up if necessary (see *"Weekly checks"*).

30 Discard any hydraulic fluid that has been bled from the system; it will not be fit for re-use.

31 Check the feel of the brake pedal. If it feels at all spongy, air must still be present in the system, and further bleeding is required. Failure to bleed satisfactorily after a reasonable repetition of the bleeding procedure may be due to worn master cylinder seals. However, check the system carefully for fluid leaks (in particular, check the rear wheel cylinders on rear drum brake models) before deciding that a master cylinder overhaul is required.

Left-hand-drive models with Teves 02 ABS

32 The procedures to bleed the brakes on left-hand-drive models fitted with Teves 02 ABS are much the same as those described for the conventional braking system used on other models. The following differences apply, however, and must be noted when bleeding the system on ABS models.

Bleeding sequence

33 If the system has been only partially disconnected, and suitable precautions were taken to minimise fluid loss, it should be necessary only to bleed that part of the system.

34 If the complete system is to be bled, then it should be done working in the following sequence:
a) *Right-hand front brake.*
b) *Left-hand front brake.*
c) *Right-hand rear brake.*
d) *Left-hand rear brake.*

Note: *When bleeding the rear brakes, an assistant working under the car should push the brake pressure regulating valve lever (where fitted) towards the rear axle.*

 Warning: Under no circumstances should the hydraulic unit bleed screws be opened.

Bleeding method

35 Ensure that the ignition is switched off, then depress and release the brake pedal twenty times to relieve the pressure in the accumulator. Fill the brake fluid reservoir to the brim before starting, refit the reservoir cap securely, and ensure that the fluid level does not drop below the minimum mark whilst the brakes are being bled.

36 Refer to paragraphs 13 to 19 and bleed the front brakes only. If preferred, a one-man brake bleeding kit may be used (paragraphs 21 to 23), but **not** a pressure-bleeding kit.

37 Before bleeding the rear brakes, first ensure that the ignition is switched off, then have an assistant depress and release the brake pedal twenty times, and then hold it down in the fully-depressed position.

38 Connect the bleed tube up to the first rear bleed screw. Have your assistant switch on the ignition, then loosen the bleed screw, and allow the fluid to flow from the circuit until the air bubbles are no longer visible. Follow the brake pedal slowly down to the floor, and hold it there - pumping the pedal should not be necessary. When no more air emerges from the bleed screw, tighten the screw and have your assistant switch off the ignition.

39 Do not allow the pump to run continuously for longer than 2 minutes at a time. If operated for longer, switch off the ignition, and allow the pump to cool for a period of 10 minutes before continuing.

40 Before proceeding, check the brake fluid level in the master cylinder, and top up if necessary.

41 Repeat the procedure in paragraphs 38 and 39 for the other rear bleed screw.

42 Finally, with all the bleed screws securely tightened, switch on the ignition and run the pump until it switches off on its own. If the pump does not switch off before 2 minutes, check the system for leaks and bleed it again from scratch.

43 On completion, top up the brake fluid level to the "MAX" level.

3 Hydraulic pipes and hoses - renewal

Note: *Refer to the note in Section 2 concerning the dangers of hydraulic fluid.*
1 If any pipe or hose is to be renewed, minimise fluid loss by first removing the master cylinder reservoir cap, then tightening it down onto a piece of polythene to obtain an airtight seal. Alternatively, flexible hoses can be sealed, if required, using a proprietary

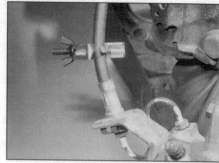

3.1 Hydraulic hose clamp fitted, to ensure minimum fluid loss

brake hose clamp **(see illustration)**; metal brake pipe unions can be plugged (if care is taken not to allow dirt into the system) or capped immediately they are disconnected. Place a wad of rag under any union that is to be disconnected, to catch any spilt fluid.

2 If a flexible hose is to be disconnected, unscrew the brake pipe union nut before removing the spring clip which secures the hose to its mounting bracket **(see illustration)**.

3 To unscrew the union nuts, it is preferable to obtain a brake pipe spanner of the correct size; these are available from most large motor accessory shops. Failing this, a close-fitting open-ended spanner will be required, though if the nuts are tight or corroded, their flats may be rounded-off if the spanner slips. In such a case, a self-locking wrench is often the only way to unscrew a stubborn union, but it follows that the pipe and the damaged nuts must be renewed on reassembly. Always clean a union and surrounding area before disconnecting it. If disconnecting a component with more than one union, make a careful note of the connections before disturbing any of them.

4 If a brake pipe is to be renewed, it can be obtained, cut to length and with the union nuts and end flares in place, from VW dealers. All that is then necessary is to bend it to shape, following the line of the original, before fitting it to the car. Alternatively, most motor accessory shops can make up brake pipes from kits, but this requires very careful measurement of the original, to ensure that the replacement is of the correct length. The safest answer is usually to take the original to the shop as a pattern.

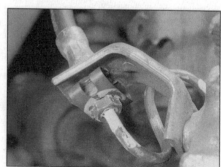

3.2 Flexible-to-rigid brake line connection showing mounting bracket and clip

3.5 Typical rigid brake lines and union connectors

5 To remove a rigid line, unscrew the union nuts at each end, prise open the clips (where fitted) and withdraw the line **(see illustration)**. On refitting, do not overtighten the union nuts. It is not necessary to exercise brute force to obtain a sound joint.

6 Ensure that the pipes and hoses are correctly routed, with no kinks, and that they are secured in the clips or brackets provided. After fitting, remove the polythene from the reservoir, and bleed the hydraulic system as described in Section 2. Wash off any spilt fluid, and check carefully for fluid leaks.

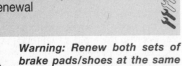

4 Front brake pads - renewal

⚠ *Warning: Renew both sets of brake pads/shoes at the same time - never renew the pads/shoes on only one wheel, as uneven braking may result. Note that the dust created by wear of the pads may contain asbestos, which is a health hazard. Never blow it out with compressed air, and do not inhale any of it. An approved filtering mask should be worn when working on the brakes. DO NOT use petrol or petroleum-based solvents to clean brake parts; use brake cleaner or methylated spirit only.*

1 Apply the handbrake, then jack up the front of the vehicle and support it on axle stands (see "*Jacking and vehicle support*"). Remove the front roadwheels.

4.10a Fit the anti-rattle springs to the hub, making sure they are correctly located . . .

4.3 On VW calipers, undo the caliper mounting bolts

2 Trace the brake pad wear sensor wiring (where fitted) back from the pads, and disconnect it from the wiring connector. Note the routing of the wiring, and free it from any relevant retaining clips. Continue as described under the relevant sub-heading.

VW calipers

3 Using a suitable Allen key or socket, slacken and remove the two caliper mounting bolts, then lift the caliper away from the brake pads and hub, and tie it to the suspension strut using a suitable piece of wire **(see illustration)**. Do not allow the caliper to hang unsupported on the flexible brake hose.

4 Withdraw the two brake pads from the swivel hub and recover the anti-rattle springs, noting their correct fitted locations. Note that the springs are different and are not interchangeable.

5 First measure the thickness of each brake pad (including the backing plate). If either pad is worn at any point to the specified minimum thickness or less, all four pads must be renewed. Also, the pads should be renewed if any are fouled with oil or grease; there is no satisfactory way of degreasing friction material, once contaminated. If any of the brake pads are worn unevenly, or are fouled with oil or grease, trace and rectify the cause before reassembly. New brake pad kits are available from VW dealers.

6 If one of the brake pads is significantly more worn than the other, it is quite likely that the caliper is partially seized. With the brake pads removed, the caliper body should be free to slide on the guide sleeves. If the action

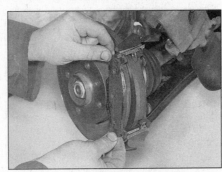

4.10b . . . and install the brake pads with their friction material facing the disc

is suspect, dismantle and clean the caliper with reference to Section 10.

7 If the brake pads are still serviceable, carefully clean them using a clean, fine wire brush or similar, paying particular attention to the sides and back of the metal backing. Clean out the grooves in the friction material (where applicable), and pick out any large embedded particles of dirt or debris. Carefully clean the pad locations in the caliper body/mounting bracket.

8 Prior to fitting the pads, check that the spacers are free to slide easily in the caliper body bushes, and are a reasonably tight fit. Brush the dust and dirt from the caliper and piston, but *do not* inhale it, as it is a health hazard. Inspect the dust seal around the piston for damage, and the piston for evidence of fluid leaks, corrosion or damage. If attention to any of these components is necessary, refer to Section 10.

9 If new brake pads are to be fitted, the caliper piston must be pushed back into the cylinder to make room for them. Either use a G-clamp or similar tool, or use suitable pieces of wood as levers. Provided that the master cylinder reservoir has not been overfilled with hydraulic fluid, there should be no spillage, but keep a careful watch on the fluid level while retracting the piston. If the fluid level rises above the "MAX" level line at any time, the surplus should be siphoned off or ejected through a plastic tube connected to the bleed screw (see Section 2). **Note:** *Do not siphon the fluid by mouth, as it is poisonous; use a syringe or an old poultry baster.*

10 Fit the new anti-rattle springs to the hub, making sure they are correctly positioned and fit the pads, and ensuring that the friction material of each pad is against the brake disc. Note that, where necessary, the pad with the wear sensor wire should be installed as the inner pad **(see illustrations)**.

11 Position the caliper over the pads, and pass the pad warning sensor wiring (where fitted) through the caliper aperture **(see illustration)**.

12 Press the caliper into position sufficiently until it is possible to install caliper mounting bolts. Tighten the mounting bolts to the specified torque setting. **Note:** *Do not exert excess pressure on the caliper, as this will*

4.11 With the pads and springs correctly located, slide the caliper back into position

9

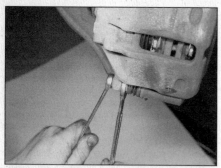

4.18 On Girling calipers, remove the lower guide pin bolt, holding the pin as shown

4.19a Pivot the caliper upwards . . .

4.19b . . . then recover the shim from the caliper piston . . .

4.20 . . . and remove the pads from the caliper mounting bracket

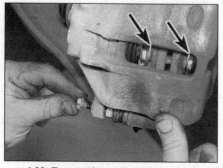

4.23 Ensure the anti-rattle springs (arrowed) are in place, then fit the new guide pin bolt

pad with the wear sensor wiring should be installed as the inner pad.

23 Refit the shim to the caliper piston. Pivot the caliper down into position, and pass the pad warning sensor wiring through the caliper aperture. If the threads of the new guide pin bolt are not already pre-coated with locking compound, apply a suitable thread-locking compound to them. Press the caliper into position whilst ensuring that the pad anti-rattle springs locate correctly with the caliper. Install the guide pin bolt, tightening it to the specified torque setting while retaining the guide pin with an open-ended spanner **(see illustration).**

24 Reconnect the brake pad wear sensor wiring connectors (where necessary) ensuring that the wiring is correctly routed.

25 Depress the brake pedal repeatedly, until the pads are pressed into firm contact with the brake disc, and normal (non-assisted) pedal pressure is restored.

26 Repeat the above procedure on the remaining front brake caliper.

27 Refit the roadwheels, then lower the vehicle to the ground and tighten the roadwheel bolts to the specified torque.

28 Check the hydraulic fluid level as described in *"Weekly checks"*.

deform the pad springs, resulting in noisy operation of the brakes.

13 Reconnect the brake pad wear sensor wiring connectors, ensuring that the wiring is correctly routed.

14 Depress the brake pedal repeatedly, until the pads are pressed into firm contact with the brake disc, and normal (non-assisted) pedal pressure is restored.

15 Repeat the above procedure on the remaining front brake caliper.

16 Refit the roadwheels, then lower the vehicle to the ground and tighten the roadwheel bolts to the specified torque.

17 New pads will not give full braking efficiency until they have bedded-in. Be prepared for this, and avoid hard braking as far as possible for the first hundred miles or so after pad renewal.

Girling caliper

18 Slacken and remove the lower caliper guide pin bolt, using a slim open-ended spanner to prevent the guide pin itself from rotating **(see illustration).** Discard the guide pin bolt - a new bolt must be used on refitting.

19 With the lower guide pin bolt removed, pivot the caliper upwards until it is clear of the brake pads and mounting bracket. Remove the shim from the caliper piston **(see illustrations).**

20 Withdraw the two brake pads from the caliper mounting bracket **(see illustration).**

21 Examine the pads and caliper as described above in paragraphs 5 to 9, substituting "guide pins" for references to spacers and bushes.

22 Install the pads in the caliper mounting bracket, ensuring that the friction material of each pad is against the brake disc. Note the

5 Rear brake pads - renewal

Note: *Refer to the warning at the start of Section 4 before starting work.*

1 Chock the front wheels, engage 1st gear (or "P"), then jack up the rear of the vehicle and support it on axle stands (see *"Jacking and vehicle support"*). Remove the rear wheels.

2 Slacken the handbrake cable and detach it from the caliper as described in Section 19.

3 Slacken and remove the caliper guide pin bolts, using a slim open-ended spanner to prevent the guide pins from rotating **(see illustration).** Discard the guide pin bolts - new bolts must be used on refitting.

4 Lift the caliper away from the brake pads, and tie it up using a suitable piece of wire **(see illustration).** Do not allow the caliper to hang unsupported on the flexible brake hose.

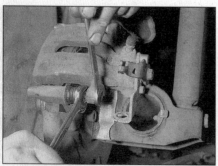

5.3 Hold the guide pin and unscrew the rear caliper guide pin bolts

5.4 Lift the caliper upwards and away . . .

5.5a . . . and remove the pads . . .

5.5b . . . and anti-rattle springs from the caliper mounting bracket

In the absence of the special tool, the piston can be screwed back into the caliper using a pair of circlip pliers

5 Withdraw the two brake pads from the caliper mounting bracket and recover the anti-rattle springs from the mounting bracket, noting their correct fitted locations **(see illustrations)**.

6 First measure the thickness of each brake pad (including the backing plate). If either pad is worn at any point to the specified minimum thickness or less, **all four** pads must be renewed. Also, the pads should be renewed if any are fouled with oil or grease; there is no satisfactory way of degreasing friction material, once contaminated. If any of the brake pads are worn unevenly, or fouled with oil or grease, trace and rectify the cause before reassembly. New brake pads are available from VW dealers.

7 If one of the brake pads is significantly more worn than the other, it is quite likely that the caliper is partially seized. With the brake pads removed, the caliper body should be free to slide on the guide sleeves. If the action is suspect, dismantle and clean the caliper with reference to Section 11.

8 If the brake pads are still serviceable, carefully clean them using a clean, fine wire brush or similar, paying particular attention to the sides and back of the metal backing. Clean out the grooves in the friction material (where applicable), and pick out any large embedded particles of dirt or debris. Carefully clean the pad locations in the caliper body/mounting bracket.

9 Prior to fitting the pads, check that the guide pins are free to slide easily in the caliper bracket, and check that the rubber guide pin gaiters are undamaged. Brush the dust and dirt from the caliper and piston, but **do not** inhale it, as it is a health hazard. Inspect the dust seal around the piston for damage, and the piston for evidence of fluid leaks, corrosion or damage. If attention to any of these components is necessary, refer to Section 11.

10 If new brake pads are to be fitted, it will be necessary to retract the piston fully into the caliper bore, by rotating it in a clockwise direction **(see Tool Tip)**. Provided that the master cylinder reservoir has not been overfilled with hydraulic fluid, there should be no spillage, but keep a careful watch on the fluid level while retracting the piston. If the

fluid level rises above the "MAX" level line at any time, the surplus should be siphoned off, or ejected through a plastic tube connected to the bleed screw (see Section 2).

> ⚠️ **Warning: Do not siphon the fluid by mouth, as it is poisonous; use a syringe or an old poultry baster.**

11 Fit the anti-rattle springs to the caliper mounting bracket, ensuring that they are correctly located. Install the pads in the mounting bracket, ensuring that each pad's friction material is against the brake disc.

12 Slide the caliper back into position over the pads.

13 If the threads of the new guide pin bolts are not already pre-coated with locking compound, apply a suitable thread-locking compound to them. Press the caliper into position, then install the bolts, tightening them to the specified torque setting while retaining the guide pin with an open-ended spanner.

14 Depress the brake pedal repeatedly, until the pads are pressed into firm contact with the brake disc, and normal (non-assisted) pedal pressure is restored.

15 Repeat the above procedure on the remaining rear brake caliper.

16 Reconnect the handbrake cables to the calipers, and adjust the handbrake as described in Section 17.

17 Refit the roadwheels, then lower the vehicle to the ground and tighten the road-wheel bolts to the specified torque setting.

18 Check the hydraulic fluid level as described in *"Weekly checks"*.

19 New pads will not give full braking efficiency until they have bedded-in. Be prepared for this, and avoid hard braking as far as possible for the first hundred miles or so after pad renewal.

6 Rear brake shoes - renewal

Note: *Refer to the warning at the start of Section 4 before starting work.*

1 Remove the brake drums (see Section 9).

2 Working carefully, and taking the necessary precautions, remove all traces of brake dust from the brake drum, backplate and shoes.

3 Measure the thickness of the friction material of each brake shoe at several points; if either shoe is worn at any point to the specified minimum thickness or less, **all four** shoes must be renewed as a set. The shoes should also be renewed if any are fouled with oil or grease; there is no way of degreasing friction material, once contaminated.

4 If any of the brake shoes are worn unevenly, or fouled with oil or grease, trace and rectify the cause before reassembly.

5 To renew the brake shoes, continue as follows. If all is well, refit the brake drum as described in Section 9.

6 Note the position of the brake shoes and springs, and mark the webs of the shoes, if necessary, to aid refitting - make a sketch of the fitted positions of the components if wished. Only work on one rear brake at a time, so that the other rear brake can be used as a guide to fitted positions.

7 Using a pair of pliers, remove the shoe retainer spring cups by depressing and turning them through 90°. With the cups removed, lift off the springs and withdraw the retainer pins **(see illustrations)**.

8 Ease the shoes out one at a time from the lower pivot point, to release the tension of the return spring, then disconnect the lower return spring from both shoes **(see illustration)**.

9 Ease the upper end of both shoes out from their wheel cylinder locations, taking care not to damage the wheel cylinder seals, and

6.7a Using pliers, twist the spring cup through 90° . . .

9

6.7b . . . then lift off the spring . . .

6.7c . . . and withdraw the retainer pin from the rear of the backplate

6.8 Unhook the shoes from the lower pivot point, and remove the lower return spring

disconnect the handbrake cable from the trailing shoe. The brake shoe assembly can then be manoeuvred out of position and away from the backplate. Do not depress the brake

6.9a Free the shoes from the wheel cylinder. Note elastic band (arrowed) used to retain pistons . . .

pedal until the brakes are reassembled; wrap a strong elastic band around the wheel cylinder pistons to retain them **(see illustrations)**.

10 Make a note of the correct fitted positions of all components **(see illustration)**, then unhook the upper return spring, and disengage the wedge key spring.

11 Unhook the tensioning spring, and remove the pushrod from the trailing shoe, together with the wedge key.

12 Examine all components for signs of wear or damage, and renew as necessary. All return springs should be renewed, regardless of their apparent condition. Although linings are available separately (without shoes) from VW dealers, renewal of the shoes complete with linings is to be preferred, unless the necessary skills and equipment are available to fit new linings to the old shoes.

13 Peel back the rubber protective caps, and check the wheel cylinder for fluid leaks or other damage; check that both cylinder pistons are free to move easily. Refer to Section 12, if necessary, for information on wheel cylinder overhaul.

14 Apply a little brake grease to the contact areas of the pushrod and handbrake lever.

15 Hook the tensioning spring into the trailing shoe. Engage the pushrod with the opposite end of the spring, and pivot the pushrod into position on the trailing shoe **(see illustrations)**.

16 Fit the wedge key between the trailing shoe and pushrod, making sure it is fitted the correct way around **(see illustration)**.

17 Locate the handbrake lever on the leading shoe in the pushrod, and fit the upper return spring using a pair of pliers **(see illustrations)**.

6.9b . . . then detach the handbrake cable and remove the shoe assembly

6.10 Prior to dismantling, note the correct fitted location of the shoe components

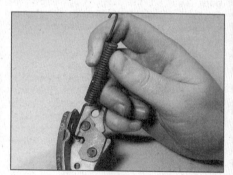

6.15a Hook the tensioning spring into the trailing shoe . . .

6.15b . . . then engage the pushrod with the opposite end of the spring . . .

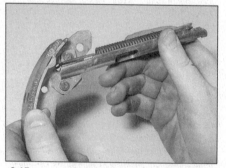

6.15c . . . and pivot the strut into position on the shoe

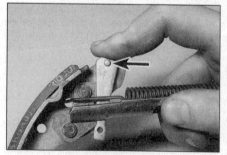

6.16 Slot the wedge key into position. Ensure raised dot (arrowed) is facing away from the shoe

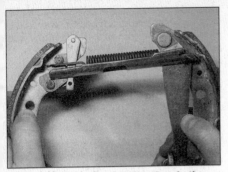

6.17a Locate the leading shoe in the pushrod . . .

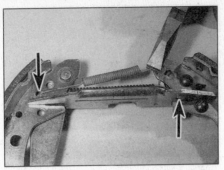

6.17b . . . and hook the upper return spring into the leading shoe and pushrod (arrowed)

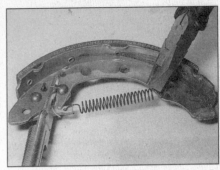

6.18 Fit the spring to the wedge key, and hook it onto the trailing shoe

18 Fit the spring to the wedge key, and hook it onto the trailing shoe **(see illustration)**.

19 Prior to installation, clean the backplate, and apply a thin smear of high-temperature brake grease or anti-seize compound to all those surfaces of the backplate which bear on the shoes, particularly the wheel cylinder pistons and lower pivot point. Do not allow the lubricant to foul the friction material.

20 Remove the elastic band fitted to the wheel cylinder, and offer up the shoe assembly.

21 Connect the handbrake cable to the handbrake lever, and locate the top of the shoes in the wheel cylinder piston slots.

22 Fit the lower return spring to the shoes, then lever the bottom of the shoes onto the bottom anchor.

23 Tap the shoes to centralise them with the backplate, then refit the shoe retainer pins and springs, and secure them in position with the spring cups.

24 Refit the brake drum as described in Section 9.

25 Repeat the above procedure on the remaining rear brake.

26 Once both sets of rear shoes have been renewed and the drums refitted, adjust the lining-to-drum clearance by repeatedly depressing the brake pedal until normal (non-assisted) pedal pressure returns.

27 Check and, if necessary, adjust the handbrake as described in Section 17.

28 On completion, check the hydraulic fluid level as described in *"Weekly checks"*.

29 New shoes will not give full braking efficiency until they have bedded-in. Be prepared for this, and avoid hard braking as far as possible for the first hundred miles or so after shoe renewal.

7 Front brake disc - inspection, removal and refitting

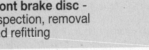

Note: *Before starting work, refer to the note at the beginning of Section 4 concerning the dangers of asbestos dust.*

Inspection

Note: *If either disc requires renewal, BOTH should be renewed at the same time, to ensure even and consistent braking. New brake pads should also be fitted.*

1 Apply the handbrake, then jack up the front of the car and support it on axle stands (see *"Jacking and vehicle support"*). Remove the appropriate front roadwheel.

2 Slowly rotate the brake disc so that the full area of both sides can be checked; remove the brake pads if better access is required to the inboard surface. Light scoring is normal in the area swept by the brake pads, but if heavy scoring or cracks are found, the disc must be renewed.

3 It is normal to find a lip of rust and brake dust around the disc's perimeter; this can be scraped off if required. If, however, a lip has formed due to excessive wear of the brake

pad swept area, then the disc's thickness must be measured using a micrometer **(see illustration)**. Take measurements at several places around the disc, at the inside and outside of the pad swept area; if the disc has worn at any point to the specified minimum thickness or less, the disc must be renewed.

4 If the disc is thought to be warped, it can be checked for run-out. Either use a dial gauge mounted on any convenient fixed point, while the disc is slowly rotated, or use feeler blades to measure (at several points all around the disc) the clearance between the disc and a fixed point, such as the caliper mounting bracket. If the measurements obtained are at the specified maximum or beyond, the disc is excessively warped, and must be renewed; however, it is worth checking first that the hub bearing is in good condition (Chapters 1 and/or 10). If the run-out is excessive, the disc must be renewed.

5 Check the disc for cracks, especially around the wheel bolt holes, and any other wear or damage, and renew if necessary.

Removal

6 On models with VW front brake calipers, remove the brake pads as described in Section 4.

7 On models with Girling front brake calipers, unscrew the two bolts securing the brake caliper mounting bracket to the swivel hub, then slide the caliper assembly off the disc. Using a piece of wire or string, tie the caliper to the front suspension coil spring, to avoid placing any strain on the brake hose.

8 Use chalk or paint to mark the relationship of the disc to the hub, then remove the screw securing the brake disc to the hub, and remove the disc **(see illustration)**. If it is tight, tap its rear face with a hide or plastic mallet.

Refitting

9 Refitting is the reverse of the removal procedure, noting the following points:
  a) *Ensure that the mating surfaces of the disc and hub are clean and flat.*
  b) *Align (if applicable) the marks made on removal, and securely tighten the disc retaining screw.*
  c) *If a new disc has been fitted, use a suitable solvent to wipe any preservative*

7.3 Measuring brake disc thickness with a micrometer

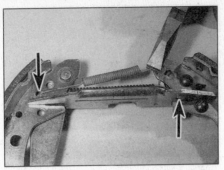

7.8 Undo the retaining screw and remove the front brake disc

9.2 Lever out the cap from the centre of the brake drum

9.3 Remove the split pin and locking cap . . .

coating from the disc, before refitting the caliper.

d) *On models with Girling brake calipers, slide the caliper into position over the disc, making sure the pads pass either side of the disc. Tighten the caliper bracket mounting bolts to the specified torque setting.*

e) *On models with VW brake calipers, refit the pads as described in Section 4.*

f) *Refit the roadwheel, then lower the vehicle to the ground and tighten the roadwheel bolts to the specified torque. On completion, repeatedly depress the brake pedal until normal (non-assisted) pedal pressure returns.*

8 Rear brake disc - inspection, removal and refitting

Note: *Before starting work, refer to the note at the beginning of Section 4 concerning the dangers of asbestos dust.*

Inspection

Note: *If either disc requires renewal, BOTH should be renewed at the same time, to ensure even and consistent braking. New brake pads should be fitted also.*

1 Firmly chock the front wheels, engage 1st gear (or "P"), then jack up the rear of the car and support it on axle stands (see "*Jacking and vehicle support*"). Remove the appropriate rear roadwheel.
2 Inspect the disc as described in Section 7.

Removal

3 Unscrew the two bolts securing the brake caliper mounting bracket in position, then slide the caliper assembly off the disc. Using a piece of wire or string, tie the caliper to the rear suspension coil spring, to avoid placing any strain on the hydraulic brake hose.
4 Using a hammer and a large flat-bladed screwdriver, carefully tap and prise the cap out of the centre of the brake disc. Renew the cap if it is disfigured during removal.
5 Extract the split pin from the hub nut, and remove the locking ring. Discard the split pin; a new one must be used on refitting.
6 Slacken and remove the rear hub nut, then slide off the toothed washer and remove the outer bearing from the centre of the disc.
7 The disc can now be slide off the stub axle.

Refitting

8 If a new disc is been fitted, use a suitable solvent to wipe any preservative coating from the disc. If necessary, install the bearing races, inner bearing and oil seal as described in Chapter 10, and thoroughly grease the outer bearing.
9 Apply a smear of grease to the disc oil seal, and slide the disc assembly onto the stub axle.
10 Fit the outer bearing and toothed thrustwasher, ensuring its tooth is correctly engaged in the axle slot.
11 Refit the hub nut, tightening it to the point where it just contacts the washer whilst rotating the brake disc to settle the hub bearings in position. Gradually slacken the hub nut until the position is found where it is just possible to move the toothed washer

from side-to-side using a screwdriver. **Note:** *Only a small amount of force should be needed to move the washer.* When the hub nut is correctly positioned, secure it in position with a new split pin.
12 Fit the cap to the centre of the brake disc, driving it fully into position.
13 Before refitting the brake caliper, make sure that both sides of the disc are completely clean. Slide the caliper into position over the disc, making sure the pads pass either side of the disc. Tighten the caliper mounting bolts to the specified torque setting.
14 Refit the roadwheel, then lower the vehicle to the ground and tighten the wheel bolts to the specified torque setting.

9 Rear brake drum - removal, inspection and refitting

Note: *Before starting work, refer to the note at the beginning of Section 4 concerning the dangers of asbestos dust.*

Removal

1 Chock the front wheels, engage 1st gear (or "P"), then jack up the rear of the vehicle and support it on axle stands (see "*Jacking and vehicle support*"). Remove the appropriate rear wheel.
2 Using a hammer and a large flat-bladed screwdriver, carefully tap and prise the cap out of the centre of the brake drum **(see illustration)**. Discard the cap if it is disfigured during removal.
3 Extract the split pin from the hub nut and remove the locking cap **(see illustration)**. Discard the split pin; a new one must be used on refitting.
4 Slacken and remove the rear hub nut, then slide off the toothed washer and remove the outer bearing from the centre of the drum **(see illustrations)**.
5 It should now be possible to withdraw the brake drum assembly from the stub axle by hand **(see illustration)**. It may be difficult to remove the drum, due to the tightness of the hub bearing on the stub axle, or due to the brake shoes binding on the inner circumference of the drum. If the bearing is tight, tap

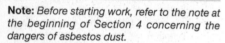

9.4a . . . then unscrew the retaining nut and remove the toothed washer

9.4b Withdraw the outer bearing . . .

9.5 . . . and remove the brake drum

9.7a Release the brake shoes by inserting a screwdriver through the drum hole . . .

9.7b . . . and levering the wedge key (arrowed) upwards

the periphery of the drum using a hide or plastic mallet, or use a universal puller, secured to the drum with the wheel bolts, to pull it off. If the brake shoes are binding, first check that the handbrake is fully released, then continue as follows.

6 Referring to Section 17, fully slacken the handbrake adjustment, to obtain maximum free play in the cable.

7 Insert a screwdriver through one of the wheel bolt holes in the brake drum, and lever up the wedge key in order to allow the brake shoes to retract fully **(see illustrations)**. The brake drum can now be withdrawn.

Inspection

Note: *If either drum requires renewal, BOTH should be renewed at the same time, to ensure even and consistent braking. New brake shoes should also be fitted.*

8 Working carefully, remove all traces of brake dust from the drum, but avoid inhaling the dust, as it is a health hazard.

9 Clean the outside of the drum, and check it for obvious signs of wear or damage, such as cracks around the roadwheel bolt holes; renew the drum if necessary.

10 Examine carefully the inside of the drum. Light scoring of the friction surface is normal, but if heavy scoring is found, the drum must be renewed. It is usual to find a lip on the drum's inboard edge which consists of a mixture of rust and brake dust; this should be scraped away, to leave a smooth surface which can be polished with fine (120- to 150-grade) emery paper. If, however, the lip is due to the friction surface being recessed by wear, then the drum must be renewed.

11 If the drum is thought to be excessively worn, or oval, its internal diameter must be measured at several points using an internal micrometer. Take measurements in pairs, the second at right-angles to the first, and compare the two, to check for signs of ovality. Provided that it does not enlarge the drum to beyond the specified maximum diameter, it may be possible to have the drum refinished by skimming or grinding; if this is not possible, the drums on both sides must be renewed. Note that if the drum is to be skimmed, BOTH drums must be refinished, to maintain a consistent internal diameter on both sides.

Refitting

12 If a new brake drum is to be installed, use a suitable solvent to remove any preservative coating that may have been applied to its interior. If necessary, install the bearing races, inner bearing and oil seal as described in Chapter 10, and thoroughly grease the outer bearing.

13 Prior to refitting, fully retract the brakes shoes by lifting up the wedge key.

14 Apply a smear of grease to the drum oil seal, and carefully slide the drum assembly onto the stub axle.

15 Fit the outer bearing and toothed thrustwasher, ensuring its tooth is correctly engaged in the axle slot.

16 Refit the hub nut, tightening it to the point where it just contacts the washer whilst rotating the brake drum to settle the hub bearings in position. Gradually slacken the hub nut until the position is found where it is just possible to move the toothed washer from side-to-side using a screwdriver. **Note:** *Only a small amount of force should be needed to move the washer.* When the hub nut is correctly positioned, refit the locking cap and secure the nut in position with a new split pin.

17 Fit the cap to the centre of the brake drum, driving it fully into position.

18 Make sure that both drums are in place, then depress the footbrake several times to operate the self-adjusting mechanism.

19 Repeat the above procedure on the remaining rear brake assembly (where necessary), then check and, if necessary, adjust the handbrake cable (see Section 17).

10.6 Holding the guide pin while unscrewing the guide pin bolt (Girling caliper)

20 On completion, refit the roadwheel(s), then lower the vehicle to the ground and tighten the wheel bolts to the specified torque.

10 Front brake caliper - removal, overhaul and refitting

Note: *Before starting work, refer to the note at the beginning of Section 2 concerning the dangers of hydraulic fluid, and to the warning at the beginning of Section 4 concerning the dangers of asbestos dust.*

Removal

1 Apply the handbrake, then jack up the front of the vehicle and support it on axle stands (see "Jacking and vehicle support"). Remove the appropriate roadwheel.

2 Minimise fluid loss by first removing the master cylinder reservoir cap, and then tightening it down onto a piece of polythene, to obtain an airtight seal. Alternatively, use a brake hose clamp, a G-clamp or a similar tool to clamp the flexible hose.

3 Clean the area around the union, then loosen the brake hose union nut.

4 Remove the brake pads as described in Section 4.

5 On models with VW brake calipers, unscrew the caliper from the end of the brake hose and remove it from the vehicle.

6 On Girling calipers, slacken and remove the caliper upper guide pin bolt, using a slim open-ended spanner to prevent the guide pin itself from rotating **(see illustration)**, then unscrew the caliper from the brake hose and remove it from the vehicle. Discard the guide pin bolt - a new bolt must be used on refitting.

Overhaul

7 With the caliper on the bench, wipe away all traces of dust and dirt, but *avoid inhaling the dust, as it is a health hazard.*

8 Withdraw the partially-ejected piston from the caliper body, and remove the dust seal.

> **HAYNES HiNT** *If the piston cannot be withdrawn by hand, it can be pushed out by applying compressed air to the brake hose union hole. Only low pressure should be required, such as is generated by a foot pump. As the piston is expelled, take great care not to trap your fingers between the piston and caliper.*

9

9 Using a small screwdriver, extract the piston hydraulic seal, taking great care not to damage the caliper bore **(see illustration)**.

10 Thoroughly clean all components, using only methylated spirit, isopropyl alcohol or clean hydraulic fluid as a cleaning medium. Never use mineral-based solvents such as

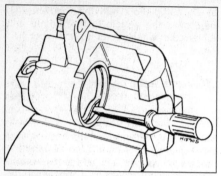

10.9 Extracting the piston seal - take care not to scratch the surface of the bore

petrol or paraffin, as they will attack the hydraulic system's rubber components. Dry the components immediately, using compressed air or a clean, lint-free cloth. Use compressed air to blow clear the fluid passages.

11 On VW calipers, withdraw the spacers from the caliper body bushes.

12 On Girling calipers, withdraw the guide pins from the caliper mounting bracket, and remove the rubber gaiters.

13 Check all components, and renew any that are worn or damaged. Check particularly the cylinder bore and piston; these should be renewed (note that this means the renewal of the complete body assembly) if they are scratched, worn or corroded in any way. Similarly check the condition of the spacers/guide pins and their bushes/bores (as applicable); both spacers/pins should be undamaged and (when cleaned) a reasonably tight sliding fit in their bores. If there is any doubt about the condition of any component, renew it.

14 If the assembly is fit for further use, obtain the appropriate repair kit; the components are available from VW dealers in various combinations.

15 Renew all rubber seals, dust covers and caps disturbed on dismantling as a matter of course; these should never be re-used.

16 On reassembly, ensure that all components are clean and dry.

17 Soak the piston and the new piston (fluid) seal in clean hydraulic fluid. Smear clean fluid on the cylinder bore surface.

18 Fit the new piston (fluid) seal, using only your fingers (no tools) to manipulate it into the cylinder bore groove. Fit the new dust seal to the piston, and refit the piston to the cylinder bore using a twisting motion; ensure that the piston enters squarely into the bore. Press the piston fully into the bore, then press the dust seal into the caliper body.

19 On VW calipers, apply the grease supplied in the repair kit (or a copper-based high-temperature brake grease or anti-seize compound) to the spacers, and insert them into their bushes.

20 On Girling calipers, apply the grease supplied in the repair kit (or a copper-based high-temperature brake grease or anti-seize compound) to the guide pins, and fit the new

gaiters. Fit the guide pins to the caliper mounting bracket, ensuring that the gaiters are correctly located in the grooves on both the sleeve and mounting bracket.

Refitting

21 Screw the caliper fully onto the flexible hose union.

22 Refit the brake pads (see Section 4).

23 Securely tighten the brake pipe union nut.

24 Remove the brake hose clamp or polythene, as applicable, and bleed the hydraulic system as described in Section 2. Note that, providing the precautions described were taken to minimise brake fluid loss, it should only be necessary to bleed the relevant front brake.

25 Refit the roadwheel, then lower the vehicle to the ground and tighten the roadwheel bolts to the specified torque.

---

11 Rear brake caliper -
removal, overhaul and refitting

Note: *Before starting work, refer to the note at the beginning of Section 2 concerning the dangers of hydraulic fluid, and to the warning at the beginning of Section 4 concerning the dangers of asbestos dust.*

Removal

1 Chock the front wheels, engage 1st gear (or "P"), then jack up the rear of the vehicle and support it on axle stands (see "*Jacking and vehicle support*"). Remove the relevant rear wheel.

2 Minimise fluid loss by first removing the master cylinder reservoir cap, and then tightening it down onto a piece of polythene, to obtain an airtight seal. Alternatively, use a brake hose clamp, a G-clamp or a similar tool to clamp the flexible hose.

3 Referring to Section 19, disconnect the handbrake inner and outer cables from the caliper lever and caliper bracket respectively.

4 Remove the brake pads as described in Section 5.

5 Clean the area around the union, then loosen the brake hose union nut. Unscrew the caliper from the end of the flexible hose and remove it from the vehicle.

Overhaul

Note: *It is not possible to overhaul the brake caliper handbrake mechanism. If the mechanism is faulty, or fluid is leaking from the handbrake lever seal, the caliper assembly must be renewed.*

6 With the caliper on the bench, wipe away all traces of dust and dirt, but avoid inhaling the dust, as it is a health hazard.

7 Using a small screwdriver, carefully prise out the dust seal from the caliper bore, taking care not to damage the piston.

8 Remove the piston from the caliper bore by rotating it in an anti-clockwise direction. This

can be achieved using a suitable pair of circlip pliers engaged in the caliper piston slots. Once the piston turns freely but does not come out any further, the piston can be withdrawn by hand.

HAYNES HINT
If the piston cannot be withdrawn by hand, it can be pushed out by applying compressed air to the brake hose union hole. Only low pressure should be required, such as is generated by a foot pump. As the piston is expelled, take care not to trap your fingers between the piston and caliper.

9 Using a small screwdriver, extract the piston hydraulic seal(s), taking care not to damage the caliper bore.

10 Withdraw the guide pins from the caliper mounting bracket, and remove the guide sleeve gaiters.

11 Thoroughly clean all components, using only methylated spirit, isopropyl alcohol or clean hydraulic fluid as a cleaning medium. Never use mineral-based solvents such as petrol or paraffin, as they will attack the hydraulic system's rubber components. Dry the components immediately, using compressed air or a clean, lint-free cloth. Use compressed air to blow clear the fluid passages.

12 Inspect all the caliper components as described in Section 10, paragraphs 13 to 16, and renew as necessary, noting that the handbrake mechanism must **not** be dismantled.

13 Soak the piston and the new piston (fluid) seal in clean hydraulic fluid. Smear clean fluid on the cylinder bore surface. Fit the new piston (fluid) seal(s), using only the fingers (no tools) to manipulate into the cylinder bore groove(s).

14 Fit the new dust seal to the piston groove, then refit the piston assembly. Turn the piston in a clockwise direction, using the method employed on dismantling, until it is fully retracted into the caliper bore. Press the dust seal into position in the caliper housing.

15 Apply the grease supplied in the repair kit (or a copper-based high-temperature brake grease or anti-seize compound) to the guide pins. Fit the new gaiters to the guide pins and fit the pins to the caliper mounting bracket, ensuring that the gaiters are correctly located in the grooves on both the pins and caliper bracket.

16 Prior to refitting, fill the caliper with fresh hydraulic fluid by slackening the bleed screw and pumping the fluid through the caliper until bubble-free fluid is expelled from the union hole.

Refitting

17 Screw the caliper fully onto the flexible hose union.

18 Refit the brake pads as described in paragraphs 10 to 12 of Section 5.

19 Securely tighten the brake pipe union nut.
20 Remove the brake hose clamp or polythene, as applicable, and bleed the hydraulic system as described in Section 2. Note that, providing the precautions described were taken to minimise brake fluid loss, it should only be necessary to bleed the relevant rear brake.
21 Connect the handbrake cable to the caliper, and adjust the handbrake as described in Section 17.
22 Refit the roadwheel, then lower the vehicle to the ground and tighten the roadwheel bolts to the specified torque. On completion, check the hydraulic fluid level as described in "Weekly checks".

12 Rear wheel cylinder - removal, overhaul and refitting

Note: *Before starting work, refer to the note at the beginning of Section 2 concerning the dangers of hydraulic fluid, and to the warning at the beginning of Section 4 concerning the dangers of asbestos dust.*

Removal

1 Remove the brake drum (see Section 9).
2 Using pliers, carefully unhook the upper brake shoe return spring, and remove it from both brake shoes. Pull the upper ends of the shoes away from the wheel cylinder to disengage them from the pistons.
3 Minimise fluid loss by first removing the master cylinder reservoir cap, and then tightening it down onto a piece of polythene, to obtain an airtight seal. Alternatively, use a brake hose clamp, a G-clamp or a similar tool to clamp the flexible hose at the nearest convenient point to the wheel cylinder.
4 Wipe away all traces of dirt around the brake pipe union at the rear of the wheel cylinder, and unscrew the union nut **(see illustration)**. Carefully ease the pipe out of the wheel cylinder, and plug or tape over its end to prevent dirt entry. Wipe off any spilt immediately.
5 Unscrew the two wheel cylinder retaining bolts from the rear of the backplate, and remove the cylinder, taking great care not to allow surplus hydraulic fluid to contaminate the brake shoe linings or ABS components, where applicable.

Overhaul

6 Brush the dirt and dust from the wheel cylinder, but take care not to inhale it.
7 Pull the rubber dust seals from the ends of the cylinder body **(see illustration)**.
8 The pistons will normally be ejected by the pressure of the coil spring, but if they are not, tap the end of the cylinder body on a piece of wood, or apply low air pressure - eg, from a foot pump - to the hydraulic fluid union hole to eject the pistons from their bores.

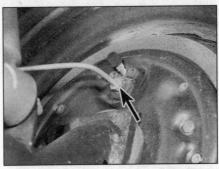

12.4 Rear brake pipe union connection (arrowed) to rear wheel cylinder

9 Inspect the surfaces of the pistons and their bores in the cylinder body for scoring, or evidence of metal-to-metal contact. If evident, renew the complete wheel cylinder assembly.
10 If the pistons and bores are in good condition, discard the seals and obtain a repair kit, which will contain all the necessary renewable items.
11 Remove the seals from the pistons, noting their correct fitted orientation. Lubricate the new piston seals with clean brake fluid, and fit them onto the pistons with their larger diameters innermost.
12 Dip the pistons in clean brake fluid, then fit the spring to the cylinder.
13 Insert the pistons into the cylinder bores using a twisting motion.
14 Fit the dust seals, and check that the pistons can move freely in their bores.

Refitting

15 Ensure that the backplate and wheel cylinder mating surfaces are clean, then spread the brake shoes and manoeuvre the wheel cylinder into position.

16 Engage the brake pipe, and screw in the union nut two or three turns to ensure that the thread has started.
17 Insert the two wheel cylinder retaining bolts, and tighten them to the specified torque. Now fully tighten the brake pipe union nut.
18 Remove the clamp from the flexible brake hose, or the polythene from the master cylinder reservoir (as applicable).
19 Ensure that the brake shoes are correctly located in the cylinder pistons, then refit the brake shoe upper return spring, using a screwdriver to stretch the spring into position.
20 Refit the brake drum (see Section 9).
21 Bleed the brake hydraulic system as described in Section 2. Providing suitable precautions were taken to minimise loss of fluid, it should only be necessary to bleed the relevant rear brake.

13 Master cylinder - removal, overhaul and refitting

Note: *Before starting work, refer to the warning at the beginning of Section 2 concerning the dangers of hydraulic fluid.*

Removal

1 Disconnect the battery negative lead. **Note:** *If the vehicle has a security-coded radio, check that you have a copy of the code number before disconnecting the battery. Refer to your VW dealer if in doubt.* For improved access, on right-hand-drive models, remove the air inlet duct as described in the relevant Part of Chapter 4; on left-hand-drive models, unbolt the coolant expansion tank and move it to one side. On engine code AFN, remove the engine top cover.

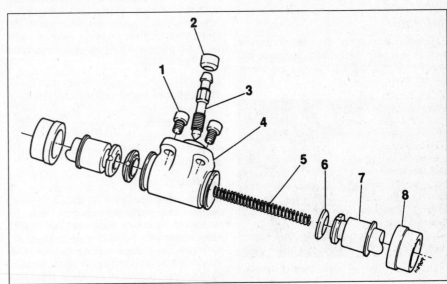

12.7 Rear wheel cylinder components

1 Retaining bolt	4 Wheel cylinder	7 Piston
2 Bleed screw cap	5 Spring	8 Dust seal
3 Bleed screw	6 Seal	

9

2 Remove the master cylinder reservoir cap, and siphon the hydraulic fluid from the reservoir. **Note:** *Do not siphon the fluid by mouth, as it is poisonous; use a syringe or an old poultry baster.* Alternatively, open any convenient bleed screw in the system, and gently pump the brake pedal to expel the fluid through a plastic tube connected to the screw (see Section 2). Disconnect the wiring plug from the brake fluid level sender unit.

3 Wipe clean the area around the brake pipe unions on the side of the master cylinder, and place absorbent rags beneath the pipe unions to catch any surplus fluid. Make a note of the correct fitted positions of the unions **(see illustration)**, then unscrew the union nuts and carefully withdraw the pipes. Plug or tape over the pipe ends and master cylinder orifices, to minimise the loss of brake fluid, and to prevent the entry of dirt into the system. Wash off any spilt fluid immediately with cold water.

4 Slacken and remove the two nuts and washers securing the master cylinder to the vacuum servo unit, then withdraw the unit from the engine compartment. Remove the O-ring from the rear of the master cylinder, and discard it.

Overhaul

5 If the master cylinder is faulty, it must be renewed. Repair kits are not available from VW dealer, so the cylinder must be treated as a sealed unit.

6 The only items which can be renewed are the mounting seals for the fluid reservoir; if these show signs of deterioration, pull off the reservoir and remove the old seals. Lubricate the new seals with clean brake fluid, and press them into the master cylinder ports. Ease the fluid reservoir into position, and push it fully home.

Refitting

7 Remove all traces of dirt from the master cylinder and servo unit mating surfaces, and fit a new O-ring to the groove on the master cylinder body.

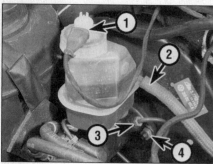

13.3 General view of brake master cylinder

Reservoir filler cap and low-level warning switch lead (1)
Clutch supply tube (2)
Brake union connections (3)
Master cylinder-to-servo retaining nut (4)

8 Fit the master cylinder to the servo unit, ensuring that the servo unit pushrod enters the master cylinder bore centrally. Refit the master cylinder mounting nuts and washers, and tighten them to the specified torque.

9 Wipe clean the brake pipe unions, then refit them to the master cylinder ports and tighten them securely.

10 Refill the master cylinder reservoir with new fluid, and bleed the complete hydraulic system as described in Section 2.

14 Brake pedal - removal and refitting

Removal

1 Disconnect the battery negative lead. **Note:** *If the vehicle has a security-coded radio, check that you have a copy of the code number before disconnecting the battery. Refer to your VW dealer if in doubt.*

2 Remove the stop-light switch (Section 21).

3 For improved access, refer to Chapter 6, and remove the clutch pedal.

4 Extract the large pedal-to-pushrod clevis pin retaining clip, and withdraw the clevis pin.

5 Move the clutch/brake pedal pivot pin fully to the right, and disengage the pedal and return spring. remove the pedal.

6 Clean the components, and check them for wear and damage. Temporarily refit the pedal, and check the bush for excessive wear. Check that the return spring and retaining clips are not damaged. Check the rubber foot pad for wear. Renew the components as necessary.

Refitting

7 Refitting is a reversal of removal, but lubricate the pivot shaft with a little multi-purpose grease. Ensure that the pedal return spring and bush are correctly located. Refit the clutch pedal and the over-centre spring as described in Chapter 6.

15 Vacuum servo unit - testing, removal and refitting

Note: *Early left-hand-drive models with ABS do not have a vacuum servo.*

Testing

1 To test the operation of the servo unit, depress the footbrake several times to exhaust the vacuum, then start the engine whilst keeping the pedal firmly depressed. As the engine starts, there should be a noticeable "give" in the brake pedal as the vacuum builds up. Allow the engine to run for at least two minutes, then switch it off. If the brake pedal is now depressed, it should feel normal, but further applications should result in the pedal feeling firmer, with the pedal stroke decreasing with each application.

2 If the servo does not operate as described, first inspect the servo unit check valve as described in Section 16. On diesel models, also check the operation of the vacuum pump as described in Section 25.

3 If the servo unit still fails to operate satisfactorily, the fault lies within the unit itself. Repairs to the unit are not possible - if faulty, the servo unit must be renewed.

Removal

Note: *On later left-hand drive models equipped with ABS, it is not possible to remove the vacuum servo unit without first removing the hydraulic unit (see Section 23). Therefore, servo unit removal and refitting should be entrusted to a VW dealer.*

4 Remove the master cylinder (Section 13).

5 On models with manual transmission, remove the clutch master cylinder as described in Chapter 6.

6 On models equipped with ABS, remove the brake pedal position sender unit (Section 23).

7 On all models, remove the heatshield (where fitted) from the front of the servo, then carefully ease the vacuum hose out from the servo unit sealing grommet.

8 From inside the vehicle, remove the stop-light switch as described in Section 21. Extract the large pedal-to-pushrod clevis pin retaining clip, and withdraw the clevis pin.

9 Undo the four retaining nuts securing the servo unit to the pedal mounting bracket, then return to the engine compartment and manoeuvre the servo unit out of position, noting the gasket which is fitted to the rear of the unit.

Refitting

10 Check the servo unit vacuum hose sealing grommet for signs of damage or deterioration, and renew if necessary.

11 Fit a new gasket to the rear of the servo unit, and reposition the unit in the engine compartment.

12 From inside the vehicle, ensure that the servo unit pushrod is correctly engaged with the brake pedal, then insert the clevis pin and secure with the retaining clip. Check the pedal is securely retained, then refit the servo unit mounting nuts and tighten them to the specified torque.

13 Carefully ease the vacuum hose back into position in the servo, taking great care not to displace the sealing grommet. Where necessary, refit the heatshield to the servo.

14 On models equipped with ABS, refit the brake pedal position sensor (see Section 23).

15 Refit the master cylinder as described in Section 13 of this Chapter. Where necessary, also refit the clutch master cylinder as described in Chapter 6.

16 Refit the stop-light switch (Section 21).

17 On completion, start the engine and check for air leaks at the vacuum hose-to-servo unit connection; check the operation of the braking system.

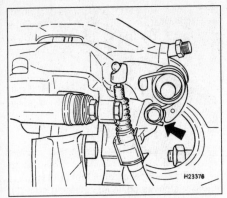

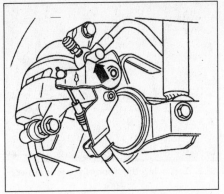

17.9a Adjust the handbrake so that the clearance between the handbrake lever and caliper (arrowed) is as stated - early rear disc brake models . . .

17.9b . . . and later rear disc brake models

16 Vacuum servo unit check valve - removal, testing and refitting

1 The check valve is in the vacuum hose from the inlet manifold to the brake servo. If the valve is to be renewed, the complete hose/valve assembly should be replaced.

Removal

2 For improved access, on right-hand-drive models, remove the air inlet duct as described in the relevant Part of Chapter 4; on left-hand-drive models, unbolt the coolant expansion tank and move it to one side. On engine code AFN, remove the engine top cover.
3 Ease the vacuum hose out of the servo unit, taking care not to displace the grommet. Note the routing of the hose, then slacken the retaining clip and disconnect the opposite end of the hose assembly from the manifold/pump and remove it from the car.

Testing

4 Examine the check valve and vacuum hose for signs of damage, and renew if necessary.
5 The valve may be tested by blowing through it in both directions; air should flow through the valve in one direction only - when blown through from the servo unit end of the valve. Renew the valve if this is not the case.
6 Examine the servo unit rubber sealing grommet for signs of damage or deterioration, and renew as necessary.

Refitting

7 Ensure that the sealing grommet is correctly fitted to the servo unit.
8 Ease the hose union into position in the servo, taking great care not to displace or damage the grommet.
9 Ensure that the hose is correctly routed, and connect it to the inlet manifold/pump, tightening its retaining clip securely.
10 On completion, start the engine and check the check valve-to-servo unit connection for signs of air leaks.

17 Handbrake - adjustment

1 To check the handbrake adjustment, first apply the footbrake firmly several times to establish correct shoe-to-drum/pad-to-disc clearance, then apply and release the handbrake several times.
2 Applying normal moderate pressure, pull the handbrake lever to the fully-applied position, counting the number of clicks emitted from the handbrake ratchet mechanism. If adjustment is correct, there should be approximately 4 to 7 clicks before the handbrake is fully applied. If this is not the case, adjust as follows.
3 Remove the handbrake lever grip and the lower trim piece as described in Section 18. Remove the rear section of the centre console as described in Chapter 11 to gain access to the handbrake cable adjusters **(see illustration 18.6)**.
4 Chock the front wheels, engage 1st gear (or "P"), then jack up the rear of the vehicle and support it on axle stands (see "Jacking and vehicle support"). Continue as described under the relevant sub-heading.

Rear drum brake models

5 Release the handbrake fully. Depress the brake pedal firmly once, then pull the handbrake lever up by four "clicks".
6 Slacken the locknuts and tighten the

adjusting sleeves equally until it is difficult to turn both rear wheels/drums. Once this is so, release the handbrake lever, and check that the wheels/hubs rotate freely. Check the adjustment by applying the handbrake fully, counting the clicks from the handbrake ratchet and, if necessary, re-adjust.
7 Once adjustment is correct, hold the adjusting sleeves and securely tighten the locknuts. Refit the centre console rear section and handbrake trim/lever grip.

Rear disc brake models

8 With the handbrake fully released, equally slacken the handbrake locknuts and adjusting sleeves until both the rear caliper handbrake levers are back against their stops. If better access is required, remove the rear roadwheels.
9 From this point, equally tighten both adjusting sleeves until both handbrake levers just move off the caliper stops. The help of an assistant will be necessary to determine the exact point when the levers lift. Ensure that the gap between each caliper handbrake lever and its stop is less than 1.5 mm, and ensure both the right- and left-hand gaps are equal **(see illustrations)**. Check that both wheels/discs rotate freely, then check the adjustment by applying the handbrake fully, counting the clicks emitted from the handbrake ratchet. If necessary, re-adjust.
10 Once adjustment is correct, hold the adjusting sleeves and securely tighten the locknuts. Refit the centre console rear section and handbrake trim/lever grip (as applicable).

18 Handbrake lever - removal and refitting

1 Chock the front and rear wheels, then engage 1st gear (or "P").
2 Remove the handbrake lever grip by pulling or levering out the securing lugs at the bottom end, and pulling the grip upwards from the lever **(see illustrations)**.
3 Withdraw the lower trim from the lever **(see illustration)**.
4 Remove the centre console rear extension, as described in Chapter 11.

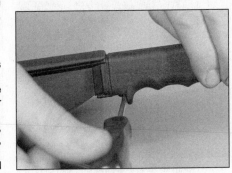

18.2a Release the securing lugs . . .

18.2b . . . and withdraw the handbrake lever grip

9

5 Unscrew and remove the cable adjuster locknut and adjuster from the cables.

6 Unscrew and remove the lever-to-floor mounting nuts, lift the cable clear, and detach the operating cables from the compensator. Disconnect the wiring from the handbrake-on warning switch (**see illustration**). Remove the lever.

7 Refit in the reverse order of removal. Adjust the cables as described in Section 17, then refit the console rear extension and associated trim fittings.

19 Handbrake cables - removal and refitting

Removal

1 Chock the front wheels, engage 1st gear (or "P"), then loosen the rear roadwheel bolts. Jack up the rear of the car and support it on axle stands (see "*Jacking and vehicle support*"). Remove the rear roadwheels.

2 Referring to Section 18, remove the handbrake lever grip and lower trim piece. Remove the rear section of the centre console as described in Chapter 11 to gain access to the handbrake adjusters. The handbrake cable consists of two sections, a right- and a left-hand section, which are linked to the lever by a compensator plate. Each section can be removed individually.

3 Slacken the relevant handbrake cable

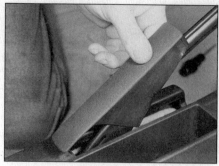

18.3 Removing the handbrake lever lower trim

locknut and adjusting sleeve to obtain maximum freeplay in the cable, and disengage the inner cable from the handbrake compensator plate.

4 On models with rear drum brakes, remove the rear brake shoes from the relevant side as described in Section 6. Release the inner cable from the brake shoe handbrake lever, then withdraw the cable from the brake backplate and remove it from underneath the vehicle (**see illustration**).

5 On models with rear disc brakes, disengage the inner cable from the caliper handbrake lever, then remove the outer cable retaining clip and detach the cable from the caliper (**see illustrations**).

6 Working back along the length of the cable, noting its correct routing, and free it from all the relevant retaining clips (**see illustration**).

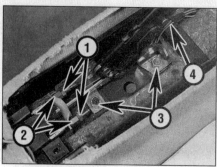

18.6 Handbrake cable locknuts (1), adjuster sleeves (2), lever retaining nuts (3) and warning light switch wiring (4)

Refitting

7 Refitting is a reversal of the removal procedure. Prior to refitting the centre console and trim, adjust the handbrake (Section 17).

20 Brake pressure regulator - general information and testing

1 The brake pressure regulator is located on the left-hand side of the rear axle, and is controlled by the vertical movement of the rear axle (**see illustrations**). The purpose of the regulator is to control the amount of braking effort to the rear wheels, in relation to the weight being carried over the rear wheels. In general, a vehicle which is lightly loaded at the rear will be

19.4 On drum brake models, remove the inner cable from the shoe operating lever and withdraw the cable from the backplate

19.5a On disc brake models, detach the inner cable from the caliper lever . . .

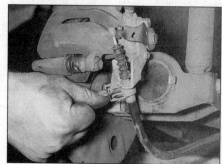

19.5b . . . then remove the retaining clip . . .

19.5c . . . and free the cable from the caliper bracket

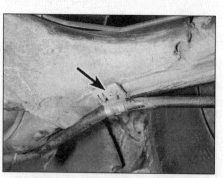

19.6 Release the retaining clip (arrowed) and detach the handbrake cable from the trailing arm

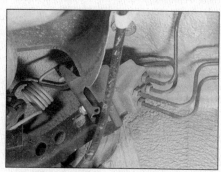

20.1a Brake pressure regulator

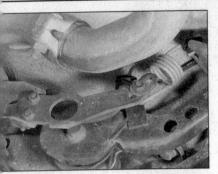

20.1b Brake pressure control spring and operating lever

more prone to rear wheel lock-up than one with significant load on board. The regulator contains a valve arrangement linked to the operating lever on the rear axle, to regulate the flow of brake fluid to the rear brakes, thus controlling the braking effort at the rear wheels. **Note:** *Later models with the Teves 20 GI anti-lock braking system do not have a mechanical brake pressure regulator - the ABS control unit contains software to regulate the rear brakes.*

2 To test the operation of the regulator, have an assistant depress the footbrake firmly, then release it quickly. With the weight of the car on the suspension, the arm on the regulator should move, indicating that the unit is not seized.

3 To test the regulator for leakage, pressure gauges must be connected to the left-hand front caliper and right-hand rear wheel cylinder or caliper, as applicable. As the equipment will not normally be available to the home mechanic, this work should be entrusted to a VW dealer.

4 The brake pressure regulator works in conjunction with the self-levelling rear suspension system (where fitted). A compressed air line connects the levelling system to the brake regulator, and whenever either the brake regulator or the compressor in the levelling system are to be detached and/or removed, the compressed air in the system must first be released. Refer to Chapter 10 for more information.

21 Stop-light switch - removal and refitting

Removal

1 The stop-light switch is located on the pedal bracket behind the facia, just above the brake pedal.

2 Disconnect the battery negative lead. **Note:** *If the vehicle has a security-coded radio, check that you have a copy of the code number before disconnecting the battery. Refer to your VW dealer if in doubt.*

3 Detach and remove the lower trim and insulation panels from the facia on driver's side.

4 Disconnect the wiring connector from the brake light switch, then twist the switch body through 90° to release it from its mounting bracket.

Refitting

5 Refit in the reverse order of removal. Check for satisfactory operation before refitting the lower facia trim panels. The stop-lights should illuminate after the brake pedal has travelled about 5 mm. If the switch is not functioning correctly, it is faulty and must be renewed; no adjustment is possible.

22 Anti-lock braking system (ABS) - general information

ABS was available as an option on all models covered in this manual, and was fitted as standard to many later models. The system comprises a hydraulic unit (which contains the hydraulic solenoid valves and accumulators), the electrically-driven return pump, and four roadwheel sensors (one fitted to each wheel), the electronic control unit (ECU) and the brake pedal position sensor. The purpose of the system is to prevent the wheel(s) locking during heavy braking. This is achieved by automatic release of the brake on the relevant wheel, followed by re-application of the brake.

The solenoids are controlled by the ECU, which itself receives signals from the four wheel sensors (one fitted on each hub), which monitor the speed of rotation of each wheel. By comparing these signals, the ECU can determine the speed at which the car is travelling. It can then use this speed to determine when a wheel is decelerating at an abnormal rate, compared to the speed of the car, and therefore predicts when a wheel is about to lock. During normal operation, the system functions in the same way as a non-ABS braking system. In addition, the brake pedal position sensor (which is fitted to the vacuum servo unit) also informs the ECU of how hard the brake pedal is being depressed.

If the ECU senses that a wheel is about to lock, it operates the relevant solenoid valve in the modulator block, which then isolates the brake caliper on the wheel which is about to lock from the master cylinder, effectively sealing-in the hydraulic pressure.

If the speed of rotation of the wheel continues to decrease at an abnormal rate, the ECU switches on the electrically-driven return pump, which pumps the hydraulic fluid back into the master cylinder, releasing pressure on the brake caliper so that the brake is released. Once the speed of rotation of the wheel returns to an acceptable rate, the pump stops; the solenoid valve opens, allowing the hydraulic master cylinder pressure to return to the caliper, which then re-applies the brake. This cycle can be carried out at up to 10 times a second.

The action of the solenoid valves and return pump creates pulses in the hydraulic circuit. When the ABS system is functioning, these pulses can be felt through the brake pedal.

The operation of the ABS system is entirely dependent on electrical signals. To prevent the system responding to any inaccurate signals, a built-in safety circuit monitors all signals received by the ECU. If an inaccurate signal or low battery voltage is detected, the ABS system is automatically shut down, and the warning light on the instrument panel is illuminated, to inform the driver that the ABS system is not operational. Normal braking should still be available, however.

If a fault does develop in the ABS system, the car must be taken to a VW dealer for fault diagnosis and repair.

The exact type of ABS fitted depends on the age of the vehicle, and on whether it is right- or left-hand-drive:

a) *Left-hand-drive models up to July 1995 were fitted with the Teves 02 system, which does not have a vacuum servo. The brake master cylinder is bolted directly onto the hydraulic unit. Bleeding the hydraulic system on these models is unique, in that the fluid pump must be run to expel the air and old brake fluid from the bleed screws - see Section 2.*

b) *Right-hand-drive models up to July 1995 were fitted with the Teves 04 system, which has a conventional vacuum servo mounted on the driver's side of the engine compartment. The brake master cylinder is mounted onto the servo, as it is on non-ABS models.*

c) *All models from July 1995 onwards were fitted with the Teves 20 GI system. This system employs a vacuum servo unit mounted on the driver's side of the engine compartment. On left-hand-drive models, the hydraulic unit is mounted directly onto the servo; on right-hand-drive models, the unit is remotely mounted. Models with the Teves 20 GI system do not have a mechanical pressure regulator on the rear axle - the ECU contains software to control the braking effort applied to the rear wheels.*

23 Anti-lock braking system (ABS) components - removal and refitting

Hydraulic unit

1 Removal and refitting of the hydraulic unit should be entrusted to a VW dealer. Great care has to be taken not to allow any fluid to escape from the unit as the pipes are disconnected. If the fluid is allowed to escape, air can enter the unit, causing air locks which cause the hydraulic unit to malfunction.

Electronic control unit (ECU)

Removal

2 On models manufactured up to July 1995, the ECU is located underneath the rear seat on the left-hand side of the car. On models manufactured after July 1995, the control unit is mounted onto the base of the hydraulic unit; on these models, the control unit cannot be removed without first removing the hydraulic unit (see paragraph 1).

9

3 Disconnect the battery negative lead. **Note:** *If the vehicle has a security-coded radio, check that you have a copy of the code number before disconnecting the battery. Refer to your VW dealer if in doubt.*

4 Lift up the left-hand rear seat cushion, and either remove the retaining screws or unclip the ECU from its mountings. Release the retaining clip and pivot the wiring connector out of position, then remove the ECU from the car.

Refitting

5 Refitting is a reversal of removal, ensuring that the ECU wiring connector is correctly and securely reconnected.

Front wheel sensor

Removal

6 Chock the rear wheels, then firmly apply the handbrake and loosen the relevant front wheel bolts. Jack up the front of the car and support it on axle stands (see *"Jacking and vehicle support"*). Remove the front roadwheel.

7 Trace the wiring back from the sensor to the connector, freeing it from all the relevant retaining clips, and disconnect it from the main loom.

8 Slacken and remove the bolt securing the sensor to the swivel hub, and remove the sensor and lead assembly from the car.

Refitting

9 Prior to refitting, apply a thin coat of multi-purpose grease to the sensor tip (VW recommend the use of lubricating paste G 000 650 - available from your dealer).

10 Ensure that the sensor and swivel hub sealing faces are clean, then fit the sensor to the hub. Refit the retaining bolt and tighten it to the specified torque.

11 Ensure that the sensor wiring is correctly routed and retained by all the necessary clips, and reconnect it to its wiring connector.

12 Refit the roadwheel, then lower the car to the ground and tighten the roadwheel bolts to the specified torque.

Rear wheel sensor

Removal

13 Chock the front wheels, engage 1st gear (or "P"), then loosen the relevant rear wheel bolts. Jack up the rear of the car and support it on axle stands (see *"Jacking and vehicle support"*). Remove the rear roadwheel.

14 Remove the sensor from the hub as described in paragraphs 7 and 8.

Refitting

15 Refit the sensor as described above in paragraphs 9 to 12.

Front reluctor rings

16 The front reluctor rings are fixed onto the rear of wheel hubs. Examine the rings for damage such as chipped or missing teeth. If renewal is necessary, the complete hub assembly must be dismantled and the rings renewed as described in Chapter 10.

Rear reluctor rings

17 The rear reluctor rings are pressed onto the inside of the rear brake drum/disc. Examine the rings for signs of damage such as chipped or missing teeth, and renew as necessary. If renewal is necessary, remove the drum/disc as described in Section 8 or 9 and take it to a VW dealer, who will have access to the necessary tools required to extract the old ring and press on the new one.

Brake pedal position sensor

Removal

18 Release the vacuum inside the servo unit by depressing the brake pedal several times. To improve access to the sensor, on right-hand-drive models, remove the master cylinder as described in Section 13; on left-hand-drive models, unbolt the coolant expansion tank and move it to one side.

19 Disconnect the battery negative lead (see paragraph 3). Trace the wiring back from the pedal position sensor, and disconnect at the connector.

20 Using a small screwdriver, carefully lever off the sensor retaining clip then withdraw the sensor from the front of the vacuum servo unit. Recover the sealing ring and circlip.

Refitting

21 If a new sensor is being fitted, note the colour of the spacer fitted to the original sensor, and fit the relevant colour spacer to the new sensor. This is vital to ensure that the correct operation of the anti-lock braking system.

22 Fit the new circlip to the groove on the front of the vacuum servo unit, positioning its end gap over the servo unit sensor lower locating slot.

23 Fit the new sealing ring to the sensor, and lubricate it with a smear of oil to aid installation.

24 Fit the sensor to the vacuum servo, aligning its locating notch with the servo unit upper groove. Push the sensor until it clicks into position, and check that it is securely retained by the circlip.

25 Refit the master cylinder or coolant expansion tank, as applicable.

26 Reconnect the sensor wiring, and connect the battery negative lead.

24.7 Ensure vacuum pump slot (arrowed) is aligned with the pump drivegear

24 Vacuum pump (diesel models) - description, removal and refitting

Description

1 The vacuum pump is mounted on the fron of the engine block, in the same position a the distributor on petrol engine models. Lik the distributor, the diesel vacuum pump i driven from the intermediate shaft.

2 The vacuum pump is required to provide vacuum supply for the servo unit. Diese engines cannot tap into the inlet manifold for vacuum supply as on petrol engines, since the manifold is not throttled.

Removal

3 Release the retaining clip, and disconnec the vacuum hose from the top of pump.

4 Slacken and remove the retaining bolt, and remove the pump retaining clamp from the cylinder block.

5 Withdraw the vacuum pump from the cylinder block, and recover the O-ring sea Discard the O-ring - a new one should be used on refitting.

Refitting

6 Fit the new O-ring to the vacuum pump and apply a smear of oil to the O-ring to aid installation.

7 Manoeuvre the vacuum pump into position making sure that the slot in the pump drivegear aligns with the dog on the pump drivegear **(see illustration)**.

8 Refit the retaining clamp and securely tighten its retaining bolt.

9 Reconnect the vacuum hose to the pump, and secure it in position with the retaining clip.

25 Vacuum pump (diesel models) - testing and overhaul

1 The operation of the braking system vacuum pump can be checked using a vacuum gauge.

2 Disconnect the vacuum pipe from the pump, and connect the gauge to the pump union using a suitable length of hose.

3 Start the engine and allow it to idle, then measure the vacuum created by the pump. As a guide, after one minute, a minimum of approximately 500 mmHg should be recorded. If the vacuum registered is significantly less than this, it is likely that the pump is faulty. However, seek the advice of a VW dealer before condemning the pump.

4 Overhaul of the vacuum pump is not possible, since no major components are available separately for it; the only spare part readily available is the pump cover sealing ring. If faulty, the complete pump assembly must be renewed.

Chapter 10
Suspension and steering

Contents

Degrees of difficulty

Easy, suitable for novice with little experience		Fairly easy, suitable for beginner with some experience		Fairly difficult, suitable for competent DIY mechanic		Difficult, suitable for experienced DIY mechanic		Very difficult, suitable for expert DIY or professional	

Specifications

General

Front suspension type	Independent, with coil spring struts incorporating telescopic shock absorbers; lower wishbones and anti-roll bar
Rear suspension type	Transverse torsion beam with trailing arms and track-correcting mountings. Coil spring struts incorporating telescopic shock absorbers
Steering type	Rack-and-pinion. Power assistance on most models

Suspension angles/wheel alignment

Front wheels:
Toe-in	0° ± 10'
Camber	1°20' ± 20'
Castor	+ 1°40' ± 30'
Maximum side-to-side difference:	
Camber	20'
Castor	30'
Track angle difference at lock of 20° left and right	-1°10' ± 30'

Rear wheels:
Camber	1°30' ± 20'
Maximum side-to-side difference	20'
Total track (at specified camber)	+ 20' ± 10'
Maximum allowable deviation	20'

Tyre pressures . . . . See end of "Weekly checks" on page 0•16

Torque wrench settings

	Nm	lbf ft
Front suspension		
Anti-roll bar connecting link nuts	20	15
Anti-roll bar mounting plate bolts	25	18
Brake splash shield bolts	10	7
Driveshaft retaining bolt:*		
M14 bolt:		
Stage 1	115	85
Stage 2	Angle-tighten a further 180°	
M16 bolt:		
Stage 1	190	140
Stage 2	Angle-tighten a further 90°	
Driveshaft retaining nut*	265	197
Strut-to-swivel hub mounting nut/bolt*	95	70
Strut upper mounting nut(s):		
Slotted nut (early models)	40	30
Conventional nuts (later models)	60	44
Subframe front mounting bolt (M12):		
Stage 1	70	52
Stage 2	Angle-tighten a further 90°	
Subframe rear mounting bolt	65	48
Vibration damper nuts	25	18
Wishbone/lower arm balljoint clamp bolt/nut	50	37
Wishbone/lower arm balljoint retaining bolts	35	26
Wishbone/lower arm pivot bolt:		
Stage 1	50	37
Stage 2	Angle-tighten a further 90°	
Wishbone/lower arm rear mounting through-bolt (M12):		
Stage 1	70	52
Stage 2	Angle-tighten a further 90°	
*Use new nut/bolt		
Rear suspension		
Brake pressure regulator mounting bracket:		
Shouldered bolts to floor	70	52
Through-bolt nut	80	59
Brake pressure regulator operating lever nut	35	26
Rear axle pivot bolt nut	80	59
Shock absorber top nut (self-locking)	25	18
Strut lower mounting nut	70	52
Strut upper mounting nut/bolt	25	18
Manual steering		
Column height adjuster lever through-bolt (left-hand thread)	22	16
Column tube bolt (left-hand thread)	22	16
Column universal joint (UJ) nuts	30	22
Steering column upper-to-lower universal joint shaft clamp bolt	25	18
Steering gear mounting clamp-to-subframe nuts	30	22
Steering gear pinion clamp bolt/nut	30	22
Steering lock housing screw	10	7
Steering wheel nut:		
With separate washer	40	30
Shouldered nut (no washer)	50	37
Track-rod adjustment locknut	50	37
Track-rod balljoint nut	35	26
Track-rod-to-steering gear locknut	50	37
Power steering (where different to manual)		
Pressure and return hose unions	30	22
Steering pump mounting and bracket retaining bolt/nuts	20	15
Steering pump pulley bolts	20	15
Track-rod-to-steering gear (use locking fluid)	70	52
Roadwheels		
Roadwheel bolts	110	81

1 General description

The front suspension is of independent, MacPherson strut and wishbone type. The strut on each side incorporates a telescopic shock absorber and coil spring **(see illustration)**. The wishbone arms are pivoted from large rubber bushes in the subframe, and are attached to the swivel hubs by a large clamped balljoint. An anti-roll bar is fitted, and is located on the wishbone arms at each end, and also at underbody mountings.

The rear suspension consists of a transverse torsion beam axle with trailing arms. The combined axle and arms pivot from large underbody mountings each side. A coil spring and shock absorber strut are located each side, between the top of the wheel arch and the axle arm at the bottom end, to control axle movement. Wedge-shaped track-corrective mountings are fitted, to provide a four-wheel steering effect when the vehicle is being cornered, and improve the handling characteristics.

A self-levelling rear suspension system is fitted to some models, and this is described in Section 13.

Rack-and-pinion steering is fitted, with power assistance on most models. The rack is mounted on a separate subframe. The steering column incorporates a telescopic collapsible section as a safety feature in the event of a collision. A height-adjustable steering column is fitted on some models.

Models from August 1992 may be equipped with an airbag mounted in the steering wheel. For details, refer to Chapter 12.

2 Front suspension strut - removal and refitting

Removal

1 Chock the rear wheels, apply the handbrake, then loosen the relevant front wheel bolts. Jack up and support the front of the car on axle stands (see *"Jacking and vehicle support"*). Remove the roadwheel on the side concerned.

2 Position a jack under the outer end of the wishbone arm for support.

3 In the engine compartment, prise the cap from the top of the strut **(see illustration)** and unscrew the self-locking nut whilst holding the piston rod stationary with an Allen key. Renew the self-locking nut once removed.

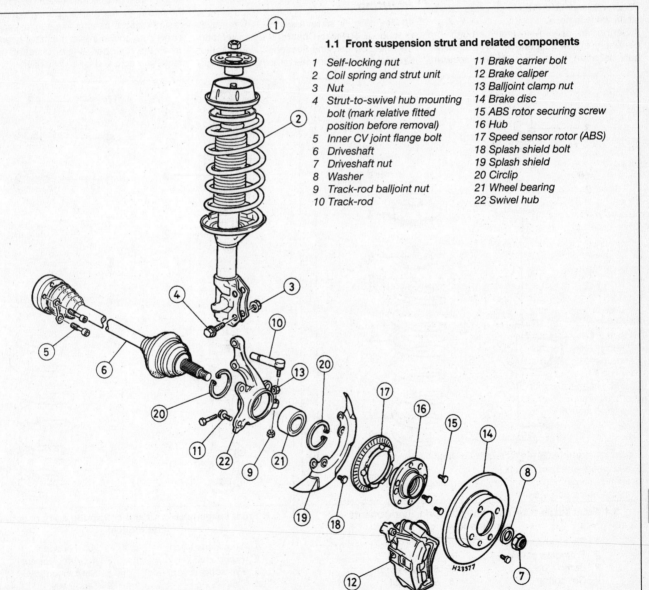

1.1 Front suspension strut and related components

1 Self-locking nut
2 Coil spring and strut unit
3 Nut
4 Strut-to-swivel hub mounting bolt (mark relative fitted position before removal)
5 Inner CV joint flange bolt
6 Driveshaft
7 Driveshaft nut
8 Washer
9 Track-rod balljoint nut
10 Track-rod
11 Brake carrier bolt
12 Brake caliper
13 Balljoint clamp nut
14 Brake disc
15 ABS rotor securing screw
16 Hub
17 Speed sensor rotor (ABS)
18 Splash shield bolt
19 Splash shield
20 Circlip
21 Wheel bearing
22 Swivel hub

10

2.3 Front suspension strut upper mounting - remove cap for access. Note Allen fitting in piston rod (arrowed)

4 Undo and remove the anti-roll bar connecting link nut (see Section 7).
5 Detach the steering track-rod end balljoint, as described in Section 22.
6 Remove the brake caliper with reference to Chapter 9, and hang it up to one side. Do not strain the fluid hose.
7 Scribe an alignment mark around the periphery of the suspension strut-to-swivel hub location lugs, to ensure accurate

positioning when refitting. Also mark the upper and lower retaining bolts to identify one from the other **(see illustration)**. This is essential, as the fitted position of the strut to swivel hub (and of the bolts) sets the camber angle. It is therefore critical that they be refitted in exactly the same position during reassembly. The bolts fitted will be 12 mm (standard) or 11 mm (alternative for adjustment). When one of each is fitted, note the position of each (top/bottom). Undo the retaining nuts, and withdraw the two bolts securing the strut at its bottom end to the swivel hub. Renew the self-locking nuts and special washers.
8 Lower the wishbone to disengage the strut from its top mounting, then prise it free from the swivel hub.
9 Note that the lower balljoint must not be detached from the wishbone without first referring to Section 6.

Refitting

10 Refitting is a reversal of the removal procedure. Refer to Chapter 9 when refitting the brake caliper, and Sections 6 and 7 in this Chapter when refitting the balljoint and anti-roll

2.7 Suspension strut-to-swivel hub bolts (arrowed) - mark relative positions before removal (see text)

bar. Tighten the retaining nuts to the specified torque. Use only new self-locking nuts with special washers to secure the strut-to-swivel hub bolts. Insert the bolts from the front of the swivel hubs. Ensure the correct realignment of the two units (as marked during removal), to ensure that the camber angle is maintained. If a new strut and/or swivel hub have been fitted, have the camber angle checked and if necessary adjusted by a VW dealer.

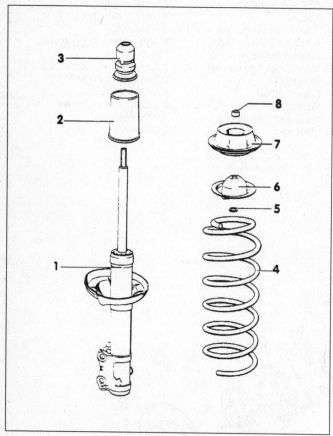

3.4 Front suspension strut and coil spring components - early models

1 Shock absorber	5 Washer
2 Protective sleeve	6 Spring seat
3 Bump stop	7 Strut bearing
4 Coil spring	8 Slotted nut

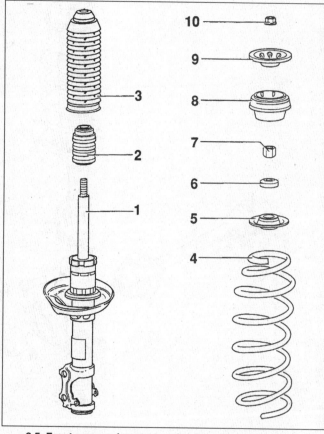

3.5 Front suspension strut and coil spring components - later models

1 Shock absorber	6 Axial bearing
2 Bump stop	7 Intermediate nut
3 Protective sleeve	8 Strut mounting
4 Coil spring	9 Stop plate
5 Spring seat	10 Self-locking nut

3 Front suspension strut and coil spring - separation and reassembly

Remove the front suspension strut as described in the previous Section.

⚠️ **Warning: Before attempting to dismantle the suspension strut, a suitable tool to hold the coil spring in compression must be obtained. Adjustable coil spring compressors are readily available, and are recommended for this operation. Any attempt to dismantle the strut without such a tool is likely to result in damage or personal injury.**

2 Support the lower end of the strut in a vice, then fit the coil spring compressor into position, and check that it is securely located.
3 Compress the spring until the upper spring seat is free of tension, then remove the nut from the top of the piston rod. On models where a slotted nut is used, a special VW tool is required. However, alternatives to the VW tool are available from tool manufacturers (eg Sykes Pickavant), or it is possible to make up your own **(see Tool Tip)**.
4 On early models, remove the strut bearing, followed by the spring seat and washer **(see illustration)**.
5 On later models, remove the stop plate and strut mounting. Remove the intermediate nut, then take off the axial bearing and spring seat **(see illustration)**.
6 Lift the coil spring from the strut with the compressor still in position. Mark the top of the spring for reference.
7 Withdraw the bump-stop components from the piston rod, noting their order of removal.
8 Move the shock absorber piston rod up and down through its complete stroke, and check that the resistance is even and smooth. If there are any signs or seizing or lack of resistance, or if fluid has been leaking

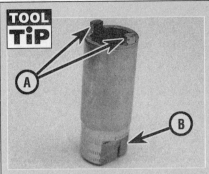

TOOL TiP

In the absence of the special VW tool, a replacement can be fabricated from a long-reach 13 mm socket. Cut the lower end of the socket to leave two teeth (A) which will engage with the slots in the strut nut, and file the upper end of the socket (B) so that it can be held with an open-ended spanner

excessively, the shock absorber/strut unit should be renewed.
9 The coil springs are normally colour-coded, and if the springs are to be renewed (it is advisable to renew both at the same time), be sure to get the correct replacement type with the identical colour code.
10 To reassemble the strut, follow the accompanying photos, beginning with illustration 3.10a. Be sure to stay in order, and carefully read the caption underneath each **(see illustrations)**.

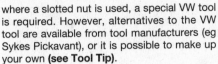

3.10a Slide the rubber damper and protective sleeve onto the strut . . .

3.10b . . . and refit the washer (where applicable) to the piston

3.10c Fit the coil spring to the strut . . .

3.10d . . . and fit the upper spring seat to the top of the spring. On later models, fit the axial bearing and intermediate nut, tightening the nut to the specified torque

3.10e Fit the strut mounting assembly (and stop plate, on later models) . . .

3.10f . . . and screw the nut onto the strut piston

3.10g Tighten the nut to the specified torque setting . . .

3.10h . . . then carefully release the compressor, ensuring the spring ends are located against the stops on the upper and lower seats

10

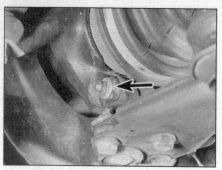

4.8a Unscrew the clamp bolt nut (arrowed) . . .

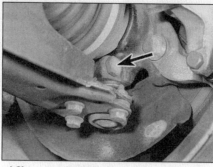

4.8b . . . and withdraw the bolt (arrowed) from the front

4 Front swivel hub - removal and refitting

Note: *The swivel hub can be removed and refitted on its own, or together with the front strut. If disconnecting the strut unit from the swivel hub, (before or after removal from the vehicle) the instructions given in paragraph 7 of Section 2 must be noted and adhered to.*

Removal

1 Firmly apply the handbrake and chock the rear wheels. Where applicable, remove the relevant front wheel trim to gain access to the driveshaft nut or bolt through the centre of the roadwheel.
2 Loosen, but do not remove, the driveshaft retaining nut or bolt. The weight of the vehicle must be on the ground, as the nut/bolt is tightened to a very high torque, and it would be dangerous to try loosening it with the vehicle raised.
3 Loosen the relevant front wheel bolts.
4 Raise the front of the vehicle and support it on axle stands (see *"Jacking and vehicle support"*). Remove the relevant front roadwheel.
5 Unscrew and remove the driveshaft nut/bolt, and recover the washer, where applicable.
6 Remove the brake caliper and disc as described in Chapter 9. The brake caliper can be tied up out of the way, leaving the hydraulic hose attached but clear of the strut.
7 Unbolt and remove the air deflector from the wishbone/lower arm.
8 Unscrew and remove the nut from the clamp bolt nut on the lower arm balljoint. Withdraw the clamp bolt, noting which direction the bolt is fitted as it is withdrawn **(see illustrations)**.
9 Refer to Section 22 and disconnect the track-rod from the swivel hub.
10 Refer to Section 7 and disconnect the anti-roll bar connecting link from the wishbone.
11 If the swivel hub is to be separated from the suspension strut, refer to paragraph 7 in Section 2, and mark the relative positions of the items described before removing the retaining bolts. Prise free the strut from the swivel hub.

12 If removing the swivel hub together with the strut, disconnect the strut at the top from the body mounting, as described in Section 2. If the suspension coil spring is still under tension, position a jack under the swivel hub to support the weight of the hub and strut; when the strut is detached at the top end from the body, lower the jack slowly to decompress the coil spring and allow the strut to be disengaged from the body.
13 Remove the swivel hub (and where applicable, the strut), withdrawing it from the driveshaft. Withdraw the hub assembly from the shaft, using a suitable puller if necessary, or carefully tap it free.

Refitting

14 Refitting is a reversal of the removal procedure. Refer to Chapter 8 for details on reconnecting the driveshaft, and Chapter 9 when refitting the brake disc and caliper. When reconnecting the suspension strut to the swivel hub, ensure that the two are correctly realigned before tightening the retaining bolts.
15 Do not fully tighten the driveshaft retaining nut/bolt or the anti-roll bar connecting link nut until after the vehicle is lowered, and with its full weight on the wheels.
16 All fastenings must be tightened to their specified torque settings.

5 Front wheel bearing - renewal

1 Remove the swivel hub, as described in the previous Section.
2 Undo the cross-head screw, and remove the brake disc.
3 Undo the retaining bolts, and remove the brake splash shield.
4 Support the swivel hub with the hub facing down, and press or drive out the hub from the housing. Remove the speed sensor on models with ABS.
5 The bearing inner race can be removed from the swivel hub using a suitable puller, but note that the bearing must be renewed once it is removed.
6 Extract the circlips, then supporting the swivel hub, press or drive out the bearing.

7 Clean the recess in the housing, then support the swivel hub and press the new bearing into position, so that it is positioned between the circlip grooves. If a tube drift is used, ensure that it butts against the bearing outer race only.
8 Press the inner bearing race onto the swivel hub, using a suitable tube drift.
9 Fit the circlips, and ensure that they are fully engaged in their grooves.
10 Refit the ABS wheel sensor to the swivel hub (where applicable), then with the swivel hub positioned and supported with its bearing shoulder facing up, press or drive the bearing housing into position.
11 Refit the splash shield and the brake disc.
12 Refit the swivel hub as described in the previous Section.
13 When the driveshaft nut/bolt and roadwheel bolts have been tightened to the specified torque, raise the car again so that the front wheels are clear of the ground. Referring to Chapter 1, Section 13 if necessary and then rotate them by hand to ensure that they turn freely, without binding. There should be no excessive lateral play.

6 Wishbone/lower arm - removal, overhaul and refitting

Removal

1 Apply the handbrake and chock the rear wheels, then loosen the relevant front roadwheel bolts. Raise and support the front of the vehicle on axle stands (see *"Jacking and vehicle support"*). Remove the relevant front roadwheel.
2 Undo the retaining bolt and detach the air deflector plate from the wishbone.
3 Position a jack under the centre of the subframe and raise it to support (not lift) the subframe.
4 Loosen the subframe rear mounting bolt on the side concerned - it should not be necessary to completely remove the bolt unless difficulty is experienced in manoeuvring out the wishbone. Unbolt and remove the wishbone rear mounting through-bolt **(see illustration)**.
5 Unbolt and detach the anti-roll bar mounting plate from the subframe and the body **(see illustration 7.4)**.
6 Unscrew the connecting link nut, and detach the anti-roll bar from the wishbone. As it is removed, note that the connecting link-to-wishbone mounting bush is fitted with its concave face towards the wishbone.
7 Unscrew and remove the wishbone/lower arm balljoint clamp bolt at the swivel hub **(see illustrations 4.8a and b)**. Note that the bolt head faces forwards. Tap the lower arm downwards to release the balljoint from the swivel hub.
8 Unscrew and remove the pivot bolt from the front inboard end of the wishbone arm (to subframe).

6.4 Subframe, wishbones and associated components

1   Wishbone/lower arm balljoint bolts
2   Wishbone/lower arm balljoint
3   Balljoint lockplate and self-locking nuts
4   Clip and lockpin
5   Air deflector plate
6   Wishbone/lower arm
7   Front pivot bush
8   Rear bush
9   Pivot bolt (M12 x 82 mm)
10 Wishbone rear mounting through-bolt (M12 x 78 mm)
11 Anti-roll bar connecting link nut
12 Washer
13 Anti-roll bar connecting link bush
14 Anti-roll bar connecting link
15 Anti-roll bar connecting link rubber bush (not separate on later models)
16 Anti-roll bar mounting plate bolt
17 Anti-roll bar mounting plate
18 Anti-roll bar mounting bush
19 Anti-roll bar
20 Subframe rear mounting bolt
21 Subframe front mounting bolt (M12 x 65 mm)
22 Vibration damper nut
23 Vibration damper
24 Subframe

9 Remove the wishbone, manoeuvring it down from the front inboard pivot, downwards and inwards from the wheel bearing, and forwards from the inboard rear mounting. It may be necessary to slightly lower the subframe to allow the wishbone to be detached at the rear inboard mounting. A suitable lever will assist in freeing the wishbone from its mountings, but take care not to damage adjacent components.

Overhaul

10 With the wishbone removed, clean it for inspection.

11 Check the balljoint for excessive wear, and check the pivot bushes for deterioration. Also examine the wishbone arm for damage and distortion. If necessary, the balljoint and bushes should be renewed.

12 To renew the balljoint, first outline its exact position on the wishbone. This is important as the relative positions of the wishbone and the balljoint are set during production, and the new balljoint must be accurately positioned when fitting it. Unscrew the nuts and remove the balljoint and clamp plate. Fit a new balljoint in the exact outline, and tighten the nuts. If fitting a new wishbone,

locate the balljoint centrally in the elongated hole.

13 To renew the front pivot bush, use a long bolt, together with a metal tube and washers, to pull the bush from the wishbone. Fit the new bush using the same method but, to ease insertion, dip the bush into soapy water first.

14 The rear mounting bonded rubber bush can be removed by prising free but, failing this, you will need to carefully cut through its rubber and steel sections to split and release it by driving it out. The latter course of action should only be necessary it if is badly corroded into position.

10

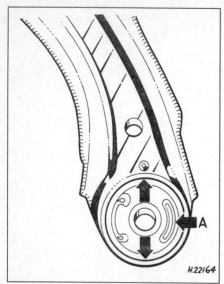

6.15 Showing wishbone rear bush fitting orientation, with arrow aligned with indent in arm, and aperture (A) towards vehicle centre

15 Press or drive the new mounting bush into position from the top end of the wishbone, but ensure that it is positioned correctly, as shown **(see illustration)**.

Refitting

16 Refitting the wishbone is a reverse of removal, noting the following points:
 a) *Delay tightening the pivot bolts until the weight of the car is on the wheels.*
 b) *Tighten all fasteners to the specified torque (where quoted).*
 c) *Refer to Section 7 when reconnecting the anti-roll bar.*
 d) *Have the front wheel alignment checked and, if necessary, adjusted on completion.*

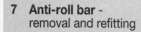

7 Anti-roll bar -
removal and refitting

Removal

1 Apply the handbrake and chock the rear wheels, then loosen the front roadwheel bolts. Raise and support the front of the vehicle on axle stands (see *"Jacking and vehicle support"*). For better access, remove the front roadwheels.
2 Position a jack centrally under the subframe and raise it to support (not lift) the subframe.
3 Loosen the subframe rear mounting bolts - it should not be necessary to completely remove the bolts unless difficulty is experienced in manoeuvring out the anti-roll bar.
4 Unscrew the retaining bolts, and detach the anti-roll bar mounting plates from the subframe and body **(see illustration)**.
5 Unscrew the connecting link nut, and detach the anti-roll bar from the wishbone each side. As they are removed, note that the

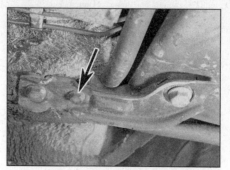

7.4 Anti-roll bar mounting plate bolt (arrowed)

connecting link-to-wishbone mounting bushes are fitted with their concave side facing the wishbone **(see illustration)**.
6 Lower the anti-roll bar, and remove it from under the vehicle.
7 Renew the anti-roll bar if it is damaged or distorted. Renew the mounting bushes if they are perished or worn.

Refitting

8 Refitting is a reversal of the removal procedure. Ensure that the connecting link mounting bushes are fitted with their concave faces towards the wishbone.

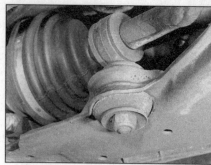

7.5 Anti-roll bar-to-wishbone connecting link

9 Do not fully tighten the retaining bolts to their specified torque settings until after the vehicle is fully lowered onto its wheels.

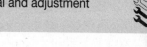

8 Rear wheel hub bearings -
renewal and adjustment

Renewal

1 The rear wheel hub bearings are housed in the rear brake drum/hub, or the rear brake disc/hub, as applicable **(see illustrations)**.

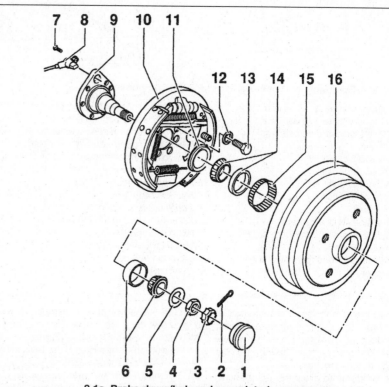

8.1a Brake drum/hub and associated components

1 Grease cap	7 Socket-head bolt	12 Dished washer
2 Split pin	8 Speed sensor (ABS only)	13 Bolt
3 Lock ring	9 Stub axle	14 Wheel bearing (inner)
4 Hexagon nut	10 Brake backplate	15 Speed sensor rotor (ABS only)
5 Thrustwasher	11 Seal ring	16 Brake drum/hub
6 Wheel bearing (outer)		

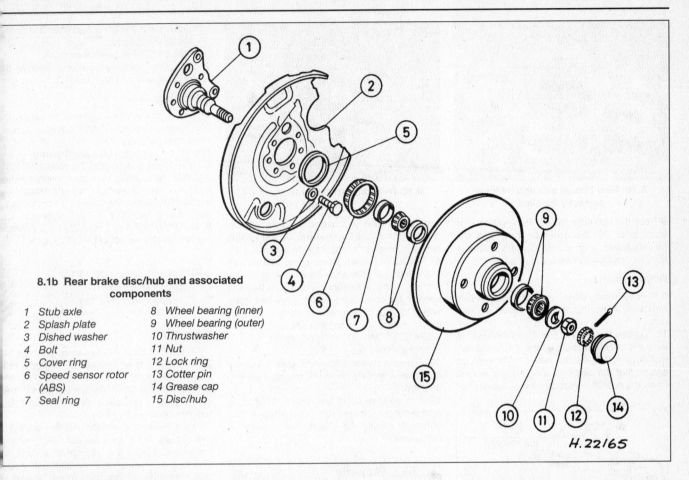

8.1b Rear brake disc/hub and associated components

1 Stub axle
2 Splash plate
3 Dished washer
4 Bolt
5 Cover ring
6 Speed sensor rotor (ABS)
7 Seal ring
8 Wheel bearing (inner)
9 Wheel bearing (outer)
10 Thrustwasher
11 Nut
12 Lock ring
13 Cotter pin
14 Grease cap
15 Disc/hub

H. 22/65

8.4 Drive the outer races out of position using a hammer and punch

Both the drum/hub and the disc/hub are removed and refitted in the same manner. Refer to Chapter 9 for removal details.

2 On disc brake models, lever off the cover ring from the rear of the hub.

3 Wipe clean the inner bearing and seal. Note the direction of fitting, then lever the seal from the hub. On models with ABS, take care not to damage the speed sensor rotor. Extract the inner bearing from the hub.

4 The races can be driven out using a suitable soft metal drift, but take care not to damage the hub or ABS speed sensor rotor (see illustration).

5 Clean the bearing race locations in the hub.

Use a tube drift of suitable diameter to drive or press the new races into position in the hub each side. Ensure that they are squarely and fully inserted (see illustration). If using the old bearings, be sure to keep the original bearings and races together. Never interchange new bearings with old races, or vice-versa.

6 Lubricate the inner bearing with grease, and insert it into position (see illustration).

7 Support the hub with its outboard face down, and carefully drive the new oil seal into position, taking care not to damage the ABS speed sensor rotor, where applicable. Lubricate the oil seal lip ready for refitting to the stub axle (see illustrations).

8.5 Drive the outer races securely into position using a socket on the outer edge

8.6 Work grease into the taper roller bearings prior to fitting them to the hub

8.7a Grease the lips of the seal, and press it into the rear of the hub

10

8.7b Rear hub oil seal and bearing correctly installed

8 Pack the hub with grease, then refit it to the stub axle. Fit the outer bearing and the thrustwasher, then screw the hub retaining nut into position by hand.

Adjustment

9 If not already done, extract the split pin, remove the locking ring and loosen the hub nut.

10 Tighten the hub nut slowly, up to the point where it only just touches the thrustwasher. Rotate the hub as the nut is tightened, to ensure that the bearings are correctly seated. Back the nut off a fraction so that the washer

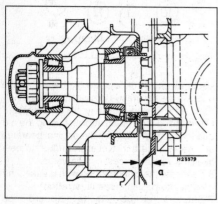

9.4 Cover ring location

a = 9.5mm

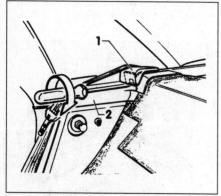

10.2 Seat belt guide removal method

1 Guide   2 Reel cover

8.10 Rear hub bearing adjustment - washer should just move

can just be seen to move when prodded with a screwdriver **(see illustration)**. Fit the locking ring and insert a new split pin to secure.

11 Beware of overtightening the hub nut, as this will cause premature bearing wear. If you are adjusting a bearing which has been in service for some time, when play has been noted, do not overtighten to compensate for wear - this is potentially dangerous and unlikely to effect anything more than a temporary solution.

12 Smear a liberal amount of grease into the cap, then carefully drive the grease cap into position.

13 If a new bearing has been fitted, it is advisable to check for play after a few hundred miles. Re-adjust the bearing if necessary.

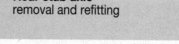

9 Rear stub axle - removal and refitting

Removal

1 Chock the front roadwheels, engage 1st gear (or "P"), then loosen the relevant rear roadwheel bolts. Raise the vehicle at the rear and support it on axle stands (see *"Jacking and vehicle support"*).

2 Refer to the appropriate Sections in Chapter 9, and proceed with the following:

a) *Remove the brake drum/hub or disc/hub (as applicable).*

b) *Remove the brake shoe assembly (drum brake models).*

10.3a Rear suspension strut upper mounting - Saloon

c) *Disconnect the brake hydraulic line from the wheel cylinder.*

d) *Disconnect the handbrake cable.*

3 Undo the retaining bolt and remove the brake backplate and stub axle.

Refitting

4 Refit in the reverse order of removal. On disc brake models, if the cover ring was removed, ensure on refitting that it i positioned as shown **(see illustration)**.

5 Refer to the appropriate Sections in Chapter 9 to refit the brake system components. Whe refitting the drum/hub or disc/hub (as applicable), adjust the wheel hub bearings as described in Section 8 of this Chapter.

6 Bleed the brake hydraulic circuit and adjust the handbrake, as described in Chapter 9.

10 Rear suspension strut and coil spring - removal and refitting

Removal

1 Chock the front roadwheels, engage 1s gear (or "P"), then loosen the relevant rea roadwheel bolts. Raise and support the vehicle at the rear on axle stands (see *"Jacking and vehicle support"*). Allow the suspension to extend fully.

2 From inside the vehicle, tilt forwards the rear seat backrest. On Estate models, release the side trim from the luggage area, and the C-pillar trim, then remove the seat belt guide When removing the belt guide, insert a screwdriver as shown **(see illustration)**, and twist it to release the guide.

3 Unbolt and detach the seat belt reel from the mounting bracket on the top of the strut Undo the two strut upper mounting bolts **(see illustrations)**.

4 Working underneath the vehicle, reach through the aperture in the trailing arm tube, and engage a spanner on the nut securing the strut bottom mounting bolt, then unscrew the bolt and remove it **(see illustration)**.

5 On models fitted with self-levelling suspension, depressurise the system as described in Section 15, then detach the ai line from the damper, and the sensor lead from the left-hand damper (where applicable).

10.3b Rear suspension strut upper mounting - Estate

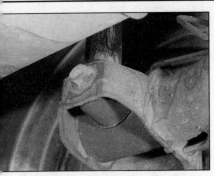

10.4 Rear suspension strut lower mounting

Disengage the strut at the bottom end, and rotate it to align the upper securing lugs of the strut with the four notches in the body. Withdraw the strut downwards (complete with coil spring) from the vehicle.

Refitting

Refit in the reverse order of removal. Ensure that the strut is correctly located at the top end, and secured by the four lugs in the body before fitting the fastening nuts and bolts. Tighten the retaining bolts to their specified torque settings, but delay full tightening of the lower mounting bolt until after the vehicle is lowered fully, and standing on its wheels.

11 Rear suspension strut and coil spring - separation and reassembly

1 The component parts of the strut and coil spring are as shown **(see illustration)**.

⚠ **Warning: Before attempting to dismantle the suspension strut, a suitable tool to hold the coil spring in compression must be obtained. Adjustable coil spring compressors are readily available, and are recommended for this operation. Any attempt to dismantle the strut without such a tool is likely to result in damage or personal injury.**

2 Fit the spring compressor, and ensure that it is fully located. Compress the spring so that the tension on the top mounting retainer is relieved.

3 Prise free the cover cap and remove the sealing O-ring.

4 Unscrew and remove the self-locking nut, then remove the dished washer, upper bush and the strut top mounting. The foam gasket on top of the mounting must be renewed.

5 Withdraw the spacer tube, the lower bush, metal cap, washer and the spring seat.

6 Lift the coil spring from the strut with the compressor still in position. Mark the top of the spring for reference.

7 Remove the bump-stop, bellows, plastic cap and packing.

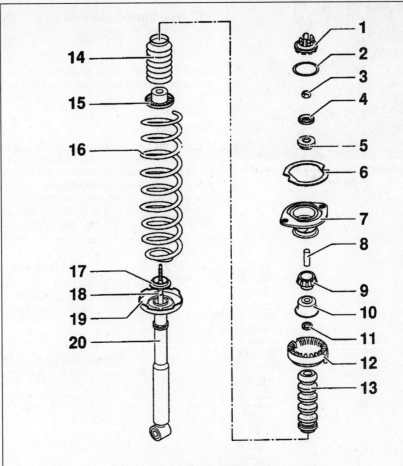

11.1 Rear suspension strut components

1 Cover cap	8 Spacer tube	15 Plastic cap
2 O-ring	9 Lower rubber bush	16 Coil spring
3 Self-locking nut	10 Metal cap	17 Spacer
4 Dished washer	11 Washer	18 Circlip
5 Upper rubber bush	12 Spring seat	19 Lower spring plate
6 Foam gasket	13 Bump stop	20 Shock absorber
7 Strut top mounting	14 Protective sleeve	

8 Note that the coil springs are colour-coded, and if renewal is necessary, check that the correct replacement is supplied for your vehicle. It is advisable to renew both rear springs at the same time, to ensure even handling characteristics.

9 Check the operation of the shock absorber in the same manner described for the front units in Section 3, paragraph 8. Renew if necessary, as the shock absorbers cannot be overhauled.

10 Reassembly of the shock absorber and coil spring is a reversal of the removal procedure. Ensure that the captive nuts are positioned in the recesses of the spring seat. The spring seat installation position must be as shown **(see illustration)**.

11 Tighten the self-locking nut to the specified torque setting. Remove the spring compressor tool before refitting the unit to the vehicle as described in Section 10.

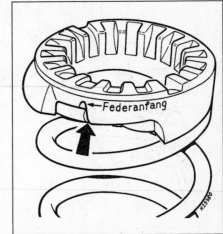

11.10 Coil spring seat correctly installed

10

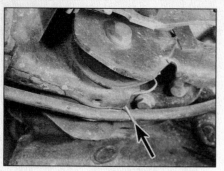

12.2 Release handbrake cable at clip (arrowed)

12 Rear torsion beam axle - removal and refitting

Note: *If the rear axle is suspected of being distorted, it must be checked in position by a VW garage, using optical alignment equipment.*

Removal

1 Chock the front wheels, engage 1st gear (or "P"), then loosen the rear roadwheel bolts. Raise and support the vehicle at the rear on axle stands (see *"Jacking and vehicle support"*). Remove the rear roadwheels.

2 Refer to Chapter 9 and disconnect the handbrake cable from each rear brake, then detach the cable from the clips securing it the axle **(see illustration)**.

3 Disconnect the brake hydraulic line fro each rear brake, and from the attachme points on the axle, referring to Chapter 9 details. Also disconnect the ABS wiring fro the wheel sensors, where applicable.

4 Position jacks or stands under the ax each side to support its weight.

5 Unbolt and remove the strut low mounting bolt each side, and detach th struts from the axle **(see illustration)**.

6 Disengage the brake pressure regulat spring from the bracket. If necessary, loose off the spring bolt, but first mark its fitte position on the bracket, to ensure corre positioning during reassembly, or th regulator adjustment will be lost.

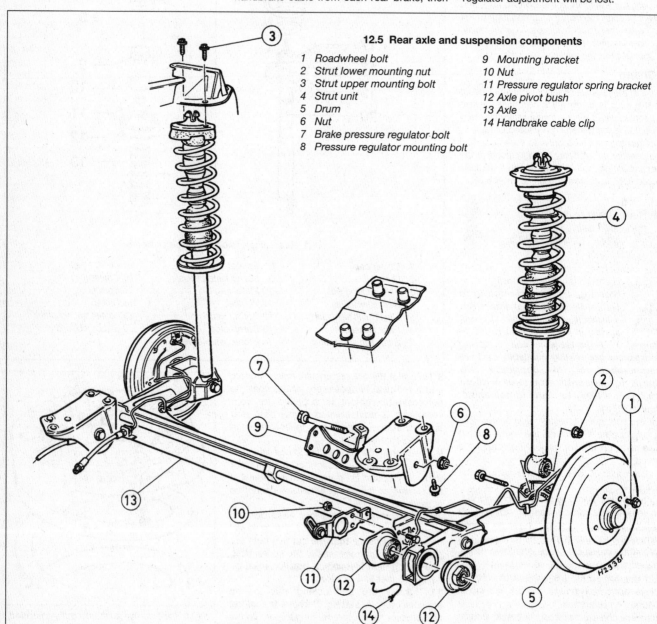

12.5 Rear axle and suspension components

1 Roadwheel bolt
2 Strut lower mounting nut
3 Strut upper mounting bolt
4 Strut unit
5 Drum
6 Nut
7 Brake pressure regulator bolt
8 Pressure regulator mounting bolt
9 Mounting bracket
10 Nut
11 Pressure regulator spring bracket
12 Axle pivot bush
13 Axle
14 Handbrake cable clip

Check that all associated fittings are clear the axle. Cover the stub axles and brake assemblies to ensure that they do not get damaged or dirty as the axle assembly is moved. Ensure that the axle is securely supported. If possible, engage the services of an assistant to help in steadying the axle assembly as it is detached and lowered from the vehicle.

Unscrew and remove the pivot bolt nut each side **(see illustration)**, then withdraw the bolts and lower the axle from the pivot/mountings. Lower and remove the axle assembly from under the vehicle.

If the mounting/pivot bushes are worn, they must be renewed. Remove the outer bush, then the inner bush, using a suitable puller. It is important that the mounting is not driven out, or else the seating would be enlarged.

10 Dip the new bushes in soapy water, to lubricate them for ease of fitting. Press each bush in from the outside with a puller, ensuring that the rubber/metal protrusions on the inner face point to the front, and the outer section points to the rear **(see illustration)**. Insert each half to the point where the conical part is in contact with the axle. Fit each half one at a time.

Refitting

1 Refitting is a reversal of the removal procedure. When the axle is raised into position, loosely assemble the retaining bolts and nuts until the axle is fully located before tightening them fully to the specified torque settings.

2 When reconnecting the brake hydraulic lines, handbrake cables and ABS wiring, ensure that everything is correctly routed and secured. Bleed the hydraulic system and adjust the handbrake as described in Chapter 9. When reconnecting the brake pressure regulator spring, its fitted position to the bracket must be as marked during removal.

13 Self-levelling suspension - description and precautions

The components and layout of the self-levelling suspension system are as shown **(see illustration)**.

With this system, the rear shock absorbers are pneumatically-controlled air spring elements, instead of the conventional hydraulic piston type. An air compressor located in the left-hand rear corner of the vehicle supplies compressed air to each rear air spring element. The compressor is a piston type unit with an electric motor. It maintains a minimum air pressure of 5 bar (70 psi) in the system. The compressor is housed in an insulated casing to reduce its operating noise.

Under normal circumstances, the system is self-levelling, but where necessary, a manual adjustment can be made by means of an adjuster wheel on the control unit. This adjustment

12.8 Rear axle pivot bolt/nut

is only required when towing or carrying an abnormal load. In normal circumstances, the adjuster wheel should be set in the "4" position to ensure the best handling characteristics.

If the compressor becomes overloaded at any time, an overload circuit breaker switches it off for a few moments, then on again. The system wiring also operates through a conventional fuse (number 4 on the main fuse/relay panel).

If the air compressor malfunctions at any time, it must be checked and repaired (or renewed, as necessary) at the earliest opportunity. As a temporary measure to restore the handling, the system air pressure can be raised (or lowered) independently by attaching an air line to the valve next to the

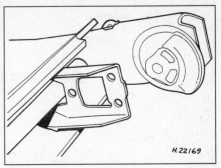

12.10 Installed position of mounting bush

control unit, and adjusting the pressure accordingly. Set the adjuster wheel to position "2" before adjusting the pressure manually.

The system switches into operation whenever the ignition is switched on, and/or when the doors, boot lid or tailgate are opened. This enables the control unit to adjust the system setting in response to any change in loading.

The system is not designed to compensate for excessive overloading. The manufacturer's maximum axle and total weights must not be exceeded.

Before working on the system or associated components, the battery must be disconnected, and the system depressurised as described in Section 15.

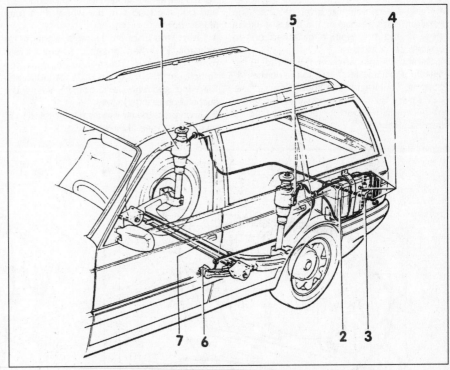

13.1 Self-levelling suspension system component locations

1 Air spring damper element
2 Pressure supply
3 Control unit
4 Distributor unit and air line system
5 Level sensor line
6 Brake pressure regulator
7 Rear axle and anti-roll bar

10

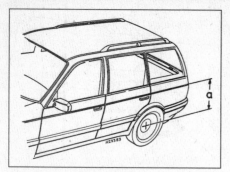

14.3 Self-levelling suspension system level check

a = 531 to 551 mm

If compressed air leaks from the system, the air spring element will rest on an internal buffer within the damper units. This will be noticeable by a hard ride and poor handling. The pneumatically-controlled brake pressure regulator will also be adversely affected. Although it is permissible to drive the vehicle in this condition, the speed must not exceed 35 mph (60 kph), and the fault in the system must be rectified as soon as possible.

14 Self-levelling suspension - level check

1 Park the vehicle on level ground. The vehicle must be unladen, the doors must be closed, and the ignition switched on (to operate the compressor).
2 Set the adjuster wheel on the control to the highest position, then turn it to the normal "4" position. Shut the tailgate/boot lid.
3 Measure the distance between the centre of the roadwheel and the body waistline rib **(see illustration)**.

4 If the level is down, check the system for any sign of leaks, but do not get confused by the hissing of air being released from the sensor on the left-hand air spring element. This occurs when the system is adjusting the height of the rear suspension.
5 A full check of the system must be entrusted to a VW dealer.

15 Self-levelling suspension - component removal and refitting

1 Before disconnecting any part of the pressure system, the air pressure in the system must first be released. To do this, first disconnect the battery earth lead, then unscrew the air pressure valve and completely release the remaining air pressure from the system. **Note:** *If the vehicle has a security-coded radio, check that you have a copy of the code number before disconnecting the battery. Refer to your VW dealer if in doubt.*

Air spring element

Removal

2 With the air pressure released from the system, remove the floor covering and the left-hand side trim from the luggage area.
3 If the left-hand air spring is being removed, detach the sensor lead at its in-line connector, and pull the lead into the wheel arch **(see illustration)**.
4 Chock the front roadwheels, engage 1st gear (or "P"), then loosen the relevant rear roadwheel bolts. Raise and support the vehicle at the rear on axle stands (see *"Jacking and vehicle support"*). Allow the suspension to extend fully.
5 Disconnect the air line from the air spring to be removed **(see illustration)**.

6 The air springs can now be detached a removed in the same manner as th described for the conventional re suspension in Section 10.

Refitting

7 Refitting is a reversal of the remov procedure. When refitting the air sprir ensure that the air line and the sensor le (where applicable) are securely attached a correctly routed before reconnecting t battery. Repressurise the system described in Section 13.

Control unit

Removal

8 Remove the left-hand side trim panel in t luggage area.
9 Detach the control unit from t compressor by pulling it free from the velc strip attachment, then detach the multi-pl connectors.

Refitting

10 Refitting is a reversal of the remov procedure.

Compressor

Removal

11 Detach the compressor earth lead fro the body.
12 Release the rubber retaining strap ar remove the air compressor unit from th wheel arch.
13 Disconnect the control unit (se paragraphs 8 and 9).
14 Separate the insulation housing ar remove the compressor.

Refitting

15 Refit in the reverse order of removal, ar repressurise the system as described Section 13.

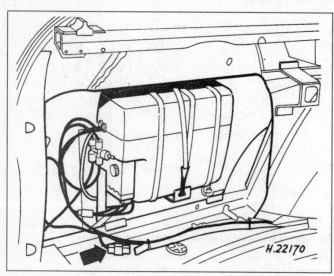

15.3 Sensor lead location - left-hand damper only

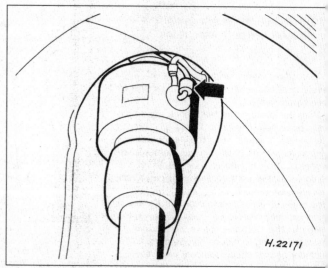

15.5 Air line-to-air spring connection - arrowed

16 Steering wheel - removal and refitting

Note: *The steering column splined adaptor, onto which the steering wheel fits, was modified in January 1989, and has a less-coarse spline than the previous type. This information should be taken into account if fitting early parts to a later vehicle, or vice-versa. Consult a VW dealer if in doubt.*

Removal

1 Set the front wheels in the straight-ahead position, and release the steering lock by inserting the ignition key. Ensure that the direction indicator lever is in the central "off" position.

Models without an airbag

2 Prise free the cover from the centre of the steering wheel. Since the cover is the horn push-button, note the location of the wires, and disconnect them from the terminals on the cover **(see illustration)**.
3 Mark the steering wheel and inner column in relation to each other, then unscrew the nut and withdraw the steering wheel. If it is tight, tap it up near the centre, using the palm of your hand, or twist it from side to side, whilst pulling upwards to release it. Remove the washer, where fitted.

Models with an airbag

4 Remove the airbag unit from the centre of the steering wheel, as described in Chapter 12.
5 Slacken and remove the retaining screws, and remove the steering column upper and lower shrouds.
6 Trace the wiring back from the airbag contact unit in the steering wheel, and disconnect it at the wiring connector.
7 Remove the steering wheel as described above in paragraphs 2 and 3.

16.2 Horn wire connections to steering wheel cover

8 With the steering wheel removed, rotate the contact unit ring slightly so its wiring connector is at the bottom (steering wheel in the straight-ahead position); this will lock the contact unit in the central position, and prevent it from being turned.

Refitting

Models without an airbag

9 Refitting is a reversal of removal, but make sure that the direction indicator lever is in its 'neutral' position, otherwise damage may occur in the cancelling arm. Engage the direction indicator lever cancelling ring tongue as the steering wheel is fitted. Tighten the retaining nut to the specified torque **(see illustrations)**.

Models with an airbag

10 Manoeuvre the wheel into position, making sure the wiring connector is correctly positioned, and engage it with the column.
11 Refit the steering wheel retaining nut, and tighten it to the specified torque setting.
12 Reconnect the contact unit wiring connector, making sure the wiring is correctly routed.
13 Refit the steering column shrouds, and securely tighten the retaining screws.
14 Refit the airbag unit as described in Chapter 12.

16.9a Engage the direction indicator cancelling ring tongue (arrowed) as the wheel is fitted . . .

17 Steering column - removal and refitting

Note: *Several of the steering column components were modified in January 1989. Most of the changes were fairly minor in nature, but two are worth mentioning. Later steering columns were increased in diameter from 20 mm to 22 mm. The later steering column splined adaptor, onto which the steering wheel fits, has a less-coarse spline than the previous type. While this information does not greatly affect any procedures in this Chapter, it should be taken into account if fitting early parts to a later vehicle, or vice-versa, as interchangeability is limited. Consult a VW dealer if in doubt.*

Removal

1 Disconnect the battery negative lead. **Note:** *If the vehicle has a security-coded radio, check that you have a copy of the code number before disconnecting the battery. Refer to your VW dealer if in doubt.*
2 Remove the steering wheel, as described in the previous Section.

16.9b . . . locate the washer . . .

16.9c . . . and tighten the retaining nut

10

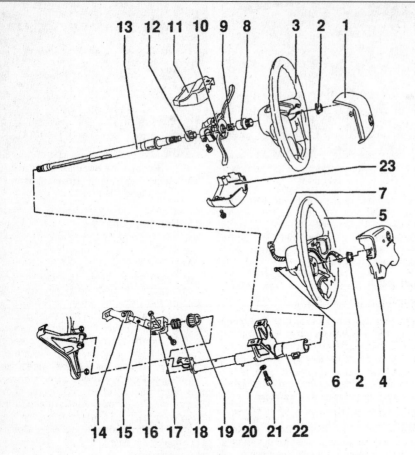

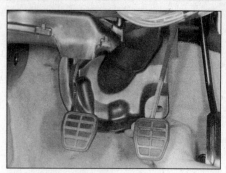

17.5 Remove the lower column/bulkhead cover

17.8 Steering column universal joint shaft clamp bolt (arrowed)

17.3 Steering column components

1 Steering wheel centre cover	7 Airbag wiring connector	14 Clamp bolt
2 Steering wheel retaining nut (with separate washer on early models)	8 Multi-splined adapter sleeve	15 Bolt
	9 Spring (with clamping washer on early models)	16 Nut
3 Steering wheel	10 Column lower switch/lock housing	17 Universal joint (UJ)
4 Airbag unit		18 Spring
5 Steering wheel (airbag type)	11 Upper trim (shroud)	19 Column lower bearing
	12 Support ring and washer	20 Washer
6 Allen bolt	13 Steering column	21 Shear bolt
		22 Column tube
		23 Lower trim (shroud)

3 If not already done, remove the screws and withdraw the steering column shrouds **(see illustration)**.

4 Remove the three screws and withdraw the combination switches. Disconnect the wiring multi-connectors.

5 Detach and remove the lower facia trim and insulation panels on the driver's side. Detach

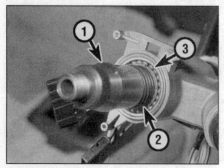

17.11a Steering column top end, showing sleeve (1), spring (2) and bearing (3)

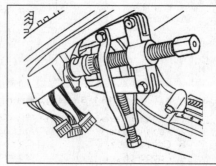

17.11b Adaptor sleeve removal method using a suitable puller

and remove the lower column/bulkhead cover **(see illustration)**.

6 Disconnect the ignition switch/steering column lock wiring connector.

7 Remove the column mounting bolts. Shear-type bolts are used - to remove them, it will be necessary to drill out the threaded portion and use a stud extractor, or tap them round with a centre-punch.

8 Unscrew and remove the column upper-to-lower universal joint shaft clamp bolt **(see illustration)**, and withdraw the column assembly from the vehicle.

9 Check the various components for excessive wear. If the column has been damaged in any way, it must be renewed as a unit.

10 Remove the ignition switch/steering column lock, as described in Chapter 12.

11 Using a suitable puller, withdraw the splined adaptor sleeve from the shaft **(see illustrations)**. If renewing the sleeve, bear in mind the information at the start of this Section.

12 If a new steering column and/or steering wheel is being fitted, bear in mind the information at the start of this Section.

13 Withdraw the column upwards through the column tube and remove it, noting the fitted positions of all components as it is removed.

14 If the steering column bottom bearing is to be renewed, drive (or draw) it out downwards from the tube. Fit the replacement bearing by driving it into position in the base of the tube, using a suitable tube drift.

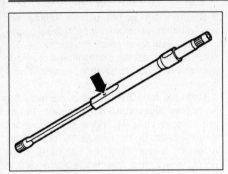

17.15 Steering column length check

Lower section lug must be visible in hole in upper section

15 To check that the column length is correct, ensure that the small lug on the lower section is aligned with the hole in the upper column section, as shown **(see illustration)**. If required, pull the sections apart up to the stop.

16 Renew any parts which are worn or suspect.

Refitting

17 Reassembly and refitting is in general a reversal of the dismantling and removal procedure, but note the following special points.

18 When assembling the top end of the column, press (or drive) the spring clamping washer (where fitted) down the shaft to the point where the spring is fully compressed.

19 Ensure that the length of the column is maintained as described in paragraph 15.

20 When fitting the multi-splined adaptor sleeve, position the sleeve over the column, and then tighten the steering wheel nut against it. Press the sleeve down to the level of the thread, remove the nut, fit a washer, and then refit and tighten the nut again so that the sleeve is pushed fully into position and tightly seated. Unscrew the nut and remove the washer.

21 Refit the ignition switch/column lock as described in Chapter 12.

22 Tighten the retaining nuts and bolts to the specified torque wrench settings. Tighten the shear-bolts until their heads break off.

23 On early models, when the steering wheel is refitted, check that the clearance between its hub face and that of the column switch is as shown **(see illustration)**. If required, tap the ignition switch/steering lock housing back so that it is in contact with the spacer sleeve.

24 On completion, ensure that the steering action, and the operation of the column switches, is satisfactory.

18 Steering column height adjuster - removal and refitting

1 The component parts of the height adjuster mechanism are as shown **(see illustration)**.

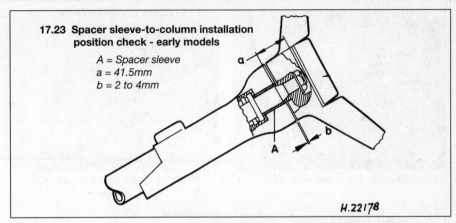

17.23 Spacer sleeve-to-column installation position check - early models

A = Spacer sleeve
a = 41.5mm
b = 2 to 4mm

H.22178

2 The adjuster mechanism components can be removed from the column after the column is lowered from the upper mounting, as described in the previous Section. Note that the lever through-bolt has a left-hand thread.

3 Any components in the height adjuster mechanism which are broken or excessively worn must be renewed.

4 When refitting the components of the adjuster, note the following points:

a) Lubricate the sliding surfaces of the adjuster.

b) When refitting the lever, tighten the through-bolt to the specified torque setting with the lever on the upper stop. Refit the securing plate after the bolt is tightened.

c) Ensure that the return springs are attached to the mounting bracket.

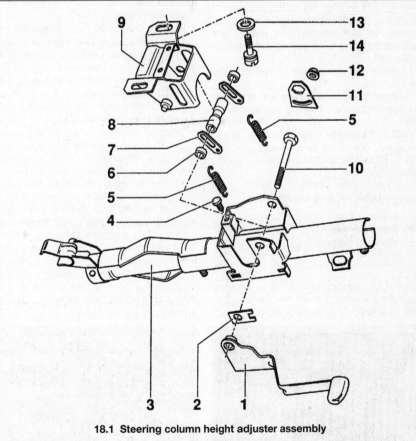

18.1 Steering column height adjuster assembly

1 Operating lever	6 Thrustwasher	11 Locking plate
2 Packing plate	7 Packing plate	12 Nut (self-locking)
3 Column tube	8 Clamping sleeve	13 Washer
4 Rubber stop	9 Mounting bracket	14 Shear-bolt
5 Return spring	10 Lever through-bolt (left-hand thread)	

10

20.2a Undo the retaining bolts . . .

20.2b . . . and remove the vibration damper

19 Steering gear bellows - renewal

1 The steering gear bellows can be removed and refitted with the steering gear unit *in situ* or removed from the vehicle.
2 Measure the exposed amount of adjustment thread showing on the inboard side of the track-rod end balljoint locknut. This will act as a guide to the adjustment position when refitting the balljoint to the rod. Loosen off the locknut, and detach the balljoint from the track-rod as described in Section 22.
3 Unscrew and remove the locking nut from the track-rod.
4 Release the retaining clips and withdraw the bellows from the steering gear and track-rod.
5 Refit in the reverse order of removal. Smear the inner bore of the bellows with lubricant prior to fitting to ease its assembly. Renew the balljoint locknuts.
6 On completion, have the front wheel alignment checked (see Section 25).

20 Steering gear - removal and refitting

Note: *If the steering gear is being removed because a knocking noise has been noted, refer to Section 21 before proceeding.*

20.8a Power steering fluid line connections at pinion . . .

Removal

1 Apply the handbrake and chock the rear wheels, then loosen the front roadwheel bolts. Raise and support the front of the vehicle on axle stands (see *"Jacking and vehicle support"*). For better access, remove the front roadwheels.
2 To improve access to the steering gear, undo the retaining bolts and remove the damper weight from the crossmember **(see illustrations)**. Support the damper as it is withdrawn (it is quite heavy).
3 Refer to Section 22, and detach the track-rod end balljoints from the swivel hub.
4 On power steering models, siphon the fluid from the system reservoir. If a suitable implement is not readily available to siphon the fluid from the system, it can be drained into a container when the hydraulic lines are detached from the steering gear.
5 Unscrew and remove the steering column upper-to-lower universal joint shaft clamp bolt **(see illustration 17.8)**. Access is restricted by the brake and fuel system components from above in the engine compartment, whilst from underneath, the exhaust system and steering components obstruct. Access to this bolt is therefore best from inside the vehicle. Detach and remove the lower facia trim and insulation panels, then release the cover from the bulkhead at the base of the column. Release the gaiter from the bulkhead on the engine side, and push it forward over the lower joint. Unscrew and remove the clamp bolt.

20.8b . . . and rack housing. The steering gear nearside mounting strap and securing bolt/nut is also shown (arrowed)

6 Support the weight of the engine and transmission, either with a hoist from above, or with a jack underneath the subframe. The latter method has the disadvantage of getting in the way in subsequent operations, so if possible use the hoist method.
7 Undo the subframe front and rear mounting bolts **(see illustration 6.4)**. Loosen, but do not remove, the wishbone rear mounting through-bolts. Do not remove the anti-roll bar mounting bolts. Lower the subframe to the point where the steering column shafts separate. As the engine is lowered, check that its associated components do not snag or damage any adjacent fittings. Do not lower it any more than is necessary.
8 On power steering models, disconnect the fluid supply and return lines from the steering gear **(see illustrations)**. Clean the connections before they are detached. Drain any fluid remaining in the system into a container for disposal. Position the lines out of the way, and seal off their ends to prevent further leakage and the possible ingress of dirt.
9 Unscrew and remove the steering gear mounting nuts from the studs in the subframe **(see illustrations)**.
10 Check that all connections are free and clear of the steering gear, then withdraw it rearwards and manoeuvre it from the vehicle.
11 If the steering gear is known to be damaged or worn beyond an acceptable level, it may have to be renewed. However, it is possible to have the steering gear overhauled - consult a VW dealer or specialist repairer for further advice.

Refitting

12 Refitting is a reversal of the removal procedure, noting the following points:

a) *Centralise the steering rack and the column shaft before connecting them. An assistant will be required to align and engage the two shafts as the subframe and engine are raised.*

b) *On power steering models, the fluid lines will also need to be connected as the unit is raised. Take care to keep the connections clean.*

c) *Tighten all fasteners to the specified torque wrench settings.*

d) *Refer to Section 22 to reconnect the track-rod ends.*

e) *On power steering models, top up the fluid level as described in "Weekly checks" and bleed the system as described in Section 23.*

f) *Finally, have the wheel alignment checked and if necessary adjusted (see Section 25).*

**20.9a Manual steering gear and associated components
(LHD shown)**

1   Mounting nut
2   Mounting clamp
3   Rubber mounting
4   Track-rod end
5   Locknut
6   Balljoint nut
7   Track-rod (RH)
8   Steering gear
9   Subframe and vibration
     damper
10 Studs
11 Universal joint nut
12 Column universal joint shaft
13 Bellows
14 Pinion clamp bolt
15 Bellows
16 Securing ring
17 Track-rod (LH)
18 Locknut

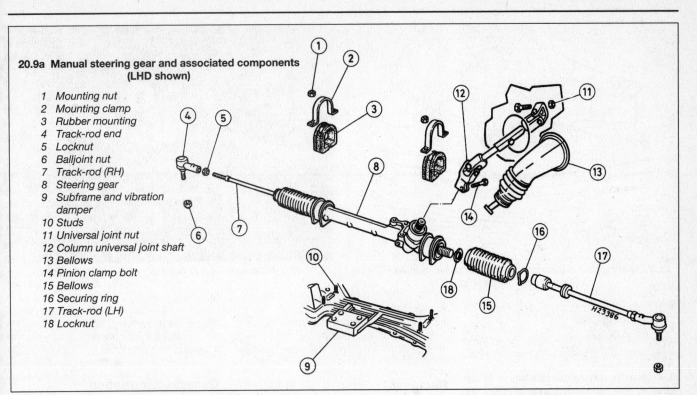

**20.9b Power steering gear and associated components
(LHD shown)**

1   Suction hose
2   Hose clip
3   Pressure hose
4   O-ring
5   Hose tie
6   Hose bracket
7   Fluid reservoir
8   Rubber ring
9   Clip
10 Reservoir cap
     (and dipstick)
11 Return flow hose
12 Balljoint nut
13 Mounting nut
14 Mounting clamp
15 Mounting rubber
16 Track-rod (RH)
17 Track-rod (LH)
18 Locknut
19 Bellows
20 Track-rod end
21 Steering gear
22 Pinion clamp bolt
23 Column universal joint shaft
24 Bellows

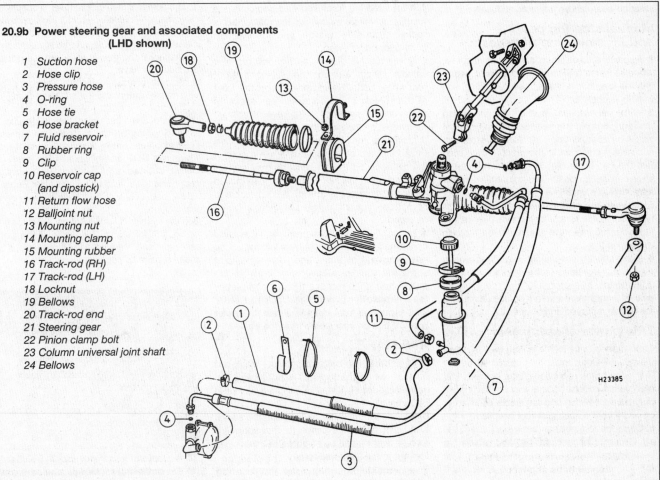

H23385

10

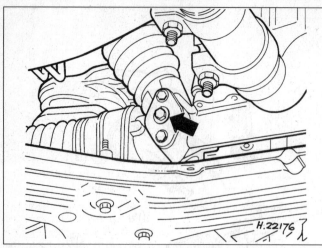

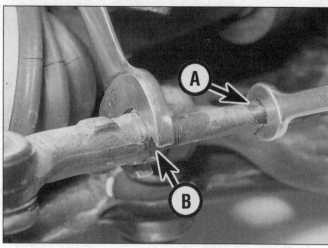

21.3 Steering gear adjustment screw - arrowed (manual steering and ZF power steering)

22.3 Hold track-rod at point (A) and loosen off nut (B)

21 Steering gear - adjustment

1 If there is any undue slackness in the steering gear, resulting in noise or rattles, the steering gear can be adjusted as follows.

Manual steering gear and ZF power steering gear

2 Apply the handbrake and chock the rear wheels. Raise and support the front of the vehicle on axle stands (see *"Jacking and vehicle support"*).
3 With the wheels in the straight-ahead position, tighten the self-locking adjustment screw by approximately 20° **(see illustration)**.
4 Lower the vehicle to the ground, then road test the car. If the steering fails to self-centre after cornering, loosen the adjustment screw a fraction at a time until it does.
5 If, when the correct self-centring point is reached, there is still excessive play in the steering, retighten the adjuster nut a fraction to take up the play.
6 If the adjustment procedures listed above do not provide satisfactory steering adjustment, it is probable that the steering gear is worn beyond an acceptable level, and it must be removed and overhauled.

TRW power steering gear

7 On models with TRW steering gear, a large-diameter locknut must be unscrewed before the adjustment screw can be turned. VW mechanics have a special tool for this, but it may be possible to find a suitable alternative, possibly from a specialist tool supplier.
8 Once the locknut has been slackened, the adjustment procedure is as given in paragraphs 2 to 6 above, remembering that the locknut must be tightened after each adjustment.

22 Track-rod end balljoints - removal and refitting

Removal

1 If the steering track-rod end balljoints are worn, play will be evident as the roadwheel is rocked from side to side, and the balljoint must then be renewed.
2 Apply the handbrake and chock the rear wheels, then loosen the relevant front roadwheel bolts. Raise and support the front of the vehicle on axle stands (see *"Jacking and vehicle support"*). Remove the front roadwheel on the side concerned.
3 Measure the distance of the exposed thread inboard of the locknut. Make a note of the distance, so that the new balljoint can be screwed on to the same position, then loosen the locknut **(see illustration)**. It is advisable to fit a new locknut if the balljoint is being renewed.
4 Loosen the balljoint nut on the side concerned, and unscrew it by a few turns - do not remove it at this stage. Use a balljoint separator tool to release the joint from the swivel hub, then remove the nut completely **(see illustration)**. With the track-rod outer joint separated from the swivel hub, the outer balljoint can be unscrewed from the track-rod.

Refitting

5 Screw the new balljoint onto the track-rod so that, when the locknut is tightened, the same amount of thread is exposed as noted on removal.
6 Reconnect the outer balljoints to the swivel hub, and tighten the nut to the specified torque wrench setting. Tighten the track-rod locknut to the specified torque.
7 On completion, have the front wheel alignment checked (see Section 25).

23 Power steering fluid - general information, draining and refilling

General information

1 The power steering fluid level is checked as described in *"Weekly checks"*. Fluid renewal is not called for by the manufacturer's maintenance schedule, and so should only be necessary if the power steering components are being removed.
2 Models produced before February 1989 use normal automatic transmission fluid (ATF) in the power steering system. Models after this date are filled with VW hydraulic oil. When topping-up the system, use the same fluid or oil as that in the system, as the two fluids are **NOT** compatible. If the system is being drained and refilled, use only the recommended fluid or oil - ie after February 1989, use only VW hydraulic oil for refilling the system.
3 If the system is in need of constant topping-up, check for signs of leakage at the pump, reservoir and steering gear hose unions and make repairs as necessary.

22.4 Balljoint separator tool in position. If joint is not being renewed, take care not to damage rubber seal (arrowed)

Draining

4 To drain the fluid from the system, detach the fluid suction hose at the pump, and drain the fluid into a container for disposal. When draining, turn the steering wheel from lock to lock to expel as much fluid as possible.

Refilling and bleeding

5 After draining off the fluid, reconnect the suction hose to the pump unit, then fill the reservoir to the top with new fluid. Restart the engine and switch off as soon as it fires, repeating the starting and stopping sequence several times; this will cause fluid to be drawn into the system quickly.

6 Watch the level of fluid, and keep adding fluid so that the reservoir is never sucked dry. When the fluid ceases to drop as a result of the start/ stop sequence, start the engine and allow it to run at idling speed.

7 Turn the steering from lock to lock several times, being careful not to leave the wheels on full lock because this will cause the pressure in the system to build up.

8 Watch the level of the fluid in the reservoir, and add fluid if necessary to keep the level at the "MAX" mark.

9 When the level stops falling and no more air bubbles appear in the reservoir, switch the engine off and fit the reservoir cap. The level of fluid will rise slightly when the engine is switched off.

10 After the vehicle is next used, re-check the fluid level as described in "Weekly checks", and top up if necessary.

24 Power steering pump - removal and refitting

Removal

1 If the power steering is suspected of malfunction, have the supply and system pressure checked by your VW dealer. The pump unit cannot be overhauled or repaired, and if defective, it must be renewed as a unit.

2 To remove the pump, first drain the system fluid, as described in the previous Section.

3 Disconnect the pressure hose from the pump.

4 Loosen the pump retaining bolts, and pivot the pump so that the drivebelt can be disconnected from the pulley.

5 Support the pump, withdraw the retaining bolts, and remove the pump.

6 If required, the fluid reservoir is easily removed by loosening off the retaining clip and lifting the unit from its bottom mounting (see illustrations).

Refitting

7 If a new pump is to be fitted, it is advisable to prime it with fluid prior to fitting, to ensure adequate lubrication during its initial stages of operation. Failure to do this could lead to a noisy pump. To prime the pump, inject the

24.6a Loosen the retaining clip . . .

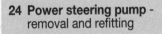

specified fluid into the fluid inlet connector on the pump, and simultaneously rotate the pump pulley. When the fluid exits from the fluid outlet (supply) connector, it is primed and ready for use.

8 Refitting is a reversal of removal, but note the following points:
a) Check the condition of the drivebelt as described in Chapter 1A or 1B, as applicable. If a new pump is being fitted, a new drivebelt should be used.
b) Tension the pump drivebelt as described in Chapter 2A or 2B, as applicable.
c) Fill the system with new oil or fluid, and then bleed the system as described in the previous Section.

25 Wheel alignment and steering angles - general information

Definitions

1 A car's steering and suspension geometry is defined in three basic settings - all angles are expressed in degrees (toe settings are also expressed as a measurement); the steering axis is defined as an imaginary line drawn through the axis of the suspension strut, extended where necessary to contact the ground.

2 Camber is the angle between each roadwheel and a vertical line drawn through its centre and tyre contact patch, when viewed from the front or rear of the car. "Positive" camber is when the roadwheels are tilted outwards from the vertical at the top; "negative" camber is when they are tilted inwards.

3 Camber angle is adjustable, and can be checked using a camber checking gauge.

4 Castor is the angle between the steering axis and a vertical line drawn through each roadwheel's centre and tyre contact patch, when viewed from the side of the car. "Positive" castor is when the steering axis is tilted so that it contacts the ground ahead of the vertical; "negative" castor is when it contacts the ground behind the vertical.

5 Castor is not adjustable, and is given for reference only; while it can be checked using a castor checking gauge, if the figure obtained

24.6b . . . and lift the reservoir from its mounting

is significantly different from that specified, the car must be taken for careful checking by a professional, as the fault can only be caused by wear or damage to the body or suspension components.

6 Toe is the difference, viewed from above, between lines drawn through the roadwheel centres and the car's centre-line. "Toe-in" is when the roadwheels point inwards, towards each other at the front, while "toe-out" is when they splay outwards from each other at the front.

7 The front wheel toe setting is adjusted by screwing the right-hand track rod in or out of its balljoint, to alter the effective length of the track rod assembly.

8 Rear wheel toe setting is not adjustable, and is given for reference only. While it can be checked, if the figure obtained is significantly different from that specified, the car must be taken for careful checking by a professional, as the fault can only be caused by wear or damage to the body or suspension components.

Checking and adjustment

Front wheel toe setting

9 Due to the special measuring equipment necessary to check the wheel alignment, and the skill required to use it properly, the checking and adjustment of these settings is best left to a VW dealer or similar expert. Note that most tyre-fitting centres now possess sophisticated checking equipment.

10 To check the toe setting, a tracking gauge must first be obtained. Two types of gauge are available, and can be obtained from motor accessory shops. The first type measures the distance between the front and rear inside edges of the roadwheels, as previously described, with the car stationary. The second type, known as a "scuff plate", measures the actual position of the contact surface of the tyre, in relation to the road surface, with the car in motion. This is achieved by pushing or driving the front tyre over a plate, which then moves slightly according to the scuff of the tyre, and shows this movement on a scale. Both types have their advantages and disadvantages, but either can give satisfactory results if used correctly and carefully.

10

25.13 Release the rubber gaiter outer clips and peel back the outer end of the gaiters (arrowed)

11 Make sure that the steering is in the straight-ahead position when making measurements.

12 If adjustment is necessary, apply the handbrake, then jack up the front of the car and support it securely on axle stands (see "*Jacking and vehicle support*"). Adjustment is made on the right-hand track rod (right- and left-hand are as seen from the driver's seat).

13 First clean the track rod threads; if they are corroded, apply penetrating fluid before starting adjustment. Release the rubber gaiter outer clips, peel back the gaiters and apply a smear of grease **(see illustration)**. This will ensure that both gaiters are free and will not be twisted or strained as their respective track rods are rotated.

14 Retain the track rod with a suitable spanner, and slacken the balljoint locknut fully. Alter the length of the track rod, by screwing them into or out of the balljoints. Rotate the track rod using an open-ended spanner fitted to the track rod flats provided; shortening the track rods (screwing them onto their balljoints) will reduce toe-in/increase toe-out.

15 When the setting is correct, hold the track rod and tighten the balljoint locknut to the specified torque setting. If after adjustment, the steering wheel spokes are no longer horizontal when the wheels are in the straight-ahead position, remove the steering wheel and reposition it (see Section 16).

16 Check that the toe setting has been correctly adjusted by lowering the car to the ground and re-checking the toe setting; re-adjust if necessary. Ensure that the rubber gaiters are seated correctly and are not twisted or strained, and secure them in position with the retaining clips; where necessary, fit a new retaining clip (refer to Section 19).

Rear wheel toe setting

17 The procedure for checking the rear toe setting is the same as described for the front setting in paragraph 10. The setting is not adjustable - see paragraph 8.

Front wheel camber angle

18 Checking and adjusting the front wheel camber angle should be entrusted to a VW dealer or other suitably-equipped specialist. Note that most tyre-fitting centres now possess sophisticated checking equipment. For reference, adjustments are made by slackening the suspension strut-to-swivel hub mounting bolts, and repositioning the swivel hub assembly.

Chapter 11
Bodywork and fittings

Contents

Degrees of difficulty

Easy, suitable for novice with little experience		**Fairly easy,** suitable for beginner with some experience		**Fairly difficult,** suitable for competent DIY mechanic		**Difficult,** suitable for experienced DIY mechanic		**Very difficult,** suitable for expert DIY or professional	

Specifications

Torque wrench settings	Nm	lbf ft
Boot lid (Saloon):		
Lock cylinder housing	7	5
Lockbolt	7	5
Striker screw	7	5
Bumper retaining bolts	82	61
Bumper retaining bracket bolts	23	17
Bumper washer jet nuts	14	10
Child bench seat mounting bolts	80	59
Door check strap bolts	7	5
Door check strap hinge	7	5
Door handle screw	7	5
Door hinge bolts	55	41
Door lock screws	20	15
Door lock striker pin	50	37
Door window regulator bolts	7	5
Lock carrier/front cross-panel retaining bolts	5	4
Seat belt anchor bolts	40	30
Seat belt front sliding plate-to-seat frame bolt	20	15
Seat belt front stalk mounting bolt	60	44
Seat belt inertia reel bolt	40	30
Seat belt rear mounting bracket nuts/bolts	23	17
Seat belt-to-height adjuster bolt	23	17
Tailgate (Estate):		
Lock and striker plate screws	23	17
Lock cylinder housing	7	5
Support strut ball stud	20	15
Support strut bracket bolts	7	5

1 General description

Two body types are produced - the four-door Saloon and the five-door Estate. The body is of all-steel construction, and incorporates calculated impact crumple zones at the front and rear, with a central safety cell passenger compartment.

During manufacture, the underbody is treated with underseal, and as a further anti-rust aid, some of the more exposed body panels are galvanised. The bumpers and wheel arch liners are plastic mouldings, for durability and strength.

2 Maintenance - bodywork and underframe

The general condition of a vehicle's bodywork is the one thing that significantly affects its value. Maintenance is easy, but needs to be regular. Neglect, particularly after minor damage, can lead quickly to further deterioration and costly repair bills. It is important also to keep watch on those parts of the vehicle not immediately visible, for instance the underside, inside all the wheel arches, and the lower part of the engine compartment.

The basic maintenance routine for the bodywork is washing - preferably with a lot of water, from a hose. This will remove all the loose solids which may have stuck to the vehicle. It is important to flush these off in such a way as to prevent grit from scratching the finish. The wheel arches and underframe need washing in the same way, to remove any accumulated mud which will retain moisture and tend to encourage rust. Paradoxically enough, the best time to clean the underframe and wheel arches is in wet weather, when the mud is thoroughly wet and soft. In very wet weather, the underframe is usually cleaned of large accumulations automatically, and this is a good time for inspection.

Periodically, except on vehicles with a wax-based underbody protective coating, it is a good idea to have the whole of the underframe

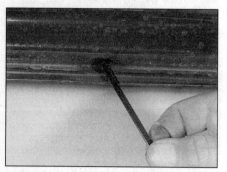

2.4 Check body drain holes are clear

of the vehicle steam-cleaned, engine compartment included, so that a thorough inspection can be carried out to see what minor repairs and renovations are necessary. Steam cleaning is available at many garages, and is necessary for the removal of the accumulation of oily grime, which sometimes is allowed to become thick in certain areas. If steam-cleaning facilities are not available, there are some excellent grease solvents available which can be brush-applied; the dirt can then be simply hosed off. Note that these methods should not be used on vehicles with wax-based underbody protective coating, or the coating will be removed. Such vehicles should be inspected annually, preferably just before Winter, when the underbody should be washed down, and any damage to the wax coating repaired. Ideally, a completely fresh coat should be applied. It would also be worth considering the use of wax-based protection for injection into door panels, sills, box sections, etc, as an additional safeguard against rust damage, where such protection is not provided by the vehicle manufacturer.

After washing paintwork, wipe off with a chamois leather to give an unspotted clear finish. A coat of clear protective wax polish will give added protection against chemical pollutants in the air. If the paintwork sheen has dulled or oxidised, use a cleaner/polisher combination to restore the brilliance of the shine. This requires a little effort, but such dulling is usually caused because regular washing has been neglected. Care needs to be taken with metallic paintwork, as special non-abrasive cleaner/polisher is required to avoid damage to the finish. Always check that the door and ventilator opening drain holes and pipes are completely clear, so that water can be drained out **(see illustration)**. Brightwork should be treated in the same way as paintwork. Windscreens and windows can be kept clear of the smeary film which often appears, by proprietary glass cleaner. Never use any form of wax or other body or chromium polish on glass.

3 Maintenance - upholstery and carpets

Mats and carpets should be brushed or vacuum-cleaned regularly, to keep them free of grit. If they are badly stained, remove them from the vehicle for scrubbing or sponging, and make quite sure they are dry before refitting. Seats and interior trim panels can be kept clean by wiping with a damp cloth. If they do become stained (which can be more apparent on light-coloured upholstery), use a little liquid detergent and a soft nail brush to scour the grime out of the grain of the material. Do not forget to keep the headlining clean in the same way as the upholstery. When using liquid cleaners inside the vehicle, do not over-wet the surfaces being cleaned. Excessive damp could

get into the seams and padded interior, causing stains, offensive odours or even rot. If the inside of the vehicle gets wet accidentally, it is worthwhile taking some trouble to dry it out properly, particularly where carpets are involved. *Do not leave oil or electric heaters inside the vehicle for this purpose.*

4 Minor body damage - repair

Repairs of minor scratches in bodywork

If the scratch is very superficial, and does not penetrate to the metal of the bodywork, repair is very simple. Lightly rub the area of the scratch with a paintwork renovator or a very fine cutting paste to remove loose paint from the scratch, and to clear the surrounding bodywork of wax polish. Rinse the area with clean water.

Apply touch-up paint to the scratch using a fine paint brush; continue to apply fine layers of paint until the surface of the paint in the scratch is level with the surrounding paintwork. Allow the new paint at least two weeks to harden, then blend it into the surrounding paintwork by rubbing the scratch area with a paintwork renovator or a very fine cutting paste. Finally, apply wax polish.

Where the scratch has penetrated right through to the metal of the bodywork, causing the metal to rust, a different repair technique is required. Remove any loose rust from the bottom of the scratch with a penknife, then apply rust-inhibiting paint to prevent the formation of rust in the future. Using a rubber or nylon applicator, fill the scratch with bodystopper paste. If required, this paste can be mixed with cellulose thinners to provide a very thin paste which is ideal for filling narrow scratches. Before the stopper-paste in the scratch hardens, wrap a piece of smooth cotton rag around the top of a finger. Dip the finger in cellulose thinners, and quickly sweep it across the surface of the stopper-paste in the scratch; this will ensure that the surface of the stopper-paste is slightly hollowed. The scratch can now be painted over as described earlier in this Section.

Repairs of dents in bodywork

When deep denting of the vehicle's bodywork has taken place, the first task is to pull the dent out, until the affected bodywork almost attains its original shape. There is little point in trying to restore the original shape completely, as the metal in the damaged area will have stretched on impact, and cannot be reshaped fully to its original contour. It is better to bring the level of the dent up to a point which is about 3 mm below the level of the surrounding bodywork. In cases where the dent is very shallow anyway, it is not worth trying to pull it out at all. If the underside of the dent is accessible, it can be hammered out gently from behind, using a mallet with a wooden or plastic head. Whilst doing this, hold a suitable block of wood firmly against the outside of the panel, to absorb the impact from the hammer blows and thus prevent a large area of the bodywork from being "belled-out".

Should the dent be in a section of the bodywork which has a double skin, or some other factor making it inaccessible from behind, a different technique is called for. Drill several small holes through the metal inside the area - particularly in the deeper section. Then screw long self-tapping screws into the holes, just sufficiently for them to gain a good purchase in the metal. Now the dent can be pulled out by pulling on the protruding heads of the screws with a pair of pliers.

The next stage of the repair is the removal of the paint from the damaged area, and from an inch or so of the surrounding "sound" bodywork. This is accomplished most easily by using a wire brush or abrasive pad on a power drill, although it can be done just as effectively by hand, using sheets of abrasive paper. To complete the preparation for filling, score the surface of the bare metal with a screwdriver or the tang of a file, or alternatively, drill small holes in the affected area. This will provide a good "key" for the filler paste.

To complete the repair, see the Section on filling and respraying.

Repairs of rust holes or gashes in bodywork

Remove all paint from the affected area, and from an inch or so of the surrounding "sound" bodywork, using an abrasive pad or a wire brush on a power drill. If these are not available, a few sheets of abrasive paper will do the job most effectively. With the paint removed, you will be able to judge the severity of the corrosion, and therefore decide whether to renew the whole panel (if this is possible) or to repair the affected area. New body panels are not as expensive as most people think, and it is often quicker and more satisfactory to fit a new panel than to attempt to repair large areas of corrosion.

Remove all fittings from the affected area, except those which will act as a guide to the original shape of the damaged bodywork (eg headlight shells etc). Then, using tin snips or a hacksaw blade, remove all loose metal and any other metal badly affected by corrosion. Hammer the edges of the hole inwards, to create a slight depression for the filler paste.

Wire-brush the affected area to remove the powdery rust from the surface of the remaining metal. Paint the affected area with rust-inhibiting paint; if the back of the rusted area is accessible, treat this also.

Before filling can take place, it will be necessary to block the hole in some way. This can be achieved with aluminium or plastic mesh, or aluminium tape.

Aluminium or plastic mesh, or glass-fibre matting, is probably the best material to use for a large hole. Cut a piece to the approximate size and shape of the hole to be filled, then position it in the hole so that its edges are below the level of the surrounding bodywork. It can be retained in position by several blobs of filler paste around its periphery.

Aluminium tape should be used for small or very narrow holes. Pull a piece off the roll, trim it to the approximate size and shape required, then pull off the backing paper (if used) and stick the tape over the hole; it can be overlapped if the thickness of one piece is insufficient. Burnish down the edges of the tape with the handle of a screwdriver or similar, to ensure that the tape is securely attached to the metal underneath.

Bodywork repairs - filling and respraying

Before using this Section, see the Sections on dent, deep scratch, rust holes and gash repairs.

Many types of bodyfiller are available, but generally speaking, those proprietary kits which contain a tin of filler paste and a tube of resin hardener are best for this type of repair which can be used directly from the tube. A wide, flexible plastic or nylon applicator will be found invaluable for imparting a smooth and well-contoured finish to the surface of the filler.

Mix up a little filler on a clean piece of card or board - measure the hardener carefully (follow the maker's instructions on the pack), otherwise the filler will set too rapidly or too slowly. Using the applicator, apply the filler paste to the prepared area; draw the applicator across the surface of the filler to achieve the correct contour and to level the surface. When a contour that approximates to the correct one is achieved, stop working the paste - if you carry on too long, the paste will become sticky and begin to "pick-up" on the applicator. Continue to add thin layers of filler paste at 20-minute intervals, until the level of the filler is just proud of the surrounding bodywork.

Once the filler has hardened, the excess can be removed using a metal plane or file. From then on, progressively-finer grades of abrasive paper should be used, starting with a 40-grade production paper, and finishing with a 400-grade wet-and-dry paper. Always wrap the abrasive paper around a flat rubber, cork, or wooden block - otherwise the surface of the filler will not be completely flat. During the smoothing of the filler surface, the wet-and-dry paper should be periodically rinsed in water. This will ensure that a very smooth finish is imparted to the filler at the final stage.

At this stage, the "dent" should be surrounded by a ring of bare metal, which in turn should be encircled by the finely "feathered" edge of the good paintwork. Rinse the repair area with clean water, until all the dust produced by the rubbing-down operation has gone.

Spray the whole area with a light coat of primer - this will show up any imperfections in the surface of the filler. Repair these imperfections with fresh filler paste or bodystopper, and again smooth the surface with abrasive paper. If bodystopper is used, it can be mixed with cellulose thinners, to form a thin paste which is ideal for filling small holes. Repeat this spray-and-repair procedure until you are satisfied that the surface of the filler, and the feathered edge of the paintwork, are perfect. Clean the repair area with clean water, and allow to dry fully.

The repair area is now ready for final spraying. Paint spraying must be carried out in a warm, dry, windless and dust-free atmosphere. This condition can be created artificially if you have access to a large indoor working area, but if you are forced to work in the open, you will have to pick your day very carefully. If you are working indoors, dousing the floor in the work area with water will help to settle the dust which would otherwise be in the atmosphere. If the repair area is confined to one body panel, mask off the surrounding panels; this will help to minimise the effects of a slight mis-match in paint colours. Bodywork fittings (eg chrome strips, door handles etc) will also need to be masked off. Use genuine masking tape, and several thickness of newspaper, for the masking operations.

Before starting to spray, agitate the aerosol can thoroughly, then spray a test area (an old tin, or similar) until the technique is mastered. Cover the repair area with a thick coat of primer; the thickness should be built up using several thin layers of paint, rather than one thick one. Using 400 grade wet-and-dry paper, rub down the surface of the primer until it is smooth. While doing this, the work area should be thoroughly doused with water, and the wet-and-dry paper periodically rinsed in water. Allow to dry before spraying on more paint.

Spray on the top coat, again building up the thickness by using several thin layers of paint. Start spraying in the centre of the repair area, and then, using a circular motion, work outwards until the whole repair area and about 2 inches of the surrounding original paintwork is covered. Remove all masking material 10 to 15 minutes after spraying on the final coat of paint.

Allow the new paint at least two weeks to harden, then, using a paintwork renovator or a very fine cutting paste, blend the edges of the paint into the existing paintwork. Finally, apply wax polish.

Plastic components

With the use of more and more plastic body components by the vehicle manufacturers (eg bumpers, spoilers, and in some cases major body panels), rectification of more serious damage to such items has become a matter of either entrusting repair work to a specialist in this field, or renewing complete components. Repair of such damage by the DIY owner is not feasible, owing to the cost of the equipment and materials required for effecting such repairs. The basic technique involves making a groove along the line of the

11

7.2 Bonnet hinge bolts. Note earth strap attached to lower bolt

crack in the plastic, using a rotary burr in a power drill. The damaged part is then welded back together, using a hot air gun to heat up and fuse a plastic filler rod into the groove. Any excess plastic is then removed, and the area rubbed down to a smooth finish. It is important that a filler rod of the correct plastic is used, as body components can be made of a variety of different types (eg polycarbonate, ABS, polypropylene).

Damage of a less serious nature (abrasions, minor cracks etc) can be repaired by the DIY owner using a two-part epoxy filler repair material which can be used directly from the tube. Once mixed in equal proportions, this is used in similar fashion to the bodywork filler used on metal panels. The filler is usually cured in twenty to thirty minutes, ready for sanding and painting.

If the owner is renewing a complete component himself, or if he has repaired it with epoxy filler, he will be left with the problem of finding a suitable paint for finishing which is compatible with the type of plastic used. At one time, the use of a universal paint was not possible, owing to the complex range of plastics met with in body component applications. Standard paints, generally speaking, will not bond to plastic or rubber satisfactorily, but professional matched paints, to match any plastic or rubber finish, can be obtained from some dealers. However, it is now possible to obtain a plastic body parts finishing kit which consists of a pre-primer treatment, a primer and coloured top coat. Full instructions are normally supplied

with a kit, but basically the method of use is to first apply the pre-primer to the component concerned, and allow it to dry for up to 30 minutes. Then the primer is applied, and left to dry for about an hour before finally applying the special-coloured top coat. The result is a correctly coloured component, where the paint will flex with the plastic or rubber, a property that standard paint does not normally possess.

5 Major body damage - repair

Where serious damage has occurred, or large areas need renewal due to neglect, it means that complete new panels will need welding-in, and this is best left to professionals. If the damage is due to impact, it will also be necessary to check completely the alignment of the bodyshell, and this can only be carried out accurately by a VW dealer using special jigs. If the body is left misaligned, it is primarily dangerous, as the car will not handle properly, and secondly, uneven stresses will be imposed on the steering, suspension and possibly transmission, causing abnormal wear, or complete failure, particularly to such items as the tyres.

6 Door rattles - tracing and rectification

1 Check first that the door is not loose at the hinges, and that the latch is holding the door firmly in position. Check also that the door lines up with the aperture in the body. If the door is out of alignment, adjust it as described in Section 23.
2 If the latch is holding the door in the correct position, but the latch still rattles, the lock mechanism is worn and should be renewed.
3 Other rattles from the door could be caused by wear in the window operating mechanism, interior lock mechanism, or loose glass channels.

7 Bonnet - removal, refitting and adjustment

Removal

1 Support the bonnet in its open position, and place some cardboard or rags beneath the corners by the hinges.
2 Mark the location of the hinges with a pencil, then loosen the four retaining bolts (see illustration).
3 Disconnect the windscreen washer tubes from the jets on the bonnet.
4 With the help of an assistant, release the stay, remove the bolts, and withdraw the bonnet from the car.

Refitting and adjustment

5 Refitting is a reversal of removal, but adjust the hinges to their original positions and check that the bonnet is level with the surrounding bodywork. If necessary, adjust the height of the bonnet front edge by screwing the rubber buffers in or out.
6 Check that the bonnet lock operates in a satisfactory manner.

8 Bonnet lock and release cable - removal and refitting

Removal

1 Raise and support the bonnet.
2 Unscrew the lock retaining screws, and lift the lock clear of the front panel. Invert the lock and detach the cable from it (see illustrations).
3 To remove the cable, undo the retaining screws and detach the release handle within the car. Release the cable from the handle (see illustration).
4 Attach a suitable length of strong cord to the inner cable at the operating lever end, then carefully pull the cable through the bulkhead and into the engine compartment. Undo the cord from the cable, and leave the cord ends exposed each side of the bulkhead.

8.2a Undo the retaining bolts . . .

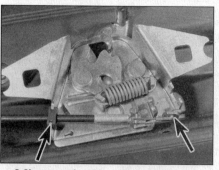

8.2b . . . and remove the bonnet lock. Invert to release cable at points indicated (arrowed)

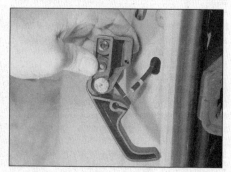

8.3 Bonnet release handle and cable

Detach the cable from the retaining clips in the engine compartment and remove it.

Refitting

5 Refit in the reverse order of removal. Tie the inner end of the cable to the exposed cord in the engine compartment, carefully pull the cable through to the release handle, then untie the cord.

6 When attaching the cable in the engine compartment, ensure that it is re-routed correctly. Check for satisfactory operation of the cable and the lock before closing the bonnet. Ensure that the bonnet locks properly when closed, and also that the safety catch operates when released.

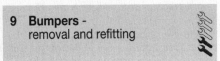

9 Bumpers - removal and refitting

Front bumper

Removal

Note: *Under no circumstances should the vehicle be driven with the front bumper and bumper brackets not securely fitted, as in this condition the front crossmember which supports the engine is no longer properly secured*

1 Undo the screws retaining the lower air inlet grille **(see illustrations)**. Release the retaining lugs, then pivot the grille down and remove it.
2 Detach and remove the spreader pins that secure the bumper to the wheel arch liner each side.
3 Where bumper-mounted foglights are fitted, detach the wiring connector from the rear of each light, referring to Chapter 12 if necessary. On later models with bumper-mounted front direction indicators, refer to Chapter 12 and disconnect the wiring from the indicator light units.
4 Unscrew and remove the bumper retaining

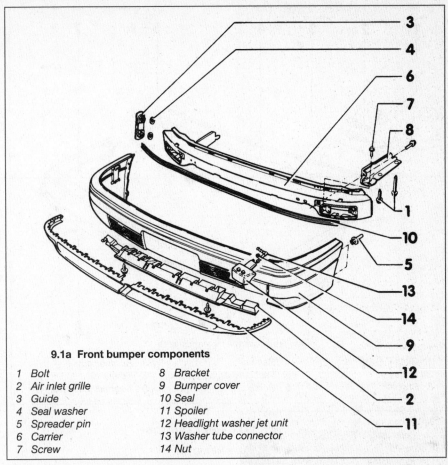

9.1a Front bumper components

1 Bolt	8 Bracket
2 Air inlet grille	9 Bumper cover
3 Guide	10 Seal
4 Seal washer	11 Spoiler
5 Spreader pin	12 Headlight washer jet unit
6 Carrier	13 Washer tube connector
7 Screw	14 Nut

bolts **(see illustration)**. Under no circumstances remove the rearmost bolt attaching the engine supporting crossmember to the body. When the bolts are removed each side, carefully withdraw the bumper unit in a parallel manner from the vehicle. Where headlight washers are fitted, pull the bumper out to the point where the washer hose can be detached from its bumper-to-crosspanel

connection before fully withdrawing the bumper.

Refitting

5 Refit in the reverse order of removal. Tighten the bumper retaining bolts to the specified torque. On completion, check for satisfactory operation of the headlight washers and/or foglights (where applicable).

9.1b Removing a lower air inlet grille screw

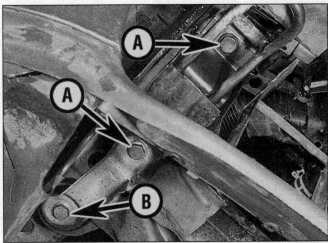

9.4 Front bumper retaining bolts (A) - do not remove bolt (B)

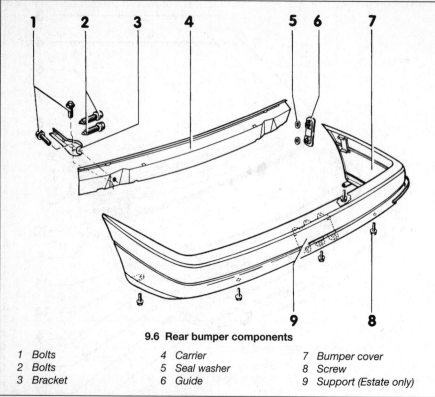

9.6 Rear bumper components

1 Bolts	4 Carrier	7 Bumper cover
2 Bolts	5 Seal washer	8 Screw
3 Bracket	6 Guide	9 Support (Estate only)

Rear bumper

Removal

6 Working underneath the vehicle, unscrew and remove the five bumper-to-underbody retaining screws **(see illustration)**.

7 Working in the luggage area, fold back the floor covering for access, then unscrew and remove the two retaining bolts each side **(see illustration)**. Remove the bumper.

9.7 Rear bumper retaining bolts

Refitting

8 Refit in the reverse order of removal. Loosely fit all retaining bolts and screws before fully tightening them. Tighten the retaining bolts to the specified torque.

10 Lock carrier/front body cross-panel - removal and refitting

Removal

1 Disconnect the battery negative lead. **Note:** *If the vehicle has a security-coded radio, check that you have a copy of the code number before disconnecting the battery. Refer to your VW dealer if in doubt.*

2 Undo the retaining bolts, and detach the bonnet lock from the panel. Move the lock (with the cable still attached) out of the way.

3 Where applicable, loosen off the retaining clip and detach the power steering fluid reservoir from the panel, and position it out of the way.

4 Remove the air inlet grille from the front bumper, as described in Section 9.

5 Referring to Chapter 12 as necessary, disconnect all the wiring connectors from the rear of the upper front light units. On later models, remove both the radiator grille and both headlight units completely (see Section 35 and Chapter 12).

6 Unscrew and remove the two bolts securing the panel to the top of the front wing each side **(see illustration)**.

7 Unscrew and remove the self-tapping screws securing the panel underneath **(see illustrations)**.

8 Unscrew and remove the retaining bolts on each side from underneath, then withdraw the lock carrier/cross-panel.

10.6 Lock carrier/cross-panel-to-front wing retaining bolts

10.7a Self-tapping screw locations (arrowed) underneath the front cross-panel

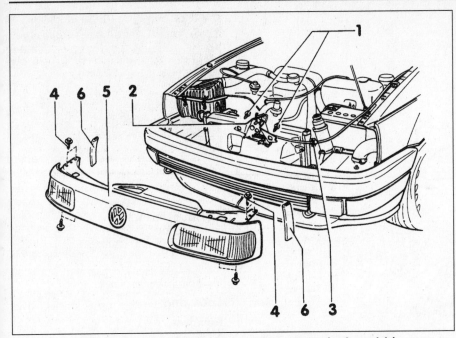

10.7b Lock carrier/front cross-panel components (early models)

1 Self-locking bolts   3 Clip   5 Lock carrier/cross-panel
2 Lock   4 Self-tapping screw   6 Edge protector strips

Refitting

9 Refit in the reverse order of removal. Check the operation of the front lights, and the bonnet lock and safety catch, on completion. Have the headlights checked for correct beam alignment (Chapter 12).

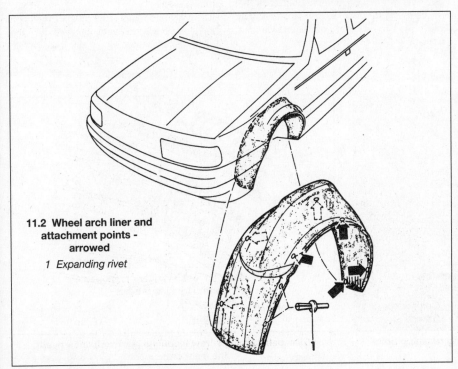

11.2 Wheel arch liner and attachment points - arrowed

1 Expanding rivet

11 Front wheel arch liners - removal and refitting

Removal

1 Chock the rear wheels, apply the handbrake, then loosen the relevant front wheel bolts. Jack up and support the front of the car on axle stands (see *"Jacking and vehicle support"*). Remove the roadwheel on the side concerned.
2 The liner is secured by expanding plastic rivets and screws, at the points indicated (**see illustration**).
3 The rivets may be of the type that have to be prised out, or they may have a central pin that has to be tapped through the rivet first, before the rivet is prised free. In either case, work carefully, as the rivets break easily, in which case they would have to be renewed. Where applicable, recover the expander pins from the rivets for re-use (the pins may fall out when the liner is removed).
4 When applicable, remove the liner securing screws.
5 Lower the liner out of position, and manoeuvre it out from under the front wing. Recover the rivet expander pins, as necessary.

Refitting

6 Refitting is a reversal of removal. Renew any fasteners which were broken on removal. When fitting the expanding-type rivets, place the rivet into position, then insert the expander pin and tap it in until the pin head is flush with the top of the rivet.

12 Boot lid - removal and refitting

Removal

1 Raise the boot lid, and disconnect the wiring connections.
2 Mark the relative fitted positions of the boot lid to its hinge on each side by profiling the hinge position on the lid with a soft lead pencil or felt tip pen.
3 Enlist the aid of an assistant to support the lid, then unscrew and remove the hinge-to-boot lid retaining bolts (**see illustration**), and lift the lid clear.

Refitting

4 Refit in the reverse order of removal. Check the lid for correct alignment, and if necessary loosen off the hinge bolts to adjust, then retighten them.

12.3 Boot lid hinge bolts

11

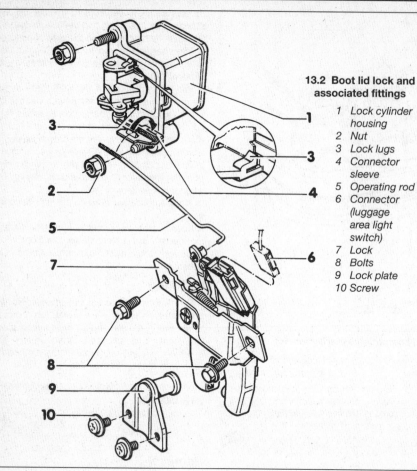

13.2 Boot lid lock and associated fittings

1 Lock cylinder housing
2 Nut
3 Lock lugs
4 Connector sleeve
5 Operating rod
6 Connector (luggage area light switch)
7 Lock
8 Bolts
9 Lock plate
10 Screw

13.3 Boot lid lock and retaining bolts

13 Boot lid lock and lock cylinder - removal and refitting

1 Where applicable, detach and remove the trim from inside the boot lid.

Lock unit

Removal

2 Disconnect the lock operating rod from the lock **(see illustration)**.
3 Mark the fitted position of the lock with a felt tip pen, then unscrew the retaining bolts **(see illustration)** and withdraw the lock unit from the boot lid. As it is withdrawn, disconnect the wiring connector for the luggage compartment light from the lock.

Refitting

4 Refit in the reverse order of removal.

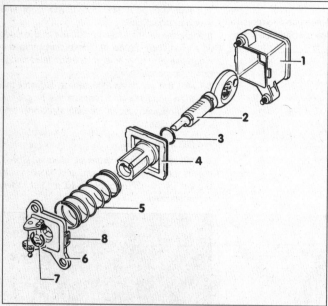

13.5a Boot lid lock cylinder components - except central locking models

1 Cylinder housing (upper)	3 Seal ring
2 Lock cylinder	4 Pushbutton
	5 Pushbutton spring

6 Cylinder housing (lower)
7 Circlip
8 Retainer

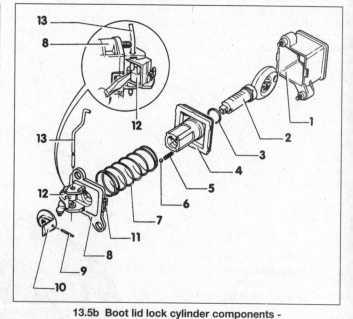

13.5b Boot lid lock cylinder components - central locking models

1 Cylinder housing (upper)
2 Lock cylinder
3 Seal ring
4 Pushbutton

5 Spring
6 Ball
7 Pushbutton spring
8 Cylinder housing (lower)

9 Spring pin
10 Eccentric
11 Retainer
12 Plastic sleeve
13 Operating rod

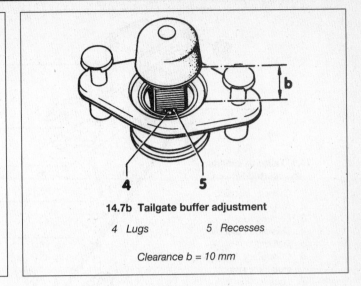

14.7a Tailgate buffer adjustment

1 *Threaded sleeve*   9 *3 mm Allen key*
2 *Spacer rib*

Clearance a = 3 mm

14.7b Tailgate buffer adjustment

4 *Lugs*   5 *Recesses*

Clearance b = 10 mm

Lock cylinder unit

Removal

5 On models with central locking, detach the operating rod by pressing lightly on the plastic side with a screwdriver in slot whilst pulling the rod from the lever **(see illustrations)**.
6 Compress the plastic retainer lugs and withdraw the cylinder from its housing.
7 To dismantle the cylinder on models without central locking, extract and remove the circlip from the cylinder groove, then withdraw the components.
8 On the central locking type cylinder, the assembly components are secured in position by a spring pin. Drive the pin out of the eccentric and cylinder, then insert the key in the lock and withdraw the components of the lock cylinder unit.

Refitting

9 Refit in the reverse order of removal, according to type. Assemble and compress the components of the cylinder unit together so that the retaining circlip or spring pin can be refitted to secure the unit components.
10 When reconnecting the operating rod on central locking models, insert the rod until it is felt to latch into the plastic slide.

14 Tailgate -
removal and refitting

Removal

1 Raise and support the tailgate. Detach and remove the tailgate trim panels.
2 Disconnect the wiring connectors to the tailgate components. Note the routing and attachment locations of the wires.
3 Mark the fitted position of each tailgate hinge using a felt tip pen.
4 Enlist the aid of an assistant to help support the tailgate, then detach the tailgate strut

each side by prising them free from their balljoints (see Section 15).
5 Unscrew and remove the tailgate retaining bolts, and lift the tailgate clear of the vehicle.

Refitting

6 Refit in the reverse order of removal. Check that the tailgate is correctly aligned before fully tightening the tailgate hinge bolts.
7 If it is found that the tailgate buffers need adjustment, carefully lever free the spreader pins from the buffer, and remove the buffer from the tailgate. Remove the rubber pad from the buffer, then using a 3 mm Allen key, turn the securing screw to the limit of the slide, then adjust the threaded sleeve to provide a 3 mm clearance as shown **(see illustration)**. The spacer rib should contact the threaded sleeve. If a new buffer is being fitted, this clearance will already be set. Pull the clamping piece out, then in again so that the lugs engage in the recesses, and the clearance between the housing and the rubber buffer is as shown **(see illustration)**. Refit the buffer, and insert the spreader pin.
8 Gently close the tailgate, then open it again. Now tighten the buffer gently to complete.

15 Tailgate support strut(s) -
removal and refitting

Removal

1 Open the tailgate and support it with a prop (or with the aid of an assistant).
2 Disconnect the strut at the top end balljoint by prising free the clip. Lift, but do not remove, the bottom joint retaining clip, to release the joint **(see illustrations)**.
3 If a strut is defective in operation, it must be renewed. Do not attempt to dismantle and repair the strut.
4 The struts are gas-filled, and if a strut is to be scrapped, it must first be made safe - this should be entrusted to a VW dealer.

Refitting

5 Refit in the reverse order of removal. Ensure that the strut is securely engaged with the balljoints, and test the operation of the tailgate to complete.

15.2a Prise free the clip from the tailgate strut at the top . . .

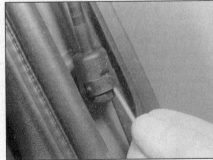

15.2b . . . and lever lower joint clip out to detach it at the bottom end

11

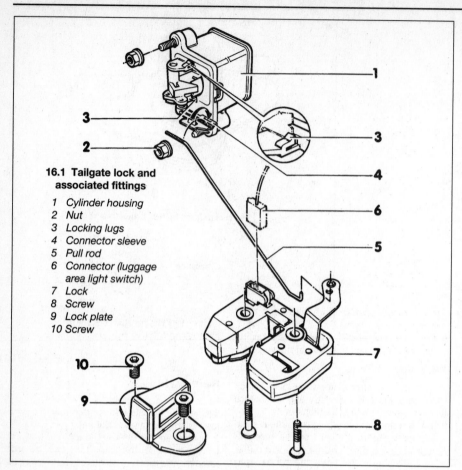

16.1 Tailgate lock and associated fittings

1 Cylinder housing
2 Nut
3 Locking lugs
4 Connector sleeve
5 Pull rod
6 Connector (luggage area light switch)
7 Lock
8 Screw
9 Lock plate
10 Screw

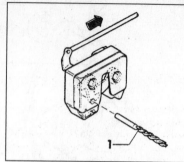

16.2 Tailgate lock setting procedure

Insert 3.2 mm diameter drill or rod into hole Pull operating rod in direction of arrow

16 Tailgate lock and lock cylinder - removal and refitting

1 Refer to Section 13 and proceed as described for the boot lid lock unit and/or the boot lid lock cylinder, as required. The lock components for Estate models are as shown (see illustration).

2 When refitting the lock unit, the operating rod must be set as follows. Insert a 3.2 mm diameter drill or rod into the hole in the lock body, and pull the operating rod as shown (see illustration). Now fit the operating rod to the lock cylinder and close the tailgate. Pull the drill or rod out of the lock body, and check the lock for satisfactory operation.

17 Door trim panel - removal and refitting

Removal

Early models

1 Unscrew and remove the door lock knob from the top of the door. Prise free the knob trim plate (see illustrations).

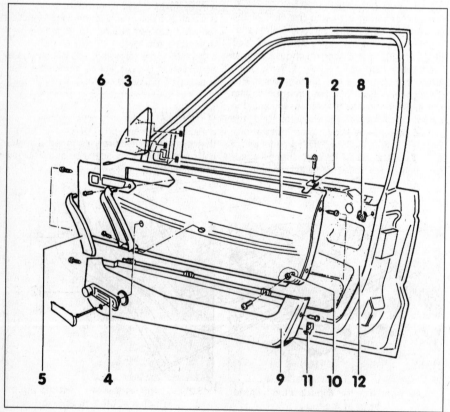

17.1a Front door trim panel components - early models

1 Lock knob
2 Trim plate
3 Trim cover
4 Window regulator handle
5 Inner door pull handle
6 Interior door latch trim plate
7 Trim panel
8 Clip
9 Door pocket
10 Sleeved nut
11 Bracket
12 Insulation sheet

17.1b Front door trim panel components - later models

1   Trim cover (or mirror adjustment switch location)
2   Door pull handle trim cover
3   Door pull handle
4   Screw
5   Screw
6   Triangular trim cover
7   Screw
8   Lock knob
9   Trim plate
10 Trim clip
11 Retaining bracket
12 Screw
13 Trim panel
14 Rubber inlay
15 Door pocket
16 Speaker cover
17 Window regulator handle

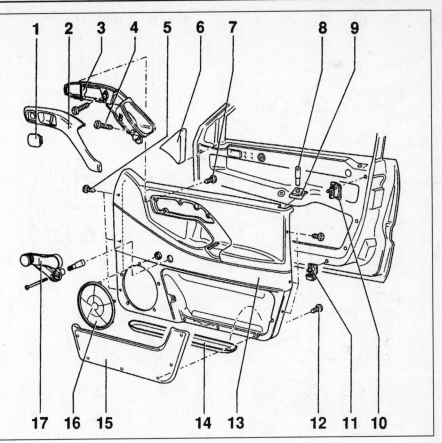

17.1c Rear door trim panel components (early models) - two-piece type shown, one-piece type similar

1   Lock knob
2   Trim plate
3   Trim cover
4   Window regulator handle
5   Inner door pull handle
6   Inner door latch trim plate
7   Trim panel
8   Clip
9   Door pocket
10 Sleeved nut
11 Bracket
12 Insulation sheet

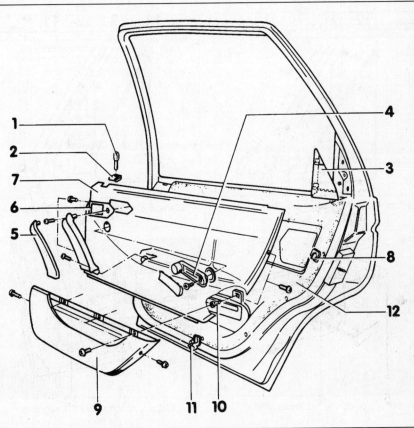

11

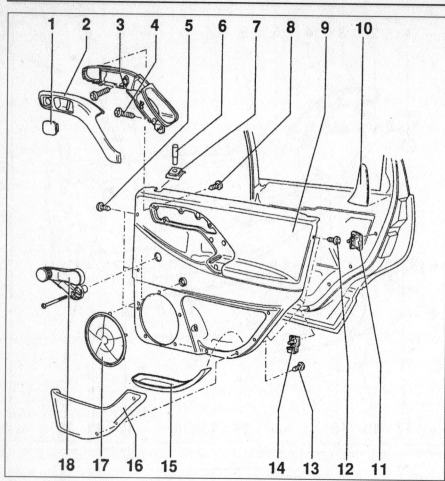

1 Trim cover (or "tweeter" speaker location)	10 Triangular trim cover
2 Door pull handle trim cover	11 Trim clip
3 Door pull handle	12 Screw
	13 Screw
4 Screw	14 Retaining bracket
5 Screw	15 Rubber inlay
6 Lock knob	16 Door pocket
7 Trim plate	17 Speaker cover
8 Screw	18 Window regulator handle
9 Trim panel	

2 Prise free and remove the triangular trim cover from the front door mirror mounting, or from the rear edge of the rear door, as applicable **(see illustrations)**.
3 On manually-operated window regulators, prise free the trim from the regulator handle, then undo the retaining screws and remove the handle. Withdraw the intermediate sleeve **(see illustrations)**.
4 Carefully prise free the trim from the inner door pull handle, then undo its retaining screws and remove the handle **(see illustrations)**.

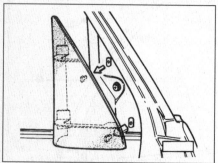

17.2a Rear door triangular trim piece removal - Saloon

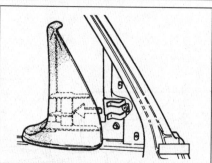

17.2b Rear door triangular trim piece removal - Estate

17.3a Prise free the handle trim . . .

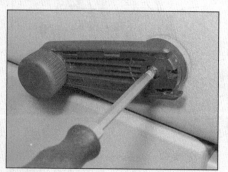

17.3b . . . undo the retaining screw . . .

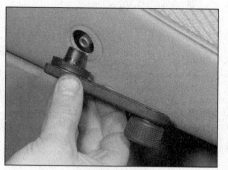

17.3c . . . withdraw the regulator handle . . .

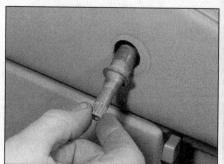

17.3d . . . and the intermediate sleeve

17.4a Prise free the trim from the inner door pull handle

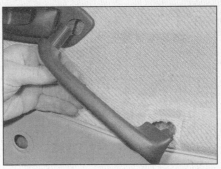

17.4b Removing the inner door pull handle

17.5 Removing the door latch trim plate

5 Slide the door latch trim plate to one side, and detach it from the trim panel **(see illustration)**. Remove the retaining screw and disengage the manual door mirror regulator control, or disconnect the electric mirror wiring, as applicable. On models with electric windows, also disconnect the switch wiring

6 Undo the main trim panel edge screws **(see illustration)**, extract the panel from the window seal slot, then lift it from the door pocket and remove it from the door.

7 Unscrew the retaining screws at each end, and remove the door pocket, where fitted **(see illustrations)**. If applicable, disconnect the speaker wiring.

8 To remove the insulation sheet, drive the expander pins through the clips, and withdraw the clips. Slide free the door lock remote control unit, and disengage the operating rod **(see illustrations)**. Carefully peel back and remove the insulation sheet from the door.

Later models

9 Pull or prise off the mirror adjustment knob from in front of the door lock handle **(see illustration)**. If no mirror adjustment is provided, prise off the trim cover from this location.

10 Prise off the outer cover from the door pull handle, and disconnect the wiring plugs from the mirror and window switches, as applicable **(see illustration)**. Unscrew and remove the screws behind the handle outer cover.

11 On models with manual window regulator handles, unclip the handle cover upwards from the base of the handle, and remove the screw now exposed. Recover the serrated washer. Pull the handle off the splines, noting its fitted position.

12 Prise off the triangular trim piece from the upper front or rear edge of the trim panel.

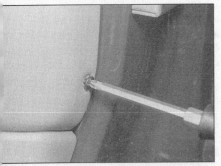

17.6 Removing a trim panel edge screw

17.7a Undo the retaining screws . . .

17.7b . . . and remove the door pocket

17.8a Drive expander pin through to release panel support clip

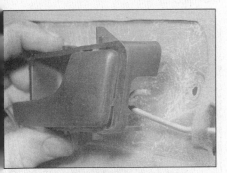

17.8b Remove the door lock remote control unit

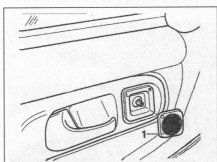

17.9 Mirror adjustment knob (1 - electric mirror type shown) removed from door trim panel

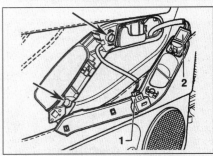

17.10 Door pull handle trim cover removed, showing wiring plugs for window switch (1) and mirror switch (2). Door pull handle retaining screw locations arrowed

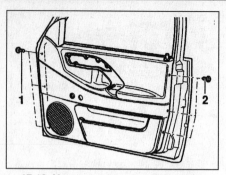

17.13 Unscrew and remove the three screws from the front (1) and rear (2) edges of the trim panel

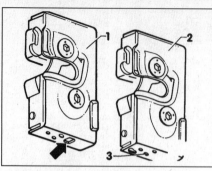

19.3 Door lock types, showing lock lever actuating hole

1 Early type lock, with large hole (arrowed)
2 Later type lock, with small hole (3)

2 Note its orientation, then carefully prise free and remove the lock connection rod.
3 Insert a suitable 3 mm diameter rod up through the appropriate access hole in the base of the lock unit, and move the operating lever to the locked position. One of two lock types will be fitted, the difference being the size of the access hole through which the 3 mm rod is inserted to trip the lock lever **(see illustration)**.
4 Undo the two retaining screws, and withdraw the lock unit from the door **(see illustrations)**. As the lock is removed, disconnect the central locking wiring connector from it, where applicable.

19.4a Undo the retaining screws . . .

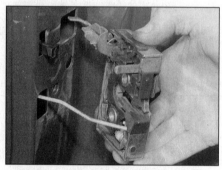

19.4b . . . and withdraw the door lock

Refitting

5 Refitting is a reversal of the removal procedure. When reconnected, check that the free travel of the door handle is between 0.1 and 1.0 mm, measured between the door lock lever and the adjuster. Rotate the adjuster to suit if required.

13 Unscrew and remove the three screws from the front and rear edges of the trim panel **(see illustration)**.
14 Lift the door trim panel up to release it from the window guide channel, and guide it over the lock knob. Where applicable, separate the wiring plugs from the speaker and immobiliser warning light, and remove the panel from the vehicle.
15 To remove the insulation sheet, refer to paragraph 8.

Refitting

16 Refit in the reverse order of removal. Renew any clips that were broken during removal. Ensure that the wiring and connections are secure and correctly routed, clear of the window regulator and latch/lock components.

18 Central locking system - general

Refer to Chapter 12.

19 Door lock - removal and refitting

Removal

1 Fully close the window. Refer to Section 17 and remove the door trim panel and the insulation sheet. Where applicable, unclip and remove the cover over the lock securing screws.

20 Door exterior handle and lock cylinder - removal and refitting

Removal

1 Remove the door inner trim panel, as described in Section 17.
2 Slide the inner lock remote control unit to the side, and disengage it from the door, then disengage the connecting rod from the remote control unit. Carefully peel back the insulation sheet from the door.
3 Unscrew and remove the retaining screw from the rear edge of the door **(see illustration)**. **Note:** *On later models, the right-hand door handle retaining screw has a **left-hand thread** (ie it unscrews **clockwise**).*
4 Detach the central locking multi-plug connector (where applicable), and detach the wire from the retaining clip.
5 Slide the handle to the rear, and disengage it from the door panel. Withdraw the handle, complete with the lock cylinder **(see illustrations)**.

20.3 Remove screw from door rear edge

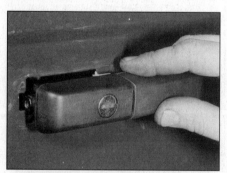

20.5a Slide the handle rearwards . . .

20.5b . . . and disengage it from the door

20.6 Door lock cylinder circlip (arrowed)

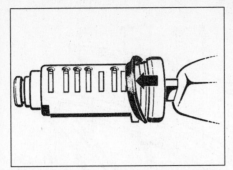

20.7a Seal position on lock cylinder before fitting

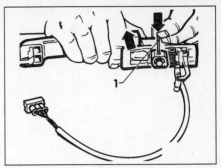

20.7b Spring and ball insertion into lock cylinder using 2.5 mm diameter rod (1)

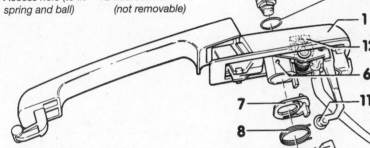

20.8 Door exterior handle and lock cylinder

1 Handle	7 Coupling plate
2 Lock cylinder	8 Spring
3 Seal ring	9 Eccentric
4 Spring	10 Circlip
5 Ball	11 Adjuster
6 Access hole (to fit spring and ball)	12 Microswitch (not removable)

6 To renew the lock cylinder, insert the key in the lock cylinder, then extract the circlip **(see illustration)** and remove the operating lever and spring. Turn the lock cylinder through 180°, then withdraw the lock cylinder and escutcheon from the handle.

7 To fit the new lock cylinder, position the seal on the cylinder as shown **(see illustration)**, with the seal slightly off its seat. Hold the door handle in the "open door" position, and insert the lock cylinder. Coat the ball with grease, and insert it together with the

spring, pushing the ball into position using a rod **(see illustration)**. With the cylinder inserted up to its stop, turn it 90° to the left.
8 The ball should be visible between the cylinder and housing. Check that the cylinder can be turned 70° in each direction, then fit the coupling plate, eccentric and spring. Press the spring ends back a little, and ensure that the spring is in contact with the housing lugs. Insert the circlip into its groove, and ensure that it is fully seated **(see illustration)**. Operate the lock, and check that it returns to its central position.

Refitting

9 Refit the door handle in the reverse order of removal. Check that the handle free play is as given in paragraph 4 of the previous Section.

21 Door window and regulator - removal and refitting

Removal

1 Remove the door trim and insulation as described in Section 17.
2 Lower the window so that the regulator is accessible through the aperture, then unscrew and remove the window-to-regulator bolts **(see illustrations)**.
3 Tilt the window down at the front, and lift it from the door **(see illustration)**.

21.2a Position the window/regulator as shown . . .

21.2b . . . then unscrew the window-to-regulator bolts

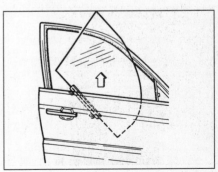

21.3 Window removal from front door

11

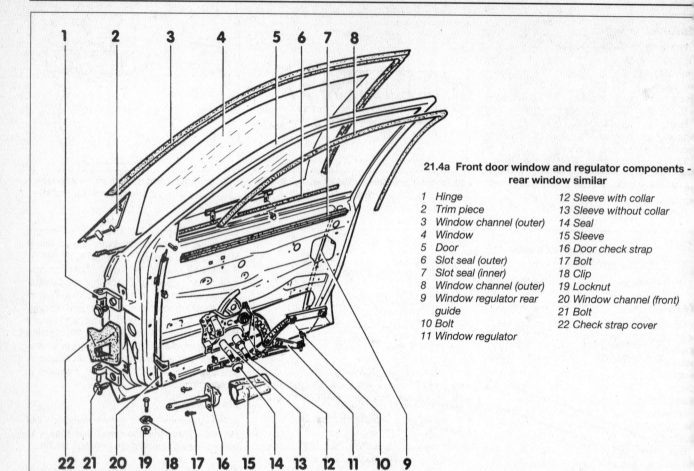

21.4a Front door window and regulator components - rear window similar

1	Hinge	12	Sleeve with collar
2	Trim piece	13	Sleeve without collar
3	Window channel (outer)	14	Seal
4	Window	15	Sleeve
5	Door	16	Door check strap
6	Slot seal (outer)	17	Bolt
7	Slot seal (inner)	18	Clip
8	Window channel (outer)	19	Locknut
9	Window regulator rear guide	20	Window channel (front)
10	Bolt	21	Bolt
11	Window regulator	22	Check strap cover

21.4b Window regulator securing bolt locations - front door

21.4c Window regulator securing bolt locations - rear door

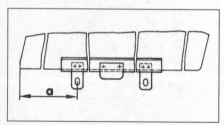

21.5a Front door window-to-lift rail position

a = 303 mm

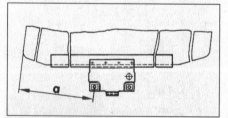

21.5b Rear door window-to-lift rail position

a = 384 mm

4 To remove the regulator, undo its retaining bolts, raise the regulator until the lugs disengage, then extract the regulator down through the door aperture (see illustrations).

Refitting

5 Refit in the reverse order of removal. When the window-to-regulator bolts are fitted, raise and lower the window before fully tightening the bolts. Ensure that the regulator is positioned as shown (see illustrations).

22 Electrically-operated windows - general information and motor renewal

General information

1 Electrically-operated windows are fitted to some models. With this system, the windows can only be raised and lowered when the ignition is switched on.

2 If a fault develops, first check that the thermal cut-out (circuit breaker) is not faulty. The location of the cut-out may be traced by referring to the wiring diagrams at the back of the book.

Motor renewal

The electric motors are attached to the window regulators. If a motor is to be removed, first refer to Section 21 and remove the regulator from the appropriate door. Disconnect the battery negative lead, referring to the Note at the start of Section 28.

Remove the eccentric disc from the regulator assembly by unscrewing the securing bolt **(see illustration)**.

The electric window motor is secured by three Torx screws **(see illustration)**. Remove the screws, separate the motor from the regulator, and disconnect the wiring plug.

Refit in the reverse order to removal.

23 Doors -
removal and refitting

Removal

On models with wiring connections in the door (central locking/electric windows/speaker leads, etc), remove the door trim and insulation panel as described in Section 17. Disconnect the wiring from the door, noting its routing. Label the wiring plugs for identification if necessary.

Unscrew the nut from the pivot pin, extract the pin and detach the door check strap **(see illustration)**.

Get an assistant to support the weight of the door, or support it with blocks. If blocks are used, make sure the door will be securely

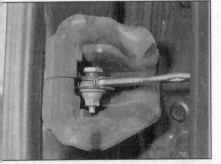

23.2 Door check strap and pivot pin

23.3 Remove the door hinge bolt (arrowed)

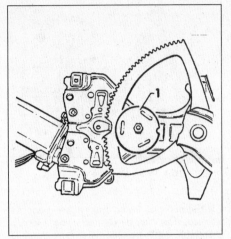

22.4 Electric window motor eccentric disc (1)

supported (it is a heavy and awkward component), and pad the blocks with some rag to prevent damage to the door. Unscrew and remove the bolts from the door hinges **(see illustration)**, then remove the door by lifting it from its hinges.

4 Clean the bolt threads with a wire brush, and the nut threads with a tap, and treat them with thread-locking fluid when refitting the door.

Refitting

5 Refitting is a reversal of the removal procedure. Ensure that any wiring to the door is correctly routed and secured.

6 On completion, shut the door and check it for closure and alignment. Unless the hinges have been disturbed, the alignment should be correct. Check the depth at which the striker enters the lock. If adjustment is required, change the number of washers fitted under the striker head **(see illustration)**.

24 Windscreen, rear window glass and rear side window glass - removal and refitting
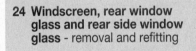

The windscreen, rear window glass, and rear side window glass are directly bonded to

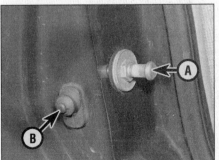

23.6 Front door striker (A) and courtesy light switch (B)

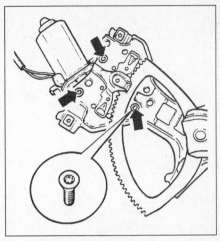

22.5 Electric window motor Torx screws (arrowed)

the metalwork. Their removal and refitting requires the use of special tools not readily available to the home mechanic. This work should therefore be left to a VW dealer, or a specialist glass replacement company.

25 Sunroof -
general

1 A sliding/tilting sunroof is fitted to some models. When fitted correctly, the roof panel in the fully closed position should be level with, or no more than 1.0 mm lower than, the roof panel, at the leading edge. The rear edge must be level with, or no more than 1.0 mm higher than, the roof panel at the rear **(see illustration)**.

2 Removal and refitting, and adjustments to the roof panel, are best entrusted to a VW garage, as specialised tools are required.

3 The sunroof panel motor can be removed and refitted as described in Chapter 12. If the motor malfunctions when the roof panel is in the open position, it can be wound shut manually. To do this, remove the interior light and its mounting panel from the roof, to provide access to the underside of the sunroof motor (see Chapter 12 for details).

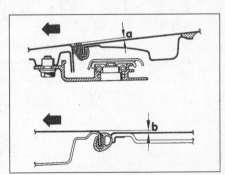

25.1 Sunroof height adjustment at front (a) and rear (b) edges; see text for details (arrow indicates front of car)

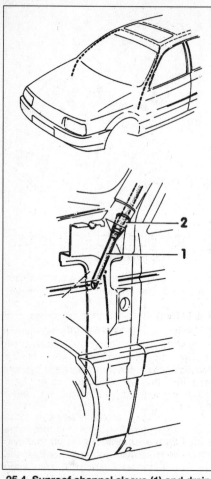

25.4 Sunroof channel sleeve (1) and drain tube (2) at base of A-pillar

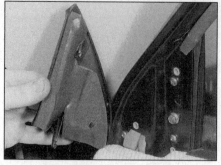

26.1 Prise free the trim . . .

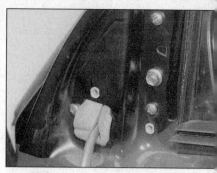

26.2a . . . for access to the mirror screws . . .

4 If the sunroof water drain hoses become blocked, they may be cleared using a length of suitable cable (speedometer drive cable is ideal). The drain tube each side terminates just below the A-pillar, behind the wheel arch liner (see illustration). Probe the tubes with the cable to ensure that they are clear, but take care not to drop the cable down the tube!

26 Door mirror - removal and refitting

Removal

1 Prise free and remove the triangular trim piece from the inside of the door (see illustration).
2 Undo the retaining screws and withdraw the mirror from the door (see illustrations).

26.2b . . . removing the door mirror

3 To completely remove the mirror, refer to Section 17 and remove the door trim panel for access to the manual mirror regulator securing screw, or to the electric mirror wiring plug, as applicable. Remove the screw or disconnect the wiring, and pull the operating cables/electrical wiring out through the top of the door.
4 If required, the mirror glass can be removed and refitted by carefully prising it free from its retaining clips, at the top, then the bottom (see illustration). Use a wide-bladed wooden or plastic wedge between the mirror glass and the housing, and take care not to crack the mirror housing.

⚠ **Warning: Wear gloves and eye protection when carrying out this operation, particularly if the mirror glass is broken.**

5 If a new mirror glass is being fitted, ensure that it is of the correct type. The mirror glass and the housing are identified for type by the trade mark on their rear/underside faces respectively.
6 To fit the glass, simply press it into position; refer to the warning above. Apply pressure carefully to the middle of the glass until it is securely located.

Refitting

7 Refitting the mirror is a reversal of the removal procedure. Check the operation of the mirror adjustment on completion.

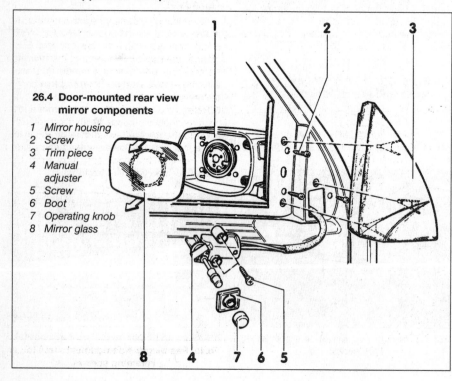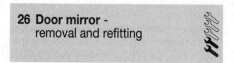

26.4 Door-mounted rear view mirror components

1 Mirror housing
2 Screw
3 Trim piece
4 Manual adjuster
5 Screw
6 Boot
7 Operating knob
8 Mirror glass

27.4 Rear console retaining screws

27 Centre console -
removal and refitting

27.5 Centre console rear extension and associated fittings

1 Manual transmission gear lever gaiter
2 Automatic transmission selector lever panel
3 Lock lugs
4 Guide
5 T-pin

Removal

1 With the handbrake on, prise open the lock tongue at the base of the handbrake grip, and pull the grip free. Withdraw the trim from the handbrake lever.
2 On manual transmission models, unscrew the gear lever knob. On automatic transmission models, undo the grub screw in the end of the lever handle, and lift the handle from the lever. On the 096 automatic transmission, note that the grub screw is smeared with locking fluid, and this makes it difficult to unscrew. When removed, the threads of the grub screw must be cleaned prior to refitting.
3 Detach the gear lever gaiter (or selector lever panel) from the console clips, and withdraw it upwards.

4 Remove the ashtray from the rear end of the console, then undo the two retaining screws in the base of the ashtray recess **(see illustration)**.
5 Remove the console rear extension by pressing down the retaining lugs at the front edge and pulling it rearwards from the console, then up and over the handbrake **(see illustration)**. Disconnect the rear ashtray illumination light lead as the unit is lifted clear.
6 Unscrew and remove the two retaining nuts at the rear of the console front section, and remove the screw each side at the front **(see illustration)**. Partially withdraw the console, detach the front ashtray illumination light lead and the cigar lighter lead, then remove the console.

Refitting

7 Refitting is a reversal of the removal procedure. When fitting the console front section into position, ensure that the two location pegs at the front engage in the facia, and that the two mounting studs are in position under the facia at the rear, before fitting the fixing nuts at the rear.

28 Facia and associated panels
- removal and refitting

Removal

1 Disconnect the battery negative lead. **Note:** *If the vehicle has a security-coded radio, check that you have a copy of the code number before disconnecting the battery. Refer to your VW dealer if in doubt.*
2 Remove the centre console, as described in the previous Section.
3 Refer to Chapter 12, and remove the instrument panel and the radio/cassette unit.
4 Undo the three retaining screws under the top edge, and the lower screws each side, then remove the oddments tray from the passenger side **(see illustrations)**.

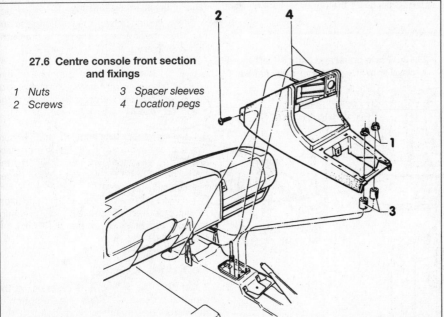

27.6 Centre console front section and fixings

1 Nuts
2 Screws
3 Spacer sleeves
4 Location pegs

28.4a Passenger side oddments tray lower retaining screws

11

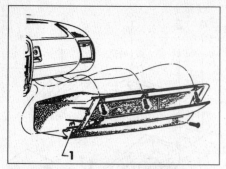

28.4b Passenger side oddments tray and fixings. Take care not to break pins (1) - left-hand-drive version shown

28.5a Removing the lower facia/oddments tray from the driver's side

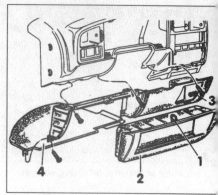

28.5b Driver's side lower facia/oddments tray and fixings - left-hand-drive version shown

1 Quick-release fitting
2 Oddments tray
3 Pins
4 Cover

28.6a Remove the heater control trim plate . . .

28.6b . . . for access to the unit retaining screws

5 Unscrew and remove the retaining screws, and remove the lower facia/oddments tray on the driver's side **(see illustrations)**. The oddments tray fixing is released by turning it through 90°.

6 Carefully prise free the trim panel from the heater control panel, then unscrew and

remove the four screws retaining the heater control panel to the facia **(see illustrations)**. Withdraw the control panel downwards, leaving the control cables attached.

7 On models equipped with a passenger side airbag, refer to Chapter 12 and remove the airbag unit.

8 The manufacturers recommend that the steering column be detached at its upper mounting and lowered out of the way. As this entails drilling out the upper shear-bolts and

renewing them during reassembly (see Chapter 10), we left the column in position, but removed the steering wheel (see Chapter 10) and found that it was still possible to remove the facia. However, access to some components in the column area is more restricted using this method.

9 Take a note of the various connections and cable harness routings, and detach the wires from their facia and associated connections. At the fusebox/relay plate, only detach those items that are attached to the instrument panel loom. The clip retainers from the instrument panel wiring loom should not be opened.

10 Prise free the plastic covers at each end of the facia panel, and undo the retaining screws **(see illustrations)**.

11 Pull out the retaining clips securing the facia at the air intake housing.

28.10a Prise free the plastic covers . . .

28.10b . . . and remove the screws at each end

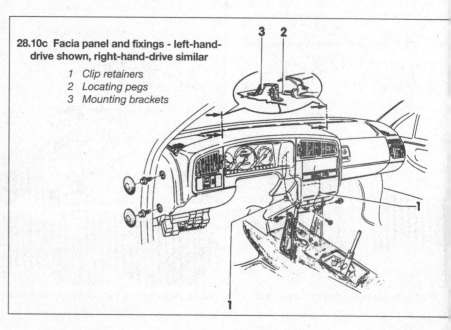

28.10c Facia panel and fixings - left-hand-drive shown, right-hand-drive similar

1 Clip retainers
2 Locating pegs
3 Mounting brackets

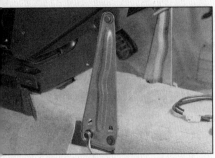

28.12 Detach facia floor-mounted support arms

12 The facia should now be held in position by the floor-mounted support arms. Enlist the aid of an assistant to support the facia, then unscrew and remove the support arm bolt at the top, and the forward bolt at the bottom (see illustration). Loosen off the rear bolt at the bottom, and pivot the arms back clear of the facia. Carefully withdraw the facia unit, checking that all fixings and wires are detached from it.

Refitting

13 Refitting is a reversal of the removal process. Ensure that the wiring harnesses are correctly re-routed before offering the facia into position. As it is fitted, guide the two locating pegs at the front of the facia into engagement with the holes in the mounting brackets. Ensure that all wiring connections are securely made. If the steering column was lowered, reconnect it as described in Chapter 10.

30.1 Interior rear view mirror removal/refitting

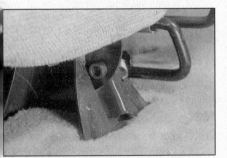

31.2 Front seat front retaining bolt

29.2a Remove the vent grille . . .

29 Glovebox -
removal and refitting

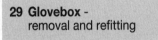

Note: *Later models equipped with a passenger side airbag do not have a glovebox.*

Removal

1 Empty the oddments tray and the glovebox.
2 Carefully pull free the air vent swivel grille, then unscrew and remove the grille housing from the facia above the glovebox (see illustrations).
3 Undo the three retaining screws (see illustration), and partially withdraw the glovebox so that the illumination light wire can be detached, then remove the glovebox.

Refitting

4 Refit in the reverse order of removal.

30 Interior mirror -
removal and refitting

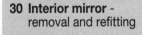

1 Rotate the mirror support arm 15° to 20°, and withdraw the mirror from the mounting (see illustration).
2 To refit, position the support arm at 15° to 20° from vertical, then turn it to the point where the lock spring is felt to engage.
3 If the mirror mounting plate becomes detached, clean away the old glue, then apply a suitable glass-to-metal glue in accordance with the glue manufacturer's instructions, and refit the mounting plate into position. Ensure

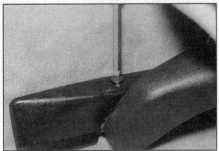

31.3a Remove the side runner trim screw (inboard runner)

29.2b . . . then undo the retaining screw and remove the grille housing

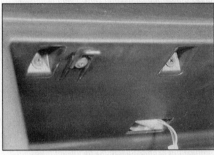

29.3 Glovebox retaining screws

that the plate is correctly orientated, so that when the mirror is fully fitted to it, the mirror support arm is vertical.

31 Seats -
removal and refitting

Front seat
Removal

1 Release the retaining clips, and pull the headrest from the seat being removed.
2 Move the seat back, and unscrew the domed nut securing the central runner and seat at the front. Withdraw the retaining bolt (see illustration).
3 Move the seat fully forwards, then undo the side runner trim screw each side. Withdraw the trim rearwards from the track. It will also be necessary to extract the flat wedge from the stop trim on the outer runner, in order to remove the stop and runner trim on that side (see illustrations).

31.3b Extract the wedge from the stop on the outer seat runner

11

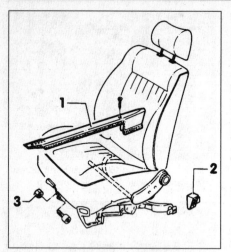

31.4 Front seat and fittings

1 Trim strip   2 Stop trim   3 Nut

4 Slide the seat to the rear, and disengage it from the runners each side. Remove it from the vehicle (see illustration).

Refitting

5 Refit the seat in the reverse order of removal.

Rear seat (non-adjustable type)

Removal

6 Pivot the backrest forwards for access, then unscrew and remove the socket-head screw each side (see illustration). Where a divided backrest is fitted, also undo the centre

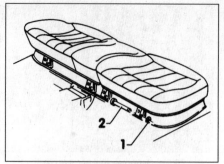

31.6 Non-adjustable rear seat, showing circlip (1) and hinge pins (2)

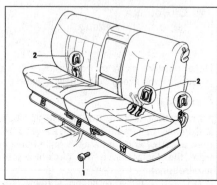

31.10 Adjustable rear seat, showing socket-head screw (1) and lock clips (2)

mounting bolt. Push the backrest downwards at an angle, and disengage it from the seat support brackets.

7 To remove the seat squab, release the circlips and withdraw the hinge pins.

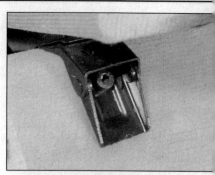

31.9 Adjustable type rear seat front mounting bolt

31.11 Underside of adjustable rear seat, showing adjuster cable and lever

Refitting

8 Refit the seat in the reverse order of removal.

Rear seat (adjustable type)

Removal

9 Undo the socket-head screws (or bolts from the front mountings (see illustration. Move the seat squab forwards, and fold dow the backrest.

10 Release the lock clips (see illustration prise the outer pivot bracket from the pin eac side, and remove the seat.

11 If required, the seat adjuster lever cable can be released by disengaging the inne cable from the runner catches and adjuste lever. Undo the nylon nuts, and detach th outer cable from the locating brackets (se illustration).

12 Refit the cable (if removed) in the revers order to removal. Ensure that the catch retur springs are fully engaged, and check th adjuster mechanism for satisfactory operatio before refitting the seat.

Refitting

13 Refit the seat in the reverse order o removal. Initially locate the lugs of the fron securing tab with the cross support.

Child bench seat

14 A child bench seat may be fitted to late Estate models (see illustration). If required we understand that the seat can be fitted t any Estate model - refer to your VW dealer.

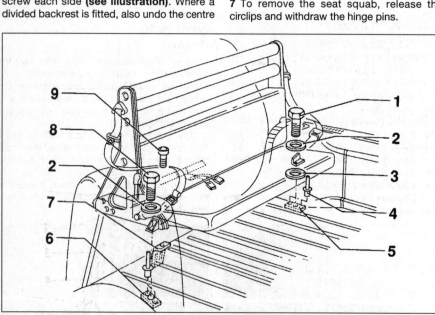

31.14 Child bench seat and fittings

1 Mounting bolt (7/16 x 25)	*5 Reinforcement plate (under luggage floor)*
2 Washer	*6 Reinforcement plate (in longitudinal member)*
3 Spacer	
4 Self-tapping screw or pop-rivet	

7 Backrest centre mounting bracket
8 Mounting bolt (7/16 x 35)
9 Screw

32 Interior trim - removal and refitting

Interior trim panels

Removal

The interior trim panels are secured using either screws or various types of trim fasteners, usually studs or clips (see illustration).

Check that there are no other panels overlapping the one to be removed; usually there is a sequence that has to be followed, and this will only become obvious on close inspection.

Remove all obvious fasteners, such as screws. If the panel will not come free, it is held by hidden clips or fasteners. These are usually situated around the edge of the panel and can be prised up to release them; note, however that they can break quite easily so replacements should be available. The best way of releasing such clips without the correct type of tool, is to use a large flat-bladed screwdriver. Note in many cases that the adjacent sealing strip must be prised back to release a panel.

When removing a panel, never use excessive force or the panel may be damaged; always check carefully that all fasteners or other relevant components have been removed or released before attempting to withdraw a panel.

Refitting

Refitting is the reverse of the removal procedure; secure the fasteners by pressing them firmly into place and ensure that all disturbed components are correctly secured to prevent rattles.

Carpets

The passenger compartment floor carpet is in one piece and is secured at its edges by screws or clips, usually the same fasteners used to secure the various adjoining trim panels.

Carpet removal and refitting is reasonably straightforward but very time-consuming because all adjoining trim panels must be removed first, as must components such as the seats, the centre console and seat belt lower anchorages.

Headlining

The headlining is clipped to the roof and can be withdrawn only once all fittings such as the grab handles, sun visors, sunroof (if fitted), windscreen and rear quarter windows and related trim panels have been removed and the door, tailgate and sunroof aperture sealing strips (as applicable) have been prised clear.

Note that headlining removal requires considerable skill and experience if it is to be carried out without damage and is therefore best entrusted to an expert.

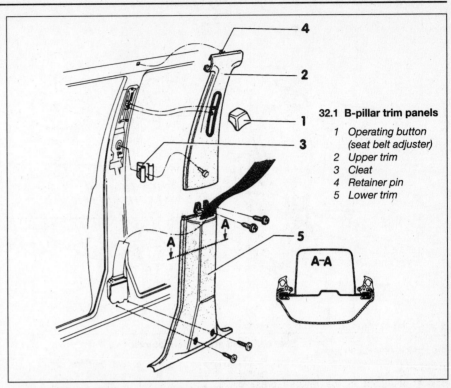

32.1 B-pillar trim panels

1 *Operating button (seat belt adjuster)*
2 *Upper trim*
3 *Cleat*
4 *Retainer pin*
5 *Lower trim*

33 Front seat belt tensioning mechanism - general information

Later models are fitted with a front seat belt tensioner system. The system is designed to instantaneously take up any slack in the seat belt in the case of a sudden frontal impact, therefore reducing the possibility of injury to the front seat occupants. Each front seat is fitted with its own system, the tensioner being situated behind the lower B-pillar trim panel (see illustration).

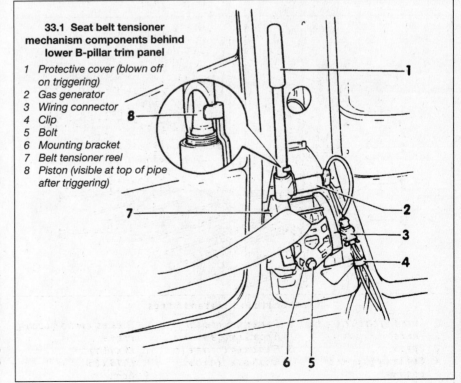

33.1 Seat belt tensioner mechanism components behind lower B-pillar trim panel

1 *Protective cover (blown off on triggering)*
2 *Gas generator*
3 *Wiring connector*
4 *Clip*
5 *Bolt*
6 *Mounting bracket*
7 *Belt tensioner reel*
8 *Piston (visible at top of pipe after triggering)*

11

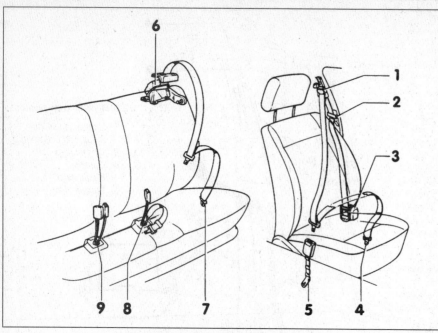

34.3a Seat belts and attachment points

1 Front belt height
  adjuster
2 Guide
3 Inertia reel

4 Front belt anchor
5 Belt stalk
6 Rear belt inertia reel
7 Rear belt anchor

8 Lap belt and single
  belt stalk
9 Double belt stalk

The seat belt tensioner is triggered by a frontal impact above a pre-determined force. Lesser impacts, including impacts from behind, will not trigger the system. The impact sensors are bolted to the chassis longitudinal members in the engine compartment.

When the system is triggered, the explosive gas in the tensioner mechanism retracts and locks the seat belt through a cable which act on the inertia reel. This prevents the seat be moving and keeps the occupant firmly position in the seat. Once the tensioner ha been triggered, the seat belt will b permanently locked and the assembly mus be renewed, together with the impac sensors.

There is a risk of injury if the system triggered inadvertently when working on th vehicle, and it is therefore strongl recommended that any work involving th seat belt tensioner system is entrusted to VW dealer. Note the following warnings befor contemplating any work on the front sea belts.

⚠ **Warning:** Do not expose th tensioner mechanism t temperatures in excess o 100° C (212° F).

Always disconnect the battery negativ lead before working on the seat belts (refe to the Note at the start of Section 28).

If the tensioner mechanism is dropped, must be renewed, even it has suffered n apparent damage.

Do not allow any solvents to come int contact with the tensioner mechanism.

Do not attempt to open the tensione mechanism as it contains explosive gas.

Tensioners must be discharged befor they are disposed of, but this task shoul be entrusted to a VW dealer.

34 Seat belts -
general

Note: On later models equipped with fron seat belt tensioners, refer to the warnings i Section 33 before working on the front sea belts.

1 Periodically check the belts for fraying o other damage. If evident, renew the belt.
2 If the belts become dirty, wipe them with damp cloth, using a little liquid detergent only
3 Check the tightness of the anchor bolts (see illustrations), and if they are eve disconnected, make quite sure that th original sequence of fitting of washers bushes, and anchor plate is retained.
4 Access to the front belt height adjuster an inertia reel units can be made by removing th trim from the B-pillar on the side concerne (see illustrations).
5 The rear seat belt anchorages can be checked by removing the rear seat squab Access to the rear seat inertia reel units (see illustrations) is made by removing the rea seat backrest and the luggage area side trim.
6 The torque wrench settings for the seat bel anchor bolts and other attachments are give in the Specifications at the start of this Chapter.
7 Never modify the seat belts, or alter the attachments to the body, in any way.

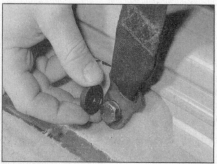

34.3b Front seat belt anchor bolt

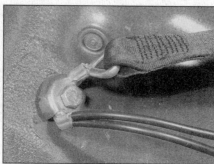

34.3c Rear seat belt anchor bolt

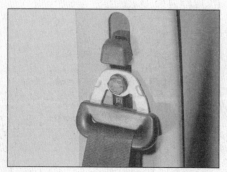

34.4a Front seat belt height adjuster

34.4b Lower B-pillar trim screws and belt guide

34.4c Front seat belt inertia reel unit and
mounting bolt

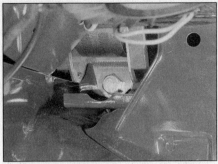

34.5a Rear seat belt inertia reel unit and
mounting bolt - Saloon model

34.5b Rear seat belt inertia reel unit and
mounting bolt - Estate model

35 Radiator grille (later models)
- removal and refitting

Removal

1 To remove the radiator grille fitted to later
models, first raise and support the bonnet.

2 Using a suitable screwdriver, carefully push
back the grille retaining lugs **(see illustration)**.
Take care not to break the lugs or damage the
grille during this operation.
3 The grille can now be manoeuvred out of
position.

Refitting

4 Refitting is a reversal of removal. Ensure
that the retaining lugs engage securely.

35.2 Radiator grille retaining lug locations
(arrowed)

Chapter 12
Body electrical system

Contents

Degrees of difficulty

	Easy, suitable for novice with little experience		Fairly easy, suitable for beginner with some experience		Fairly difficult, suitable for competent DIY mechanic		Difficult, suitable for experienced DIY mechanic		Very difficult, suitable for expert DIY or professional

Specifications

System type	12 volt, negative earth

Bulbs

	Wattage
Brake light (separate)	21
Brake and tail lights	21/5
Foglight (rear)	21
Headlights:	
Single bulb	60/55 (H4 type)
Twin bulbs	55 (H1 type)
Indicators	21
Number plate light	5
Reversing light	21
Sidelights	4
Tail light (separate)	5

Wiper blades

Type:	
Front	Champion X53
Rear (Estate)	Champion X41

Torque wrench settings

	Nm	lbf ft
Airbag unit securing screws (driver's side)	9	7
Rear window wiper mounting bolts	5	4
Rear window wiper mounting bracket bolts	5	4
Windscreen wiper arm nuts	16	12
Windscreen wiper connecting lever nut	7	5
Windscreen wiper crank arm/connecting rod nut	22	16
Windscreen wiper frame bolt	5	4
Wiper arm nut	16	12
Wiper arm spacer nut	7	5

12

1 General information and precautions

Warning: Before carrying out any work on the electrical system, read through the precautions given in "Safety first!" at the beginning of this manual, and in Chapter 5.

The electrical system is of 12-volt negative earth type. Power for the lights and all electrical accessories is supplied by a lead/acid type battery which is charged by the alternator.

This Chapter covers repair and service procedures for the various electrical components not associated with the engine. Information on the battery, alternator and starter motor can be found in Chapter 5A.

It should be noted that prior to working on any component in the electrical system, the battery negative terminal should first be disconnected to prevent the possibility of electrical short-circuits and/or fires. **Note:** *If the vehicle has a security-coded radio, check that you have a copy of the code number before disconnecting the battery. Refer to your VW dealer if in doubt.*

2 Electrical fault-finding - general information

Note: *Refer to the precautions given in "Safety first!" and in Chapter 5 before starting work. The following tests relate to testing of the main electrical circuits, and should not be used to test delicate electronic circuits (such as anti-lock braking systems), particularly where an electronic control unit is used.*

General

A typical electrical circuit consists of an electrical component, any switches, relays, motors, fuses, fusible links or circuit breakers related to that component, and the wiring and connectors which link the component to both the battery and the chassis. To help to pinpoint a problem in an electrical circuit, wiring diagrams are included at the end of this Chapter.

Before attempting to diagnose an electrical fault, first study the appropriate wiring diagram to obtain a complete understanding of the components included in the particular circuit concerned. The possible sources of a fault can be narrowed down by noting if other components related to the circuit are operating properly. If several components or circuits fail at one time, the problem is likely to be related to a shared fuse or earth connection.

Electrical problems usually stem from simple causes, such as loose or corroded connections, a faulty earth connection, a blown fuse, a melted fusible link, or a faulty relay (refer to Section 3 for details of testing relays). Visually inspect the condition of all fuses, wires and connections in a problem circuit before testing the components. Use the wiring diagrams to determine which terminal connections will need to be checked in order to pinpoint the trouble-spot.

The basic tools required for electrical fault-finding include a circuit tester or voltmeter (a 12-volt bulb with a set of test leads can also be used for certain tests); a self-powered test light (sometimes known as a continuity tester); an ohmmeter (to measure resistance); a battery and set of test leads; and a jumper wire, preferably with a circuit breaker or fuse incorporated, which can be used to bypass suspect wires or electrical components. Before attempting to locate a problem with test instruments, use the wiring diagram to determine where to make the connections.

To find the source of an intermittent wiring fault (usually due to a poor or dirty connection, or damaged wiring insulation), a "wiggle" test can be performed on the wiring. This involves wiggling the wiring by hand to see if the fault occurs as the wiring is moved. It should be possible to narrow down the source of the fault to a particular section of wiring. This method of testing can be used in conjunction with any of the tests described in the following sub-Sections.

Apart from problems due to poor connections, two basic types of fault can occur in an electrical circuit - open-circuit, or short-circuit.

Open-circuit faults are caused by a break somewhere in the circuit, which prevents current from flowing. An open-circuit fault will prevent a component from working, but will not cause the relevant circuit fuse to blow.

Short-circuit faults are caused by a "short" somewhere in the circuit, which allows the current flowing in the circuit to "escape" along an alternative route, usually to earth. Short-circuit faults are normally caused by a breakdown in wiring insulation, which allows a feed wire to touch either another wire, or an earthed component such as the bodyshell. A short circuit fault will normally cause the relevant circuit fuse to blow.

Finding an open-circuit

To check for an open-circuit, connect one lead of a circuit tester or voltmeter to either the negative battery terminal or a known good earth.

Connect the other lead to a connector in the circuit being tested, preferably nearest to the battery or fuse.

Switch on the circuit, bearing in mind that some circuits are live only when the ignition switch is moved to a particular position.

If voltage is present (indicated either by the tester bulb lighting or a voltmeter reading, as applicable), this means that the section of the circuit between the relevant connector and the battery is problem-free.

Continue to check the remainder of the circuit in the same fashion.

When a point is reached at which no voltage is present, the problem must lie between that point and the previous test point with voltage. Most problems can be traced to a broken, corroded or loose connection.

Finding a short-circuit

To check for a short-circuit, first disconnect the load(s) from the circuit (loads are the components which draw current from a circuit, such as bulbs, motors, heating elements, etc).

Remove the relevant fuse from the circuit, and connect a circuit tester or voltmeter to the fuse connections.

Switch on the circuit, bearing in mind that some circuits are live only when the ignition switch is moved to a particular position.

If voltage is present (indicated either by the tester bulb lighting or a voltmeter reading, as applicable), this means that there is a short-circuit.

If no voltage is present, but the fuse still blows with the load(s) connected, this indicates an internal fault in the load(s).

Finding an earth fault

The battery negative terminal is connected to "earth:"- the metal of the engine/transmission and the car body - and most systems are wired so that they only receive a positive feed, the current returning through the metal of the car body. This means that the component mounting and the body form part of that circuit. Loose or corroded mountings can therefore cause a range of electrical faults, ranging from total failure of a circuit, to a puzzling partial fault. In particular, lights may shine dimly (especially when another circuit sharing the same earth point is in operation), motors (eg. wiper motors or the radiator cooling fan motor) may run slowly, and the operation of one circuit may have an apparently unrelated effect on another. Note that on many vehicles, earth straps are used between certain components, such as the engine/transmission and the body, usually where there is no metal-to-metal contact between components due to flexible rubber mountings, etc.

To check whether a component is properly earthed, disconnect the battery and connect one lead of an ohmmeter to a known good earth point. Connect the other lead to the wire or earth connection being tested. The resistance reading should be zero; if not, check the connection as follows.

If an earth connection is thought to be faulty, dismantle the connection and clean back to bare metal both the bodyshell and the wire terminal or the component earth connection mating surface. Be careful to remove all traces of dirt and corrosion, then use a knife to trim away any paint, so that a clean metal-to-metal joint is made. On reassembly, tighten the joint fasteners securely; if a wire terminal is being refitted, use serrated washers between the terminal and the bodyshell to ensure a clean and secure connection. When the connection is remade, prevent the onset of corrosion in the future by applying a coat of petroleum jelly or silicone-based grease or by spraying on (at regular intervals) a proprietary ignition sealer or a water dispersant lubricant.

3 Fuses and relays - general information

Main fuses

1 The fuses are located on a single panel in the lower facia on the driver's side.

2 Access to the fuses is gained either by lifting off and removing the oddments tray from the lower facia, or by simply pulling open the cover panel on later models **(see illustrations)**.

3 The main fuses are located in a row below the relays. The fuses are numbered, and the circuits which they protect are listed on the rear face of the oddments tray or panel **(see illustrations)**. A list of fuses also appears on page 12•26 at the end of this Chapter.

4 On some models (depending on specification), some additional fuses are located in separate holders above the main fuses or above the relays.

5 To remove a fuse, first switch off the circuit concerned (or the ignition), then pull the fuse out of its terminals. Plastic tweezers are supplied next to the fuse/relay panel to remove the fuses for inspection and renewal. The wire within the fuse should be visible; if the fuse is blown it will be broken or melted.

6 Always renew a fuse with one of an identical rating; never use a fuse with a different rating from the original or substitute anything else. Never renew a fuse more than once without tracing the source of the trouble. The fuse rating is stamped on top of the fuse; note that the fuses are also colour-coded for easy recognition.

7 If a new fuse blows immediately, find the cause before renewing it again; a short to earth as a result of faulty insulation is most

3.2a On early models, unclip and remove the oddments tray for access to the fuses

likely. Where a fuse protects more than one circuit, try to isolate the defect by switching on each circuit in turn (if possible) until the fuse blows again. Always carry a supply of spare fuses of each relevant rating on the vehicle, a spare of each rating should be clipped into the base of the fusebox.

Fusible links

8 On diesel models, the glow plug electrical supply circuit is protected by a fusible link. The link is located in the engine compartment, either above the brake servo or on the glow plug control unit next to the washer reservoir. If this link has melted, this indicates a serious wiring fault - renewing the link should **not** be attempted without first diagnosing the reason why it failed.

9 Prior to renewing the link, first ensure that the ignition switch is turned off. Ensure that the driver's door is securely shut - the door switch is used to operate the glow plug system on models with the AAZ engine. Unclip the cover to gain access to the metal link. Slacken the retaining screws, then slide the link out of position.

10 Fit the new link (noting the information given in paragraphs 6 and 7) then tighten its retaining screws securely and clip the cover into position.

Relays

11 The relays are of sealed construction, and cannot be repaired if faulty. The relays are of the plug-in type, and may be removed by pulling directly from their terminals. On some

3.2b On later models, the fuses are accessed by pulling open the cover panel

of the relays located behind the facia, it is necessary to prise the two plastic clips outwards before removing the relay.

12 If a circuit or system controlled by a relay develops a fault and the relay is suspect, operate the system; if the relay is functioning, it should be possible to hear it click as it is energised. If this is the case, the fault lies with the components or wiring of the system. If the relay is not being energised, then either the relay is not receiving a main supply or a switching voltage, or the relay itself is faulty. Testing is by the substitution of a known good unit, but be careful; while some relays are identical in appearance and in operation, others look similar but perform different functions.

13 To renew a relay, first ensure that the ignition switch is off. The relay can then simply be pulled out from the socket and the new relay pressed in.

Fuse/relay panel

14 The fuse/relay panel can be removed by pressing the retaining clip each side so that the engagement pins can be pulled from the recess in the support. The clips can then be swung forward and pulled free from the relay panel pins **(see illustration)**. Withdraw the fuse/relay unit by prising out the support arms to release the panel pins from the holes in the support arms, and pull the unit free.

3.3a Fuse and relay panel

3.3b Fuse number/circuit identification table on reverse side of cover panel/oddments tray

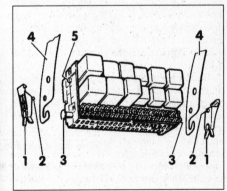

3.14 Fuse and relay unit

1 Securing clips   4 Support arms
2 Retaining pins   5 Pin
3 Plate pins

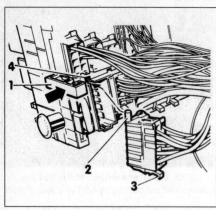

3.15 Multi-plug installation to fuse/relay panel

1 Locking slide   3 Retaining lug
2 Lock pins   4 Lock pin recess

15 To detach the multi-pin plug from the rear of the fuse/relay panel, grip and pull the retainer slide out about 5 mm. Press the multi-pin plug securing lug to release the relay panel socket **(see illustration)**.

16 When refitting the plugs, ensure that they are fitted as far in as possible, and that the securing lugs engage. Fit the lock slide against its stop (all of the plugs must be fully engaged to enable the slide to fully enter and lock in position).

4 Ignition switch/steering column lock - removal and refitting

Removal

1 Disconnect the battery negative lead (refer to Section 1).

2 Remove the steering wheel as described in Chapter 10.

3 Remove the steering column combination switch as described in Section 5.

4 Pull and withdraw the clamping ring, spring and contact ring from the column **(see illustration)**.

5 Undo the retaining screws from the lock housing clamp, then withdraw the lock housing up the column and remove it.

6 To renew the lock, mark the housing at the points indicated **(see illustration)**, then carefully drill a 3 mm diameter hole to a depth of 3 mm at the point of the 'a' to 'b' intersection. Drill the housing until the cylinder lock spring is visible, then press the spring in, and pull out the lock cylinder. The shank end of the drill is ideal to compress the spring with.

Refitting

7 Insert the new lock cylinder into position in the housing. As it is fitted, turn the key gently in the cylinder to engage the cylinder onto its stop.

8 Refit the housing to the column in the reverse order of removal. Where the column does not project fully from the tube, pull it further up by fitting a nut and spacer washer onto the column, and tighten the washer against the housing to pull the column up so that it projects.

9 Refer to Section 5 to refit the steering column combination switch.

10 Refer to Chapter 10 to refit the steering wheel.

5 Steering column combination switch - removal and refitting

Removal

1 Disconnect the battery negative lead (refer to Section 1).

2 Refer to Chapter 10 and remove the steering wheel.

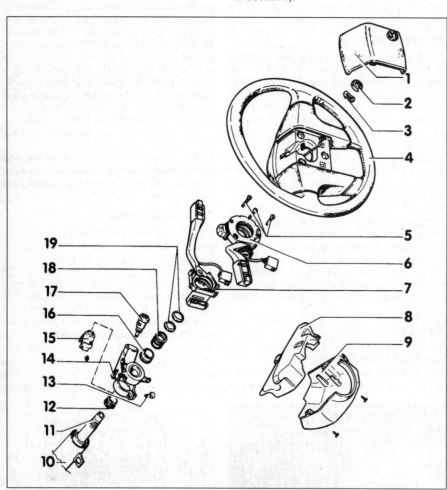

4.4 Ignition switch/steering column lock components

1 Steering wheel cover and horn button (non-airbag type shown)	6 Indicator switch	13 Lock housing screws
	7 Wiper/washer switch	14 Steering lock housing
2 Nut	8 Upper shroud	15 Ignition switch
3 Spring washer	9 Lower shroud	16 Contact ring
4 Steering wheel	10 Column tube	17 Lock cylinder
5 Column switch screws	11 Column	18 Spring
	12 Support ring	19 Clamp ring

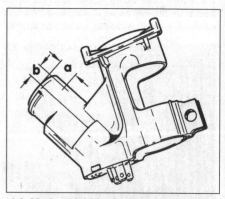

4.6 Mark and drill column lock housing at intersection of "a" and "b"

a = 12 mm   b = 10 mm

3 Undo the two retaining screws (from underneath) and remove the upper and lower column shrouds **(see illustration)**.
4 Undo the three retaining screws and remove the indicator switch, and detach the wiring connector from it **(see illustrations)**.
5 Withdraw the wiper switch, and detach its wiring connector **(see illustration)**.

Refitting

6 Refitting is a reversal of the removal procedure. Ensure that the wiring connections are securely made. Check for satisfactory operation on completion.

6 Switches - removal and refitting

Facia switch

1 Using a small screwdriver or similar tool, carefully prise the switch out of the facia **(see illustrations)**.
2 Disconnect the multi-plug from the rear of the switch.
3 Refitting is a reversal of removal.

Courtesy light switches

4 Prise off the rubber cover.
5 Unscrew the cross-head screw.
6 Carefully withdraw the switch from the body aperture **(see illustration)**. Disconnect the wiring and remove the switch. Make sure that the wiring does not drop back into the aperture by using tape or string to secure it.
7 Refitting is a reversal of removal.

5.3 Removing the steering column shrouds

5.4b ... and remove the indicator switch

5.4a Undo the retaining screws . . .

5.5 Wiper/washer switch removal

Electric door mirror adjuster switch

8 Slide the trim panel to the side and remove it from the door panel.

9 Detach the wiring connector **(see illustration)**. Compress the retaining lugs on the underside of the switch and push it from the trim panel.
10 Refit in the reverse order of removal.

Sunroof control switch

Early models

11 Use a small screwdriver or a similar tool and carefully prise free the switch from the roof panel, then release the wiring connector **(see illustration)**.

Later models

12 Using a small screwdriver, prise out the interior light/switch console from the roof panel. Release the switch locating lugs **(see illustration)**, push the switch out of the console panel and disconnect the wiring plug.

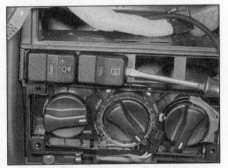
6.1a Carefully lever the underside of the switch (early type shown) . . .

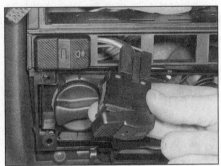
6.1b . . . and release it from the facia panel

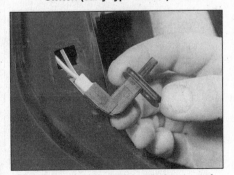
6.6 Door courtesy light switch removal

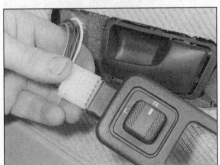
6.9 Door mirror adjuster switch wiring plug removal

6.11 Sunroof control switch removal - early models

12

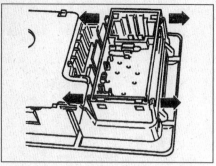

6.12 Sunroof control switch removal - later models

6.15 Handbrake warning switch location (arrowed)

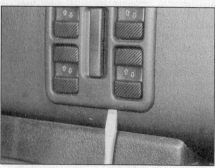

6.18a Prise free the window switch from the lower door trim (early models) . . .

All models

13 Refit in the reverse order of removal.

Handbrake warning switch

14 Remove the centre console as described in Chapter 11.

15 Undo the cross-head screw and remove the switch from the lever **(see illustration)**. On some models the switch may be secured by a rivet, in which case the rivet will need to be drilled out to remove the switch. This may necessitate removing the handbrake lever to allow access - refer to Chapter 9 for details.

16 Detach the wiring connector from the switch.

17 Refit in the reverse order of removal.

Door-mounted electric window switches

Early models

18 Carefully prise free the switch panel from the lower door trim as shown and detach the wiring connectors **(see illustrations)**.

Later models

19 Prise free the upper section of the inner door pull handle, and detach the wiring connector. Depress the switch retaining tabs and remove the switch **(see illustration)**.

All models

20 Refitting is a reversal of removal.

Stop-light switch

21 Refer to Chapter 9.

Steering column combination switch

22 Refer to Section 5.

Rotary lighting switch - later models

23 Insert a thin blade or feeler gauge between the top of the lighting switch panel and the driver's air vent. Press the retaining tab to the right and withdraw the lighting switch panel from the facia. Detach the wiring connector. The instrument lighting and headlight range control switches can now be unclipped and removed from the panel as necessary.

24 Refitting is a reversal of removal.

7 Exterior light bulbs - renewal

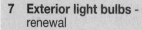

1 Whenever a bulb is renewed, note the following points:

a) *Disconnect the battery negative lead before starting work (see Section 1).*
b) *Remember that if the light has just been in use, the bulb may be extremely hot.*
c) *Always check the bulb contacts and holder, ensuring that there is clean metal-to-metal contact between the bulb and its live(s) and earth. Clean off any corrosion or dirt before fitting a new bulb.*
d) *Wherever bayonet-type bulbs are fitted,*

6.18b . . . and detach the wiring connector

e) *ensure that the live contact(s) bear firmly against the bulb contact.*
f) *Always ensure that the new bulb is of the correct rating and that it is completely clean before fitting it; this applies particularly to headlight/foglight bulbs (see below).*

Headlight

2 When working on the right-hand headlight, on models equipped with air conditioning, undo the refrigerant hose securing clip screw from the wing drain channel, then lift the hose and position it out of the way. Where necessary for improved access, pull free and detach the air inlet duct from the front of the air cleaner, and position it out of the way **(see illustration)**.

Early models

3 Rotate the domed rear cap to the left and detach it from the unit housing **(see illustration)**.

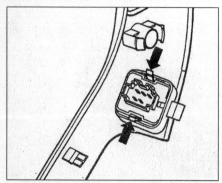

6.19 Depress the switch retaining tabs and release the window switch - later models

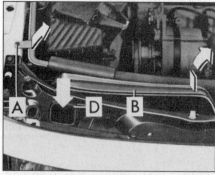

7.2 Headlight bulb renewal on models with air conditioning

A *Refrigerant hose securing screw*
B *Air inlet*
D *Bulb access hole*

7.3 Headlight rear cover cap showing orientation marks

7.4 Detach the wiring connector . . .

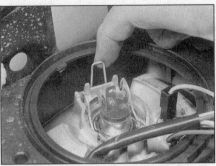

7.5a . . . release the retaining clip . . .

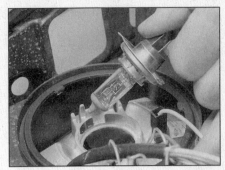

7.5b . . . and withdraw the bulb from the headlight

7.7a Depress the retaining tongue in the direction of the arrow . . .

7.7b . . . then withdraw the cover panel from the vehicle

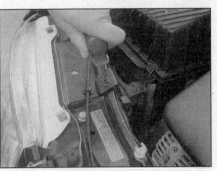

7.7c To access the main beam bulb, undo the securing screw . . .

7.7d . . . then release the retaining lugs from their locations and withdraw the cover panel

4 Working through the bulb access hole in the lock carrier if necessary, pull free the wiring connector from the bulbholder (see illustration).

5 Release the wire retaining clip and withdraw the bulb (see illustrations).

6 Refitting is a reversal of removal. Do not touch the glass of the new bulb with bare fingers. If the glass is accidentally touched, clean it with methylated spirit.

Later models

7 When working on the right-hand headlight, the top cover must be removed by releasing the lug at the air cleaner housing and depressing the tongue on the lock carrier/cross-panel. Release the retaining lugs and manoeuvre the panel out from the front of the vehicle. If the main beam bulb is being

renewed, remove the screw from the top cover. Release the retaining lugs and manoeuvre the panel out from the front of the vehicle (see illustrations).

8 Separate main and dipped beam bulbs are fitted on later models. Identify which bulb is to be worked on, then unclip and remove the relevant cover from the rear of the headlight. The outer cover is for dipped beam (and sidelights), the inner cover for the main beam bulb (see illustrations).

9 Disconnect the wiring plug from the rear of the bulb, then unhook the bulb retaining wire clip and withdraw the bulb from the rear of the headlight (see illustration).

10 Refitting is a reversal of removal. Do not touch the glass of the new headlight bulb with bare fingers. If the glass is accidentally touched, clean it with methylated spirit.

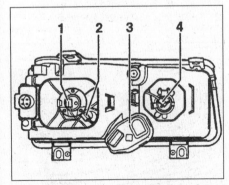

7.8a Headlight rear cover details on later models

1 Dipped beam   3 Headlight range
   bulb   control motor
2 Sidelight bulb   4 Main beam bulb

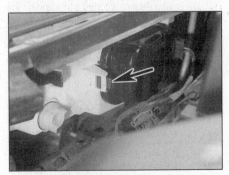

7.8b Headlight rear cover retaining clip (arrowed) - one either side

7.8c Squeeze together the retaining clips and release the headlight rear cover

12

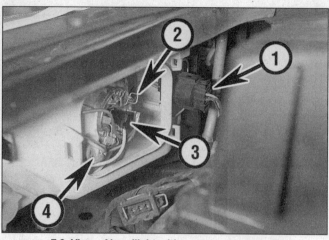

7.9 View of headlight with rear cover removed

7.12a Detach the wiring connector . . .

1 Headlight wiring plug   3 Bulb wiring plug
2 Bulb retaining wire clip   4 Sidelight bulbholder

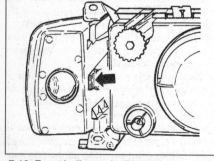

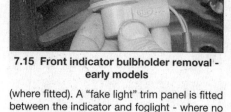

7.12b . . . and extract the sidelight bulb
and holder - early models

7.12c Sidelight bulbholder (arrowed) on
later models

7.15 Front indicator bulbholder removal -
early models

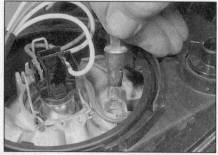

7.16 Front indicator locking tab - press in
direction of arrow to release

7.19 Prising out the trim panel next
to the indicator light -
model without front foglight shown

Front sidelight

11 Remove the plastic cover from the rear of the headlight. On later models, unclip and remove the outermost cover for access to the sidelight bulb **(see illustration 7.9)**.
12 On early models, disconnect the wiring plug, then extract the bulbholder from the reflector. On later models, the bulbholder and wiring are removed together **(see illustrations)**.
13 Depress and twist the bulb to remove it.
14 Refitting is a reversal of removal.

Front direction indicator

Early models

15 The bulbholder is located outboard of the headlight rear cover in the engine compartment. Turn the bulbholder on the rear of the light anti-clockwise and remove it **(see illustration)**. Depress and twist the bulb to remove it from the bulbholder.
16 The light unit may be removed after first removing the headlight housing (Section 9). Depress the locking tab on the inboard side of the light unit to separate it from the headlight **(see illustration)**.
17 Refitting is a reversal of removal.

Later models

18 The direction indicator is located in the front bumper, outboard of the front foglights

(where fitted). A "fake light" trim panel is fitted between the indicator and foglight - where no front foglight is fitted, the trim panel is that much larger.
19 Using a suitable screwdriver, prise out the trim panel for access to the light unit securing screw **(see illustration)**.
20 Remove the securing screw **(see illustration)** and withdraw the direction indicator light unit from the front bumper. Disconnect the wiring connector. Twist off the light unit rear cover for access to the bulb.
21 Refitting is a reversal of removal.

7.20 Indicator light unit securing
screw (arrowed) -
model with front foglight shown

Direction indicator side repeater light

22 Push the lens down and then tilt it out at the top to release the lens. Extract the bulb from the holder **(see illustration)**.

23 To remove the light unit, partially remove the wheel arch liner for access (refer to Chapter 11). Disconnect the wiring connector in the engine compartment and feed the wiring through, together with the bulbholder.

24 Refitting is a reversal of removal.

Front foglight

Early models

25 Using a flat-bladed screwdriver, prise the expander pins from the frame plugs **(see illustration)**, then press the plugs from the frame and remove the frame.

26 Unscrew and remove the three retaining screws and withdraw the light unit **(see illustration)**.

27 Prise free the protector cap from the rear of the light unit, then detach the wiring connector, unhook the spring clip and extract the halogen type bulb **(see illustration)**.

28 Refit in the reverse order of removal. Do not touch the glass of the new bulb with bare fingers. If the glass is accidentally touched, clean it with methylated spirit. When inserting the bulb, the lug in the reflector must engage with the bulb plate recess.

29 On completion, check the light for satisfactory operation. If necessary, vertical adjustment to the beam can be made by

7.22 Direction indicator side repeater light lens separated from bulbholder

turning the adjuster screw at the side of the lens, below the single light unit retaining screw **(see illustration)**. No provision is made for horizontal adjustment.

Later models

30 Using a suitable screwdriver, prise out the trim panel between the foglight and the direction indicator for access to the foglight securing screws **(see illustration)**.

31 Remove the two securing screws and withdraw the foglight unit from the front bumper. Note that the third, lowest screw is the beam adjustment screw. Disconnect the wiring connector. Twist off the light unit rear cover for access to the bulb.

32 The bulb is retained by a wire clip, similar to that used in the headlight bulbs. Squeeze together the two "ears" of the wire clip and extract the bulb **(see illustration)**.

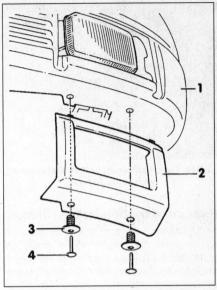

7.25 Front foglight attachment details - early models

1 Bumper cover
2 Frame
3 Frame securing plugs
4 Expander pins

33 On completion, check the light for satisfactory operation. If necessary, vertical adjustment to the beam can be made by turning the adjuster screw at the base of the lens **(see illustration)**. No provision is made for horizontal adjustment.

7.26 Front foglight removal

7.27 Front foglight bulb removal

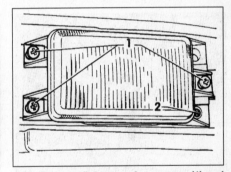

7.29 Front foglight securing screws (1) and beam adjustment screw (2) - early models

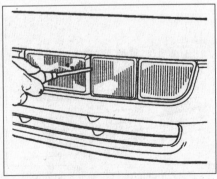

7.30 Prising out the trim panel between the foglight and direction indicator light

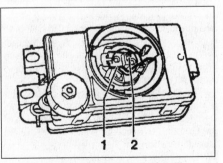

7.32 Front foglight bulb details

1 Bulb retaining wire clip
2 Foglight bulb

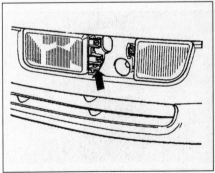

7.33 Foglight beam vertical adjustment screw (arrowed)

12

7.34a Rear combination light bulbholder removal - Saloon

7.34b Rear combination light bulbholder removal from boot lid - Saloon

7.35 Rear combination light unit retaining nuts (arrowed) - Saloon

Rear combination lights - Saloon

34 Unclip the inner trim panel from the boot lid or from the inside of the boot, as applicable, and pivot it back out of the way of the light unit. Depress the retaining clips and withdraw the combination bulbholder. Press and untwist the bulb from the holder (see illustrations).

35 To remove the light unit, remove the bulbholder unit as described above, then unscrew and remove the retaining nuts (see illustration). Remove the light unit.

36 Refit in the reverse order of removal, and then check for the satisfactory operation of all rear lights.

Rear combination lights - Estate

37 Detach the tailgate access cover or open the access flap from the rear luggage area trim on the side concerned. Compress the right- and left-hand retaining clips towards the centre of the light unit, and withdraw the bulbholder (see illustration). Press and untwist the bulb to remove it.

38 To remove the light unit, undo the retaining nuts and withdraw the unit from the body (see illustration).

39 Refit in the reverse order of removal. If the brake/tail light bulb is difficult to fit, turn it 180° before fitting. Check the rear lights for satisfactory operation on completion.

Number plate light

40 The number plate lights are located in the boot lid or tailgate, just above the number plate. For better access to the retaining screws, open the boot lid or tailgate. Undo the two retaining screws and remove the relevant number plate light unit (see illustration).

41 Extract the bulb and holder from the light unit (see illustration), and then remove the bulb from its holder.

42 Refit in the reverse order of removal, and check the light for satisfactory operation.

Rear lights - boot lid or tailgate-mounted

43 To renew these bulbs, first open the boot lid or tailgate.

44 Release the retaining catch and open the access panel in the boot lid or tailgate trim panel (see illustration).

45 Squeeze together the retaining clips either side of the bulbholder, and remove it from its location (see illustration). Press and twist the bulbs to remove from the bulbholder.

46 Refit in the reverse order of removal, and check the light for satisfactory operation.

7.37 Rear combination light bulbholder removal from tailgate - Estate

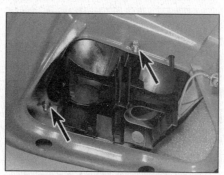

7.38 Rear combination light unit showing retaining nuts (arrowed) to tailgate - Estate

7.40 Remove the number plate light unit . . .

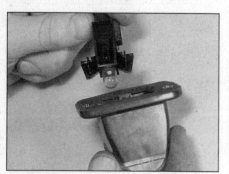

7.41 . . . and extract the bulb and holder

7.44 Open the access panel in the boot lid or tailgate trim panel . . .

7.45 . . . then release the bulbholder and withdraw it for access to the bulbs

8.2a Front-mounted interior light with lens removed for access to bulb

8.2b Interior light unit - side-mounted

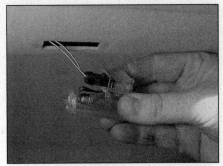
8.2c Interior light unit - rear-mounted

8 Interior light bulbs - renewal

1 Whenever a bulb is renewed, note the following points:
a) Disconnect the battery negative lead before starting work (see Section 1).
b) Remember that if the light has just been in use, the bulb may be extremely hot.
c) Always check the bulb contacts and holder, ensuring that there is clean metal-to-metal contact between the bulb and its live(s) and earth. Clean off any corrosion or dirt before fitting a new bulb.
d) Wherever bayonet-type bulbs are fitted, ensure that the live contact(s) bear firmly against the bulb contact.
e) Always ensure that the new bulb is of the correct rating and that it is completely clean before fitting it.

Interior/reading lights

2 One of two methods will be required to gain access to the interior light bulbs, depending on model. Either prise free the lens from the light housing, or prise out the light housing itself (it may then be necessary to release the reflector or bulbholder from the rear of the light unit). Remove the bulb from its holder in the housing (see illustrations).
3 Refit in the reverse order of removal.

Luggage area and glovebox lights

4 Prise free the light lens/unit and extract the festoon bulb from its holder (see illustration).

5 Refit in the reverse order of removal, and check for satisfactory operation.

Sunvisor/vanity mirror light

6 Prise free the lens from the sunvisor. The festoon bulbs can be extracted from their holders in the visor (see illustration).
7 Refit in the reverse order of removal.

Instrument panel bulbs

8 Remove the instrument panel as described in Section 10.
9 To remove an LED warning light "bulb", remove the LED bracket, then pull the "bulb" free (see illustrations).
10 To remove an illumination bulb, untwist or pull out the holder and extract the bulb from it (see illustrations).

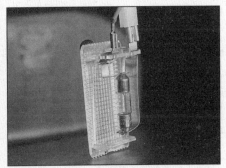
8.4 Luggage area/glovebox type light and bulb

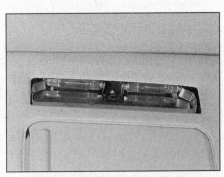
8.6 Sunvisor/vanity mirror bulbs (lens removed)

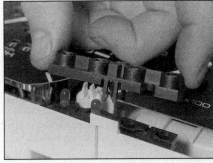
8.9a Instrument panel LED bracket removal

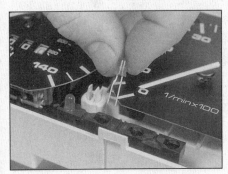
8.9b LED "bulb" removal from the instrument panel

8.10a Instrument panel illumination bulbs - twist and pull to remove this type ...

8.10b ... grip and pull this type

12

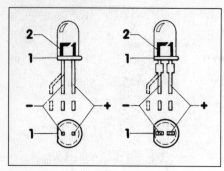

8.11 LED "bulbs" showing correct orientation for fitting

1 Flat on diode housing
2 Large pole in diode housing
Note: The negative (-) pole is sometimes angled

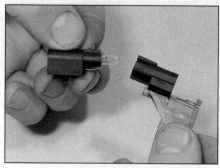

8.12 Cigar lighter illumination bulb removal

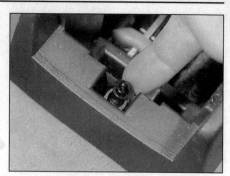

8.14 Ashtray bulbholder removal

11 Refit in the reverse order of removal. When inserting an LED "bulb", check that it is orientated as shown **(see illustration)**.

Cigar lighter illumination bulb

12 Refer to Section 12 and remove the cigar lighter and the central console panel in which it is mounted. Leaving the cigar lighter in the panel, pull free the bulbholder from the rear of the lighter, and extract the bulb from the holder **(see illustration)**.
13 Refit in the reverse order of removal.

Ashtray illumination bulb

14 Prise free the bulbholder from the trim/console panel **(see illustration)**. Pull free the bulb from its holder.
15 Refit in the reverse order of removal.

High-level stop-light bulbs

16 Working inside the car (Saloon models) or outside the car with the tailgate open (Estate models), press in the two retaining tabs either side of the bulbholder and release the bulbholder from the light unit **(see illustration)**.
17 The LED "bulbs" can now be extracted and renewed as necessary **(see illustration 8.11)**.

Switch illumination bulbs

18 Switch illumination bulbs are usually built into the switch itself, and cannot be renewed separately. Refer to Section 6 and remove the switch - bulb renewal should then be self-evident, if it is possible; otherwise, renew the switch.

Heater control panel illumination bulb

19 Refer to Chapter 3, Section 12.

9 Headlights - removal, refitting and beam adjustment

Removal

1 To remove the headlight, refer to Section 7 as necessary and detach the wiring connectors from the rear of the headlight.

Early models

2 Unscrew and remove the four retaining bolts along the top edge of the headlight housing **(see illustration)**, and remove the housing.
3 Undo the four retaining screws **(see illustration)** and remove the headlight unit from the housing.
4 If required, the reflector can be separated from the housing. To achieve this, carefully

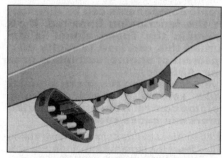

8.16 High-level stop-light bulbholder removal - press retaining tabs inwards to release

lever free the housing-to-lens retaining clips, and detach the lens **(see illustration)**. Rotate the headlight adjusters to the point where the reflector can be removed. Remove the bulbs (head and sidelights) and detach the earth.

Later models

5 Refer to Chapter 11 and remove the radiator grille.
6 Using a suitable screwdriver, carefully prise the trim cap at the side of the headlight forwards, and remove it **(see illustration)**.
7 Remove the securing bolt and pull forward the trim strip below the headlight **(see illustration)**. To completely remove the trim strip, the bolt on the other side of the vehicle must also be removed.

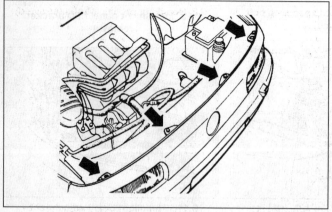

9.2 Headlight housing securing screws

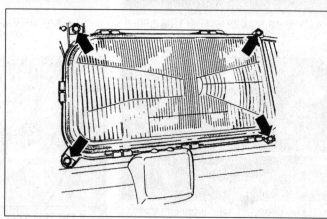

9.3 Headlight securing screws (arrowed)

8 Remove the four retaining bolts **(see illustration)** and withdraw the headlight from the vehicle.

Refitting

9 Reassembly and refitting is a reversal of the removal procedure. On completion check for satisfactory operation, and have the headlight beam adjustment checked as soon as possible (see below).

Beam adjustment

10 Accurate adjustment of the headlight beam is only possible using optical beam setting equipment, and this work should therefore be carried out by a VW dealer or suitably equipped workshop.

11 For reference, the headlights can be adjusted using the adjuster assemblies fitted to the top of each light unit **(see illustrations)**.

12 Some models are equipped with an electrically operated headlight beam adjustment system which is controlled through the switch in the facia. On these models, ensure that the switch is set to the basic (–) position before adjusting the headlight aim.

13 On models fitted with a self-levelling suspension system, the levelling system control knob must be set in the No 4 position. If the vehicle has previously been driven with the setting control in any other position, the adjuster knob must first be turned to the No 2 position (electronic off) with the ignition on. The system will then set itself at the normal level setting. From this point, do not further load or unload the vehicle until after the headlights are adjusted.

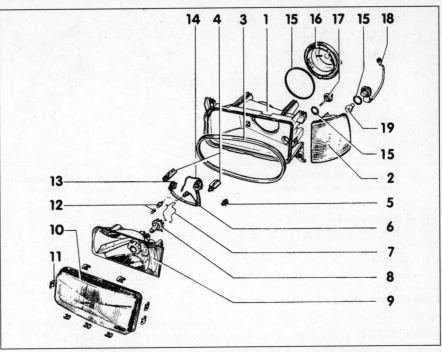

9.4 Headlight unit and associated components - early models

1 Headlight housing (left-hand)
2 Indicator housing (left-hand)
3 Seal
4 Adjuster thread
5 Securing clips
6 Wiring loom
7 Spring clip
8 Bulb (halogen) for headlight
9 Reflector
10 Lens
11 Retaining clip
12 Bulbholders (sidelight)
13 Multi-point connector
14 Connector sleeve for reflector earth
15 Seal
16 Cap
17 Connector rod
18 Indicator wiring
19 Indicator bulb

9.6 Remove the trim cap from the side of the headlight by prising it forwards

9.7 Headlight trim strip securing bolt (arrowed)

9.8 Headlight retaining bolts (arrowed)

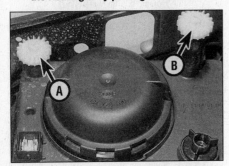

9.11a Headlight adjusters seen from behind the headlight unit (early type)

A Horizontal adjuster   B Vertical adjuster

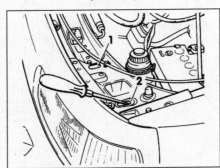

9.11b Headlight beam adjustment - horizontal setting (1) and vertical setting (2) - early models

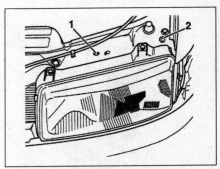

9.11c Headlight beam adjustment - vertical setting (1) and horizontal setting (2) - later models

10.3 Removing the instrument panel surround - early models

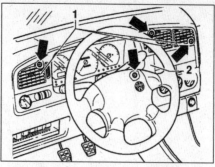

10.7 Instrument panel surround securing screws - arrowed (later models)

1 Vent grilles   2 Trim panel

10.8a Undo the retaining screws (A) - note instrument cover panel screws (B) . . .

10 Instrument panel -
removal and refitting

1 Disconnect the battery negative lead (refer to Section 1).
2 Remove the steering wheel as described in Chapter 10.

Early models

3 Undo the two retaining screws and remove the instrument panel surround (see illustration).

Later models

4 Remove the three vent grilles from the driver's side and central vent housings.
5 Remove the rotary lighting switch (Section 6).
6 Unclip the trim panel immediately behind the left-hand side of the steering wheel.

7 Remove four screws - one behind each vent grille, and one behind the trim panel removed in paragraph 6 - and take out the instrument panel surround (see illustration).

All models

8 Unscrew and remove the instrument panel securing screw each side, then withdraw the unit, easing it free from the right-hand side. When sufficiently withdrawn, detach the wiring multi-connectors from the rear face of the panel, and also the multi-function indicator (MFI) pressure hose (where applicable), then remove the panel. On early models without an electronic speedometer, the speedometer cable will automatically disengage as the panel is withdrawn (see illustrations).

9 Refitting is a reversal of the removal procedure. As the panel is relocated into position, guide the speedometer cable into engagement.

11 Instruments -
removal and refitting

1 Remove the instrument panel (Section 10).
2 Remove the cover retaining screw each side, then carefully lever the trim cover-to-housing clips, and detach the cover (see illustration).
3 The instruments are secured in position by clips or screws (see illustrations). Release the clips or undo the screws as applicable to remove the instruments. Take care not to damage the printed circuit when working on the panel.

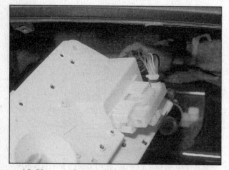

10.8b . . . then withdraw the panel and detach the wiring

10.8c Speedometer cable end fitting at speedometer

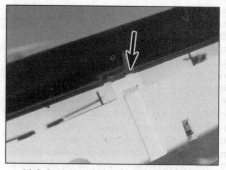

11.2 Instrument panel trim cover-to-housing clip (arrowed)

11.3a Releasing the retaining clips . . .

11.3b . . . to remove the tachometer

11.3c Unscrew the speedometer retaining screws (electronic speedometer fitted to later models is a push-fit in the panel)

11.4 Instrument panel components - multi-function indicator (MFI) type

1 Trim cover
2 Fuel gauge
3 MFI unit
4 Coolant temperature gauge
5 Voltage stabiliser
6 Tachometer (clock on lower-specification models) and oil pressure warning control unit
7 Speedometer
8 Hall sender
9 MFI pressure sender
10 Warning lights - right
11 Warning lights - left
12 Printed circuit
13 Bulbs/holders for dash illumination
14 Housing
15 Contact plate for Hall sender
16 Speedometer cable cap

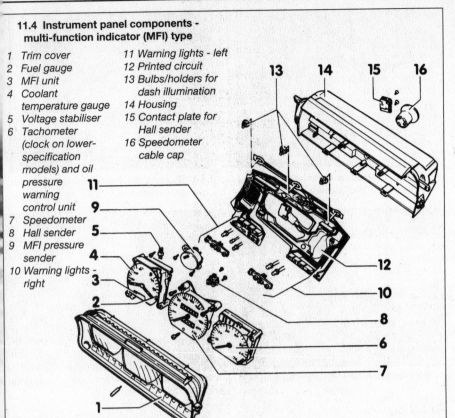

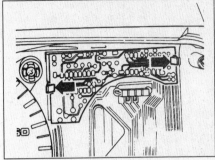

11.5 Oil pressure warning control unit and retaining lugs - arrowed

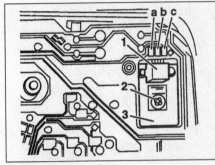

11.6 Instrument panel voltage stabiliser, showing wiring connections (a, b and c)

1 Voltage stabiliser
2 Retaining screw
3 Heat sink

4 Where fitted, the multi-function indicator and Hall sender units can be removed after undoing their retaining screws. The Hall sender is secured to the rear face of the speedometer **(see illustration)**.

5 To remove the oil pressure warning control unit, remove the analogue clock or tachometer, then prise back the lugs and remove the unit from the printed circuit **(see illustration)**.

6 To remove the voltage stabiliser, undo the retaining screw and withdraw the unit. When refitting this unit, ensure that the three connector pins are correctly engaged and the retaining screw tightly fitted **(see illustration)**.

7 The contact plate for the Hall (or induction) sender is attached to the speedometer cable

cap, and can be removed by undoing the two retaining screws. When refitting this unit, thread the printed circuit so that it does not crease, and secure it so that it cannot slip. Ensure that the plate is clamped under the speedometer cable connector before tightening the retaining screws.

8 The speedometer cable connector can be removed by turning it from the locked position to the released position, then pulling it free **(see illustration)**. Refit in the reverse order to removal.

9 To remove the printed circuit, detach and remove the instruments, the multi-function indicator pressure sender and contact plate as previously described. Compress the spreader lugs that retain the connector strip,

and carefully pull free and remove the connector strip and the printed circuit. Refit in the reverse order to removal.

12 Cigar lighter - removal and refitting

Removal

1 Refer to Chapter 11 and remove the centre console. As the console is withdrawn, detach the wiring connector from the rear of the lighter **(see illustration)**.

2 Carefully prise free the trim piece from the front of the lighter panel **(see illustration)**.

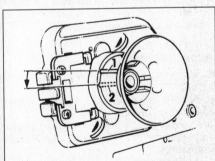

11.8 Speedometer cable connector showing the locked (1) and released (2) positions

12.1 Withdraw console and detach wiring connector . . .

12.2 . . . remove trim piece

12.3a Press securing lug . . .

12.3b . . . to allow cigar lighter to be withdrawn

13.3a Undo the retaining nut . . .

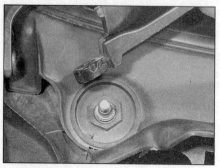

13.3b . . . and remove the wiper arm

13.7 Windscreen wiper motor plastic cover

13.8 Windscreen wiper motor and wiring connection

3 Insert a small screwdriver blade into the lighter body, and depress the retaining tags whilst pushing the lighter unit out from the rear **(see illustrations)**.

Refitting

4 Refit in the reverse order of removal.

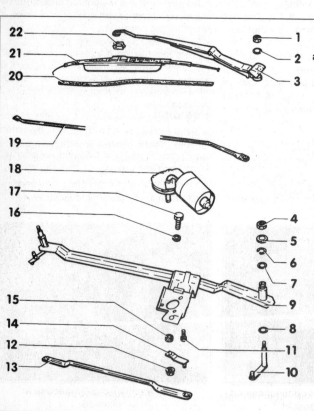

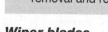

13.10a Windscreen wiper motor and associated components - early models

1 Nut
2 Washer
3 Wiper arm
4 Spindle nut
5 Plastic washer
6 Snap ring
7 O-ring
8 Spring washer
9 Wiper frame
10 Lever
11 Wiper motor mounting bolt
12 Nut
13 Connecting rod
14 Crank
15 Rubber spacer
16 Washer
17 Wiper motor mounting plate bolt
18 Wiper motor
19 Connecting rod
20 Wiper rubber
21 Wiper blade
22 Retaining clip

13 Windscreen wiper components - removal and refitting

Wiper blades

1 Refer to *"Weekly checks"*.

Wiper arms

2 If the wipers are not in their parked position, switch on the ignition, and allow the motor to automatically "park".
3 Before removing an arm, mark its "parked" position on the glass with a strip of adhesive tape. Prise off the cover and unscrew the spindle nut **(see illustrations)**. Remove the washer and ease the arm from the spindle by rocking it slowly from side to side.
4 Refitting is a reversal of removal, but before tightening the spindle nuts, position the wiper blades as marked before removal.

Wiper motor

5 Disconnect the battery negative lead (refer to Section 1).
6 Remove the wiper arms as described in paragraphs 2 and 3.
7 Where applicable, unhook the plastic cover and remove it from the motor **(see illustration)**.
8 Disconnect the wiring plug from the wiper motor **(see illustration)**.
9 Undo the wiper frame-to-body nuts (at the wiper arm driveshafts) and unscrew the motor

**13.10b Windscreen wiper motor and associated components -
later models**

1 Rubber spacer
2 Washer
3 Wiper motor
   mounting plate
   plastic nut
4 Wiper motor
   mounting bolt
5 Wiper blade
6 Wiper arm
7 Cover
8 Wiper arm
   securing nut
9 Washer
10 Spindle nut
11 Circlip
12 Washer
13 O-ring
14 Wiper frame
15 Spring washer
16 Spring washer
17 Lever
18 Connecting rod
19 Wiper motor
20 Connecting rod
21 Crank
22 Nut

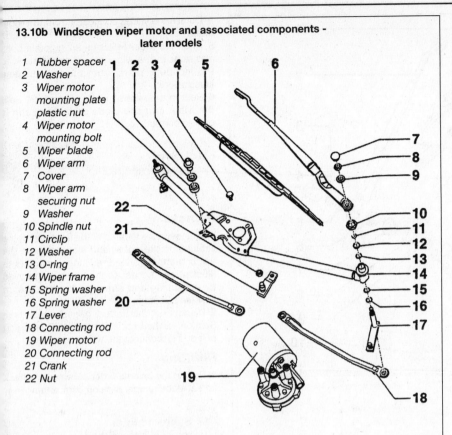

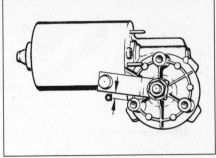

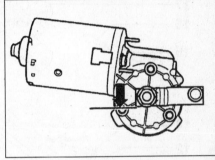

**13.11a Windscreen wiper motor crank arm
in "parked" position for refitting -
early models**

a = 5 mm

**13.11b Windscreen wiper motor crank arm
in "parked" position for refitting -
later models**

mounting plate nut/bolt. Withdraw the wiper
motor and mounting frame assembly.
10 If required, unbolt and remove the motor
from the frame. If the assembly is to be
completely dismantled, note the fitted order of
all washers and spacers, etc **(see
illustrations)**.
11 Refit in the reverse order of removal.
Lubricate the connecting rod bearings with a
little molybdenum disulphide grease. If a new
wiper motor is being fitted, the crank arm
must be positioned in the "parked" position
(see illustrations).
12 On completion, check for satisfactory
operation.

14 Washer system -
   general

1 All models are fitted with a windscreen
washer system. Estate models also have a
tailgate washer, and some models are fitted
with headlight washers.
2 The fluid reservoir for the windscreen
washer (and where applicable, for the
headlight and tailgate washers) is located in
the engine compartment on the left-hand
side. The fluid pump is attached to the side of
the reservoir body **(see illustration)**.

3 The reservoir fluid level must be regularly
topped up with proper washer fluid containing
an antifreeze agent, but not cooling system
antifreeze - see "Weekly checks".
4 The supply hoses are attached by rubber
couplings to their various connections, and if
required, can be detached by simply pulling
them free from the appropriate connector
(see illustrations).
5 The washer jets can be cleaned and
adjusted using a needle. When adjusted
correctly, the jets should be aimed at a point
just above the centre of the wiper swept area.
6 The headlight washer jets are best adjusted
using the VW tool, and should therefore be
entrusted to a VW garage to set.

14.2 Washer reservoir and pump unit

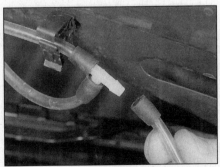

**14.4a Washer hoses and connections on
underside of bonnet**

**14.4b Washer hose connection at
bulkhead**

12

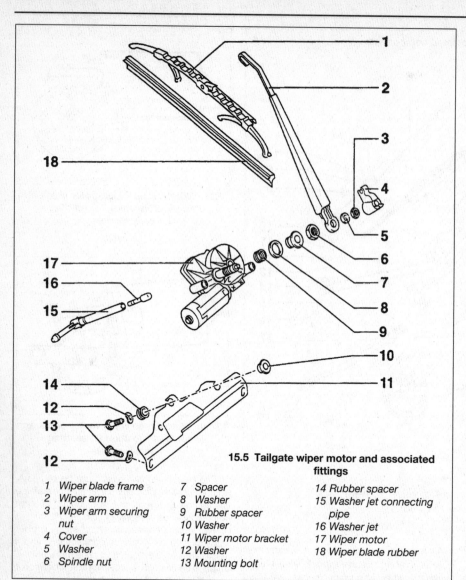

15.5 **Tailgate wiper motor and associated fittings**

1 Wiper blade frame	7 Spacer	14 Rubber spacer
2 Wiper arm	8 Washer	15 Washer jet connecting
3 Wiper arm securing	9 Rubber spacer	pipe
nut	10 Washer	16 Washer jet
4 Cover	11 Wiper motor bracket	17 Wiper motor
5 Washer	12 Washer	18 Wiper blade rubber
6 Spindle nut	13 Mounting bolt	

15 Tailgate wiper motor - removal and refitting

1 Disconnect the battery negative lead, with reference to Section 1.

2 Open the tailgate and detach the trim panel from it. Prise free the plastic compression clips, then their bush clips, using a suitable forked tool - take care not to damage the trim or the clips.

3 Remove the wiper arm and blade as described in Section 13, then unscrew the spindle nut. Remove the nut and washers.

4 Detach the wiring connector from the wiper motor.

5 Undo the wiper motor mounting plate bolts and remove the wiper motor, complete with the mounting plate, from the tailgate (**see illustration**).

6 Refit in the reverse order of removal. Refit the wiper arm and blade so that the arm is parked correctly.

16 Horns - removal and refitting

Removal

1 The horns are located at the front end of the vehicle, on the right-hand side between the front bumper and the inner wing (**see illustration**). Access to the horns is improved by unclipping and removing the wheel arch liner (see Chapter 11).

2 Disconnect the battery negative lead (see Section 1), then undo the horn unit retaining bolt and disconnect the wiring connector.

Refitting

3 Refit in the reverse order of removal. Check for satisfactory operation on completion.

17 Sunroof motor - removal and refitting

Closing sunroof manually

1 If the motor malfunctions when the roof panel is in the open position, it can be wound shut manually. To do this, prise out the interior light and its mounting panel from the roof, to provide access to the underside of the sunroof motor.

2 Insert a screwdriver into the slot in the motor drive, push it upwards, and wind the roof shut by hand (**see illustration**).

Motor removal

3 Ensure that the sunroof is fully closed - refer to paragraphs 1 and 2 if the motor has failed. Disconnect the battery negative lead (refer to Section 1).

4 If not already done, prise out the interior light and its mounting panel from the roof. Disconnect the wiring plugs from the light and sunroof switch, and remove the light. To remove the motor trim panel, undo the two retaining screws, then push the panel towards the windscreen and unclip it at the front edge from the headlining.

5 Undo the retaining screws and remove the motor. As it is withdrawn, detach the wiring connections.

6 Refit in the reverse order of removal, noting the following points:
 a) Smear the drive pinion with a little grease before engaging the motor with the cables.

16.1 **Horn location showing mounting bracket**

17.2 **Insert screwdriver as shown to close sunroof manually**

b) As with removal, it is important that the roof panel be in the closed position to ensure correct engagement. If the motor was activated whilst it was removed, or if a new motor is being fitted, it must be set for correct engagement before fitting. To do this, connect up the switch wire to it and operate the motor so that it is set at the closed position (see illustration). By operating the motor via the operating switch, the motor pinion turns can be counted and the motor set in the closed position ready for fitting.

c) Check for satisfactory operation on completion.

18 Central locking system - general information and component renewal

1 Most models are equipped with a central door locking system, which automatically locks all doors and the rear tailgate/boot lid in unison with the manual locking of either front door. The system is operated by a bi-pressure pump, which supplies vacuum to lock the doors, and pressure to unlock them (see

17.6 Sunroof motor pinion adjustment positions

1 Sunroof switch
2 Sunroof motor pinion
A (end stop of tilt operation) to 0: two turns
B (end stop of sliding operation) to 0:nine turns
0 Closed position

illustrations). Apart from the central locking positioners and the bi-pressure pump, the door locks are identical to those on models without central locking - see Chapter 11.

2 Should the system develop a fault, the condition and security of the hoses should first be checked. A leak will cause the bi-pressure pump to run longer than five seconds, and if it runs for thirty-five seconds, an internal control unit will automatically switch it off.

Positioner units

3 Access to the central locking positioner units is made after removing the trim from the door, boot lid, tailgate or luggage area (as applicable) - see Chapter 11.
4 Compress the retaining clip and detach the wire from the positioner (see illustration).

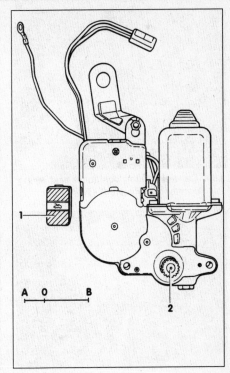

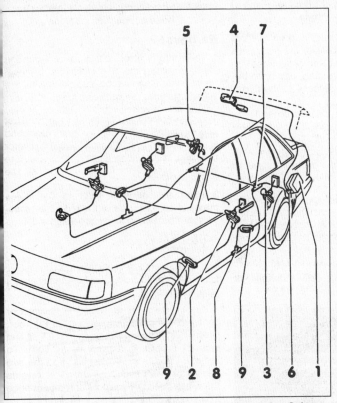

18.1a Central locking system circuit and components - Saloon

1 Bi-pressure pump	4 Boot lid positioner	7 T-piece
2 Front door positioner	5 Fuel tank flap positioner	8 T-piece
3 Rear door positioner	6 T-piece	9 Pipe connector (from February 1989)

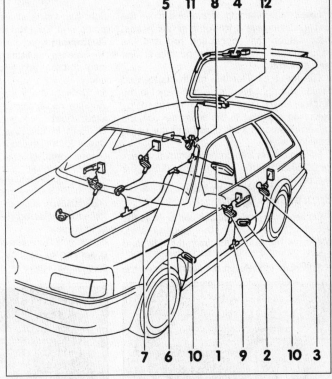

18.1b Central locking system circuit and components - Estate

1 Bi-pressure pump	5 Fuel tank flap positioner	10 Pipe connection (from February 1989)
2 Front door positioner	6 T-piece	11 Foam rubber tube
3 Rear door positioner	7 T-piece	12 Bellows tube
4 Tailgate positioner	8 T-piece	
	9 T-piece	

12

18.4 Central locking positioner and wiring connector (arrowed) - front door

18.5a Undo the retaining screws . . .

18.5b . . . disconnect the connecting rod . . .

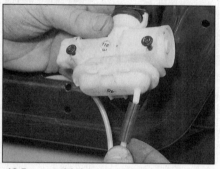

18.5c . . . withdraw the locking positioner and detach the hose

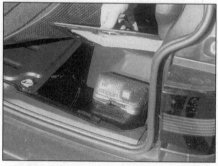

18.9 Central locking bi-pressure pump location - Estate

18.11 Bi-pressure pump showing insulation housing, wiring connector and hose connection - Saloon

5 Loosen the retaining screws and move the unit to disengage it from the screw heads, then detach the connecting rod and the vacuum hose. Remove the positioner unit **(see illustrations)**.
6 The fuel tank filler flap control is located behind the right-hand side trim panel in the luggage area, and can be removed by detaching the hose to the positioner unit, the flap-to-positioner control rod and the single retaining screw.
7 Refit in the reverse order of removal. Check for satisfactory operation before refitting the trim panel(s).

Bi-pressure pump

8 On Saloon models, detach and remove the left-hand side trim in the luggage area. Withdraw the pump unit from the left-hand side.
9 On Estate models, lift the floor cover on the

right-hand side at the rear, and lift out the pump unit from the recess in the floor **(see illustration)**.
10 Release the retaining strap, and open the insulating container for access to the pump unit.
11 Detach the wiring connector and the vacuum hose, and remove the pump **(see illustration)**.
12 Refit in the reverse order of removal. Check for satisfactory operation of the pump before refitting the insulation and trim panel/floor cover.

19 Radio - removal and refitting

Note: *This Section applies only to standard-fit audio equipment.*

Removal

1 The radio is fitted with special mounting clips, requiring the use of special removal tools, which should be supplied with the vehicle, or may be obtained from an in-car entertainment specialist. Alternatively, it may be possible to make up some removal tools **(see illustration)**.
2 Disconnect the battery negative lead - refer to Section 1.

Early models

3 Insert the removal rods in the holes provided on each side of the radio front face, so that the spring clips are released **(see illustration)**.

Later models

4 Slide the removal tools into the slots either side of the radio front panel until they locate **(see illustration)**.

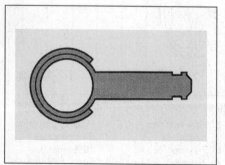

19.1 Later-type radio removal tool

19.3 Radio/cassette unit withdrawal using special rods

19.4 Slide the removal tools into the slots in the radio front panel, and pull out the unit

All models

Withdraw the radio from the mounting case, then disconnect the loudspeaker, supply and aerial plugs. Some radio units also have a fuse fitted on the rear face (see illustration).

Refitting

Refitting is a reversal of removal, but push the radio fully into its case until the spring clips are engaged. If the radio is of the security code type, it will be necessary to enter the code number before switching on the radio.

20 Radio aerial - removal and refitting

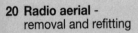

Front wing-mounted aerial

Removal

1 Refer to Chapter 11 and remove the front wheel arch liner on the side concerned.
2 Unscrew the aerial support bracket bolt (see illustration).
3 Depending on aerial type, it may be possible to disconnect the wiring from the base of the aerial for improved access to the nut. If this is not the case, hold the wiring to one side as the nut is unscrewed.
4 If the aerial lead cannot be disconnected from the aerial, it will now be necessary to

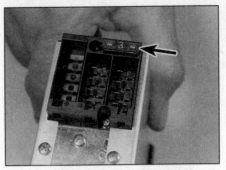

19.5 Radio/cassette wiring block connector - note fuse (arrowed)

remove the radio/cassette unit from the facia (see Section 19). Disconnect the aerial lead from the rear of the radio/cassette, and tie a piece of string securely to it. Returning to the front wing, carefully withdraw the aerial and lead through. As far as possible, note the routing of the cable as it is withdrawn. When the lead emerges, untie the string and leave it in position, so that the string can be used to draw the aerial lead back into the vehicle when refitting.
5 If the aerial lead can be disconnected from the aerial, unplug it and tie the lead up out of the way so that it cannot fall irretrievably back into the vehicle.

Refitting

6 Refitting is a reversal of removal. Where applicable, use the string to draw the aerial

20.2 Radio aerial and support bracket bolt - arrowed (under front wing)

lead through into the vehicle. Tighten the aerial support bolt securely, noting that the bracket provides the aerial earth connection, and so needs to be clean and tight. Refit the wheel arch liner as described in Chapter 11.

Roof-mounted aerial

7 Gaining access to the aerial mounting involves lowering the headlining at the rear. Removing the headlining is not normally a task to be undertaken lightly, and this job may have to be entrusted to a VW dealer. If you are satisfied that this can be accomplished easily, the procedure is otherwise very similar to the wing-mounted aerial. The roof-mounted aerial components are as shown - the aerial lead is in two sections, joined behind the facia panel at the right-hand windscreen pillar (see illustration).

Rear window-mounted aerial

8 On some models, the aerial is a "ribbon element" type, affixed to the rear window (directly above the heated rear window element). To assist reception, an amplifier is fitted (see illustration). In the event of the element being damaged, repairs or renewal should be referred to a VW garage.
9 If required, the amplifier can be removed by detaching the wiring and aerial cable connectors from the unit, then undoing the retaining screw (which also secures the unit earth lead). Refit in the reverse order of removal. Ensure that all connections are securely made, and that the earth lead connection is clean.

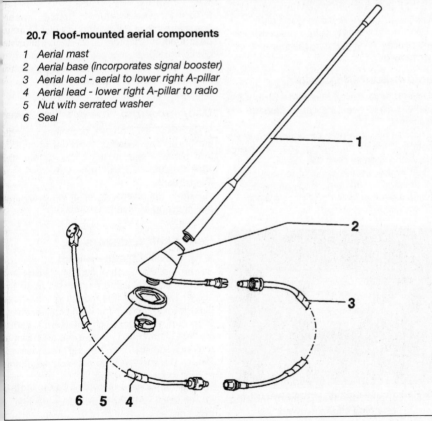

20.7 Roof-mounted aerial components

1 Aerial mast
2 Aerial base (incorporates signal booster)
3 Aerial lead - aerial to lower right A-pillar
4 Aerial lead - lower right A-pillar to radio
5 Nut with serrated washer
6 Seal

20.8 Rear window aerial amplifier unit

12

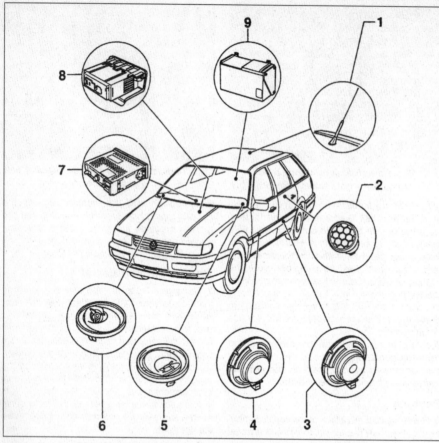

21.5a Early-type door-mounted "bass" speaker showing three of the four retaining screws behind (arrowed)

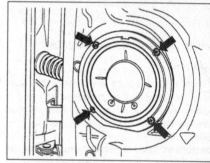

21.5b Later-type door-mounted speaker screws (arrowed) are removed from the front

21.1 Speaker and audio equipment locations - later models

1 Roof aerial
2 Treble speaker ("tweeter")
3 Full-range ("bass") speaker
4 Full-range ("bass") speaker
5 Treble speaker ("tweeter")
6 Treble speaker ("tweeter")
7 Radio/cassette unit
8 Cassette storage box
9 CD autochanger

21 Speakers - removal and refitting

1 Depending on model, the speakers may be fitted at either end of the facia, in the front and rear door trim panels, and in the parcel shelf or rear side trim panel (see illustration).

Facia-mounted speaker

2 Using a screwdriver, carefully lever out the speaker grille. Take care not to damage the facia panel.
3 The speaker can now be prised out of its location. Detach the wiring connector and remove the speaker from the vehicle.
4 Refit in the reverse order of removal. Note any direction-of-fitting markings on the rear of the speaker.

Door-mounted "bass" speaker

5 To remove a door-mounted "bass" speaker, remove the appropriate door trim as described in Chapter 11. Where applicable, unclip the speaker cover from the door trim panel. Undo the retaining screws, detach the wiring connectors and remove the speaker (see illustrations).

Door-mounted "tweeter" speaker

6 Carefully lever off the door inner handle surround. The "tweeter" speaker is clipped into place - release the clips, detach the wiring and remove the speaker (see illustration).
7 Refit in the reverse order of removal. Note any direction-of-fitting markings on the rear of the speaker.

Rear shelf speakers

8 To remove the shelf-mounted speaker on Saloon models, reach under the speaker and compress its retaining clips, then push the speaker up through the mounting panel (see illustrations). Detach the wiring connections.
9 To remove a rear shelf speaker on Estate models, detach and remove the side trim in the luggage area on the side concerned. Detach the speaker from the mounting panel and disconnect the wiring.
10 Refit in the reverse order of removal. Note any direction-of-fitting markings on the rear of the speaker.

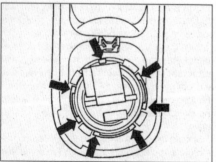

21.6 Door-mounted "tweeter" speaker retaining clips (arrowed)

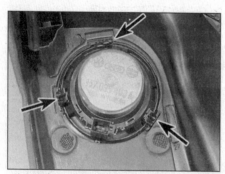

21.8a Rear shelf speaker (Saloon) showing retaining clips (arrowed)

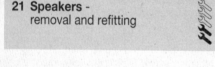

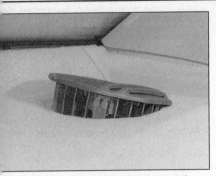

21.8b Rear shelf speaker removal (Saloon)

22 Airbag system -
general information and precautions

Warning: Before carrying out any operations on the airbag system, disconnect the battery negative terminal. When operations are complete, make sure no one is inside the vehicle when the battery is reconnected.

Note that the airbag(s) must not be subjected to temperatures in excess of 90°C (194°F). When the airbag is removed, ensure that it is stored the correct way up to prevent possible inflation.

Do not allow any solvents or cleaning agents to contact the airbag assemblies. They must be cleaned using only a damp cloth.

The airbags and control unit are both sensitive to impact. If either is dropped or damaged they should be renewed.

Disconnect the airbag control unit wiring plug prior to using arc-welding equipment on the vehicle.

Both a driver's and passenger's airbag were fitted as standard to later models in the Passat range; on other models they were available as an optional extra. Models fitted with a driver's side airbag have the word AIRBAG stamped on the airbag unit, which is fitted to the centre of the steering wheel. Models also equipped with a passenger's side airbag also have the word AIRBAG stamped on the passenger's end of the facia, in place of the glovebox. The airbag system comprises of the airbag unit (complete with gas generator), an impact sensor, the control unit and a warning light in the instrument panel.

The airbag system is triggered in the event of a heavy frontal impact above a predetermined force; depending on the point of impact. The airbag is inflated within milliseconds, and forms a safety cushion between the driver and the steering wheel or (where applicable) the passenger and the facia. This prevents contact between the upper body and the wheel/facia, and therefore greatly reduces the risk of injury. The airbag then deflates almost immediately.

Every time the ignition is switched on, the airbag control unit performs a self-test. The self-test takes approximately 3 seconds, and during this time the airbag warning light on the facia is illuminated. After the self-test has been completed, the warning light should go out. If the warning light fails to come on, remains illuminated after the initial 3-second period, or comes on at any time when the vehicle is being driven, there is a fault in the airbag system. The vehicle should then be taken to a VW dealer for examination at the earliest possible opportunity.

23 Airbag system components - removal and refitting

Note: *Refer to the warnings in Section 22 before carrying out the following operations.*
1 Disconnect the battery negative terminal (see Section 1).

Driver's side airbag

Note: *New airbag retaining screws will be required on refitting.*
2 For improved access, slacken and remove the retaining screws, and remove the steering column upper and lower shrouds.
3 Slacken and remove the two Allen screws from the rear of the steering wheel, rotating the wheel as necessary to gain access to the screws.
4 Return the steering wheel to the straight-ahead position, then carefully lift the airbag assembly away from the steering wheel and disconnect the wiring connector from the rear of the unit. Note that the airbag must not be knocked or dropped, and should be stored the correct way up with its padded surface uppermost.
5 On refitting, reconnect the wiring connector and seat the airbag unit in the steering wheel, making sure the wire does not become trapped. Fit the new retaining screws and tighten them securely. Switch on the ignition, **then** reconnect the battery negative lead.

Passenger side airbag

6 Slacken and remove the passenger side lower facia panel retaining screws. Move the panel downwards to release its upper retaining clips, and remove it from the facia.
7 Unscrew the retaining screws, situated along the lower edge of the airbag.
8 Move the airbag assembly downwards to disengage the upper locating pegs from the mounting frame. Remove the airbag unit from the facia, disconnecting the wiring connector as it becomes accessible. Recover the guides from the airbag mounting frame.
9 On refitting, ensure that the guides are correctly seated in the mounting frame then manoeuvre the airbag into position and reconnect the wiring connector.

10 Locate the airbag pegs into the guides then refit the retaining screws, tightening them securely.
11 Refit the lower facia panel.
12 Switch on the ignition, **then** reconnect the battery negative lead.

Airbag control unit

13 No information on the airbag control unit was available at the time of writing.

Airbag wiring contact unit

14 Remove the steering wheel as described in Chapter 10.
15 Taking care not to rotate the contact unit, undo the three retaining screws and remove it from the steering wheel.
16 On refitting, fit the unit to the steering wheel and securely tighten its retaining screws. If a new contact unit is being fitted, cut the cable-tie which is fitted to prevent the unit accidentally rotating.
17 Refit the steering wheel as described in Chapter 10.

24 Anti-theft alarm system - general information

Note: *This information is applicable only to the anti-theft alarm system fitted by VW as standard equipment.*

Later models are fitted with an anti-theft alarm system as standard equipment. The alarm has switches on all the doors (including the tailgate/boot lid), the bonnet and the ignition switch. If the tailgate/boot lid, bonnet or any of the doors are opened or the ignition switch is switched on whilst the alarm is set, the alarm horn will sound and the hazard warning lights will flash. The alarm also has an immobiliser function which makes the ignition (petrol models) or fuel supply system (diesel models) inoperable whilst the alarm is triggered.

The alarm is set using the key in the driver's or passenger's front door lock. Simply hold the key in the locking position until the warning light near the driver's door lock button starts to flash. The alarm system will then start to monitor its various switches approximately 30 seconds later.

With the alarm set, if the tailgate/boot lid is unlocked, the lock switch sensing will automatically be switched off but the door and bonnet switches will still be active. Once the tailgate/boot lid is shut and locked again, the switch sensing will be switched back on again.

Should the alarm system become faulty, the vehicle should be taken to a VW dealer for examination. They will have access to a special diagnostic tester which will quickly trace any fault present in the system.

12

25 Heated front seat components - removal and refitting

Heater mats

1 On models equipped with heated front seats, a heater pad is fitted to both the seat back and the seat cushion. Renewal of either heater mat involves peeling back the upholstery, removing the old mat, sticking the new mat in position and then refitting the upholstery. Note that upholstery removal and refitting requires considerable skill and experience if it is to be carried out successfully and is therefore best entrusted to your VW dealer. In practice, it will be very difficult for the home mechanic to carry out the job without ruining the upholstery.

Heated seat switches

2 Disconnect the battery negative lead (see Section 1).

3 Using a suitable flat-bladed screwdriver carefully prise out the small blanking plate from the side of the switch assembly.

4 Carefully prise the switch assembly out of position and disconnect its wiring connector.

5 Refitting is the reverse of removal.

Key to wiring diagrams

No.	Description
A	Battery
B	Starter
C	Alternator
C1	Voltage regulator
D	Ignition switch
E	Lighting switch
E1	Lighting switch
E2	Indicator switch
E3	Hazard warning lamp switch
E4	Headlamp dip and flasher switch
E9	Fresh air blower switch
E15	Heated rear window switch
E19	Parking lamp switch
E20	Instrument/dash panel lighting control
E22	Intermittent wiper switch
E23	Foglamp switch
E39	Electric window isolation switch
E40	Electric window switch, front left
E41	Electric window switch, right
E43	Mirror adjustment switch
E45	CCS switch
E48	Mirror adjustment changeover switch
E52	Electric window switch, rear left, in door
E53	Electric window switch, rear left
E54	Electric window switch, rear right, in door
E55	Electric window switch, rear right
E81	Electric window switch, front right
E86	Recall button for multi-function indicator
E102	Headlamp range adjuster
E109	Memory switch for multi-function indicator
F	Brake lamp switch
F1	Oil pressure switch
F2	Door contact switch, front left
F3	Door contact switch, front right
F4	Reversing lamp switch
F5	Boot lamp switch
F8	Kickdown switch
F9	Handbrake warning switch
F10	Door contact switch, rear left
F11	Door contact switch, rear right
F18	Radiator fan thermoswitch
F22	Oil pressure switch
F25	Throttle valve switch
F26	Thermotime switch
F34	Brake fluid level warning-contact
F35	Thermotime switch for inlet manifold pre-heater
F36	Clutch pedal switch
F47	Brake pedal switch
F59	Central locking switch
F60	Idle switch

No.	Description
F66	Low coolant level switch
F81	Full-throttle switch
F87	Fan run-on thermoswitch
F93	Diaphragm pressure switch
F96	Altitude sender
F114	Central locking switch (passenger's door)
F130	Pressure switch for fuel pump run-on
F131	Positioning unit for central locking, front left
F132	Positioning unit for central locking, rear left
F133	Positioning unit for central locking, front right
F134	Positioning unit for central locking, rear right
F166	Part throttle switch for EGR
G	Fuel gauge sender
G1	Fuel gauge
G2	Coolant temperature sender
G3	Coolant temperature gauge
G4	Firing point sender
G5	Rev counter
G6	Fuel pump
G8	Oil temperature sender
G17	Ambient air temperature sensor
G19	Potentiometer for airflow meter
G21	Speedometer
G22	Speedometer sender, Hall sender on gearbox
G23	Fuel pump
G27	Engine temperature sensor
G28	Engine speed sensor
G32	Coolant low level sensor
G39	Lambda probe with heater
G40	Hall sender
G42	Inlet air temperature sender
G54	Speed sender for multi-function indicator/radio (GALA)/cruise control
G55	Pressure sender for multi-function indicator
G61	Knock sensor 1
G62	Coolant temperature sender unit
G66	Knock sensor 2
G68	Road speed sender
G69	Throttle valve potentiometer
G70	Air mass meter
G72	Inlet manifold temperature sender
G74	CO potentiometer
G79	Accelerator position sender
G80	Needle lift sender
G81	Fuel temperature sender
G127	Throttle valve potentiometer
G149	Modulating piston movement sender

No.	Description
H	Horn control
H1	Dual-tone horn
H3	Oil pressure warning buzzer
H11	Oil pressure warning buzzer
J2	Indicator/hazard warning flasher relay
J4	Dual-tone horn relay
J5	Foglamp relay
J6	Voltage stabiliser
J17	Fuel pump relay
J30	Rear wash/wipe relay
J31	Intermittent wash/wipe relay
J52	Glow plug relay
J59	Relief relay (for X-contact)
J81	Inlet manifold preheater relay
J88	Electronic ignition control unit in plenum chamber, left
J104	ABS control unit
J114	Oil pressure warning control unit
J119	Multi-function indicator
J120	Control unit for coolant shortage indicator
J138	Control unit for radiator fan run-on
J139	Electric windows control unit
J152	Side light warning buzzer
J159	Control unit for Idle speed stabilisation and overrun cut off, above relay plate
J169	Control unit for Digifant in plenum chamber, left
J176	Current supply for Digifant control unit
J179	Glow period control unit, on additional carrier, behind dash panel, left
J202	Mono-Jetronic control unit
J204	KE-Motronic control unit, in plenum chamber, right
J206	Fuel pump run-on relay
J208	Relay for lambda probe heater
J220	Control unit for Motronic in plenum chamber, centre
J248	Diesel direct injection system control unit, in plenum chamber, right
J257	Mono-Motronic control unit, in plenum chamber, right
J285	Control unit with display unit in dash panel insert
J317	Voltage supply relay, terminal 30
J325	Coolant heater relay, on bulkhead, left
J338	Throttle valve control part
J359	Low heater output relay is printed out
J360	High heater output relay is printed out
J361	Simos control unit, in plenum chamber, right
J362	Immobiliser control unit, behind dash panel, left
J363	Simos current supply relay

No.	Description
K1	Main beam warning lamp
K2	Alternator warning lamp
K3	Oil pressure warning lamp
K4	Sidelight warning lamp
K5	Turn indicator warning lamp
K6	Hazard warning lamp indicator lamp
K7	Dual circuit brakes/handbrake warning lamp
K10	Heated rear window warning lamp
K13	Rear foglamp warning lamp
K28	Coolant temperature/low level warning lamp
K29	Glow period warning lamp
K55	Turn indicator warning lamp, left
K83	Self-diagnosis warning lamp
K94	Turn indicator warning lamp, right
L1	Twin filament headlamp bulb, left
L2	Twin filament headlamp bulb, right
L8	Clock lighting
L9	Lighting switch lamp
L10	Dash insert lamp
L15	Ashtray lighting
L16	Fresh air controls lamp
L19	Gear selector indicator light bulb
L28	Cigarette lighter lamp
L39	Heated rear window switch lamp
L40	Foglamp switch lamp
L46	Rear foglamp bulb, left
L48	Rear ashtray lamp
L53	Electric window switch lamp
L66	Cassette storage lamp
L75	Digital display light
M1	Parking lamp, left
M2	Tail lamp, right
M3	Parking lamp, right
M4	Tail lamp, left
M5	Indicator, front left
M6	Indicator, rear left
M7	Indicator, front right
M8	Indicator, rear right
M9	Brake light bulb, left
M10	Brake light bulb, right
M16	Reversing lamp, left
M17	Reversing lamp, right
M18	Indicator side repeater lamp, left
M19	Indicator side repeater lamp, right
M21	Stop/tail lamp, left
M22	Stop/tail lamp, right
N	Ignition coil
N9	Warm-up valve
N10	Temperature sensor
N17	Cold start valve
N18	EGR valve
N23	Series resistance for fresh air blower
N24	Series resistance with overheating fuse
N30	Fuel injector, cylinder No 1
N31	Fuel injector, cylinder No 2
N32	Fuel injector, cylinder No 3
N33	Fuel injector, cylinder No 4
N34	Injector series resistance
N35	Mirror adjustment solenoid, driver's side
N41	TCI-H control unit
N42	Mirror adjustment solenoid, passenger's side
N51	Inlet manifold preheater element

No.	Description
N65	Overrun cut-off valve
N70	Final output stage for ignition system
N71	Control valve for idle stabilisation
N73	Differential pressure regulator
N75	Boost pressure limitation solenoid valve
N79	Heater element (crankcase breather)
N80	Solenoid valve, activated charcoal filter
N108	Commencement of injection valve
N109	Fuel cut-off valve
N113	Windscreen washer jets heater
N114	Ignition firing point adjustment control valve
N115	Solenoid cut-off valve, activated charcoal system
N123	Positioner for idle speed boost
N146	Quantity adjuster
N152	Ignition transformer
N156	Inlet manifold change over valve
N157	Ignition transformer output stage
N161	Two-way valve for exhaust gas recirculation
N165	Positioner for commencement of injection
O	Distributor
P	Spark plug connector
Q	Spark plug
Q6	Glow plug
Q7	Coolant heater elements
R	Connection for radio
S24	Overheating fuse
S39	Glow plug strip fuse, on bulkhead, left
S43	Electric windows fuse
S78	Coolant pump fuse
S104	Radiator fan fuse
S105	Radiator fan fuse
S109	Coolant heater element strip fuse
T1	Single connector, various locations
T1a	Single connector, various locations
T1b	Single connector, behind relay plate
T1c	Single connector, various locations
T1d	Single connector, behind relay plate
T1e	Single connector, behind relay plate
T1f	Single connector, various locations
T1g	Single connector, various locations
T1h	Single connector, various locations
T1i	Single connector, behind relay plate
T1k	Single connector, various locations
T1l	Single connector, in plenum chamber, right
T1n	Single connector, near left headlamp
T1o	Single connector, behind dash panel, centre
T1r	Single connector, behind relay plate
T1s	Single connector, behind relay plate
T1t	Single connector, under rear seat, centre
T1u	Single connector, near coil
T1v	Single connector, behind relay plate
T1w	Single connector, various locations
T1x	Single connector, near ignition coil
T1y	Single connector, self-diagnosis connector, behind console
T2	2-pin connector, various locations
T2a	2-pin connector, various locations
T2b	2-pin connector, various locations

No.	Description
T2c	2-pin connector, various locations
T2d	2-pin connector, various locations
T2e	2-pin connector, various locations
T2f	2-pin connector, various locations
T2g	2-pin connector, various locations
T2h	2-pin connector, various locations
T2i	2-pin connector, behind relay plate
T2j	2-pin connector, near exhaust manifold
T2k	2-pin connector, behind relay plate
T2l	2-pin connector, left of bulkhead
T2m	2-pin connector, various locations
T2n	2-pin connector, behind relay plate
T2p	2-pin connector, behind relay plate
T2r	2-pin connector, on fresh air blower series resistance
T2s	2-pin connector, in boot, left
T2x	2-pin connector, various locations
T2y	2-pin connector, various locations
T2z	2-pin connector, various locations
T3	3-pin connector, various locations
T3a	3-pin connector, various locations
T3b	3-pin connector, near front interior lamp
T3c	3-pin connector, various locations
T3d	3-pin connector, various locations
T3e	3-pin connector
T3f	3-pin connector
T3g	3-pin connector, various locations
T3h	3-pin connector, various locations
T3i	3-pin connector, left of engine compartment
T3m	3-pin connector, various locations
T3n	3-pin connector, various locations
T3p	3-pin connector, front passenger's door
T3q	3-pin connector, front passenger's door
T4	4-pin connector, near exhaust manifold
T4a	4-pin connector, various locations
T4b	4-pin connector, behind relay plate
T4c	4-pin connector, behind steering column trim
T4d	4-pin connector, under steering column trim
T4e	4-pin connector, left headlamp
T4f	4-pin connector, various locations
T4h	4-pin connector, behind steering column trim
T4l	4-pin connector, behind relay plate
T5	5-pin connector, various locations
T5a	5-pin connector, various locations
T5b	5-pin connector, behind steering column trim
T5c	5-pin connector, behind steering column trim
T5d	5-pin connector, in tailgate/bootlid
T5e	5-pin connector
T5f	5-pin connector, near relay plate in left A-pillar
T6	6-pin connector, various locations
T6a	6-pin connector, various locations
T6b	6-pin connector, various locations
T6e	6-pin connector, left of bulkhead
T6f	6-pin connector, behind relay plate
T6l	6-pin connector
T6m	6-pin connector, in B-pillar
T6n	6-pin connector, in B-pillar
T7a	7-pin connector, behind steering column trim

12

No.	Description	No.	Description	No.	Description
T8	8-pin connector, various locations	TV14	Self-diagnosis function box, behind console	V50	Water pump
T8a	8-pin connector	TV17	Door contact switch junction box, above relay plate	V59	Washer pump
T8b	8-pin connector			V60	Throttle valve positioner
T8c	8-pin connector	U1	Cigarette lighter	V69	Central locking pump control unit
T12	12-pin connector	V	Windscreen wiper motor	W	Interior lamp, front
T16	16-pin connector	V2	Fresh air blower	W3	Boot lamp
T17	17-pin connector	V5	Windscreen washer pump	W6	Glovebox lamp
T18	18-pin connector	V7	Radiator fan	W11	Reading lamp, rear left
T24	24-pin conector, on cylinder head, left	V12	Wiper motor	W12	Reading lamp, rear right
T28	28-pin connector, various locations	V14	Window motor, left	W15	Interior lamp
T28a	28-pin connector, on cylinder head, left	V15	Window motor, right	X	Number plate lamp
T45	45-pin connector	V17	Mirror adjustment motor, driver's	Y2	Digital clock
T42	42-pin connector, on cylinder head, left	V25	Mirror adjustment motor, passenger's	Y4	Trip recorder
T38	38-pin connector	V26	Window motor, rear left	Z1	Heated rear window
T68	68-pin connector	V27	Window motor, rear right	Z4	Heated mirror, driver's
TV2	Terminal 30 junction, behind relay plate	V48	Positioning motor for headlamp range control, left	Z5	Heated mirror, passenger's
TV5	Terminal 15a junction box, above relay plate			Z20	Windscreen washer jet heater
		V49	Positioning motor for headlamp range control, left	Z21	Windscreen washer jet heater, right
TV13	Speed signal junction, above relay plate				

Earth connections

1	Battery earth strap	80	Instrument loom	138	Motronic loom
2	Gearbox earth strap	86	Rear loom	139	Motronic loom
12	Near battery	89	Electric window loom	156	Diesel direct injection loom
14	Gearbox	94	Digifant loom	159	Digifant loom
15	Cylinder head	98	Bootlid/tailgate loom	173	Mono-Motronic loom
16	Cylinder head cover	101	Headlamp range control loom	174	Mono-Motronic loom
17	Inlet manifold	105	Central locking loom	182	Engine loom
18	Cylinder block	117	Mono-Jetronic loom	193	Radiator fan loom
29	Near cylinder head/exhaust manifold	119	Headlamp loom	204	Digifant loom
30	Relay plate	120	Headlamp loom	217	Glow plug system loom
40	Under rear seat, right	125	Headlamp loom	220	Engine loom
43	Bottom of right A-pillar	126	Mono-Jetronic loom	221	Engine loom
50	Left of boot	128	Interior lamp loom	224	Lighting switch loom
51	Left of boot	129	Dual-tone horn loom	246	Simos loom

Positive connections

A11	Instrument loom	E30	Engine loom	Q13	Electric window loom
C10	Headlamp loom	F25	Diesel direct injection system loom	Q15	Electric window loom
C11	Radiator fan loom	F26	Diesel direct injection system loom	Q16	Electric window loom
C12	Headlamp loom	F29	Glow plug loom	Q17	Electric window loom
C13	Dual-tone horn loom	F30	Glow plug loom	Q18	Electric window loom
C14	Heated washer jet loom	F31	Diesel direct injection system loom	R4	Interior lamp/door contact switch loom
C19	Headlamp loom	F32	Diesel direct injection system loom	R28	Rear loom
C20	Headlamp loom	G1	Digifant loom	S1	Central locking loom
D98	Engine loom	G2	Digifant loom	S2	Central locking loom
E3	Mono-Jetronic loom	G3	Cable sleeve, injectors	S3	Central locking loom
E5	Mono-Jetronic loom	G4	Cable sleeve, injectors	W2	Rear loom
E6	Motronic loom	H20	Diagnostic loom	W9	Rear loom
E10	Mono-Jetronic loom	H21	Diagnostic loom	W10	Rear loom
E11	Mono-Jetronic loom	K21	Radiator fan loom	Y1	Interior lamp loom
E12	Mono-Motronic loom	N2	Headlamp range control loom	Z	Mirror adjustment/heating loom
E13	Mono-Motronic loom	Q9	Electric window loom		

Fuses (Typical)

No.	Rating (A)/Colour	Circuit protected	No.	Rating (A)/Colour	Circuit protected
1	10/Red	Dip beam (left-hand)	13	10/Red	Horn, radiator fan run-on
2	10/Red	Dip beam (right-hand)	14	10/Red	Reversing lights, mirrors, heated washer jets, seat heating, thermotronic sensor, gearshift illumination (automatic)
3	10/Red	Instrument panel and number plate lighting			
4	15/Blue	Rear wiper, sunroof, self-levelling control unit *	15	10/Red	Engine electronics
5	15/Blue	Windscreen wiper motor, front and rear washers	16	15/Blue	Warning lights, multi-function indicator, glove box light
6	20/Yellow	Blower unit, air conditioner	17	10/Red	Indicators
7	10/Red	Side and tail light (right-hand)	18	20/Yellow	Fuel pump, lambda probe
8	10/Red	Side and tail light (left-hand)	19	30/Green	Radiator fan, air conditioner
9	20/Yellow	Heated rear window, rear view mirror heating	20	20/Yellow	Brake lights, cruise control system
10	15/Blue	Foglights and rear foglights	21	15/Blue	Interior/luggage compartment lights, cigarette lighter, clock, central locking, multi-function indicator
11	10/Red	Main beam (left-hand) and warning light			
12	10/Red	Main beam (right-hand)	22	10/Red	Radio

Note that the self-levelling system compressor has a circuit breaker, which in the event of an overload switches of automatically, then switches on again after a few seconds

Alternator, Battery, Starter

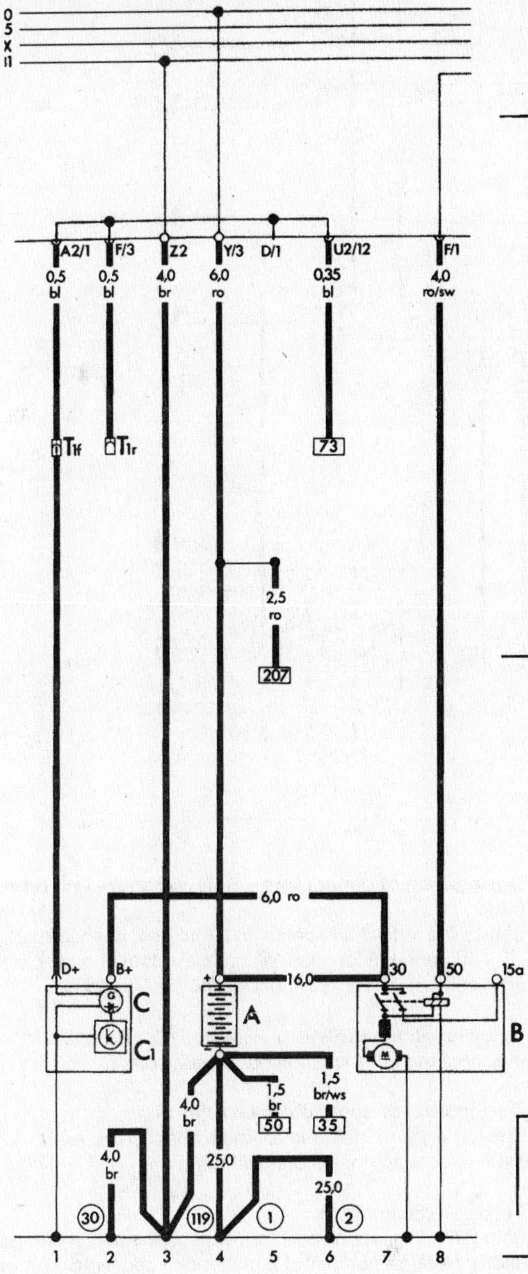

Designation for current circuit illustrated

Relay plate with fuse box indicated
by grey area

Wire colours

ge = yellow
ws = white
ro = red
li = lilac
bl = blue
gr = grey
gn = green
br = brown
sw = black

Consumer circuit with wire routing
All switches and contacts are shown in the "off" position.

Vehicle earth
Numbers in circles show the location on the vehicle
(see legend).

Current track No.
Makes it easier to find the connections.

Legend
In all current flow diagrams the same parts designations
are used for similar components: e.g. Always A for battery

A – Battery
B – Starter
C – Alternator
C 1 – Voltage regulator
T 1f – Single connector, engine compartment, right
T 1r – Single connector
1 – Earth strap, battery – body
2 – Earth strap, gearbox – body
30 – Earth point – 1 – next to relay plate
119 – Earth connection – 1 –, in headlight wiring loom

12

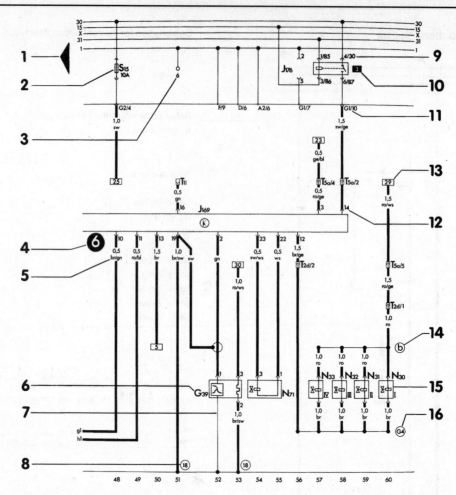

1 – **Arrow** indicates the next current circuit relevant to current flow diagram

2 – **Designation of a fuse**
e.g. fuse No. 15 (10 amps.) in fuse box

3 – **Measuring points on the relay plate**

4 – **Measuring points for fault finding programmes**
The numbers in the black circles can be found in a diagram, or in a fault finding programme current flow diagram.

5 – **Wire cross-section** (in mm²) **and wire colours**
(Abbreviations are explained in colour key next to current flow diagram).

6 – **Part designation**
Using the legend you can identify the part referred to.

7 – **Internal connections** (thin lines)
These connections are not always to be found in the form of wires. Internal connections are however current carrying connections. They make it possible to trace the flow of current inside the components and wiring looms.

8 – **Designation of earth point or earth connection in wiring loom**
Location of earth points in the vehicle are indicated in the legend or in which wiring loom these permanent connections can be found.

9 – **Designation of connectors – Relays/control unit on relay plate**
Shows the individual contact in a multi-pin connector e.g. 4/30
4 = contact 4 at location ❸ on relay plate or relay carrier
30 = contact 30 on relay/control unit

10 – **Relay location number**
Indicates the relay location on the relay plate.

11 – **Designation of connectors on relay plate**
Shows wiring of multi-pin or single connectors, e.g. G 1/10 – multi-pin connector G1 contact 10.

12 – **Terminal designation**
With the designation which appears on the actual component and/or terminal number of a multi-point connector

13 – **Wire continuation**
Numbers in frame indicate in which current track the wire is continued.

14 – **Continuation of internal connections**
Letters indicate where in the next part of the current flow diagram the connection continues.

15 – **Symbol for components (see pages 12•29 and 12•30)**

16 – **Designation of connection in wiring loom**
The legend indicates in which wiring loom these permanent connections can be found.

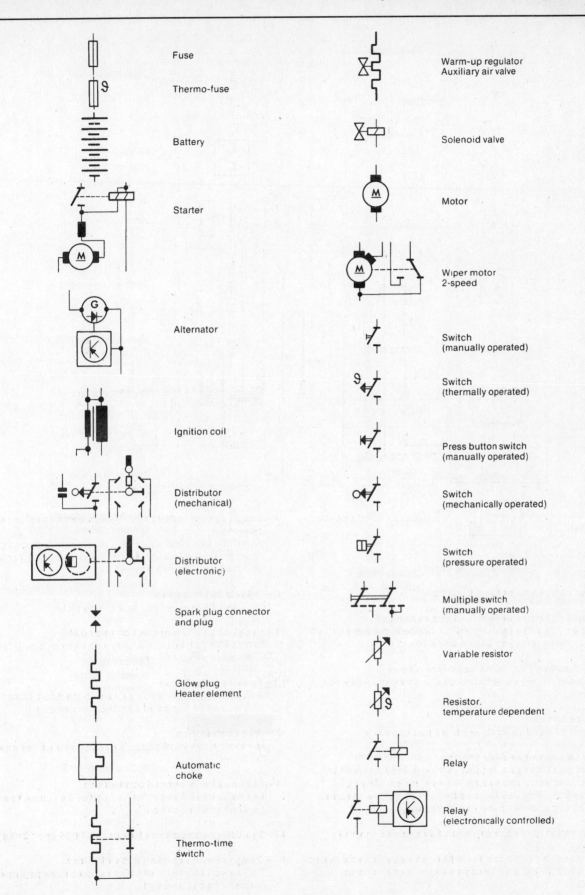

Fuse

Thermo-fuse

Battery

Starter

Alternator

Ignition coil

Distributor (mechanical)

Distributor (electronic)

Spark plug connector and plug

Glow plug Heater element

Automatic choke

Thermo-time switch

Warm-up regulator Auxiliary air valve

Solenoid valve

Motor

Wiper motor 2-speed

Switch (manually operated)

Switch (thermally operated)

Press button switch (manually operated)

Switch (mechanically operated)

Switch (pressure operated)

Multiple switch (manually operated)

Variable resistor

Resistor. temperature dependent

Relay

Relay (electronically controlled)

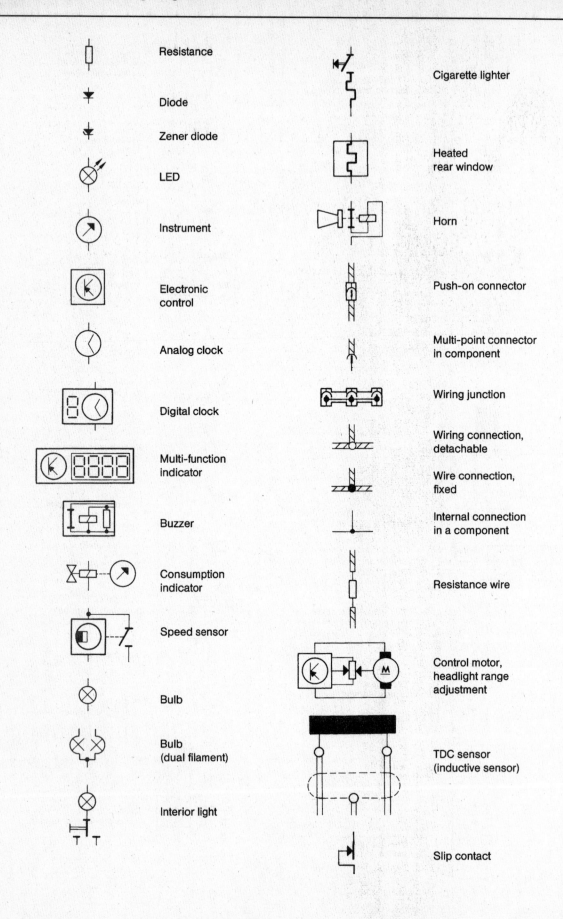

Resistance	Cigarette lighter
Diode	Heated rear window
Zener diode	Horn
LED	Push-on connector
Instrument	Multi-point connector in component
Electronic control	Wiring junction
Analog clock	Wiring connection, detachable
Digital clock	Wire connection, fixed
Multi-function indicator	Internal connection in a component
Buzzer	Resistance wire
Consumption indicator	Control motor, headlight range adjustment
Speed sensor	TDC sensor (inductive sensor)
Bulb	
Bulb (dual filament)	
Interior light	Slip contact

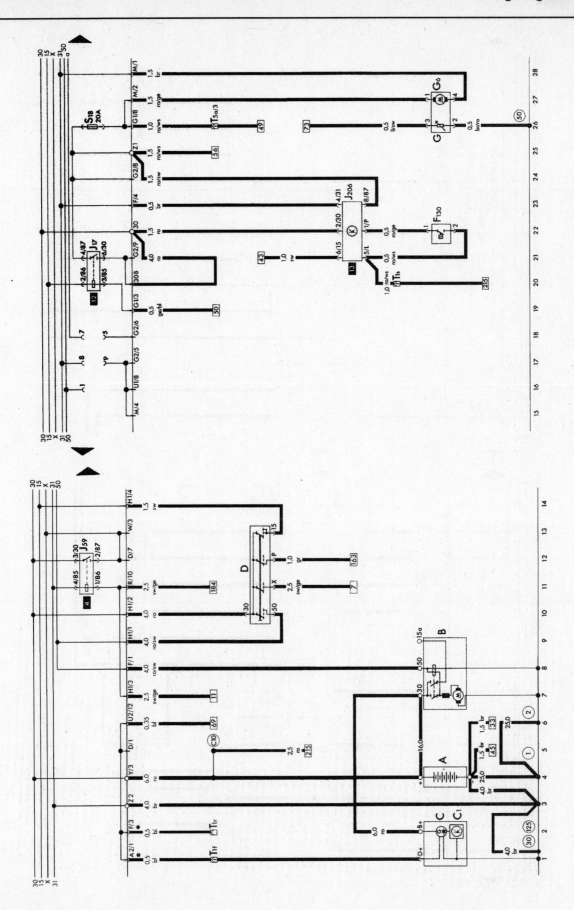

Fuel supply system - All models up to 1994

Alternator, Battery, Starter and Ignition switch - All models up to 1994

12

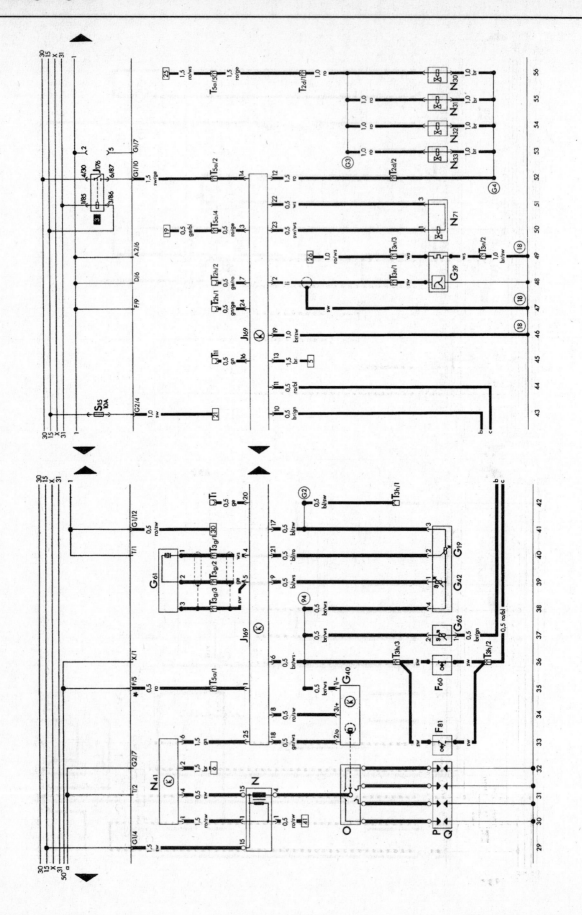

Digifant control, Lamda probe, Injectors - Models up to 1994

Ignition system, Digifant control unit, Knock sensor - Models up to 1994

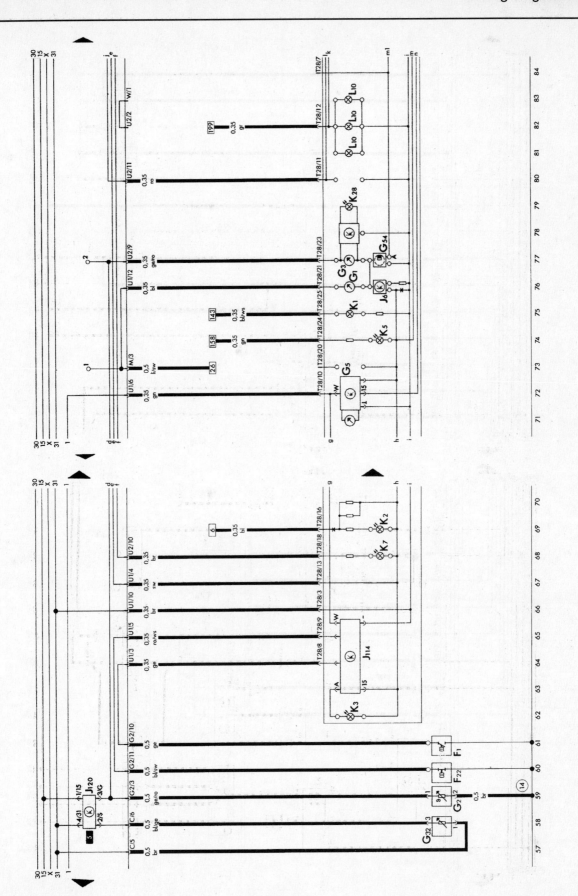

Dash panel insert, Rev. counter, Fuel and coolant temperature gauges -
All models up to 1994

Coolant shortage indicator, Optical and acoustic oil pressure warning -
All models up to 1994

12

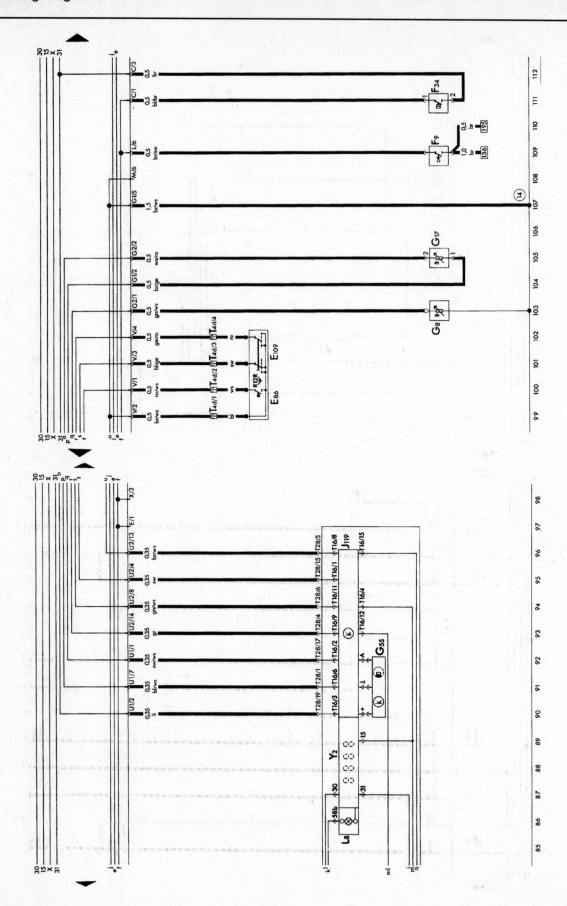

Switch and sender for multi-function indicator - All models up to 1994

Multi-function indicator - All models up to 1994

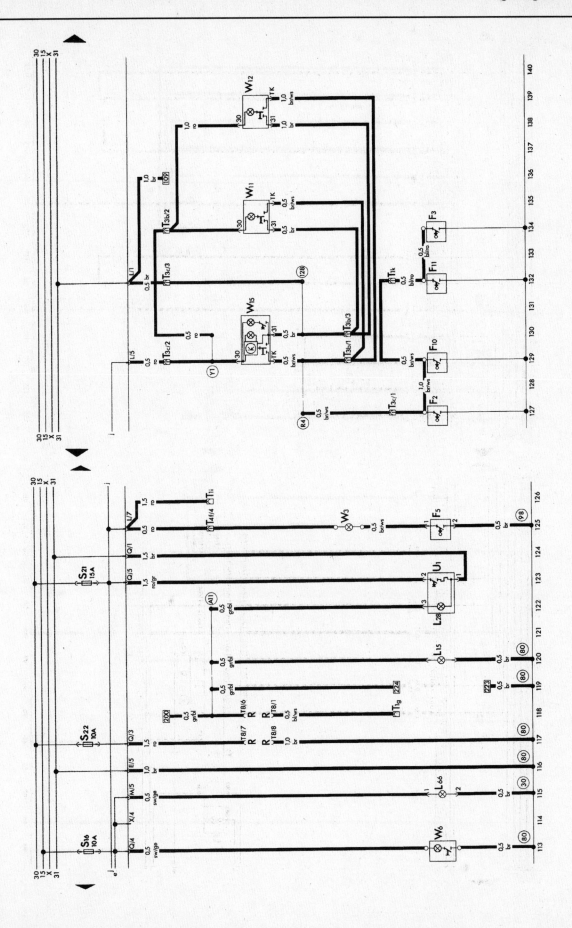

Interior light, Rear reading lights - All models up to 1994

Glove box light, Cigarette lighter, Boot light, Radio connection, Ashtray light,
Cassette storage light - All models up to 1994

12

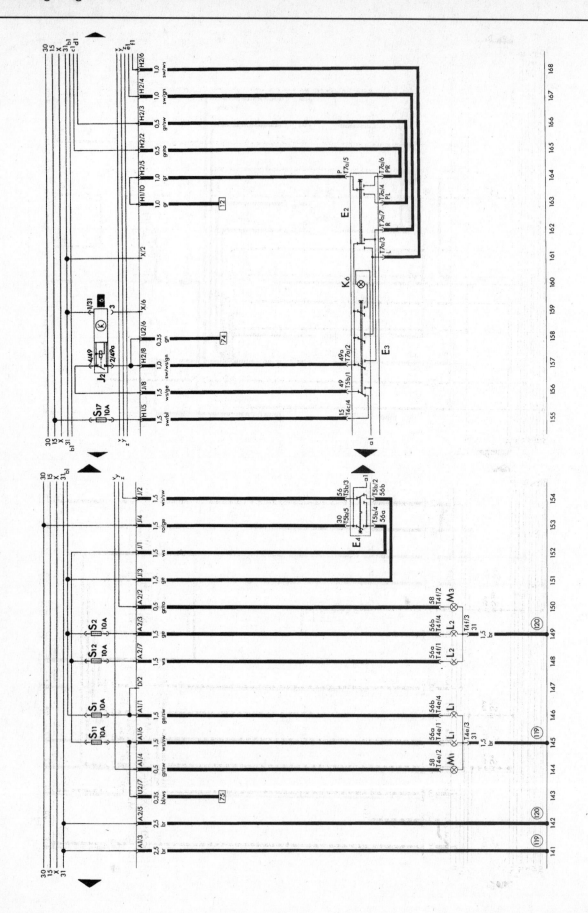

Turn signals and emergency lights system, Parking light switch -
All models up to 1994

Headlights and Sidelights - All models up to 1994

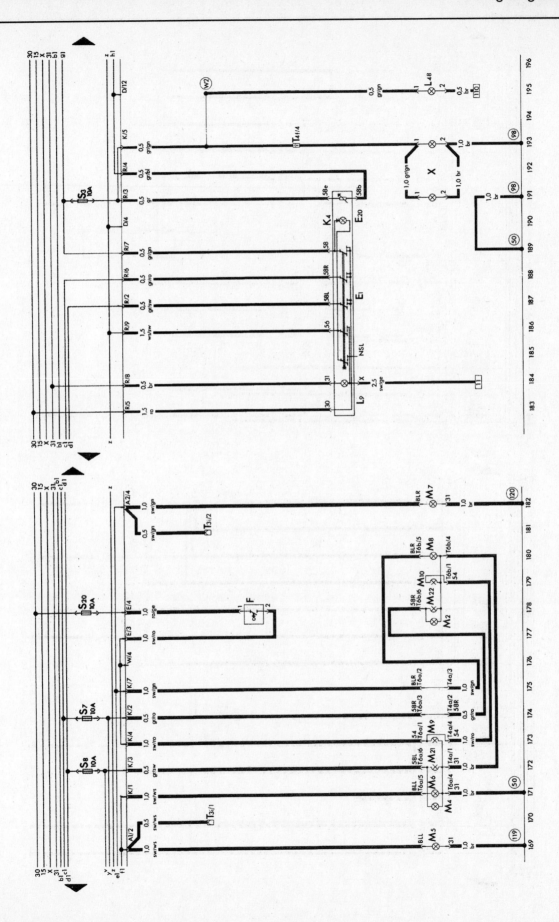

Lighting switch, Number plate lights, Rear ashtray light - All models up to 1994

Turn signals, Brake lights and Tail lights - All models up to 1994

12

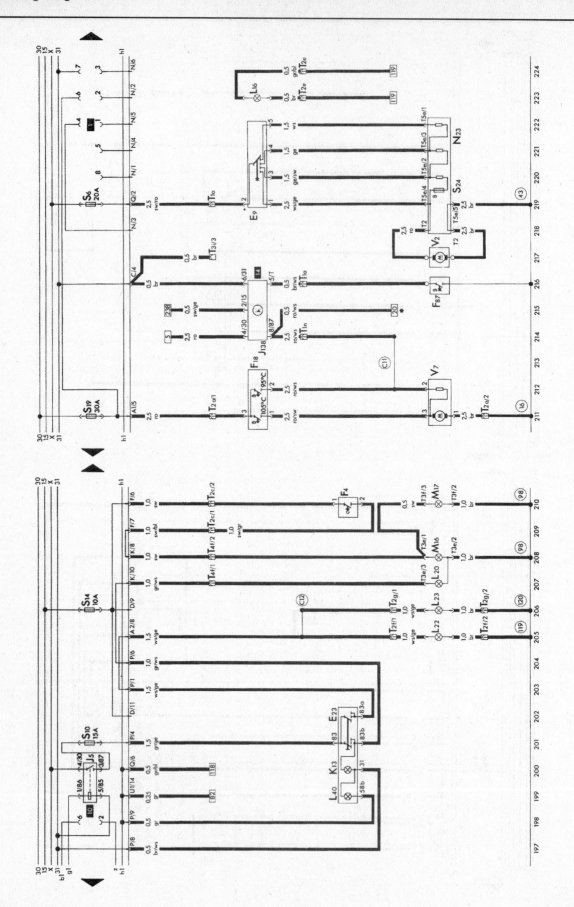

Radiator fan, Fresh air blower - All models up to 1994

Front and rear foglights, Reversing lights - All models up to 1994

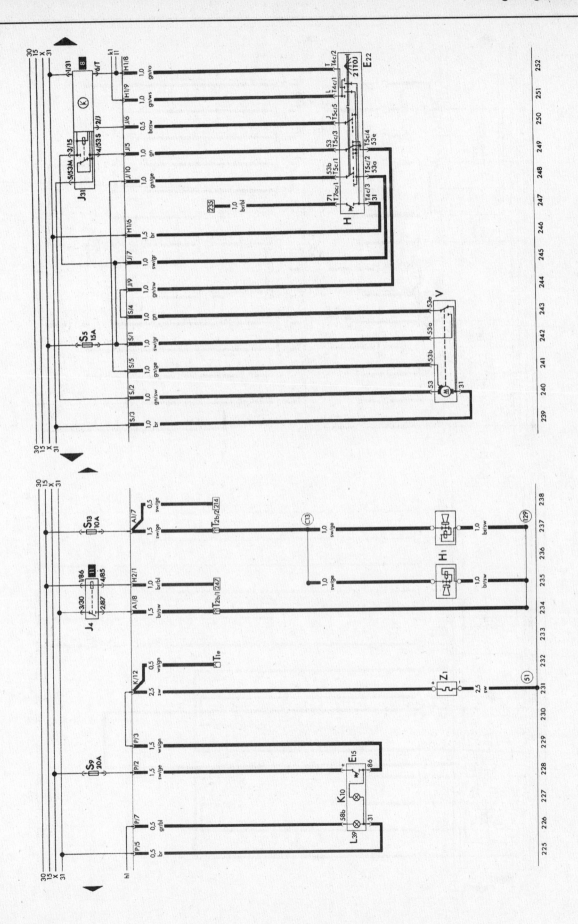

Windscreen wiper and washer - All models up to 1994

Heated rear window, Dual tone horn - All models up to 1994

12

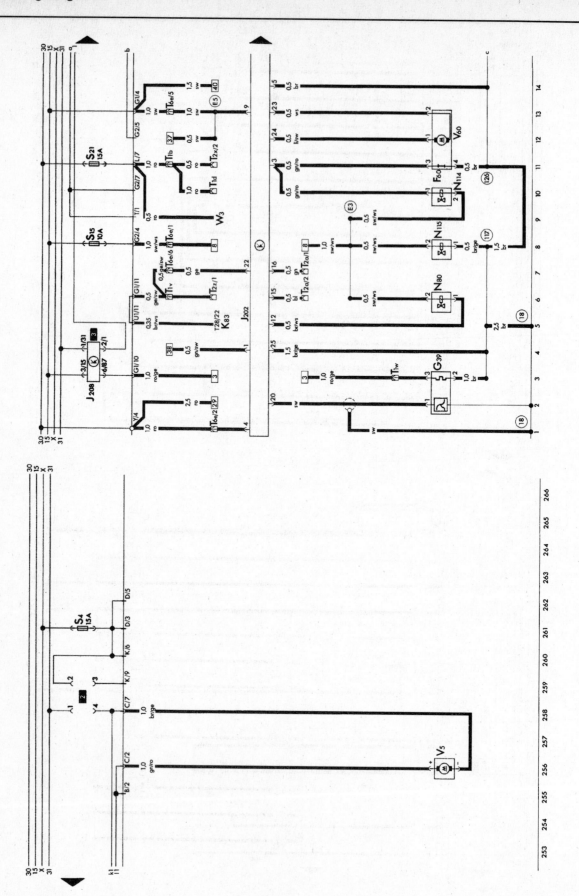

Fuel injection system, Lambda probe - Mono-jetronic models up to 1994

Windscreen washer - All models up to 1994

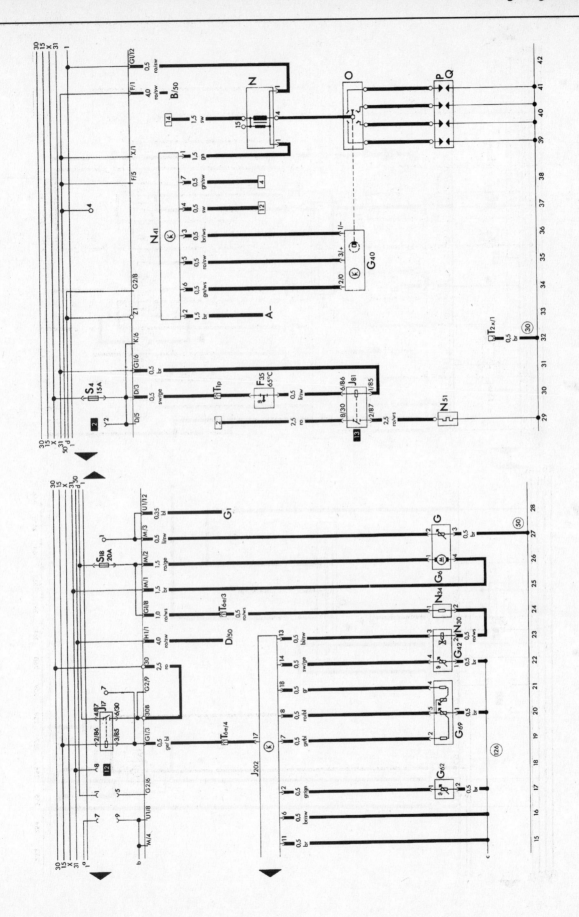

Intake manifold preheating, Ignition system - Mono-jetronic models up to 1994

Fuel injection system, Fuel supply system - Mono-jetronic models up to 1994

12

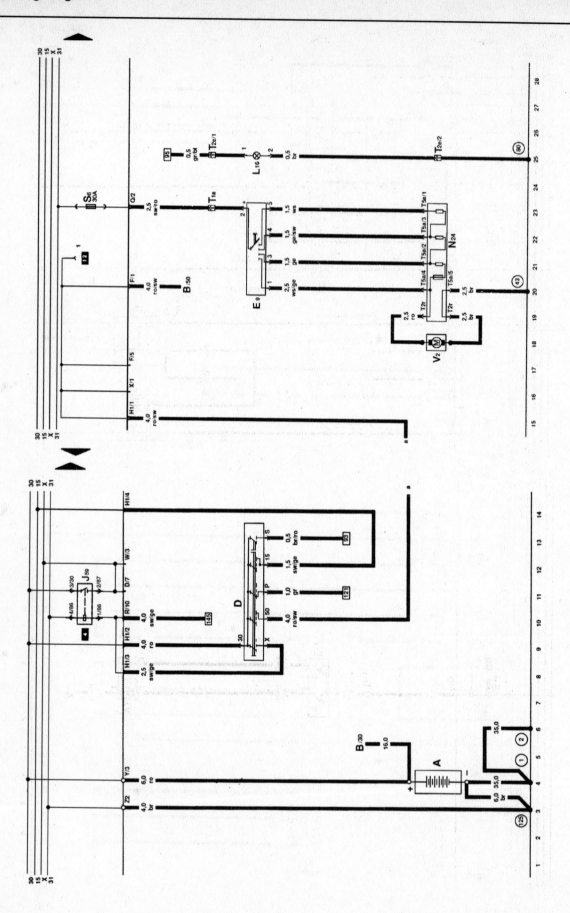

Fresh air blower - All models from 1994

Battery, Ignition/starter switch - All models from 1994

Alternator, Starter, Intake manifold pre-heating - Engine code AAM and ABS from 1994

2-stage radiator cooling fan - Engine code AAM and ABS from 1994

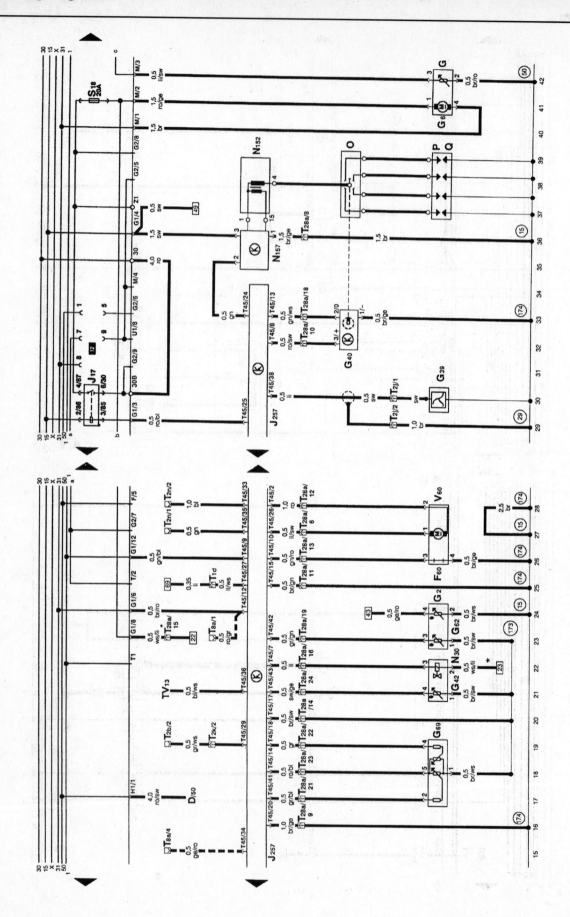

Control unit, Lambda probe, Ignition system, Fuel supply system - Engine code AAM and ABS from 1994

Control unit, Throttle valve potentiometer, Injector, Throttle valve positioner - Engine code AAM and ABS from 1994

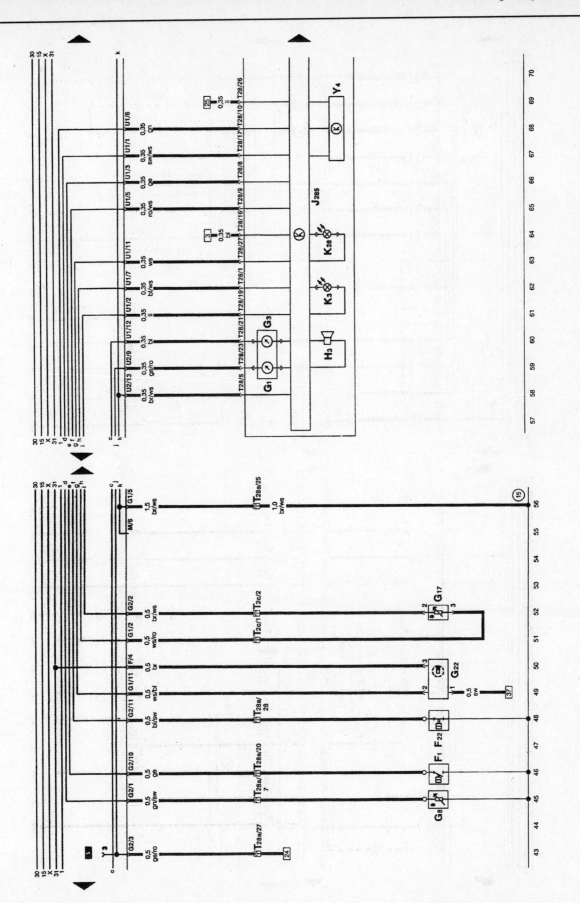

Dash panel insert, Oil pressure and coolant temperature warning, fuel gauge and
Trip recorder - Engine code AAM and ABS from 1994

Multi-function indicator sender, Speedometer sender, Oil pressure switch -
Engine code AAM and ABS from 1994

12

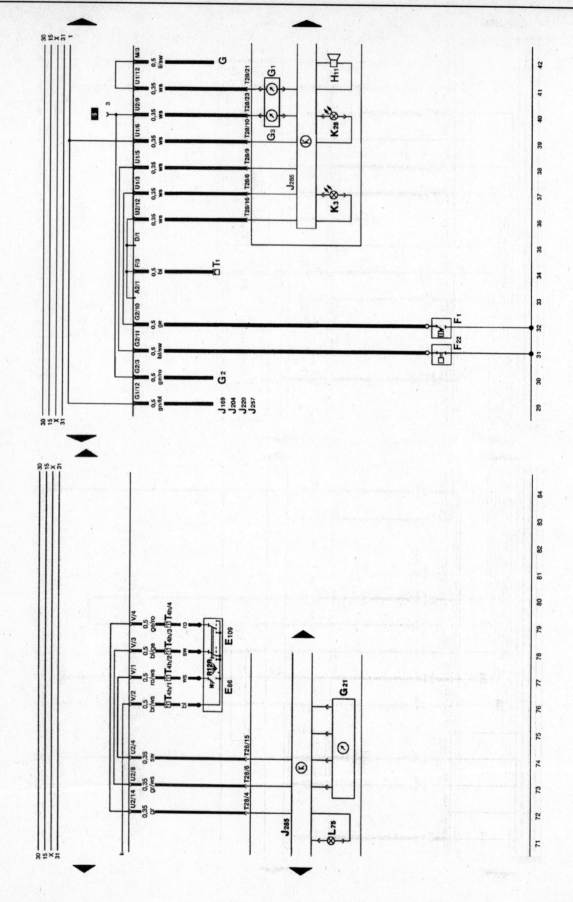

Dash panel insert, Fuel gauge, Coolant shortage and Temperature gauge/warning, optical and acoustic Oil pressure warning - All models from 1994

Dash panel insert, Speedometer, Multi-function indicator switch - Engine code AAM and ABS from 1994

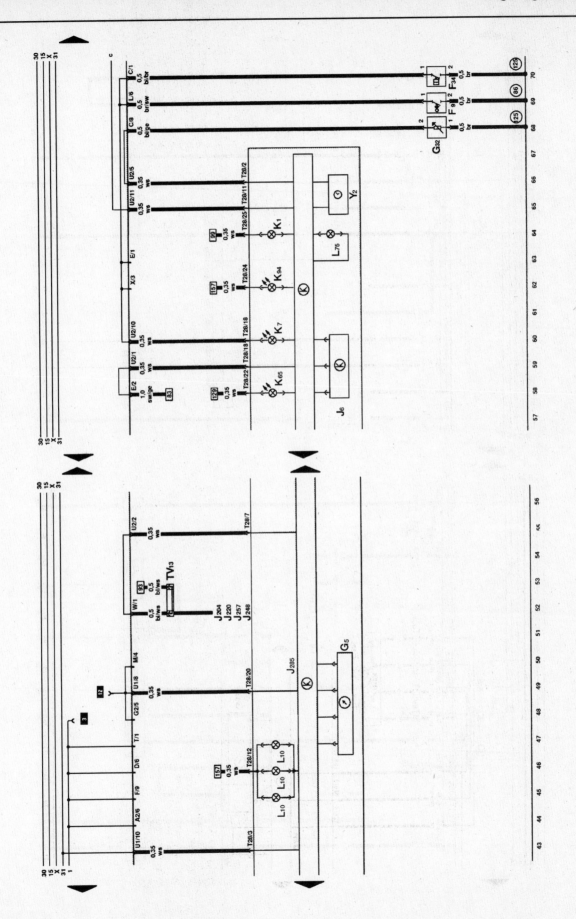

Dash panel insert, Digital clock, Handbrake warning and Brake fluid level switch,
Coolant shortage warning - All models from 1994

Dash panel insert, Rev. counter - All models from 1994

12

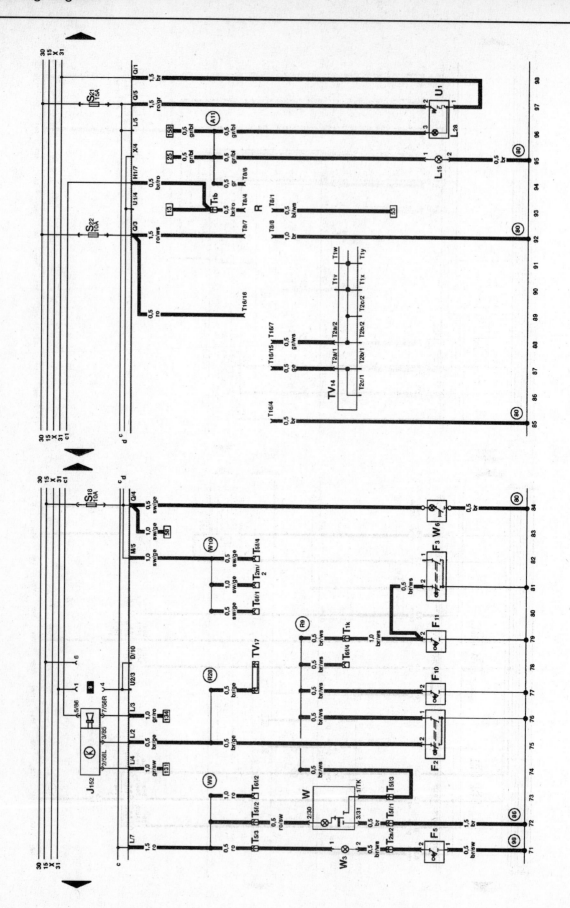

Self-diagnosis junction box, Radio connection, Ashtray light, Cigarette lighter - All models from 1994

Interior lights, Luggage compartment lights, Glove box light, Side light warning indicator - All models from 1994

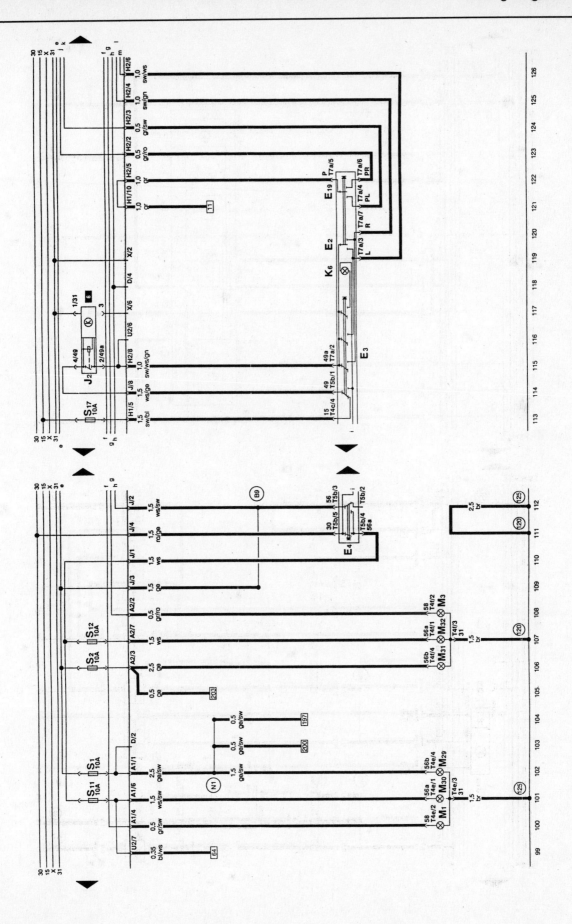

Turn signals and Hazard warning lights, Parking light switch

Headlights, Sidelights, Dipped beam and Flasher switch

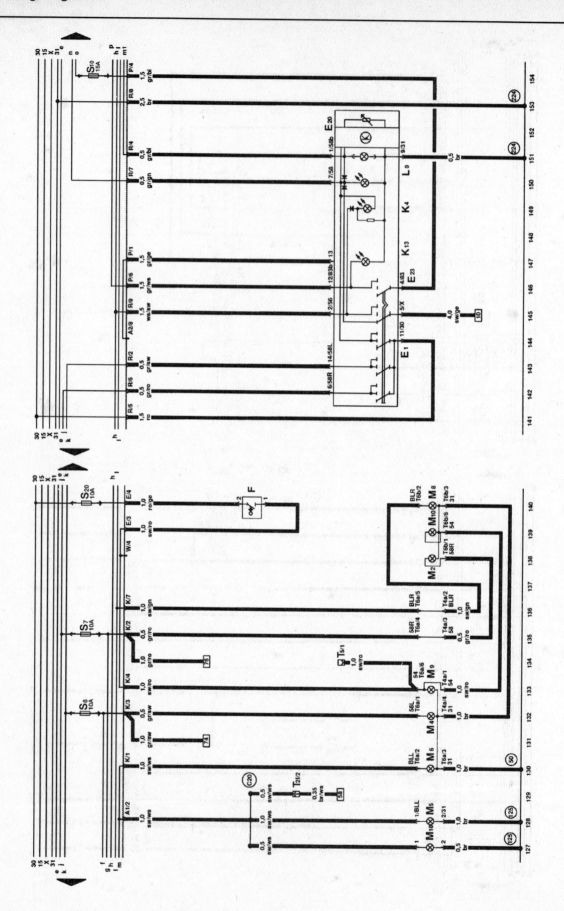

Lighting switch - All models from 1994

Turn signals, Brake lights and Tail lights - All models from 1994

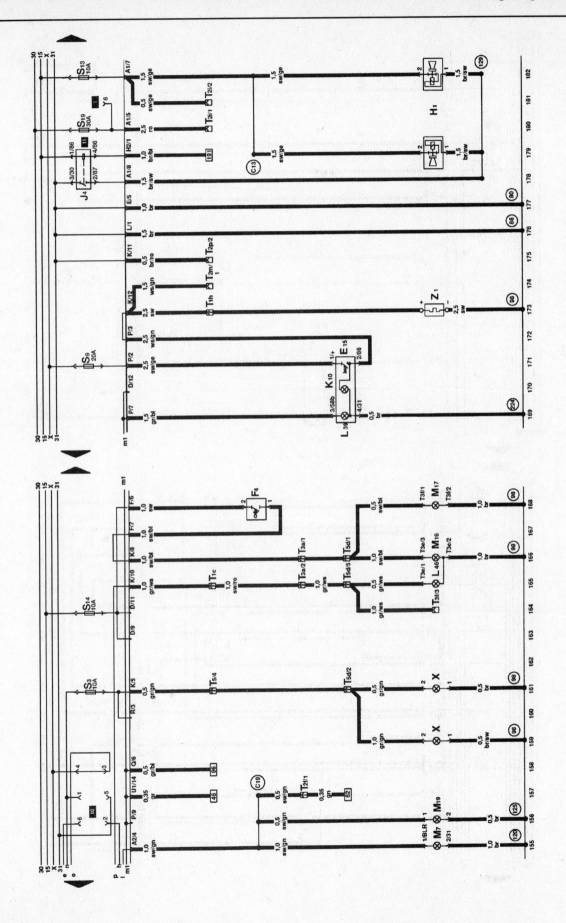

Heated rear window, Dual tone horn - All models from 1994

Rear foglights, Reversing lights, Number plate lights - All models from 1994

12

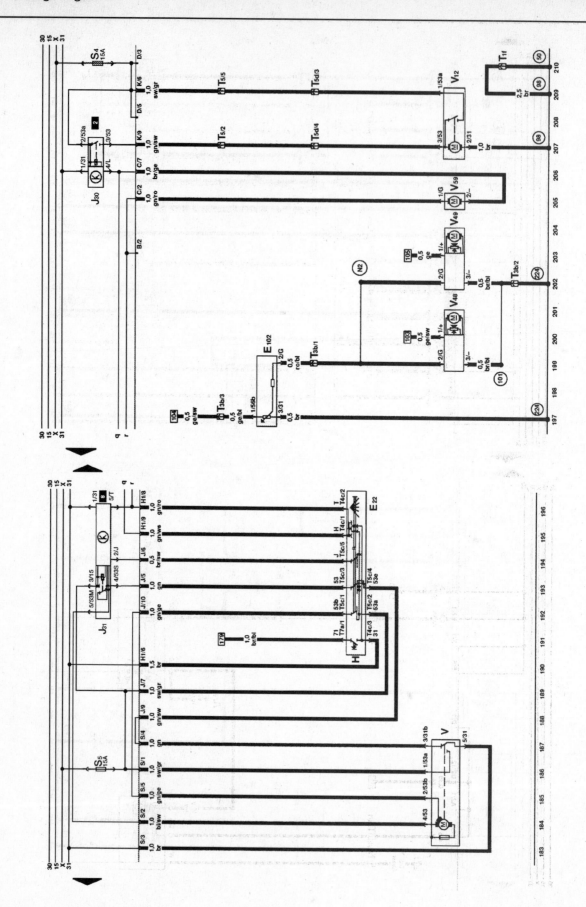

Headlight range control, Rear window wash/wipe system - All models from 1994

Windscreen wash/wipe system - All models from 1994

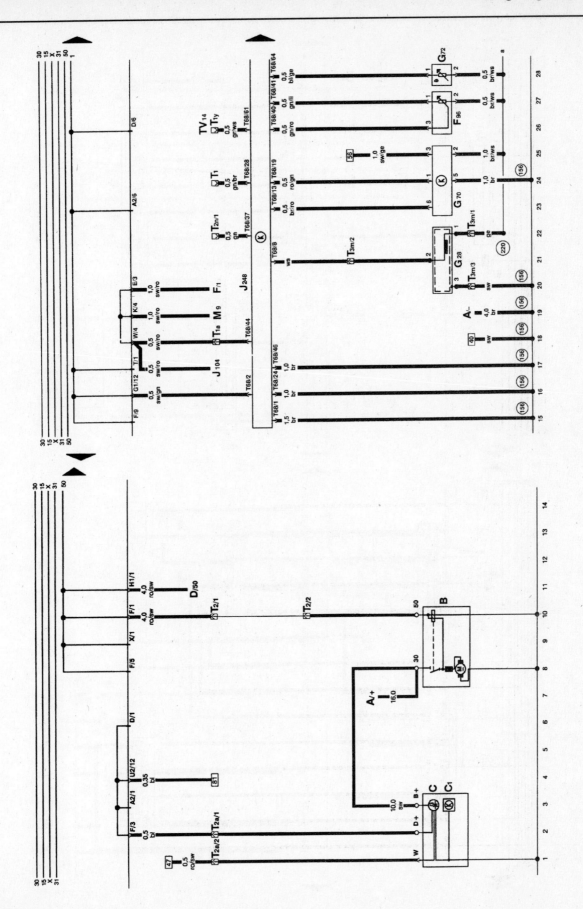

Direct injection system control unit - Diesel (engine code 1Z) from 1994

Alternator, Starter - Diesel (engine code 1Z) from 1994

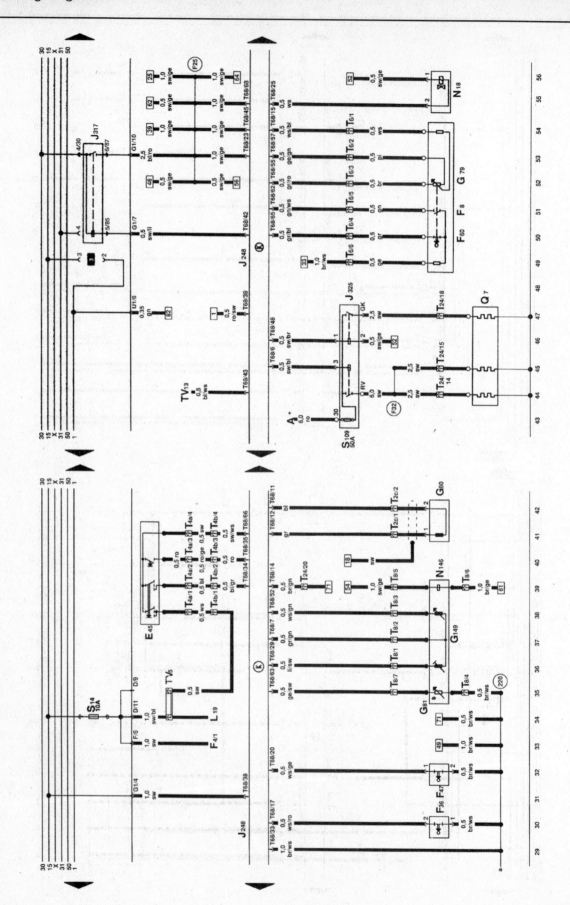

Direct injection system control unit (continued) –
Diesel (engine code 1Z) from 1994

Direct injection system control unit (continued) –
Diesel (engine code 1Z) from 1994

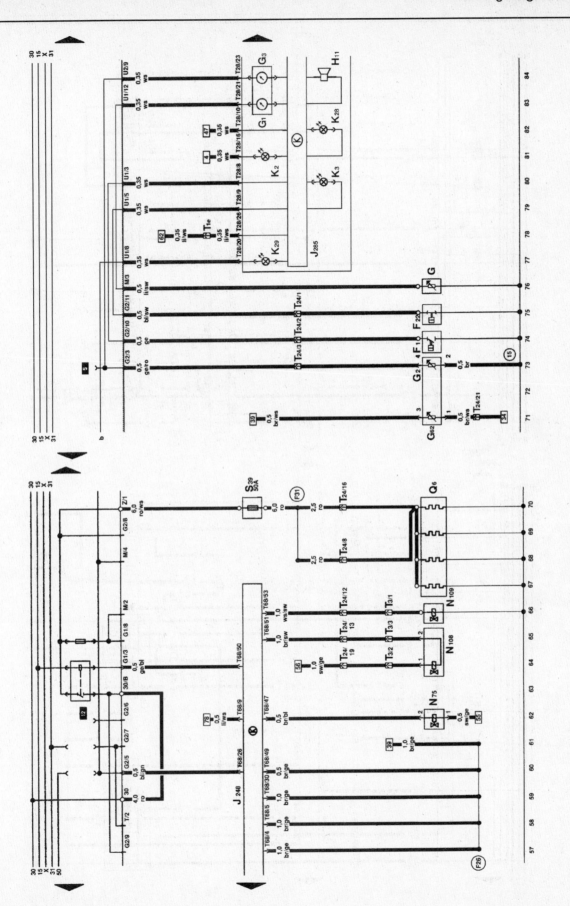

Dash panel insert, Coolant shortage/temperature warning, Oil pressure warning, Fuel gauge - Diesel (engine code 1Z) from 1994

Direct injection system control unit (continued) - Diesel (engine code 1Z) from 1994

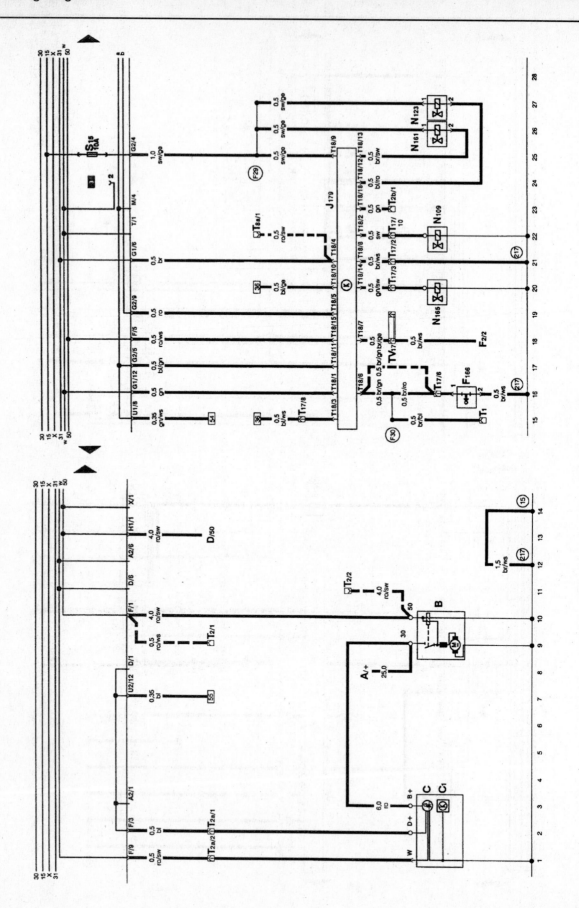

Glow plug system, fuel cut-off, EGR - Diesel (engine code AAZ) from 1994

Alternator, Starter - Diesel (engine code AAZ) from 1994

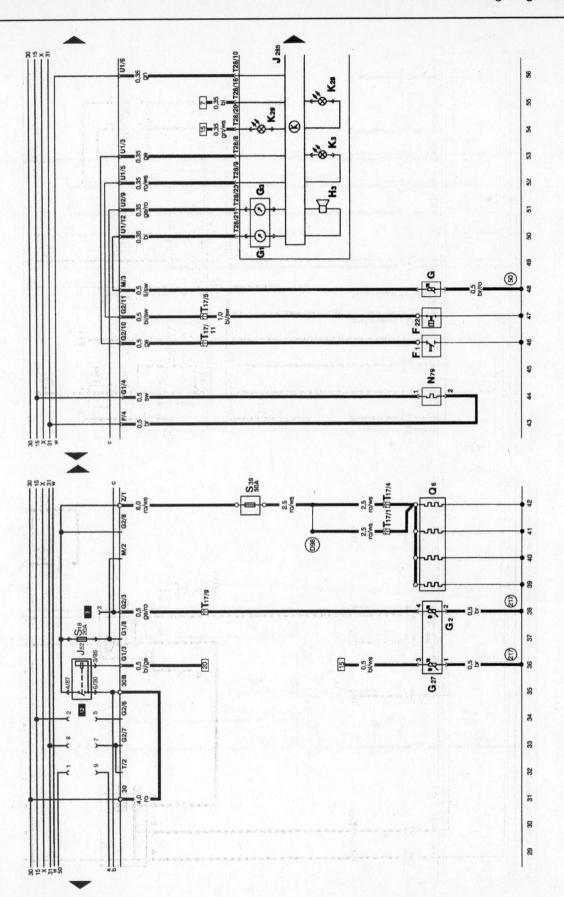

Dash panel insert, Coolant shortage/temperature warning, Oil pressure warning,
Fuel gauge - Diesel (engine code AAZ) from 1994

Glow plugs, Coolant temperature sensor -
Diesel (engine code AAZ) from 1994

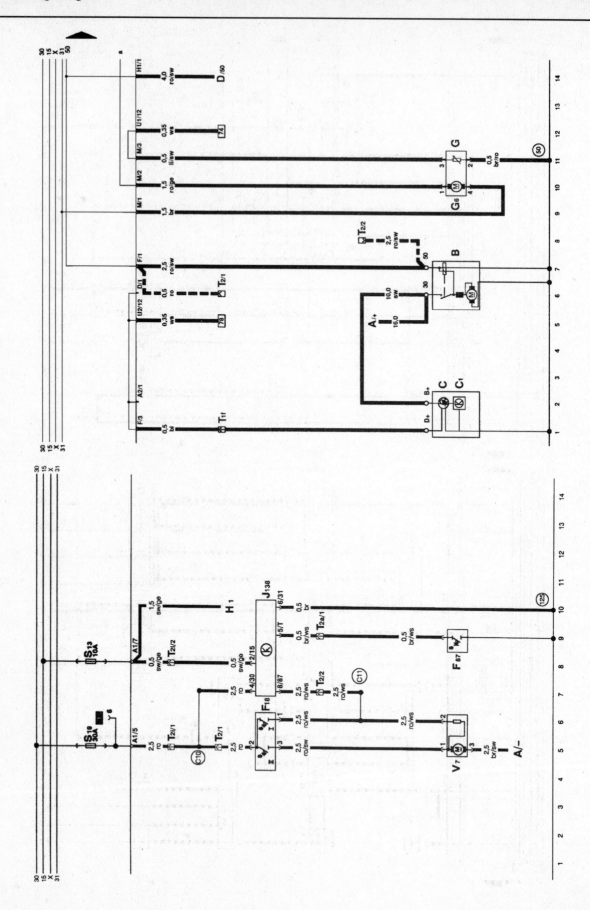

Alternator, Starter, Fuel supply system - Engine code 2E from 1994

Radiator cooling fan - Engine code 2E from 1994

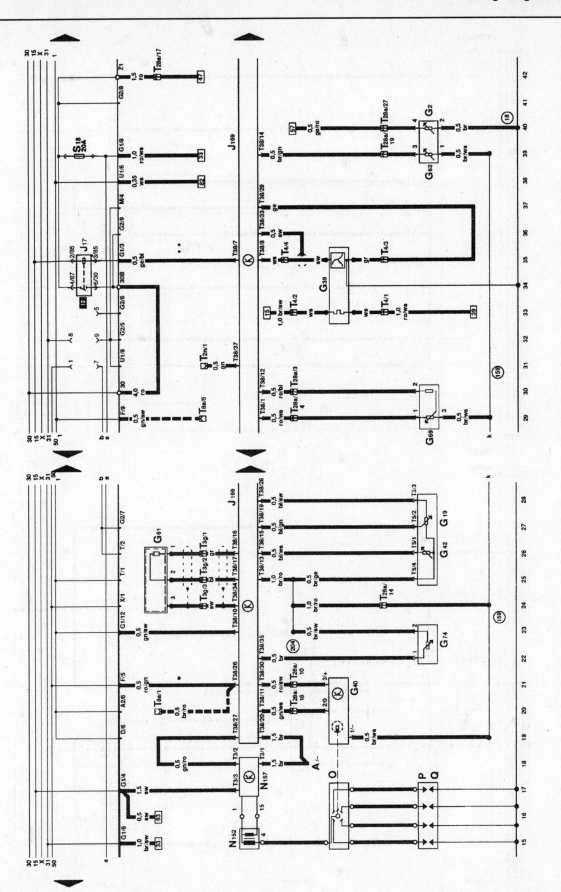

Digifant control unit, Lambda probe, Throttle valve potentiometer, Coolant temperature gauge - Engine code 2E from 1994

Ignition system, Digifant control unit, Knock sensor, Coolant temperature sensor, CO potentiometer - Engine code 2E from 1994

12

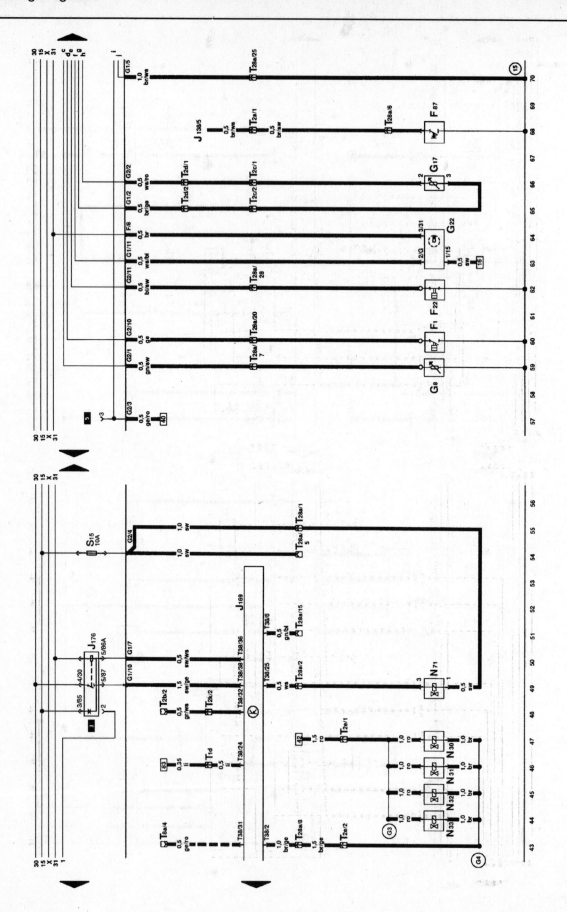

Digifant control unit, Injectors, Idling stabilisation valve - Engine code 2E from 1994   Multi-function indicator sender, Speedometer sender and Oil pressure switch - Engine code 2E from 1994

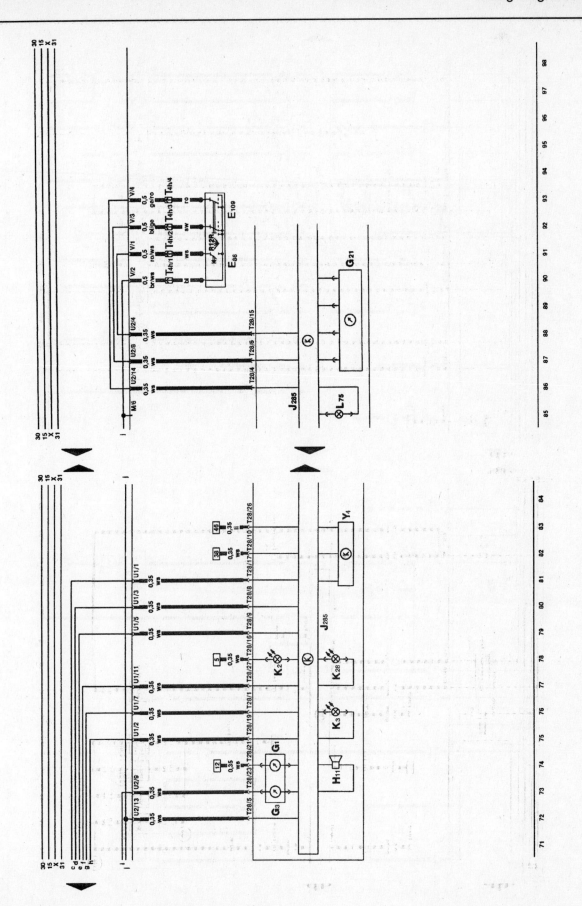

Dash panel insert, Speedometer, Multi-function switch - Engine code 2E from 1994

Dash panel insert, Coolant shortage/temperature warning, Oil pressure warning, Fuel gauge, Trip recorder - Engine code 2E from 1994

12

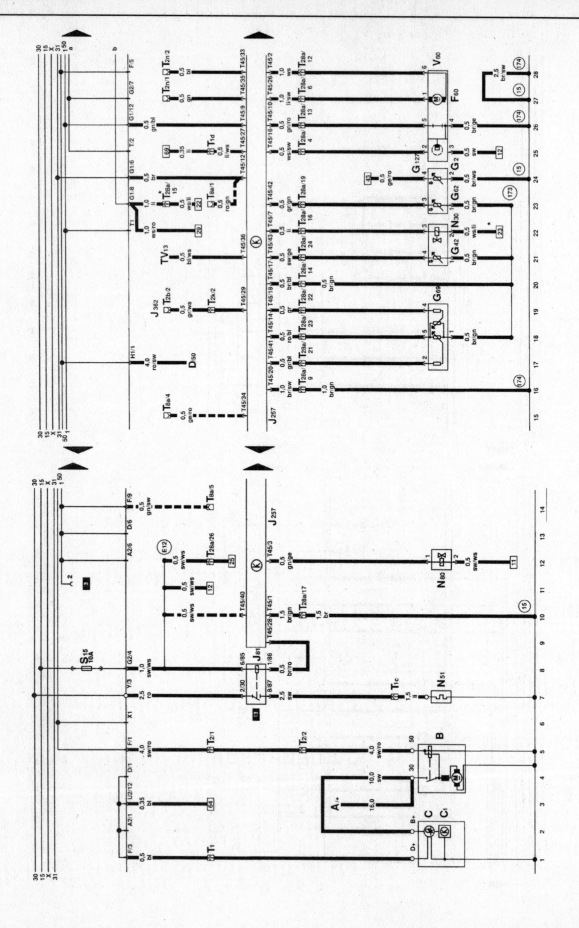

Control unit, Throttle valve potentiometer, Injector, Throttle valve positioner -
Engine code ADZ from 1994

Alternator, Starter, Manifold pre-heating, Fuel injection control unit -
Engine code ADZ from 1994

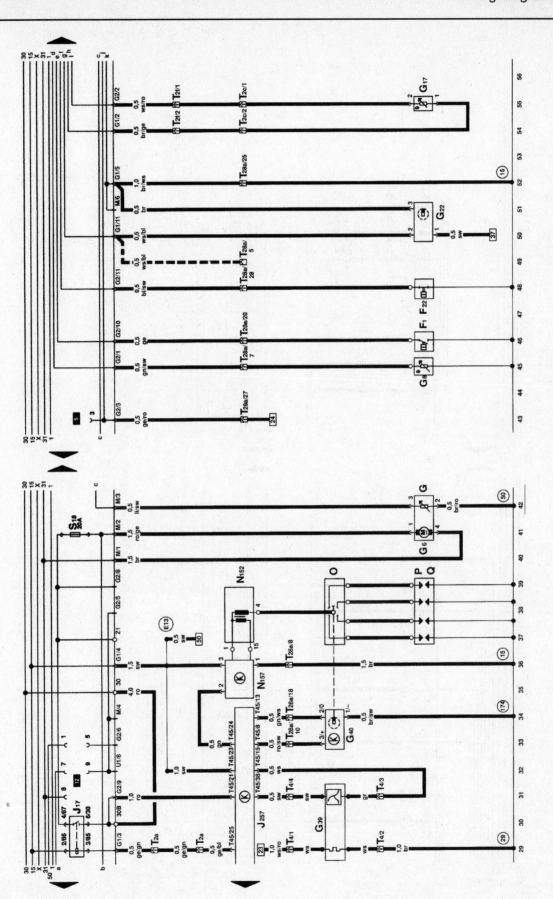

Multi-function indicator sender, Speedometer sender, Oil pressure switch -
Engine code ADZ from 1994

Control unit, Lambda probe, Ignition system, Fuel supply system -
Engine code ADZ from 1994

12

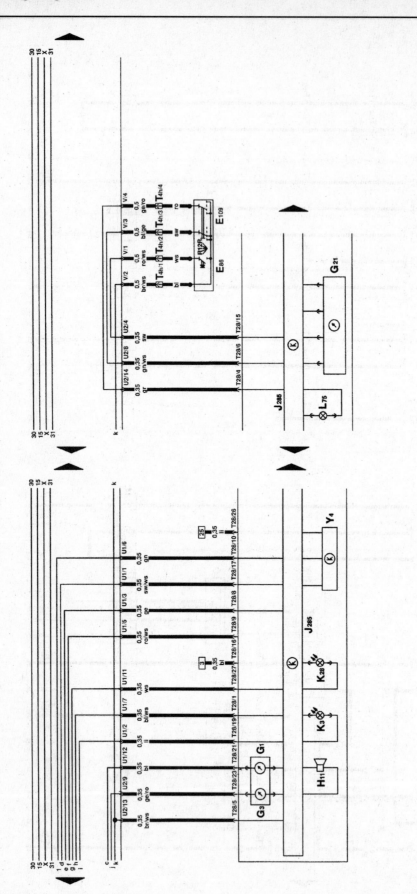

Dash panel insert, Speedometer, Multi-function indicator switch – Engine code ADZ from 1994

Dash panel insert, Coolant shortage/temperature warning, Oil pressure warning, Fuel gauge, Trip recorder – Engine code ADZ from 1994

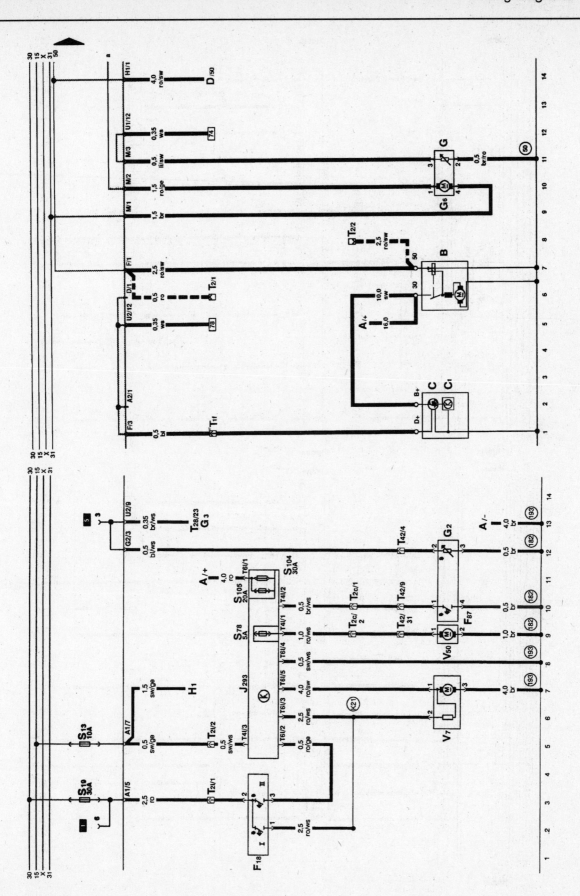

Alternator, Starter, Fuel pump, Fuel gauge sender - Simos fuel injection models from 1994

Radiator fan, Coolant pump, Coolant temperature gauge sender, Fan run-on thermoswitch - Simos fuel injection models from 1994

12

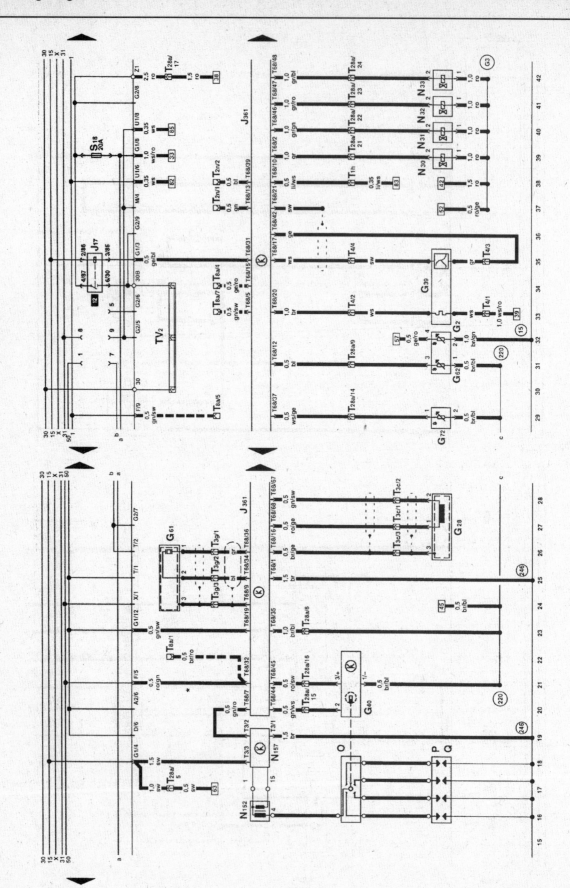

Control unit, Lambda probe, Coolant temperature sender, Injectors, Manifold temperature sensor - Simos fuel injection models from 1994

Control unit, Ignition system, Engine speed sensor, Knock sensor - Simos fuel injection models from 1994

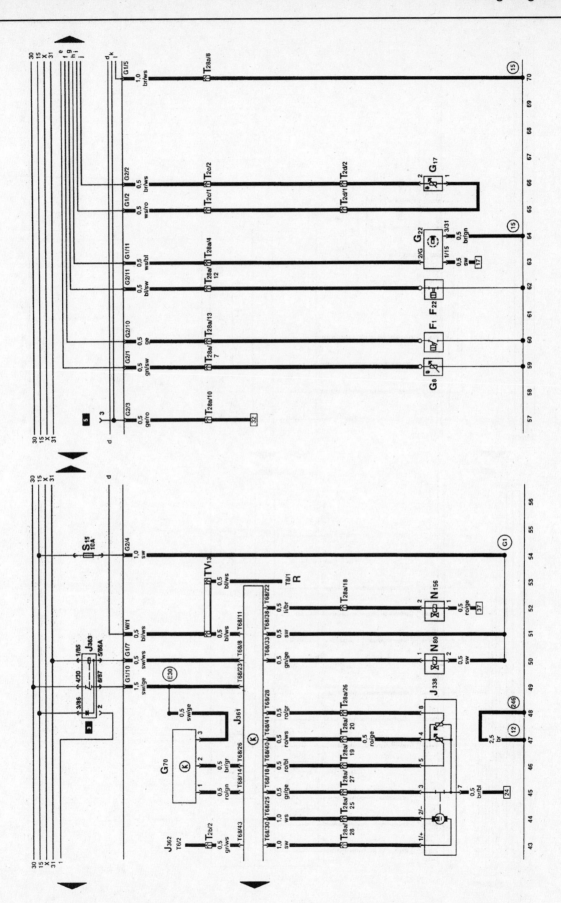

Control unit, Air mass meter, Throttle valve control part, Charcoal filter solenoid   Oil temperature sender, Oil pressure switch, Speedometer sender, air temperature
valve - Simos fuel injection models from 1994   sensor - Simos fuel injection models from 1994

12

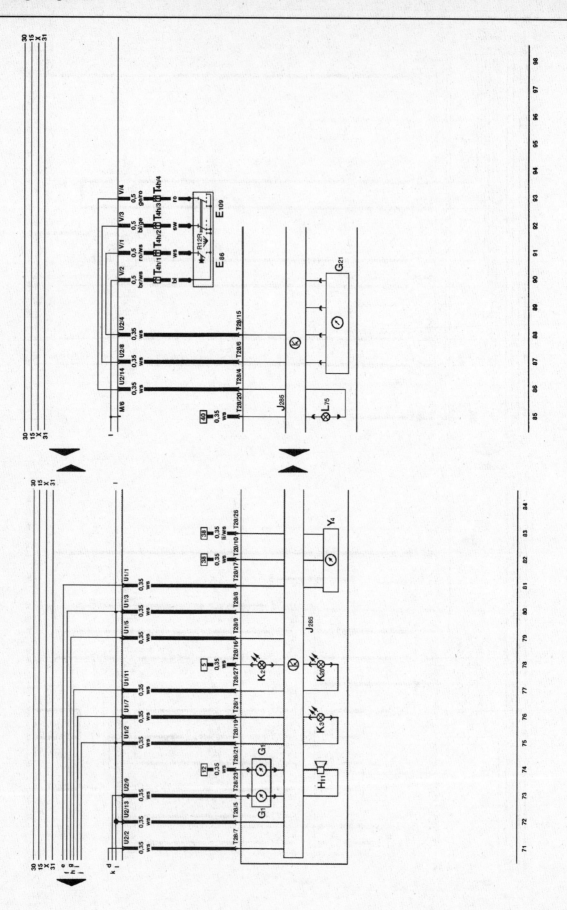

Dash panel insert, Oil pressure warning, Trip recorder, Coolant warning, Fuel gauge
- Simos fuel injection models from 1994

Dash panel insert, Speedometer, Multi-function indicator switch -
Simos fuel injection models from 1994

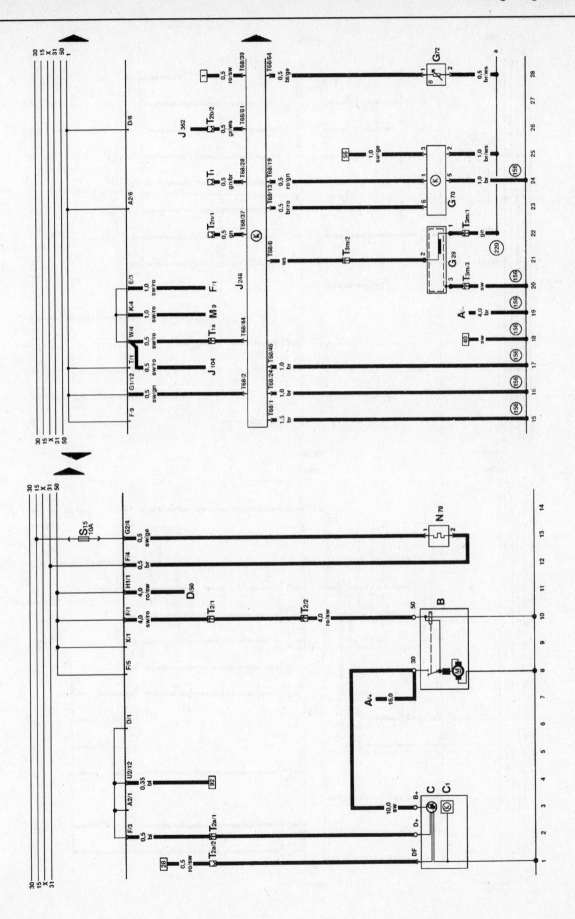

Engine management control unit - Diesel (engine code AFN)

Alternator, Starter - Diesel (engine code AFN)

12

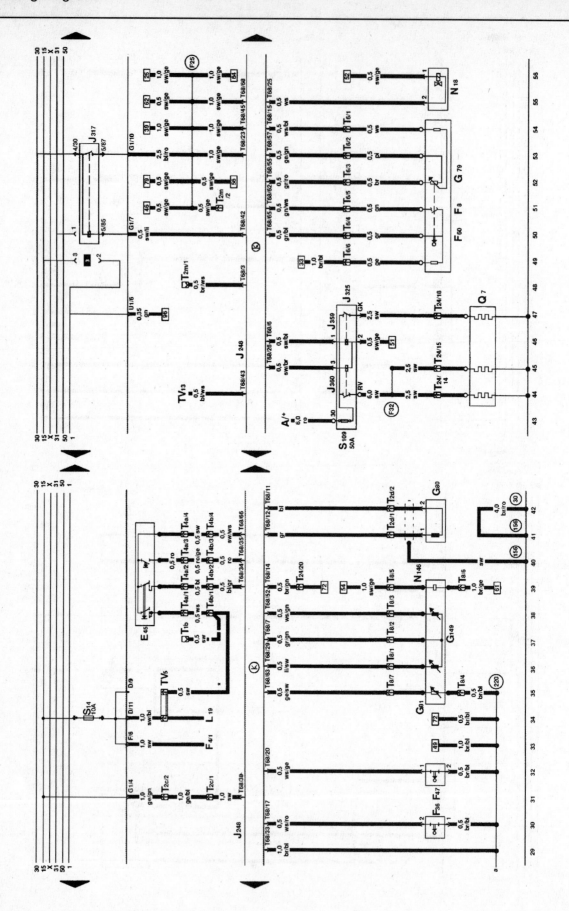

Engine management control unit (continued) - Diesel (engine code AFN)

Engine management control unit (continued) - Diesel (engine code AFN)

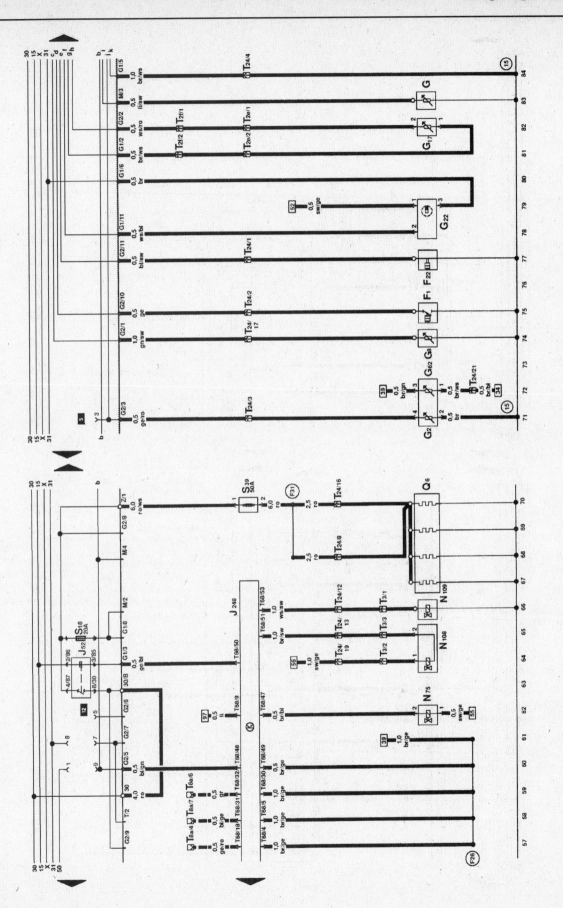

Multi-function indicator sender, Speedometer sender, Oil pressure switch, Coolant temperature gauge sender - Diesel (engine code AFN)

Engine management control unit (continued) - Diesel (engine code AFN)

12

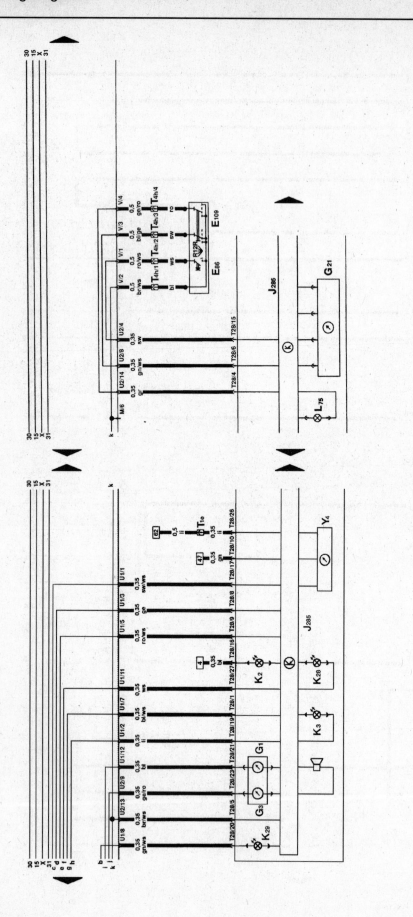

Dash panel insert, Speedometer, Multi-function indicator switch - Diesel (engine code AFN)

Dash panel insert Coolant shortage/temperature gauge, Oil pressure warning, Fuel gauge, Trip recorder - Diesel (engine code AFN)

Dimensions and weights

Note: *All figures are approximate, and may vary according to model. Refer to manufacturer's data for exact figures.*

Dimensions

	Up to 1994	1994 on
Overall length:		
Saloon models	4575 mm	4605 mm
Estate models	4575 mm	4595 mm
Overall width:		
Excluding mirrors	1705 mm	1720 mm
Including mirrors	N/A	1960 mm
Overall height (unladen):		
Saloon models	1430 mm	1430 mm
Estate models:		
With roof rails or roof aerial	1500 mm	1485 mm
Without roof rails or roof aerial	1460 mm	1445 mm
Wheelbase	2625 mm	2625 mm

Weights

Kerb weight	1125 to 1285 kg*
Maximum gross vehicle weight**	1650 to 1820 kg*
Maximum roof rack load	75 kg
Maximum towing weight**	
Braked trailer	1200 kg
Unbraked trailer	550 to 650 kg*
Maximum trailer nose weight	85 kg

*Depending on model and specification.
**Refer to VW dealer for exact recommendations.

Conversion factors

Length (distance)

Inches (in)	x 25.4	= Millimetres (mm)	x 0.0394	= Inches (in)
Feet (ft)	x 0.305	= Metres (m)	x 3.281	= Feet (ft)
Miles	x 1.609	= Kilometres (km)	x 0.621	= Miles

Volume (capacity)

Cubic inches (cu in; in³)	x 16.387	= Cubic centimetres (cc; cm³)	x 0.061	= Cubic inches (cu in; in³)
Imperial pints (Imp pt)	x 0.568	= Litres (l)	x 1.76	= Imperial pints (Imp pt)
Imperial quarts (Imp qt)	x 1.137	= Litres (l)	x 0.88	= Imperial quarts (Imp qt)
Imperial quarts (Imp qt)	x 1.201	= US quarts (US qt)	x 0.833	= Imperial quarts (Imp qt)
US quarts (US qt)	x 0.946	= Litres (l)	x 1.057	= US quarts (US qt)
Imperial gallons (Imp gal)	x 4.546	= Litres (l)	x 0.22	= Imperial gallons (Imp gal)
Imperial gallons (Imp gal)	x 1.201	= US gallons (US gal)	x 0.833	= Imperial gallons (Imp gal)
US gallons (US gal)	x 3.785	= Litres (l)	x 0.264	= US gallons (US gal)

Mass (weight)

Ounces (oz)	x 28.35	= Grams (g)	x 0.035	= Ounces (oz)
Pounds (lb)	x 0.454	= Kilograms (kg)	x 2.205	= Pounds (lb)

Force

Ounces-force (ozf; oz)	x 0.278	= Newtons (N)	x 3.6	= Ounces-force (ozf; oz)
Pounds-force (lbf; lb)	x 4.448	= Newtons (N)	x 0.225	= Pounds-force (lbf; lb)
Newtons (N)	x 0.1	= Kilograms-force (kgf; kg)	x 9.81	= Newtons (N)

Pressure

Pounds-force per square inch (psi; lbf/in²; lb/in²)	x 0.070	= Kilograms-force per square centimetre (kgf/cm²; kg/cm²)	x 14.223	= Pounds-force per square inch (psi; lbf/in²; lb/in²)
Pounds-force per square inch (psi; lbf/in²; lb/in²)	x 0.068	= Atmospheres (atm)	x 14.696	= Pounds-force per square inch (psi; lbf/in²; lb/in²)
Pounds-force per square inch (psi; lbf/in²; lb/in²)	x 0.069	= Bars	x 14.5	= Pounds-force per square inch (psi; lbf/in²; lb/in²)
Pounds-force per square inch (psi; lbf/in²; lb/in²)	x 6.895	= Kilopascals (kPa)	x 0.145	= Pounds-force per square inch (psi; lbf/in²; lb/in²)
Kilopascals (kPa)	x 0.01	= Kilograms-force per square centimetre (kgf/cm²; kg/cm²)	x 98.1	= Kilopascals (kPa)
Millibar (mbar)	x 100	= Pascals (Pa)	x 0.01	= Millibar (mbar)
Millibar (mbar)	x 0.0145	= Pounds-force per square inch (psi; lbf/in²; lb/in²)	x 68.947	= Millibar (mbar)
Millibar (mbar)	x 0.75	= Millimetres of mercury (mmHg)	x 1.333	= Millibar (mbar)
Millibar (mbar)	x 0.401	= Inches of water (inH₂O)	x 2.491	= Millibar (mbar)
Millimetres of mercury (mmHg)	x 0.535	= Inches of water (inH₂O)	x 1.868	= Millimetres of mercury (mmHg)
Inches of water (inH₂O)	x 0.036	= Pounds-force per square inch (psi; lbf/in²; lb/in²)	x 27.68	= Inches of water (inH₂O)

Torque (moment of force)

Pounds-force inches (lbf in; lb in)	x 1.152	= Kilograms-force centimetre (kgf cm; kg cm)	x 0.868	= Pounds-force inches (lbf in; lb in)
Pounds-force inches (lbf in; lb in)	x 0.113	= Newton metres (Nm)	x 8.85	= Pounds-force inches (lbf in; lb in)
Pounds-force inches (lbf in; lb in)	x 0.083	= Pounds-force feet (lbf ft; lb ft)	x 12	= Pounds-force inches (lbf in; lb in)
Pounds-force feet (lbf ft; lb ft)	x 0.138	= Kilograms-force metres (kgf m; kg m)	x 7.233	= Pounds-force feet (lbf ft; lb ft)
Pounds-force feet (lbf ft; lb ft)	x 1.356	= Newton metres (Nm)	x 0.738	= Pounds-force feet (lbf ft; lb ft)
Newton metres (Nm)	x 0.102	= Kilograms-force metres (kgf m; kg m)	x 9.804	= Newton metres (Nm)

Power

Horsepower (hp)	x 745.7	= Watts (W)	x 0.0013	= Horsepower (hp)

Velocity (speed)

Miles per hour (miles/hr; mph)	x 1.609	= Kilometres per hour (km/hr; kph)	x 0.621	= Miles per hour (miles/hr; mph)

Fuel consumption*

Miles per gallon (mpg)	x 0.354	= Kilometres per litre (km/l)	x 2.825	= Miles per gallon (mpg)

Temperature

Degrees Fahrenheit = (°C x 1.8) + 32   Degrees Celsius (Degrees Centigrade; °C) = (°F - 32) x 0.56

It is common practice to convert from miles per gallon (mpg) to litres/100 kilometres (l/100km), where mpg x l/100 km = 282

Spare parts are available from many sources, including maker's appointed garages, accessory shops, and motor factors. To be sure of obtaining the correct parts, it may sometimes be necessary to quote the vehicle identification number. If possible, it can also be useful to take the old parts along for positive identification. Items such as starter motors and alternators may be available under a service exchange scheme - any parts returned should always be clean.

Our advice regarding spare part sources is as follows.

Officially-appointed garages

This is the best source of parts which are peculiar to your car, and are not otherwise generally available (eg badges, interior trim, certain body panels, etc). It is also the only place at which you should buy parts if the vehicle is still under warranty.

Accessory shops

These are very good places to buy materials and components needed for the maintenance of your car (oil, air and fuel filters, spark plugs, light bulbs, drivebelts, oils and greases, brake pads, touch-up paint, etc). Parts like this sold by a reputable shop are of the same standard as those used by the car manufacturer.

Motor factors

Good factors will stock all the more important components which wear out comparatively quickly and can sometimes supply individual components needed for the overhaul of a larger assembly. They may also handle work such as cylinder block reboring, crankshaft regrinding and balancing, etc.

Tyre and exhaust specialists

These outlets may be independent or members of a local or national chain. They frequently offer competitive prices when compared with a main dealer or local garage, but it will pay to obtain several quotes before making a decision. Also ask what 'extras' may be added to the quote - for instance, fitting a new valve and balancing the wheel are both often charged on top of the price of a new tyre.

Other sources

Beware of parts or materials obtained from market stalls, car boot sales or similar outlets. Such items are not invariably sub-standard, but there is little chance of compensation if they do prove unsatisfactory. In the case of safety-critical components such as brake pads there is the risk not only of financial loss but also of an accident causing injury or death.

Vehicle identification

Modifications are a continuing and unpublicised process in vehicle manufacture, quite apart from major model changes. Spare parts manuals and lists are compiled upon a numerical basis, the individual vehicle identification numbers being essential to correct identification of the component concerned.

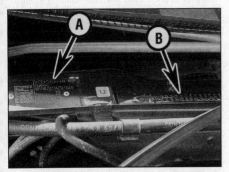

Type plate (A) and chassis number (B)

When ordering spare parts, always give as much information as possible. Quote the car model, year of manufacture, body and engine numbers as appropriate.

The type plate and chassis number may be found in the engine compartment, on top of the bulkhead **(see illustration)**. On some models, this information may appear on the passenger door pillar. Later models also have the chassis number on a small plate on the top of the facia panel ("visible VIN") **(see illustration)**.

The vehicle data sticker (which contains the vehicle identification number (VIN), engine and transmission code letters, and paint codes) is located on the left of the rear cross-panel in the boot on Saloon models, and on the left of

the spare wheel well on Estate models.

The engine number is situated on the cylinder block (on some models, it can also be found on a sticker attached to the timing belt cover) and can be found in the following locations:

a) *Petrol engines - stamped on the front of the cylinder block, directly below the cylinder head mating surface (see illustration).*

b) *Diesel engines - stamped on the front of the cylinder block, between the injection pump and vacuum pump (see illustration).*

Note: *The first part of the engine number gives the engine code - eg "AAZ".*

Chassis number on later models is visible through the windscreen

Type plate/chassis number (1) and petrol engine number (2) locations

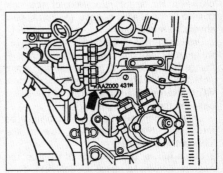

Engine number location - diesel models (arrowed)

Whenever servicing, repair or overhaul work is carried out on the car or its components, observe the following procedures and instructions. This will assist in carrying out the operation efficiently and to a professional standard of workmanship.

Joint mating faces and gaskets

When separating components at their mating faces, never insert screwdrivers or similar implements into the joint between the faces in order to prise them apart. This can cause severe damage which results in oil leaks, coolant leaks, etc upon reassembly. Separation is usually achieved by tapping along the joint with a soft-faced hammer in order to break the seal. However, note that this method may not be suitable where dowels are used for component location.

Where a gasket is used between the mating faces of two components, a new one must be fitted on reassembly; fit it dry unless otherwise stated in the repair procedure. Make sure that the mating faces are clean and dry, with all traces of old gasket removed. When cleaning a joint face, use a tool which is unlikely to score or damage the face, and remove any burrs or nicks with an oilstone or fine file.

Make sure that tapped holes are cleaned with a pipe cleaner, and keep them free of jointing compound, if this is being used, unless specifically instructed otherwise.

Ensure that all orifices, channels or pipes are clear, and blow through them, preferably using compressed air.

Oil seals

Oil seals can be removed by levering them out with a wide flat-bladed screwdriver or similar implement. Alternatively, a number of self-tapping screws may be screwed into the seal, and these used as a purchase for pliers or some similar device in order to pull the seal free.

Whenever an oil seal is removed from its working location, either individually or as part of an assembly, it should be renewed.

The very fine sealing lip of the seal is easily damaged, and will not seal if the surface it contacts is not completely clean and free from scratches, nicks or grooves. If the original sealing surface of the component cannot be restored, and the manufacturer has not made provision for slight relocation of the seal relative to the sealing surface, the component should be renewed.

Protect the lips of the seal from any surface which may damage them in the course of fitting. Use tape or a conical sleeve where possible. Lubricate the seal lips with oil before fitting and, on dual-lipped seals, fill the space between the lips with grease.

Unless otherwise stated, oil seals must be fitted with their sealing lips toward the lubricant to be sealed.

Use a tubular drift or block of wood of the appropriate size to install the seal and, if the seal housing is shouldered, drive the seal down to the shoulder. If the seal housing is unshouldered, the seal should be fitted with its face flush with the housing top face (unless otherwise instructed).

Screw threads and fastenings

Seized nuts, bolts and screws are quite a common occurrence where corrosion has set in, and the use of penetrating oil or releasing fluid will often overcome this problem if the offending item is soaked for a while before attempting to release it. The use of an impact driver may also provide a means of releasing such stubborn fastening devices, when used in conjunction with the appropriate screwdriver bit or socket. If none of these methods works, it may be necessary to resort to the careful application of heat, or the use of a hacksaw or nut splitter device.

Studs are usually removed by locking two nuts together on the threaded part, and then using a spanner on the lower nut to unscrew the stud. Studs or bolts which have broken off below the surface of the component in which they are mounted can sometimes be removed using a stud extractor. Always ensure that a blind tapped hole is completely free from oil, grease, water or other fluid before installing the bolt or stud. Failure to do this could cause the housing to crack due to the hydraulic action of the bolt or stud as it is screwed in.

When tightening a castellated nut to accept a split pin, tighten the nut to the specified torque, where applicable, and then tighten further to the next split pin hole. Never slacken the nut to align the split pin hole, unless stated in the repair procedure.

When checking or retightening a nut or bolt to a specified torque setting, slacken the nut or bolt by a quarter of a turn, and then retighten to the specified setting. However, this should not be attempted where angular tightening has been used.

For some screw fastenings, notably cylinder head bolts or nuts, torque wrench settings are no longer specified for the latter stages of tightening, "angle-tightening" being called up instead. Typically, a fairly low torque wrench setting will be applied to the bolts/nuts in the correct sequence, followed by one or more stages of tightening through specified angles.

Locknuts, locktabs and washers

Any fastening which will rotate against a component or housing during tightening should always have a washer between it and the relevant component or housing.

Spring or split washers should always be renewed when they are used to lock a critical component such as a big-end bearing retaining bolt or nut. Locktabs which are folded over to retain a nut or bolt should always be renewed.

Self-locking nuts can be re-used in non-critical areas, providing resistance can be felt when the locking portion passes over the bolt or stud thread. However, it should be noted that self-locking stiffnuts tend to lose their effectiveness after long periods of use, and should then be renewed as a matter of course.

Split pins must always be replaced with new ones of the correct size for the hole.

When thread-locking compound is found on the threads of a fastener which is to be re-used, it should be cleaned off with a wire brush and solvent, and fresh compound applied on reassembly.

Special tools

Some repair procedures in this manual entail the use of special tools such as a press, two or three-legged pullers, spring compressors, etc. Wherever possible, suitable readily-available alternatives to the manufacturer's special tools are described, and are shown in use. In some instances, where no alternative is possible, it has been necessary to resort to the use of a manufacturer's tool, and this has been done for reasons of safety as well as the efficient completion of the repair operation. Unless you are highly-skilled and have a thorough understanding of the procedures described, never attempt to bypass the use of any special tool when the procedure described specifies its use. Not only is there a very great risk of personal injury, but expensive damage could be caused to the components involved.

Environmental considerations

When disposing of used engine oil, brake fluid, antifreeze, etc, give due consideration to any detrimental environmental effects. Do not, for instance, pour any of the above liquids down drains into the general sewage system, or onto the ground to soak away. Many local council refuse tips provide a facility for waste oil disposal, as do some garages. If none of these facilities are available, consult your local Environmental Health Department, or the National Rivers Authority, for further advice.

With the universal tightening-up of legislation regarding the emission of environmentally-harmful substances from motor vehicles, most vehicles have tamperproof devices fitted to the main adjustment points of the fuel system. These devices are primarily designed to prevent unqualified persons from adjusting the fuel/air mixture, with the chance of a consequent increase in toxic emissions. If such devices are found during servicing or overhaul, they should, wherever possible, be renewed or refitted in accordance with the manufacturer's requirements or current legislation.

OIL CARE
FOLLOW THE CODE
OIL BANK LINE
0800 66 33 66

Note: It is antisocial and illegal to dump oil down the drain. To find the location of your local oil recycling bank, call this number free.

The jack supplied with the vehicle tool kit should only be used for changing the roadwheels - see "Wheel changing" at the front of this manual. When carrying out any other kind of work, raise the vehicle using a hydraulic (or "trolley") jack, and always supplement the jack with axle stands positioned under the vehicle jacking points.

When using a hydraulic jack or axle stands, always position the jack head or axle stand head under one of the relevant jacking points.

To raise the front and/or rear of the vehicle, use the jacking/support points at the front and rear ends of the door sills, indicated by the rectangular or triangular depressions in the sill panel (see illustrations). Position a block of wood with a groove cut in it on the jack head to prevent the vehicle weight resting on the sill edge; align the sill edge with the groove in the wood so that the vehicle weight is spread evenly over the surface of the block. Supplement the jack with axle stands (also

with slotted blocks of wood) positioned as close as possible to the jacking points.

Do not jack the vehicle under any other part of the sill, sump, floor pan, or any of the steering or suspension components. With the vehicle raised, an axle stand should be positioned beneath the vehicle jack location point on the sill.

Never work under, around, or near a raised vehicle, unless it is adequately supported on stands.

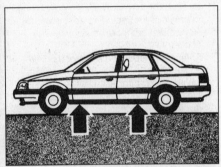

Front and rear jacking points (arrowed)

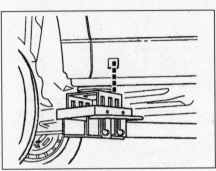

Front jacking/support point

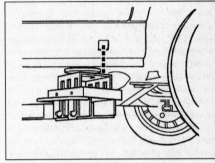

Rear jacking/support point

Radio/cassette unit anti-theft system - precaution

The radio/cassette unit fitted by VW may be equipped with a built-in security code, to deter thieves. If the power source to the unit is cut, the anti-theft system will activate. Even if the power source is immediately reconnected, the

unit will not function until the correct security code has been entered. Therefore, if you do not know the correct code, DO NOT disconnect the battery negative lead, or remove the radio/cassette unit from the vehicle. The exact

procedure for reprogramming a unit which has been disconnected from its power supply varies from model to model. Consult the radio booklet which should have been supplied with the vehicle for specific details.

Introduction

A selection of good tools is a fundamental requirement for anyone contemplating the maintenance and repair of a motor vehicle. For the owner who does not possess any, their purchase will prove a considerable expense, offsetting some of the savings made by doing-it-yourself. However, provided that the tools purchased meet the relevant national safety standards and are of good quality, they will last for many years and prove an extremely worthwhile investment.

To help the average owner to decide which tools are needed to carry out the various tasks detailed in this manual, we have compiled three lists of tools under the following headings: *Maintenance and minor repair, Repair and overhaul,* and *Special.* Newcomers to practical mechanics should start off with the *Maintenance and minor repair* tool kit, and confine themselves to the simpler jobs around the vehicle. Then, as confidence and experience grow, more difficult tasks can be undertaken, with extra tools being purchased as, and when, they are needed. In this way, a *Maintenance and minor repair* tool kit can be built up into a *Repair and overhaul* tool kit over a considerable period of time, without any major cash outlays. The experienced do-it-yourselfer will have a tool kit good enough for most repair and overhaul procedures, and will add tools from the *Special* category when it is felt that the expense is justified by the amount of use to which these tools will be put.

Maintenance and minor repair tool kit

The tools given in this list should be considered as a minimum requirement if routine maintenance, servicing and minor repair operations are to be undertaken. We recommend the purchase of combination spanners (ring one end, open-ended the other); although more expensive than open-ended ones, they do give the advantages of both types of spanner.

- [ ] *Combination spanners:*
  Metric - 8 to 19 mm inclusive
- [ ] *Adjustable spanner - 35 mm jaw (approx.)*
- [ ] *Spark plug spanner (with rubber insert) - petrol models*
- [ ] *Spark plug gap adjustment tool - petrol models*
- [ ] *Set of feeler gauges*
- [ ] *Brake bleed nipple spanner*
- [ ] *Screwdrivers:*
  Flat blade - 100 mm long x 6 mm dia
  Cross blade - 100 mm long x 6 mm dia
  Torx - various sizes (not all vehicles)
- [ ] *Combination pliers*
- [ ] *Hacksaw (junior)*
- [ ] *Tyre pump*
- [ ] *Tyre pressure gauge*
- [ ] *Oil can*
- [ ] *Oil filter removal tool*
- [ ] *Fine emery cloth*
- [ ] *Wire brush (small)*
- [ ] *Funnel (medium size)*
- [ ] *Sump drain plug key (not all vehicles)*

Repair and overhaul tool kit

These tools are virtually essential for anyone undertaking any major repairs to a motor vehicle, and are additional to those given in the *Maintenance and minor repair* list. Included in this list is a comprehensive set of sockets. Although these are expensive, they will be found invaluable as they are so versatile - particularly if various drives are included in the set. We recommend the half-inch square-drive type, as this can be used with most proprietary torque wrenches.

The tools in this list will sometimes need to be supplemented by tools from the *Special* list:

- [ ] *Sockets (or box spanners) to cover range in previous list (including Torx sockets)*
- [ ] *Reversible ratchet drive (for use with sockets)*
- [ ] *Extension piece, 250 mm (for use with sockets)*
- [ ] *Universal joint (for use with sockets)*
- [ ] *Flexible handle or sliding T "breaker bar" (for use with sockets)*
- [ ] *Torque wrench (for use with sockets)*
- [ ] *Self-locking grips*
- [ ] *Ball pein hammer*
- [ ] *Soft-faced mallet (plastic or rubber)*
- [ ] *Screwdrivers:*
  Flat blade - long & sturdy, short (chubby), and narrow (electrician's) types
  Cross blade - long & sturdy, and short (chubby) types
- [ ] *Pliers:*
  Long-nosed
  Side cutters (electrician's)
  Circlip (internal and external)
- [ ] *Cold chisel - 25 mm*
- [ ] *Scriber*
- [ ] *Scraper*
- [ ] *Centre-punch*
- [ ] *Pin punch*
- [ ] *Hacksaw*
- [ ] *Brake hose clamp*
- [ ] *Brake/clutch bleeding kit*
- [ ] *Selection of twist drills*
- [ ] *Steel rule/straight-edge*
- [ ] *Allen keys (inc. splined/Torx type)*
- [ ] *Selection of files*
- [ ] *Wire brush*
- [ ] *Axle stands*
- [ ] *Jack (strong trolley or hydraulic type)*
- [ ] *Light with extension lead*
- [ ] *Universal electrical multi-meter*

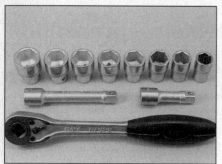

Sockets and reversible ratchet drive

Brake bleeding kit

Torx key, socket and bit

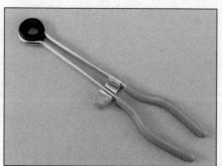

Hose clamp

Angular-tightening gauge

Special tools

The tools in this list are those which are not used regularly, are expensive to buy, or which need to be used in accordance with their manufacturers' instructions. Unless relatively difficult mechanical jobs are undertaken frequently, it will not be economic to buy many of these tools. Where this is the case, you could consider clubbing together with friends (or joining a motorists' club) to make a joint purchase, or borrowing the tools against a deposit from a local garage or tool hire specialist. It is worth noting that many of the larger DIY superstores now carry a large range of special tools for hire at modest rates.

The following list contains only those tools and instruments freely available to the public, and not those special tools produced by the vehicle manufacturer specifically for its dealer network. You will find occasional references to these manufacturers' special tools in the text of this manual. Generally, an alternative method of doing the job without the vehicle manufacturers' special tool is given. However, sometimes there is no alternative to using them. Where this is the case and the relevant tool cannot be bought or borrowed, you will have to entrust the work to a dealer.

- ☐ Angular-tightening gauge
- ☐ Valve spring compressor
- ☐ Valve grinding tool
- ☐ Piston ring compressor
- ☐ Piston ring removal/installation tool
- ☐ Cylinder bore hone
- ☐ Balljoint separator
- ☐ Coil spring compressors (where applicable)
- ☐ Two/three-legged hub and bearing puller
- ☐ Impact screwdriver
- ☐ Micrometer and/or vernier calipers
- ☐ Dial gauge
- ☐ Stroboscopic timing light
- ☐ Dwell angle meter/tachometer
- ☐ Fault code reader
- ☐ Cylinder compression gauge
- ☐ Hand-operated vacuum pump and gauge
- ☐ Clutch plate alignment set
- ☐ Brake shoe steady spring cup removal tool
- ☐ Bush and bearing removal/installation set
- ☐ Stud extractors
- ☐ Tap and die set
- ☐ Lifting tackle
- ☐ Trolley jack

Buying tools

Reputable motor accessory shops and superstores often offer excellent quality tools at discount prices, so it pays to shop around.

Remember, you don't have to buy the most expensive items on the shelf, but it is always advisable to steer clear of the very cheap tools. Beware of 'bargains' offered on market stalls or at car boot sales. There are plenty of good tools around at reasonable prices, but always aim to purchase items which meet the relevant national safety standards. If in doubt, ask the proprietor or manager of the shop for advice before making a purchase.

Care and maintenance of tools

Having purchased a reasonable tool kit, it is necessary to keep the tools in a clean and serviceable condition. After use, always wipe off any dirt, grease and metal particles using a clean, dry cloth, before putting the tools away. Never leave them lying around after they have been used. A simple tool rack on the garage or workshop wall for items such as screwdrivers and pliers is a good idea. Store all normal spanners and sockets in a metal box. Any measuring instruments, gauges, meters, etc, must be carefully stored where they cannot be damaged or become rusty.

Take a little care when tools are used. Hammer heads inevitably become marked, and screwdrivers lose the keen edge on their blades from time to time. A little timely attention with emery cloth or a file will soon restore items like this to a good finish.

Working facilities

Not to be forgotten when discussing tools is the workshop itself. If anything more than routine maintenance is to be carried out, a suitable working area becomes essential.

It is appreciated that many an owner-mechanic is forced by circumstances to remove an engine or similar item without the benefit of a garage or workshop. Having done this, any repairs should always be done under the cover of a roof.

Wherever possible, any dismantling should be done on a clean, flat workbench or table at a suitable working height.

Any workbench needs a vice; one with a jaw opening of 100 mm is suitable for most jobs. As mentioned previously, some clean dry storage space is also required for tools, as well as for any lubricants, cleaning fluids, touch-up paints etc, which become necessary.

Another item which may be required, and which has a much more general usage, is an electric drill with a chuck capacity of at least 8 mm. This, together with a good range of twist drills, is virtually essential for fitting accessories.

Last, but not least, always keep a supply of old newspapers and clean, lint-free rags available, and try to keep any working area as clean as possible.

Micrometers

Dial test indicator ("dial gauge")

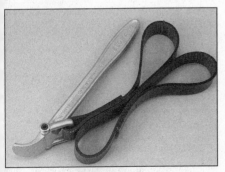

Strap wrench

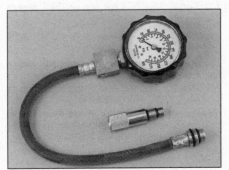

Compression tester

Fault code reader

This is a guide to getting your vehicle through the MOT test. Obviously it will not be possible to examine the vehicle to the same standard as the professional MOT tester. However, working through the following checks will enable you to identify any problem areas before submitting the vehicle for the test.

Where a testable component is in borderline condition, the tester has discretion in deciding whether to pass or fail it. The basis of such discretion is whether the tester would be happy for a close relative or friend to use the vehicle with the component in that condition. If the vehicle presented is clean and evidently well cared for, the tester may be more inclined to pass a borderline component than if the vehicle is scruffy and apparently neglected.

It has only been possible to summarise the test requirements here, based on the regulations in force at the time of printing. Test standards are becoming increasingly stringent, although there are some exemptions for older vehicles. For full details obtain a copy of the Haynes publication Pass the MOT! (available from stockists of Haynes manuals).

An assistant will be needed to help carry out some of these checks.

The checks have been sub-divided into four categories, as follows:

1 Checks carried out **FROM THE DRIVER'S SEAT**

2 Checks carried out **WITH THE VEHICLE ON THE GROUND**

3 Checks carried out **WITH THE VEHICLE RAISED AND THE WHEELS FREE TO TURN**

4 Checks carried out on **YOUR VEHICLE'S EXHAUST EMISSION SYSTEM**

1 Checks carried out **FROM THE DRIVER'S SEAT**

Handbrake

☐ Test the operation of the handbrake. Excessive travel (too many clicks) indicates incorrect brake or cable adjustment.
☐ Check that the handbrake cannot be released by tapping the lever sideways. Check the security of the lever mountings.

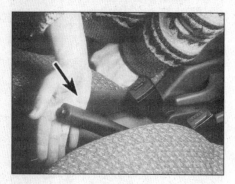

Footbrake

☐ Depress the brake pedal and check that it does not creep down to the floor, indicating a master cylinder fault. Release the pedal, wait a few seconds, then depress it again. If the pedal travels nearly to the floor before firm resistance is felt, brake adjustment or repair is necessary. If the pedal feels spongy, there is air in the hydraulic system which must be removed by bleeding.

☐ Check that the brake pedal is secure and in good condition. Check also for signs of fluid leaks on the pedal, floor or carpets, which would indicate failed seals in the brake master cylinder.
☐ Check the servo unit (when applicable) by operating the brake pedal several times, then keeping the pedal depressed and starting the engine. As the engine starts, the pedal will move down slightly. If not, the vacuum hose or the servo itself may be faulty.

Steering wheel and column

☐ Examine the steering wheel for fractures or looseness of the hub, spokes or rim.
☐ Move the steering wheel from side to side and then up and down. Check that the steering wheel is not loose on the column, indicating wear or a loose retaining nut. Continue moving the steering wheel as before, but also turn it slightly from left to right.
☐ Check that the steering wheel is not loose on the column, and that there is no abnormal

movement of the steering wheel, indicating wear in the column support bearings or couplings.

Windscreen and mirrors

☐ The windscreen must be free of cracks or other significant damage within the driver's field of view. (Small stone chips are acceptable.) Rear view mirrors must be secure, intact, and capable of being adjusted.

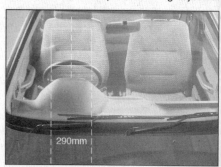

290mm

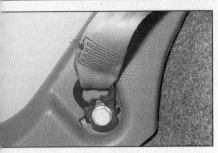

Seat belts and seats

Note: *The following checks are applicable to all seat belts, front and rear.*

☐ Examine the webbing of all the belts (including rear belts if fitted) for cuts, serious fraying or deterioration. Fasten and unfasten each belt to check the buckles. If applicable, check the retracting mechanism. Check the security of all seat belt mountings accessible from inside the vehicle.

☐ The front seats themselves must be securely attached and the backrests must lock in the upright position.

Doors

☐ Both front doors must be able to be opened and closed from outside and inside, and must latch securely when closed.

2 Checks carried out WITH THE VEHICLE ON THE GROUND

Vehicle identification

☐ Number plates must be in good condition, secure and legible, with letters and numbers correctly spaced – spacing at (A) should be twice that at (B).

☐ The VIN plate and/or homologation plate must be legible.

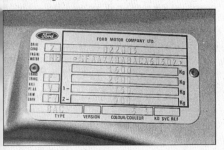

Electrical equipment

☐ Switch on the ignition and check the operation of the horn.

☐ Check the windscreen washers and wipers, examining the wiper blades; renew damaged or perished blades. Also check the operation of the stop-lights.

☐ Check the operation of the sidelights and number plate lights. The lenses and reflectors must be secure, clean and undamaged.

☐ Check the operation and alignment of the headlights. The headlight reflectors must not be tarnished and the lenses must be undamaged.

☐ Switch on the ignition and check the operation of the direction indicators (including the instrument panel tell-tale) and the hazard warning lights. Operation of the sidelights and stop-lights must not affect the indicators - if it does, the cause is usually a bad earth at the rear light cluster.

☐ Check the operation of the rear foglight(s), including the warning light on the instrument panel or in the switch.

Footbrake

☐ Examine the master cylinder, brake pipes and servo unit for leaks, loose mountings, corrosion or other damage.

☐ The fluid reservoir must be secure and the fluid level must be between the upper (A) and lower (B) markings.

Steering and suspension

☐ Inspect both front brake flexible hoses for cracks or deterioration of the rubber. Turn the steering from lock to lock, and ensure that the hoses do not contact the wheel, tyre, or any part of the steering or suspension mechanism. With the brake pedal firmly depressed, check the hoses for bulges or leaks under pressure.

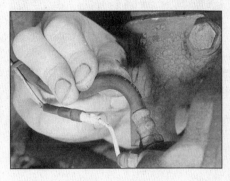

Steering and suspension

☐ Have your assistant turn the steering wheel from side to side slightly, up to the point where the steering gear just begins to transmit this movement to the roadwheels. Check for excessive free play between the steering wheel and the steering gear, indicating wear or insecurity of the steering column joints, the column-to-steering gear coupling, or the steering gear itself.

☐ Have your assistant turn the steering wheel more vigorously in each direction, so that the roadwheels just begin to turn. As this is done, examine all the steering joints, linkages, fittings and attachments. Renew any component that shows signs of wear or damage. On vehicles with power steering, check the security and condition of the steering pump, drivebelt and hoses.

☐ Check that the vehicle is standing level, and at approximately the correct ride height.

Shock absorbers

☐ Depress each corner of the vehicle in turn, then release it. The vehicle should rise and then settle in its normal position. If the vehicle continues to rise and fall, the shock absorber is defective. A shock absorber which has seized will also cause the vehicle to fail.

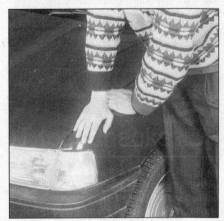

Exhaust system

☐ Start the engine. With your assistant holding a rag over the tailpipe, check the entire system for leaks. Repair or renew leaking sections.

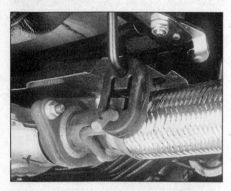

3 Checks carried out
WITH THE VEHICLE RAISED AND THE WHEELS FREE TO TURN

Jack up the front and rear of the vehicle, and securely support it on axle stands. Position the stands clear of the suspension assemblies. Ensure that the wheels are clear of the ground and that the steering can be turned from lock to lock.

Steering mechanism

☐ Have your assistant turn the steering from lock to lock. Check that the steering turns smoothly, and that no part of the steering mechanism, including a wheel or tyre, fouls any brake hose or pipe or any part of the body structure.
☐ Examine the steering rack rubber gaiters for damage or insecurity of the retaining clips. If power steering is fitted, check for signs of damage or leakage of the fluid hoses, pipes or connections. Also check for excessive stiffness or binding of the steering, a missing split pin or locking device, or severe corrosion of the body structure within 30 cm of any steering component attachment point.

Front and rear suspension and wheel bearings

☐ Starting at the front right-hand side, grasp the roadwheel at the 3 o'clock and 9 o'clock positions and shake it vigorously. Check for free play or insecurity at the wheel bearings, suspension balljoints, or suspension mountings, pivots and attachments.
☐ Now grasp the wheel at the 12 o'clock and 6 o'clock positions and repeat the previous inspection. Spin the wheel, and check for roughness or tightness of the front wheel bearing.

☐ If excess free play is suspected at a component pivot point, this can be confirmed by using a large screwdriver or similar tool and levering between the mounting and the component attachment. This will confirm whether the wear is in the pivot bush, its retaining bolt, or in the mounting itself (the bolt holes can often become elongated).

☐ Carry out all the above checks at the other front wheel, and then at both rear wheels.

Springs and shock absorbers

☐ Examine the suspension struts (when applicable) for serious fluid leakage, corrosion, or damage to the casing. Also check the security of the mounting points.
☐ If coil springs are fitted, check that the spring ends locate in their seats, and that the spring is not corroded, cracked or broken.
☐ If leaf springs are fitted, check that all leaves are intact, that the axle is securely attached to each spring, and that there is no deterioration of the spring eye mountings, bushes, and shackles.

☐ The same general checks apply to vehicles fitted with other suspension types, such as torsion bars, hydraulic displacer units, etc. Ensure that all mountings and attachments are secure, that there are no signs of excessive wear, corrosion or damage, and (on hydraulic types) that there are no fluid leaks or damaged pipes.
☐ Inspect the shock absorbers for signs of serious fluid leakage. Check for wear of the mounting bushes or attachments, or damage to the body of the unit.

Driveshafts (fwd vehicles only)

☐ Rotate each front wheel in turn and inspect the constant velocity joint gaiters for splits or damage. Also check that each driveshaft is straight and undamaged.

Braking system

☐ If possible without dismantling, check brake pad wear and disc condition. Ensure that the friction lining material has not worn excessively, (A) and that the discs are not fractured, pitted, scored or badly worn (B).

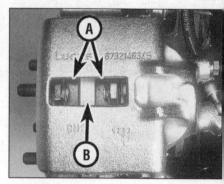

☐ Examine all the rigid brake pipes underneath the vehicle, and the flexible hose(s) at the rear. Look for corrosion, chafing or insecurity of the pipes, and for signs of bulging under pressure, chafing, splits or deterioration of the flexible hoses.
☐ Look for signs of fluid leaks at the brake calipers or on the brake backplates. Repair or renew leaking components.
☐ Slowly spin each wheel, while your assistant depresses and releases the footbrake. Ensure that each brake is operating and does not bind when the pedal is released.

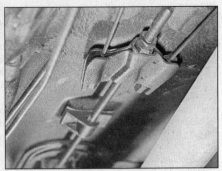

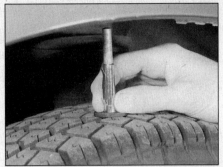

□ Examine the handbrake mechanism, checking for frayed or broken cables, excessive corrosion, or wear or insecurity of the linkage. Check that the mechanism works on each relevant wheel, and releases fully, without binding.

□ It is not possible to test brake efficiency without special equipment, but a road test can be carried out later to check that the vehicle pulls up in a straight line.

Fuel and exhaust systems

□ Inspect the fuel tank (including the filler cap), fuel pipes, hoses and unions. All components must be secure and free from leaks.

□ Examine the exhaust system over its entire length, checking for any damaged, broken or missing mountings, security of the retaining clamps and rust or corrosion.

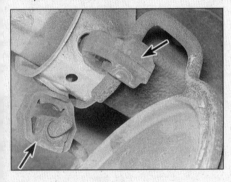

Wheels and tyres

□ Examine the sidewalls and tread area of each tyre in turn. Check for cuts, tears, lumps, bulges, separation of the tread, and exposure of the ply or cord due to wear or damage. Check that the tyre bead is correctly seated on the wheel rim, that the valve is sound and

properly seated, and that the wheel is not distorted or damaged.

□ Check that the tyres are of the correct size for the vehicle, that they are of the same size and type on each axle, and that the pressures are correct.

□ Check the tyre tread depth. The legal minimum at the time of writing is 1.6 mm over at least three-quarters of the tread width. Abnormal tread wear may indicate incorrect front wheel alignment.

Body corrosion

□ Check the condition of the entire vehicle structure for signs of corrosion in load-bearing areas. (These include chassis box sections, side sills, cross-members, pillars, and all suspension, steering, braking system and seat belt mountings and anchorages.) Any corrosion which has seriously reduced the thickness of a load-bearing area is likely to cause the vehicle to fail. In this case professional repairs are likely to be needed.

□ Damage or corrosion which causes sharp or otherwise dangerous edges to be exposed will also cause the vehicle to fail.

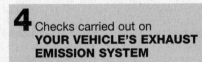

4 Checks carried out on YOUR VEHICLE'S EXHAUST EMISSION SYSTEM

Petrol models

□ Have the engine at normal operating temperature, and make sure that it is in good tune (ignition system in good order, air filter element clean, etc).

□ Before any measurements are carried out, raise the engine speed to around 2500 rpm, and hold it at this speed for 20 seconds. Allow

the engine speed to return to idle, and watch for smoke emissions from the exhaust tailpipe. If the idle speed is obviously much too high, or if dense blue or clearly-visible black smoke comes from the tailpipe for more than 5 seconds, the vehicle will fail. As a rule of thumb, blue smoke signifies oil being burnt (engine wear) while black smoke signifies unburnt fuel (dirty air cleaner element, or other carburettor or fuel system fault).

□ An exhaust gas analyser capable of measuring carbon monoxide (CO) and hydrocarbons (HC) is now needed. If such an instrument cannot be hired or borrowed, a local garage may agree to perform the check for a small fee.

CO emissions (mixture)

□ At the time of writing, the maximum CO level at idle is 3.5% for vehicles first used after August 1986 and 4.5% for older vehicles. From January 1996 a much tighter limit (around 0.5%) applies to catalyst-equipped vehicles first used from August 1992. If the CO level cannot be reduced far enough to pass the test (and the fuel and ignition systems are otherwise in good condition) then the carburettor is badly worn, or there is some problem in the fuel injection system or catalytic converter (as applicable).

HC emissions

□ With the CO emissions within limits, HC emissions must be no more than 1200 ppm (parts per million). If the vehicle fails this test at idle, it can be re-tested at around 2000 rpm; if the HC level is then 1200 ppm or less, this counts as a pass.

□ Excessive HC emissions can be caused by oil being burnt, but they are more likely to be due to unburnt fuel.

Diesel models

□ The only emission test applicable to Diesel engines is the measuring of exhaust smoke density. The test involves accelerating the engine several times to its maximum unloaded speed.

Note: *It is of the utmost importance that the engine timing belt is in good condition before the test is carried out.*

□ Excessive smoke can be caused by a dirty air cleaner element. Otherwise, professional advice may be needed to find the cause.

Engine   1

- [ ] Engine fails to rotate when attempting to start
- [ ] Engine rotates, but will not start
- [ ] Engine difficult to start when cold
- [ ] Engine difficult to start when hot
- [ ] Starter motor noisy or excessively-rough in engagement
- [ ] Engine starts, but stops immediately
- [ ] Engine idles erratically
- [ ] Engine misfires at idle speed
- [ ] Engine misfires throughout the driving speed range
- [ ] Engine hesitates on acceleration
- [ ] Engine stalls
- [ ] Engine lacks power
- [ ] Engine backfires
- [ ] Oil pressure warning light illuminated with engine running
- [ ] Engine runs-on after switching off
- [ ] Engine noises

Cooling system   2

- [ ] Overheating
- [ ] Overcooling
- [ ] External coolant leakage
- [ ] Internal coolant leakage
- [ ] Corrosion

Fuel and exhaust systems   3

- [ ] Excessive fuel consumption
- [ ] Fuel leakage and/or fuel odour
- [ ] Excessive noise or fumes from exhaust system

Clutch   4

- [ ] Pedal travels to floor - no pressure or very little resistance
- [ ] Clutch fails to disengage (unable to select gears)
- [ ] Clutch slips (engine speed increases, with no increase in vehicle speed)
- [ ] Judder as clutch is engaged
- [ ] Noise when depressing or releasing clutch pedal

Manual transmission   5

- [ ] Noisy in neutral with engine running
- [ ] Noisy in one particular gear
- [ ] Difficulty engaging gears
- [ ] Jumps out of gear
- [ ] Vibration
- [ ] Lubricant leaks

Automatic transmission   6

- [ ] Fluid leakage
- [ ] Transmission fluid brown, or has burned smell
- [ ] General gear selection problems
- [ ] Transmission will not downshift (kickdown) with accelerator pedal fully depressed
- [ ] Engine will not start in any gear, or starts in gears other than Park or Neutral
- [ ] Transmission slips, shifts roughly, is noisy, or has no drive in forward or reverse gears

Driveshafts   7

- [ ] Clicking or knocking noise on turns (at slow speed on full-lock)
- [ ] Vibration when accelerating or decelerating

Braking system   8

- [ ] Vehicle pulls to one side under braking
- [ ] Noise (grinding or high-pitched squeal) when brakes applied
- [ ] Excessive brake pedal travel
- [ ] Brake pedal feels spongy when depressed
- [ ] Excessive brake pedal effort required to stop vehicle
- [ ] Judder felt through brake pedal or steering wheel when braking
- [ ] Brakes binding
- [ ] Rear wheels locking under normal braking

Suspension and steering systems   9

- [ ] Vehicle pulls to one side
- [ ] Wheel wobble and vibration
- [ ] Excessive pitching and/or rolling around corners, or during braking
- [ ] Wandering or general instability
- [ ] Excessively-stiff steering
- [ ] Excessive play in steering
- [ ] Lack of power assistance
- [ ] Tyre wear excessive

Electrical system   10

- [ ] Battery will not hold a charge for more than a few days
- [ ] Ignition/no-charge warning light remains illuminated with engine running
- [ ] Ignition/no-charge warning light fails to come on
- [ ] Lights inoperative
- [ ] Instrument readings inaccurate or erratic
- [ ] Horn inoperative, or unsatisfactory in operation
- [ ] Windscreen/tailgate wipers inoperative, or unsatisfactory in operation
- [ ] Windscreen/tailgate washers inoperative, or unsatisfactory in operation
- [ ] Electric windows inoperative, or unsatisfactory in operation
- [ ] Central locking system inoperative, or unsatisfactory in operation

Introduction

The vehicle owner who does his or her own maintenance according to the recommended service schedules should not have to use this section of the manual very often. Modern component reliability is such that, provided those items subject to wear or deterioration are inspected or renewed at the specified intervals, sudden failure is comparatively rare. ults do not usually just happen as a result of en failure, but develop over a period of Major mechanical failures in particular ally preceded by characteristic

symptoms over hundreds or even thousands of miles. Those components which do occasionally fail without warning are often small and easily carried in the vehicle.

With any fault-finding, the first step is to decide where to begin investigations. Sometimes this is obvious, but on other occasions, a little detective work will be necessary. The owner who makes half a dozen haphazard adjustments or replacements may be successful in curing a fault (or its symptoms), but will be none the

wiser if the fault recurs, and ultimately may have spent more time and money than was necessary. A calm and logical approach will be found to be more satisfactory in the long run. Always take into account any warning signs or abnormalities that may have been noticed in the period preceding the fault - power loss, high or low gauge readings, unusual smells, etc - and remember that failure of components such as fuses or spark plugs may only be pointers to some underlying fault.

These pages provide an easy-reference guide to the more common problems which may occur during the vehicle's life. These problems and their possible causes are grouped under headings such as Engine, Cooling system, etc. The Chapter and/or Section which deals with the problem is also shown in brackets. Whatever the fault, certain basic principles apply. These are as follows:

Verify the fault. This is simply a matter of being sure you know exactly what the symptoms are before starting work. This is particularly important if you are investigating a fault for someone else, who may not have described it very accurately.

Don't overlook the obvious. For example, if it won't start, is there fuel in the tank? (Don't take anyone else's word on this particular point, and don't trust the fuel gauge either!) If an electrical fault is indicated, look for loose or broken wires before digging out the test gear.

Cure the disease, not the symptom. Substituting a flat battery with a fully-charged one will get you off the hard shoulder, but if the underlying cause is not attended to, the new battery will go the same way. Similarly, changing oil-fouled spark plugs (petrol models) for a new set will get you moving again, but remember that the reason for the fouling (if it wasn't simply an incorrect grade of plug) will have to be established and corrected.

Don't take anything for granted. Particularly, don't forget that a "new" component may itself be defective (especially if it's been rattling around in the boot for months), and don't leave components out of a fault diagnosis sequence just because they are new or recently-fitted. When you do finally diagnose a difficult fault, you'll probably realise that all the evidence was there from the start.

1 Engine

Engine fails to rotate when attempting to start

- [ ] Battery terminal connections loose or corroded ("*Weekly checks*").
- [ ] Battery discharged or faulty (Chapter 5A).
- [ ] Broken, loose or disconnected wiring in the starting circuit (Chapter 5A).
- [ ] Defective starter solenoid or switch (Chapter 5A).
- [ ] Defective starter motor (Chapter 5A).
- [ ] Starter pinion or flywheel ring gear teeth loose or broken (Chapters 2A, 2B, 2C and 5A).
- [ ] Engine earth strap broken or disconnected (Chapter 5A).

Engine rotates, but will not start

- [ ] Fuel tank empty.
- [ ] Battery discharged (engine rotates slowly) (Chapter 5A).
- [ ] Battery terminal connections loose or corroded ("*Weekly checks*").
- [ ] Immobiliser or anti-theft alarm system fault (Chapter 12).
- [ ] Ignition components damp or damaged - petrol models (Chapters 1A and 5B).
- [ ] Ignition timing incorrect (Chapter 5B)
- [ ] Broken, loose or disconnected wiring in the ignition circuit - petrol models (Chapter 5B).
- [ ] Worn, faulty or incorrectly-gapped spark plugs - petrol models (Chapter 1A).
- [ ] Preheating system faulty - diesel models (Chapter 5C).
- [ ] Fuel injection system fault - petrol models (Chapter 4A or 4B).
- [ ] Fuel cut-off ("stop") solenoid faulty - diesel models (Chapter 4C).
- [ ] Air in fuel system - diesel models (Chapter 4C).
- [ ] Major mechanical failure (eg camshaft drive) (Chapter 2A, 2B or 2C).

Engine difficult to start when cold

- [ ] Battery discharged (Chapter 5A).
- [ ] Ignition timing incorrect (Chapter 5B)
- [ ] Battery terminal connections loose or corroded ("*Weekly checks*").
- [ ] Worn, faulty or incorrectly-gapped spark plugs - petrol models (Chapter 1A).
- [ ] Preheating system faulty - diesel models (Chapter 5C).
- [ ] Fuel injection system fault - petrol models (Chapter 4A or 4B).
- [ ] Other ignition system fault - petrol models (Chapter 5B).
- [ ] Fast idle valve incorrectly adjusted - diesel models (Chapter 4C).
- [ ] Low cylinder compressions (Chapter 2A or 2B).

Engine difficult to start when hot

- [ ] Air filter element dirty or clogged (Chapter 1).
- [ ] Fuel injection system fault - petrol models (Chapter 4A or 4B).
- [ ] Low cylinder compressions (Chapter 2A or 2B).
- [ ] Ignition timing incorrect (Chapter 5B)

Starter motor noisy or excessively-rough in engagement

- [ ] Starter pinion or flywheel ring gear teeth loose or broken (Chapters 2A, 2B and 5A).
- [ ] Starter motor mounting bolts loose or missing (Chapter 5A).
- [ ] Starter motor internal components worn or damaged (Chapter 5A).

Engine starts, but stops immediately

- [ ] Loose or faulty electrical connections in the ignition circuit - petrol models (Chapter 5B).
- [ ] Vacuum leak at the throttle body or inlet manifold - petrol models (Chapter 4A or 4B).
- [ ] Blocked injector/fuel injection system fault - petrol models (Chapter 4A or 4B).

Engine idles erratically

- [ ] Air filter element clogged (Chapter 1).
- [ ] Vacuum leak at the throttle body, inlet manifold or associated hoses - petrol models (Chapter 4A or 4B).
- [ ] Worn, faulty or incorrectly-gapped spark plugs - petrol models (Chapter 1A).
- [ ] Uneven or low cylinder compressions (Chapter 2A or 2B).
- [ ] Camshaft lobes worn (Chapter 2A or 2B).
- [ ] Timing belt incorrectly tensioned (Chapter 2A or 2B).
- [ ] Blocked injector/fuel injection system fault - petrol models (Chapter 4A or 4B).
- [ ] Faulty injector(s) - diesel models (Chapter 4C).

Engine misfires at idle speed

- [ ] Worn, faulty or incorrectly-gapped spark plugs - petrol models (Chapter 1A).
- [ ] Faulty spark plug HT leads - petrol models (Chapter 5B).
- [ ] Vacuum leak at the throttle body, inlet manifold or associated hoses - petrol models (Chapter 4A or 4B).
- [ ] Blocked injector/fuel injection system fault - petrol models (Chapter 4A or 4B).
- [ ] Faulty injector(s) - diesel models (Chapter 4C).
- [ ] Distributor cap cracked or tracking internally - petrol models (where applicable) (Chapter 5B).
- [ ] Uneven or low cylinder compressions (Chapter 2A or 2B).
- [ ] Disconnected, leaking, or perished crankcase ventilation hoses (Chapter 4D).

1 Engine (continued)

Engine misfires throughout the driving speed range

- ☐ Fuel filter choked (Chapter 1).
- ☐ Fuel pump faulty, or delivery pressure low - petrol models (Chapter 4A or 4B).
- ☐ Fuel tank vent blocked, or fuel pipes restricted (Chapter 4A, 4B or 4C).
- ☐ Vacuum leak at the throttle body, inlet manifold or associated hoses - petrol models (Chapter 4A or 4B).
- ☐ Worn, faulty or incorrectly-gapped spark plugs - petrol models (Chapter 1A).
- ☐ Faulty spark plug HT leads - petrol models (Chapter 5B).
- ☐ Faulty injector(s) - diesel models (Chapter 4C).
- ☐ Distributor cap cracked or tracking internally - petrol models (where applicable) (Chapter 5B).
- ☐ Faulty ignition coil - petrol models (Chapter 5B).
- ☐ Uneven or low cylinder compressions (Chapter 2A or 2B).
- ☐ Blocked injector/fuel injection system fault - petrol models (Chapter 4A or 4B).

Engine hesitates on acceleration

- ☐ Worn, faulty or incorrectly-gapped spark plugs - petrol models (Chapter 1A).
- ☐ Vacuum leak at the throttle body, inlet manifold or associated hoses - petrol models (Chapter 4A or 4B).
- ☐ Blocked injector/fuel injection system fault - petrol models (Chapter 4A or 4B).
- ☐ Faulty injector(s) - diesel models (Chapter 4C).

Engine stalls

- ☐ Vacuum leak at the throttle body, inlet manifold or associated hoses - petrol models (Chapter 4A or 4B).
- ☐ Fuel filter choked (Chapter 1).
- ☐ Fuel pump faulty, or delivery pressure low - petrol models (Chapter 4A or 4B).
- ☐ Fuel tank vent blocked, or fuel pipes restricted (Chapter 4A, 4B or 4C).
- ☐ Blocked injector/fuel injection system fault - petrol models (Chapter 4A or 4B).
- ☐ Faulty injector(s) - diesel models (Chapter 4C).

Engine lacks power

- ☐ Timing belt incorrectly fitted or tensioned (Chapter 2A or 2B).
- ☐ Fuel filter choked (Chapter 1).
- ☐ Ignition timing incorrect (Chapter 5B)
- ☐ Fuel pump faulty, or delivery pressure low - petrol models (Chapter 4A or 4B).
- ☐ Uneven or low cylinder compressions (Chapter 2A or 2B).
- ☐ Worn, faulty or incorrectly-gapped spark plugs - petrol models (Chapter 1A).
- ☐ Vacuum leak at the throttle body, inlet manifold or associated hoses - petrol models (Chapter 4A or 4B).
- ☐ Blocked injector/fuel injection system fault - petrol models (Chapter 4A or 4B).
- ☐ Faulty injector(s) - diesel models (Chapter 4C).
- ☐ Injection pump timing incorrect - diesel models (Chapter 4C).
- ☐ Brakes binding (Chapters 1 and 9).
- ☐ Clutch slipping (Chapter 6).

Engine backfires

- ☐ Timing belt incorrectly fitted or tensioned (Chapter 2A or 2B).
- ☐ Vacuum leak at the throttle body, inlet manifold or associated hoses - petrol models (Chapter 4A or 4B).
- ☐ Blocked injector/fuel injection system fault - petrol models (Chapter 4A or 4B).
- ☐ Ignition timing incorrect (Chapter 5B).

Oil pressure warning light illuminated with engine running

- ☐ Low oil level, or incorrect oil grade ("Weekly checks").
- ☐ Worn engine bearings and/or oil pump (Chapter 2C).
- ☐ High engine operating temperature (Chapter 3).
- ☐ Oil pressure relief valve defective (Chapter 2A or 2B).
- ☐ Oil pick-up strainer clogged (Chapter 2A or 2B).

Engine runs-on after switching off

- ☐ Excessive carbon build-up in engine (Chapter 2C).
- ☐ High engine operating temperature (Chapter 3).
- ☐ Fuel injection system fault - petrol models (Chapter 4A or 4B).
- ☐ Faulty fuel cut-off ("stop") solenoid - diesel models (Chapter 4C).

Engine noises

Pre-ignition (pinking) or knocking during acceleration or under load

- ☐ Ignition timing incorrect/ignition system fault - petrol models (Chapter 5B).
- ☐ Incorrect grade of spark plug - petrol models (Chapter 1A).
- ☐ Incorrect grade of fuel (Chapter 1).
- ☐ Vacuum leak at the throttle body, inlet manifold or associated hoses - petrol models (Chapter 4A or 4B).
- ☐ Excessive carbon build-up in engine (Chapter 2C).
- ☐ Blocked injector/fuel injection system fault - petrol models (Chapter 4A or 4B).

Whistling or wheezing noises

- ☐ Leaking inlet manifold or throttle body gasket - petrol models (Chapter 4A or 4B).
- ☐ Leaking exhaust manifold gasket or pipe-to-manifold joint (Chapter 4A, 4B or 4C).
- ☐ Leaking vacuum hose (Chapters 4, 5B and 9).
- ☐ Blowing cylinder head gasket (Chapter 2A or 2B).

Tapping or rattling noises

- ☐ Worn valve gear or camshaft (Chapter 2A or 2B).
- ☐ Ancillary component fault (water pump, alternator, etc) (Chapters 3, 5A, etc).

Knocking or thumping noises

- ☐ Worn big-end bearings (regular heavy knocking, perhaps less under load) (Chapter 2C).
- ☐ Worn main bearings (rumbling and knocking, perhaps worsening under load) (Chapter 2C).
- ☐ Piston slap (most noticeable when cold) (Chapter 2C).
- ☐ Ancillary component fault (water pump, alternator, etc) (Chapters 3, 5A, etc).

2 Cooling system

Overheating

- [ ] Insufficient coolant in system ("*Weekly checks*").
- [ ] Auxiliary drivebelt broken or incorrectly-adjusted (Chapter 1 or 2).
- [ ] Thermostat faulty (Chapter 3).
- [ ] Radiator core blocked, or grille restricted (Chapter 3).
- [ ] Electric cooling fan or thermoswitch faulty (Chapter 3).
- [ ] Pressure cap faulty (Chapter 3).
- [ ] Ignition timing incorrect/ignition system fault - petrol models (Chapter 5B).
- [ ] Inaccurate temperature gauge sender unit (Chapter 3).
- [ ] Airlock in cooling system (Chapter 1).

Overcooling

- [ ] Thermostat faulty (Chapter 3).
- [ ] Inaccurate temperature gauge sender unit (Chapter 3).

External coolant leakage

- [ ] Deteriorated or damaged hoses or hose clips (Chapter 1).
- [ ] Radiator core or heater matrix leaking (Chapter 3).
- [ ] Pressure cap faulty (Chapter 3).
- [ ] Water pump seal leaking (Chapter 3).
- [ ] Boiling due to overheating (Chapter 3).
- [ ] Core plug leaking (Chapter 2C).

Internal coolant leakage

- [ ] Leaking cylinder head gasket (Chapter 2A or 2B).
- [ ] Cracked cylinder head or cylinder bore (Chapter 2A or 2B).

Corrosion

- [ ] Infrequent draining and flushing (Chapter 1).
- [ ] Incorrect coolant mixture or inappropriate coolant type ("*Lubricants and fluids*" and Chapter 1).

3 Fuel and exhaust systems

Excessive fuel consumption

- [ ] Air filter element dirty or clogged (Chapter 1).
- [ ] Fuel injection system fault - petrol models (Chapter 4A or 4B).
- [ ] Faulty injector(s) - diesel models (Chapter 4C).
- [ ] Ignition timing incorrect/ignition system fault - petrol models (Chapter 5B).
- [ ] Tyres under-inflated ("*Weekly checks*").

Fuel leakage and/or fuel odour

- [ ] Damaged or corroded fuel tank, pipes or connections (Chapter 4).

Excessive noise or fumes from exhaust system

- [ ] Leaking exhaust system or manifold joints (Chapters 1 and 4).
- [ ] Leaking, corroded or damaged silencers or pipe (Chapters 1 and 4).
- [ ] Broken mountings causing body or suspension contact (Chapter 1).

4 Clutch

Pedal travels to floor - no pressure or very little resistance

- [ ] Broken clutch cable - cable-operated clutch (Chapter 6).
- [ ] Cable automatic adjuster faulty - cable-operated clutch (Chapter 6).
- [ ] Hydraulic fluid level low/air in the hydraulic system - hydraulically-operated clutch ("*Weekly checks*" or Chapter 6).
- [ ] Broken clutch release bearing or fork (Chapter 6).
- [ ] Broken diaphragm spring in clutch pressure plate (Chapter 6).

Clutch fails to disengage (unable to select gears)

- [ ] Cable automatic adjuster faulty - cable-operated clutch (Chapter 6).
- [ ] Faulty master/slave cylinder - hydraulically-operated clutch (Chapter 6).
- [ ] Hydraulic fluid level too high - hydraulically-operated clutch ("*Weekly checks*" or Chapter 6)
- [ ] Clutch disc sticking on gearbox input shaft splines (Chapter 6).
- [ ] Clutch disc sticking to flywheel or pressure plate (Chapter 6).
- [ ] Faulty pressure plate assembly (Chapter 6).
- [ ] Clutch release mechanism worn or incorrectly assembled (Chapter 6).

Clutch slips (engine speed increases, with no increase in vehicle speed)

- [ ] Cable automatic adjuster faulty - cable-operated clutch (Chapter 6).
- [ ] Hydraulic fluid level too high - hydraulically-operated clutch ("*Weekly checks*" or Chapter 6)
- [ ] Clutch disc linings excessively worn (Chapter 6).
- [ ] Clutch disc linings contaminated with oil or grease (Chapter 6).
- [ ] Faulty pressure plate or weak diaphragm spring (Chapter 6).

Judder as clutch is engaged

- [ ] Clutch disc linings contaminated with oil or grease (Chapter 6).
- [ ] Clutch disc linings excessively worn (Chapter 6).
- [ ] Clutch cable sticking or frayed - cable-operated clutch (Chapter 6).
- [ ] Faulty or distorted pressure plate or diaphragm spring (Chapter 6).
- [ ] Worn or loose engine or gearbox mountings (Chapter 2A or 2B).
- [ ] Clutch disc hub or gearbox input shaft splines worn (Chapter 6).

Noise when depressing or releasing clutch pedal

- [ ] Worn clutch release bearing (Chapter 6).
- [ ] Worn or dry clutch pedal bushes (Chapter 6).
- [ ] Faulty pressure plate assembly (Chapter 6).
- [ ] Pressure plate diaphragm spring broken (Chapter 6).
- [ ] Broken clutch disc cushioning springs (Chapter 6).

5 Manual transmission

Noisy in neutral with engine running

☐ Input shaft bearings worn (noise apparent with clutch pedal released, but not when depressed) (Chapter 7A).*
☐ Clutch release bearing worn (noise apparent with clutch pedal depressed, possibly less when released) (Chapter 6).

Noisy in one particular gear

☐ Worn, damaged or chipped gear teeth (Chapter 7A).*

Difficulty engaging gears

☐ Clutch fault (Chapter 6).
☐ Worn or damaged gearchange linkage/cable (Chapter 7A).
☐ Incorrectly-adjusted gearchange linkage/cable (Chapter 7A).
☐ Worn synchroniser units (Chapter 7A).*

Jumps out of gear

☐ Worn or damaged gearchange linkage/cable (Chapter 7A).
☐ Incorrectly-adjusted gearchange linkage/cable (Chapter 7A).
☐ Worn synchroniser units (Chapter 7A).*
☐ Worn selector forks (Chapter 7A).*

Vibration

☐ Lack of oil (Chapter 1).
☐ Worn bearings (Chapter 7A).*

Lubricant leaks

☐ Leaking differential output oil seal (Chapter 7A).
☐ Leaking housing joint (Chapter 7A).*
☐ Leaking input shaft oil seal (Chapter 7A).*

Although the corrective action necessary to remedy the symptoms described is beyond the scope of the home mechanic, the above information should be helpful in isolating the cause of the condition, so that the owner can communicate clearly with a professional mechanic.

6 Automatic transmission

Note: *Due to the complexity of the automatic transmission, it is difficult for the home mechanic to properly diagnose and service this unit. For problems other than the following, the vehicle should be taken to a dealer service department or automatic transmission specialist. Do not be too hasty in removing the transmission if a fault is suspected, as most of the testing is carried out with the unit still fitted.*

Fluid leakage

☐ Automatic transmission fluid is usually dark in colour. Fluid leaks should not be confused with engine oil, which can easily be blown onto the transmission by airflow.
☐ To determine the source of a leak, first remove all built-up dirt and grime from the transmission housing and surrounding areas using a degreasing agent, or by steam-cleaning. Drive the vehicle at low speed, so airflow will not blow the leak far from its source. Raise and support the vehicle, and determine where the leak is coming from. The following are common areas of leakage:
a) Oil pan (Chapter 1 and 7B).
b) Dipstick tube (Chapter 1 and 7B).
c) Transmission-to-fluid cooler pipes/unions (Chapter 7B).

Transmission neutral fluid brown, or has burned smell

☐ Transmission fluid level low, or fluid in need of renewal (Chapter 1).

General gear selection problems

☐ Chapter 7B deals with checking and adjusting the selector cable on automatic transmissions. The following are common problems which may be caused by a poorly-adjusted cable:

a) Engine starting in gears other than Park or Neutral.
b) Indicator panel indicating a gear other than the one actually being used.
c) Vehicle moves when in Park or Neutral.
d) Poor gear shift quality or erratic gear changes.
☐ Refer to Chapter 7B for the selector cable adjustment procedure.

Transmission will not downshift (kickdown) with accelerator pedal fully depressed

☐ Low transmission fluid level (Chapter 1).
☐ Incorrect selector cable adjustment (Chapter 7B).

Engine will not start in any gear, or starts in gears other than Park or Neutral

☐ Incorrect selector cable adjustment (Chapter 7B).

Transmission slips, shifts roughly, is noisy, or has no drive in forward or reverse gears

☐ There are many probable causes for the above problems, but the home mechanic should be concerned with only one possibility - fluid level. Before taking the vehicle to a dealer or transmission specialist, check the fluid level and condition of the fluid as described in Chapter 1. Correct the fluid level as necessary, or change the fluid and filter if needed. If the problem persists, professional help will be necessary.

7 Driveshafts

Clicking or knocking noise on turns (at slow speed on full-lock)

☐ Lack of constant velocity joint lubricant, possibly due to damaged [gaiter] (Chapter 8).
☐ [Worn] outer constant velocity joint (Chapter 8).

Vibration when accelerating or decelerating

☐ Worn inner constant velocity joint (Chapter 8).
☐ Bent or distorted driveshaft (Chapter 8).

8 Braking system

Note: *Before assuming that a brake problem exists, make sure that the tyres are in good condition and correctly inflated, that the front wheel alignment is correct, the front wheels are balanced, and that the vehicle is not loaded with weight in an unequal manner. Apart from checking the condition of all pipe and hose connections, any faults occurring on the anti-lock braking system should be referred to a VW dealer for diagnosis.*

Vehicle pulls to one side under braking

- ☐ Worn, defective, damaged or contaminated brake pads/shoes on one side (Chapters 1 and 9).
- ☐ Seized or partially-seized front brake caliper/wheel cylinder piston (Chapters 1 and 9).
- ☐ A mixture of brake pad/shoe lining materials fitted between sides (Chapters 1 and 9).
- ☐ Brake caliper or backplate mounting bolts loose (Chapter 9).
- ☐ Worn or damaged steering or suspension components (Chapters 1 and 10).

Noise (grinding or high-pitched squeal) when brakes applied

- ☐ Brake pad or shoe friction lining material worn down to metal backing (Chapters 1 and 9).
- ☐ Excessive corrosion of brake disc or drum. (May be apparent after the vehicle has been standing for some time (Chapters 1 and 9).
- ☐ Foreign object (stone chipping, etc) trapped between brake disc and shield (Chapters 1 and 9).

Excessive brake pedal travel

- ☐ Inoperative rear brake self-adjust mechanism - drum brakes (Chapters 1 and 9).
- ☐ Faulty master cylinder (Chapter 9).
- ☐ Air in hydraulic system (Chapters 1 and 9).
- ☐ Faulty vacuum servo unit (Chapter 9).

Brake pedal feels spongy when depressed

- ☐ Air in hydraulic system (Chapters 1 and 9).
- ☐ Deteriorated flexible rubber brake hoses (Chapters 1 and 9).
- ☐ Master cylinder mounting nuts loose (Chapter 9).
- ☐ Faulty master cylinder (Chapter 9).

Excessive brake pedal effort required to stop vehicle

- ☐ Faulty vacuum servo unit (Chapter 9).
- ☐ Faulty vacuum pump - diesel models (Chapter 9).
- ☐ Disconnected, damaged or insecure brake servo vacuum hose (Chapter 9).
- ☐ Primary or secondary hydraulic circuit failure (Chapter 9).
- ☐ Seized brake caliper or wheel cylinder piston(s) (Chapter 9).
- ☐ Brake pads or brake shoes incorrectly fitted (Chapters 1 and 9).
- ☐ Incorrect grade of brake pads or brake shoes fitted (Chapters 1 and 9).
- ☐ Brake pads or brake shoe linings contaminated (Chapters 1 and 9).

Judder felt through brake pedal or steering wheel when braking

- ☐ Excessive run-out or distortion of discs/drums (Chapters 1 and 9).
- ☐ Brake pad or brake shoe linings worn (Chapters 1 and 9).
- ☐ Brake caliper or brake backplate mounting bolts loose (Chapter 9).
- ☐ Wear in suspension or steering components or mountings (Chapters 1 and 10).
- ☐ Vibration through pedal - Anti-lock Braking System (ABS) in operation - no fault (models with ABS).

Brakes binding

- ☐ Seized brake caliper or wheel cylinder piston(s) (Chapter 9).
- ☐ Incorrectly-adjusted handbrake mechanism (Chapter 9).
- ☐ Faulty master cylinder (Chapter 9).

Rear wheels locking under normal braking

- ☐ Rear brake shoe linings contaminated (Chapters 1 and 9).
- ☐ Faulty brake pressure regulator (Chapter 9).

9 Suspension and steering

Note: *Before diagnosing suspension or steering faults, be sure that the trouble is not due to incorrect tyre pressures, mixtures of tyre types, worn tyres, or binding brakes.*

Vehicle pulls to one side

- ☐ Defective or worn tyre (*"Weekly checks"*).
- ☐ Excessive wear in suspension or steering components (Chapters 1 and 10).
- ☐ Incorrect front wheel alignment (Chapter 10).
- ☐ Accident damage to steering or suspension components (Chapter 1).

Wheel wobble and vibration

- ☐ Front roadwheels out of balance (vibration felt mainly through the steering wheel) (*"Weekly checks"*).
- ☐ Rear roadwheels out of balance (vibration felt throughout the vehicle) (*"Weekly checks"*).
- ☐ Roadwheels damaged or distorted (*"Weekly checks"*).
- ☐ Faulty, worn or damaged tyre (*"Weekly checks"*).
- ☐ Worn steering or suspension joints, bushes or components (Chapters 1 and 10).
- ☐ Wheel bolts loose (Chapter 1).

Excessive pitching and/or rolling around corners, or during braking

- ☐ Defective shock absorbers (Chapters 1 and 10).
- ☐ Broken or weak spring and/or suspension component (Chapters 1 and 10).
- ☐ Worn or damaged anti-roll bar or mountings (Chapter 10).

Wandering or general instability

- ☐ Incorrect front wheel alignment (Chapter 10).
- ☐ Worn steering or suspension joints, bushes or components (Chapters 1 and 10).
- ☐ Roadwheels out of balance (*"Weekly checks"*).
- ☐ Faulty or damaged tyre (*"Weekly checks"*).
- ☐ Wheel bolts loose (Chapter 1).
- ☐ Defective shock absorbers (Chapters 1 and 10).

Excessively-stiff steering

- ☐ Incorrect power steering fluid level (*"Weekly checks"*).
- ☐ Lack of steering gear lubricant (Chapter 10).
- ☐ Seized track rod end balljoint or suspension balljoint (Chapters 1 and 10).
- ☐ Broken or incorrectly-adjusted auxiliary drivebelt - power steering (Chapter 1).
- ☐ Incorrect front wheel alignment (Chapter 10).
- ☐ Steering rack or column bent or damaged (Chapter 10).

9 Suspension and steering (continued)

Excessive play in steering

- ☐ Worn steering column intermediate shaft universal joint (Chapter 10).
- ☐ Worn steering track rod end balljoints (Chapters 1 and 10).
- ☐ Worn rack-and-pinion steering gear (Chapter 10).
- ☐ Worn steering or suspension joints, bushes or components (Chapters 1 and 10).

Lack of power assistance

- ☐ Broken or incorrectly-adjusted auxiliary drivebelt (Chapter 1 or 2).
- ☐ Incorrect power steering fluid level ("*Weekly checks*").
- ☐ Restriction in power steering fluid hoses (Chapter 1).
- ☐ Faulty power steering pump (Chapter 10).
- ☐ Faulty rack-and-pinion steering gear (Chapter 10).

Tyre wear excessive

Tyres worn on inside or outside edges

- ☐ Tyres under-inflated (wear on both edges) ("*Weekly checks*").
- ☐ Incorrect camber or castor angles (wear on one edge only) (Chapter 10).

- ☐ Worn steering or suspension joints, bushes or components (Chapters 1 and 10).
- ☐ Excessively-hard cornering.
- ☐ Accident damage.

Tyre treads exhibit feathered edges

- ☐ Incorrect toe setting (Chapter 10).

Tyres worn in centre of tread

- ☐ Tyres over-inflated ("*Weekly checks*").

Tyres worn on inside and outside edges

- ☐ Tyres under-inflated ("*Weekly checks*").

Tyres worn unevenly

- ☐ Tyres/wheels out of balance ("*Weekly checks*").
- ☐ Excessive wheel or tyre run-out ("*Weekly checks*").
- ☐ Worn shock absorbers (Chapters 1 and 10).
- ☐ Faulty tyre ("*Weekly checks*").

10 Electrical system

Note: *For problems associated with the starting system, refer to the faults listed under "Engine" earlier in this Section.*

Battery will not hold a charge for more than a few days

- ☐ Battery defective internally (Chapter 5A).
- ☐ Battery terminal connections loose or corroded ("*Weekly checks*").
- ☐ Auxiliary drivebelt worn or incorrectly adjusted (Chapter 1 or 2).
- ☐ Alternator not charging at correct output (Chapter 5A).
- ☐ Alternator or voltage regulator faulty (Chapter 5A).
- ☐ Short-circuit causing continual battery drain (Chapters 5A and 12).

Ignition/no-charge warning light remains illuminated with engine running

- ☐ Auxiliary drivebelt broken, worn, or incorrectly adjusted (Chapter 1).
- ☐ Alternator brushes worn, sticking, or dirty (Chapter 5A).
- ☐ Alternator brush springs weak or broken (Chapter 5A).
- ☐ Internal fault in alternator or voltage regulator (Chapter 5A).
- ☐ Broken, disconnected, or loose wiring in charging circuit (Chapter 5A).

Ignition/no-charge warning light fails to come on

- ☐ Warning light bulb blown (Chapter 12).
- ☐ Broken, disconnected, or loose wiring in warning light circuit (Chapter 12).
- ☐ Alternator faulty (Chapter 5A).

Lights inoperative

- ☐ Bulb blown (Chapter 12).
- ☐ Corrosion of bulb or bulbholder contacts (Chapter 12).
- ☐ Blown fuse ("*Weekly checks*" or Chapter 12).
- ☐ Faulty relay (Chapter 12).
- ☐ Broken, loose, or disconnected wiring (Chapter 12).
- ☐ Faulty switch (Chapter 12).

Instrument readings inaccurate or erratic

Instrument readings increase with engine speed

- ☐ Faulty voltage stabiliser (Chapter 12).

Fuel or temperature gauges give no reading

- ☐ Faulty gauge sender unit (Chapters 3 and 4A, 4B or 4C).
- ☐ Wiring open-circuit (Chapter 12).
- ☐ Faulty gauge (Chapter 12).

Fuel or temperature gauges give continuous maximum reading

- ☐ Faulty gauge sender unit (Chapters 3 and 4A, 4B or 4C).
- ☐ Wiring short-circuit (Chapter 12).
- ☐ Faulty gauge (Chapter 12).

Horn inoperative, or unsatisfactory in operation

Horn operates all the time

- ☐ Horn push either earthed or stuck down (Chapter 12).
- ☐ Horn cable-to-horn push earthed (Chapter 12).

Horn fails to operate

- ☐ Blown fuse ("*Weekly checks*" or Chapter 12).
- ☐ Cable or cable connections loose, broken or disconnected (Chapter 12).
- ☐ Faulty horn (Chapter 12).

Horn emits intermittent or unsatisfactory sound

- ☐ Cable connections loose (Chapter 12).
- ☐ Horn mountings loose (Chapter 12).
- ☐ Faulty horn (Chapter 12).

Windscreen/tailgate wipers inoperative, or unsatisfactory in operation

Wipers fail to operate, or operate very slowly

- ☐ Wiper blades stuck to screen, or linkage seized or binding ("*Weekly checks*" or Chapter 12).
- ☐ Blown fuse ("*Weekly checks*" or Chapter 12).
- ☐ Cable or cable connections loose, broken or disconnected (Chapter 12).
- ☐ Faulty relay (Chapter 12).
- ☐ Faulty wiper motor (Chapter 12).

Wiper blades sweep over too large or too small an area of the glass

- ☐ Wiper arms incorrectly positioned on spindles (Chapter 12).
- ☐ Excessive wear of wiper linkage (Chapter 12).
- ☐ Wiper motor or linkage mountings loose or insecure (Chapter 12).

Wiper blades fail to clean the glass effectively

- ☐ Wiper blade rubbers worn or perished ("*Weekly checks*").
- ☐ Wiper arm tension springs broken, or arm pivots seized (Chapter 12).
- ☐ Insufficient windscreen washer additive to adequately remove road film ("*Weekly checks*").

Windscreen/tailgate washers inoperative, or unsatisfactory in operation

One or more washer jets inoperative

- ☐ Blocked washer jet (Chapter 1).
- ☐ Disconnected, kinked or restricted fluid hose (Chapter 12).
- ☐ Insufficient fluid in washer reservoir ("*Weekly checks*").

Washer pump fails to operate

- ☐ Broken or disconnected wiring or connections (Chapter 12).
- ☐ Blown fuse ("*Weekly checks*" or Chapter 12).
- ☐ Faulty washer switch (Chapter 12).
- ☐ Faulty washer pump (Chapter 12).

Washer pump runs for some time before fluid is emitted from jets

- ☐ Faulty one-way valve in fluid supply hose (Chapter 12).

Electric windows inoperative, or unsatisfactory in operation

Window glass will only move in one direction

- ☐ Faulty switch (Chapter 12).

Window glass slow to move

- ☐ Regulator seized or damaged, or in need of lubrication (Chapter 11).
- ☐ Door internal components or trim fouling regulator (Chapter 11).
- ☐ Faulty motor (Chapter 11).

Window glass fails to move

- ☐ Blown fuse ("*Weekly checks*" or Chapter 12).
- ☐ Faulty relay (Chapter 12).
- ☐ Broken or disconnected wiring or connections (Chapter 12).
- ☐ Faulty motor (Chapter 11).

Central locking system inoperative, or unsatisfactory in operation

Complete system failure

- ☐ Blown fuse ("*Weekly checks*" or Chapter 12).
- ☐ Faulty relay (Chapter 12).
- ☐ Broken or disconnected wiring or connections (Chapter 12).
- ☐ Faulty bi-pressure pump (Chapter 11).

Latch locks but will not unlock, or unlocks but will not lock

- ☐ Broken or disconnected latch operating rods or levers (Chapter 11).
- ☐ Faulty relay (Chapter 12).
- ☐ Faulty bi-pressure pump (Chapter 11).

One solenoid/motor fails to operate

- ☐ Broken or disconnected wiring or connections (Chapter 12).
- ☐ Faulty operating assembly (Chapter 11).
- ☐ Broken, binding or disconnected latch operating rods or levers (Chapter 11).
- ☐ Fault in door latch (Chapter 11).

A

ABS (Anti-lock brake system) A system, usually electronically controlled, that senses incipient wheel lockup during braking and relieves hydraulic pressure at wheels that are about to skid.

Air bag An inflatable bag hidden in the steering wheel (driver's side) or the dash or glovebox (passenger side). In a head-on collision, the bags inflate, preventing the driver and front passenger from being thrown forward into the steering wheel or windscreen.

Air cleaner A metal or plastic housing, containing a filter element, which removes dust and dirt from the air being drawn into the engine.

Air filter element The actual filter in an air cleaner system, usually manufactured from pleated paper and requiring renewal at regular intervals.

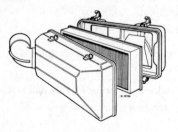

Air filter

Allen key A hexagonal wrench which fits into a recessed hexagonal hole.

Alligator clip A long-nosed spring-loaded metal clip with meshing teeth. Used to make temporary electrical connections.

Alternator A component in the electrical system which converts mechanical energy from a drivebelt into electrical energy to charge the battery and to operate the starting system, ignition system and electrical accessories.

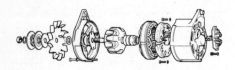

Alternator (exploded view)

Ampere (amp) A unit of measurement for the flow of electric current. One amp is the amount of current produced by one volt acting through a resistance of one ohm.

Anaerobic sealer A substance used to prevent bolts and screws from loosening. Anaerobic means that it does not require oxygen for activation. The Loctite brand is widely used.

Antifreeze A substance (usually ethylene glycol) mixed with water, and added to a vehicle's cooling system, to prevent freezing of the coolant in winter. Antifreeze also contains chemicals to inhibit corrosion and the formation of rust and other deposits that would tend to clog the radiator and coolant passages and reduce cooling efficiency.

Anti-seize compound A coating that reduces the risk of seizing on fasteners that are subjected to high temperatures, such as exhaust manifold bolts and nuts.

Anti-seize compound

Asbestos A natural fibrous mineral with great heat resistance, commonly used in the composition of brake friction materials. Asbestos is a health hazard and the dust created by brake systems should never be inhaled or ingested.

Axle A shaft on which a wheel revolves, or which revolves with a wheel. Also, a solid beam that connects the two wheels at one end of the vehicle. An axle which also transmits power to the wheels is known as a live axle.

Axle assembly

Axleshaft A single rotating shaft, on either side of the differential, which delivers power from the final drive assembly to the drive wheels. Also called a driveshaft or a halfshaft.

B

Ball bearing An anti-friction bearing consisting of a hardened inner and outer race with hardened steel balls between two races.

Bearing

Bearing The curved surface on a shaft or in a bore, or the part assembled into either, that permits relative motion between them with minimum wear and friction.

Big-end bearing The bearing in the end of the connecting rod that's attached to the crankshaft.

Bleed nipple A valve on a brake wheel cylinder, caliper or other hydraulic component that is opened to purge the hydraulic system of air. Also called a bleed screw.

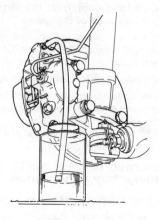

Brake bleeding

Brake bleeding Procedure for removing air from lines of a hydraulic brake system.

Brake disc The component of a disc brake that rotates with the wheels.

Brake drum The component of a drum brake that rotates with the wheels.

Brake linings The friction material which contacts the brake disc or drum to retard the vehicle's speed. The linings are bonded or riveted to the brake pads or shoes.

Brake pads The replaceable friction pads that pinch the brake disc when the brakes are applied. Brake pads consist of a friction material bonded or riveted to a rigid backing plate.

Brake shoe The crescent-shaped carrier to which the brake linings are mounted and which forces the lining against the rotating drum during braking.

Braking systems For more information on braking systems, consult the *Haynes Automotive Brake Manual*.

Breaker bar A long socket wrench handle providing greater leverage.

Bulkhead The insulated partition between the engine and the passenger compartment.

C

Caliper The non-rotating part of a disc-brake assembly that straddles the disc and carries the brake pads. The caliper also contains the hydraulic components that cause the pads to pinch the disc when the brakes are applied. A caliper is also a measuring tool that can be set to measure inside or outside dimensions of an object.

Camshaft A rotating shaft on which a series of cam lobes operate the valve mechanisms. The camshaft may be driven by gears, by sprockets and chain or by sprockets and a belt.

Canister A container in an evaporative emission control system; contains activated charcoal granules to trap vapours from the fuel system.

Canister

Carburettor A device which mixes fuel with air in the proper proportions to provide a desired power output from a spark ignition internal combustion engine.

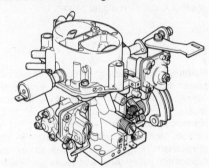

Carburettor

Castellated Resembling the parapets along the top of a castle wall. For example, a castellated balljoint stud nut.

Castellated nut

Castor In wheel alignment, the backward or forward tilt of the steering axis. Castor is positive when the steering axis is inclined rearward at the top.

Catalytic converter A silencer-like device in the exhaust system which converts certain pollutants in the exhaust gases into less harmful substances.

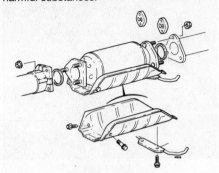

Catalytic converter

Circlip A ring-shaped clip used to prevent endwise movement of cylindrical parts and shafts. An internal circlip is installed in a groove in a housing; an external circlip fits into a groove on the outside of a cylindrical piece such as a shaft.

Clearance The amount of space between two parts. For example, between a piston and a cylinder, between a bearing and a journal, etc.

Coil spring A spiral of elastic steel found in various sizes throughout a vehicle, for example as a springing medium in the suspension and in the valve train.

Compression Reduction in volume, and increase in pressure and temperature, of a gas, caused by squeezing it into a smaller space.

Compression ratio The relationship between cylinder volume when the piston is at top dead centre and cylinder volume when the piston is at bottom dead centre.

Constant velocity (CV) joint A type of universal joint that cancels out vibrations caused by driving power being transmitted through an angle.

Core plug A disc or cup-shaped metal device inserted in a hole in a casting through which core was removed when the casting was formed. Also known as a freeze plug or expansion plug.

Crankcase The lower part of the engine block in which the crankshaft rotates.

Crankshaft The main rotating member, or shaft, running the length of the crankcase, with offset "throws" to which the connecting rods are attached.

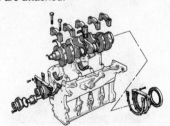

Crankshaft assembly

Crocodile clip See Alligator clip

D

Diagnostic code Code numbers obtained by accessing the diagnostic mode of an engine management computer. This code can be used to determine the area in the system where a malfunction may be located.

Disc brake A brake design incorporating a rotating disc onto which brake pads are squeezed. The resulting friction converts the energy of a moving vehicle into heat.

Double-overhead cam (DOHC) An engine that uses two overhead camshafts, usually one for the intake valves and one for the exhaust valves.

Drivebelt(s) The belt(s) used to drive accessories such as the alternator, water pump, power steering pump, air conditioning compressor, etc. off the crankshaft pulley.

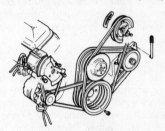

Accessory drivebelts

Driveshaft Any shaft used to transmit motion. Commonly used when referring to the axleshafts on a front wheel drive vehicle.

Driveshaft

Drum brake A type of brake using a drum-shaped metal cylinder attached to the inner surface of the wheel. When the brake pedal is pressed, curved brake shoes with friction linings press against the inside of the drum to slow or stop the vehicle.

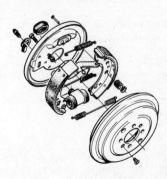

Drum brake assembly

E

EGR valve A valve used to introduce exhaust gases into the intake air stream.

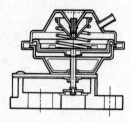

EGR valve

Electronic control unit (ECU) A computer which controls (for instance) ignition and fuel injection systems, or an anti-lock braking system. For more information refer to the *Haynes Automotive Electrical and Electronic Systems Manual.*

Electronic Fuel Injection (EFI) A computer controlled fuel system that distributes fuel through an injector located in each intake port of the engine.

Emergency brake A braking system, independent of the main hydraulic system, that can be used to slow or stop the vehicle if the primary brakes fail, or to hold the vehicle stationary even though the brake pedal isn't depressed. It usually consists of a hand lever that actuates either front or rear brakes mechanically through a series of cables and linkages. Also known as a handbrake or parking brake.

Endfloat The amount of lengthwise movement between two parts. As applied to a crankshaft, the distance that the crankshaft can move forward and back in the cylinder block.

Engine management system (EMS) A computer controlled system which manages the fuel injection and the ignition systems in an integrated fashion.

Exhaust manifold A part with several passages through which exhaust gases leave the engine combustion chambers and enter the exhaust pipe.

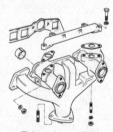

Exhaust manifold

F

Fan clutch A viscous (fluid) drive coupling device which permits variable engine fan speeds in relation to engine speeds.

Feeler blade A thin strip or blade of hardened steel, ground to an exact thickness, used to check or measure clearances between parts.

Feeler blade

Firing order The order in which the engine cylinders fire, or deliver their power strokes, beginning with the number one cylinder.

Flywheel A heavy spinning wheel in which energy is absorbed and stored by means of momentum. On cars, the flywheel is attached to the crankshaft to smooth out firing impulses.

Free play The amount of travel before any action takes place. The "looseness" in a linkage, or an assembly of parts, between the initial application of force and actual movement. For example, the distance the brake pedal moves before the pistons in the master cylinder are actuated.

Fuse An electrical device which protects a circuit against accidental overload. The typical fuse contains a soft piece of metal which is calibrated to melt at a predetermined current flow (expressed as amps) and break the circuit.

Fusible link A circuit protection device consisting of a conductor surrounded by heat-resistant insulation. The conductor is smaller than the wire it protects, so it acts as the weakest link in the circuit. Unlike a blown fuse, a failed fusible link must frequently be cut from the wire for replacement.

G

Gap The distance the spark must travel in jumping from the centre electrode to the side

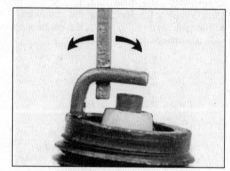

Adjusting spark plug gap

electrode in a spark plug. Also refers to the spacing between the points in a contact breaker assembly in a conventional points-type ignition, or to the distance between the reluctor or rotor and the pickup coil in an electronic ignition.

Gasket Any thin, soft material - usually cork, cardboard, asbestos or soft metal - installed between two metal surfaces to ensure a good seal. For instance, the cylinder head gasket seals the joint between the block and the cylinder head.

Gasket

Gauge An instrument panel display used to monitor engine conditions. A gauge with a movable pointer on a dial or a fixed scale is an analogue gauge. A gauge with a numerical readout is called a digital gauge.

H

Halfshaft A rotating shaft that transmits power from the final drive unit to a drive wheel, usually when referring to a live rear axle.

Harmonic balancer A device designed to reduce torsion or twisting vibration in the crankshaft. May be incorporated in the crankshaft pulley. Also known as a vibration damper.

Hone An abrasive tool for correcting small irregularities or differences in diameter in an engine cylinder, brake cylinder, etc.

Hydraulic tappet A tappet that utilises hydraulic pressure from the engine's lubrication system to maintain zero clearance (constant contact with both camshaft and valve stem). Automatically adjusts to variation in valve stem length. Hydraulic tappets also reduce valve noise.

I

Ignition timing The moment at which the spark plug fires, usually expressed in the number of crankshaft degrees before the piston reaches the top of its stroke.

Inlet manifold A tube or housing with passages through which flows the air-fuel mixture (carburettor vehicles and vehicles with throttle body injection) or air only (port fuel-injected vehicles) to the port openings in the cylinder head.

J

Jump start Starting the engine of a vehicle with a discharged or weak battery by attaching jump leads from the weak battery to a charged or helper battery.

L

Load Sensing Proportioning Valve (LSPV) A brake hydraulic system control valve that works like a proportioning valve, but also takes into consideration the amount of weight carried by the rear axle.

Locknut A nut used to lock an adjustment nut, or other threaded component, in place. For example, a locknut is employed to keep the adjusting nut on the rocker arm in position.

Lockwasher A form of washer designed to prevent an attaching nut from working loose.

M

MacPherson strut A type of front suspension system devised by Earle MacPherson at Ford of England. In its original form, a simple lateral link with the anti-roll bar creates the lower control arm. A long strut - an integral coil spring and shock absorber - is mounted between the body and the steering knuckle. Many modern so-called MacPherson strut systems use a conventional lower A-arm and don't rely on the anti-roll bar for location.

Multimeter An electrical test instrument with the capability to measure voltage, current and resistance.

N

NOx Oxides of Nitrogen. A common toxic pollutant emitted by petrol and diesel engines at higher temperatures.

O

Ohm The unit of electrical resistance. One volt applied to a resistance of one ohm will produce a current of one amp.

Ohmmeter An instrument for measuring electrical resistance.

O-ring A type of sealing ring made of a special rubber-like material; in use, the O-ring is compressed into a groove to provide the sealing action.

O-ring

Overhead cam (ohc) engine An engine with the camshaft(s) located on top of the cylinder head(s).

Overhead valve (ohv) engine An engine with the valves located in the cylinder head, but with the camshaft located in the engine block.

Oxygen sensor A device installed in the engine exhaust manifold, which senses the oxygen content in the exhaust and converts this information into an electric current. Also called a Lambda sensor.

P

Phillips screw A type of screw head having a cross instead of a slot for a corresponding type of screwdriver.

Plastigage A thin strip of plastic thread, available in different sizes, used for measuring clearances. For example, a strip of Plastigage is laid across a bearing journal. The parts are assembled and dismantled; the width of the crushed strip indicates the clearance between journal and bearing.

Plastigage

Propeller shaft The long hollow tube with universal joints at both ends that carries power from the transmission to the differential on front-engined rear wheel drive vehicles.

Proportioning valve A hydraulic control valve which limits the amount of pressure to the rear brakes during panic stops to prevent wheel lock-up.

R

Rack-and-pinion steering A steering system with a pinion gear on the end of the steering shaft that mates with a rack (think of a geared wheel opened up and laid flat). When the steering wheel is turned, the pinion turns, moving the rack to the left or right. This movement is transmitted through the track rods to the steering arms at the wheels.

Radiator A liquid-to-air heat transfer device designed to reduce the temperature of the coolant in an internal combustion engine cooling system.

Refrigerant Any substance used as a heat transfer agent in an air-conditioning system. R-12 has been the principle refrigerant for many years; recently, however, manufacturers have begun using R-134a, a non-CFC substance that is considered less harmful to

the ozone in the upper atmosphere.

Rocker arm A lever arm that rocks on a shaft or pivots on a stud. In an overhead valve engine, the rocker arm converts the upward movement of the pushrod into a downward movement to open a valve.

Rotor In a distributor, the rotating device inside the cap that connects the centre electrode and the outer terminals as it turns, distributing the high voltage from the coil secondary winding to the proper spark plug. Also, that part of an alternator which rotates inside the stator. Also, the rotating assembly of a turbocharger, including the compressor wheel, shaft and turbine wheel.

Runout The amount of wobble (in-and-out movement) of a gear or wheel as it's rotated. The amount a shaft rotates "out-of-true." The out-of-round condition of a rotating part.

S

Sealant A liquid or paste used to prevent leakage at a joint. Sometimes used in conjunction with a gasket.

Sealed beam lamp An older headlight design which integrates the reflector, lens and filaments into a hermetically-sealed one-piece unit. When a filament burns out or the lens cracks, the entire unit is simply replaced.

Serpentine drivebelt A single, long, wide accessory drivebelt that's used on some newer vehicles to drive all the accessories, instead of a series of smaller, shorter belts. Serpentine drivebelts are usually tensioned by an automatic tensioner.

Serpentine drivebelt

Shim Thin spacer, commonly used to adjust the clearance or relative positions between two parts. For example, shims inserted into or under bucket tappets control valve clearances. Clearance is adjusted by changing the thickness of the shim.

Slide hammer A special puller that screws into or hooks onto a component such as a shaft or bearing; a heavy sliding handle on the shaft bottoms against the end of the shaft to knock the component free.

Sprocket A tooth or projection on the periphery of a wheel, shaped to engage with a chain or drivebelt. Commonly used to refer to the sprocket wheel itself.

Starter inhibitor switch On vehicles with an

automatic transmission, a switch that prevents starting if the vehicle is not in Neutral or Park.

Strut See MacPherson strut.

T

Tappet A cylindrical component which transmits motion from the cam to the valve stem, either directly or via a pushrod and rocker arm. Also called a cam follower.

Thermostat A heat-controlled valve that regulates the flow of coolant between the cylinder block and the radiator, so maintaining optimum engine operating temperature. A thermostat is also used in some air cleaners in which the temperature is regulated.

Thrust bearing The bearing in the clutch assembly that is moved in to the release levers by clutch pedal action to disengage the clutch. Also referred to as a release bearing.

Timing belt A toothed belt which drives the camshaft. Serious engine damage may result if it breaks in service.

Timing chain A chain which drives the camshaft.

Toe-in The amount the front wheels are closer together at the front than at the rear. On rear wheel drive vehicles, a slight amount of toe-in is usually specified to keep the front wheels running parallel on the road by offsetting other forces that tend to spread the wheels apart.

Toe-out The amount the front wheels are closer together at the rear than at the front. On front wheel drive vehicles, a slight amount of toe-out is usually specified.

Tools For full information on choosing and using tools, refer to the *Haynes Automotive Tools Manual*.

Tracer A stripe of a second colour applied to a wire insulator to distinguish that wire from another one with the same colour insulator.

Tune-up A process of accurate and careful adjustments and parts replacement to obtain the best possible engine performance.

Turbocharger A centrifugal device, driven by exhaust gases, that pressurises the intake air. Normally used to increase the power output from a given engine displacement, but can also be used primarily to reduce exhaust emissions (as on VW's "Umwelt" Diesel engine).

U

Universal joint or U-joint A double-pivoted connection for transmitting power from a driving to a driven shaft through an angle. A U-joint consists of two Y-shaped yokes and a cross-shaped member called the spider.

V

Valve A device through which the flow of liquid, gas, vacuum, or loose material in bulk may be started, stopped, or regulated by a movable part that opens, shuts, or partially obstructs one or more ports or passageways. A valve is also the movable part of such a device.

Valve clearance The clearance between the valve tip (the end of the valve stem) and the rocker arm or tappet. The valve clearance is measured when the valve is closed.

Vernier caliper A precision measuring instrument that measures inside and outside dimensions. Not quite as accurate as a micrometer, but more convenient.

Viscosity The thickness of a liquid or its resistance to flow.

Volt A unit for expressing electrical "pressure" in a circuit. One volt that will produce a current of one ampere through a resistance of one ohm.

W

Welding Various processes used to join metal items by heating the areas to be joined to a molten state and fusing them together. For more information refer to the *Haynes Automotive Welding Manual*.

Wiring diagram A drawing portraying the components and wires in a vehicle's electrical system, using standardised symbols. For more information refer to the *Haynes Automotive Electrical and Electronic Systems Manual*.

Note: *References throughout this index are in the form - "Chapter number" • "Page number"*

Haynes Manuals – The Complete List

Title	Book No.
ALFA ROMEO	
Alfa Romeo Alfasud/Sprint (74 - 88) up to F	0292
Alfa Romeo Alfetta (73 - 87) up to E	0531
AUDI	
Audi 80 (72 - Feb 79) up to T	0207
Audi 80, 90 (79 - Oct 86) up to D & Coupe (81 - Nov 88) up to F	0605
Audi 80, 90 (Oct 86 - 90) D to H & Coupe (Nov 88 - 90) F to H	1491
Audi 100 (Oct 82 - 90) up to H & 200 (Feb 84 - Oct 89) A to G	0907
Audi 100 & A6 Petrol & Diesel (May 91 - May 97) H to P	3504
Audi A4 (95 - Feb 00) M to V	3575
AUSTIN	
Austin/MG/Rover Maestro 1.3 & 1.6 (83 - 95) up to M	0922
Austin/MG Metro (80 - May 90) up to G	0718
Austin/Rover Montego 1.3 & 1.6 (84 - 94) A to L	1066
Austin/MG/Rover Montego 2.0 (84 - 95) A to M	1067
Mini (59 - 69) up to H	0527
Mini (69 - Oct 96) up to P	0646
Austin/Rover 2.0 litre Diesel Engine (86 - 93) C to L	1857
BEDFORD	
Bedford CF (69 - 87) up to E	0163
Bedford/Vauxhall Rascal (86 - Oct 94) C to M	3015
BMW	
BMW 316, 320 & 320i (4-cyl) (75 - Feb 83) up to Y	0276
BMW 320, 320i, 323i & 325i (6-cyl) (Oct 77 - Sept 87) up to E	0815
BMW 3-Series (Apr 91 - 96) H to N	3210
BMW 3- & 5-Series (sohc) (81 - 91) up to J	1948
BMW 520i & 525e (Oct 81 - June 88) up to E	1560
BMW 525, 528 & 528i (73 - Sept 81) up to X	0632
CITROEN	
Citroën 2CV, Ami & Dyane (67 - 90) up to H	0196
Citroën AX Petrol & Diesel (87 - 97) D to P	3014
Citroën BX (83 - 94) A to L	0908
Citroën C15 Van Petrol & Diesel (89 - Oct 98) F to S	3509
Citroën CX (75 - 88) up to F	0528
Citroën Saxo Petrol & Diesel (96 - 01) N to X	3506
Citroën Visa (79 - 88) up to F	0620
Citroën Xantia Petrol & Diesel (93 - 98) K to S	3082
Citroën XM Petrol & Diesel (89 - 98) G to R	3451
Citroën Xsara (97 - 00) R to W	3751
Citroën ZX Diesel (91 - 98) J to S	1922
Citroën ZX Petrol (91 - 98) H to S	1881
Citroën 1.7 & 1.9 litre Diesel Engine (84 - 96) A to N	1379
FIAT	
Fiat 500 (57 - 73) up to M	0090
Fiat Bravo & Brava (95 - 00) N to W	3572
Fiat Cinquecento (93 - 98) K to R	3501
Fiat Panda (81 - 95) up to M	0793
Fiat Punto Petrol & Diesel (94 - Oct 99) L to V	3251
Fiat Regata (84 - 88) A to F	1167
Fiat Tipo (88 - 91) E to J	1625
Fiat Uno (83 - 95) up to M	0923
Fiat X1/9 (74 - 89) up to G	0273

Title	Book No.
FORD	
Ford Capri II (& III) 1.6 & 2.0 (74 - 87) up to E	0283
Ford Capri II (& III) 2.8 & 3.0 (74 - 87) up to E	1309
Ford Escort (Sept 80 - Sept 90) up to H	0686
Ford Escort & Orion (Sept 90 - 97) H to P	1737
Ford Escort Mk II Mexico, RS 1600 & RS 2000 (75 - 80) up to W	0735
Ford Fiesta (76 - Aug 83) up to Y	0334
Ford Fiesta (Aug 83 - Feb 89) A to F	1030
Ford Fiesta (Feb 89 - Oct 95) F to N	1595
Ford Fiesta Petrol & Diesel (Oct 95 - 97) N to R	3397
Ford Granada (Sept 77 - Feb 85) up to B	0481
Ford Granada & Scorpio (Mar 85 - 94) B to M	1245
Ford Ka (96 - 99) P to T	3570
Ford Mondeo Petrol (93 - 99) K to T	1923
Ford Mondeo Diesel (93 - 96) L to N	3465
Ford Orion (83 - Sept 90) up to H	1009
Ford Sierra 4 cyl. (82 - 93) up to K	0903
Ford Sierra V6 (82 - 91) up to J	0904
Ford Transit Petrol (Mk 2) (78 - Jan 86) up to C	0719
Ford Transit Petrol (Mk 3) (Feb 86 - 89) C to G	1468
Ford Transit Diesel (Feb 86 - 99) C to T	3019
Ford 1.6 & 1.8 litre Diesel Engine (84 - 96) A to N	1172
Ford 2.1, 2.3 & 2.5 litre Diesel Engine (77 - 90) up to H	1606
FREIGHT ROVER	
Freight Rover Sherpa (74 - 87) up to E	0463
HILLMAN	
Hillman Avenger (70 - 82) up to Y	0037
HONDA	
Honda Accord (76 - Feb 84) up to A	0351
Honda Civic (Feb 84 - Oct 87) A to E	1226
Honda Civic (Nov 91 - 96) J to N	3199
HYUNDAI	
Hyundai Pony (85 - 94) C to M	3398
JAGUAR	
Jaguar E Type (61 - 72) up to L	0140
Jaguar MkI & II, 240 & 340 (55 - 69) up to H	0098
Jaguar XJ6, XJ & Sovereign; Daimler Sovereign (68 - Oct 86) up to D	0242
Jaguar XJ6 & Sovereign (Oct 86 - Sept 94) D to M	3261
Jaguar XJ12, XJS & Sovereign; Daimler Double Six (72 - 88) up to F	0478
JEEP	
Jeep Cherokee Petrol (93 - 96) K to N	1943
LADA	
Lada 1200, 1300, 1500 & 1600 (74 - 91) up to J	0413
Lada Samara (87 - 91) D to J	1610
LAND ROVER	
Land Rover 90, 110 & Defender Diesel (83 - 95) up to N	3017
Land Rover Discovery Petrol & Diesel (89 - 98) G to S	3016
Land Rover Series IIA & III Diesel (58 - 85) up to C	0529
Land Rover Series II, IIA & III Petrol (58 - 85) up to C	0314
MAZDA	
Mazda 323 (Mar 81 - Oct 89) up to G	1608

Title	Book No.
Mazda 323 (Oct 89 - 98) G to R	3455
Mazda 626 (May 83 - Sept 87) up to E	0929
Mazda B-1600, B-1800 & B-2000 Pick-up (72 - 88) up to F	0267
MERCEDES BENZ	
Mercedes-Benz 190, 190E & 190D Petrol & Diesel (83 - 93) A to L	3450
Mercedes-Benz 200, 240, 300 Diesel (Oct 76 - 85) up to C	1114
Mercedes-Benz 250 & 280 (68 - 72) up to L	0346
Mercedes-Benz 250 & 280 (123 Series) (Oct 76 - 84) up to B	0677
Mercedes-Benz 124 Series (85 - Aug 93) C to K	3253
Mercedes-Benz C-Class Petrol & Diesel (93 - Aug 00) L to W	3511
MG	
MGA (55 - 62)*	0475
MGB (62 - 80) up to W	0111
MG Midget & AH Sprite (58 - 80) up to W	0265
MITSUBISHI	
Mitsubishi Shogun & L200 Pick-Ups (83 - 94) up to M	1944
MORRIS	
Morris Ital 1.3 (80 - 84) up to B	0705
Morris Minor 1000 (56 - 71) up to K	0024
NISSAN	
Nissan Bluebird (May 84 - Mar 86) A to C	1223
Nissan Bluebird (Mar 86 - 90) C to H	1473
Nissan Cherry (Sept 82 - 86) up to D	1031
Nissan Micra (83 - Jan 93) up to K	0931
Nissan Micra (93 - 99) K to T	3254
Nissan Primera (90 - Aug 99) H to T	1851
Nissan Stanza (82 - 86) up to D	0824
Nissan Sunny (May 82 - Oct 86) up to D	0895
Nissan Sunny (Oct 86 - Mar 91) D to H	1378
Nissan Sunny (Apr 91 - 95) H to N	3219
OPEL	
Opel Ascona & Manta (B Series) (Sept 75 - 88) up to F	0316
Opel Ascona (81 - 88) (Not available in UK see Vauxhall Cavalier 0812)	3215
Opel Astra (Oct 91 - Feb 98) (Not available in UK see Vauxhall Astra 1832)	3156
Opel Calibra (90 - 98) (See Vauxhall/Opel Calibra Book No. 3502)	
Opel Corsa (83 - Mar 93) (Not available in UK see Vauxhall Nova 0909)	3160
Opel Corsa (Mar 93 - 97) (Not available in UK see Vauxhall Corsa 1985)	3159
Opel Frontera Petrol & Diesel (91 - 98) (See Vauxhall/Opel Frontera Book No. 3454)	
Opel Kadett (Nov 79 - Oct 84) up to B	0634
Opel Kadett (Oct 84 - Oct 91) (Not available in UK see Vauxhall Astra & Belmont 1136)	3196
Opel Omega & Senator (86 - 94) (Not available in UK see Vauxhall Carlton & Senator 1469)	3157
Opel Omega (94 - 99) (See Vauxhall/Opel Omega Book No. 3510)	
Opel Rekord (Feb 78 - Oct 86) up to D	0543
Opel Vectra (Oct 88 - Oct 95) (Not available in UK see Vauxhall Cavalier 1570)	3158
Opel Vectra Petrol & Diesel (95 - 98) (Not available in UK see Vauxhall Vectra 3396)	3523

* Classic reprint

Title	Book No.
PEUGEOT	
Peugeot 106 Petrol & Diesel (91 - 01) J to X	1882
Peugeot 205 Petrol (83 - 97) A to P	0932
Peugeot 206 Petrol and Diesel (98 - 01) S to X	3757
Peugeot 305 (78 - 89) up to G	0538
Peugeot 306 Petrol & Diesel (93 - 99) K to T	3073
Peugeot 309 (86 - 93) C to K	1266
Peugeot 405 Petrol (88 - 97) E to P	1559
Peugeot 405 Diesel (88 - 96) E to N	3198
Peugeot 406 Petrol & Diesel (96 - 97) N to R	3394
Peugeot 505 (79 - 89) up to G	0762
Peugeot 1.7/1.8 & 1.9 litre Diesel Engine (82 - 96) up to N	0950
Peugeot 2.0, 2.1, 2.3 & 2.5 litre Diesel Engines (74 - 90) up to H	1607
PORSCHE	
Porsche 911 (65 - 85) up to C	0264
Porsche 924 & 924 Turbo (76 - 85) up to C	0397
PROTON	
Proton (89 - 97) F to P	3255
RANGE ROVER	
Range Rover V8 (70 - Oct 92) up to K	0606
RELIANT	
Reliant Robin & Kitten (73 - 83) up to A	0436
RENAULT	
Renault 5 (Feb 85 - 96) B to N	1219
Renault 9 & 11 (82 - 89) up to F	0822
Renault 18 (79 - 86) up to D	0598
Renault 19 Petrol (89 - 94) F to M	1646
Renault 19 Diesel (89 - 95) F to N	1946
Renault 21 (86 - 94) C to M	1397
Renault 25 (84 - 92) B to K	1228
Renault Clio Petrol (91 - May 98) H to R	1853
Renault Clio Diesel (91 - June 96) H to N	3031
Renault Espace Petrol & Diesel (85 - 96) C to N	3197
Renault Fuego (80 - 86) up to C	0764
Renault Laguna Petrol & Diesel (94 - 00) L to W	3252
Renault Mégane & Scénic Petrol & Diesel (96 - 98) N to R	3395
ROVER	
Rover 213 & 216 (84 - 89) A to G	1116
Rover 214 & 414 (89 - 96) G to N	1689
Rover 216 & 416 (89 - 96) G to N	1830
Rover 211, 214, 216, 218 & 220 Petrol & Diesel (Dec 95 - 98) N to R	3399
Rover 414, 416 & 420 Petrol & Diesel (May 95 - 98) M to R	3453
Rover 618, 620 & 623 (93 - 97) K to P	3257
Rover 820, 825 & 827 (86 - 95) D to N	1380
Rover 3500 (76 - 87) up to E	0365
Rover Metro, 111 & 114 (May 90 - 98) G to S	1711
SAAB	
Saab 90, 99 & 900 (79 - Oct 93) up to L	0765
Saab 900 (Oct 93 - 98) L to R	3512
Saab 9000 (4-cyl) (85 - 95) C to N	1686
SEAT	
Seat Ibiza & Cordoba Petrol & Diesel (Oct 93 - Oct 99) L to V	3571
Seat Ibiza & Malaga (85 - 92) B to K	1609

Title	Book No.
SKODA	
Skoda Estelle (77 - 89) up to G	0604
Skoda Favorit (89 - 96) F to N	1801
Skoda Felicia Petrol & Diesel (95 - 99) M to T	3505
SUBARU	
Subaru 1600 & 1800 (Nov 79 - 90) up to H	0995
SUZUKI	
Suzuki SJ Series, Samurai & Vitara (4-cyl) (82 - 97) up to P	1942
Suzuki Supercarry (86 - Oct 94) C to M	3015
TALBOT	
Talbot Alpine, Solara, Minx & Rapier (75 - 86) up to D	0337
Talbot Horizon (78 - 86) up to D	0473
Talbot Samba (82 - 86) up to D	0823
TOYOTA	
Toyota Carina E (May 92 - 97) J to P	3256
Toyota Corolla (Sept 83 - Sept 87) A to E	1024
Toyota Corolla (80 - 85) up to C	0683
Toyota Corolla (Sept 87 - Aug 92) E to K	1683
Toyota Corolla (Aug 92 - 97) K to P	3259
Toyota Hi-Ace & Hi-Lux (69 - Oct 83) up to A	0304
TRIUMPH	
Triumph Herald (59 - 71) up to K*	0010
Triumph TR2, TR3, TR3A, TR4 & TR4A (52 - 67)*	0028
Triumph TR5 & 6 (67 - 75)*	0031
Triumph Spitfire (62 - 81) up to X	0113
Triumph Stag (70 - 78) up to T	0441
VAUXHALL	
Vauxhall Astra (80 - Oct 84) up to B	0635
Vauxhall Astra & Belmont (Oct 84 - Oct 91) B to J	1136
Vauxhall Astra (Oct 91 - Feb 98) J to R	1832
Vauxhall/Opel Calibra (90 - 98) G to S	3502
Vauxhall Carlton (Oct 78 - Oct 86) up to D	0480
Vauxhall Carlton & Senator (Nov 86 - 94) D to L	1469
Vauxhall Cavalier 1600, 1900 & 2000 (75 - July 81) up to W	0315
Vauxhall Cavalier (81 - Oct 88) up to F	0812
Vauxhall Cavalier (Oct 88 - 95) F to N	1570
Vauxhall Chevette (75 - 84) up to B	0285
Vauxhall Corsa (Mar 93 - 97) K to R	1985
Vauxhall/Opel Frontera Petrol & Diesel (91 - Sept 98) J to S	3454
Vauxhall Nova (83 - 93) up to K	0909
Vauxhall/Opel Omega (94 - 99) L to T	3510
Vauxhall Vectra Petrol & Diesel (95 - 98) N to R	3396
Vauxhall/Opel 1.5, 1.6 & 1.7 litre Diesel Engine (82 - 96) up to N	1222
VOLKSWAGEN	
Volkswagen Beetle 1200 (54 - 77) up to S	0036
Volkswagen Beetle 1300 & 1500 (65 - 75) up to P	0039
Volkswagen Beetle 1302 & 1302S (70 - 72) up to L	0110
Volkswagen Beetle 1303, 1303S & GT (72 - 75) up to P	0159

Title	Book No.
Volkswagen Golf & Bora Petrol & Diesel (April 98 - 00) R to X	3727
Volkswagen Golf & Jetta Mk 1 1.1 & 1.3 (74 - 84) up to A	0716
Volkswagen Golf, Jetta & Scirocco Mk 1 1.5, 1.6 & 1.8 (74 - 84) up to A	0726
Volkswagen Golf & Jetta Mk 1 Diesel (78 - 84) up to A	0451
Volkswagen Golf & Jetta Mk 2 (Mar 84 - Feb 92) A to J	1081
Volkswagen Golf & Vento Petrol & Diesel (Feb 92 - 96) J to N	3097
Volkswagen LT vans & light trucks (76 - 87) up to E	0637
Volkswagen Passat & Santana (Sept 81 - May 88) up to E	0814
Volkswagen Passat Petrol & Diesel (May 88 - 96) E to P	3498
Volkswagen Polo & Derby (76 - Jan 82) up to X	0335
Volkswagen Polo (82 - Oct 90) up to H	0813
Volkswagen Polo (Nov 90 - Aug 94) H to L	3245
Volkswagen Polo Hatchback Petrol & Diesel (94 - 99) M to S	3500
Volkswagen Scirocco (82 - 90) up to H	1224
Volkswagen Transporter 1600 (68 - 79) up to V	0082
Volkswagen Transporter 1700, 1800 & 2000 (72 - 79) up to V	0226
Volkswagen Transporter (air-cooled) (79 - 82) up to Y	0638
Volkswagen Transporter (water-cooled) (82 - 90) up to H	3452
VOLVO	
Volvo 142, 144 & 145 (66 - 74) up to N	0129
Volvo 240 Series (74 - 93) up to K	0270
Volvo 340, 343, 345 & 360 (76 - 91) up to J	0715
Volvo 440, 460 & 480 (87 - 97) D to P	1691
Volvo 740 & 760 (82 - 91) up to J	1258
Volvo 850 (92 - 96) J to P	3260
Volvo 940 (90 - 96) H to N	3249
Volvo S40 & V40 (96 - 99) N to V	3569
Volvo S70, V70 & C70 (96 - 99) P to V	3573
AUTOMOTIVE TECHBOOKS	
Automotive Air Conditioning Systems	3740
Automotive Brake Manual	3050
Automotive Carburettor Manual	3288
Automotive Diagnostic Fault Codes Manual	3472
Automotive Diesel Engine Service Guide	3286
Automotive Electrical and Electronic Systems Manual	3049
Automotive Engine Management and Fuel Injection Systems Manual	3344
Automotive Gearbox Overhaul Manual	3473
Automotive Service Summaries Manual	3475
Automotive Timing Belts Manual – Austin/Rover	3549
Automotive Timing Belts Manual – Ford	3474
Automotive Timing Belts Manual – Peugeot/Citroën	3568
Automotive Timing Belts Manual – Vauxhall/Opel	3577
Automotive Welding Manual	3053
In-Car Entertainment Manual (3rd Edition)	3363

* Classic reprint

CL11.3/01

Preserving Our Motoring Heritage

< The Model J Duesenberg Derham Tourster. Only eight of these magnificent cars were ever built – this is the only example to be found outside the United States of America

Almost every car you've ever loved, loathed or desired is gathered under one roof at the Haynes Motor Museum. Over 300 immaculately presented cars and motorbikes represent every aspect of our motoring heritage, from elegant reminders of bygone days, such as the superb Model J Duesenberg to curiosities like the bug-eyed BMW Isetta. There are also many old friends and flames. Perhaps you remember the 1959 Ford Popular that you did your courting in? The magnificent 'Red Collection' is a spectacle of classic sports cars including AC, Alfa Romeo, Austin Healey, Ferrari, Lamborghini, Maserati, MG, Riley, Porsche and Triumph.

A Perfect Day Out

Each and every vehicle at the Haynes Motor Museum has played its part in the history and culture of Motoring. Today, they make a wonderful spectacle and a great day out for all the family. Bring the kids, bring Mum and Dad, but above all bring your camera to capture those golden memories for ever. You will also find an impressive array of motoring memorabilia, a comfortable 70 seat video cinema and one of the most extensive transport book shops in Britain. The Pit Stop Cafe serves everything from a cup of tea to wholesome, home-made meals or, if you prefer, you can enjoy the large picnic area nestled in the beautiful rural surroundings of Somerset.

> John Haynes O.B.E., Founder and Chairman of the museum at the wheel of a Haynes Light 12.

< Graham Hill's Lola Cosworth Formula 1 car next to a 1934 Riley Sports.

The Museum is situated on the A359 Yeovil to Frome road at Sparkford, just off the A303 in Somerset. It is about 40 miles south of Bristol, and 25 minutes drive from the M5 intersection at Taunton.

Open 9.30am - 5.30pm (10.00am - 4.00pm Winter) 7 days a week, *except Christmas Day, Boxing Day and New Years Day*

Special rates available for schools, coach parties and outings Charitable Trust No. 292048